Intergroup Cognition
and Intergroup Behavior

Applied Social Research

Marlene Turner and Anthony Pratkanis, Series Editors

Sedikides/Schopler/Insko • Intergroup Cognition and Intergroup Behavior

Intergroup Cognition
and Intergroup Behavior

Edited by

Constantine Sedikides
John Schopler
Chester A. Insko
University of North Carolina at Chapel Hill

 LAWRENCE ERLBAUM ASSOCIATES, PUBLISHERS
1998   Mahwah, New Jersey   London

Copyright © 1998 by Lawrence Erlbaum Associates, Inc.
All rights reserved. No part of this book may be reproduced in any form, by photostat, microform, retrieval
system, or any other means, without the prior written
permission of the publisher.

Lawrence Erlbaum Associates, Inc., Publishers
10 Industrial Avenue
Mahwah, New Jersey 07430

Library of Congress Cataloging-in-Publication-Data

Intergroup cognition and intergroup behavior / edited by
Constantine Sedikides, John Schopler, Chester A. Insko
   p. cm.
      Includes bibliographical references and index.
      ISBN 0-8058-2055-8. —ISBN 0-8058-2056-6 (pbk.)
      I. Intergroup relations. 2. Social interaction. 3. Social
psychology. 4. Cognition. I. Sedikides, Constantine. II.
Schopler, John. III. Insko, Chester A.
      HM132.I49 1997
      302.3—dc21
                                              97-1712
                                                 CIP

Books published by Lawrence Erlbaum Associates are printed
on acid-free paper, and their bindings are chosen for strength
and durability.

Printed in the United States of America
10   9   8   7   6   5   4   3   2   1

*To John W. Thibaut and Thomas M. Ostrom
Influential Colleagues and Friends*

Contents

Introduction

Social psychology has maintained a keen interest in issues related to intergroup behavior, such as ingroup favoritism, prejudice, and discrimination. The field has also been preoccupied with ways to reduce prejudice and discrimination. For example, intergroup contact has been offered as an important vehicle for prejudice and discrimination reduction.

Since the early 1980s, the social cognitive perspective has gained acceptance in social psychology. This perspective has been applied to the study of intergroup relations. Theoretical advances have been made regarding such issues as the representation of information about in-group and outgroup members, the structural properties of stereotypes, the relation between cognitive representation and judgment, and the ways in which cognition, affect, and motivation influence interactively the perception, judgment, and memory of in-group and outgroup members.

This edited volume seeks to bring these two traditions together. The volume focuses on the interplay between cognition and behavior in intergroup settings. What are the complex and multifaceted ways in which intergroup cognition and intergroup behavior are related? How does intergroup cognition (e.g., stereotypes, judgments, memories) influence intergroup behavior (e.g., in-group favoritism, discrimination, social movements)? How does intergroup behavior change intergroup cognition? What are the roles of affect, motivational processes, and social context? How effective can change in intergroup cognition be in altering intergroup behavior? These are the general questions this volume addresses.

Part I focuses on two conceptual issues that surround the study of intergroup cognition and behavior. The chapter by Schaller, Rosell, and Asp (chap. 1) discusses the relative merits of parsimony and pluralism for a full understanding of the relation between intergroup cognition and behavior. The chapter considers three prototypic perspectives: the rationalization approach, the social categorization approach, and the information-processing approach. Each perspective has made unique contributions to this relation. However, the pluralistic integration of the three perspectives is likely to be the most promising. On that premise, the authors propose a pluralistic model and evaluate its applicability and potential. The chapter by Wilder and Simon (chap. 2) is concerned with conceptualizations of the construct "group." *Groups* have been defined both categorically (in terms of similarities among group members) and dynamically (in terms of interactions among groups members). These definitions have guided much of the research on intergroup and intragroup processes. The chapter authors increase awareness on the part of researchers that adoption of a given definition influences the researchers' assumptions, as well as interpretations of group members' cognitions and behavior.

Part II clarifies the meanings of *intergroup cognition* and *behavior* by pitting them against *individual cognition* and *behavior*. What is special about groups, compared to individuals, that gives way to the emergence of differing cognitions and behavior? In chapter 3, Hamilton, Sherman, and Lickel argue that perceivers expect an individual to be more coherent and organized than a group. That is, individuals are expected to be higher than groups in entitativity. In fact, both individuals and groups lie on an entitativity continuum, and perceivers' cognition and behavior toward them are a function of this continuum. Insko and Schopler (chap. 4) point out a fundamental difference between perception of and behavior toward individuals and groups: Groups are distrusted more than individuals. For example, people expect and remember more competitive group-on-group than one-on-one interactions. More important, people behave more competitively when interacting with another group than when interacting with another individual. Distrust can be the result of processes such as increased self-consciousness, subjective perceptions of evaluative scrutiny, and informational uncertainty. Beside distrust, however, there can be another explanation for the heightened degree of competitiveness between groups than between individuals: Belonging to an entitative (i.e., highly cohesive) group is likely associated with loss of personal control (Insko, Schopler, and Sedikides, chap. 5).

Part III focuses on the perceptual and judgmental processes that influence intergroup cognition and behavior. Chapters 6, 7 and 8 discuss judgmental processes. In general, outgroups are perceived as more homogenous than ingroups. Also, outgroups are perceived as having more covarying features than ingroups. What are the judgmental consequences of such perceptions? According to Linville and Fischer (chap. 6), perceivers are more likely to (a) generalize stereotypes about the outgroup to individual outgroup members, (b) generalize stereotype-consistent (but not stereotype-inconsistent) information from the individual to the outgroup, and (c) make more extreme evaluations of the outgroup. Furthermore, perceivers are less likely to classify a stereotype-inconsistent person as a member of the outgroup. The behavioral repercussions of these judgmental processes may extend to several domains, such as hiring decisions and intergroup conflict.

Biernat, Vescio, and Manis (chap. 7) want to know how judgment standards affect behavior. They claim that judgment standards pertaining to a social group are activated by the stereotype of that group. These standards are then applied to evaluate the behavior of individual group members. Standards shift depending on the groups. Consider learning that Pat "shoved someone." This behavior would be labeled as "moderately aggressive" when Pat is a man, but "very aggressive" when Pat is a woman. This has implications for behavior. Perceivers may be more likely to want to associate with Pat the man than with Pat the woman.

How do stereotypes affect judgments and behavior? By supplying the perceiver with a ready-made cause-and-effect structure, Wittenbrink, Park, and Judd argue (chap. 8). This structure is applied to the construal of group members' behaviors. As a result, these behaviors acquire a configuration that would not be there had the stereotype been absent. The configuration resembles a person type. The person type will guide behavior, such as anticipation of future interaction and behavioral confirmation.

Part IV is concerned with social contextual mechanisms that impact on intergroup cognition and behavior. How do person types and, more generally, stereotypes produce behavioral confirmation on the part of others (e.g., outgroup members)? Claire and Fiske (chap. 9) tackle this question by emphasizing three major social contextual variables: shared beliefs about the target individual, the individual's knowledge that is relevant to the interaction, and the relationship between the interactants.

Social context (e.g., another group) can sometimes threaten a group's resources or security. Under such circumstances, members of the threatened group may develop paranoid cognition: They may overfocus their attention to the perceived threat, ruminate about it, become hypervigilant, and overscrutinize it. These phenomena is the subject of Kramer and Messick's treatise (chap. 10). Social context can also determine what type of self, individual versus collective, will be activated and guide behavior. The individual self will guide individual behavior, such as social mobility strategies, whereas the collective self will guide collective action, such as participation in social movements. Simon (chap. 11) discusses these issues, as well as why members of low-status minorities are more likely to define themselves in terms of the individual than the collective self—a process that retards social movement. Awareness of common fate may be an antidote to this tendency.

Social context is of paramount importance in intergroup conflict. Levine, Moreland, and Ryan (chap. 12) discuss how social context (i.e., group socialization) affects both the efforts of two competing groups to increase their membership and intragroup relations. Group socialization depends on evaluation (an assessment on the part of the member and the group of how satisfactory their relationship is), commitment (a judgment of whether the relationship is more rewarding than past, present, or future relationships), and role transition (criteria for changes in the relationship). These variables indicate the complex interplay of cognition, affect, and behavior in influencing intra- and intergroup processes.

Part V focuses on ways in which socially undesirable intergroup cognitions (e.g., stereotypes) and behaviors (e.g., discrimination) can be reduced. Bodenhausen, Macrae, and Garst (chap. 13) emphasize three conditions: awareness of such cognitions, motivation to avoid such behaviors, and availability of cognitive resources to do so. Dovidio, Gaertner, Isen, Rust, and Guerra (chap. 14) add another variable: positive affect. Positive affect reduces discriminatory behavior against an outgroup, provided that the relation between the two groups is neutral, ambiguous, or cooperative. Hewstone and Lord (chap. 15) add several other prerequisites: (a) The target individual needs to behave positively, (b) The target needs to be a typical outgroup member, (c) the domain on which the target excels has to be perceived as a representing the target's social group, (d) the target must not be perceived as an exception to his or her group, (e) no individuating information about the target should be given that detracts from the domain on which the target excels, and (f) the target must be associated strongly with the group to which the target belongs. Finally, Miller, Urban, and Vanman (chap. 16) discuss the important role that membership in multiple groups (crossed categorization) plays in the reduction of unwanted intergroup cognition and behavior.

Part VI contains a single chapter by Mackie and Smith (chap. 17). These authors comment on the chapters of this volume in the context of a broad overview of the relation between intergroup cognition and behavior. In conclusion, the edited volume acknowledges the emerging trend toward integrating social-cognitive concepts and techniques with the study of intergroup behavior. The volume explores the reciprocal relation between intergroup cognition and intergroup behavior. We hope the effort will instigate further research into the subtleties of this relation. The time has come for a more lively dialogue among researchers in the areas of intergroup cognition and intergroup behavior.

—Constantine Sedikides
John Schopler
Chester A. Insko
University of North Carolina at Chapel Hill

I

Intergroup Cognition and Intergroup Behavior: Conceptual Issues

1

Parsimony and Pluralism in the Psychological Study of Intergroup Processes

Mark Schaller
University of British Columbia

Michelle Ceynar Rosell
Charles H. Asp
University of Montana

> *"Among those verses of the poet Archilochus that have survived one can read this line: "The fox knows many things, but the hedgehog knows only one big thing." The same is true of researchers. So long as they are describing, one sees them exploring aggressively, like the fox, the numerous trails that criss-cross the topology of society. . . . As soon as this researcher assumes the task of explaining the corpus of results arrived at, everything changes. Like the hedgehog, he involuntarily rolls up in a ball and sticks out his spines, that is, he rejects what clashes with and contradicts his own views.*
> —Serge Moscovici (1988/1993, p. 2)

> *Seek simplicity and distrust it.*
> —Alfred North Whitehead (1920/1964, p. 163)

Several centuries after Archilochus mused on the fox and the hedgehog, but still more than 2,000 years ago, Aristotle offered his own, more formal and extensive contemplations about the nature of knowledge. Powerful as Aristotelian thought was, however, it had fallen from favor by the 5th century A.D. Augustinian mysticism began to overshadow Aristotelian philosophy, and philosophical investigation of the natural world was neglected in favor of theological inquiry into God's will. In the 13th century, Thomas Aquinas exhumed the relative objectivism of Aristotle, and attempted to synthesize it with Augustinian thought. Aquinas and several succeeding generations of

3

"Thomists" constructed sophisticated theories about the nature of God's creation and what it revealed about His will.

William of Ockham (1290–1349) reacted strongly against this integrative Thomist practice of "natural theology." A Franciscan theologian, Ockham advised that the intrusion of Aristotelian ideas into Augustinian theology did a grave injustice to Christian faith. But Ockham was not merely a theologian; he was a logician as well. His critique was based, in part, on the powerful logical premise that complex, sophisticated explanations are unnecessary if a simpler one exists to explain the same phenomena. Ockham suggested that there was no need to construct elaborate theories about the makeup of natural things; all that was necessary was to acknowledge that God willed things into existence.

This brief (and greatly oversimplified) snapshot of Ockham's theological philosophy illustrates an aspect of Ockham's logical philosophy, for which he is far better known within scientific circles today: the principle of parsimony. "Entities are not to be multiplied beyond necessity." "What can be done with fewer is done in vain with more." These and related aphorisms are embodied by the logical tool that scientists know as "Ockham's razor."

There is perhaps no more treasured implement in the scientist's conceptual toolbox than Ockham's razor. Scientists working in all areas encounter complex phenomena and interrelated processes. It is difficult, if not impossible, to consider fully every strand of these elaborate webs. It is no surprise that we are tempted again and again to unsheathe Ockham's razor—to put its fine blade to whatever conceptual knot confronts us, and to pare our explanations for the workings of the natural world to their simplest form. Confronted with the complex reality lurking behind every empirical question, the diversity-loving fox becomes a razor-wielding hedgehog.

This chapter discusses the use of Ockham's razor in the domain of intergroup processes. Specifically, it considers the consequences of the quest for parsimony in theories about the origins of group stereotypes, prejudice, and discrimination. Ultimately, it argues, a complete understanding of these origins demands a more diverse and integrative understanding of the dynamic interactions among intergroup cognition, behavior, and context.

CAUSES AND CONSEQUENCES OF THE USE OF OCKHAM'S RAZOR

First, it may be instructive to consider the concept of *parsimony* more generally. Why does one crave conceptual simplicity? What are the consequences of this ambition?

The Psychological and Logical Roots of Parsimony

When explaining their everyday world, people generally prefer simpler explanations over more complex ones (Read & Marcus-Newhall, 1993). These preferences may result from fundamental motives for structure, closure, and control (Burger & Cooper, 1979; Neuberg & Newsom, 1993; Webster & Kruglanski, 1994). Just as these motives play a role in the acquisition and interpretation of social knowledge (including stereotypes; Schaller, Boyd, Yohannes, & O'Brien, 1995), so too they influence the development of scientific theories (Kruglanski, 1989, 1994). Thus, the appeal of parsimony in science may be less logical than it is psychological (Kuhn, 1957; Russell, 1929). Kuhn (1957) stated plainly that parsimonious explanations appeal to an "aesthetic sense, and that alone" (p. 181).

Of course, even if the desire for parsimony is merely a reflection of the makeup of the human psyche, this need not undermine the logical or scientific value of Ockham's razor. Ignoble motives of scientists have often been observed to serve science well (Hull, 1988). There may be logical and empirical advantages to parsimonious explanations (Popper, 1934/1959). For instance, Forster and Sober (1994) suggested that the choice between scientific explanations "has nothing to do with simplicity and everything to do with predictive accuracy" (p. 28); they offered evidence that simpler explanations can afford more accurate predictions of empirical results. Similarly, psychometricians have suggested that, compared with models with more parameters, parsimonious models offer more precise estimates and better fits to empirical data sets (Bentler & Mooijaart, 1989; Mulaik et al., 1989).

These pragmatic perspectives on parsimony are somewhat narrow in their focus, however. Their goal is to fit theoretical explanation to a particular set of empirical data. Indeed, Sober (1990) advised that "the justification of parsimony must be local and subject matter specific" (p. 92). Certainly, scientists want to be able to explain individual data sets; but science also needs to collectively explain all the sets of empirical data that have accumulated on a phenomenon—to enhance the fit between theoretical explanation and the *variety* of things as they are experienced in the world (Kant, 1781/1900). An overreliance on Ockham's razor can lead to a worldview that leaves out too much reality.

Thus, like Archilochus' fox, we wish to explore broadly and describe in detail our diverse natural world. Yet like the hedgehog, we prefer to interpret this world in simple, elementary terms. Scientists struggle to attain the delicate balance between the competing goals of descriptive completeness and explanatory coherence. One way that this balance appears to be realized is through *pluralism* (Fiske & Schweder, 1986).

Parsimony Breeds Pluralism

A typical scenario in the social sciences fits the following pattern: Theory A is sufficient to explain Data Set A' (and so to add Theory B to the mix is superfluous). Theory B is sufficient to explain Data Set B' (and so to add Theory A to the mix is similarly superfluous). But neither Theory A nor Theory B by itself can explain the joint existence of Data Sets A' and B'. As a result, both Theories A and B are necessary to account for the variety of data relevant to a particular phenomenon. In a sense, both theories are insufficient; in another sense, both theories are necessary.

Thus, we find ourselves contending with the existence of multiple theories that address narrowly defined facets of a particular phenomenon. Each theory may be parsimonious in its own right, but none can completely explain the full range of relevant phenomena that exist in the real world or across the multiple data sets in the scientific literature. Parsimony breeds pluralism. A hedgehog may know only one big thing, but there is rarely only a single razor-wielding hedgehog in the field. This consequence of parsimony is readily apparent in the psychological literature on stereotypes, prejudice, and discrimination.

OCKHAM'S RAZOR IN THE STUDY
OF INTERGROUP PROCESSES

Decades of scientific inquiry reveal that the origins of stereotypes, prejudice, and discrimination are multifarious and complex. How do psychologists deal with this complexity? Often, they simply overlook it. Consider three prototypical perspectives.

The Rationalization Approach: The Priority
of Discrimination

In *The Nature of Prejudice*, Allport (1958) observed, "Many people did not vote for Al Smith in the presidential election of 1928 because he was a Catholic. Yet the reason they gave was that he was 'uncouth' " (pp. 164–165). Allport suggested that, "the rationalizing and justifying function of a stereotype exceeds its function as a reflector of group attributes" (p. 192). His analysis implies a causal priority to discrimination: Prejudice toward and stereotypes about group members result from discriminatory behavior.

Many forms of discrimination are directed by historical events or cultural norms. People kill members of other groups during times of war. People enslave members of other groups. Different groups occupy different roles in any given culture. Given the powerful motive for cognitive consistency (Abelson, Aronson, McGuire, Newcomb, Rosenberg, & Tannenbaum, 1968; Cialdini, Trost, & Newsom, 1995), people may seek to rationalize their own acts of discrimination (Lerner & Miller, 1978) and justify existing systems of discrimination (Jost & Banaji, 1994). Stereotypes and prejudice result. For instance, Hoffman and Hurst (1990) found that gender stereotypes can result simply from a process through which people attempt to explain or justify normative divisions of labor that assign men and women to different roles.

The Social Categorization Approach: The Priority of Prejudice

In 1971, the results of a series of experiments exploring the consequences of categorizing people into groups (Tajfel, Billig, Bundy, & Flament, 1971) were published. Several years later, Turner (1978) summarized the findings as follows: "Tajfel et al. (1971) have reported that the variable of social categorization *per se* is sufficient as well as necessary to induce forms of ingroup favouritism against the outgroup. . . . The *mere* perception by subjects (Ss) that they belonged to two separate groups seemed sufficient to cause intergroup discrimination" (p. 101; italics original). This line of research established social categorization as a key concept in the study of intergroup relations, and provided the empirical foundation for Social Identity Theory (Tajfel & Turner, 1979) and related theoretical models (e.g., Brewer, 1979; Turner, Hogg, Oakes, Reicher, & Wetherell, 1987).

A central tenet of this theoretical perspective holds that group categorization, coupled with the motivation for a positive self-concept, leads group members to evaluate their own groups more positively than outgroups. This prejudice, in turn, accounts for discriminatory behavior favoring ingroups over outgroups, and may lead to the emergence of stereotypic perceptions about outgroup members. For instance, Schaller and Maass (1989) found that, under conditions of minimal group categorization, prejudicial evaluations of groups led to stereotypic recall of group information.

Social categorization also influences perceptions of variability within groups. Research on perceived intragroup variability has demonstrated that members of real groups view their ingroup to be more heterogeneous than relevant outgroups (Ostrom & Sedikides, 1992). The same phenomenon occurs among novel groups — groups with which people have had no prior experience (e.g., Mackie, Sherman, & Worth, 1993; Wilder, 1984). Thus, another hallmark of stereotypes—the tendency to view "them" as all alike—can be interpreted as resulting from mere categorization.

The appeal of the social categorization approach lies not only in its conceptual parsimony, but also in its empirical economy. Researchers may employ the so-called "minimal group paradigm," randomly assigning participants to novel groups with which they have no history, and about which they have virtually no information. The processes proposed to lead to prejudice, discrimination, and stereotyping can be examined in explicit isolation from any preexisting group prejudices, and from any historically or culturally relevant intergroup context.

The Information-Processing Approach:
The Priority of Stereotypes

In 1976, the results of two experiments (Hamilton & Gifford, 1976) were published suggesting that "the differential perception of majority and minority groups could result solely from the cognitive mechanisms involved in processing information about stimulus events that differ in their frequencies of co-occurrence" (p. 392, Abstract). This widely cited article exposed psychologists to a fascinating stereotyping phenomenon—the "distinctiveness-based illusory correlation" effect, as it is typically called. This article exemplified a different perspective on the development of stereotypes, prejudice, and discrimination: Cognitive information processing directly determines the formation of group stereotypes, which in turn can lead to the emergence of prejudice and discrimination. In fact, later research (Schaller & Maass, 1989) provided direct evidence that, under the conditions identified by Hamilton and Gifford (1976), stereotypic perceptions caused prejudicial evaluations, and not the reverse.

The information-processing perspective has propelled a number of other hypotheses concerning the development of stereotypes, and their relation to prejudice and discrimination. For instance, erroneous stereotypes about disadvantaged groups can result from perceivers' failure to sufficiently use complex statistical reasoning strategies or decision-making rules when drawing group inferences from observations of group members' behavior (Allison, Mackie, & Messick, 1996; Mackie, Allison, Worth, & Asuncion, 1992; Schaller, Asp, Rosell, & Heim, 1996; Schaller & O'Brien, 1992). In addition, cognitive mechanisms of memory storage and recall are implicated in the tendency to perceive groups—particularly groups to which one does not belong—as excessively homogeneous (e.g., Linville, Fischer, & Salovey, 1989; Park & Hastie, 1987).

Emergent within this perspective has been a different sort of "minimal group" methodological paradigm. In much of the research conducted within this tradition, research participants are presented with information describing novel, hypothetical groups about whom they have no prior information whatsoever. They do not even have the minimal information resulting from knowledge of their own affiliation. Information processing proceeds unencumbered by preexisting beliefs, values, or desires about the groups in question. The processes proposed to lead to stereotyping, prejudice, and discrimination are examined in explicit isolation from the psychological consequences of social categorization.

The Pros and Cons of Pluralistic Parsimony

Figure 1.1 provides a schematic summary of the three perspectives just reviewed. Each perspective provides a simple, parsimonious explanation for the origins of stereotypes, prejudice, and discrimination. But they differ in the psychological mechanisms proposed to account for the emergence of these phenomena, and for the causal relations between the phenomena.

Because of their fundamental differences in focus, the different perspectives on intergroup processes offer complementary perspectives. All of these processes and more may contribute to the positive correlations observed

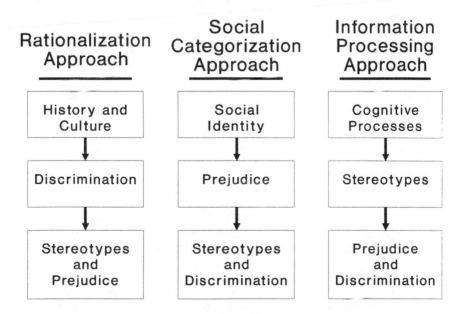

FIG. 1.1. Three parsimonious perspectives on the development and interrelations of stereotypes, prejudice, and discrimination.

among stereotypes, prejudice, and discrimination (Dovidio, Brigham, Johnson, & Gaertner, 1996). Although any single perspective on intergroup processes might be considered conceptually parsimonious, the scientific body of knowledge on the subject is anything but simple. In the study of intergroup cognition and behavior, the quest for parsimony has yielded plurality and diversity.

Although the multiplicity of conceptual perspectives might rankle those who aspire toward a single, simple, unified theory of intergroup processes, this pluralism is by no means bad. From the perspective of scientific evolution, it is perhaps not only inevitable, but valuable. If science proceeds through a process of epistemological evolution (Campbell, 1974; Hull, 1988; Popper, 1972), conceptual and methodological diversity is fundamental and necessary to scientific progress (Cronbach, 1986; Feyerabend, 1975; Schaller, Crandall, Stangor, & Neuberg, 1995). Tolerance—even encouragement—for multiple perspectives is vital to any science.

However, consumers of science expect scientific theories to interpret narrow slices of the world as it might be, as well as describe and predict the natural world as it is. To the extent that a particular scientific explanation of intergroup processes fails to describe or predict any of the varieties of actual intergroup behavior, that scientific explanation is judged inadequate. A number of authors have noted the limitations inherent in reductionist approaches to stereotypes, prejudice, and discrimination (Rothbart & Lewis, 1994; Spears, Oakes, Ellemers, & Haslam, 1997; Stangor & Schaller, 1996; Tajfel, 1981). Just as researchers have challenged the minimalism of Social Identity Theory (Insko & Schopler, 1987; Schiffman & Wicklund, 1992), so too Social Identity theorists have criticized the information-processing perspective for its apparent neglect of "social reality" (Oakes, Haslam, & Turner, 1994; Tajfel, 1981; Turner et al., 1987). Each of the three parsimonious perspectives considered earlier leaves out a lot of reality. Disaffection for reductionist theories is an encouraging sign that a more integrated, pluralist perspective may be emerging. Without dismissing the hedgehog from the scientific enterprise, the fox may nonetheless be in ascendancy.

NEW SHAVINGS FROM THE OLD RAZOR: TOWARD A PLURALISTIC INTEGRATION

To explain intergroup behavior in the natural world (not just the laboratory), a conceptual model of intergroup processes may have to simultaneously embrace the multiple perspectives that we have considered.

The Language of Integration: Cognition, Behavior, and Context

How might we begin to forge some conceptually coherent integration among the various, ostensibly distinct perspectives? As a first step, it might be useful to challenge the use of "stereotypes," "prejudice," and "discrimination" as conceptually distinct aspects of intergroup relations.

It has become increasingly difficult to maintain firm definitional boundaries among *stereotypes*, *discrimination*, and *prejudice*. Each term connotes multiple meanings. For instance, *stereotypes* has been defined both as cognitive structures that are stored in individual minds, as well as consensual beliefs that are shared between individuals and stored in contextual structures (Ashmore & Del Boca, 1981; Stangor & Schaller, 1996). *Discrimination* may refer to the actions of individuals, but may also be "institutional" and embedded in broader social structures, such as voting rights or property ownership laws (Jones, 1972). The multiple meanings problem is particularly profligate when considering prejudice. *Prejudice* may be construed variously as feelings one has toward a group or the expression of those feelings; it may refer to mental structures, such as attitudes, or to the manner in which people cognitively process information about groups (von Hippel, Sekequaptewa, & Vargas, 1995). The issue of multiple meanings is further complicated by the considerable conceptual overlap among stereotypes, prejudice, and discrimination. For instance, although stereotypes has often been defined strictly in terms of knowledge, beliefs, or perceptions of groups, and prejudice more often has referred to affect-laden evaluations of groups, recent research has suggested that affective components are attached to stereotypes as well (Stangor & Lange, 1993).

These definitional complexities suggest that a more fruitful way to integrate different theoretical perspectives might be to draw different conceptual lines. A bit of reflection reveals that the three theoretical perspectives considered earlier all concern the relations among intergroup cognition, intergroup behavior, and intergroup context.

Intergroup cognition refers to thoughts, motives, or other mental processes that concern groups (especially distinctions between groups) and that occur within the individual. *Intergroup behavior* refers to communications and actions that concern groups and that occur at an interpersonal level. (i.e., group-relevant processes that occur between persons, rather than within persons). Finally, *intergroup context* refers to situations, contexts, and cultural structures relevant to groups.

Intergroup context is implicated in all three of these parsimonious theoretical approaches discussed earlier. The rationalization approach suggests that context (historical events and/or cultural structures) influences behaviors directed toward group members, and that these behaviors in turn influence intergroup cognitions. The social categorization approach suggests that the context in which one finds oneself (a member of a group in relation to other groups) leads to certain individual-level cognitive processes and/or structures. These intergroup cognitions may then influence other aspects of cognition, as well as behavior directed toward group members. The information-processing approach also begins with context — in this case, the structure of the perceived social environment (e.g., the relative size of different groups that are perceived). The structure of the perceived environment interacts with the manner in which that information is processed to produce cognitive structures, which in turn may influence other aspects of cognition as well as behavior.

This exercise does more than merely decant old wine into newly labeled bottles. It provides a rudimentary framework that may help us forge an integration among the traditionally separate perspectives on the origins of intergroup phenomena. This framework (see Fig. 1.2) is simple in some respects, but complex in others. It is broad in scope, attending to individual-level phenomena (intergroup cognition), interpersonal-level phenomena (intergroup behavior), and cultural-level phenomena (intergroup context). It is also dynamic, explicitly recognizing the bidirectional causal relations among cognition, behavior, and context. These relations are discussed in four steps. First, some of the complicated relations among different aspects of individual-level cognitions relevant to groups are considered. Second, the reciprocal relations between individual-level cognitions and interpersonal-

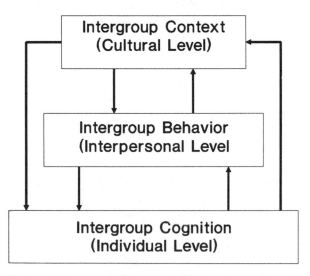

FIG. 1.2. Dynamic bidirectional relations among intergroup cognition, behavior, and context.

level intergroup behaviors are considered. Third, the effects of cultural-level group contexts on intergroup cognitions and behavior are considered. Finally, the manner in which individual-level cognitions and interpersonal behavior influence and even construct these cultural-level intergroup contexts is considered.

Relations Among Different Aspects of Intergroup Cognition

Although the social categorization approach has placed a priority on prejudice and the information-processing approach has placed a priority on stereotypes, cognitive processes lie at the heart of both. These cognitive processes are distinct, but they are related.

Encoding and recall phenomena are central to the information-processing approach, and yet recall for group information is influenced by social categorization. For instance, Howard and Rothbart (1980) found that a perceiver's own group membership guided the manner in which group-relevant information was encoded, and thus affected the type of group-relevant information that was later recalled. The paradigmatic cognitive phenomenon of stereotype formation — the "distinctiveness-based illusory correlation" effect demonstrated by Hamilton and Gifford (1976) — is fundamentally altered by social categorization. The enhanced recall associated with non-normative, minority group behavior (Hamilton, Dugan, & Trolier, 1985) disappears when perceivers are members of one of the perceived groups (Schaller & Maass, 1989). Not only does social categorization influence the outcomes of the cognitive mechanisms underlying stereotype development, but it also alters the nature of the cognitive mechanisms that operate in the first place (Schaller & Maass, 1989).

Social categorization also impacts reasoning processes that influence stereotype formation. Schaller (1992) found that people are especially likely to engage in simplistic reasoning, and thus are especially likely to form erroneous group stereotypes if those stereotypes reflect positively on one's ingroup. However, if simplistic reasoning results in stereotypes reflecting negatively on one's ingroup, then people are more likely to engage in complex reasoning. Thus, when perceivers of groups are members of groups, the reasoning processes underlying stereotype development become tools that are used strategically to satisfy group-based prejudices.

Finally, there is evidence that a perceiver's own group membership influences the specific dimensions along which a person attempts to differentiate between groups. Uninvolved perceivers tend to develop stereotypes defined primarily by those traits or characteristics that most strongly differentiate groups from one another (Ford & Stangor, 1992). This is not the case for people who actually belong to one of those groups. Instead, their emerging group stereotypes are influenced strongly by whether a group-differentiating trait casts their ingroup in a positive or negative light (Ford, 1993). Again, the cognitive processes underlying stereotype formation serve the specific epistemic motives that are aroused by social categorization.

Just as social categorization influences cognitive processing of social information, the opposite is true as well. People belong to numerous social categories, and the act of fitting a person to a category is not simply a static, reflexive process (see Miller, Urban, & Vanman, chap. 16, this volume). The social categories in which we place ourselves and others are, at least in part, psychological constructions; these constructions are dependent on a number of cognitive processes (Brewer, 1988, 1991; Simon, 1993; Smith & Zarate, 1992). At the very least, the categorization process is influenced by those categories that are most chronically accessible in memory (Sedikides & Skowronski, 1991). For example, self-schemas are likely to influence categorization processes, particularly the categories in which people are likely to place themselves (Markus, 1977). People who have strong feminine gender schemas, for example, tend to remember more feminine attributes and ascribe more feminine qualities to themselves (Markus, Crane, Bernstein, & Siladi, 1982).

Self-schemas also influence our perceptions of others (Sedikides & Skowronski, 1994), in part because of their effects on the way we categorize others. Fong and Markus (1982) found that people seek out information about others that is related to their own self-schemas. People who are either very shy or very outgoing are likely to categorize others according to their degree of extraversion; people who are "aschematic" on this trait are less likely to categorize others according to this dimension. In a related vein, Stangor, Lynch, Duan, and Glass (1992) found that racially prejudiced people are more likely to use race to categorize others, compared with nonprejudiced perceivers.

Relations Between Intergroup Cognition and Intergroup Behavior

The rapprochement between isolated theoretical perspectives becomes more apparent when one considers the reciprocal relations between cognitions about groups and behavior toward group members.

The effects of intergroup cognition on behavior are well documented. Attitudes concerning racial outgroups influence one's behavior toward members of those outgroups (McConahay, 1983; McConahay & Hough,

1976). The activation from memory of particular social categories influences actual behavior toward those individuals (Herr, 1986). Chronic category-based expectations of others exert effects on our behavior toward them, as well as their behavior toward us (Darley & Fazio, 1980; Jussim, 1986; Word, Zanna, & Cooper, 1974). More recent research reveals how these behavioral confirmation effects are responsive to yet another layer of intergroup cognition — individual-level motives and goals (Neuberg, 1995; Snyder, 1992). Other recent lines of work also reveal how different levels of cognitive processes may interact in complicated ways in predicting behavior toward members of other groups (e.g., Devine, 1989).

Reciprocally, intergroup behavior influences intergroup cognition in a multitude of ways that go well beyond the rationalization process discussed earlier. Much recent work reveals the impact of group-relevant communication behaviors. For example, the use of derogatory slurs in interpersonal speech appears to have several distinct consequences on cognitions relevant to those groups. Compared with value-neutral group descriptions, emotionally laden slurs may make negative group prototypes or characteristics more accessible from memory (Greenberg & Pyszczynski, 1985), and may influence one's perception of norms concerning intergroup behavior (Crandall, Thompson, Sakalli, & Schiffhauer, 1995). These immediate cognitive consequences may affect other forms of intergroup cognition, such as interpretation of a person's behavior and impression formation, and may ultimately influence behavior toward that person or other members of derogated outgroups.

Other aspects of interpersonal communication behavior also influence intergroup cognitions. People may strategically choose to use certain pronouns when describing groups (e.g., *we* vs. *they*; *us* vs. *them*) to symbolically identify with or distance themselves from a certain group (Cialdini et al., 1976). It is likely that these communication strategies do not merely reflect the speaker's temporary self-categorization, but also influence listeners' perceptions and impressions of the speaker and the groups about which the speaker speaks (Perdue, Dovidio, Gurtman, & Tyler, 1990). Finally, people use more abstract words than when describing undesirable ingroup and desirable outgroup behaviors (Maass, Milesi, Zabbini, & Stahlberg, 1995; Maass, Salvi, Arcuri, & Semin, 1989). This "linguistic intergroup bias" reflects individual-level cognitive processes that reinforce the speaker's existing intergroup cognitions, and also are likely to influence the intergroup cognitions of listeners.

Effects of Context on Intergroup Cognition and Behavior

The relations between intergroup cognition and behavior cannot be fully understood in the absence of context. Individual-level cognitions and interpersonal behaviors are constrained by local situations, as well as by broader cultural and historical structures.

The effects of local context on intergroup cognitions and behaviors have been reviewed extensively elsewhere (Oakes et al., 1994; Turner et al., 1987), and thus needs little elaboration. A few examples suffice to demonstrate that the various aspects of intergroup cognition and behavior considered earlier are context-dependent. An individual's social context influences the extent to which ethnicity, gender, sex, and other categorical characteristics define a person's spontaneous self-concept (Hogg & Turner, 1987; McGuire, McGuire, & Cheever, 1986; McGuire, McGuire, Child, & Fujioka, 1978). Context may also influence the manner in which we categorize others (e.g., by imposing cognitive constraints that reduce the accessibility from memory of certain social categories; Gilbert & Hixon, 1991).

Situations that promote intergroup cooperation (or competition) may also affect self- and other categorization, and may ultimately affect beliefs, attitudes, and feelings about in- and outgroups (Gaertner, Mann, Dovidio, Murrell, & Pomare, 1990; see also Dovidio, Gaertner, Isen, Rust, & Guerra, chap. 14, this volume). In fact, any situation promoting intergroup contact is likely to have effects on intergroup cognitions. The tendency to perceive outgroups as highly homogeneous (Ostrom & Sedikides, 1992) occurs, in part, because of the relatively infrequent contact with outgroup members, compared with ingroup members (Brigham & Malpass, 1985; Linville, Fischer, & Salovey, 1989). Increased interpersonal contact and familiarity with a group facilitates attention to finer intragroup distinctions (Tanaka & Taylor, 1991; Zebrowitz, Montepare, & Lee, 1993), and may increase perceptions of intragroup variability.

Local situations promoting contact among groups are imbedded in a broader historical context, and are dependent on cultural structures that may be either explicit (e.g., laws governing racial integration of schools) or implicit (e.g., nonrandom geographic distributions of immigrant populations). Societal-level "experiments" designed to alter these structures have had a direct impact on interpersonal interactions among members of different groups, and in some cases (although here things become more complicated) on individual-level cognitions as well (Aronson, Stephan, Sikes, Blaney, & Snapp, 1978; Cook, 1985; Hewstone & Brown, 1986; Miller & Brewer, 1984).

Other cultural-level structures also exert influences on intergroup cognition and behavior, such as structures governing relative group status and power. The relative power of ingroups and outgroups affects the ways in which individuals process information about and behave toward ingroup and outgroup members (Fiske, 1993; Sachdev & Bourhis, 1991; see also Claire & Fiske, chap. 9, this volume).

One's status as a member of a minority or majority group is also dictated by historical and/or cultural contexts. Minority or majority status is defined by population demographics, and exerts a powerful and pervasive influence on individual-level cognitive and motivational processes. For instance, the various cognitive processes underlying the "distinctiveness-based illusory correlation" effect (Fiedler, 1991; Hamilton & Gifford, 1976), are fundamentally based on this distinction. There is growing evidence that people cognitively process group information differently, depending on the relative size of the group (Mullen, 1991; Mullen & Johnson, 1995). Majority and minority group members may also differ in the strength of their motives related to self-categorization and social identity (Gerard & Hoyt, 1974). In addition, contrary to the usual "outgroup homogeneity effect," Simon (1992; Simon & Brown, 1987) found that members of minority groups perceive their ingroup to be more homogeneous than relevant outgroups.

In general, it is worth noting that historical events create an ever-changing intergroup context against which specific groups are perceived by individuals. Haslam, Turner, Oakes, McGarty, and Hayes (1992) found that Australians' beliefs about Americans changed over time due to changing frames of reference provided by historical events. Prior to the Gulf War, Americans were judged against the comparison standard of the Soviet Union. Against this standard, Americans were perceived to be aggressive. However, during the Gulf War, the standard against which Americans were judged shifted and the national character of the United States was now compared to that of Iraq. Against this new standard, Americans were judged to be less aggressive than before, although, ironically, the United States was actively engaged in an international conflict.

Cognition, Behavior, and the Evolution of Intergroup Contexts

The relation between social context and individual/interpersonal psychology is marked by "bottom–up" and "top–down" processes. Not only do cultural-level intergroup contexts exert important influences on intergroup cognition and behavior, but these "lower level" phenomena help shape the emergence and evolution of those cultural structures. According to Moscovici's theory of "social representations" (Farr & Moscovici, 1984; Moscovici, 1988/1993), the norms, values, politics, and other consensually shared knowledge structures that define society emerge from and are sustained by the thoughts, feelings, and interactions of individuals. In essence, society is invented by its people.

A related perspective can be culled from the dynamical systems theories, which are popular in biology, economics, and computer science (Kauffman, 1992; Lewin, 1992) and are beginning to be applied toward understanding human social behavior (Vallacher & Nowak, 1994). For instance, Latané and his colleagues (Latané, 1996; Nowak, Szamrej, & Latané, 1990) have shown in both computer simulations and empirical studies that public opinion and attitudinal norms emerge spontaneously over time—the result of simple rules governing the individual-level processes of attitude change and the interpersonal dynamics of persuasion.

A dynamic, evolutionary approach may be a particularly valuable tool in understanding the emergence of and changes in consensually shared stereotypes and normative structures supporting prejudice and discrimination (Schaller & Latané, 1996). This approach provides a conceptual paradigm within which it may be possible to address questions about variables that are typically ignored within a purely individual-level psychology of intergroup relations. What processes and variables influence the relative distribution of different beliefs about groups? What processes and variables influence the rate of change in beliefs about groups? What processes and variables influence the pattern of change in beliefs about groups?

In attempting to answer these questions, this approach may offer a novel perspective on classic questions about the functions and contents of intergroup cognitions and behaviors. For instance, although much theory and research reveals that stereotypes and prejudices serve epistemic and esteem-related functions for individuals (Stangor & Schaller, 1996), that work does not explain why some beliefs are more likely to perpetuate across space and time than others. Two different stereotypes may be equally functional to the individual in terms of filling epistemic and esteem-related needs, but one of those stereotypes may never be shared consensually whereas the other might spread quickly through a population. Why? According to a dynamic systems approach, the answer lies, in part, in the causes and consequences of interpersonal communication. Beliefs that are better suited to be communicated from one person to another are more "adaptive" (i.e., are more likely to be propagated rather than dying with the death of the carrier). Any aspect of a stereotype that facilitates communication enhances the likelihood that the stereotype will propagate through a human population. In this sense, stereotypes serve a function not only to the people who hold them, but also to themselves—not unlike "selfish genes" in certain theories of biological evolution (Dawkins, 1976).

More generally, this perspective indicates that, through the mediating role of interpersonal communication, individual cognitions and motives may influence cultural-level structure and processes that in turn influence the perceptions of, cognitions about, and behavior toward groups and group members. The portrait emerging is that of an evolving social landscape that is responsive to self-organizing processes analogous to those of biological ecosystems (Schaller & Latané, 1996). The real-world origins of intergroup cognitions and behaviors might best be understood within this dynamic, evolutionary perspective.

THE FOX AND THE HEDGEHOG REVISITED

Despite the opposition of Ockham and the almost-complete segregation of theology and science in Western culture, integrations between Aristotelian philosophy and Augustinian theology remain with us today in various forms. We find one example in the prestigious Gifford Lectures that are given regularly at Aberdeen, Scotland, and are devoted to the subject of "Natural Theology" — the reading of God's mind as expressed in the works of nature. In 1985, physicist Freeman Dyson offered a series of Gifford Lectures under the title "In Praise of Diversity." In one lecture, Dyson (1988) echoed Archilocus in offering a simple distinction between two types of scientists — unifiers and diversifiers:

> Unifiers are people whose driving passion is to find general principles which will explain everything. They are happy if they can leave the universe looking a little simpler than they found it. Diversifiers are people whose passion is to explore details. . . . They are happy if they can leave the universe a little more complicated than they found it. (pp. 44–45)

Dyson suggested that physicists tend to be unifiers, whereas biology is the natural domain of diversifiers (see Feist, 1994, for evidence supporting Dyson's hunch).

Where does that leave the social scientist? Psychologists and social scientists in general have aspired to the conceptual methods of physics, the idol of objectivism, the hardest of hard sciences. It is not surprising, then, that social scientists have held Ockham's razor in such reverence and have tended toward the reductionist habits of the hedgehog. But the topics of study in psychology are more closely descended from the biological rather than the physical sciences. Certainly this is true for the study of intergroup cognition and behavior. In studying these phenomena, it is sometimes blinding to follow the model of physics too closely. Instead of aspiring to model ourselves after our chosen Godfather of physics, we might best pattern ourselves after our true Grandfather of biology. While still maintaining a sacred space in our conceptual toolbox for Ockham's razor, we might clutch it a little less tightly and wield it a little more carefully. At the very least, it is worthwhile to be wary of our natural inclination toward hedgehoggery. The pluralistic perspective of the fox appears to be a minimal necessity if we are to most accurately and completely describe what goes on in the natural world of intergroup cognition and behavior.

ACKNOWLEDGMENT

Preparation of this chapter was supported by a MONTS grant from the Montana Science and Technology Alliance. We appreciate the support.

REFERENCES

Abelson, R. P., Aronson, E., McGuire, W. J., Newcomb, T. M., Rosenberg, M. J., & Tannenbaum, P. H. (Eds.). (1968). *Theories of cognitive consistency: A sourcebook.* Chicago: Rand McNally.

Allison, S. T., Mackie, D. M., & Messick, D. M. (1996). Outcome biases in social perception: Implications for dispositional inference, attitude change, stereotyping, and social behavior. In M. Zanna (Ed.), *Advances in experimental social psychology* (Vol. 28, pp. 53–93). San Diego: Academic Press.

Allport, G. W. (1958). *The nature of prejudice.* New York: Doubleday Anchor. (Original work published 1954)

Aronson, E., Stephan, C., Sikes, J., Blaney, N., & Snapp, M. (1978). *The jigsaw classroom.* Beverly Hills, CA: Sage.

Ashmore, R. D., & Del Boca, F. K. (1981). Conceptual approaches to stereotypes and stereotyping. In D. L. Hamilton (Ed.), *Cognitive processes in stereotyping and intergroup behavior* (pp. 1–35). Hillsdale, NJ: Lawrence Erlbaum Associates.

Bentler, P. M., & Mooijaart, A. (1989). Choice of structural model via parsimony: A rationale based on precision. *Psychological Bulletin, 106,* 315–317.

Brewer, M. B. (1979). In-group bias in the minimal intergroup situation: A cognitive-motivational analysis. *Psychological Bulletin, 86,* 307–324.

Brewer, M. B. (1988). A dual process model of impression formation. In T. K. Srull & R. S. Wyer, Jr. (Eds.), *Advances in social cognition* (Vol. 1, pp. 1–36). Hillsdale, NJ: Lawrence Erlbaum Associates.

Brewer, M. B. (1991). The social self: On being the same and different at the same time. *Personality and Social Psychology Bulletin, 17,* 475–482.

Brigham, J. C., & Malpass, R. S. (1985). The role of experience and contact in the recognition of faces of own- and other-race persons. *Journal of Social Issues, 41*(3), 139–156.

Burger, J. M., & Cooper, H. M. (1979). The desirability of control. *Motivation and Emotion, 3,* 381–393.

Campbell, D. T. (1974). Evolutionary epistemology. In P. A. Schilpp (Ed.), *The philosophy of Karl R. Popper* (pp. 413–463). LaSalle, IL: Open Court.

Cialdini, R. B., Borden, R. J., Thorne, A., Walker, M. R., Freeman, S., & Sloane, L. R. (1976). Basking in reflected glory: Three (football) field studies. *Journal of Personality and Social Psychology, 34,* 406–415.

Cialdini, R. B., Trost, M. R., & Newsom, J. T. (1995). Preference for consistency: The development of a valid measure and the discovery of surprising behavioral implications. *Journal of Personality and Social Psychology, 69,* 318–328.

Cook, S. W. (1985). Experimenting on social issues: The case of school desegregation.

American Psychologist, 40, 452–460.

Crandall, C. S., Thompson, E, A., Sakalli, N., & Schiffhauer, K. L. (1995). *Creating hostile environments: Name-calling and social norms.* Unpublished manuscript, University of Kansas.

Cronbach, L. J. (1986). Social inquiry by and for Earthlings. In D. W. Fiske & R. A. Schweder (Eds.), *Metatheory in social science: Pluralisms and subjectivities* (pp. 83–107). Chicago: University of Chicago Press.

Darley, J. M., & Fazio, R. H. (1980). The origin of self-fulfilling prophecies in a social interaction sequence. *American Psychologist, 35,* 867–881.

Dawkins, R. (1976). *The selfish gene.* Oxford, England: Oxford University Press.

Devine, P. G. (1989). Stereotypes and prejudice: Their automatic and controlled components. *Journal of Personality and Social Psychology, 56,* 5–18.

Dovidio, J. F., Brigham, J. C., Johnson, B. T., & Gaertner, S. L. (1996). Stereotyping, prejudice, and discrimination: Another look. In C. N. Macrae, C. Stangor, & M. Hewstone (Eds.), *Stereotypes and stereotyping* (pp. 276–319). New York: Guilford.

Dyson, F. (1988). *Infinite in all directions.* New York: Harper & Row.

Farr, R. M., & Moscovici, S. (1984). *Social representations.* Cambridge, England: Cambridge University Press.

Feist, G. J. (1994). Personality and working style predictors of integrative complexity: A study of scientists' thinking about research and teaching. *Journal of Personality and Social Psychology, 67,* 474–484.

Feyerabend, P. (1975). *Against method.* London, England: New Left.

Fiedler, K. (1991). The tricky nature of skewed frequency tables: An information loss account of distinctiveness-based illusory correlations. *Journal of Personality and Social Psychology, 60,* 24–36.

Fiske, D. W., & Schweder, R. A. (1986). *Metatheory in social science: Pluralisms and subjectivities.* Chicago: University of Chicago Press.

Fiske, S. T. (1993). Controlling other people: The impact of power on stereotyping. *American Psychologist, 48,* 621–628.

Fong, G. T., & Markus, H. (1982). Self-schemas and judgments about others. *Social Cognition, 1,* 191–205.

Ford, T. E. (1993). *The role of epistemic motivation and attribute diagnosticity in stereotype formation.* Unpublished manuscript.

Ford, T. E., & Stangor, C. (1992). The role of diagnosticity in stereotype formation: Perceiving group means and variances. *Journal of Personality and Social Psychology, 63,* 356–367.

Forster, M., & Sober, E. (1994). How to tell when simpler, more unified or less *ad hoc* theories will provide more accurate predictions. *British Journal for the Philosophy of Science, 45,* 1–35.

Gaertner, S. L., Mann, J. A. Dovidio, J. F., Murrell, A. J., & Pomare, M. (1990). How does cooperation reduce intergroup bias? *Journal of Personality and Social Psychology, 59,* 692–704.

Gerard, H. B., & Hoyt, M. F. (1974). Distinctiveness of social categorization and attitude toward ingroup members. *Journal of Personality and Social Psychology, 29,* 836–842.

Gilbert, D. T., & Hixon, J. G. (1991). The trouble of thinking: Activation and application of stereotypic beliefs. *Journal of Personality and Social Psychology, 60*(4), 509–517.

Greenberg, J., & Pyszczynski, T. (1985). The effects of an overheard ethnic slur on evaluations of the target: How to spread a social disease. *Journal of Experimental Social Psychology, 21,* 61–72.

Hamilton, D. L., Dugan, P. M., & Trolier, T. K. (1985). The formulation of stereotypic beliefs: Further evidence for distinctiveness-based illusory correlations. *Journal of Personality and Social Psychology, 48,* 5–17.

Hamilton, D. L., & Gifford, R. K. (1976). Illusory correlation in interpersonal perception: A cognitive basis of stereotypic judgments. *Journal of Experimental Social Psychology, 12*, 392–407.

Haslam, S. A., Turner, J. C., Oakes, P. J., McGarty, C., & Hayes, B. K. (1992). Context-dependent variation in social stereotyping: 1. The effects of intergroup relations as mediated by social change and frame of reference. *European Journal of Social Psychology, 22*, 3–20.

Herr, P. M. (1986). Consequences of priming: Judgment and behavior. *Journal of Personality and Social Psychology, 51*, 1106–1115.

Hewstone, M., & Brown, R. (1986). Contact is not enough: An intergroup perspective on the "Contact Hypothesis." In M. Hewstone & R. J. Brown (Eds.), *Contact and conflict in intergroup encounters* (pp. 1–44). London: Basil Blackwell.

Hoffman, C., & Hurst, N. (1990). Gender stereotypes: Perception or rationalization. *Journal of Personality and Social Psychology, 58*, 197–208.

Hogg, M. A., & Turner, J. C. (1987). Intergroup behavior, self-stereotyping, and the salience of social categories. *British Journal of Social Psychology, 26*, 325–340.

Howard, J. W., & Rothbart, M. (1980). Social categorization and memory for ingroup and outgroup behavior. *Journal of Personality and Social Psychology, 38*, 301–310.

Hull, D. L. (1988). *Science as a process*. Chicago: University of Chicago Press.

Insko, C. A., & Schopler, J. (1987). Categorization, competition, and collectivity. In C. Hendrick (Ed.), *Review of personality and social psychology* (pp. 213–251). Newbury Park, CA: Sage.

Jones, J. M. (1972). *Prejudice and racism*. Reading, MA: Addison-Wesley.

Jost, J. T., & Banaji, M. R. (1994). The role of stereotyping in system-justification and the production of false consciousness. *British Journal of Social Psychology, 33*, 1–27.

Jussim, L. (1986). Self-fulfilling prophecies: A theoretical and integrative review. *Psychological Review, 93*, 429–445.

Kant, I. (1900). *Critique of pure reason*. New York: Wiley. (Original work published 1781)

Kauffman, S. (1992). *The origins of order*. Oxford, England: Oxford University Press.

Kruglanski, A. W. (1989). *Lay epistemics and human knowledge: Cognitive and motivational bases*. New York: Plenum.

Kruglanski, A. W. (1994). The social-cognitive bases of scientific knowledge. In W. R. Shadish & S. Fuller (Eds.), *The social psychology of science* (pp. 197–213). New York: Guilford.

Kuhn, T. S. (1957). *The structure of scientific revolutions*. Chicago: University of Chicago Press.

Latané, B. (1996). Dynamic social impact: The creation of culture by communication. *Journal of Communication, 46*(4), 13–25.

Lerner, M. J., & Miller, D. T. (1978). Just world research and the attribution process: Looking back and ahead. *Psychological Bulletin, 85*, 1030–1051.

Lewin, R. (1992). *Complexity: Life at the edge of chaos*. New York: Macmillan.

Linville, P. W., Fischer, G. W., & Salovey, P. (1989). Perceived distributions of the characteristics of in-group and out-group members: Empirical evidence and a computer simulation. *Journal of Personality and Social Psychology, 57*, 165–188.

Maass, A., Milesi, A., Zabbini, S., & Stahlberg, D. (1995). Linguistic intergroup bias: Differential expectancies or in-group protection? *Journal of Personality and Social Psychology, 68*, 116–126.

Maass, A., Salvi, D., Arcuri, L., & Semin, G. (1989). Language use in intergroup contexts: The linguistic intergroup bias. *Journal of Personality and Social Psychology, 57*, 981–993.

Mackie, D. M., Allison, S. T., Worth, L. T., & Asuncion, A. G. (1992). The generalization of outcome-biased counter-stereotypic inferences. *Journal of Experimental Social Psychology, 28*, 43–64.

Mackie, D. M., Sherman, J. W., & Worth, L. T. (1993). On-line and memory-based processes in group variability judgments. *Social Cognition, 11*, 44–69.

Markus, H. (1977). Self-schemata and processing information about the self. *Journal of Personality and Social Psychology, 35*, 63–78.

Markus, H., Crane, M., Bernstein, S., & Siladi, M. (1982). Self-schemas and gender. *Journal of Personality and Social Psychology, 42*(1), 38–50.

McConahay, J. B. (1983). Modern racism and modern discrimination: The effects of race, racial attitudes, and context on simulated hiring decisions. *Personality and Social Psychology Bulletin, 9*, 551–558.

McConahay, J. B., & Hough, J. C., Jr. (1976). Symbolic racism. *Journal of Social Issues, 32*(2), 23–45.

McGuire, W. J., McGuire, C. V., & Cheever, J. (1986). The self in society: Effects of social contexts on the sense of self. *British Journal of Social Psychology, 25*, 259–270.

McGuire, W. J., McGuire, C. V., Child, P., & Fujioka, T. (1978). Salience of ethnicity in the spontaneous self-concept as a function of one's ethnic distinctiveness in the social environment. *Journal of Personality and Social Psychology, 36*, 511–520.

Miller, N., & Brewer, M. B. (Eds.). (1984). *Groups in contact: The psychology of desegregation*. New York: Academic Press.

Moscovici, S. (1993). *The invention of society*. Cambridge, England: Polity. (Original work published 1988)

Mulaik, S. A., James, L. R., Van Alstine, J., Bennett, N., Lind, S., & Stilwell, C. D. (1989). An evaluation of goodness-of-fit indices for structural equation models. *Psychological Bulletin, 105*, 430–445.

Mullen, B. (1991). Group composition, salience, and cognitive representations: The phenomenology of being in a group. *Journal of Experimental Social Psychology, 27*, 297–323.

Mullen, B., & Johnson, C. (1995). Cognitive representation in ethnophaulisms and illusory correlation in stereotyping. *Personality and Social Psychology Bulletin, 21*, 420–433.

Neuberg, S. L. (1995). Social motives and expectancy-tinged social interactions. In R. M. Sorrentino & E. T. Higgins (Eds.), *Handbook of motivation and cognition* (Vol. 3, pp. 225–261). New York: Guilford.

Neuberg, S. L., & Newsom, J. T. (1993). Personal need for structure: Individual differences in chronic motivation to simplify. *Journal of Personality and Social Psychology, 65*, 113–131.

Nowak, A., Szamrej, J., & Latané, B. (1990). From private attitude to public opinion: A dynamic theory of social impact. *Psychological Review, 97*, 362–376.

Oakes, P. J., Haslam, S. A., & Turner, J. C. (1994). *Stereotyping and social reality*. Oxford: Basil Blackwell.

Ostrom, T. M., & Sedikides, C. (1992). Out-group homogeneity effects in natural and minimal groups. *Psychological Bulletin, 112*, 536–552.

Park, B., & Hastie, R. (1987). Perception of variability in category development: Instance-versus abstraction-based stereotypes. *Journal of Personality and Social Psychology, 53*, 621–635.

Perdue, C. W., Dovidio, J. F., Gurtman, M. B., & Tyler, R. B. (1990). Us and them: Social categorization and the process of intergroup bias. *Journal of Personality and Social Psychology, 59*, 475–486.

Popper, K. (1959). *The logic of scientific discovery*. New York: Basic Books. (Original work published 1934)

Popper, K. (1972). *Objective knowledge: An evolutionary approach*. Oxford, England: Clarendon.

Read, S. J., & Marcus-Newhall, A. (1993). Explanatory coherence in social explanations: A parallel distributed processing account. *Journal of Personality and Social Psychology, 65*, 429–447.

Rothbart, M., & Lewis, S. (1994). Cognitive processes and intergroup relations: A historical perspective. In P. G. Devine, D. L. Hamilton, & T. M. Ostrom (Eds.), *Social cognition: Impact on social psychology* (pp. 347–382). San Diego: Academic Press.

Russell, B. (1929). *Mysticism and logic.*

Sachdev, I., & Bourhis, R. Y. (1991). Power and status differentials in minority and majority group relations. *European Journal of Social Psychology, 21*, 1–24.

Schaller, M. (1992). Ingroup favoritism and statistical reasoning in social inference: Implications for formation and maintenance of group stereotypes. *Journal of Personality and Social Psychology, 63*, 61–74.

Schaller, M., Asp, C. H., Rosell, M. C., & Heim, S. J. (1996). Training in statistical reasoning inhibits the formation of erroneous group stereotypes. *Personality and Social Psychology Bulletin, 22*, 829–844.

Schaller, M., Boyd, C., Yohannes, J., & O'Brien, M. (1995). The prejudiced personality revisited: Personal need for structure and formation of erroneous group stereotypes. *Journal of Personality and Social Psychology, 68*, 544–555.

Schaller, M., Crandall, C. S., Stangor, C., & Neuberg, S. L. (1995). "What kinds of social psychology experiments are of value to perform": A comment on Wallach and Wallach (1994). *Journal of Personality and Social Psychology, 69*, 611–618.

Schaller, M., & Latané, B. (1996). Dynamic social impact and the evolution of social representations. A natural history of stereotypes. *Journal of Communication, 46*(4), 64–71.

Schaller, M., & Maass, A. (1989). Illusory correlation and social categorization: Toward an integration of motivational and cognitive factors in stereotype formation. *Journal of Personality and Social Psychology, 56*, 709–721.

Schaller, M., & O'Brien, M. (1992). "Intuitive analysis of covariance" and group stereotype formation. *Personality and Social Psychology Bulletin, 18*, 776–785.

Schiffman, R., & Wicklund, R. A. (1992). The minimal group paradigm and its minimal psychology: On equating social identity with arbitrary group membership. *Theory and Psychology, 2*, 29–50.

Sedikides, C., & Skowronski, J. J. (1991). The law of cognitive structure activation. *Psychological Inquiry, 2*, 169–184.

Sedikides, C., & Skowronski, J. J. (1994). The self in impression formation: Trait centrality and social perception. *Journal of Experimental Social Psychology, 29*, 347–357.

Simon, B. (1992). The perception of ingroup and outgroup homogeneity: Re-introducing the intergroup context. In W. Stroebe & M. Hewstone (Eds.), *European review of social psychology* (Vol. 3, pp. 1–30). Chichester, England: Wiley.

Simon, B. (1993). On the asymmetry in the cognitive construal of ingroup and outgroup: A model of egocentric social categorization. *European Journal of Social Psychology, 23*, 131–147.

Simon, B., & Brown, R. (1987). Perceived intragroup homogeneity in minority–majority contexts. *Journal of Personality and Social Psychology, 53*, 703–711.

Smith, E. R., & Zarate, M. A. (1992). Exemplar-based model of social judgment. *Psychological Review, 99*(1), 3–21.

Snyder, M. (1992). Motivational foundations of behavioral confirmation. In M. P. Zanna (Ed.), *Advances in experimental social psychology* (Vol. 25, pp. 67–114). San Diego: Academic Press.

Sober, E. (1990). Let's razor Ockham's razor. In D. Knowles (Ed.), *Explanation and its limits* (pp. 73–93). Cambridge, England: Cambridge University Press.

Spears, R., Oakes, P. J., Ellemers, N., & Haslam, S. A. (1997). *The social psychology of stereotyping and group life.* Oxford, England: Basil Blackwell.

Stangor, C., & Lange, J. (1993). Cognitive representations of social groups: Advances in conceptualizing stereotypes and stereotyping. In M. Zanna (Ed.), *Advances in experimental social psychology* (Vol. 26, pp. 357–416). San Diego: Academic Press.

Stangor, C., Lynch, L., Duan, C., & Glass, B. (1992). Categorization of individuals on the basis of multiple social features. *Journal of Personality and Social Psychology*, *62*, 207–281.

Stangor, C., & Schaller, M. (1996). Stereotypes as individual and collective representations. In C. N. Macrae, C. Stangor, & M. Hewstone (Eds.), *Stereotypes and stereotyping* (pp. 3–37). New York: Guilford.

Tajfel, H. (1981). *Human groups and social categories: Studies in social psychology*. Cambridge, England: Cambridge University Press.

Tajfel, H. (1982). The social psychology of intergroup relations. *Annual Review of Psychology*, *33*, 1–39.

Tajfel, H., Billig, M., Bundy, R. P., & Flament, C. (1971). Social categorization and intergroup behavior. *European Journal of Social Psychology*, *1*, 149–177.

Tajfel, H., & Turner, J. C. (1979). An integrative theory of intergroup conflict. In W. G. Austin & S. Worchel (Eds.), *The social psychology intergroup relations* (pp. 33–47). Monterey, CA: Brooks/Cole.

Tanaka, J. W., & Taylor, M. (1991). Object categories and expertise: Is the basic level in the eye of the beholder? *Cognitive Psychology*, *23*, 457–482.

Turner, J. (1978). Social categorization and social discrimination in the minimal group paradigm. In H. Tajfel (Ed.), *Differentiation between social groups* (pp. 101–140). London: Academic Press.

Turner, J. C., Hogg, M. A., Oakes, P. J., Reicher, S., & Wetherell, M. S. (1987). *Rediscovering the social group: A self-categorization theory*. Oxford: Basil Blackwell.

Vallacher, R., & Nowak, A. (1994). *Dynamical systems in social psychology*. New York: Academic Press.

von Hippel, W., Sekaquaptewa, D., & Vargas, P. (1995). On the role of encoding processes in stereotype maintenance. In M. Zanna (Ed.), *Advances in experimental social psychology* (Vol. 27, pp. 177–254). San Diego: Academic Press.

Webster, D. M., & Kruglanski, A. W. (1994). Individual differences in need for cognitive closure. *Journal of Personality and Social Psychology*, *67*, 1049–1062.

Whitehead, A. N. (1964). *The concept of nature*. Cambridge, England: Cambridge University Press. (Original work published 1920)

Wilder, D. A. (1986). Social categorization: Implications for creation and reduction of intergroup bias. In L. Berkowitz (Ed.), *Advances in experimental social psychology* (Vol. 19, pp. 291–355). Orlando, FL: Academic Press.

Word, C. O., Zanna, M. P., & Cooper, J. (1974). The nonverbal mediation of self-fulfilling prophecies in interracial interaction. *Journal of Experimental Social Psychology*, *10*, 109–120.

Zebrowitz, L. A., Montepare, J. M., & Lee, H. K. (1993). They don't all look alike: Individuated impressions of other racial groups. *Journal of Personality and Social Psychology*, *65*, 85–101.

2

Categorical and Dynamic Groups: Implications for Social Perception and Intergroup Behavior

David Wilder
Andrew F. Simon
Rutgers University

"Die Grenzen meiner Sprache bedeuten die Grenzen meinter Welt."

"The limits of my language meun the limits of my world."
— Ludwig Wittgenstein (1922, p. 148)

"When I use a word, . . . it means just what I choose it to mean — neither more nor less."
— Humpty Dumpty
(Carroll, *Through the Looking Glass*, 1872/1982, p. 184)

Let us begin with the well-worn observation that the words we use to represent reality help to create that reality. Philosophers and eggheads ranging from Wittgenstein to Humpty Dumpty have pointed to the ambiguity that is created when words are called on to represent reality. Two people may use the same word to mean somewhat different things, and, of course, two people may use different words to mean the same thing. In this manner, any conversation is partly a negotiation, in which the parties must establish a common meaning to proceed with their business. To cite an extreme but apt example, consider the difficulty in conversing across language and culture. Even when an apparently adequate translation is found for a particular word, that translation may miss subtleties of nuance. Moreover, a common culture and language does not guarantee clarity of meaning. For example, within our academic department, the meaning of familiar words such as *psychology* and *science* varies substantially among the faculty.

To the extent that language is ambiguous, it can be a Pandora's box, unleashing misunderstanding and confusion in our social relations. With the exception of proper nouns, which refer to specific, concrete objects, most words represent categories of objects, actions, and modifiers that do not have a single isomorphic relationship with the reality we perceive through our senses. For example, the proper name *Empire State Building* refers to a particular structure in New York City; when people use that word, the referent is unambiguous. (Even someone who has never seen the Empire State Building would recognize the term as refering to a concrete object.) But the word *skyscraper* may conjure different images for different persons, and may be defined differently, not only across persons but by the same person across contexts. For someone raised in a rural setting, a structure 200 feet tall might seem to pierce the heavens, whereas the same building would appear to be a mere pustile to the city dweller.

To counter the ambiguity of everyday language, scientists have operationalized key words in the conduct of their research. Thus, in reporting an experiment, they dutifully explain how they have defined critical words in terms of the behaviors or operations performed in the experiment. Eventually, generalizations are made from specific research findings to a more comprehensive, theoretical conclusion. At that point, researchers cross the Rubicon from definitions with precise physical referents to theoretical constructs open to multiple interpretations. For example, *aggression* may be defined as a shock administered to a hapless victim via a flip of a switch on a control panel. But after conducting our research, we will be tempted to make a general statement about aggression in humans or a statement about the causes of aggression beyond the behaviors observed in our experiment. At that point, we introduce ambiguity. Others who read the word *aggression* outside the context of a flipped switch will conjure different images and definitions. Of course, all of this has been said before. We begin with these observations to set the stage for discussing a word that has been used frequently in social psychology with different meanings — *group*.

The argument developed in this chapter is that the term *group* has been used differently at different times by both lay persons and social psychologists. We propose that most definitions of *group* possess one or both of the following criteria: (a) groups are defined by similarities among the members (categorical definition), or (b) groups are defined by interaction among members (dynamic definition). These two means of defining a group influence both the knowledge base about groups and the behavior toward members of groups. In developing this argument, this chapter begins with a consideration of how *group* has been defined by lay persons and social psychologists.

DEFINING A GROUP

A portion of the definition of *group* found in a standard dictionary reads as follows: "1. An assemblage of persons or objects; aggregation. . . . 2. Two or more figures that make up a unit or a design, as in sculpture or painting. 3. A number of individuals or things considered together because of certain similarities" (Morris, 1976, p. 582). Additional entries in the definition of *group* are more esoteric, refering to linguistic, military, and mathematical applications of group. Examination of the entries cited earlier reveals two common features of everyday usage of the word *group*: A group is a unit and members of a group are similar to one another. Before turning to social-psychological definitions of *group*, one other characteristic of group should be noted. *Group* can be used as either a singular or plural collective noun. Again, quoting from *The American Heritage Dictionary*, "A singular verb occurs when the persons or things in question are considered as one or as acting as one, or when they are related by membership in a class or category. A plural verb is possible when 'group' refers to persons thought of as acting individually" (1976, p. 582). This grammatical point is mentioned because it parallels a dualism in the usage of *group* in social-psychological research and statistical analyses. Sometimes we treat a group as a tag placed on a collection of individuals, and our interest is in the behavior of individuals (individual level of analysis). At other times, we treat a group as an emergent unit, and we talk about the group, as a whole, as the basic unit of analysis (group level).

An overview of the various definitions of *group* employed by social psychologists reveals a tale not unlike that of the blind men trying to describe an elephant by touching only one part of the animal. Although definitions vary from writer to writer, each appears reasonable in its context and, at least on the surface, would appear to be describing the same entity. We review a few of these definitions, focusing on some of the more prominent names in social-psychological research.

Allport (1924) offered the following definition of *group* in his classic social psychology text: " . . . we may define a group as any aggregate consisting of two or more persons who are assembled to perform some task, to deliberate upon some proposal or topic of interest, or to share some affective experience of common appeal" (p. 260). Note the use of the word *assembled* and the idea of common fate (or experience) that permeates Allport's definition.

McDougall (1920), another noteworthy early psychologist, wrote that there is " . . . one condition that may raise the behaviour of a temporary and unorganised crowd to a higher plane, namely the presence of a clearly defined common purpose in the minds of all its members" (p. 67). Although Allport and McDougall had lively disagreements about the properties of

groups (e.g., group mind), they did agree that a common purpose distinguished a group from an aggregate of persons.

Both Campbell (1958) and Homans (1950) emphasized the importance of
a boundary in the definition of *group*. Homans posited that the " . . .
definition of a group implies, and is meant to imply, that the group has a
boundary . . . " (p. 86). Others have focused on the perception of a
"relationship" among members, which may or may not necessitate interaction (Bales, 1953; Krech & Crutchfield, 1948; Lewin, 1948).

The requirement of "interdependence" is central to some social psychologists (Cartwright & Zander, 1968; Cattell, 1951; Newcomb, 1963; Thibaut
& Kelley, 1959). Lewin (1951) regarded a group as a dynamic whole, and
stated that a definition of *group* should be based on the interdependence
among the members. "The essence of a group is not the similarity or
dissimilarity of its members, but their interdependence" (Lewin, 1948, p.
84). Similarly, Fiedler (1967) argued that a group is " . . . a set of
individuals who share a common fate, that is, who are interdependent in the
sense that an event which affects one member is likely to affect all" (p. 6).

Other researchers consider "interaction" among members to be a critical
characteristic of groups (Bales, 1950; Homans, 1950; Merton, 1957;
Newcomb, 1963). Shaw (1981) defined a *group* as follows: "Two or more
persons who are interacting with one another in such a manner that each
person influences and is influenced by each other person" (p. 454). After a
thoughtful overview of types of social aggregates ranging from a passive
audience to a large organization, McGrath (1984) defined *groups* as " . . .
those social aggregates that involve mutual awareness and potential mutual
interaction" (p. 7).

Finally, Asch (1952) distinguished between a group as " . . . a collection
of units that, although different from one another, possess some property
in common" and a group " . . . the members of which are interdependent"
(p. 260). The latter type of group has emergent "group properties." We end
this brief survey with Asch's definition because it brings us full circle to the
dictionary definition with which we began. Like *The American Heritage
Dictionary*, Asch made the distinction between groups based on *similarity*
and groups based on interdependence.

HISTORY OF GROUP RESEARCH

Research on small-group behavior by American social psychologists en-
joyed its greatest popularity in the group dynamics movement of the 1950s
and 1960s (Bales, 1950; Cartwright & Zander, 1968; Steiner, 1972; Zander,
1979). If one were to point to a single piece of research that sowed the seed

of group research in this country, Zander argued that it would be the Lewin, Lippitt, and White (1939) investigation of leadership style and group climate. Certainly Lewin's field theory provided a compelling argument for studying individual behavior in groups. Lewin believed that a person's behavior was determined by the forces present in that person's phenomenological field or life space at the moment. Nothing could be more in the present than the activities of others about him or her.

In addition to Lewin and his influential students, the rise of group research in the United States can be attributed, in part, to the advent of World War II. Knowledge of how people interact in groups was thought to be helpful both in the immediate sense of fostering more effective military units and in the long-term sense of encouraging a better peacetime society that might, through social engineering, avoid the mistakes of the present and past generations, which had always known major wars. The idea that the study of groups may prove socially beneficial was not confined to university laboratories. In 1947, the National Training Laboratory for Group Development was established to teach methods of facilitating change in organizations and the application of group research to applied settings (Back, 1972).

As Steiner (1974) and Zander (1979) pointed out, the 1950s and 1960s were a heyday for experimental small-group research in mainstream American social psychology. By the end of the 1960s, however, group research appeared to be in decline. Zander noted several reasons for this, including some practical difficulties in conducting group research, whether in a field or laboratory setting. Group research usually requires more resources (e.g., participants, materials, lab space, assistants) and is more vulnerable to mishaps (e.g., a mistake can affect multiple sets of data) than research with one subject at a time. In addition, some of the constructs used in group research have been difficult to pin down (e.g., cohesion).

In his analysis of the decline of group research in leading, mainstream social-psychology journals, Steiner (1974) proposed a more subtle, molar explanation. He argued that fluctuations in interest may reflect a response to changes in society. Thus, an increase in group research after World War II was triggered by concerns about how to improve social interaction both in combat units and, more generally, in society as a whole. Because of the lag between societal input and research output, the full effect of this influence was not visible until the late 1950s and the 1960s. By that time, social focus moved to an increasing emphasis on the individual. In response to this swing of the pendulum, social research began moving away from groups to the individual, as evidenced by the rise of attribution and social cognition as dominant research paradigms. Levine and Moreland (1990) offered evidence consistent with an argument that the decline in group research reflects changing "tastes," rather than a dissatisfaction with groups, per se, as a topic of study. They noted that group research is alive and well in areas outside of mainstream experimental social psychology. There are thriving research programs in organizational psychology and business school settings.

Moreland, Hogg, and Hains (1994) reviewed publication data in the three top American social-psychology journals: *Journal of Personality and Social Psychology, Journal of Experimental Social Psychology*, and *Personality and Social Psychology Bulletin*. As part of their informative review, they reported a curvilinear trend for publication of group research. Group research declined during the 1970s, but has risen again in the 1990s. They attributed this increase in interest largely to applications of social cognition to group topics (most notably stereotypes), and to the social categorization work initiated by Tajfel and his colleagues. Based on the findings of Moreland et al., it would appear that the increase in group research reported in some major social-psychology journals is not a revival of the "good old religion" of the 1950s and 1960s. Rather it is a different sort of group research — one that has attempted to apply the methods and interests of social cognition (e.g., Fiske & Taylor, 1984; Hamilton, 1981) beyond the individual to the group. That combined with the overlapping interest of social categorization researchers (e.g., Oakes, Haslam, & Turner, 1994; Turner, Hogg, Oakes, Reicher, & Wetherell, 1987) accounts for the lion's share of any resurgence of group research in mainstream social psychology during the 1990s.

Indeed, we suspect that group research involving interacting groups has not shown a strong resurgence in experimental social psychology. To get an indication of the state of group research involving interacting, dynamic (as distinct from categorical) groups, we examined the number of publications from January 1994 through September 1995 in the *Journal of Personality and Social Psychology — Interpersonal Behavior and Group Processes* (JPSP) and the *Journal of Experimental Social Psychology* (JESP). These are the two most prominent American journals that publish predominantly experimental social psychology. Of the 60 articles published during that time period in the groups section of JPSP, 15 involved interacting groups as part of the methodology. This is the section of JPSP to which group research is normally sent. Of the 46 articles published during the same period in JESP, only 6 involved interacting groups.

We wish to propose another reason why group research declined toward the end of the 1960s. The chill in small-group research can be traced to a tilt in the axis of social psychology from the study of interpersonal interaction, based heavily on behaviorism as a world view, to intrapersonal dynamics using an information-processing metaphor. This change in research focus was not precipitous. Certainly, group research never ceased even during the bleak years that spawned Steiner's (1974, 1986) lament.

The two most influential catalysts for this shift in research focus from "out there" (interaction) to "in here" (cognitions) were Festinger's (1957) dissonance theory and Heider's (1958) attribution model. These works, along with the influence of the new look in perception (Bruner, 1958; Tajfel, 1969), turned the rudder of social-psychological research, and the field began to move away from theories based on learning models (e.g., Yale communication model of attitude change, social exchange theories). A fundamental premise of behaviorism is that the subject matter for psychology is overt behavior (i.e., actions that can be publicly observed). Reality for the behaviorist is "out there," beyond the individual in the public world. The proper subject for group researchers, therefore, is interaction among members of a group. Most group research during the 1950s and 1960s involved interactions among group members (e.g., work on cohesion, leadership, conformity), as epitomized by *Group Dynamics*, the collected bible of small-group research edited by Cartwright and Zander (1968).

In the late 1960s and 1970s "reality" moved inside the head due to the impact of cognitive consistency theories (Abelson, Aronson, McGuire, Newcomb, Rosenberg, & Tannenbaum, 1968), attribution theories (Heider, 1958; Jones & Davis, 1965; Kelley, 1967), and the serial information-processing paradigm borrowed from cognitive psychology. Social psychologists became increasingly concerned with how people process social information, and how their representations of social information influence subsequent action. This shift in the epicenter of social research moved social reality from out there to inside the head. Groups increasingly became a construct that perceivers use to organize their social world, rather than an independent reality of its own. For some of us, it was important to understand when individuals perceive themselves to be group members and how their group identities affect their judgments of others. Answering those questions did not require a live, interacting group. Indeed, from the vantage point of social cognition, the individual is the fundamental unit of analysis; what is of chief concern is how individuals perceive and process information. A social group is simply one more source of information to be noticed, interpreted, and responded to.

TWO DEFINITIONS OF GROUP

Returning to the distinction between a group defined on the basis of interaction versus similarity, it seems that the former definition is more akin to how groups were conceived of and studied in the 1950s and 1960s during the heyday of group dynamics. Nevertheless, a definition based on similarity is closer to that used when groups are studied from the perspective of social cognition and social categorization research. So what? As Humpty Dumpty might say, "What's the harm in defining a group as one chooses so long as it's stated clearly?" To which Ludwig Wittgenstein might reply, "How you define a group affects what you learn about groups." What, then, are some implications of defining a group in terms of "similarity" versus "interaction"?

Categorical Definition: Groups Based on Similarity

When similarity is the criterion used for group membership, the term *group* is used in the same manner as the term *category*. In other words, membership is determined by the possession of specified characteristics by which the universe of persons is split into two classes: those who possess the characteristics (group members) and those who do not (nonmembers). Some of the implications of defining a group this way are as follows:

1. Membership is determined by shared properties or characteristics of the members. These shared characteristics often reflect stable traits or desires of the members.

2. The individual member is a hologram of the category. That is, the category is replicated within the individual by the latter's possession of the critical criteria for membership. If the category membership of an individual is known, then characteristics of that person, relevant to the category, can be inferred. If an individual is known to be a member of a group, then general characteristics of that group can be inferred from that particular individual.

3. The group is the sum of its individual members. Because of this, it cannot have properties not already possessed by its members (e.g., Allport, 1924).

4. Because the group is based on judgments of similarity among members, a perceiver may construct a group with or without the participation of the target members. In other words, the existence of a group is in the mind of the beholder. It is a cognitive construct resulting from the abstraction of similarity among persons.

5. As cognitive constructs, groups are created as a means to simplify the social world (cognitive miser concept). When persons are perceived as members of a group, there can be a loss of individual or personal information about them. Similarities within the category are accentuated. Therefore, "group-level" perceptions can be less detailed than "individual-level" perceptions (Tajfel & Turner, 1979). However, there can also be a

gain of information following categorization when characteristics common to the group are attributed to them (Oakes et al., 1995).

Propositions 1–3 follow from the treatment of a group as a category, much like nonhuman categories, such as animals, vegetables, and minerals. Proposition 4 reflects the phenomenological basis of the categorical conceptualization of group. Because groups are cognitive constructs, reality for the group is in the mind of the perceiver. The physical existence of a group "out there," although important, is less critical than its existence "in the head." For example, from a social identity perspective, a group exists when persons perceive some common identity, regardless of whether it is recognized as such by others. Proposition 5 addresses a motivational basis for categorizing persons into groups on the basis of similarity, and describes two apparently opposite consequences of the categorization process. The former refers to instances in which details about an individual are discounted or overlooked as a result of being categorized into the group. The latter proposition refers to instances in which little may be known about the individual, so expectations associated with the social category generate additional information about the person.

Dynamic Definition: Groups Based on Interaction

When interaction is used as the criterion for group membership, a different set of propositions is generated from those listed for a categorical definition of *group*. The following propositions are organized in a parallel manner to the list for "groups based on similarity:"

1. Groups arise out of the relationship among members. Group membership is determined by the interaction (behavior) of the members. Membership is not determined by the possession of dispositional properties, traits, or motivations on the part of the individual members.
2. The goodness-of-fit of a specific member is determined by how well that person fits into the structure of the group, much as the fit of a puzzle piece is determined by how well it locks into place with other pieces. Thus, similarity among members is not necessary. Inferences from a specific group member to the group cannot be made with the same assurance as when membership is based on similarity (category definition of group). The individual is not a replication of the group. Inferences from knowledge of the typical group member cannot be made to a specific member with the same assurance as when membership is based on similarity.

3. The group is greater than the sum of its parts. Characteristics may emerge from the interaction among members that are not present in any individual member (Asch, 1952; McDougall, 1920).

4. Because groups result from interaction among individuals, groups exist "out there." Perceptions of dynamic groups are more closely bound to the stimulus field and less likely to be distorted by perceiver expectations. Dynamic groups are not created by perceiver attempts to employ cognitive shortcuts to minimize effort.

A comparison of the propositions from the "group as a category" and "group as a dynamic entity" perspectives reveals some clear differences in conceptualization of groups. The dynamic perspective considers group membership to be a condition that emerges from the interaction of individuals. Although individuals may be drawn together by a common purpose or even behavioral similarities, it is their interaction that creates a structured interdependence. How alike the individuals are in terms of appearance, beliefs, and behavior is not critical. However, for the category-based conception of group, specification of a set of characteristics held in common by all members is essential to the definition of group. This differentiation is reminiscent of Lewin's (1935) distinction between Aristotelian and Galilean modes of scientific thought.

Lewin argued that Aristotelian thought is characterized by explanations based on categorization. Explanations are based on sorting and classifying objects on the basis of similarity and regularity. For the Aristotelian thinker, the regular and the frequent are lawful, whereas the individual exception is a chance event. Phenotypic or surface similarities are sufficient for forming categories. The nature of an element is expressed in the characteristics common to it and other members of its category. What Lewin described as Aristotelian thought appears to be quite similar to what we have called a *categorical* conceptualization of groups.

In contrast, Galilean thought is characterized by an examination of the relationship among underlying or genotypic variables. Neither regularity nor frequency is necessary for lawfulness. The individual exception is as lawful as the regular. The actions of an element in any situation are determined not by the intrinsic nature of that element (e.g., traits, dispositions), but by the set of forces in the extant field. Behavior is a function of the interaction of the elements present in the field at that moment. Thus, Galilean thought appears to be quite similar to what we have called a *dynamic* conceptualization of groups.

In distinguishing between Aristotelian and Galilean thought, Lewin argued for the superiority of the latter as a scientific tool. We do not suggest that a dynamic conceptualization of groups is necessarily superior to one based on categorization. But we do suggest that a dynamic definition is different from a categorical one, and that those differences have implica-tions for social perception. We also do not suggest that these styles of thought are mutually exclusive. For example, one may judge persons to be members of a common group on the basis of their interaction (dynamic definition), and from that judgment infer similarities among those members (categorical definition). Some years ago, Wilder (1978) reported that merely labeling persons as a *group* is sufficient to trigger assumptions of similarity and common causality. In those experiments, subjects heard the opinions of persons who either were labeled as members of a common group or were described as an aggregate. In comparison to the noncategorized aggregate, group members were judged to be more similar to one another, and their behavior was attributed more to the influence of one another.

Implications for Social Perception and Behavior

A categorical conception of group bases group membership on similarity. By definition, members of the group must possess those characteristics important for group membership; otherwise they are excluded from the category. An implication of categorical reasoning is that knowledge of one member of the group is sufficient to know the essential characteristics of other group members. By comparison, a dynamic conception of group bases group membership on the relationship among the parties. Member-ship is contingent on the interaction and structure that emerges from that interaction (e.g., norms, roles). Thus, knowledge of the properties and traits of one member does not guarantee similar knowledge of other members. Indeed, group members may share nothing other than their common effort to achieve a goal. We turn to three quite different examples to illustrate our point: stereotypes, intergroup contact, and baseball.

Stereotypes. Consider the distinction between perceiving a person as a group member or as an individual. This distinction has been talked about in various guises for a number of years. Tajfel (1978) proposed that persons can be perceived along a continuum ranging from interpersonal to inter-group. At one extreme, we may regard another (or ourselves) as a unique individual independent of social groups. At the other extreme we may regard another as a deindividuated representative of a social category or group; someone who is interchangeable with other members of that group. Whether perceptions are at the individual or group level depends on a variety of factors, including the salience of cues associated with relevant groups to which the target may be assigned, the similarity of the target to others about him or her, and constraints placed on the ability of the perceiver to process information about the target (Fiske & Taylor, 1984; Wilder, 1993; Wilder & Simon, 1996).

We propose a different approach to the individual–group distinction. Persons are likely to be viewed as individuals when we actively interact with them. Our judgments of them are then guided by the outcome of that interaction. The personal, individual-level relationship we have with them does not arise from greater knowledge of them, per se, but from the process of interaction. In other words, we do not view them as unique individuals because we have compared their traits/behaviors with stereotypes of a social category and found a mismatch (Fiske & Neuberg, 1990). Rather, we judge them to be unique because our interaction with them creates a social structure with meaning for us (e.g., conversation about plans for dinner, committee decision). It is that interaction that structures the field, thereby obviating categorical judgments. Certainly, at a later time we may reflect on an interaction and treat it in a passive, categorical manner. For instance, one may think back on a conversation and say to oneself that one's partner's comments reflected his or her membership in a social group. But while the conversation is occurring, one's judgments are guided by the interaction. The two people comprise the social field of the moment.

However, when we make judgments about others from afar or on the basis of passive observation (as is often the case in laboratory experiments guided by a social-cognitive perspective), we are more likely to rely on social categories to sort others and to construct a meaningful scenario in which to act. In other words, we employ more Aristotelian thinking, sorting others on the basis of their similarities/dissimilarities to us and to each another. Judgments about them are made on the basis of their match with social categories (groups) and the expectations (stereotypes) we have about those social categories. It seems that much of the stereotype literature fits this format. Participants view information about a target person (ranging from a direct statement of categorical membership to more subtle category-relevant actions of the target) and are then asked to make judgments, from which an assessment of their use of stereotypes is made. (See Hamilton & Sherman, 1994, for a comprehensive review of the social cognition approach to stereotype research.)

Are we arguing, then, that persons do not use stereotypes to guide their interactions? No, not exactly. We would agree with the current consensus that stereotypes do affect social perception and behavior (Greenwald & Banaji, 1995; Hamilton & Sherman, 1994). But we also maintain that stereotypes reflect categorical thinking, and are most likely to affect social perception and behavior when we are engaged in categorical thought. When we contemplate an interaction with someone, particularly someone about whom we know little other than surface information (e.g., gender, occupation), our initial response to that person will be in terms of the social categories to which the individual belongs. That initial response can certainly influence the course of subsequent interaction. But once interaction has begun and we are actively involved in a dynamic relationship, the relationship is the structure that guides our cognitions and subsequent actions. General stereotypes of the social category become relatively unimportant compared with the live interaction. In our view, stereotypes (categorical judgments) have greater impact on expectations of future behavior and recall of past behavior than on the present, dynamic interaction that engulfs the individual.

Intergroup Contact. As another example of the influence of one's conception of groups (as categories or dynamic entities), consider the checkered history of intergroup contact as a balm for bias. Contact with members of a disliked out group can produce a positive change in attitudes and beliefs toward that group, providing that the contact experience is positive and the contact persons are considered to be fairly typical of others in the outgroup (Allport, 1954; Amir, 1969; Hewstone & Brown, 1986; Wilder, 1984; Wilder, Simon, & Faith, 1996). Nevertheless, contact under the most favorable conditions does not guarantee success (see Amir, 1969; Brewer & Miller, 1988, for a list of those conditions). One argument for the success of contact is based on a warmed-over amalgamation of learning and cognitive consistency theories (Wilder, 1986). Pleasant, productive experience with specific members of a disliked social group promotes a positive evaluation of those persons. Furthermore, to the extent that those pleasant members are viewed as typical of others in their group, the benefits of positive contact should generalize to the group as a whole.

We offer another reason that contact with specific group members does not easily generalize to attitudes and beliefs about the entire group. When intergroup contact occurs in a face-to-face setting, the participants are often encouraged to interact in cooperative pursuit of a common goal (e.g., Sherif, 1966; Worchel & Austin, 1986). Their interaction defines a dynamic group (the contact group), and the beneficial effects of that interaction are attributed to the interplay of the specific individuals. The outgroup is simply not present as a category in their field. Only when they step out of the interaction and are asked (by others or, perhaps, through self-reflection) to make some judgment about the outgroup as a whole are they likely to make an associative or consistent inference from the successful interaction to category-based attributes (such as stereotypes) of the entire outgroup. In short, the generalization that researchers seek from specific contact experiences must be induced; to get it, a shift must occur from the dynamic interaction that was experienced to a categorical inference. For this reason, we suspect that contact, no matter how positive, will always suffer poor generalization. The best bet for contact as a strategy is to expect little, and therefore employ multiple contact experiences to net a modest change — a point Sherif (1966) made in his ground-breaking summer camp experiments.

Baseball.   A couple of years ago, we conducted a study of attributions people make to explain the behavior of baseball players (Wilder & Simon, 1997). This research was triggered by a fortuitous conjunction of one author's involvement as a little league coach and his interest in attributions that observers make about group behavior. Subjects for this study were students who were split into two conditions on the basis of whether they identified themselves as baseball fans. All subjects were shown a short videotape of excerpts from major league baseball games. After each excerpt, the subjects were asked to make an attribution about why a particular player acted the way he did. They indicated the extent to which a player's actions appeared to reflect his disposition (ability), effort, difficulty of the task, and influence of his teammates. It was found that fans differed from nonfans in the extent to which they attributed a player's behavior to his disposition and to the influence of his team. Nonfans were more likely than fans to attribute good or bad performance to disposition; the latter were more likely to attribute performance to the actions of the team as a whole. These data suggest that nonfans perceived the baseball team as a social category—a collection of individuals who share common traits and whose behavior reflects those traits (in this case, baseball skills). By contrast, fans perceived the baseball team as a dynamic group—an interacting set of individuals who, although all possessing baseball talents, differed in specific abilities and whose behavior reflected their interdependence in playing the game. Although both fans and nonfans saw the same stimulus material, their interpretation of it was influenced by the kind of group schema each used to organize the ballteam.

Lab Experiment.   Leaving the baseball diamond for the lab, we conducted an experiment that more directly examined differences in group perception that occur when groups are perceived as categorical versus dynamic units (Wilder & Simon, 1997). Participants in this study viewed a videotape of a group of alleged pre-law students who met regularly to discuss current legal issues. In the meeting shown on the videotape, four members of the pre-law group expressed their opinions about a legal case. Although all four opinions were similar, each person offered different arguments so that their views were not identical. Half of the participants in the experiment viewed a tape on which the pre-law group was described as a collection of individuals with similar interests (categorical group condition). The four members gave their opinions one at a time, and the camera focused only on the speaker.

In the other condition (dynamic group), participants viewed a tape of the same four group members giving the same opinions. This time the camera focused on the entire group, and group members expressed only part of their opinions before turning the floor over to another person. Although the content of the messages was the same in both conditions, there was a perception of more interaction in the dynamic group condition. Later, participants made attributions about the causes of the group members' opinions. Participants showed a significantly stronger dispositional attribution for the similar opinions of the members of the categorical group than for the similar opinions of the dynamic group. They also made a significantly stronger attribution to the influence of the group (i.e., group pressure and desire to benefit the group) for the similar opinions expressed by the members of the dynamic group than for the same behavior in the categorical group.

These findings parallel the survey of the baseball fans and nonfans. Persons who perceive a group as a category (nonfans in the baseball study and participants in the categorical group condition in the lab experiment) attributed common behavior to the dispositional similarity of the members. This finding fits well with Propositions 2 and 3 about categorical groups. Because the group was defined by the similarities of the members, common action among the members was judged to be a manifestation of those common dispositions. However, persons who perceived the group as a dynamic entity (fans in the baseball study and participants in the dynamic group conditon in the lab experiment) attributed common behavior to the influence of the interacting group members. This finding fits with Propositions 2 and 3 about dynamic groups. Because the group was defined by the interaction of the members, common action among members was attributed to that interaction, rather than to properties of the persons.

CONCLUSIONS

This chapter distinguished two ways in which lay persons and researchers have defined a group. Groups are sometimes defined by similarities among the members — in the same way in which nonsocial categories of objects are defined (categorical definition). Groups are also sometimes defined by interaction among the members (dynamic definition). In making this distinction, we are not contending that one or the other is the preferred way to define a social group. However, the schema (categorical vs. dynamic) we use to conceptualize a group influences the assumptions we make about the group members and the interpretations we place on their actions.

To return to where we began with Messieurs Dumpty and Wittgenstein, how we define a word has significant impact on the reality that we construct with it. This chapter has suggested that lay persons and researchers use the term *group* in multiple ways, two of which (group as category, group as dynamic unit) have differing implications for the questions we pose and the answers we generate about groups. Clearly, many of these ideas are speculative and have been designed more to raise questions about how we think of groups than to provide definitive answers.

Of particular interest to us are implications of people's conceptualization of groups for the interpretation they give to group members' behavior in an intergroup context. For instance, assumptions of similarity among group members may be quite diagnostic for categorical groups, but inaccurate for dynamic groups. To the extent that we, as perceivers, are lazy and treat all groups as composed of similar others, we assume greater homogeneity and engage in greater stereotyping than may be warranted by the actual relationship among those group members. This argument suggests that a careful consideration of our assumptions about groups is warranted for accurate social perception. As sages have consistently cautioned us, better knowledge of ourselves fosters better knowledge of others.

REFERENCES

Abelson, R. P., Aronson, E., McGuire, W. J., Newcomb, T. M., Rosenberg, M. J., & Tannenbaum, P. H. (1968). *Theories of cognitive consistency.* Chicago: Rand McNally.

Allport, F. H. (1924). *Social psychology.* Boston: Houghton Mifflin.

Allport, G. W. (1954). *The nature of prejudice.* Garden City, NY: Doubleday Anchor.

Amir, Y. (1969). Contact hypothesis in ethnic relations. *Psychological Bulletin, 71,* 319–341.

Asch, S. E. (1952). *Social psychology.* Englewood Cliffs, NJ: Prentice-Hall.

Back, K. (1972). *Beyond words.* New York: Russel Sage Foundation.

Bales, R. F. (1950). A set of categories for the analysis of social group interaction. *American Sociological Review, 15,* 257–263.

Brewer, M. B., & Miller, N. (1988). Contact and cooperation: When do they work? In P. A. Katz & D. A. Taylor (Eds.), *Eliminating racism: Profiles in controversy* (pp. 315–326). New York: Plenum.

Bruner, J. S. (1958). Social psychology and perception. In E. E. Maccoby, T. M. Newcomb, & E. L. Hartley (Eds.), *Readings in social psychology* (pp. 85–94). New York: Holt, Rinehart and Winston.

Campbell, D. T. (1958). Common fate, similarity and other indices of the status of aggregates of persons as social entities. *Behavioral Science, 3,* 14–25.

Carroll, L. (1982). *The complete illustrated works of Lewis Carroll.* London: Chancellor Press. (Original work published 1872)

Cartwright, D., & Zander, A. (1968). *Group dynamics* (3rd ed.). New York: Harper & Row.

Cattell, R. B. (1951). New concepts for measuring leadership in terms of group syntality. *Human Relations, 4,* 161–184.

Festinger, L. (1957). *A theory of cognitive dissonance.* Stanford, CA: Stanford University Press.

Fiedler, F. E. (1967). *A theory of leadership effectiveness.* New York: McGraw-Hill.

Fiske, S. T., & Neuberg, S. L. (1990). A continuum of impression formation, from category-based to individuating processes: Influences of information and motivation on attention and interpretation. In M. Zanna (Ed.), *Advances in experimental social psychology* (Vol. 23, pp. 1–74). San Diego: Academic Press.

Fiske, S. T., & Taylor, S. E. (1984). *Social cognition.* Reading, MA: Addison-Wesley.

Greenwald, A. G., & Banaji, M. R. (1995). Implicit social cognition: Attitudes, self-esteem, and stereotypes. *Psychological Review, 102*, 4-27.

Hamilton D. L. (Ed.). (1981). *Cognitive processes in stereotyping and intergroup behavior*. Hillsdale, NJ: Lawrence Erlbaum Associates.

Hamilton, D. L., & Sherman, J. W. (1994). Stereotypes. In R. S. Wyer & T. K. Srull (Eds.), *Handbook of social cognition* (Vol. 2, pp. 1-68). Hillsdale, NJ: Lawrence Erlbaum Associates.

Heider, F. (1958). *The psychology of interpersonal relations*. New York: Wiley.

Hewstone, M., & Brown, R. (Eds.). (1986). *Contact and conflict in intergroup encounters*. New York: Basil Blackwell.

Homans, G. C. (1950). *The human group*. New York: Harcourt.

Jones, E. E., & Davis, K. E. (1965). From acts to dispositions: The attribution process in person perception. In L. Berkowitz (Ed.), *Advances in experimental social psychology* (Vol. 2, pp. 219-266). New York: Academic Press.

Kelley, H. H. (1967). Attribution theory in social psychology. In D. Levine (Ed.), *Nebraska symposium on motivation* (Vol. 15, pp. 192-238). Lincoln, NE: University of Nebraska Press.

Krech, D., & Crutchfield, R. S. (1948). *Theory and problems of social psychology*. New York: McGraw-Hill.

Levine, J. M., & Moreland, R. L. (1990). Progress in small group research. *Annual Review of Psychology, 41*, 585-634.

Lewin, K. (1935). *A dynamic theory of personality*. New York: McGraw-Hill.

Lewin, K. (1948). *Resolving social conflicts*. New York: Harper.

Lewin, K. (1951). *Field theory in social science*. New York: Harper.

Lewin, K., Lippitt, R., & White, R. (1939). Patterns of aggressive behavior in experimentally created "social climates." *Journal of Social Psychology, 10*, 271-299.

McDougall, W. (1920). *The group mind* (2nd ed,), New York: G. P. Putnam's Sons.

McGrath, T. E. (1984). *Groups: Interaction and performance*. Englewood Cliffs, NJ: Prentice-Hall.

Merton, R. K. (1957). *Social theory and social structure* (rev. ed.). Glencoe, IL: The Free Press.

Moreland, R. L., Hogg, M. A., & Hains, S. C. (1994). Back to the future: Social psychological research on groups. *Journal of Experimental Social Psychology, 30*, 527-555.

Morris, W. (Ed.). (1976). *The American heritage dictionary of the English language*. Boston: Houghton Mifflin.

Newcomb, T. M. (1963). Social psychological theory: Integrating individual and social approaches. In E. P. Hollander & R. G. Hunt (Eds.), *Current perspectives in social psychology* (pp. 7-20). New York: Oxford University Press.

Oakes, P. J., Haslam, S. A., & Turner, J. C. (1994). *Stereotyping and social reality*. Oxford: Basil Blackwell.

Shaw, M. E. (1981). *Group dynamics: The psychology of small group behavior* (3rd ed.). New York: McGraw-Hill.

Sherif, M. (1966). *Group conflict and co-operation: Their social psychology*. London: Routledge & Kegan Paul.

Steiner, I. D. (1972). *Group process and productivity*. New York: Academic Press.

Steiner, I. D. (1974). Whatever happened to the group in social psychology? *Journal of Experimental Social Psychology, 10*, 94-108.

Steiner, I. D. (1986). Paradigms and groups. In L. Berkowitz (Ed.), *Advances in experimental social psychology* (Vol. 19, pp.251-289). San Diego, CA: Academic Press.

Tajfel, H. (1969). Cognitive aspects of prejudice. *Journal of Social Issues, 25*, 79-97.

Tajfel, H. (1978). *Differentiation between social groups: Studies in the social psychology of intergroup relations*. New York: Academic Press.

Tajfel, H., & Turner, J. C. (1979). An integrative theory of intergroup conflict. In W. G. Austin & S. Worchel (Eds.), *The social psychology of intergroup relations*. Monterey, CA: Brooks/Cole.

Thibaut, J. W., & Kelley, H. H. (1959). *The social psychology of groups*. New York: Wiley.

Turner, J. C., Hogg, M. A., Oakes, P. J., Reicher, S. D., & Wetherell, M. S. (1987). *Rediscovering the social group: A self-categorization theory*. Oxford: Basil Blackwell.

Wilder, D. A. (1978). Perceiving persons as a group: Effects on attributions of causality and beliefs. *Social Psychology, 1*, 13–23.

Wilder, D. A. (1984). Intergroup contact: The typical member and the exception to the rule. *Journal of Experimental Social Psychology, 20*, 177–194.

Wilder, D. A. (1986). Social categorization: Implications for creation and reduction of intergroup bias. In L. Berkowitz (Ed.), *Advances in experimental social psychology* (Vol. 19, pp. 291–355). San Diego, CA: Academic Press.

Wilder, D. A. (1993). The role of anxiety in facilitating stereotypic judgments of out-group behavior. In D. Mackie & D. Hamilton (Eds.), *Affect, cognition, and stereotyping: Interactive processes in group perception* (pp. 87–109). San Diego, CA: Academic Press.

Wilder, D. A., & Simon, A. F. (1996). Incidental and integral affect as triggers of stereotyping. In R. M. Sorrentino & E. T. Higgins (Eds.), *Handbook of motivation and cognition* (Vol. 3, pp. 397–422). New York: Guilford.

Wilder, D. A., & Simon, A. F. (1997). *Groups as categories and dynamic entities: Initial research*. Manuscript in preparation.

Wilder, D. A., Simon, A. F., & Faith, M. (1996). Enhancing the impact of counterstereotypic information: Dispositional attributions for deviance. *Journal of Personality and Social Psychology, 71*, 276–287.

Wittgenstein, L. (1922). *Tractatus logico-philosophicus*.

Worchel, S., & Austin, W. G. (Eds.). (1986). *The social psychology of intergroup relations* (2nd ed.). Monterey, CA: Brooks/Cole.

Zander, A. (1979). The study of group behavior during four decades. *Journal of Applied Behavioral Science, 30*, 272–282.

II

Interindividual Versus Intergroup Cognition and Behavior

3

Perceiving Social Groups: The Importance of the Entitativity Continuum

David L. Hamilton
University of California, Santa Barbara

Steven J. Sherman
Indiana University

Brian Lickel
University of California, Santa Barbara

In our everyday lives, we encounter people all the time and in all kinds of situations. We are continuously perceiving and interacting with others. Even when we are alone, we spend much of our time thinking about others. We also regularly encounter groups of people in all kinds of social settings. We talk about, worry about, joke about, and anticipate being with these groups. We sometimes value them, we sometimes hate them. Sometimes we see individuals as individuals, sometimes we see them as group members. What leads us to perceive "groupness" in a collection of individuals? Certainly we do not see every aggregate of individuals as a meaningful group; we rarely think of the collection of persons waiting to board an airplane as possessing the quality of "groupness." Yet we do think of people as belonging to a group under a remarkable variety of circumstances.

This chapter is concerned with these issues. It begins by presenting a theoretical analysis of the similarities and differences in the way perceivers form impressions of individuals and of groups, and it briefly summarizes the evidence pertinent to the issues raised in that analysis. The discussion then focuses specifically on the perception of groups, examining some implications of our analysis for questions of when and how we perceive collections of persons to be groups. In doing so, this chapter also considers the relationship between the *perception* of groupness by observers and the *definition* of groupness by social scientists.

IMPRESSIONS OF INDIVIDUALS AND
GROUPS: A PROCESS COMPARISON

A Theoretical Analysis

Perceiving, understanding, and knowing others involves the perceiver in active processing and use of information. When we meet an individual, we immediately begin the process of forming an impression of that person (Asch, 1946). Similarly, perhaps, when we see a gathering of people, and we immediately begin to evolve a conception of what that group is like. Or do we?

Although at first glance these may seem to be fairly commonplace observations, a little thought on these matters quickly leads to a number of puzzling questions, the answers to which are not immediately obvious. Do we always develop conceptions of the individuals and groups of people that we encounter? Are we just as likely to develop a conception of a group as we are to form an impression of an individual? When we do, are the same psychological processes involved in forming those individual and group impressions?

In a recent article (Hamilton & Sherman, 1996), we examined how perceivers process information about group members and how conceptions of groups are formed from that information. In doing so, we analyzed the similarities and differences in the way perceivers develop conceptions of groups and impressions of individuals. We developed a set of principles that summarize the way impressions of individuals are formed, and we then evaluated the evidence regarding the development of conceptions of groups in light of those principles. Because the present chapter grows out of this analysis, we begin by briefly summarizing our development of these points.

Our analysis of the impression formation process was organized around a "fundamental postulate" that we proposed as underlying this entire process: "The perceiver assumes unity in the personalities of others. Persons are seen as coherent entities." Given this assumption, the perceiver's task in forming an impression of a person becomes that of comprehending and understanding the basic themes that comprise the person's individuality.

From that fundamental postulate, we derived several important principles specifying processes that characterize the impression formation process. These include the following: (a) From the information acquired, the perceiver spontaneously makes inferences about the dispositions that characterize the person's personality, (b) the perceiver assumes that the person will manifest consistency across time and situations, (c) the information acquired about the person is used to develop an organized impres-

sion of the person, and (d) the perceiver strives to resolve any inconsistencies in the information acquired about the person. Despite being presented
as sweeping generalizations, these principles provide a viable overview of
what is known about the impression formation process. In fact, there at
least some evidence in the impression formation literature to support each
of these principles (cf. Hamilton & Sherman, 1996).

Having presented this postulate and set of principles, we then analyzed
whether the same principles apply when perceivers develop conceptions of
groups from information they acquire about group members. Our analysis
was based on a "fundamental assumption" that perceivers do not expect the
same degree of unity and coherence in a group that they do in an individual
person. If this assumption is correct, and if all of the processes summarized
in the four principles presented earlier derive from that expectation of unity
and coherence, then it follows that the process of developing group
conceptions should be characterized by those processes to a lesser degree
than is evidenced in forming impressions of individuals.

Between-Target Differences

The heart of our analysis, then, was to examine the evidence relevant to this
comparison of how individual and group impressions are formed. This
section briefly highlights some of this evidence (for a more thorough review,
see Hamilton & Sherman, 1996).

Principle 1: Spontaneous Inferences/On-Line Processing.   When perceiving an individual, the perceiver attempts to understand the dispositions
of the person. Inferences about a person's characteristics are made spontaneously and judgments are made on-line as information about the person is
processed (Carlston & Skowronski, 1994; Hastie & Park, 1986; Uleman,
1987). In contrast, because perceivers do not expect the same degree of
coherence in groups, they are less likely to form impressions on-line.
Instead, judgments about the characteristics of groups are more likely to be
memory-based, made only when directly called for and based on whatever
events the perceiver can access from memory. Evidence from our research
supports this difference in processing for individuals and groups (McConnell, Sherman, & Hamilton, 1994, 1997; Sanbonmatsu, Sherman, & Hamilton, 1987; Susskind, Maurer, Thakkar, Sherman, & Hamilton, 1994).
Compared with individual targets, strong impressions of groups are less
likely to form spontaneously as the information is processed.

Principle 2: Expectations of Consistency.   Perceivers expect consistency in target persons. They expect the personality of an individual to

remain consistent across time and situation. However, if perceivers expect less unity and coherence in group targets, then they should be less inclined to expect consistency in the behaviors of group members. Although few studies have examined this issue, recent results support this proposition (Park, DeKay, & Kraus, 1994; Weisz & Jones, 1993).

Principle 3: Organization of Impressions. The assumption that perceivers spontaneously organize information about the target person was at the core of Asch's (1946) view of impression formation. Research on person memory has shown that perceivers organize person information according to trait themes, evaluative implications, or perceived goals (Hamilton, Driscoll, & Worth, 1989; Hamilton, Katz, & Leirer, 1980; Hoffman, Mischel, & Mazze, 1981; Srull & Wyer, 1989). Consistent with our analysis of between-target differences, Wyer, Bodenhausen, and Srull (1984) found that perceivers integrate items of information into an organized representation to a greater extent for an individual target than for a group target (particularly for behaviors that were evaluatively relevant to subjects' prior impression-based expectancies about the target).

Principle 4: Processing Inconsistent Information. Our proposal that perceivers assume more coherence in the behavior and dispositions of individuals than of groups has important implications for how people deal with behavior that does not fit easily into an impression of an individual or group target. Research on person memory has shown that, when confronted with an inconsistency in a person's behavior, perceivers (a) spend more time processing the incongruent behavior compared with expectancy-congruent behavior, (b) generate causal explanations for the incongruent behavior, and (c) exhibit better memory for incongruent than congruent behaviors. Consistent with our analysis, research has shown that each of these effects is less likely to occur for a group target than for an individual target. First, Stern, Marrs, Millar, and Cole (1984) found that when the target was an individual, participants spent longer reading incongruent than congruent behaviors. However, when each statement referred to a different member of an unidentified group, this difference in processing time for congruent and incongruent behaviors disappeared. Second, Hastie (1984) showed that when the target was an individual, perceivers spontaneously generated causal explanations for incongruent behaviors to a greater degree than they did for congruent behaviors. Susskind et al. (1997) replicated this finding when the target was an individual, but found that when the behaviors referred to members of a group, the tendency to generate causal explanations for incongruent behavior was no longer evident. Thus, expectancy-incongruent information triggers attributional thinking for individual targets, but not for group targets. Finally, a number of studies have found that perceivers show heightened recall of expectancy-incongruent behavior when it pertains to an individual target, whereas this effect is strongly attenuated when the target is a group (Srull, 1981; Srull, Lichtenstein, & Rothbart, 1985; Stern et al., 1984).

In summary, the research summarized by Hamilton and Sherman (1996) provides considerable evidence for the contention that the same information is processed differently as a function of whether it describes an individual or members of a group. These differences follow from and support our fundamental assumption that perceivers hold differing expectancies about the degree of unity and coherence that typically characterize individual and group targets.

Within-Target Variations

Beyond these between-target differences, we can also consider variation within a type of target (individual or group) in the extent to which these processes are engaged. In our theoretical perspective, this variation derives from the same foundation on which those between-target differences were based: expectations of unity and coherence in the target. Thus, in addition to the difference in "default" expectancies about individual and group targets noted earlier, perceivers may also differentiate among (individual or group) targets about whom they hold differing expectations of unity, organization, and consistency. Thus, for example, we expect more internal structure and behavioral consistency from the leader of an important organization than we do from a person diagnosed as borderline manic-depressive. Similarly, a well-trained military unit is a more tightly organized, cohesive group than is a once-a-month book club.

Campbell (1958) introduced the term *entitativity* to refer to the degree to which a group is perceived as having this property of "groupness," of being an entity, and he specifically noted that groups vary in the extent to which they are seen as possessing entitativity. Thus, this concept becomes of central importance for our analysis, in that variation in perceived entitativity will thereby determine the extent to which impression formation processes become significantly engaged as information about group members is acquired and used.

We have investigated whether perceptions of the entitativity of a group of people influence the way in which information about group members is processed, organized, and used in forming impressions of that group (McConnell et al., 1997). In these experiments, entitativity of group targets was manipulated through instructions that generated differing expectations about the degree of consistency and similarity that existed among the various group members. When perceivers expected high entitativity, they engaged in on-line impression formation, attempting to arrive at an integrated impression of the group as the information about its members was being presented (as reflected in several dependent measures, including both memory and judgment data). However, when the group target was presented in a way that suggested low entitativity, perceivers did not form integrated impressions and produced results more typical for group targets, as described in the preceding section. Similarly, McConnell et al. (1997) manipulated expectancies about the consistency of an individual target's behaviors. When expectancies of consistency were strong, subjects formed clear and integrated impressions, typical of the findings described for individual targets in the preceding section. However, when expectancies for an individual's consistency were low, a different pattern of results was obtained. In fact, by undermining perceivers' default expectancies of consistency in an individual target, we produced results that more strongly resembled findings typically obtained for group targets (as described previously).

In summary, the concept of entitativity can apply to both individual and group targets; for each type of target, perceived entitativity can influence the way in which impressions of that target are formed (see also McConnell et al., 1994). As documented in our between-target analysis, perceivers expect greater unity or entitativity in individual compared with group targets, and this creates general processing differences for the two types of targets. As these within-target variations indicate, differences in perceivers' expectations about individuals or groups can produce parallel differences in information processing and impression formation.

Hamilton and Sherman's (1996) analysis compared the processing of information in forming impressions of individual and group targets. The remainder of this chapter focuses on groups as targets of social perception. It considers in more detail the variation among groups in the extent to which they are perceived as having entitativity, as possessing "groupness," and examines the variables that contribute to the perception of entitativity. The chapter then discusses the ways that theorists and researchers studying groups have defined what a *group* is, and what elements contribute to a group being a group. Finaly, the chapter considers the extent to which social perceivers rely on those same cues and information about groups in their perceptions of group entitativity.

COMPLEXITIES IN UNDERSTANDING
PERCEIVED ENTITATIVITY

The concept of entitativity and the variation among groups in the extent to which they are perceived as possessing this attribute are at the core of our analysis. Therefore, we introduce the concept of an *Entitativity Continuum* along which groups are perceived as varying. The Entitativity Continuum is of central importance because the perception of a group's position along that continuum will determine the nature of the information processing that transpires as the observer acquires, processes, and uses information about the group and its members.

A useful way to appreciate the variation of groups along the Entitativity Continuum is by introducing several well-chosen examples of collections of people. Consider the extent to which each one qualifies as a group, and why (or why not):

1. An urban street gang is a relatively small and tightly knit group. The members of the group share a number of features (age, locale, socioeconomic status [SES], ethnic background, etc.), they all know each other well, and they have extensive interaction with each other. Continued membership in the group assumes a high degree of commitment, and leaving the group is difficult and can be dangerous.

2. The thousands of members of the Democratic Party are bound together by certain ill-defined ideological principles that are of varying significance to its members. They are heterogeneous on virtually every imaginable attribute, and most have never met each other. Degree of commitment and length of group membership vary considerably among the members, and leaving the group is a matter of personal choice with little consequence. Still, some members devote most of their lives to the welfare of the group.

3. The Philadelphia Phillies baseball team consists of a limited number of group members who share a variety of attributes (gender, approximate age, athletic ability, etc.) and spend at least part of the year in intense collaborative effort. Most members have had a brief history of association with the group. Although momentary involvement in the group may be quite strong, one's allegiance can easily be shifted to another team (a current outgroup) with virtually no consequence, and this can occur as result of either personal choice (free agency) or action by the group power structure (trade).

4. Americans of Polish descent have in common one defining characteristic of national ancestry. Many members of this group also share cultural similarities that derive from that heritage, although many others do not. Some identify quite strongly with that heritage, feeling strong bonds with relatives in "the old country," including some whom they have never met (and never will); others do not. Although such identification may vary considerably among group members, changing this group membership is not possible.

5. Consider a task force of engineers working together to develop a new computer system for improved airplane guidance and tracking—a project that is of considerable financial importance to the contract research company by whom they are employed. There is an appointed leader of the task force, and different individual members (or subsets of members) are responsible for developing different aspects of the overall plan. The members of the task force have been working together on this project for several months. They therefore know each other very well, and they respect each other's unique contributions to the combined effort. Each of them also realizes that failure to win the contract for this project may ultimately lead to layoffs for some (perhaps even most) members of the group.

6. Imagine the following scene. It's a hot summer day in a city in the American South in 1955. In the lobby of the city hall, there are two lines of persons waiting their turn for a drink at water fountains. One line is longer than the other. The lines move relatively quickly, so no one is in line for very long. Within either line, no one knows more than 1–2 other persons. Having quenched their thirst, people go their respective ways. A sign over one water fountain says "Colored" and a sign over the other fountain says "Whites Only."

All of these scenarios portray collectives of persons that, to most observers, would be considered to be groups. They obviously vary in a number of properties, a point to which we return later. First, however, consider two other scenarios that have many elements in common with the features portrayed in the preceding examples, but that describe aggregates of persons that, to most observers, would not qualify as meaningful groups.

7. A man enters his local bank and notices that two lines of people have formed, each waiting to be served. One line, the longer one, consists of people waiting to make deposits or withdrawals. The second, shorter line consists of people waiting to gain access to their safe deposit boxes. Fortunately for the customers, both lines move fairly quickly, so no one has to stand in line for very long. Within each line, few if any people know each other. Having completed their business, the people go their respective ways.

8. In a nearly full movie theater, someone notices smoke coming from behind the screen. Suddenly it is very important for everyone to leave the theater. Quickly but calmly, this large gathering of strangers moves toward the exits in an orderly, almost coordinated fashion, everyone having the same goal in mind. A few individuals spontaneously take charge, guiding people toward the appropriate exits. Fortunately, everyone manages to get outside without panic or personal injury.

These examples describe very different types of social settings involving collectives of people. With the exception of the last two examples, these collectives would be considered by most observers to be *groups* in some sense of that term. Yet these capsules describe groups that are characterized and held together by very different properties. As the last two examples illustrate, not all collections of persons are perceived to be meaningful groups. We shall see, however, that it can be difficult to specify the properties that differentiate these collectivities from others in whom we more readily perceive an element of groupness.

BASES OF PERCEIVED ENTITATIVITY

Although the question of what constitutes "groupness" seems fundamental to understanding intergroup perceptions, we know relatively little about the conditions that foster perceptions of groupness. A number of candidates have, however, been proposed. In discussing them, we refer to the scenarios we created earlier in considering the extent to which each property is useful in identifying conditions that contribute to the perception of entitativity.

Perceived Entitativity Based on Group Features

Campbell (1958) sought to address the question of when an aggregate of individuals is perceived as a group. His approach was to apply principles of perceptual organization, derived from research on object perception, to understanding how group entitativity is perceived. That is, Campbell argued, several cues are used by the visual system to identify when several stimulus elements are part of the same physical entity; he suggested that social perceivers may use the same types of cues in their perceptions of human "elements" that sometimes, but not always, are members of a social entity. The three primary cues he suggested follow.

Proximity. In perceptions of the physical world, elements that exist in close proximity to each other are likely to be seen as parts of the same object or organization. Similarly, a collection of individuals may be more likely to be seen as a group when those persons are physically proximal to each other. For example, proximity may contribute to perceiving entitativity in the urban street gang, the Phillies, the project task force, and the racial groups in line at water fountains. However, to the extent that members of the Democratic Party or Polish Americans are perceived as a group, such perceptions would not be based on proximity, indicating that proximity is not a necessary precondition. Moreover, the examples of the lines at the bank and the people exiting the movie theater, both of which include physical proximity, indicate that proximity is not a sufficient condition for perceiving groupness either.

Similarity.   Physical stimuli that are similar to each other are more likely to be perceived as part of the same entity. In the same vein, it seems plausible that perceived similarity may enhance the likelihood that persons will be perceived as comprising a group. In fact, virtually all of the groups described in our scenarios are characterized by some form of similarity among members. However, the bases of similarity vary widely in these examples, including race (water fountain lines), age (street gang, Phillies), national heritage (Polish Americans), education (engineers), abilities (Phillies), and beliefs (Democrats, at least in theory). Other appearance cues — the Phillies' uniforms, identifying dress codes of gang members — may also enhance the perception of similarity, and thereby contribute to perceived entitativity. However, similarity does not guarantee perceived groupness. If everyone in line at the bank happened to be male, would they then be perceived as a group? It seems unlikely.

Common Fate.   Physical elements that are seen as moving together in the same direction are perceived as members of the same physical entity. Similarly, it may be that persons whose activities are oriented toward the same end, and who therefore share a common fate, will be more likely to be perceived as a group. This feature is most apparent in the example of the task force of engineers whose plan may or may not be approved; but it is also relevant to sports teams (Phillies), and gang members, and is starkly revealed in discriminatory practices (different water fountains for African Americans and Whites). However, the people who had to quickly exit the movie theater because of fire shared, at least temporarily, a common fate as well. Again, common fate is neither sufficient to nor necessary for the perception of entitativity.

In addition to proximity, similarity, and common fate, Campbell (1958) suggested other possible cues to group entitativity, again drawing on principles of perceptual organization. These included goodness of form and "resistance to intrusion," which may have counterparts in social perception as organization among members and permeability of group boundaries. In our illustrative scenarios, some of the groups are highly organized (the project task force, the Phillies), whereas others clearly are not (Polish Americans, Democrats). Similarly, some groups can be joined or left with relative ease (Democrats), some only with difficulty or risk (street gangs, task force members), and in some cases such changes are virtually impossible (groups based on racial or national descent).

Campbell's analysis is highly original and intriguing. It suggests a number of possible perceptual cues that the social perceiver may use in inferring that an aggregate of individual persons possesses the quality of entitativity—that they comprise a social group. Nevertheless, none of these features is perfectly correlated with entitativity.

Perceived Entitativity Based on Natural Kind Status

Labels for social groups often have important effects on impressions of, reaction to, and behavior toward those groups. Rothbart and Taylor (1992) wondered why our labels for social categories possess such power, and they noted that group labels vary greatly in the strength of these effects. They accounted for these differences in terms of the distinction between natural kinds and artifacts. The concepts of "natural kinds" and "artifacts" were introduced as a way of making an important distinction among category types (Gelman, 1988; Keil, 1989). Natural kinds are objects that exist in the world independently of the behavior and beliefs of humans (e.g., giraffes, calcium). Artifacts are categories of things that reflect the operation of human needs, wishes, and constructions (e.g., chairs, umbrellas). Natural kinds are perceived as possessing underlying essences that serve to make the category unique and distinctive. In contrast, artifacts are seen as sharing only superficial and function-related properties.

Although the distinction between natural kinds and artifacts was developed to apply to nonsocial categories, Rothbart and Taylor (1992) applied this distinction to social categories, arguing that different social groups are viewed as natural kinds to a greater or lesser extent. Just as we argued that social groups differ in the degree to which they are seen as possessing entitativity, Rothbart and Taylor proposed that there is a continuum of "natural kindness" along which social groups are seen to vary. Just as the perception of the degree of entitativity of a group is important for processing information about and developing impressions of that group (Hamilton & Sherman, 1996), so too is the extent to which a group is perceived as a natural kind important in terms of the way we think about and represent that group and its members.

Rothbart and Taylor (1992) identified two dimensions that are most relevant to the perception of groups as natural kinds: inductive potential and unalterability. *Inductive potential* refers to the fact that membership in a natural kind category allows for inferences about a wide variety of attributes and qualities. Some social categories (e.g., race, occupation) are perceived as high in inductive potential, and thus allow for the prediction of diverse and important knowledge about group members. Other social categories (e.g., literature preferences, first name) have little inductive potential. *Unalterability* refers to the ease or difficulty of changing one's category status. Gender and race are highly unalterable, whereas one's political affiliation or hobby is easily changeable. Unalterability is similar to Campbell's (1958) conception of the impenetrability of group boundaries, which he cited as a possible indicator of entitativity.

Which social categories are most likely to be perceived as having natural kind status? According to Rothbart and Taylor, the answer is categories that are judged as high in both inductive potential and unalterability. They proposed that similarity in surface characteristics (e.g., physical appearance) is the most important element for perceptions of both high inductive potential and high unalterability. Physical similarity is used as an indication that group membership has rich inductive potential, and that the group has some essence or core quality. In addition, groups bound together by physical similarity give the suggestion that group membership is highly unalterable. Rothbart and Taylor (1992) suggested that race and gender are the social groupings that have the highest degree of natural kind status, and therefore are the groups most strongly perceived as having core properties or essences—the properties that give these groups meaning and identity. The importance of race and gender in the stereotyping and prejudice literature attests to the perception of these social categories as natural kinds.

In some respects, the concept of natural kindness is similar to our concept of entitativity. The perceiver's belief in a fundamental essence for a social group and a belief in an underlying coherence, consistency, and unity for the attributes of the group members resemble our conception of entitativity. Just as inductive potential is one of the important dimensions of a social category that is relevant to its perception as a natural kind, inductive potential would seem to be a key aspect of entitativity. When group membership is indicative of many traits, abilities, beliefs, and goals, it seems likely that perceived entitativity is high. However, which of these is cause and which is effect is not so clear. Rothbart and Taylor maintained that it is the perception of high inductive potential that leads to the judgment of natural kind status. We too would see the perception of inductive potential as a factor leading to the perceived entitativity of a group. However, we would also maintain that the perception of high entitativity for a group (however that perception is arrived at) will increase the degree of inductive potential regarding inferences about group members.

Rothbart and Taylor's second dimension for the judgment of natural kind status is unalterability. However, we do not regard perceived unalterability as a crucial precursor to the perception of entitativity in a social group. Membership in a fraternity or the Philadelphia Phillies is easily alterable, yet these two groups are quite high in entitativity; they are perhaps higher than social groupings such as gender or nationality, which are characterized by unalterability, but where perceptions of unity and coherence are limited by the size and diversity of the membership.

Finally, Rothbart and Taylor (1992) have argued that groups that are seen as natural kinds will be perceived as relatively homogeneous. However, we (Hamilton & Sherman, 1996) have argued that entitativity and perceived homogeneity are not necessarily related. Outgroups are generally perceived as more homogeneous than are ingroups (the outgroup homogeneity effect), and yet the groups to which we belong and with which we identify (our ingroups) are more likely to be seen as possessing a high degree of entitativity—as having an identity and cohesiveness. As we noted in the preceding subsection, perceptions of similarity or homogeneity are but one element that can contribute to the perception of group entitativity. The group's history, the shared goals of its members, and their interdependence seem likely to play much stronger roles in perceived entitativity than is the extent to which a group is perceived as a natural kind.

Perceived Entitativity Based on Group Size

Mullen (1991) has argued that the relative size of a group can fundamentally influence the way the group is perceived. Is it possible that group size is a key variable that influences the perception of entitativity? Mullen summarized evidence showing that, as the size of a group increases, (a) conformity and social loafing of group members increase, (b) perceived consensus of group members decreases, (c) ingroup bias decreases, and (d) perceived variability of the group decreases. Based on these findings, he concluded that group size is an important determinant of a wide array of effects.

Mullen (1991) explained these effects by proposing that the relative size of a group influences the group's salience to perceivers: As group size decreases, the group's salience increases. He argued that the differential salience of majority and minority groups influences the nature of representations that perceivers develop of these groups. Specifically, he proposed that perceivers develop prototype-based representations of minority groups and exemplar-based representations of majority groups. These representational differences then lead perceivers to process information about majority and minority groups in fundamentally different ways, adopting a simpler, more heuristic processing style when processing information about minority group members.

Although intrigued by Mullen's analyses, we have reservations about his conceptual framework as a means of understanding entitativity. First, although small groups may sometimes be more salient than large groups, this is not always the case. Even when it is, the salience due to differences in group size will not invariably influence perceptions of entitativity. For example, two of our scenarios described two lines of people of differing size. In the bank example, although one line of customers was larger than the other, this difference by itself would not lead observers to view either line as a group or to perceive them as differing in entitativity. Moreover, although the lines at the "Colored" and "White" drinking fountains are perceived as groups having entitativity, it seems unlikely that this perception is based on the fact that one group happens to be smaller than the other. It also seems possible that some effects that Mullen ascribes to salience based on group size instead reflect general expectancies about the nature of minority and majority groups. Brewer, Weber, and Carini (1995) held constant the number of majority and minority persons viewed by experimental participants, yet they found that knowledge of majority/minority status affected perceived entitativity. Thus, information pertaining to minority group members was processed differently, even when they were not themselves a salient minority.

Second, in contrast to the view that perceivers engage in simpler, more heuristic processing for minority group targets than for majority group targets, and that this difference relates to perceived entitativity, the evidence we have reviewed (Hamilton & Sherman, 1996) suggests that perceivers do *not* process information about highly entitative targets (persons or groups) in a simple and heuristic fashion. Rather, perceivers seem to process information more extensively and attend to inconsistencies in behavior to a greater extent for such targets. Therefore, if minority groups did have higher entitativity than majority groups, we would argue that perceivers process information regarding minority groups in a less, not more, heuristic fashion.

Given these considerations, we question the degree to which group size, in and of itself, drives perceivers' perceptions of entitativity. Group size may be correlated with entitativity, but it is undoubtedly correlated with other important variables as well. For example, members of small groups probably have more interpersonal interaction with each other and are more interdependent than are members of large groups. It is variables such as these, not group size per se, that are likely to influence the perception of entitativity.

Functional Bases of Perceived Entitativity

In each of the preceding discussions of bases of perceived entitativity, the analysis has focused on properties of the group being perceived — whether they be perceptual cues, structural properties, or the identification of a group as reflecting a "natural kind" category. In all of these cases, the perception of entitativity is driven by properties of the group — by stimulus features that are "out there" (or at least believed to be out there). As such, perceptions of entitativity should be stable across both time and perceivers. That is, the perceived entitativity of a group should not fluctuate dramatically, and there should be some reasonable level of consensus among observers about a group's entitativity. In a word, from these perspectives, perceived entitativity is driven by group-based properties.

In contrast to these approaches, Brewer and Harasty (1996) highlighted the role of perceiver variables in group perception, including individual differences as well as transitory motivational and contextual determinants. Perceiving a group as a group can, then, be influenced by the perceiver's currently activated expectancies and affective states, and may be beneficial to meeting the perceiver's needs and goals. Because of this emphasis, we refer to this approach as a *functional* perspective on the bases of perceived entitativity.

Brewer and Harasty (1996) discussed a variety of factors that might influence the perception of groupness. For example, the ease or difficulty of the information-processing task faced by perceivers can influence the way information about group members is organized and stored in memory, and can thereby influence perceptions of the group as a whole (Rothbart, Fulero, Jensen, Howard, & Birrell, 1978). Similarly, the perceiver's processing goals can influence the way information about group members is encoded and represented in memory, including the extent to which group members are represented as a unit and the extent of consistency perceived among group members (Park, DeKay, & Kraus, 1994; Seta & Hayes, 1994). Information about ingroup and outgroup members may be represented in memory differently, not only as a function of properties of the information acquired about group members (Park & Rothbart, 1982; Park, Ryan, & Judd, 1992), but also as a function of the relationship between the groups (Brewer, Weber, & Carini, 1995) and the perceiver's motives and goals (Simon, 1993). Finally, there may be individual differences among perceivers in their proclivity to see coherence and structure in groups.

It seems to us that Brewer and Harasty's (1996) approach to the perceived entitativity of groups represents a nice parallel to Brewer's (1991) optimal distinctiveness theory. That theory emphasized the importance of conflicting needs for inclusion and differentiation in determining ingroup identification, and argued that social identity represents a reconciliation of these two needs. The relative importance of these two needs can enhance or diminish an individual's need to feel part of a meaningful ingroup. Parallel concerns may influence the perception of groupness in others. Just as an individual might focus on a need for belonging or a need for distinctiveness at different times, so too might one, at different times, focus on the coherence, structure, and unity of a group versus the lack of similarity and consistency among its members. In fact, to the extent that one's functional focus is more on the need for inclusion, one is more likely to perceive an ingroup as high in entitativity. However, at different times, when one's focus is on the need for uniqueness, that same ingroup might be perceived as rather low in entitativity. Thus, both of these approaches to the perception of groups emphasize the motivations that increase or decrease the amount of groupness that is perceived in a collection of people.

PERCEIVED ENTITATIVITY: A THEORETICAL PERSPECTIVE

Earlier we presented descriptions of several social collectivities that most people would consider *groups,* at least in some sense of that word: Few would doubt that street gangs, political parties, baseball teams, work groups, and people sharing racial, national, religious, and other forms of ethnic heritage are commonly perceived as meaningful groups. Equally obvious is the fact that there are many circumstances when perceivers see aggregates of persons without thinking of them as a group. What is it that binds certain of these collectives together such that we endow them with the quality of being a group? Given that we perceive an aggregate of persons to constitute a group, *how much* entitativity do we see the group as having, and why? How do we determine where any given group falls along the Entitativity Continuum?

In reviewing possible conceptual frameworks for thinking about these questions, we were struck by the variety of properties and concepts that seem relevant to an analysis of possible bases of perceived entitativity: the size of the group; its history and longevity; the permeability of its boundaries; its potential as a "natural kind" category; the similarity, proximity, interdependence, familiarity, and common fate of the group's members; and so on. All of them seem to be factors that plausibly would influence the perception of entitativity in groups, and indeed we submit that all of them contribute to that perception. But which among them are more important, and which are less influential?

Answering these questions is difficult for (at least) two reasons. First, the necessary empirical work has not yet been done, so any answer at this point must be largely speculative. Second, although all of these variables may influence perceived entitativity, many of them undoubtedly are intercorrelated to a substantial degree across a range of actual groups. Members of small groups are more likely to be familiar with each other, have face-to-face interactions, and share physical proximity than are members of large groups. Ethnic groups often have rather impermeable boundaries, and their members are likely to have physical similarities, share history and heritage, and perhaps be subject to common fate. Given these relationships, efforts to tease apart the unique contribution of any given feature or property will be difficult. Moreover, as indicated in our earlier discussion, although these properties may contribute to the perception of entitativity, for most of them it is clear that they are neither necessary nor sufficient conditions for perceiving entitativity.

Nevertheless, we venture the opinion that there is one variable on which groups differ that is a primary clue to any given group's degree of entitativity. We propose that the most useful indicator of a group's position along the Entitativity Continuum is the extent to which it possesses organization and structure among its members. In particular, the presence of organization in a group clearly implies entitativity. Such organization may be reflected in several ways: a hierarchical structure within the group, a differentiation of roles and functions among its members, purposive integration of activity, and/or clear differentials in leadership, power, status, and responsibility. These properties may be manifested in different ways in different groups. For example, a military unit possesses these features explicitly, with relatively little tolerance for variation in or violation of the defined structure; in a family, these properties may be more implicit, with greater tolerance for improvisation, but they are typically present nevertheless (in fact, when they are not present, we often refer to a "dysfunctional" family—and perceive it as less entitative as a consequence). Our main point is that groups that manifest cues reflecting organization and structure will be perceived as entitative units.

Interestingly, Asch (1952) advanced a similar position some 45 years ago:

> We do not see a group of men merely according to proximity, distribution, or similarity of its members. A marching platoon is more than a visually perceived unit; it is an organization with psychological properties. . . . We grasp the coordination of [its members'] movements as a demonstration of group discipline, an ordering of their separate wills in subordination to a common purpose. We see the platoon as a strong or a threatening formation. The quality of power it reveals is a consequence of the knowledge of its purpose and of the manner in which it is held together. (p. 224)

In another example, Asch observed, "A picket line in front of a plant has a quality of unity that is a product of its organization" (p. 225). We can do no better than Asch's descriptions in conveying the important role of organization in the perception of entitativity.

The groups portrayed in the scenarios presented earlier reflect varying degrees of organization and, we submit, reflect comparable variation in perceived entitativity. At the high end of the Entitativity Continuum, the task force working on the computer system is a well-structured group, and the street gang has leaders and followers, established norms, and other characteristics of group structure and organization. Similarly, the Phillies have clear differentiation of roles among its members, and their success depends on their effectiveness in performing in an organized, coordinated fashion. All of these groups convey a clear sense of groupness, and hence lead to the perception of entitativity. The Democratic Party has a formal organizational structure that implies an entitative character, although it often functions in a manner that suggests an intermediate degree of organization (at best). Other groups convey this characteristic to lesser degrees. Despite their similarities in national heritage or race, neither the Polish Americans nor the racial groups in the water fountain lines have an organized nature, and hence do not possess entitativity to the same extent as the preceding examples. Finally, at the low end of the Entitativity Continuum are the aggregates of persons described in the bank lines and in the movie theater. These collectives possess an organized nature to a minimal (at best) extent, and hence are not seen as having entitativity—as being "real" groups. In summary, the extent to which groups possess organization and structure seems to define their positions on the Entitativity Continuum.

In characterizing the social perceiver, it may seem odd to suggest that racial, gender, or ethnic groups, about whom stereotypes are so widespread, are not perceived as highly entitative groups. Certainly they would be considered meaningful groups (in some sense) by most observers. Moreover, the history of intergroup relations is replete with examples wherein such groups have been identified and treated as singular groups—in which "they" all look alike and "they" are all treated (i.e., discriminated against) in the same way. In this light, it is important to emphasize that we are discussing groups that vary considerably along the Entitativity Continuum; our analysis suggests that large categories based on race, gender, national origin, and so on probably have an intermediate place along this continuum.

Although categories such as race and gender may not be extremely high in entitativity, these social categories have been identified as being high in "natural kindness," as discussed earlier (Rothbart & Taylor, 1992). That is, gender and race groups are perceived as having a core or essence, and these groups are high in inductive potential. Thus, members of one of these groups can be perceived as "all alike," and it is not surprising that stereotyping and prejudice are widespread with regard to racial, ethnic, and gender groups. However, just because all members of a grouping are perceived as sharing essential qualities and as similar in many important respects does not mean that a collection of these individuals will be highly entitative. The individuals comprising a group may be quite similar with regard to physical characteristics, personalities, and abilities, and yet a group of such individuals need not be cohesive, organized, structured, or interdependent. It is these qualities that, in our analysis, define and determine entitativity. Moreover, it is not clear that knowledge about race or gender groups becomes represented in memory in such an organized fashion, or that violations of expectancies typically lead to efforts to explain such inconsistencies among group members. Thus, we must distinguish between the perception of entitativity in groups and other seemingly related but distinct concepts, such as the perception of a group as a natural kind and the perception of homogeneity within a group (Hamilton & Sherman, 1996).

Does this focus on a group's organization mean that the other determinants of perceived entitativity that we discussed earlier are unimportant? Certainly not. All of these bases of perceived entitativity (i.e., similarity, appearance of a natural kind, salience due to minority status, etc.) contribute to the perception of unity and coherence among group members. Any group that possesses one of these features will be perceived as entitative to some degree, but in our view it will be perceived as more so if it also appears to be (or is expected to be) an organized group. However, a group that clearly has an organized and purposive manner need not have highly similar, proximal, or salient members to be perceived as having high entitativity. It is in this sense that we view perceived organization as having a differentially impactful role in evaluating a group's position along the Entitativity Continuum.

GROUPS AND THE PERCEPTION OF GROUPS

Groups and Categories

The preceding analysis of the perception of entitativity leads to another important observation. Our emphasis on the importance of a group's apparent organization and structure in the perception of its entitativity is consistent with theorizing by scholars concerned with understanding the nature of groups. In particular, the social psychological literature on groups has always had a somewhat narrower definition of *groups* than has the literature on perceptions of groups. Although a broad range of definitions of the term *group* has been offered (see Cartwright & Zander, 1968, pp. 46–48 for a sampling and discussion of such definitions), most authors include some mention of interdependence, organization, and/or role differentiation among the group's members.

The importance of these features of the definition of a group pertains to a distinction between groups, defined in this way, and the kinds of groups of interest to researchers who study intergroup perceptions, stereotyping, and the like. This distinction was clearly articulated in one of the early, and highly influential, textbooks on social psychology, Krech and Crutchfield's (1948) *Theory and Problems of Social Psychology,* where the authors stated that "A group does not merely mean individuals characterized by some similar property. Thus, for example, a collection of Republicans or farmers or Negroes or blind men is not a *group.* These collections may be called *classes* of people. The term *group,* on the other hand, refers to two or more people who bear an *explicit psychological relationship to one another"* (p. 18; italics in original). The same point was nicely illustrated by Lewin (1948) in the following passage:

> Similarity between persons merely permits their classification, their subsumption under the same abstract concept, whereas belonging to the same social group means concrete, dynamic interrelations among persons. A husband, a wife, and a baby are less similar to each other, in spite of their being a strong natural group, than the baby is to other babies, or the husband to other men, or the wife to other women. Strong and well-organized groups, far from being fully homogeneous, are bound to contain a variety of different sub-groups and individuals. It is not similarity or dissimilarity that decides whether two individuals belong to the same or different groups, but social interaction or other types of interdependence. A group is best defined as a dynamic whole based on interdependence rather than similarity. (p. 184)

This emphasis on the importance of organization, differentiation of roles, and pursuit of a common purpose as defining properties of a group continues in more contemporary definitions of groups among researchers in the group dynamics tradition (e.g., McGrath, 1984). Collections of persons that lack these properties, including people of the same gender or ethnicity, are viewed as classes or, in more contemporary terms, social categories.

In contrast to these perspectives on what constitutes a group is virtually any book, chapter, or article on the perception of groups, intergroup perception, or stereotyping. In this literature, those social categories — membership in which may be defined by nothing more than sharing a single feature, such as skin color, gender, or national heritage — are considered meaningful groups simply because they are so commonly perceived in everyday social life as meaningful groups. Perceivers have richly developed beliefs about such groups, and our language and everyday conversation are filled with references to them. In this view, then, women, Hungarians, African Americans, and gays all qualify as meaningful groups, despite the fact that many members of these groups will never even encounter each other.

Thus, the term *group* has two distinct meanings: one meaning that is

preferred by scholars, who seek to understand the properties and functioning of small, interactive groups, and another, much broader meaning
that is used by social perception researchers and that seems commonplace in
everyday parlance. At one level, the distinction seems to be a mere semantic
difference that social psychologists have lived with for decades. Aside from
occasional alcohol-induced, late-night ideological arguments at confer-
ences, it is not a distinction that arouses much passion. Everyone understands that when one researcher talks about group decision making and
another talks about a stereotype of a group, the term *group* is referring to
quite different entities in the two cases.

However, by considering the placement of these social entities along the
Entitativity Continuum, the present analysis offers a potentially unifying
framework for understanding these distinctions. Consistent with emphases
prevalent in the groups dynamics tradition, we view groups characterized by
organization, interdependence, and purposiveness as being distinctly high in
entitativity, and we believe that perceivers see them as such. From our
perspective, the perception that a group possesses this degree of entitativity
typically induces information-processing mechanisms that we earlier identified as being characteristic of forming impressions of individuals: on-line
inferences and evaluations, organized representation of information, surprise and attributional processing when a member's behavior clearly violates
expectations about the group, and so on (Hamilton & Sherman, 1996;
McConnell et al., 1994, 1997). These groups are perceived to be the
well-integrated (as well as differentiated) units that group dynamics researchers have always said they are.

What, then, about the large "social categories" that are the life-blood of
the intergroup perception researcher? We would argue that these "categories" of people are indeed groups, if for no other reason than they are
uniformly perceived as such by virtually everyone (the group dynamics
researcher being the lone possible exception). If they were not perceived as
meaningful entities, everything from wars between countries to debates
about affirmative action would be far less prevalent in our world and our
society. Thus, we view these groups as possessing moderate to high
entitativity, although not as high as the organized, interdependent groups
described earlier.

An Emerging Unification?

Our analysis based on the Entitativity Continuum has grown out of our
attempt to understand how perceivers detect "groupness" in their perceptions of social aggregates. Our proposed Entitativity Continuum stands in
contrast to the distinction between groups and nongroups, which has been

the focus of much discussion in the group dynamics literature. However, it happens that ideas paralleling our proposals can be found in the more recent writings of some group theorists in their analyses of the nature of and differences among social groups. Consider, for example, the following comments from Moreland (1987):

> An analysis of group formation raises several complex issues. One such issue involves the meaning of the term "group." In order to determine whether a group has formed, someone must be able to specify what a group is. Unfortunately, there is little agreement among social psychologists about the "essential" characteristics of small groups. . . . And it seems unlikely that anyone will produce a definitive listing of those characteristics anytime soon. Perhaps we should abandon these efforts to distinguish groups from non-groups and consider instead a hypothetical dimension of "groupness" that is relevant to every set of persons. Group formation could then be regarded as a *continuous* phenomenon involving the movement of a set of persons along that dimension, rather than as a *discontinuous* phenomenon involving the transformation of a nongroup into a group. (p. 81; italics in original)

Moreland's conception of a continuous dimension along which groups vary directly parallels our conception of an Entitativity Continuum along which groups are perceived. We believe that the correspondence between these two conceptualizations offers a hope for an emerging unification between research on the analysis of groups and research on the perception of groups. The benefits and limitations of such a unification cannot be fully anticipated at this point, but the prospect of such integration between research on group perception and group behavior justifies, in our view, efforts in this direction.

Earlier we discussed a variety of cues that the perceiver might use to infer the extent of a group's "groupness" or entitativity. We might think of the perceiver's task in terms of a Brunswikian lens model, as shown in Fig. 3.1. In the figure, X_1-X_5 represent variables that contribute to the groupness or entitativity of a group, and that also might serve as cues for inferring entitativity. P represents the observer's perception of entitativity based on those cues, and G represents the group's actual level of entitativity. The lines connecting the cues (X_i) with P represent the extent to which the perceiver uses these cues in inferring entitativity, and are called *cue utilization coefficients* (r_{cu}). The extent to which those variables are actually associated with groupness are *validity coefficients* (r_v). To the extent that perceivers' *use* of the available cues (cue utilization coefficients) matches their *usefulness* as valid indicators of groupness (validity coefficients), the perceivers' judgments of entitativity will be accurate (r_a).

As Moreland (1987) noted, there is no "definitive listing" of "essential

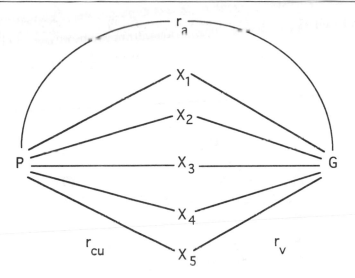

FIG. 3.1. The lens model.

characteristics" of groups. Nevertheless, various authors have provided lists of candidates. For example, in his textbook on group dynamics, Forsyth (1990) identified several characteristics that define groups, including interdependence among members, shared goals, interaction among members, relatively small size of group, cohesiveness, shared goals, and (of particular relevance to our analysis) group structure. It is interesting that these characteristics correspond quite closely to several of the features of social aggregates discussed earlier as possible cues to entitativity. The degree of correspondence between the characteristics perceivers use as cues to entitativity and the characteristics that actually define groupness is, at this juncture, unknown.

Such an analysis, of course, assumes that we have a suitable criterion measure of the extent to which any group is indeed a group. Unfortunately, group researchers have had difficulty agreeing on such a criterion. Consequently, research assessing the accuracy of perceivers' judgments of group formation has been scarce. In one of the few research programs attempting to investigate this question, Freeman (1992; Freeman & Webster, 1994) studied the interaction patterns of a number of individuals in particular settings over an extended time. These participants were then asked to make judgments about the extent of interaction among pairs of individuals and to sort individuals into groups. The findings of these studies suggest that (a) subjects' reports of interaction patterns (group formation) correspond at a reasonable level to the actual patterns of interaction that occurred among these persons, but that (b) subjects' judgment data reflect some degree of simplification and exaggeration of the observed interaction patterns. Freeman's research is quite useful as a first step toward developing the bridge between group behavior and group perception. Moreover, his findings are fascinating in their suggestion that observers are reasonably accurate while simultaneously manifesting some degree of bias in their mental representations of the groups they observe. Thus, there can be discrepancies between what a group is and how it is perceived.

CONCLUSION: ORGANIZATION, THE ENTITATIVITY CONTINUUM, AND THE PERCEPTION OF INDIVIDUALS AND GROUPS

Our theoretical analysis has generated two central propositions. First, building on previous conceptualizations (Campbell, 1958; Hamilton & Sherman, 1996), we postulated that groups are perceived as existing along an Entitativity Continuum. Second, we postulated that the most important element in the social perceiver's inference about the degree of a group's entitativity is the extent to which the group is an organized entity. A group is more "groupy" when the structural relations among its parts are clearly evident—when it has identifiable leaders, differentiation of roles and functions, established norms, and the like. As was developed earlier in this chapter (and more extensively in Hamilton & Sherman, 1996), the extent to which a group is perceived as being entitative has direct implications for a number of important principles of information processing that will guide the way information about the group and its members will be processed and utilized. Specifically, the perception of entitativity leads to spontaneous, on-line inferences and evaluations, organized representation of acquired information in memory, efforts toward resolution of inconsistencies, and expectations for consistency in the group's performance and the behaviors of its members. Thus, the perception of a group's entitativity has substantial ramifications for a number of aspects of group perception.

Our analysis goes beyond previous efforts to address these issues in postulating the central role of perceived group organization in determining perceptions of entitativity. In our view, the perception of a group as an organized unit is a primary basis for perceivers inferring that the group is indeed a meaningful group. In concluding this chapter, we draw attention to two benefits of this emphasis on perceived organization.

One benefit of the emphasis on the importance of perceiving a group as an organized entity brings us back to our original goal in examining the processes underlying perceptions of groups. As we discussed earlier, the purpose of Hamilton and Sherman's (1996) analysis was to compare the processes mediating perceptions of individuals and of groups—or more specifically, to examine the similarities and differences in how impressions of individuals and conceptions of groups are formed. Based on the extensive literature on forming impressions of individuals, we postulated that perceivers expect an individual to be an organized, coherent unit, and therefore seek to form an impression of the person that identifies and represents his or her primary characteristics in a coherent manner. We then hypothesized that social perceivers expect such coherence in groups to a lesser degree, and found in the literature numerous empirical findings consistent with this view. These observations led us to emphasize the importance of the Entitativity Continuum, which underlies perceptions of both individuals and groups. To the extent that groups are perceived as possessing, or are expected to possess, coherence and organization, they will be perceived as being high in entitativity, and the commonly observed differences in processing information about individual and group targets, based on a priori assumptions about target entitativity, will be diminished. In identifying perceived organization of the target as the primary element underlying this continuum, we have brought the analysis of group perception once again into line with the perception of individual targets, which rests heavily on the assumption that individuals' personalities are unified and organized.

The second benefit of our approach, developed in this chapter, extends this perspective to the interface between group perception and group behavior. In highlighting the importance of a group's organization and structure for the perception of that group, our analysis establishes ties to previous analyses in the group literature regarding the definition of *groupness*. In essence, we view the social perceiver as intuitively engaging in analyses that parallel those of the social scientist, who tries to understand what groups are and what their properties are. Social aggregates are viewed as varying along the Entitativity Continuum, and both the perceiver and the social scientist use information about their properties to understand their placement along that continuum. Given that the literatures on group perception and group process have remained somewhat distinct from each other, this potential bridge may offer some benefits for future analyses and rapprochement.

ACKNOWLEDGMENT

Preparation of this chapter was supported, in part, by NIMH Grant MH-40058. Brian Lickel was supported by a NSF Graduate Fellowship.

REFERENCES

Asch, S. E. (1946). Forming impressions of personality. *Journal of Abnormal and Social Psychology, 41*, 258–290.

Asch, S. E. (1952). *Social psychology.* New York: Oxford University Press.

Brewer, M. B. (1991). The social self: On being the same and different at the same time. *Personality and Social Psychology Bulletin, 17*, 475–482.

Brewer, M. B., & Harasty, A. S. (1996). Seeing groups as entities: The role of perceiver motivation. In R. Sorrentino & E. T. Higgins (Eds.), *Handbook of motivation and cognition Vol. 3: The interpersonal context* (pp. 347–370). New York: Guilford.

Brewer, M. B., Weber, J. G., & Carini, B. (1995). Person memory in intergroup contexts: Categorization versus individuation. *Journal of Personality and Social Psychology, 69*, 29–40.

Campbell, D. T. (1958). Common fate, simiiarity, and other indices of the status of aggregates of persons as social entities. *Behavioral Science, 3*, 14–25.

Carlston, D. E., & Skowronski, J. J. (1994). Savings in the relearning of trait information as evidence for spontaneous inference generation. *Journal of Personality and Social Psychology, 66*, 840–856.

Cartwright, D., & Zander, A. (1968). Groups and group membership: Introduction. In D. Cartwright & A. Zander (Eds.), *Group dynamics: Research and theory* (3rd ed., pp. 45–62). New York: Harper & Row.

Forsyth, D. R. (1990). *An introduction to group dynamics.* Pacific Grove, CA : Brooks/Cole.

Freeman, L. C. (1992). Filling in the blanks: A theory of cognitive categories and the structure of social affiliation. *Social Psychology Quarterly, 55*, 118–127.

Freeman, L. C., & Webster, C. M. (1994). Interpersonal proximity in social and cognitive space. *Social Cognition, 12*, 223–247.

Gelman, S. A. (1988). The development of induction within natural kind and artifact categories. *Cognitive Psychology, 20*, 65–95.

Hamilton, D. L., Driscoll, D. M., & Worth, L. T. (1989). Cognitive organization of impressions: Effects of incongruency in complex representations. *Journal of Personality and Social Psychology, 57*, 925–939.

Hamilton, D. L., Katz, L. B., & Leirer, V. O. (1980). Organizational processes in impression formation. In R. Hastie, T. M. Ostrom, E. B. Ebbesen, R. S. Wyer, Jr., D. L. Hamilton, & D. E. Carlston (Eds.), *Person memory: The cognitive basis of social perception* (pp. 121–153). Hillsdale, NJ: Lawrence Erlbaum Associates.

Hamilton, D. L., & Sherman, S. J. (1996). Perceiving persons and groups. *Psychological Review, 103*, 336–355.

Hastie, R. (1984). Causes and effects of causal attribution. *Journal of Personality and Social Psychology, 46*, 44–56.

Hastie, R., & Park, B. (1986). The relationship between memory and judgment depends on whether the judgment task is memory-based or on-line. *Psychological Review, 93*, 258–268.

Hoffman, C., Mischel, W., & Mazze, K. (1981). The role of purpose in the organization of information about behavior: Trait-based versus goal-based categories in person cognition. *Journal of Personality and Social Psychology, 40*, 211–225.

Keil, F. C. (1989). *Concepts, kinds, and cognitive development.* Cambridge, MA: MIT Press.

Krech, D., & Crutchfield, R. C. (1948). *Theory and problems of social psychology.* New York: McGraw-Hill.

Lewin, K. (1948). *Resolving social conflicts.* New York: Harper.

McConnell, A. R., Sherman, S. J., & Hamilton, D. L. (1994). The on-line and memory-based aspects of individual and group target judgments. *Journal of Personality and Social Psychology*, *67*, 173-185.

McConnell, A. R., Sherman, S. J., & Hamilton, D. L. (1997). Target entitativity: Implications for information processing about individual and group targets. *Journal of Personality and Social Psychology*, *72*, 750-762.

McGrath, J. E. (1984). *Groups: Interaction and performance*. Englewood Cliffs, NJ: Prentice-Hall.

Moreland, R. L. (1987). The formation of small groups. In C. Hendrick (Ed.), *Group processes: Review of personality and social psychology* (Vol. 8., pp. 80-110). Newbury Park, CA: Sage.

Mullen, B. (1991). Group composition, salience, and cognitive representations: The phenomenology of being in a group. *Journal of Experimental Social Psychology*, *27*, 297-323.

Park, B., DeKay, M. L., & Kraus, S. (1994). Aggregating social behavior into person models: Perceiver-induced consistency. *Journal of Personality and Social Psychology*, *66*, 437-459.

Park, B., & Rothbart, M. (1982). Perception of out-group homogeneity and levels of social categorization: Memory for the subordinate attributes of in-group and out-group members. *Journal of Personality and Social Psychology*, *42*, 1051-1068.

Park, B., Ryan, C. S., & Judd, C. M. (1992). Role of meaningful subgroups in explaining differences in perceived variability for in-groups and out-groups. *Journal of Personality and Social Psychology*, *63*, 553-567.

Rothbart, M., Fulero, S., Jensen, C., Howard, J., & Birrell, P. (1978). From individual to group impressions: Availability heuristics in stereotype formation. *Journal of Experimental Social Psychology*, *14*, 237-255.

Rothbart, M., & Taylor, M. (1992). Social categories and social reality: Do we view social categories as natural kinds? In G. R. Semin & K. Fiedler (Eds.), *Language, interaction and social cognition* (pp. 11-36). Newbury Park, CA: Sage.

Sanbonmatsu, D. M., Sherman, S. J., & Hamilton, D. L. (1987). Illusory correlation in the perception of individuals and groups. *Social Cognition*, *5*, 1-25.

Seta, C. E., & Hayes, N. (1994). The influence of impression formation goals on the accuracy of social memory. *Personality and Social Psychology Bulletin*, *20*, 93-101.

Simon, B. (1993). On the asymmetry in the cognitive construal of ingroup and outgroup: A model of egocentric social categorization. *European Journal of Social Psychology*, *23*, 131-147.

Srull, T. K. (1981). Person memory: Some tests of associative storage and retrieval models. *Journal of Experimental Psychology: Human Learning and Memory*, *7*, 440-462.

Srull, T. K., Lichtenstein, M., & Rothbart, M. (1985). Associative storage and retrieval processes in person memory. *Journal of Experimental Psychology: Learning, Memory, and Cognition*, *11*, 316-345.

Srull, T. K., & Wyer, R. S., Jr. (1989). Person memory and judgment. *Psychological Review*, *96*, 58-83.

Stern, L. D., Marrs, S., Millar, M. G., & Cole, E. (1984). Processing time and the recall of inconsistent and consistent behaviors of individuals and groups. *Journal of Personality and Social Psychology*, *47*, 253-262.

Susskind, J., Maurer, K. L., Thakkar, V., Sherman, J. W., & Hamilton, D. L. (1997). *Perceiving individuas and groups: Expectancies, inferences, and causal attributions*. Unpublished manuscript, University of California, Santa Barbara.

Uleman, J. S. (1987). Consciousness and control: The case of spontaneous trait inferences. *Personality and Social Psychology Bulletin*, *13*, 337-354.

Weisz, C., & Jones, E. E. (1993). Expectancy disconfirmation and dispositional inference: Latent strength of target-based and category-based expectancies. *Personality and Social*

Psychology Bulletin, 19, 563–573.

Wyer, R. S., Bodenhausen, G. V., & Srull, T. K. (1984). The cognitive representation of persons and groups and its effect on recall and recognition memory. *Journal of Experimental Social Psychology, 20,* 445–469.

4

Differential Distrust of Groups and Individuals

Chester A. Insko
John Schopler
University of North Carolina at Chapel Hill

One of the classic issues in social science concerns whether decent people are prone to behave indecently when banded together in a group (G. Allport, 1985). Our approach to this issue involves a contrast between interindividual and intergroup behavior in the context of a matrix game (typically a prisoner's dilemma game [PDG]), in which communication between players is allowed (Insko, Schopler, Hoyle, Dardis, & Graetz, 1990; Insko et al., 1987, 1988, 1992, 1993, 1994; McCallum et al., 1985; Schopler, Insko, Graetz, Drigotas, & Smith, 1991; Schopler et al., 1993, 1994, 1995). The majority of these studies were conducted in a suite in which individuals or groups were located in different "home" rooms that were connected to a central room. After examining a version of a PDG matrix provided for a given trial, individuals or group representatives (or in some instances entire groups) went to the central room to discuss possible action with their opponent (or opponents) and then returned to their home rooms, where a choice was made. In the groups condition, the choice was made by the group as a whole. The final decision was recorded on a form, which was carried back to the central room and given to the experimenter. The experimenter announced the decisions by the two individuals or the two groups, and distributed the money that had been earned. Although there were a few studies involving just one trial, typically the procedure was repeated for 10 trials.

All of these referenced studies found a statistically significant and descriptively large tendency for intergroup relations to be more competitive or less cooperative than interindividual relations. This phenomenon is labeled a *discontinuity effect*. Interindividual–intergroup discontinuity is the tendency, in the context of moderately noncorrespondent outcomes, for relations among groups to be more competitive, or less cooperative, than relations among individuals. Three terms in this definition require comment: *discontinuity, group,* and *noncorrespondent outcomes.*

The term *discontinuity* as a label for the difference between groups and individuals was suggested by our late colleague John Thibaut, a collaborator in and co-author of several of the early discontinuity experiments. Thibaut was impressed by Brown's (1954) discussion of LeBon (1895), and in particular of Brown's statement that "The quality of mob behavior has always required explanation because of its apparent discontinuity with the private characters of the individuals involved" (p. 843). Such historical precedent, however, has not impressed some commentators, who have argued that a discontinuity requires that there be more than two points, and that we have only the contrast of interindividual relations with intergroup relations. In fact, we do have unpublished research demonstrating that two-on-two relations are markedly more competitive than one-on-one relations, with three-on-three and four-on-four relations producing progressively smaller increases. There is indeed a discontinuity between interindividual and intergroup relations involving the smallest possible group size. But aside from such evidence, we still believe that Brown's use of the term *discontinuity* in the context of only two points was appropriate because the observed differences in behavior were out of proportion to expectations.

Second, consider the term *group*. As this term is used in the prior statement, it means nothing more than an aggregate or set of individuals. Clearly, however, the term *group* can also be used to imply a set of individuals who have a sense of perceived "oneness" or "entitativity" (Campbell, 1958). Indeed, we would like to be able to argue that the existence of discontinuity provides face valid evidence for the existence of groups in this more psychological sense. However, to avoid circularity, it is necessary to use the term *group* in two different senses. Group in the sense of an aggregate or set of individuals is assumed in the definition of *discontinuity*. The existence of discontinuity, however, provides evidence for the existence of groups in the more psychological meaning of the term.

Third, consider the reference to "noncorrespondent outcomes." According to Kelley and Thibaut's (1978), the pattern of outcomes in a matrix can vary from perfectly correspondent to perfectly noncorrespondent. For matrices with symmetric outcomes for both players, this dimension is indexed by the simple correlation between the outcomes for the two players. With the PDG, and with other mixed-motive matrices that we have investigated, this correlation is moderately negative. For such matrices, there is conflict of interest. It is for such matrices, and situations described by such matrices, for which we believe the discontinuity effect is most likely to occur. There is less reason to expect a discontinuity effect with matrices that are perfectly noncorrespondent (-1). With such matrices (as illustrated by a tug of war), there is no satisfactory way to be cooperative, and this is equally true of groups and individuals. Likewise with correspondent matrices and situations described by such matrices, outcomes can be maximized only through coordination of responses, and this is also equally true for groups and individuals. Whether the degree of noncorrespondence makes a difference within the broad range from 0 down to but not including -1 is a matter that is currently being investigated.

Conversations with our social-psychology colleagues (as well as communications from commentators) occasionally have revealed the misconception that groups are more competitive than individuals in all circumstances. Clearly, this is not the case. To repeat, we believe that discontinuity is most likely for situations such as the PDG, which involve moderately noncorrespondent outcomes. This assertion suggests a further question. Just how common are such situations? Although this is an interesting and important question, we have no definitive answer. We are impressed, however, by the fairly sizable number of situations that can be modeled by a PDG array. These include Brown's (1965) analysis of escape and acquisitive panic situations, as well as entrapment situations, along with Axelrod's (1984) emphasis on reciprocity opportunities, such as in the trench warfare in World War I or the federal congress after the early 1800s — when turnover decreased and the opportunity for reciprocity increased. Finally, the rules governing production payoffs can also conform to a PDG array, as in Erev, Bornstein, and Galili's (1993) demonstration with orange pickers. Although more such situations could be enumerated, it is obviously the case that we do not know the relative frequency with which such choices confront groups or individuals.

A DISCONTINUITY PERSPECTIVE ON THE EARLY HISTORY OF SOCIAL PSYCHOLOGY

A concern with the contrast between the individual and group played a prominent role in the early history of social psychology. For example, LeBon (1895), whose group-mind analysis of crowd behavior was very influential, phrased the issue in a typical way: "Isolated he may be a cultivated individual; in a crowd he is a barbarian, that is, a creature acting by instinct" (p. 35). Such a contrast of the individual and group can, in fact, be traced back to Plato's *Republic*. As G. Allport (1985) pointed out, Plato feared democracy because of his belief that democracy involved rule by irrational mobs; "Had every Athenian citizen been a Socrates, every Athenian assembly would still have been a mob" (p. 22). Among American social scientists, F. Allport (1924) is well known for having rejected the concept of the *group mind*. It is perhaps less well known, however, that in his later years he referred to the problem of the relation of the individual and the collective as the master problem of social psychology (F. Allport, 1962).

Nevertheless, from a discontinuity perspective, F. Allport shared with other great thinkers an uncritical acceptance of a poorly phrased issue. It is evident that individuals who are totally alone cannot engage in the kind of morally questionable behavior that was of concern to LeBon. Aggressive, competitive behavior directed toward others requires at least one other person. When individuals are totally alone, they can eat, sleep, daydream, and, of most interest, work on tasks. This is precisely why experimental work on social psychology's "master problem" focused on task performance—social facilitation; (Triplett, 1897), individual versus group problem solving (Shaw, 1932), social loafing (Latané, Williams, & Harkins, 1979), or brainstorming (Osborn, 1957).

We certainly do not mean to imply that research on social facilitation, brainstorming, and so on is not interesting or important. We do believe, however, that, if the issue is to determine the difference between individual and group responses to social stimuli, the contrast cannot involve the isolated individual. The minimal social unit must be the dyad, and the basic comparison must be between the dyad and intergroup behavior. F. Allport (1920) was, of course, heavily involved in research on social facilitation. However, if it had occurred to him to contrast interindividual behavior with intergroup behavior, one can well imagine that the subsequent history of social psychology might have been rather different.

As LeBon's quote referring to the "isolated" individual makes clear, it wasn't just the American social psychologists who failed to conceptualize the issue adequately. LeBon himself had not conceptualized his own problem adequately. G. Allport (1985) offered an interesting perspective on this issue. G. Allport did not criticize his brother, Floyd, or other American social psychologists, but did point out that a contemporary of LeBon's, Sighele who had become involved in a dispute with LeBon over priority of ideas, had, in fact, conceptualized the issue in terms of comparison with the dyad. Referring to Sighele, Allport stated: "No other social psychologist seems to have focused his work at the basic level of the dyad, and then tested his views in relation to progressively larger groupings. The idea is a good one" (p. 23). We obviously agree.[1]

THREE HYPOTHESES

Counting published and unpublished studies, we have obtained the discontinuity effect over two dozen times. Discontinuity effects have been obtained under many conditions: when the groups contained two, three, or four persons; when the groups were all female or all male; when the intergroup contact involved only representatives or all group members; when the monetary values in the matrix were equated per individual or were exactly equal in the individuals and groups conditions; when the matrix payoff values were increased by a factor of 10 or were not so increased; when the low values in the matrices were negative or positive; when the matrices were symmetric, giving the players equal power, or not symmetric, giving the players unequal power; and when the matrix was of a PDG, mutual-fate control (MFC), or n-person variety.[2]

Given the reliability and the magnitude of the effect, we suspect that it is multiply determined. Three different hypotheses have been formulated to account for the discontinuity effect. Each hypothesis focuses on a different difference between interindividual and intergroup relations. The schema-based distrust (or fear) hypothesis is based on the tendency to distrust other groups more than other individuals. The social-support-for-shared-self-interest (or greed) hypothesis is based on the ability of group members to provide each other with social support for immediate self-interest, in contrast to the lack of such social support available to individuals. Finally, the identifiability hypothesis is based on the participant's assumption that, in an interindividual relationship, the opponent will be able to assign responsibility to oneself if a self-interested choice is made, and the participant's assumption that in an intergroup setting the opponent's ability to assign personal responsibility for self-interested behavior is somewhat limited. Membership in a group provides a shield of anonymity.

---

[1]We find it interesting that Sighele, like Plato, believed that democracy, because of its reliance upon groups of people, was an evil. Allport (1985) pointed out that some of Sighele's ideas "laid one of the cornerstones for later fascistic ideology" (p. 23).

[2]One exception to the prior list of generalities relates to an unequal power matrix (Schopler et al., 1991). Our only study of this issue found that males did not show a discontinuity effect on a second block of five trials. Also, although we have not directly investigated this matter, we have the impression that discontinuity effects are smaller (individuals more competitive, groups less competitive) with matrices containing very small amounts of money—possibly because individuals are less concerned with appearing selfish, and groups see little in the immediate situation to make them fearful or greedy.

COGNITION (DIFFERENTIAL DISTRUST) AND
BEHAVIOR (DISCONTINUITY EFFECT)

We believe that cognitive processes play an important role in all three of the prior hypotheses. Because we have devoted more time to exploring the cognitive basis for the fear hypothesis, however, we restrict further discussion mainly to that issue. In the interest of clarity, let us state that we conceive of differential distrust of groups and individuals as cognition and the discontinuity effect as behavior.

We measure differential distrust by assessing participants' beliefs about, expectations of, discussion of, and memories for intergroup and interpersonal interactions. We measure the discontinuity effect with choices on the PDG matrix, with choices on n-person variations of the PDG matrix, with choices on a three-alternative variation of the PDG matrix, and with intergroup or interindividual interactions recorded by participants in the course of a 1-week period.

It is our contention that the discontinuity effect is partially rooted in the members' ethnocentric schema of an outgroup. The anticipation of interacting with another group instigates learned beliefs or expectations that intergroup relations are competitive, unfriendly, deceitful, and aggressive. The term *schema* is defined as a set of beliefs serving to organize and guide memory for past events and expectations regarding future events.

EVIDENCE FOR THE DIFFERENTIAL DISTRUST
OF GROUPS AND INDIVIDUALS

PDG-Alt Choices

Consider the PDG matrix in Fig. 4.1. That this is a PDG matrix can be verified easily by the fact that there are symmetric choices in which the outcomes of the column player, for example, decrease in rank order across cells from upper right to upper left to lower right to lower left. A further requirement is that the average of the outcomes in the lower left to upper right cells is less than the outcome in the upper left cell. The reason for this requirement is to discourage players from cooperating by taking turns making X and Z choices.[3]

---

[3]A more detailed definition of a PDG is contained in the matrix analysis suggested by Kelley and Thibaut (1978). In their view, a PDG contains a mutual fate-control component,

X   Z

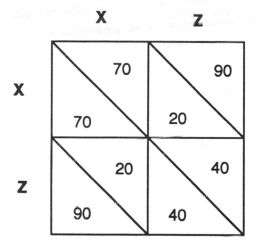

FIG. 4.1. A PDG matrix.

Consider a situation in which both players have selected X, the cooperative choice, on a PDG matrix. Why might either player choose Z on the following trial? There are at least two plausible motives. One motive for the Z choice is the self-interest, or greed, associated with receiving the highest possible outcome (90 in the Fig. 4.1 matrix). However, another equally plausible motivation is the fear of receiving the lowest possible outcome (20 in the Fig. 4.1 matrix). Theoretically, self-interest, or greed, is based on the expectation that the opponent is likely to choose X, and is therefore vulnerable, but fear, or distrust, is based on the expectation that the opponent is likely to choose Z, and is therefore dangerous.

By way of clarification, self-interest can involve either a desire to maximize own outcomes (*max own* in the language of Kelley and Thibaut) or to obtain higher outcomes than the opponent (*max rel* in the language of Kelley and Thibaut). (A desire to obtain higher outcomes than the opponent is commonly expressed as a desire to win.) Likewise, fear can involve either a desire to avoid minimizing outcomes or to avoid receiving a lower outcome than the opponent. (A desire to avoid receiving a lower outcome than the opponent is commonly expressed as a desire to avoid losing.) Thus, the distinction between *max own* and *max rel* cross-cuts, and is not confounded with, the distinction between greed and fear. This point clarifies that greed implies either the tangible outcomes emphasized by Campbell (1965), the relativistic outcomes emphasized by Tajfel (1978), or both (see Insko et al., 1992, for an empirical investigation of this issue).

which is discordant with and larger than the reflexive-control component in an outcome array that contains no behavior-control component.

For present purposes, the important point is that the Z choice in the PDG involves a confound of fear and greed motives. In an attempt to avoid the confound, we have developed a new matrix — a three-choice matrix labeled a *PDG-Alt matrix*. With the PDG-Alt matrix, the distrustful player has an alternative to the Z choice, which is referred to as "withdrawal." An example of a PDG-Alt matrix is presented in Fig. 4.2. Note that the four corners of this 3 X 3 matrix constitute a PDG. For the remaining cells, which describe a center cross, the outcomes for both players are exactly halfway between the upper left and lower right cells. On a PDG-Alt matrix, choosing Y, or withdrawal, guarantees an intermediate outcome without regard for the opponent's choice. Given the expectation that the opponent will choose Z, the Y choice is thus the rational, or outcome-maximizing, choice. However, with such a matrix, the Z choice clearly flows from greed-based motivation. If a player chooses Z on the PDG-Alt matrix, and thus avoids the safe Y choice, it is plausible that the motivation is more likely greed-based than fear-based.

The first investigation of the PDG-Alt matrix was conducted by Insko et al. (1990). This study included a comparison of the PDG and PDG-Alt matrices. Like many other discontinuity studies, it involved the use of representatives for trial-by-trial communication, extensive initial instructions in the meaning of the matrix choices, two practice trials in which outcomes were points and not money, and 10 trials in which outcomes were money. The most important results are presented in Table 4.1.

The means in Table 4.1 are for the choices of two individuals or two groups over 10 trials, and thus have a potential range from 0 to 20. For the Z or "competitive" choices given in the first row, it is clear that groups have

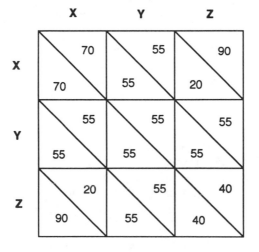

FIG. 4.2. A PDG-Alt matrix.

TABLE 4.1

Competitive Choices, Cooperative Choices, 2-Trial Tactical Withdrawal
Choices, 2-Trial Noncombative Choices, n-Trial Tactical Choices, and
n-Trial Noncombative Choices in the Insko et al. (1990) Experiment

| | PDG | | PDG-Alt | |
Choices	Individuals	Groups	Individuals	Groups
Competitive	1.00	10.14	1.75	4.50
Cooperative	19.00	9.86	17.36	10.43
2-Trial tactical withdrawal			0.28	2.57
2-Trial noncombative withdrawal			0.60	2.50

Note. Because there were 10 trials and either two individuals or two groups making choices on each trial, each of the choice types has a possible range from 0 to 20. (From "Individual-Group Discontinuity as a Function of Fear and Greed" by C. A. Insko, J. Schopler, R. H. Hoyle, G. J. Dardis, and K. A. Graetz, 1990, *Journal of Personality and Social Psychology, 58,* p. 74.) Copyright 1990 by the American Psychological Association. Reprinted by permission.

markedly higher means than do individuals. This is true for the PDG, where the Z choice is one of two possible choices; it is also true for the PDG-Alt, where the Z choice is one of three possible choices. The significant discontinuity effect on the PDG-Alt matrix is consistent with the possibility that part of the motivational basis for the discontinuity effect is greed or self-interest. A possible objection to such a conclusion is that the Z choices are really an attempt to restore equality by the group, which happened to get behind the opponent due to some accidental combination of choices in the more complex intergroup situation. To address this possibility, the data were rescored for Trials 2–10 to only count those competitive choices for which a group or individual was ahead in earnings on the prior trial or trials. The data again revealed that groups chose Z more than did individuals. This was true for the PDG as well as PDG-Alt. The second row of Table 4.1 gives the means for the X, or cooperative, choices. These means clearly indicate that, for both the PDG and the PDG-Alt, individuals cooperated more than did groups.

Given our present concern with fear, the most relevant results are those for the Y, or withdrawal, choices. However, due to a potential ambiguity in the meaning of a withdrawal choice, an overall analysis of withdrawal was not conducted. Instead, withdrawal choices were dichotomized. Consider a player who chose to compete on the PDG-Alt matrix. What is this player likely to do on the following trial? Unless that player is convinced of the opponent's willingness to forgive, the rational choice would appear to be withdrawal. In fact, a detailed examination of the data indicated that, following a competitive choice, groups did, indeed, tend to withdraw. Certainly, such withdrawal is arguably based on fear of the opponent's competitive intent. However, if a group decided to compete and follow the competitive choice with a withdrawal choice, the withdrawal choice is more plausibly interpreted as an aspect of an overall offensive strategy, and is thus more greed-based than fear-based. Informal monitoring of group discussions revealed no instances in which groups explicitly expressed what should be done following a given trial. Still, a conservative approach to the data is to differentiate those withdrawal choices that occurred immediately following an own competitive choice on the last practice trial or any of Trial 1–9 from those withdrawal choices that did not follow an immediately prior competitive choice. Withdrawal choices that did not follow an immediately prior competitive choice were labeled "2-trial noncombative withdrawal choices," and withdrawal choices that did follow an immediately prior competitive choice were labeled "2-trial tactical withdrawal choices." The means given in the third and fourth rows of Table 4.1 indicate that groups engaged in both types of withdrawal more than did individuals.[4]

The prior results provide compelling evidence that at least part of the discontinuity effect is due to a greater distrust of the opponent by groups than by individuals. Still, such an interpretation is based on the assumption that withdrawal not preceded by a competitive choice is fear-based. One way to eliminate the necessity of such an assumption is to have groups and individuals play the PDG-Alt for only one trial with full knowledge that there will be only one trial. With such a situation, all tactical concern with sequences of choices would be ruled out, and it would be more obvious that a withdrawal choice is indeed fear-based. Such an approach was taken in an experiment by Schopler et al. (1993).

There are two potential problems with conducting an experiment involving only one trial. The first potential problem relates to the practice trials. Given the importance of the practice trials in familiarizing participants with the choice combinations of the matrix, how does one conduct an experiment that has only one meaningful trial? The solution was to have the individuals and groups play their practice trials against the experimenter. There were three such practice trials. On each trial, the experimenter chose a different one of the three alternatives.

The second potential problem relates to possible unreliability of data from only one trial. Aside from interest in sequence effects, the main reason for conducting multiple trials is to increase reliability. To address this

---

[4]Consider a group, or individual, who decides to compete and then withdraw on all subsequent trials. Again, it is arguable that withdrawal in the context of such a long-term tactic should be considered more greed-based then fear-based. Accordingly, the withdrawal choices were recategorized so as to differentiate withdrawal preceded either by a competitive choice or by any number of withdrawal choices back to a competitive choice from all other occurrences of withdrawal. The former withdrawal choices were labeled "n-trial tactical withdrawal choices," and the later withdrawal choices were labeled "n-trial noncombative withdrawal choices." For both n-trial types of withdrawal, the means were significantly larger for groups than for individuals.

potential problem, we had the groups and individuals play three trials, but each trial was played against a different opponent. To accomplish this, four players (groups or individuals) were required in a given session. The players, whether groups or individuals, were labeled *A, B, C,* and *D.* Thus, on Trial 1, *A* was paired with *B* and *C* with *D*; on Trial 2, *A* was paired with *C* and *B* with *D*; on Trial 3, *A* was paired with *D* and *C* with *B.* For a given session, there were 12 choices (four players times three trials), with each choice being against a different opponent. Mean number of competitive, cooperative, and withdrawal choices are given in Table 4.2. With each choice, there is a potential range from 0 to 12. The means for competitive and cooperative choices, given in the first two rows, indicate that groups competed more and cooperated less than did individuals.

As it turned out, our initial concern with the possible unreliability of data obtained from a single trial was not warranted. Subsequent research with groups and individuals playing a single trial against a single opponent yielded results generally consistent with those described earlier for single trials with multiple opponents. Two additional, one-trial experiments (Insko et al., 1993; Schopler et al., 1995) revealed that groups withdrew more than did individuals. It is worth emphasizing that there was only one trial, and that participants knew from the beginning of the interaction that there was to be only one trial. One of these experiments (Insko et al., 1993) investigated the effect of communication on withdrawal; it is discussed in more detail later.

PDG-Alt Choices With and Without Communication

Typically we have studied discontinuity with explicit trial-by-trial communication. Sometimes the communication between groups has occurred

TABLE 4.2
Competitive Choices, Cooperative Choices, and Withdrawal Choices
in the Schopler et al. (1993) Experiment

	Individuals		Groups	
Choices	Males	Females	Males	Females
Competitive	1.4	0.4	6.1	2.9
Cooperative	9.6	11.0	1.4	6.0
Withdrawal	1.0	0.6	4.5	3.1

Note. Each of the three choices has a possible range from 0 to 12. (From "Individual–Group Discontinuity: Further Evidence for Mediation by Fear and Greed" by J. Schopler, C. A. Insko, K. A. Graetz, S. Drigotas, V. A. Smith, and K. Dahl, 1993, *Personality and Social Psychology Bulletin, 19,* p. 423.) Copyright 1993 by the Society for Personality and Social Psychology. Reprinted by permission.

through representatives, sometimes by having all of the participants in one group meet with all of the participants in the other group, and sometimes through the use of an intercom. One frequent result of the discussions is an agreement to cooperate on the next trial, or at least an assertion by one side or the other that they will cooperate on the next trial. For example, Insko et al. (1994) found that, with tape-recorded discussions that occurred through an intercom in an experiment with two n-person versions of the PDG, there were agreements to cooperate on the first trial for 76% of the individual sessions and for 61% of the group sessions. On the second and last trials, there were agreements to cooperate on 80.1% of the individual sessions and on 61% of the group sessions. As it turned out, significantly more of the individuals than the groups kept the agreements. For present purposes, however, the important point is that both individuals and groups communicated cooperative intent. Roughly comparable results were obtained by Schopler et al. (1995) in a one-trial experiment with the PDG-Alt. Coding of tape-recorded intercom discussion indicated that there was a consensus to cooperate in 85% of the group sessions and in 76% of the individual sessions.

We have argued that people have a schema that leads them to distrust an outgroup. Trustworthiness and expertness are the two classic components of source credibility (Hovland, Janis, & Kelley, 1953), and research (Walster, Aronson, & Abrahams, 1966) has demonstrated that the trustworthiness of a source does have an impact on the persuasive impact of a communication. Thus, if there is a schema dictating distrust of an outgroup, the presence or absence of communication between groups should have a smaller impact on cooperativeness than should the presence or absence of communication between individuals. Stated differently, the implication of the schema-based distrust hypothesis is that communication between individuals should produce a greater increase in cooperativeness than should communication between groups.

The predicted groups versus individuals by communication versus no communication interaction for the cooperative responses was tested by Insko et al. (1993). Their experiment involved the PDG-Alt in a one-trial situation, in which communication between two groups and between two individuals was or was not possible. The group members sat in one room, but, in the communication condition, were able to communicate with the other group through a common microphone. Each participant in the individuals' condition also sat in a room equipped with a microphone.

With the PDG-Alt matrix, a decrease in cooperativeness between individuals who do not communicate could be associated with either an increase in competitiveness or withdrawal. For the following reason, an increase in withdrawal was predicted. Consistent with the social support for shared self-interest, or greed, hypothesis, under some circumstances group members are able to overcome normative pressures against acting selfishly by the social support they provide each other. Individuals have no such social support. Thus, if individuals do not cooperate, they should withdraw. Therefore, it was predicted that the absence of communication should produce a greater increase in withdrawal for individuals than for groups. This is a groups versus individuals by communication versus no communication interaction for withdrawal.

As the means in Table 4.3 indicate, both the predictions for cooperative choices and for withdrawal choices were supported. Consistent with the schema-based distrust hypothesis, the means in the first row for cooperative choices indicate that communication produced a greater increase for individuals than for groups. In fact, the descriptively small increase for groups was not statistically significant. Consistent with the assumption that social support facilitates the overcoming of the appearance of selfishness, the means in the second row for withdrawal choices indicate that the absence of communication produced a greater increase for individuals than for groups. Finally, what about competitive choices? No effect for communication was predicted, and none was obtained. The means in the third row indicate that there was more competition between groups than between individuals.

Aside from the support for our theoretical ideas, the obtained results are interesting from another perspective. Upon learning about our research, some of our colleagues have quite reasonably inquired why it is that we routinely obtain such high rates of cooperation between individuals, in view of the fact that the older PDG literature found an abundance of competition between individuals. Referring to this older literature, for example, Oskamp and Perlman (1965) stated that, "investigators have uniformly found a relatively low level of cooperation (typically 20% to 40%) and a

TABLE 4.3
Competitive Choices, Cooperative Choices, and Withdrawal Choices in the
Insko et al. (1993) Experiment

| | Individuals | | | | Groups | | | |
| | Communication | | No Communication | | Communication | | No Communication | |
Choices	Males	Females	Males	Females	Males	Females	Males	Females
Cooperative	1.94	1.92	1.29	0.88	0.38	0.75	0.33	0.43
Withdrawal	0.00	0.00	0.57	0.92	0.63	0.42	0.33	1.00
Competitive	0.06	0.08	0.14	0.21	1.00	0.83	1.33	0.58

Note. Because each pair of groups or individuals has two possible choices, scores for all choices have a potential range from 0 to 2. (From "The Role of Communication in Interindividual–Intergroup Discontinuity" by C. A. Insko, J. Schopler, S. M. Drigotas, K. Graetz, J. Kennedy, C. Cox, and G. Bornstein, 1993, *Journal of Conflict Resolution, 37,* p. 123.) Copyright 1993 by Sage Publications. Reprinted by permission.

decreasing amount of cooperation as the game is continued for intermediate lengths" (p. 360, italics in original). There are, in fact, numerous differences between our research and this older literature. For example, we have never used Deutsch's (1958, 1960) individualistic set; we have not used points, poker chips, or "imaginary money" as outcomes; we have always taken great care to instruct participants in the meaning of the various matrix choices, and to enable participants to play initial practice trials; and, most importanct, we have always used trial-by-trial communication between individuals (and also between groups). Most of the older PDG literature did not permit communication between players. Of the few studies that did permit communication, the communication was frequently restricted in some way. In some studies, the communication occurred only after some trials (Scodel, Minas, Ratoosh, & Lipetz, 1959); in some studies, the participants passed notes (Terhune, 1968); in some studies, the participants selected which experimentally supplied notes they wished to send (Radlow & Weidner, 1966); and in some studies, the notes could only be sent in one direction (Loomis, 1959). Wichman (1972) argued that such variation in procedure is one of the factors accounting for the inconsistency in the literature, and that it is preferable to investigate communication as it normally occurs. Wichman found that with face-to-face communication, individuals cooperated 87% of the time—a percentage within the range of results that we have repeatedly obtained.

Beliefs

The definition of term *schema* includes a set of beliefs serving to organize and guide memory for past events and expectations regarding future events. But do we have any evidence that people, in fact, have beliefs indicating that outgroups are competitive and untrustworthy? A study by Hoyle, Pinkley, and Insko (1989) obtained such evidence. Participants marked 50 personality trait adjectives according to whether the traits characterized typical interindividual relations or, in a different condition, typical intergroup relations. Participants were given illustrations of interindividual or intergroup pairs (e.g., a member of one fraternity and a member of another fraternity, or two fraternities). Separate factor analyses of the two conditions yielded similar factor structures: one factor, labeled *agreeableness,* that loaded with traits such as cooperative, trustworthy, and helpful; and a second factor, labeled *abrasiveness,* that loaded with traits such as competitive, boastful, and domineering. Mean scores on the two factors indicated that interindividual relations were perceived as higher than intergroup relations on the agreeableness factor and lower on the abrasiveness factor.

Expectancies

We have postulated that the outgroup schema guides expectations of future events. Indeed, the fear hypothesis is based on the assumption that participants expect that a group opponent is more likely to be competitive than is an individual opponent. But do we have evidence that such a difference in expectancies exists? The results of three studies (Hoyle et al., 1989; Insko et al., 1993; Schopler et al., 1995) provide an affirmative answer to this question.

In addition to the previously described study of the different beliefs regarding outgroups and other individuals, Hoyle et al. completed a second study that investigated expectancies. This second study had participants rate the expected characteristics of an anticipated series of interactions using the scales in the described agreeableness and abrasiveness factors. Six participants located in separate rooms (three on either side of a suite) were given different expectations regarding interaction with the participants on the opposite side of the suite. One independent variable related to whether the three participants on one side of the suite expected to remain in their individual rooms or move to a common, group room. A second independent variable related to whether the three participants on the other side of the suite were expected to remain in their individual rooms or move to a common, group room. Other than to characterize the interactions as involving "everyday social situations," the nature of the interaction settings or contexts were not described, and indeed no such interactions occurred. Rather, participants were simply asked to rate the expected interaction on the scales in the agreeableness and brasiveness factors. An analysis of variance (ANOVA) revealed no significant effects for whether the participants anticipated being alone or in a group. However, there was a main effect for the anticipation of interacting with another individual or a group. Anticipated interaction with a group produced higher scores on the abrasiveness factor than did interaction with an individual. Although the effect on the agreeableness factor was in the anticipated direction, that effect was not significant.

In the research cited earlier, anticipated interaction with an outgroup resulted in more expected competitiveness, but not less expected cooperativeness, than did interaction with an individual. These data suggest that competitiveness and cooperativeness are not conceptualized as a single bipolar dimension, but rather as two separate dimensions—a conclusion consistent with the Hoyle et al. (1989) result that cooperativeness and competitiveness loaded on two different factors. The data suggest that the outgroup schema more obviously includes expected competitiveness than unexpected cooperativeness. This conclusion is consistent with the results of a second study (Insko et al., 1993).

The Insko et al. study is the previously described study that tested and confirmed the prediction that communication between individuals would produce a greater increase in cooperativeness than would communication between groups (see Table 4.3). Recall that this experiment involved one trial with the PDG-Alt matrix. For present purposes, the relevant results relate to the expected competitiveness and cooperativeness of the opponent. The expectancy assessment asked participants to divide 100 points among the three PDG-Alt alternatives according to the likelihood that the opponent had chosen or would choose X, Y, or Z. This assessment was taken either immediately after the practice trials or immediately after the choice, but before feedback as to the opponent's choice. Note that the "after-choice" assessment did occur before learning of the opponent's choice. Note also that because the "before-choice" assessment occurred before the opportunity for communication, no effect for the communication manipulation could have occurred in that condition. For present purposes, we ignore the results for expected withdrawal and focus on the results for expected competition, and cooperation (see Table 4.4).

These results contain some complex interactions. Initially, consider the results for groups versus individuals and the interaction of groups versus individuals with assessment order. Consistent with prediction, groups expected more competition than did individuals (see the first row). These results are in contrast to those for expected cooperativeness (see Row 2 of Table 4.4), where the overall tendency of individuals to expect more cooperativeness, relative to groups, was significant only in the after-assessment condition. Consistent with the Hoyle et al. (1989) results, there was no effect for expected cooperativeness before the choice. Recall that in

TABLE 4.4
Expected Competition and Expected Cooperation
in the Insko et al. (1993) Experiment

	Individuals				Groups			
	Communication		No Communication		Communication		No Communication	
Expectancy	Before	After	Before	After	Before	After	Before	After
Competition	29.86	13.93	25.00	23.65	31.64	37.78	37.89	33.97
Cooperation	33.88	76.39	35.54	35.56	28.95	41.67	26.33	20.44

Note. The expectancy scores have a potential range from 0 to 100. However, because participants did not always respond to each of the three expectancy ratings with numbers that totaled 100 (e.g., 33, 33, 33), the column sums tend to deviate somewhat from 100. (From "The Role of Communication in Interindividual–Intergroup Discontinuity" by C. A. Insko, J. Schopler, S. M. Srigotas, K. Graetz, J. Kennedy, C. Cox, and G. Bornstein, 1993, *Journal of Conflict Resolution, 37,* p. 126.) Copyright 1993 by Sage Publications. Reprinted by permission.

the Hoyle et al. study, all of the data were collected before the choice (which, in fact, did not occur).

The finding that, with the before-assessment, the difference between groups and individuals is only present for the expectation of competitiveness can be used as leverage for a related issue. This issue has to do with whether the expectation of a difference between groups and individuals is due just to the groups condition, just to the individuals condition, or both. Is the difference between groups and individuals due to the expected competitiveness and noncooperativeness of groups, to the expected cooperativeness and noncompetitiveness of individuals, or both? In formulating a group schema, we have assumed that the difference is mainly due to the expected competitiveness and noncooperativeness of groups.

There is an abundance of evidence that people think more readily in terms of positive-confirming-promotive instances than in terms of negative-disconfirming-preventive instances — a tendency initially identified by Hovland (1952), but more recently empirically documented by McGuire and McGuire (1991). It is interesting that McGuire and McGuire obtained evidence that this difference is due both to ability and to "proclivity."

For groups, perceived competitiveness is confirming and perceived cooperativeness is disconfirming, whereas for individuals, perceived cooperativeness is confirming and perceived competitiveness is disconfirming. Thus, the fact that opponents who are groups differ from opponents who are individuals in expected competitiveness, but not in expected cooperativeness, implies that this difference is due to perceived movement of groups away from individuals, rather than to perceived movement of individuals away from groups. Such a conclusion is, of course, consistent with our interpretation of that difference as due to a group schema, rather than to an individual schema.

Finally, turning to the effect of the presence or absence of communication, recall that the postulated lack of trustworthiness associated with the group schema led to the prediction that communication between groups would be less credible and consequently less convincing than communication between individuals. But if this is true, communication between individuals should lead to a decrease in expected competitiveness relative to that seen with communication between groups. However, because it was only the "after" assessment that could detect any effect of the communication, the prediction was of a groups versus individuals by communication versus no-communication by before-assessment versus after-assessment interaction. This interaction was significant. As can be seen in Row 1 of Table 4.4, the tendency for communication to decrease expected competitiveness more for individuals than for groups occurred only with the after assessment. For individuals, communication decreased expected competitiveness from 23.65 to 13.93; for groups, communication increased expected competitiveness nonsignificantly from 33.97 to 37.78.

The third experiment with expectancies data (Schopler et al., 1995) also involved one trial with the PDG-Alt matrix, but assessed expectancies only after the choice (but still before learning of the opponent's choice). The results indicate that individuals expected less competition, more cooperation, and less withdrawal than did groups. Means on a 100-point scale for comparable conditions are approximately the same as those in Table 4.4. For the comparable communication condition, for example, expected competitiveness was 17.2 for individuals and 36.8 for groups.

Pre-Choice Discussion and Post-Choice Reasons

A fourth category of evidence concerning the differential distrust of groups and individuals comes from the content of the prechoice discussion between groups and between individuals. If groups are more prone to distrust each other than are individuals, it is to be expected that discussions between groups will include more statements of distrust than will discussions between individuals. This matter was investigated in two studies (Insko et al., 1994; Schopler et al., 1995), in which communication occurred through an intercom. In the Insko et al. study, which involved two different n-person versions of the PDG, judges coded the tape-recorded discussions for both explicit statements of distrust (e.g., "I don't trust you") and implicit statements of distrust (e.g., "Don't cheat on this"). The mean number of both types of distrust (or fear) statements was significantly higher for groups than for individuals. Because comparable results were obtained for explicit and implicit statements, the two types of statements were combined into one index in the Schopler et al. study. This study, which involved a one-trial test with the PDG-Alt, again found that there were significantly more distrust statements in discussions between groups than in discussions between individuals.

For individuals, of course, the discussions with the opponent were the only discussions that occurred. For groups, however, there were also "within" discussions. Because individuals had no such discussions, a comparison with groups is not possible. However, it is possible to correlate number of within-group distrust statements with the groups' choices. An earlier study by Insko et al. (1990) had found that, for within-group distrust coded from tape-recorded discussions across 10 trials with the PDG, the correlation with cooperative choices was -.59. More distrust was associated with fewer cooperative choices. Such a correlation provided reason to hope for a general relationship between the number of within-group distrust statements and the matrix choices that were made. As it turned out, however, neither the Insko et al. (1994) study with n-person games nor the Schopler et al. (1995) study with the PDG-Alt obtained significant correlations between the number of within-group statements of distrust and the matrix choices. In retrospect, we believe that the hope for such correlations was naive. If a group reaches consensus very quickly on the untrustworthiness of the other group, the within-group discussion may contain few statements of distrust. However, if there is disagreement regarding the trustworthiness of the other group, there may be extended discussion and numerous statements of distrust. Hence, we now believe that number of within-group distrust statements is a poor index of the final group consensus. This is particularly true in studies such as Schopler et al. (1995), which involved only one trial, or Insko et al. (1994), which involved two trials. In studies such as Insko et al. (1990), which involved 10 trials, total number of distrust statements may indeed be a correlate of matrix choices. With multiple trials and multiple choices, there is more reason for choices to be justified with multiple statements of distrust.

After the initial analysis of the Schopler et al. (1995) data, it occurred to us that in simply coding for the number of distrust statements we ignored statements of trust. Although the number of trust statements was relatively small, statements of explicit trust (e.g., "I trust you") and implicit trust ("They said they would choose X so why don't we as well?") did occur. Collapsing explicit and implicit trust into one index yielded a surprisingly high correlation of $+.70$ with cooperative choices. (Also the mean number of trust statements was significantly lower in the discussion between groups than in the discussion between individuals.) Given the prior argument that number of within-group distrust statements is a poor index of overall distrust, why is there such a strong relationship between number of trust statements and cooperative choices? The answer may have something to do with the lower frequency of trust statements, plus the fact that in approximately half of the groups making trust statements, those statements were made after the group had decided to cooperate, and thus appeared to be a justification for the cooperative choice.

Overall, the discussion data reveal more distrust and fewer trust statements in discussion between groups than in discussion between individuals, and a complex relationship between discussion within groups and the final decision. With one or two trials, number of distrust statements is not related to the cooperative choice, but number of trust statements is so related. With multiple trials, there may be a relation between number of distrust statements and number of cooperative choices.

Although the discussion data provide some support for the fear-based group-schema hypothesis, the results are not totally consistent. The problem is that we do not fully understand the dynamics of the group decision-making process. Although we lack such understanding, we do have evidence for each participant's own stated reason for his or her decision. This evidence comes from a postexperimental questionnaire that asked participants to state the reasons why they had chosen X (cooperation), Y (withdrawal), or Z (competition). Such an assessment of retrospective reasons was taken in the Schopler et al. (1995) study with a single trial on the PDG-Alt. Coding of the open-ended responses revealed an abundance of differences between group and individual sessions. Compared with individuals, groups reported more retrospective greed, distrust, and deceit, and less retrospective trust, concern with maximizing joint outcomes, and concern with fairness. Of equal interest are the correlations among distrust, trust, and greed and each of the three PDG-Alt choices. Because the correlation matrix contains nine correlations, a Bonferroni criterion of .005 (.05/9 = .005) was used to evaluate the significance of the correlations. Using this criterion, six of the nine correlations were large enough to be significant. These are the correlations of distrust with cooperative choices (-.48), distrust with withdrawal choices (.50), trust with cooperative choices (.82), trust with competitive choices (-.58), greed with cooperative choices (-.52), and greed with competitive choices (.90). These results are in good agreement with the fear hypothesis (and also with the greed hypothesis), and provide some reassurance that our inconsistent results for within-group discussion should not be construed as fatal to the fear hypothesis.

Memory

The previously described results indicate that participants both believe and expect relations between groups to be more competitive than relations between individuals. Why is this the case? One possibility is that some aspect of the experimental setting or instructions contained cues suggesting such a difference. Another possibility is that participants recall intergroup relations as more competitive than interindividual relations.

Three experiments, all reported in Pemberton, Insko, and Schopler (1996), have been conducted. The first two experiments required participants to recall and describe in brief phrases intergroup interactions or, in a different condition, interindividual interactions. Subsequently, participants were asked to go back through their lists and rate these interactions on the scales in the Hoyle et al. (1989) abrasiveness and agreeableness factors.

Examples of recalled intergroup interactions were: "staff meeting between our store and the Pittsboro store," "church groups at camp," "UNC vs. Duke basketball game," "the band vs. the athletes," and "Pro-Life vs. Pro-Choice groups." Examples of recalled interindividual interactions were: "Christine and I talking at the mall," "LaToya and I contemplating not going downstairs for the fire alarm," "Shannon and I camping last weekend," and "stranger and I stuck in the elevator."

Consistent with the Hoyle et al. results, there were no significant effects on any of the scales in the agreeableness factor in either of the first two experiments. However, there were significant results for all of the scales in the abrasiveness factor in both experiments. Table 4.5 contains the means for the abrasiveness scales in the second experiment. Note that for each of the scales, intergroup relations were rated as higher than the interindividual relations. Note also that these differences remained even when the interactions relating to sports and games were removed from the data set. This was also true in the first experiment, which had results similar to those in Table 4.5.

The third experiment followed a different procedure, in which participants recalled interactions in one of four categories: cooperative interindividual, competitive intergroup, cooperative interindividual, and competitive intergroup. Thus, the experiment included two between-participant factors: cooperative versus competitive interactions and interindividual versus intergroup interactions. The dependent variable was simply the number of recalled interactions. Unlike in the first two experiments, participants did not rate the recalled interactions. In their research on positive and negative thoughts, McGuire and McGuire (1991) considered this more directive approach to be an assessment of ability and the less constraining approach of Experiments 1 and 2 to be an assessment of proclivity.

TABLE 4.5

Mean Ratings on the Abrasiveness Factor in Experiment 2 of Pemberton, Insko, and Schopler (1996)

	All Interactions		Interactions Excluding Sports/Games	
Scale	Groups	Individuals	Groups	Individuals
Proud	4.81	3.32	4.74	3.09
Aggressive	4.61	3.16	4.06	2.95
Competitive	4.80	3.21	4.28	2.84
Overconfident	4.56	2.68	4.05	2.43
Demanding	4.55	3.33	4.47	3.20
Boastful	4.61	2.82	4.07	2.56
Domineering	4.70	2.79	4.37	2.61
Mean	4.68	3.03	4.29	2.81

Note. All ratings are on a scale ranging from 1 (*definitely did not apply*) to 7 (*definitely did apply*). (From "Memory for and Experience of Differential Competitive Behavior of Individuals and Groups" by M. J. Pemberton, C. A. Insko, and J. Schopler, 1996, *Journal of Personality and Social Psychology, 71*, p. 955.) Copyright 1996 by the American Psychological Association. Reprinted by permission.

Mean numbers of recalled interactions are graphed in Fig. 4.3. An ANOVA revealed two significant effects. First, there was a main effect indicating that more interindividual than intergroup interactions were recalled. Second, and more important, there was an interaction indicating that the proportion of competitive to cooperative interactions was greater for intergroup than for interindividual interactions. Follow-up simple-effect tests indicated that more competitive ($M = 7.67$) than cooperative ($M = 5.48$) intergroup interactions were recalled, and marginally more cooperative ($M = 12.41$) than competitive ($M = 10.41$) interpersonal interactions were recalled. A further analysis that included a within-participants variable of whether the interactions were, or were not, sports/games related revealed no significant effects for that variable.

All three experiments converge in suggesting that participants recall intergroup relations as relatively more competitive than interindividual relations, and that this relative difference holds even for interactions that are *not* related to sports or games. It is plausible that the belief that intergroup relations are more competitive than interindividual relations, and the expectancy that intergroup relations will be more competitive than interindividual relations, can be attributed to the fact that people generally recall intergroup relations as being more competitive than interindividual relations.

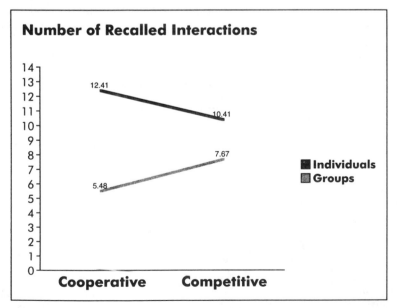

FIG. 4.3. Number of recalled interactions in the third experiment of Pemberton, Insko, and Schopler (1996).

Yes, But Is It a Schema?

The five categories of evidence indicate that participants make PDG-Alt choices indicative of more distrust of groups than of individuals, that participants believe groups to be more competitive than individuals, that participants expect groups to be more competitive than individuals, that participants express more distrust of groups than of individuals, and that participants remember groups as being more competitive than individuals. This evidence for differential distrust of groups and individuals makes a preliminary case for the existence of an outgroup schema. Recall that *schema* means a set of beliefs serving to organize and guide memory for past events and expectations regarding future events. Our use of the term *schema* overlaps with Bartlett's (1932) use of the term to refer to " . . . organized representation of past behavior and experience that guided an individual in construing new experience" (Markus & Zajonc, 1985, p. 144), and also with Hastie's (1981) second meaning of the term as a template or filing system.

Despite postulating such a schema, we do not possess definitive evidence for its existence. Definitive evidence for a schema is most obviously provided by evidence from a situation in which it is clear that the obtained results cannot be accounted for simply by different experiences. At the same time, it should be recognized that in generally postulating distrust of outgroups we are hardly asserting a novel idea. For example, Campbell (1967) pointed out that "If most or all groups are in fact ethnocentric, then it becomes an 'accurate' stereotype to accuse an outgroup of some aspects of ethnocentrism" (p. 823). Campbell went on to describe a "universal" outgroup stereotype, " . . . of which each ingroup might accuse each outgroup, or some outgroup, or the average outgroup" (p. 823). From the perspective of the observer, this universal stereotype of the outgroup includes egotism and immorality, as well as clannishness, dishonesty, competitiveness, and hostility toward the observer's ingroup. An interesting historical illustration of schemalike expectations occurs in Plato's *Republic*, where Polemarchus defends a traditional maxim of Greek morality that "justice consists of helping one's friends and harming one's enemies" (Plato, 1941). It is also of interest that, before formulating social identity theory, Tajfel (1970) interpreted the results of early mere categorization experiments as flowing from a learned " 'generic norm' of behavior toward outgroups," a norm that dictates that we "act in a manner that discriminates against the outgroup and favors the ingroup" (pp. 98–99). Also, Doise (1969) reported that, before any interaction, subjects attribute fewer cooperative motives to the opposing group than to themselves or to their own group members. From a somewhat different perspective, Sears (1983) postulated a person-positivity bias—a bias that should lead to the more favorable evaluation of individuals than of groups (see Miller & Felicio, 1990, for supporting evidence).

WHY ARE INTERGROUP RELATIONS RECALLED AS MORE COMPETITIVE?

The three studies described earlier provide consistent evidence that intergroup relations are recalled as more competitive than interindividual relations. What is responsible for this difference? One simple possibility is that participants have experienced intergroup relations as more competitive than interindividual relations. We approached this issue by using a modified version of the Rochester Interaction Record (RIR; Reis & Wheeler, 1991). We completed two experiments (Pemberton et al., 1996).

RIR Experiment 1

Procedure, Predictions, and Examples. Our interest was in determining whether, in the course of one week, intergroup interactions were perceived as more competitive than interindividual interactions. In order for participants to understand how to classify their interactions, we distinguished among five different types of experiences: one-on-one interactions, within-group interactions, one-on-group interactions, group-on-one interactions, and group-on-group interactions. One-on-group and group-on-one interactions are distinguished by whether the participant interacts with a group or whether a group in which the participant is a member interacts with an individual. Participants were not given a conceptual definition of the term *group;* rather, the meaning of the term was conveyed through examples.

Participants classified their interactions and then rated them on separate competitiveness and cooperativeness scales. We expected no differences among the five interaction types on the cooperativeness scale. For the competitiveness scale, however, we predicted that the three interactions involving groups (one-on-group, group-on-one, group-on-group) would be rated as more competitive than the two interactions that were not with groups (one-on-one, within-group). Because our theoretical framework provided no basis for expecting a difference between one-on-one and within-group interactions, no difference was predicted for that contrast. Although we expected a difference among the three types of interactions with groups, this prediction was not confirmed.

Because many participants did not record instances of each of the three types of interactions with groups, we followed a two-stage data analytic strategy. In Stage 1, we conducted a five-level analysis consistent with the planned contrasts. This analysis used only data for those participants who recorded instances of each of the five interaction types. In Stage 2, we conducted a three-level analysis by collapsing the three interactions with groups into one category. Most participants did, in fact, have at least one interaction involving a group. Only the results for the five-level analysis are described because the three-level analysis yielded results consistent with those of the five-level analysis.

Examples of one-on-one interactions were: "ping-pong last evening" and "staying overnight at Mark's." Examples of within-group interactions were: "talking with Aaron and Todd" and "joke contest between my brothers, cousins, and I." Examples of one-on-group interactions were: "meeting with strength coaches to prepare for the game" and "ran into some of my girlfriends at a bar." Examples of group-on-one interactions were: "my old girlfriend and I spoke to an acquaintance in passing" and "Bob, Jeff, and I interviewing football player." Examples of group-on-group interactions were: "four of us met another group on Franklin Street" and "intramural soccer game."

Results: Competitiveness and Cooperativeness. Mean competitiveness and cooperativeness ratings are given in Table 4.6. In line with past results for beliefs, expectancies, and memories, there were no significant effects for rated cooperativeness. For competitiveness, the differences among the five conditions are not descriptively large (Column 1 of Table 4.6). However, the planned contrast of the mean of all three types of interactions with a group and the mean of one-on-one and within-group interactions revealed a significant difference. Interactions with a group

TABLE 4.6
Mean Competitiveness and Cooperativeness Ratings for the Five-Level
Analysis of the First RIR Experiment in Pemberton, Insko, and Schopler
(1996)

	All Interactions		Interactions Excluding Sports/Games	
Level	*Competitiveness*	*Cooperativeness*	*Competitiveness*	*Cooperativeness*
One-on-One	2.23	5.31	2.21	5.31
Within-Group	2.85	5.29	2.75	5.33
One-on-Group	2.48	5.34	2.46	5.30
Group-on-One	2.81	5.42	2.78	5.45
Group-on-Group	3.62	4.71	3.26	4.76

Note. All ratings are on a 7-point scale, with high numbers indicating the most competitiveness or cooperativeness. (From "Memory for and Expeience of Differential Competitive Behavior of Individuals and Groups" by M. J. Pemberton, C. A. Insko, and J. Schopler, 1996, *Journal of Personality and Social Psychology, 71,* p. 959.) Copyright 1996 by the American Psychological Association. Reprinted by permission.

(one-on-group, group-on-one, group-on-group) in general were rated as more competitive. No other contrasts were significant. As can be seen from the means in Table 4.6, when the data were reanalyzed with all interactions relating to sports or games eliminated the results remained essentially unchanged.

Results: Memory. The obtained results suggest that a possible reason for the tendency to recall intergroup relations as more competitive than interindividual relations is that participants experience intergroup relations as being more competitive than interindividual relations. However, although differences in competitiveness exist between the perceptions of intergroup and interpersonal interactions, the differences for the memory data are descriptively larger than the differences for the RIR data.

This issue was directly addressed by asking participants, after the week of recording data, to recall as many of their one-on-one, group-on-one, one-on-group, and group-on-group interactions as they could, and then to rate these interactions for competitiveness. Mean competitiveness ratings for recalled interactions were 2.92 for one-on-one and 4.59 for groups. For recorded interactions, the comparable competitiveness ratings were 2.34 for one-on-one and 3.45 for groups. The difference for the recalled data between one-on-one and groups was significantly larger than the difference for recorded data.

RIR Experiment 2

Procedure. The procedure for the second RIR experiment differed from the first; rather than rating each of the five types of social interactions (one-on-one, within-group, one-on-group, group-on-one, group-on-group) for competitiveness and cooperativeness, participants categorized each of the five types of interactions as either competitive or cooperative. Thus, the dependent variable was simply the number of recorded interactions in each of the 10 categories over 1 week. Note that the difference between the two RIR studies parallels the difference between the first two and the third recall studies described earlier (Pemberton et al., 1996). As in the first RIR experiment, the results of the three-level anlaysis are similar to those of the five-level analylsis, and only the results of the five-level analysis are described here.

Results. Mean numbers of interactions are given in Table 4.7. There were two significant main effects: the cooperative–competitive main effect and the interaction type main effect. The cooperative–competitive main effect indicates that more cooperative than competitive interactions were

TABLE 4.7

Numbers and Percentages of Competitive and Cooperative Interactions in
the Five-Level Analysis of the Second RIR Experiment in Pemberton,
Insko, and Schopler (1996)

	All Interactions		Interactions Excluding Sports/Games	
Level	Competitive	Cooperative	Competitive	Cooperative
One-on-One	3.94(8.2%)	44.44(91.9%)	3.58(7.0%)	47.50(92.9%)
Males only	5.00(12.6%)	34.50(87.3%)	3.00(7.1%)	39.25(92.9%)
Females only	3.30(6.1%)	50.40(93.9%)	3.88(7.0%)	51.63(93.0%)
Within-Group	2.63(12.4%0	18.50(87.6%)	2.25(11.6%)	17.17(88.4%)
Males only	4.00(12.8%)	27.33(87.1%)	3.00(11.5%)	23.00(88.5%)
Females only	1.80(12.0%)	13.20(88.0%)	1.88(11.7%)	14.25(88.3%)
One-on-Group	1.25(23.8%)	4.00(76.%)	1.08(17.8%)	5.00(82.2%)
Males only	1.67(27.8%)	4.33(72.2%)	1.25(18.5%)	5.50(81.5%)
Females only	1.00(20.8%)	3.80(79.2%)	1.00(17.4%)	4.75(82.6%)
Groups-on-One	0.56(15.5%)	3.06(84.5%)	0.58(13.4%)	3.75(86.6%)
Males only	0.33(18.1%)	1.33(80.1%)	0.25(16.7%)	1.25(83.3%)
Females only	0.70(14.6%)	4.10(85.4%)	0.75(13.0%)	5.00(87.0%)
Group-on-Group	1.25(39.2%)	1.94(60.8%)	0.58(21.8%)	2.08(78.2%)
Males only	2.50(65.3%)	1.33(34.7%)	0.75(42.9%)	1.00(57.1%)
Females only	0.50(17.9%)	2.30(82.1%)	0.50(16.0%)	2.63(84.0%)

Note. From "Memory for and Experience of Differential Competitive Behavior of Individuals and Groups" by M. J. Pemberton, C. A. Insko, and J. Schopler, 1996, *Journal of Personality and Social Psychology, 71,* p. 962. Copyright 1996 by the American Psychological Association. Reprinted by permission.

recorded. The interaction type main effect indicates that more interactions were recorded for one-on-one than for within-group, and more for one-on-one and within-group combined than for the three group conditions combined. More important, the statistical interaction of the cooperative-competitive variable and the type of interaction variable was significant. Breaking down that interaction by the planned contrasts indicated that interactions with groups were relatively more competitive than interactions one-on-one or within-groups. Furthermore, there were relatively more competitive than cooperative interactions within-group than one-on-one. Although the methodology was somewhat different, the first RIR experiment did not result in a difference in the rated competitiveness of one-on-one and within-group interactions. As can be seen in Table 4.7, the results remain largely the same after all recorded interactions relating to sport or games were removed from the data. The tendency for groups to be more competitive than individuals is not restricted to sports.[5]

---

[5]A further result is the triple interaction involving gender. The tendency for one-on-one and within-group interactions to be relatively more competitive than interactions with groups was significant for both males and females; however, the patterns differed somewhat. One-on-one

Conclusions

The two RIR experiments agree in suggesting that interaction with groups are perceived as more competitive than are interactions with individuals. Furthermore, they indicate that this generalization applies even when attention is restricted to interactions that do not involve sports or games. Thus, the data strongly suggest that one reason why intergroup relations are recalled as being more competitive than interindividual relations is that intergroup relations are experienced as being more competitive than interindividual relations.

However, as described earlier, the first RIR experiment found that participants recalled the intergroup interactions relative to the interindividual interactions as being even more competitive than what they had previously recorded. Such results obviously suggest that the tendency to remember intergroup interactions as more competitive than interindividual interactions is not just a function of experience. To the extent that this is true, there may indeed be an outgroup schema.

GROUPS ARE NOT ALWAYS MORE COMPETITIVE THAN INDIVIDUALS

An examination of Table 4.7 makes it clear that in some instances individuals compete and in many instances groups cooperate. Thus, it would be clearly inaccurate to conclude that groups "invariably" compete, although Rabbie and Lodewijkx (1994) attributed such a conclusion to us. It was argued here and elsewhere (Insko et al., 1993; Schopler & Insko, 1992) that Kelley and Thibaut's (1978) index of correspondence provides a basis for predicting when groups will or will not compete more than individuals. Theoretically, the situations in which groups cooperate should be ones in which outcomes are positively correlated, and the situations in which individuals compete should be ones in which outcomes are perfectly, or almost perfectly, negatively correlated.

INTERINDIVIDUAL–INTERGROUP DISCONTINUITY IN A NONLABORATORY CONTEXT

Although we initially framed the two RIR experiments as investigations of one possible explanation of the tendency to recall intergroup interactions as

---

interactions were seen as relatively more cooperative for females than for males, and group-on-group interactions were seen as relatively more competitive for males than for females (see Table 4.7).

being more competitive than interindividual interactions, an alternative framing as a demonstration of discontinuity without a matrix, and indeed without a laboratory context, is also possible. Such an alternative framing, however, raises the issue as to whether the distinction between the situations that the participants categorized as interindividual and those categorized as intergroup is confounded with some other variable that is responsible for the difference in reported competitiveness. Insofar as we frame the RIR results as providing one possible explanation for the tendency to recall intergroup relations as being more competitive than interindividual relations, the issue of a possible confounding variable is arguably less relevant. However, to the extent that we frame the RIR results as providing evidence for a nonlaboratory demonstration of the discontinuity effect, the issue of a possible confounding variable merits serious consideration.

One possible confounding variable in the RIR studies is familiarity. Perhaps the interindividual situations involve more familiar participants than do the intergroup situations, and perhaps this difference in familiarity is responsible for the lesser perceived competitiveness of interindividual than intergroup situations. This possibility was anticipated after the first RIR study, but prior to the second. In the second RIR study, participants rated their familiarity with the other individual or group in each of the categorized social situations. The data indeed revealed greater familiarity with the "other" in the interindividual situation than in the intergroup situation. However, the data did not reveal that cooperative and competitive interactions differed in familiarity. In fact, there was a descriptive trend in the opposite direction (i.e., for competitive interactions to be with relatively more familiar others). It is, of course, still possible that some other confounding variable may account for the results, but for now we will tentatively interpret the two RIR studies as providing nonlaboratory evidence for interindividual–intergroup discontinuity.

SUMMARY

We have reviewed five categories of evidence indicating that other groups are distrusted more than other individuals. The first cateogry relates to the choices that participants make with a PDG-Alt matrix. Four studies obtained evidence indicating that, on such a matrix, groups withdraw more than individuals. The second category relates to beliefs regarding intergroup and interindividual relations. One study found that participants believe that intergroup compared with interindividual relations are more competitive. The third category relates to expectations of the opponent's choice before completion of the first trial. Three studies found that there is a greater expectation of competition when the opponent is a group than when the opponent is an individual. One of these studies further demonstrated that what is crucial is not whether the participant is alone or in a group, but whether the opponent is an individual or a group. The fourth category relates to the coding of tape-recorded discussions that occurred prior to the PDG-Alt choices and from postexperimental statements as to reasons for PDG-Alt choices. Two studies found that discussions between groups produced a greater number of coded distrust statements than did discussions between individuals; and one study found that, relative to individuals, group members made a greater number of distrust statements as retrospective reasons for PDG-Alt choices. The fifth and final category relates to participants' memories for one-on-one and group interactions. Three studies found that recalled group-on-group interactions were more competitive than recalled one-on-one interactions.

Further research investigated the possibility that different memories for one-on-one and group interactions are a function of different experiences. Participants kept 1-week diaries, in which they recorded and rated the competitiveness of one-on-one, within-group, one-on-group, group-on-one, and group-on-group interactions. It was found that one-on-one and within-group interactions were rated as less competitive than all interactions involving groups. These findings were supported in a second study, in which participants simply recorded the occurrence of cooperative or competitive one-on-one, within-group, one-on-group, group-on-one, or group-on-group interactions. The first study also found that the difference in competitiveness between recalled one-on-one interactions and interactions with groups was even larger than the comparable difference for the previously recorded interactions — thereby providing support for the hypothesized outgroup schema that is responsible for the differential distrust of groups and individuals.

ACKNOWLEDGMENT

Work on this chapter was supported by NIMH grant MH53258 to the authors.

REFERENCES

Allport, F. H. (1920). The influence of the group upon association and thought. *Journal of Experimental Psychology, 3*, 159–182.
Allport, F. H. (1924). *Social psychology*. Boston: Houghton Mifflin.
Allport, F. H. (1962). A structuronomic concept of behavior: Individual and collective: 1.

Structural theory and the master problem of social psychology. *Journal of Abnormal and Social Psychology*, *64*, 1-30.

Allport, G. W. (1985). The historical background of social psychology. In G. Lindzey & E. Aronson (Eds.), *The handbook of social psychology* (Vol. 1, pp. 1-46). New York: Random House.

Axelrod, R. (1984). *The evolution of cooperation*. New York: Basic Books.

Bartlett, F. C. (1932). *Remembering: A study in experimental and social psychology*. Cambridge, England: Cambridge University Press.

Brown, R. (1954). Mass phenomena. In G. Linzey (Ed.), *Handbook of social psychology* (Vol. 2, pp. 833-876). Cambridge, MA: Addison-Wesley.

Brown, R. (1965). *Social psychology*. New York: The Free Press.

Campbell, D. T. (1958). Common fate, similarity, and other indices of the status of aggregates of persons as social entities. *Behavioral Science, 3*, 14-25.

Campbell, D. T. (1965). Ethnocentrism and other altruistic motives. In D. Levine (Ed.), *Nebraska symposium on motivation* (Vol. 13, pp. 283-311). Lincoln, NE: University of Nebraska Press.

Campbell, D. T. (1967). Stereotypes and perception of group differences. *American Psychologist, 22*, 817-829.

Deutsch, M. (1958). Trust and suspicion. *Journal of Conflict Resolution, 2*, 267-279.

Deutsch, M. (1960). The effect of motivational orientation upon threat and suspicion. *Human Relations, 13*, 123-139.

Doise, W. (1969). Stratégie de jeu á lintérieu et entre des groupes de nationalités différentes. *Bulletin du Centre d'Études et Recherches Psychotechniques, 18*, 13-26.

Erev, I., Bornstein, G., & Galili, R. (1993). Constructive intergroup competition as a solution to the free rider problem: A field experiment. *Journal of Experimental Social Psychology, 29*, 463-478.

Hastie, R. (1981). Schematic principles on human memory. In T. E. Higgins, C. Herman, & M. P. Zanna (Eds.), *Social cognition: The Ontario symposium on personality and social psychology* (Vol. 1). Hillsdale, NJ: Lawrence Erlbaum Associates.

Hovland, C. I. (1952). A "communication" analysis of concept learning. *Psychological Review, 59*, 461-472.

Hovland, C. I., Janis, I. L., & Kelley, H. H. (1953). *Communication and persuasion*. London: Oxford University Press.

Hoyle, R. H., Pinkley, R. L., & Insko, C. A. (1989). Perceptions of behavior: Evidence of differing expectations for interpersonal and intergroup interactions. *Personality and Social Psychology Bulletin, 15*, 365-376.

Insko, C. A., Hoyle, R. H., Pinkley, R. L., Hong, G., Slim, R., Dalton, G., Lin, Y., Ruffin, P. P., Dardis, G. J., Bernthal, P. R., & Schopler, J. (1988). Individual-group discontinuity: The role of a consensus rule. *Journal of Experimental Social Psychology, 24*, 505-519.

Insko, C. A., Pinkley, R. L., Hoyle, R. H., Dalton, B., Hong, G., Slim, R., Landry, P., Holton, B., Ruffin, P. F., & Thibaut, J. (1987). Individual-group discontinuity: The role of intergroup contact. *Journal of Experimental Social Psychology, 23*, 250-267.

Insko, C. A., Schopler, J., Drigotas, S. M., Graetz, K., Kennedy, J., Cox, C., & Bornstein, G. (1993). The role of communication in interindividual-intergroup discontinuity. *Journal of Conflict Resolution, 37*, 108-138.

Insko, C. A., Schopler, J., Graetz, K. A., Drigotas, S. M., Currey, K. P., Smith, S. L., Brazil, D., & Bornstein, G. (1994). Interindividual-intergroup discontinuity in the Prisoner's Dilemma Game. *Journal of Conflict Resolution, 38*, 87-116.

Insko, C. A., Schopler, J., Hoyle, R. H., Dardis, G. J., & Graetz, K. A. (1990). Individual-group discontinuity as a function of fear and greed. *Journal of Personality and Social Psychology, 58*, 68-79.

Insko, C. A., Schopler, J., Kennedy, J. F., Dahl, K. R., Graetz, K. A., & Drigotas, S. M.

(1992). Individual-group discontinuity from the differing perspectives of Campbell's realistic group conflict theory and Tajfel and Turner's social identity theory. *Social Psychology Quarterly, 55*, 272–291.

Kelley, H. H., & Thibaut, J. W. (1978). *Interpersonal relations.* New York: Wiley.

Latané, B., Williams, K., & Harkins, S. (1979). Many hands make light the work: The causes and consequences of social loafing. *Journal of Personality and Social Psychology, 37*, 822–832.

LeBon, G. (1895). *Psychologie des foules. [The crowd].* London: Unwin.

Loomis, J. L. (1959). Communication, the development of trust and cooperative behavior. *Human Relations, 12*, 305–315.

Markus, H., & Zajonc, R. B. (1985). The cognitive perspective in social psychology. In G. Lindzey & E. Aronson (Eds.), *The handbook of social psychology*, (3rd ed., pp. 137–230). New York: Random House.

Miller, C. T., & Felicio, D. M. (1990). Person-positivity bias: Are individuals liked better than groups? *Journal of Experimental Social Psychology, 26*, 408–420.

McCallum, D. M., Harring, K., Gilmore, R., Drenan, S., Chase, J., Insko, C. A., & Thibaut, J. (1985). Competition between groups and between individuals. *Journal of Experimental Social Psychology, 21*, 301–320.

McGuire, W. J., & McGuire, C. V. (1991). The content, structure, and operation of thought systems. In R. S. Wyer, Jr. & T. K. Srull (Eds.), *Advances in social cognition* (pp. 1–78). Hillsdale, NJ: Lawrence Erlbaum Associates.

Osborn, A. F. (1957). *Applied imagination.* New York: Scribner's.

Oskamp, S., & Perlman, D. (1965). Factors affecting cooperation in a prisoner's dilemma game. *Journal of Conflict Resolution, 9*, 359–374.

Pemberton, M. B., Insko, C. A., & Schopler, J. (1996). Memory for and exprience of differential competitive behavior of individuals and groups. *Journal of Personality and Social Psychology, 71*, 953–966.

Plato. (1941). *The republic of Plato* (F. Cornford, Trans.). Oxford, England: Oxford University Press.

Rabbie, J. M., & Lodewijkx, H. G. M. (1994). Conflict and aggression: An individual-group continuum. In B. Markovsky, K. Heimer, & J. O'Brien (Eds.), *Advances in group processes* (Vol. 11, pp. 139–174). Greenwich, CT: JAI.

Radlow, R., & Weidner, M. F. (1966). Unenforced commitments in "cooperative" and "noncooperative" constant-sum games. *Journal of Conflict Resolution, 10*, 497–505.

Reis, H. R., & Wheeler, L. (1991). Studying social interaction with the Rochester Interaction Record. In M. P. Zanna (Ed.), *Advances in experimental social psychology* (Vol. 24, pp. 269–318). New York: Academic Press.

Schopler, J., & Insko, C. A. (1992). The discontinuity effect in interpersonal and intergroup relations: Generality and mediation. In W. Stroebe & M. Hewstone (Eds.), *European review of social psychology* (Vol. 3, pp. 121–151). Chichester, England: Wiley.

Schopler, J., Insko, C. A., Currey, D., Smith, S., Brazil, D., Riggins, T., Gaertner, L., & Kilpatrick, S. (1994). The survival of a cooperative tradition in the intergroup discontinuity context. *Motivation and Emotion, 18*, 301–315.

Schopler, J., Insko, C. A., Drigotas, S. M., Wieselquist, J., Pemberton, M., & Cox, C. (1995). The role of identifiablity in the reduction of interindividual-intergroup discontinuity. *Journal of Experimental Social Psychology.*

Schopler, J., Insko, C. A., Graetz, K. A., Drigotas, S. M., & Smith, V. A. (1991). The generality of the individual-group discontinuity effect: Variations in positivity-negativity of outcomes, players' relative power, and magnitude of outcomes. *Personality and Social Psychology Bulletin, 17*, 612–624.

Schopler, J., Insko, C. A., Graetz, K. A., Drigotas, S. M., Smith, V. A., & Dahl, K. (1993). Individual-group discontinuity: Further evidence for mediation by fear and greed. *Person-*

ality and Social Psychology Bulletin, 19, 419–431.

Scodel, A., Minas, J. S., Ratoosh, P., & Lipetz, M. (1959). Some descriptive aspects of two-person non-zero-sum games. Journal of Conflict Resolution, 3, 114–119.

Sears, D. (1983). The person-positivity bias. Journal of Personality and Social Psychology, 44, 233–250.

Shaw, C. (1932). A comparison of individuals and small groups in the rational solution of complex problems. American Journal of Psychology, 54, 491–504.

Tajfel, H. (1970). Experiments in intergroup discrimination. Scientific American, 223(5), 96–102.

Tajfel, H. (1978). Interindividual behaviour and intergroup behaviour. In H. Tajfel (Ed.), Differentiation between social groups (pp. 27–60). London: Academic Press.

Terhune, K. W. (1968). Motives, situation, and interpersonal conflict within prisoner's dilemma. Journal of Personality and Social Psychology Monograph Supplement, 8 (3, Part 2), 1–24.

Triplett, N. (1897). The dynamogenic factors in pacemaking and competition. American Journal of Psychology, 9, 507–533.

Walster, E., Aronson, E., & Abrahams, D. (1966). On increasing the persuasiveness of a low prestige communicator. Journal of Experimental Social Psychology, 2, 325–342.

Wichman, H. (1972). Effects of isolation and communication cooperation in a two-person game. In L. S. Wrightsman, Jr., J. O'Connor, & N. J. Baker (Eds.), Cooperation and competition: Readings on mixed-motive games (Vol. 1, pp. 197–205). Belmont, CA: Brooks/Cole.

5

Personal Control, Entitativity, and Evolution

Chester A. Insko
John Schopler
Constantine Sedikides
University of North Carolina at Chapel Hill

In 1958, Campbell coined the term *entitativity* to refer to the perception of any aggregate of objects as a unit, or as an entity. As we and many other social psychologists use the term, it refers to the perception of an aggregate of individuals as a social group. Horwitz and Rabbie (1982) credited Lewin (1948) with an earlier interest in the perception of entitativity in this more social-psychological sense. Lewin attempted to "raise the consciousness" of Jewish adolescents by arguing that the most important determinant of who belongs to what groups is not the degree of similarity among the individuals, but rather "interdependence of fate" (p. 184). According to Horwitz and Rabbie, Lewin had been influenced by his experiences in Europe, where some people were treated as Jewish even though they had not previously considered themselves to be Jewish.

It is apparent that neither Lewin nor Campbell believed that demographic categories per se were sufficient for the creation of entitativity. We agree with this view. However, Tajfel (1978) clearly believed that mere categorization was sufficient to induce "genuine awareness of membership in separate and distinct groups" (p. 35). Tajfel's evidence has been critically evaluated elsewhere (Insko & Schopler, 1987).

A DISCONTINUITY APPROACH TO ENTITATIVITY

Relations between groups are more competitive, or less cooperative, than relations between individuals, in the context of moderately noncorrespondent outcomes. We termed this phenomenon *interindividual–intergroup discontinuity* (Insko & Schopler, chap. 4, this volume). In this definition, we use the term *group* to mean nothing more than a set of individuals. Our basic assumption is that, if discontinuity exists, a set of individuals is, in fact, a psychologically real group; that is, when a set of three individuals competes with another set of three individuals to a greater degree than single individuals compete with single individuals, the two sets of three individuals are, in fact, groups.[1] Note that this approach uses behavior (i.e., discontinuity) to provide a *marker* for the existence of a particular type of cognition (i.e., entitativity).

ENTITATIVITY AS PARTIAL LOSS OF PERSONAL CONTROL

Three experiments have followed the discontinuity-implies-entitativity line of reasoning (Insko et al., 1987, 1988, 1994). These experiments both illustrate the complexity of the problem and suggest that entitativity flows from loss of personal control.

The Insko et al. (1987) experiment was conducted in a seven-room suite, in which three rooms opened onto either side of a long central room. This suite of rooms had previously been used to demonstrate that, when each of the three participants located in the separate rooms on one side of the suite repeatedly "played" the prisoner's dilemma game (PDG) one-on-one with the three participants located in the separate rooms on the other side of the suite, the interaction was far more cooperative than when the three participants on one side of the suite were moved to a single room and required to reach consensus regarding how they should interact with the set of similarly arranged participants on the other side of the suite. A major intent of the Insko et al. experiment was to create an intermediate condition between the extremes of one-on-one and three-on-three interactions. In this outcome interdependence condition, the three participants located in separate rooms on each side of the suite were informed that they would be

---

[1]Although we believe that using the occurrence of discontinuity as evidence for entitativity is reasonable, it is worth noting that our research has focused on the prisoner's dilemma game (PDG), in which (a) the cooperative choice involves a confound of maximizing equal outcomes and maximizing the joint sum of outcomes, and (b) the competitive choice involves a confound of maximizing own outcomes and maximizing the relative difference between own and other outcomes. The use of other matrices (e.g., Multiple Alternative Matrices [MAMs]; Bornstein et al., 1983) might reveal a different pattern of differences between intergroup and interindividual relations. (For further discussion of this issue, see Insko & Schopler, 1987.)

sharing equally their earnings with the two other participants on the same side of the suite.

However, the results indicate that there was no significant difference between the individuals condition and the outcome interdependence condition over the 10 trials. With 10 trials and two choices per trial, there were 20 possible cooperative choices. In the individuals condition, males made 19.09 and females made 18.27 cooperative choices, whereas in the outcome interdependence condition, males made 18.72 and females made 18.27 cooperative choices. The similar high rates of cooperation were, however, significantly different from two different groups conditions: a "group-rep" condition, in which the groups communicated with each other through representatives (8.78 for males and 10.00 for females), and a "group-all" condition, in which groups communicated with each other by all members of one group meeting with all members of the other group (11.64 for males and 13.90 for females). In all conditions, the communication occurred during each of the 10 trials. The group-all condition produced significantly more cooperation than the group-rep condition. But the important point is that both conditions differed from the individuals and outcome interdependence conditions, which, as indicated, did not differ from each other.

The Insko et al. (1988) experiment examined the issue further by creating even more intermediate conditions. The first condition was the outcome interdependence condition of the Insko et al. (1987) experiment. The second condition was a contact condition, in which the three participants on each side of the suite were moved to the same room. In all other respects, however, everything was the same as the outcome interdependence condition (i.e., the participants on the same side of the suite shared earnings, could not talk to each other, and interacted one-on-one with a participant on the other side of the suite). The third condition was a discussion condition. This condition was the same as the contact condition, except that the three participants in the same room on one side of the suite could talk to each other. The fourth condition was a consensus condition. In this condition, the three participants on each side of the suite were required to reach consensus regarding their PDG choices. However, they still met one-on-one with their opposite number on the other side of the suite. The final condition was the group-all condition of the Insko et al. (1987) experiment. This condition differs from the consensus condition only in that the three participants on each side collectively, rather than singly, meet with the three participants on the other side of the suite. In terms of the number of cooperative choices over the 10 trials, the means were as follows: 17.00 in the outcome interdependence condition, 17.47 in the contact condition, 16.59 in the discussion condition, 10.67 in the consensus condition, and 9.94 in the group-all condition. The outcome interdependence, contact, and discussion conditions did not differ from each other, nor did the group-all and consensus conditions differ from each other. However, the latter two "groups" conditions did differ from the former three "individuals" conditions. The consensus and group-all conditions produced the least cooperation.

Insko et al. (1988) interpreted these results as indicating that a consensus rule was necessary for the production of between-group competitiveness, and thus entitativity. This interpretation, however, was rather naive because of the failure to think beyond the immediate experimental situation to other situations, in which it is obvious that between-group competitiveness can occur in the absence of a within-group consensus requirement. The Insko et al. (1994) experiment clearly made this point. This experiment involved two different n-person versions of the PDG. Six participants were again located in separate rooms, three on either side of the experimental suite. In the individuals condition, each participant on one side of the suite used an intercom to talk to one participant on the other side of the suite. In the groups condition, the three participants on a given side of the suite first used the intercom to talk within group, then to talk between groups to participants on the other side of the suite, and finally to talk within group for a second time. In the groups condition, each participant was given a promissory note worth $2.10, and was asked to make a decision as to whether to "invest" that note. In the context of the n-person games, "invest" is a euphemism for compete. The rules of the two games, the details of which need not concern us here, generally indicated that the group that invested more notes would earn more money than the other group, but that the groups would jointly earn the most money if no one invested. The important point is that the procedural rules of the games dictated that each group member lost a degree of control to his or her group. In the individuals condition, such control was not lost because each individual controlled (all) three notes.

The results indicate, consistently with a discontinuity perspective, that the groups invested more notes than did the individuals. A further unexpected result, however, related to a manipulation of the presence or absence of a consensus requirement within the groups condition. Half of the participants in the groups condition operated under a consensus rule and half did not, and the presence or absence of this rule had no significant effect on the obtained results. Such results make it clear that discontinuity and entitativity can occur in the absence of a consensus rule.

Insko et al. (1994) interpreted these results as indicating that not outcome interdependence, not a consensus rule, but procedural interdependence is necessary for entitativity. Thibaut and Walker (1975) used the term *procedure* in their discussion of procedural justice to mean a set of rules that can differ in the extent to which the person gives up control. For example, they described the inquisitorial system as a procedure through which "nearly all of the control in the hearing process is allocated to the decision maker," and the adversarial system as a procedure "in which most of the control of the process is exercised by the parties through their attorneys" (p. 27). With the n-person PDGs, the rules of the game, the procedure, dictated that each group member was partially controlled by the decisions of the fellow group members. Thus, procedural interdependence is a set of rules or circumstances that involves a partial loss of personal control.

But why then did the consensus rule produce intergroup competitiveness in the Insko et al. (1988) experiment? The answer is that, with the simpler PDG, a loss of personal control was confounded with the presence of the consensus rule. Evidence consistent with this interpretation comes from the reported results for assessments taken on the postexperimental questionnaire (see Table 5.1). Questions that asked for ratings of the extent to which own side was perceived as a group and the extent to which other side was perceived as a group tracked the matrix choice results only partially because these ratings were higher in the discussion condition than in the interdependence and contact conditions, and the matrix choices were equally cooperative in these conditions (see the first three rows of Table 5.1). However, a rating of self-control of earnings tracked the matrix choice results exactly (see Row 4 of Table 5.1). There was significantly less rated control in the consensus and group-all conditions than in the interdependence, contact, and discussion conditions. Based on these results, we propose that entitativity involves a partial loss of personal control.

TABLE 5.1
Number of Cooperative Choices, and Rated Extent to Which Participants on Own Side of the Suite Acted as if They Were a Group, Participants on Other Side of the Suite Acted as if They Were a Group, and There Was Self-Control of Earnings in the Interdependence, Contact, Discussion, Consensus, and Group-All Conditions

Variable	Interdependence	Contact	Discussion	Consensus	Group-All
Cooperative choices	17.00	17.47	16.59	10.67	9.94
Own side as group	3.23	3.38	6.46	8.38	8.39
Other side as group	3.66	3.69	5.08	6.12	6.47
Self-control of earnings	5.95	6.15	6.29	5.32	5.35

Note. Number of cooperative choices has a possible range from 0 to 20; all ratings were on a 9-point scale, in which high numbers indicate a greater effect. (From "Individual–Group Discontinuity: The Role of a Consensus Rule" by C. A. Insko, R. H. Hoyle, R. L. Pinkley, G. Hong, R. Slim, G. Dalton, Y. Lin, P. P. Ruffin, G. J. Dardis, P. R. Bernthal, and J. Schopler, 1988, *Journal of Experimental Social Psychology, 24,* pp. 505–519.) Copyright 1988 by Academic Press. Reprinted by permission.

A POSSIBLE EVOLUTIONARY BASIS FOR DIFFERENTIAL DISTRUST OF GROUPS AND INDIVIDUALS

One explanation of interindividual–intergroup discontinuity is the perception of greater distrust of other groups than of other individuals (Insko & Schopler, chap. 4, this volume). Although it may appear as "something of a stretch," we believe that a plausible evolutionary argument can be made for such differential distrust, and that this argument is consistent with an interpretation of entitativity as a partial loss of personal control. The first step in our speculation is accepting the arguments of many scholars (Baumeister & Leary, 1995; Caporael & Brewer, 1991; Leakey, 1978; Stevens & Fiske, 1996) that there is survival value in being social, or that there is survival value in trusting and cooperating with other individuals.

Biological Selection at the Individual Level

Sedikides and Skowronski (1997) argued that "the evolution from Homo habilis to Homo erectus was partly a consequence of the challenges that the ancestral savanna niche posed to the latter species" (p. 20). They cited Fox's (1980) assertion that the movement from an arboreal background to the savanna put *Homo erectus* in competition with other species possessing greater stature, speed, strength, and ferocity. They quoted with approval Fox's statement that "ultimate success can only lie in the very helplessness of the original creature" (p. 175), and then stated "That *Homo erectus* was physically ill equipped to be a hunter is a cornerstone of our evolutionary argument" (p. 20). Sedikides and Skowronski maintained that, because isolated individuals were unlikely to survive, there was selection for those individuals who were socially oriented. The advantage of within-group cooperation included increased efficiency in hunting, sharing of the surplus food that resulted from the successful hunting of big game, improved vigilance in the detection of and warning about predators, and improved defense against predators through "predator mobbing."

We find such an argument plausible. On the savanna, there was indeed survival value in being social, in trusting other individuals, in cooperating with other individuals. However, from a discontinuity perspective, the problem is to explain why the survival value of being social did not generalize from between-individual and within-group relations to between-group relations. One might assume that many of the reasons for cooperative relations between individuals, or within a group, would also apply to relations between groups. It could be argued that cooperation between groups would improve defense against predators, improve vigilance in the detection of and warning of predators, facilitate the sharing of food, and increase the efficiency of hunting.

Why might the argument regarding the survival value of being social have only limited application to relations between groups? One reason is that the advantage of cooperation between groups in achieving increased efficiency in hunting and allowing for the sharing of available food would less obviously apply when there is an insufficiency of food, or at least an insufficiency of food in a given locale. With a sufficiency of game and edible vegetation, a more optimal division of labor made possible by between-group cooperation would indeed increase outcomes. With an insufficiency of food, however, there would more likely be noncorrespondent outcomes (Kelley & Thibaut, 1978), in which it would not be possible for both groups to obtain sufficient food.

An obvious complexity here has to do with just how much available food any individual or group would regard as sufficient. Because of the social support that group members provide each other for being greedy and possessive, it is quite likely that group-judged sufficiency would be considerably more expansive than would individual judged sufficiency. To the extent that this is true, between-group relations should be even more problematic than between-individual relations.

The argument that selection for trust and cooperation between individuals, or within a group, does not apply to relations between groups when there is a judged insufficiency of food is reminiscent of Campbell's (1965) realistic group-conflict theory. Campbell argues that it is competition over "real" resources such as territory or possessions that is responsible for the development of outgroup rejection and distrust. Implicit in Campbell's position is the assumption that the "real" resources do not exist (or are not perceived to exist) in a sufficient amount.

A further matter beyond the sufficiency of available food relates to the problem of optimal group size. Consider a situation in which one group that is hunting in a given territory is confronted with another group that wishes to move into the same territory. Even if cooperation between the groups would facilitate hunting efficiency, there would be an increase in the difficulty of coordinating activities between groups, or activities among twice as many people, as well as a reduction in the effort of individual group members as the number of people increased (Karau & Williams, 1993; Steiner, 1972). Thus, the coordination cost and motivational loss associated with a large number of people may still be further reasons why the survival value of being social applies only to relatively small group sizes.

Finally, the argument that the survival value of being social does not readily generalize from between-individual relations to between-group relations is supported by an even more basic biological fact. This is the fact that procreation (except in the case of rape), and thus the survival of the species. is dependent on cooperation between individuals. There is a survival value for between-individual relations that is obviously absent for between-group relations. This is a difference that existed even before our ancestors foresook the forest for the savanna.

Biological Selection at the Group Level

The prior argument that the survival value of being social does not generalize from between-individual to between-group relations assumes implicitly that evolutionary selection operates at the individual level. What about the possibility that evolutionary selection also operates at the group level? This is the kind of possibility that may initially strike many individually oriented psychologists as metaphysically spooky. However, Wilson and Sober (1994) gave an example of how group selection might operate in a completely reasonable manner. They described an archipelago in which the individual islands are populated by rabbits. On one of the islands, a mutant arises that grazes more efficiently, and thus at the individual level is better adapted. However, the proliferation of this new strain leads to overgrazing, and thus the eventual demise of the entire group of rabbits populating this one island. Wilson and Sober noted that what happens parallels the tragedy of the commons (Hardin, 1968) and prisoner's dilemma outcome arrays (Rapoport & Chammah, 1965). Wilson and Sober argued that "fit populations replace unfit populations in the same sense that fit rabbits replace unfit rabbits within populations" (p. 589). Wilson and Sober's position is this: Just as individuals can be "vehicles" for genes, groups can be "vehicles" for individuals. By a "vehicle," they mean any circumstance that produces "shared fate," as is illustrated by the metaphor of a rowing crew in which everyone is "in the same boat" (p. 591).

Except to indicate that Wilson and Sober's complete theory is based on "natural selection that operates on a nested hierarchy of units" (p. 585)—genes, individuals, groups, and metapopulations—further details are left to the interested reader. For present purposes, the most relevant question concerns whether it is reasonable to suppose that group-level selection could have operated so as to produce selection for distrust between groups. We believe that such a question can be answered in the affirmative.

Two extremes of between-group orientation are militaristic hostility on the one hand and pacifistic docility on the other. We suspect that a group that adopted either one of these orientations would be unlikely to survive in the long run.

Consider a group that, because of superior numbers, tactics, or weapons, is able to adopt a successful militaristic, imperialistic orientation toward other groups. For several reasons we believe that in the long run such a group would eventually meet its "Waterloo." The eventual demise of such a group might occur for any of at least three reasons. The first reason is that the success of the militaristic group would motivate other groups to join forces against the "common enemy." The second reason is that continued military success might eventually lead to overly long lines of communication and resupply—a consideration that obviously applies more to groups with a fixed home territory than to nomadic groups. The third and final reason is that, given the capacity of humans for creativity and invention, particularly in the face of necessity, sooner or later some opposing group would develop even more superior tactics and/or weapons.

Even if a group were successful in conquering its opponents, however, we believe that in the long run such a group would have difficulty maintaining its power, and thus its hostile orientation toward other groups. One reason relates to the interdependence that would eventually develop between the conquering group and the conquered/enslaved groups. To the extent that the dominant group became dependent on the enslaved groups for the necessities of life, the power of the dominant group would not be "usable" (Thibaut & Kelley, 1959), and the tendency to dominate would be undermined. Second, in the long run, absolute power over conquered groups would lead to a lower level of prosperity than will trade between free groups (Insko et al., 1983). Third and finally, the high probability of sexual relations between the conquered and enslaved groups would eventually lead to a genetic drift away from the conquered group's predisposition to dominate other groups.

The opposite of the tendency to orient with hostility to another group is the tendency to adopt a pacifistic orientation toward opposing groups. We also think that this orientation will not lead to long-term survival at the group level: opposing groups would dominate. However, between the extremes of militarism and pacifism there is a middle ground that involves a wariness toward and distrust of other groups. Groups that adopt this orientation are the most likely to survive. If this is true, there is indeed a biological predisposition toward distrust of groups other than one's own.

IMPLICATION FOR ENTITATIVITY

We have argued that the Wilson and Sober (1994) position has an implication for group-level selection of a biological predisposition to distrust other groups. There is, however, a further implication regarding the perception of entitativity, or the perception of separate individuals as a group. In the present context, the important point is that Wilson and

Sober's position regarding group-level selection seems more compatible with Lewin's than Tajfel's position: that is, it appears that Wilson and Sober's emphasis on "shared fate" or "being in the same boat" is more like Lewin's emphasis on "interdependence of fate" than Tajfel's emphasis on categorization.[2] This issue becomes important if it is indeed the case that biological evolution has created a cognitive predisposition toward the perception of entitativity—a predisposition that corresponds to the circumstance resulting in group-level selection.

An obvious problem is that Wilson and Sober argued for group-level selection without being very precise about what they meant by the term *group*. The metaphor of "being in the same boat" is just that—a metaphor. Reasoning backward, one might suppose that a group is some kind of arrangement among organisms, such that breeding within the unit is permitted but that breeding among units is discouraged.

Therefore, Wilson and Sober's position could be interpreted as assuming that a group is an arrangement that restricts freedom or limits personal control. We, of course, have proposed that entitativity also involves a loss of freedom or control. It is no accident that the two conceptions of groups relate to partial loss of personal control. In fact, given the tendency toward efficient evolutionary adaptation, it would be remarkable if perceived entitativity were based on one kind of group and group selection were based on an entirely different kind of group.

We have argued that groups restrict the personal control of individual members. But how far can these restrictions go? Obviously, they can vary from extreme to low. Extreme loss of personal control is likely to lead to either helplessness (Seligman, 1975) or corrective action toward restoring control (e.g., being hypervigilant toward group leaders, disputing the authority of group leaders, or deserting the group; Fiske, Morling, & Steven, 1996). However, low levels of personal control loss may not be sufficient for entitativity to occur. Thus, our argument is that moderate or partial levels of control are most likely to form the basis for entitativity and are most likely to have formed the basis for group selection.

The present chapter concludes with a clarification. Herein, entitativity was discussed from the perspective of the actor, or the person who is a member of a group. However, Hamilton, Sherman, and Lickel (chap. 3, this volume) discussed entitativity, as did Campbell (1958), from the perspective of an external observer. We believe that the two approaches are complementary. We argued that members of high entitativity groups have given up a degree of personal freedom and control. Hamilton et al. argued that high entitativity groups are groups that observers perceive as well

---

[2]There is, of course, no dispute regarding whether categorization is necessary for perceived entitativity; the dispute regards whether categorization is sufficient.

organized and highly structured. Hence, it is likely that highly organized and structured groups are groups in which the members have relatively limited freedom and control.

However, there is one potential inconsistency between the two approaches. We argued that, from the group members' perspective, entitativity will not necessarily be present if personal loss of control is excessive. To illustrate this point, group members (e.g., members of an authoritarian political party or organization) may become disgruntled and cease progressively to identify with the group (i.e., may perceive the ingroup as lower in entitativity) as the group tightens up its rules, adds new and even more stringent rules, and increases its control over its members. However, according to the Hamilton et al. argument, a strong and rigid organizational structure would result in excessive control of a group over its members, which, in turn, would lead an external observer to infer that the group is high in entitativity. Thus, in reference to the prior example, the implication of the Hamilton et al. argument is that the more a group rigidifies its structure, the higher in entitativity the group will be perceived by external observers. These are testable hypotheses that we hope future research considers seriously.

ACKNOWLEDGMENT

Work on this chapter was supported by NIMH grant MH 53258.

REFERENCES

Baumeister, R. F., & Leary, M. R. (1995). The need to belong: Desire for interpersonal attachments as a fundamental human motivation. *Psychological Bulletin, 117*, 497–529.

Bornstein, G., Crum, L., Wittenbraker, J., Harring, K., Insko, C. A., & Thibaut, J. (1983). On the measurement of social orientations in the minimal group paradigm. *European Journal of Social Psychology, 13*, 321–350.

Campbell, D. T. (1958). Common fate, similarity, and other indices of the status of aggregates of persons as social entities. *Behavioral Science, 3*, 14–25.

Campbell, D. T. (1965). Ethnocentrism and other altruistic motives. In D. Levine (Ed.), *Nebraska symposium on motivation* (Vol. 13, pp. 283–311). Lincoln, NE: University of Nebraska Press.

Caporael, L. R., & Brewer, M. B. (1991). Reviving evolutionary psychology: Biology meets society. *Journal of Social Issues, 47*, 187–195.

Fiske, S. T., Morling, B., & Stevens, L. E. (1996). Controlling self and others: A theory of anxiety, mental control, and social control. *Personality and Social Psychology Bulletin, 22*, 115–123.

Fox, R. (1980). *The red lamp of incest*. New York: E. P. Dutton.

Hardin, G. (1968). The tragedy of the commons. *Science, 162*, 1243–1248.

Horwitz, M., & Rabbie, J. M. (1982). Individuality and membership in the intergroup system. In H. Tajfel (Ed.), *Social identity and intergroup relations* (pp. 241-274). New York: Cambridge University Press.

Insko, C. A., Gilmore, R., Drenan, S., Lipsitz, A., Moehle, D., & Thibaut, J. (1983). Trade versus expropriation in open groups: A comparison of two types of social power. *Journal of Personality and Social Psychology, 44,* 977-999.

Insko, C. A., Hoyle, R. H., Pinkley, R. L., Hong, G., Slim, R., Dalton, G., Lin, Y., Ruffin, P. P., Dardis, G. J., Bernthal, P. R., & Schopler, J. (1988). Individual-group discontinuity: The role of a consensus rule. *Journal of Experimental Social Psychology, 24,* 505-519.

Insko, C. A., Pinkley, R. L., Hoyle, R. H., Dalton, B., Hong, G., Slim, R., Landry, P., Holton, B., Ruffin, P. F., & Thibaut, J. (1987). Individual-group discontinuity: The role of intergroup contact. *Journal of Experimental Social Psychology, 23,* 250-267.

Insko, C. A., & Schopler, J. (1987). Categorization, competition and collectivity. In C. Hendrick (Ed.), *Review of personality and social psychology: Group processes* (Vol. 8, pp. 213-251). New York: Sage.

Insko, C. A., Schopler, J., Graetz, K. A., Drigotas, S. M., Currey, K. P., Smith, S. L., Brazil, D., & Bornstein, G. (1994). Interindividual-intergroup discontinuity in the Prisoner's Dilemma Game. *Journal of Conflict Resolution, 38,* 87-116.

Karau, S. J., & Williams, K. D. (1993). Social loafing: A meta-analytic review and theoretical integration. *Journal of Personality and Social Psychology, 65,* 681-706.

Kelley, H. H., & Thibaut, J. W. (1978). *Interpersonal relations.* New York: Wiley.

Leakey, R. E. (1978). *People of the lake: Mankind and its beginnings.* New York: Avon.

Lewin, K. (1948). *Resolving social conflicts.* New York: Harper & Row.

Rapoport, A., & Chammah, A. M. (1965). *Prisoner's dilemma: A study in conflict and cooperation.* Ann Arbor, Michigan: University of Michigan Press.

Sedikides, C., & Skowronski, J. J. (1997). The symbolic self in evolutionary context. *Personality and Social Psychology Review, 1,* 80-102.

Seligman, M. E. P. (1975). *Helplessness: On depression, development, and death.* San Francisco: Freeman.

Steiner, I. D. (1972). *Group process and productivity.* New York: Academic Press.

Stevens, L. E., & Fiske, S. T. (1996). Motivation and cognition in social life: A social survival perspective. *Social Cognition, 13,* 189-214.

Tajfel, H. (1978). Interindividual behaviour and intergroup behaviour. In H. Tajfel (Ed.), *Differentiation between social groups* (pp. 27-60). London: Academic Press.

Thibaut, J., & Walker, L. (1975). *Procedural justice.* New York: Wiley.

Thibaut, J. W., & Kelley, H. H. (1959). *The social psychology of groups.* New York: Wiley.

Wilson, D. S., & Sober, E. (1994). Reintroducing group selection to the human behavioral sciences. *Behavioral and Brain Sciences, 17,* 585-654.

III

Processes Affecting Intergroup Cognition and Intergroup Behavior: Perceptual and Judgmental Processes

6

Group Variability and Covariation: Effects on Intergroup Judgment and Behavior

Patricia W. Linville
Gregory W. Fischer
Duke University

Social categories provide an essential tool for simplifying and making sense of the complex social environment in which we live. By assigning others to various social categories (e.g., adult, female, lawyer), we develop and apply mental rules that allow us to learn from past situations and generalize to new ones. In doing so, however, we run the risk of oversimplifying and overgeneralizing. As useful as it is to identify common properties of the members of a group, it is also essential to make distinctions. Thus, recent research on stereotyping and intergroup behavior has looked beyond simple perceptions of group stereotypes to examine ways in which people perceive variability and make distinctions among members of a group.

In addition to this functional argument, there are other reasons why it is important to understand how perceptions of group variability affect intergroup perception and behavior. First, people make reasonably accurate estimates of group variability, which suggests that they encode variability information and access it when needed (Judd, Ryan, & Park, 1991; Nisbett & Kunda, 1985). Second, perceptions of group variability influence inferences, evaluations, and behavior toward group members (e.g., Linville, 1982; Linville & Fischer, 1993b; Linville & Jones, 1980; Nisbett, Krantz, Jepson, & Kunda, 1983; Park & Hastie, 1987; Quattrone & Jones, 1980). Both findings support the functional argument regarding the importance of perceived variability.

Third, despite their general ability to detect group variability, people's perceptions of variability are biased. The most common bias is outgroup homogeneity: People perceive less variability in their outgroups than in comparable ingroups (e.g., Judd & Park, 1988; Linville, 1982; Linville, Fischer, & Salovey, 1989; Linville & Jones, 1980; Park & Rothbart, 1982; Quattrone & Jones, 1980). This outgroup homogeneity bias appears somewhat independent of ingroup favoritism, thus highlighting the relative contribution of various cognitive and social-motivational processes. In other cases, however, when social identity needs are strongly tied to group membership, people sometimes show an opposite ingroup homogeneity bias (Brown & Wootton-Millward, 1993; Simon, 1992a; Simon & Brown, 1987).

Fourth, understanding how people perceive group variability is important in understanding basic issues in social categorization. Research on group variability has stimulated lively debates regarding competing models and approaches to social categorization (e.g., prototype vs. exemplar categorization; online vs. memory-based processing; cognitive vs. social-motivational influences). For a summary of these debates, see *Annual Review of Psychology* articles by Brewer and Kramer (1985), Hilton and von Hippel (1996), Messick and Mackie (1989), Sherman, Judd, and Park (1989), and Schneider (1991).

Fifth, understanding perceived group variability is central to understanding stereotyping. For example, Hamilton and Sherman (1994) opened their handbook chapter on stereotyping with five questions: What is a stereotype? How do people develop stereotypes? When and how are they used? Why do they persist? How can we change them? The answer to each of these questions depends on how people incorporate knowledge of variability in their judgments and behavior.

Finally, to the extent that perceiving an outgroup as homogeneous contributes to greater conflict, stereotyping, and prejudice toward outgroup members, then creating experiences that lead to more differentiated impressions of outgroups may contribute to better intergroup relations, as well as to better decisions about individuals whose group identity is salient (e.g., decisions about hiring, promotion, and firing).

In short, perceived group variability appears to play an important role in intergroup judgment and behavior. At least 12 reviews of perceived group variability have appeared since 1986 (e.g., Hamilton & Sherman, 1994; Hilton & von Hippel, 1996; Linville & Fischer, 1993a; Linville, Salovey, & Fischer, 1986; Messick & Mackie, 1989; Mullen & Hu, 1989; Ostrom & Sedikides, 1992; Park, Judd, & Ryan, 1991; Quattrone, 1986; Sedikides & Ostrom, 1993; Simon, 1992a; Wilder 1986). In 1993, a special edition of *Social Cognition* was devoted to the topic.

This chapter continues this tradition. However, it departs from past reviews in two ways: by placing more emphasis on the consequences of perceived group variability, and by discussing new research on perceived covariation among the features of group members and its consequences for judgment. This chapter begins by reviewing research on outgroup homogeneity. It reviews empirical findings, discusses proposed mechanisms, and describes several formal models. The next section discusses consequences — how differences in perceived group variability affect generalization, categorization, extremity of judgment, and stereotype revision. The third section discusses a new bias, the *outgroup covariation effect*, in which people tend to perceive greater covariation among the features of outgroup members (Linville, Fischer, & Yoon, 1996). The fourth section shows an important consequence of perceived covariation — the *covariation extremity effect*. Greater perceived covariation among features leads to more extreme judgments about group members. It also presents a framework linking familiarity with a group to both perceived covariation among pairs of features and extremity of overall judgments about group members. The final section suggests future research topics dealing with behavioral consequences of perceived variability and covariation.

PERCEIVED GROUP VARIABILITY

People Usually Perceive Less Variability Among Outgroup Members

Most research on perceived group variability has focused on testing the outgroup homogeneity hypothesis — that outgroup members perceive a group to be more homogeneous than do ingroup members. The effect appears to be quite robust across a variety natural groups, including profession, nationality, race, religion, age, college major, and sorority-fraternity affiliation. It also appears to be robust across a variety of variability measures.

Investigators have used a wide variety of group homogeneity measures, including judgments of the overall similarity of group members (Mackie & Asuncion, 1990; Park & Rothbart, 1982), number of group subtypes created (Brewer & Lui, 1984; Linville, 1982; Park, Ryan, & Judd, 1992), and dimensional complexity (Linville & Jones, 1980; Linville, 1982). Each of these types of measures implicitly or explicitly concerns patterns or sets of feature values. The typical finding with each of these types of measures is *outgroup homogeneity* — people perceive outgroups as more homogeneous than comparable ingroups.

The predominant focus of recent research has been on measures of perceived variability and stereotypicality with respect to single features, such as intelligence or likability. Measures of *single-feature variability* include the range, standard deviation, and perceived differentiation (*Pd*) of a feature (e.g., Jones, Wood, & Quattrone, 1981; Linville et al., 1989; Park & Judd, 1990). The typical finding is that people perceive their outgroups to be less variable along single features than their ingroups (for reviews see Brewer, 1993; Linville, 1997; Linville & Fischer, 1993a; Messick & Mackie, 1989; Mullen & Hu, 1989; Ostrom & Sedikides, 1992; Park, Judd, & Ryan, 1991; Sedikides & Ostrom, 1993). As noted earlier, an ingroup homogeneity effect arises in some cases where people identify strongly with their ingroup (Simon, 1992a). We discuss this in a later section on causes of perceived variability.

Measures of single-feature stereotypicality reflect the extent to which members of a group are perceived to display the stereotypic features of the group (Park & Judd, 1990; Park & Rothbart, 1982). Because these measures are based on the means of distributions, not their variances, we have argued that such measures are not measures of variability in the usual statistical sense (Linville & Fischer, 1993a; see also Simon, 1995). Indeed, Park and Judd (1990) found that measures of stereotypicality were uncorrelated with dispersion measures of variability. The typical finding with these measures is an *outgroup stereotypicality effect* — people view their outgroups as being more stereotypic than their ingroups (e.g., Park & Judd, 1990; Park & Rothbart, 1982). Judd, Park, Ryan, Brauer, and Kraus (1995) documented one interesting exception involving race. African-American college students viewed White students as more stereotypic than themselves, as one would expect from the outgroup stereotypicality effect. White students, however, showed no outgroup stereotypicality bias. Instead, they also perceived Whites to be more stereotypic. Judd et al. suggested that White youths are learning to deemphasize ethnic differences, whereas African-American youths increasingly value ethnic pride and ethnic differences.

Models of Perceived Variability

Research on group variability has served as a catalyst for research on more basic questions regarding how knowledge of groups is mentally represented and processed. This has led researchers to take cognitive models of categorization more seriously. Two types of models have been considered: property abstraction models (including prototype models), in which category properties are actively abstracted "online"; and multiple exemplar models, in which category exemplars are stored and then retrieved as needed to make judgments about the category.

Property Abstraction Models.   Because earlier work on perceptions of social groups focused mainly on group stereotypes, social psychologists relied mainly on simple prototype models (Posner & Keele, 1968), in which a group is represented by a list of prototypic features (i.e., the stereotype) that are actively abstracted online as the perceiver encounters exemplars of the category. For example, a typical prototype of a football player might be, "Football players are big, strong, quick, fit, and highly aggressive." The traditional prototype model is limited because it fails to represent the variability that perceivers see within the category. For example, one may believe that, although most football players are big and strong, others are small but very fast. Thus, more recent abstraction models, such as Fried and Holyoak's (1984) category density model, assume that people form online abstractions of both the mean and variance of each category-relevant feature.

Park and Judd (Judd & Park, 1988; Park & Judd, 1990) proposed a prototype-plus-exemplars model to account for the outgroup homogeneity effect. They suggested that judgments of outgroup variability are based on online abstractions of variability, whereas judgments of ingroup variability are based on online variability abstractions plus information from ingroup exemplars that are retrieved from memory. The intuition behind the model is that consideration of ingroup exemplars will add to the perceived variability of the ingroup. This model is supported by their finding that perceived ingroup variability was significantly correlated with the variability of retrieved ingroup members, but perceived outgroup variability was not correlated with retrieval of outgroup members (Park & Judd, 1990).

Kraus, Ryan, Judd, Hastie, and Park (1993) proposed a new property abstraction model, in which perceivers engage in an online abstraction process to construct mental frequency distributions over the levels of each category-relevant attribute. According to this model, the outgroup homogeneity effect occurs because ingroup members are classified along more finely grained attribute levels than outgroup members (e.g., five vs. two attribute levels).

Multiple Exemplar Models.   Within cognitive psychology, property abstraction models of categorization have generally given way to multiple exemplar and distributed memory models (Estes, 1993; Kruschke, 1992; McClelland & Rumelhart, 1985; Medin, 1989). One impetus for turning to exemplar models in representing categories was their natural ability to deal with people's knowledge of the variability within a category. In these models, category knowledge consists of a set of exemplars representing specific instances or subtypes of the category. With this representation, judgments of variability are made by activating a set of category exemplars in memory, then estimating the variability of each feature in this activated set (Linville, 1997; Linville & Fischer, 1993a; Linville, Fischer, & Salovey, 1989; Linville et al., 1986).

According to exemplar models, judgment is a memory-based process, in which specific instances and subtypes play a key role (Smith & Zarate, 1992). Linville et al. (1989) developed PDIST, a computer simulation model of how people generate perceived distributions of category features from a set of exemplars stored in memory. PDIST relies on a probe-echo mechanism like that proposed by Hintzman (1986), but extends Hintzman's model by adding judgment processes needed to construct a perceived distribution of a category feature. For example, suppose the task is to estimate a distribution of the intelligence of football players. To perform this task in PDIST, one would construct a set of memory probes to retrieve relevant exemplars. When a memory probe is formed in working memory (e.g., "high intelligence, football player"), it activates in parallel a set of traces in long-term memory. Each trace is activated in proportion to its similarity to the probe. The set of activated traces is called the *echo*. The strength of the echo reflects the number and strengths of the traces activated by the probe. PDIST uses the relative strengths of these echoes to construct a perceived distribution of the characteristics of group members. For example, suppose the memory probe "low intelligence, football player" evokes a strong echo, whereas the probes "average intelligence, football player" and "high intelligence, football player" evoke weak and very weak echoes, respectively. In these cases, PDIST will form a distribution in which most football players are low in intelligence, a few are average in intelligence, and fewer still are high in intelligence. From this one may infer that the typical football player is low in intelligence, and that football players do not vary much in this regard.

According to PDIST and most other exemplar models, retrieval is a parallel and implicit process that need not be accessible to consciousness. Thus, retrieval may involve a large number of exemplars without time or cognitive resource concerns, and it may not be revealed by traditional recall measures (Hintzman, 1986). As a consequence, although exemplar processes are memory-based, they do not necessarily predict a correlation between judged variability and the exemplars that are explicitly recalled (see Smith & Zarate, 1992).

How do exemplar models account for the outgroup homogeneity effect? It follows from basic principles of statistical sampling theory that the larger the size of a random sample, the larger the variability of that sample. Thus, to the extent that perceivers have been exposed to representative samples of category exemplars, the greater the number of retrieved exemplars, the greater the perceived variability of the group. Because people tend to be more familiar with their ingroup, they store and retrieve more exemplars of the ingroup. Thus, greater familiarity with the ingroup will lead a multiple exemplar process like PDIST to perceive the outgroup as more homogeneous. (Exemplar models are also compatible with several other mechanisms discussed in the next section on mechanisms underlying outgroup homogeneity.)

Several types of evidence support the PDIST model (Linville, Fischer, & Salovey, 1989). First, perceived variability was greater for the ingroup in cases where participants were more familiar with the ingroup (age, nationality), but not in cases where participants were equally familiar with the ingroup and outgroup (gender). Second, people who had more contact with a group perceived greater variability within the group. Third, perceived variability increased over time as group members had more contact with one another (perceived variability of class members increased over the semester). Fourth, a computer simulation of the PDIST model revealed that it reproduced each of these results. Greater familiarity with a simulated group led to greater perceived variability. Finally, Mackie, Sherman, and Worth's (1993) reaction time study supported the hypothesis that judgments of group variability were memory-based. This favors exemplar models like PDIST over online abstraction models.

Mechanisms Contributing to Perceived Outgroup Homogeneity

Familiarity. We have already discussed one informational mechanism that leads to greater perceived variability for ingroups — greater familiarity with the ingroup. Other things being equal, greater familiarity means that a perceiver is likely to encounter a more varied set of exemplars of a group, which should lead to a more differentiated and variable representation of a group (Linville, 1982; Linville et al., 1989). Empirical evidence supports this link. For Irish and American students, perceived outgroup variability correlated 0.49 with the number of outgroup members they had met and 0.40 with the number they knew well (Linville & Fischer, 1993a). Similarly, for Hindu and Muslim students, quantity of contact with the outgroup was the best predictor of perceived outgroup variability (Islam & Hewstone, 1993). Other factors also contribute to the outgroup homogeneity effect.

Prototype-First Learning. Park and Hastie (1987) contrasted perceived variability under two different learning conditions. In the prototype-first condition, participants first saw information about the prototypic features of a group, and then were shown specific exemplars of the group. In the exemplars-first condition, participants first saw the exemplars of the group, then were shown the group prototype. Those in the prototype-first condition perceived less variability. Park and Hastie suggested that people typically learn about outgroups via a prototype-first process, whereas they learn about ingroups via an exemplars-first process. If so, this is a second informational bias that contributes to outgroup homogeneity.

Second-Hand Exemplars. Knowledge of social groups is based, in part, on first-hand exemplars encountered in direct observation or interaction with group members, and, in part, on second-hand exemplars conveyed in media images, books, or aural descriptions by friends and family members. Linville and Fischer (1993a) proposed that second-hand exemplars frequently represent widely shared stereotypes about groups, whereas first-hand exemplars more truly reflect the diversity within social groups. They suggested that because second-hand exemplars constitute a relatively greater proportion of people's knowledge of outgroups, people tend to perceive less variability among outgroup members.

Attention to Individuating Versus Shared Features. The preceding mechanisms involve differences in people's knowledge of ingroups and outgroups. A second class of mechanisms concerns how people process that information. Park and Rothbart (1982) showed that people are more likely to attend to *individuating features* of ingroup than outgroup members. After reading stories, people were equally likely to recall the genders of male and female protagonists, but more likely to recall the occupation (an individuating feature) of members of their gender ingroup. By definition, individuating features display greater variability, so this memory/attention bias contributes to the greater perceived variability of ingroups. A related finding is that memory of ingroups is organized by person, whereas memory of outgroups is organized in terms of attributes of the group (Ostrom, Carpenter, Sedikides, & Li, 1993; Sedikides, 1996). Again, individuating information appears more salient for ingroups.

Incentives to Make Distinctions. A third type of mechanism concerns incentives. Because people usually interact more with members of their ingroup, they often have greater incentives to distinguish among ingroup members (Linville et al., 1986, 1989). Making more distinctions leads to greater perceived variability. This hypothesis is consistent with the Kraus et al. (1993) finding that people use more levels per feature for ingroups than outgroups. It is also consistent with a broader theme in research on adaptive decision making—namely, that people expend more effort on information processing when the benefits of expending the effort are high relative to the effort involved (Payne, Bettman, & Johnson, 1993).

Social Identity. Several recent theoretical contributions to the homogeneity field have been inspired by social identity concepts (e.g., Tajfel, 1978, 1982). In Brewer's (1991, 1993) optimal distinctiveness theory, perceived group variability is subject to motivational forces associated with needs for self-identity and differentiation from others. Optimal distinctiveness involves identifying with social categories in such a way as to achieve a balance between feeling assimilated and feeling differentiated from others. In a large, highly inclusive ingroup, the need to differentiate oneself (me vs. us comparison) leads one to perceive the ingroup as heterogeneous. In a small, distinctive or exclusive ingroup, the need to identify with the ingroup (us vs. them comparison) leads one to perceive the ingroup as homogeneous. Thus, strong identification with the ingroup should lead to greater perceived *ingroup homogeneity,* rather than the more typical outgroup homogeneity.

Simon, Brown, and their colleagues (e.g., Brown & Wootton-Millward, 1993; Simon, 1992a; Simon & Brown 1987; Simon & Pettigrew, 1990) have demonstrated that ingroup homogeneity effects often occur in situations where social identity needs are strong (see also Mullen & Hu, 1989). Further, ingroup homogeneity effects are most likely to arise on attributes that are relevant to the group identity (Kelly, 1989; Simon, 1992b). For example, nurses showed an ingroup homogeneity effect for nurse-related attributes, but an outgroup homogeneity effect for doctor-relevant attributes (Brown & Wootton-Millward, 1993). Members of a British political party showed an ingroup homogeneity effect for attitudes central to the party's ideology (e.g., private health care), but an outgroup homogeneity effect for personality traits (e.g., loyal; Kelly, 1989). These findings indicate that outgroup homogeneity is not as universal as we once thought, and suggest that social identity needs influence perceived variability.

Bartsch and Judd (1993; Judd & Bartsch, 1995) disputed whether group identity is the source of the ingroup homogeneity effect because demonstrations of the effect have confounded strong social identity with the minority status of the ingroup. Bartsch and Judd presented data that they interpreted as showing that smaller ingroup size is the key to the ingroup homogeneity effect, when it occurs. Simon (1995) and Haslam and Oakes (1995) disputed Bartsch and Judd's findings and conclusions. Despite controversy about the locus of the effect, it is clear that the combination of small ingroup size and strong social identity can lead to ingroup homogeneity.

Other Factors. A variety of other factors also influence perceived group variability. Perceived group homogeneity depends on temporal factors, such as degree of socialization of a group's identity or amount of time with a group (Brown & Wootton-Millward, 1993; Linville et al., 1989).

The relationship between an ingroup and an outgroup is also important, particularly the relative power and advantaged–disadvantaged status of the groups (Brewer, 1993; Brown & Wootton-Millward, 1993; Linville et al., 1989; Lorenzi-Cioldi, Eagly, & Stewart, 1995; Sedikides, in press). For example, both males and females tend to see females as more homogeneous, which may be interpreted in terms of men's greater status and power (Lorenzi-Cioldi et al., 1995).

In short, the outgroup homogeneity effect is multiply determined by greater familiarity with the ingroup, prototype-first learning for the outgroup, relatively greater exposure to second-hand exemplars of the outgroup, greater incentives to make distinctions among ingroup members, and greater attention to individuating features of ingroup members. Further, exceptions to outgroup homogeneity are also multiply determined. Exceptions are especially likely in cases where the ingroup serves important social identity needs, or where one is not more familiar with one's ingroup.

CONSEQUENCES OF PERCEIVED VARIABILITY

If one looks broadly at the consequences of ingroup–outgroup status, the literature is full of behavioral consequences (e.g., Dovidio & Gaertner, 1986). If one looks at the consequences of perceived group variability, however, the literature is quite limited. Although the field has made substantial progress in research on measures, determinants, and different categorization models of variability, we have largely ignored the consequences of perceived group variability, and almost entirely ignored overt behavioral outcomes. For this reason, our discussion of the consequences of perceived group variability focuses primarily on effects on judgments. Judgments are important in their own right, and are often direct precursors to behavior. Research has shown that perceiving a group as more homogeneous (e.g., the outgroup) influences several aspects of stereotyping and group perception, including categorization, generalization, inference, and evaluation.

Variability Effects on Generalization

Generalizations from a group to an individual group member have important implications for behavior. When we make such generalizations, we respond to individuals as if they were typical of the group as a whole. Generalizations from an individual to the group are important because they may serve to modify group stereotypes that can then be used to guide behavior toward individual group members. Overgeneralizing from one instance may lead to false inferences about the prototypic characteristics of the group as a whole.

The laws of probability imply that the more homogeneous a group, the more one should generalize from individual to group and from group to individual. In the first case, if a group is homogeneous, information about the characteristics of a single group member are quite informative about the prototypic features of the group. This is not the case for a highly variable group. In the second case, if a group is homogeneous and we know its prototypic features, we can generalize these to an individual group member with relatively high confidence. With a highly variable group, however, such generalizations are subject to greater uncertainty. Empirical studies support both predictions.

Generalizing From Individuals to Groups. Quattrone and Jones (1980) predicted that, because people tend to perceive outgroups to be more homogeneous, they should make stronger generalizations from the behavior of a single group member to the group as a whole when the group is an outgroup. Princeton and Rutgers students viewed a tape of either a Princeton or a Rutgers student making a choice during a psychology experiment (e.g., to wait alone or with others). Then they estimated the proportion of students from that university who would make the same decision as the one they observed. As predicted, participants made stronger generalizations about their outgroup. Princeton students made stronger generalizations about Rutgers students, and Rutgers students made stronger generalizations about Princeton students.

Nisbett and his colleagues reported similar results (Nisbett, Krantz, Jepson, & Kunda, 1983) when they manipulated the perceived variability of the group. In the low-variability condition, they instructed participants to contemplate the central tendency of the group, thus making the homogeneity of the group more salient. Following this manipulation, participants made stronger generalizations from one member to the group as a whole.

Park and Hastie (1987) took a more direct approach by manipulating the actual variability of a group. They exposed participants to either a high- or low-variance set of training exemplars. These training stimuli were behavioral descriptions prescaled in terms of intelligence and sociability. In a subsequent generalization task, participants made inferences about other characteristics of the group. For instance, they were told that one group member was honest (according to a personality inventory), and were asked to estimate what percent of the group was similarly honest. When the new trait was evaluatively consistent with the original group stereotype, participants made stronger generalizations when the group was homogeneous. However, when the new trait was evaluatively inconsistent with the original group stereotype, participants made weaker generalizations when the group was homogeneous. In short, when a group is homogeneous, people are more likely to generalize stereotype-consistent information about an individual to the group as a whole, and less likely to generalize counterstereotypic information about an individual to the group (Park & Hastie, 1987).

Rehder and Hastie (1996) recently obtained similar results in generalizations over time. Participants were shown a set of group exemplars from 1985, and were asked to make mean and 95% confidence range estimates. Then they were shown one, two, or three new exemplars from the group in 1995, and were asked to make new mean and range estimates for 1995. The more variable the 1985 training set, the less people changed their beliefs about the mean (and range) of the 1995 distribution. Again, greater group variability reduced the degree to which people changed their beliefs in light of new data about individual group members.

Generalizing From Group to Individual. A similar hypothesis arises for generalizations from the group to an individual. When a group is homogeneous, people should be more likely to apply group attributes (e.g., the group stereotype) to an individual member. Surprisingly, this prediction has received less attention. There is clear evidence that people frequently generalize group stereotypes to individual group members. For example, Krueger and Rothbart (1988) showed that people judge a male to be more aggressive than a female when each performs the same aggressive act. There is also evidence that the stronger one's group stereotype, the more likely one is to apply it to individual members. Ryan, Judd, and Park (1996) showed that the more stereotypic one's perceptions of Asian Americans or African Americans, the more one generalized a group stereotype to individual members who performed ambiguous actions. Thus, greater stereotypicality led to greater group-to-individual generalization. Greater perceived group variability moderated this effect, reducing the tendency to generalize group stereotypes to individual members. This supports the hypothesis that greater perceived homogeneity leads to stronger group-to-individual generalization of stereotypes.

Lambert (1995; Lambert & Wyer, 1990) showed that typicality plays an important role in group-to-individual generalizations when the group is homogeneous. When a group is homogeneous, typicality plays a "gatekeeper" role. If an idividual group member performs an act typical of the group, perceivers use the group to infer other qualities of that individual. If the member performs an atypical act, no such inferences are made. For example, people liked an individual who performed an act that was typical of a homogeneous, liked group, and disliked an individual who performed an act that was typical of a homogeneous, disliked group. When the group was heterogeneous, however, typicality had no effect. Instead, liking judgments only depended on how much perceivers liked the group and the action.

Variability Effects on Categorization

Before one can apply a group stereotype to an individual, one must first categorize the individual as a member of the group. In some cases, this is obvious (e.g., gender), but in others it is not, especially when there are several bases for classification. Basic categorization research has shown that the greater the variability of a category, the more likely a somewhat atypical new exemplar is to be classified as an instance of the category (for reviews, see Medin, 1989; Smith & Medin, 1981). Similar effects arise in judgments of social category membership. In the Park and Hastie (1987) study described earlier, participants were exposed to a set of training stimuli from either a high- or low-variance category. Then they judged whether new exemplars were members of the category. They were more likely to classify a person with atypical group attributes as a member of the group when the group was high in variance. In a related finding, Lambert (1995) showed that people were quicker to judge an atypical member to be atypical when the group was low in variance. This indicates that atypical outgroup members are less likely to be classified as members of the group, thus reinforcing outgroup homogeneity.

Variability Effects on Extremity of Judgment

Linville and Jones (1980; Linville, 1982) developed a model of social judgment in which dimensional complexity plays a key role. A more complex representation of a category is one with more independent features. Thus, greater complexity entails making greater distinctions among the members and subtypes of a category, which is closely akin to variability. We hypothesized that greater dimensional complexity would lead to less extreme overall judgments about members of a category. Why? The more distinct features one uses to represent members of a category, the more likely one is to perceive category members as good in some respects but bad in others, which will tend to moderate overall judgments. This leads to the complexity extremity hypothesis—the less complex one's thinking about a group, the more extreme one's overall evaluations of individual members. To test this hypothesis, we further assumed that because people generally have greater contact with their ingroups, they should form more complex representations of ingroups. Thus, they should make more extreme overall judgments about outgroup members. The Linville and Jones (1980) results support this outgroup extremity prediction. White participants read and evaluated several law school applications, some weak and some strong, that contained incidental information on the race of the applicant. When evaluating a strong application, White participants rated an African-

American applicant higher than a comparable White applicant. When evaluating a weak application, they rated an African-American applicant lower than a comparable White applicant. Thus, White students were more extreme when rating applicants from their racial outgroup.

Linville (1982) obtained similar results using age as the group variable. When reading a favorable vignette, young people rated an older male more positively than a comparable young male. When reading an unfavorable vignette, they rated an older male more negatively than a comparable younger one. Similarly, Linville and Salovey (1982) found that older people rated vignettes about young people more extremely than identical vignettes about older people. In short, both young and older people rated members of their outgroup more extremely than they rated members of their ingroup. At the individual level, those less complex in their thinking about the category of older adults were more extreme in their ratings of specific older targets ($r = -0.65$). They were both more positive about the favorable older person and more negative about the unfavorable older person (Linville, 1982). Finally, when complexity was manipulated by drawing people's attention to two versus six features of stimuli, such as features of chocolate chip cookies (or law school essays), those attending to fewer features made more extreme evaluations — more positive about the cookies (essays) they liked most and more negative about the cookies (essays) they liked least (Linville, 1982; Linville & Jones, 1980).

In short, the complexity-extremity effect emerges when complexity is measured as an individual difference variable, manipulated by ingroup-outgroup membership, or manipulated by directing people's attention to a small or large number of features. Greater complexity in one's mental representation of a category leads to less extreme overall judgments about individual members. Because people tend to have less complex representations of outgroups, they tend to make more extreme judgments about outgroup members.

Variability Effects on Stereotypes

As noted earlier, there is a large literature indicating that group stereotypes can influence judgments about individual group members, especially when relatively little is known about the individual (Krueger & Rothbart, 1988). Perceptions of group variability have important effects on the development, maintenance, modification, and application of stereotypes. Consider the following questions posed by Hamilton and Sherman (1994) in their handbook chapter on stereotyping. First, what is a stereotype? Research on group variability suggests that the concept of a group stereotype should be modified to include not only the central tendency of a group, but also the variability of the group.

Second, how do people develop stereotypes? Our earlier discussions of prototype-first learning (Park & Hastie, 1987) and second-hand exemplars (Linville & Fischer, 1993a) suggest that learning from abstracted group stereotypes or subtypes facilitates developing strong stereotypes, whereas learning from individual group exemplars facilitates developing a differentiated representation of the group. However, Ford and Stangor (1992) found that when people learn from exemplars, they are most likely to form stereotypes about features that display low within-group variance. Such features are more diagnostic of the group.

Third, when and how are stereotypes used? As we saw earlier, a group stereotype is most likely to be applied to an individual member when the stereotype is strong (Ryan, Judd, & Park, 1996), the group is homogeneous (Lambert, 1995; Lambert & Wyer, 1990; Ryan, Judd, & Park, 1996), the individual performs an act typical of a homogeneous group (Lambert, 1995; Lambert & Wyer, 1990), and relatively little is known about the individual (Krueger & Rothbart, 1988).

Finally, why do stereotypes persist, and how can we change them? Again, research on group variability and categorization provides some important insights. When a group is homogeneous, a counter stereotypic new exemplar is unlikely to be classified as an instance of the group (Park & Hastie, 1987). Thus, homogeneous groups are relatively impervious to change by exposure to atypical exemplars. In contrast, a counterstereotypical exemplar is more likely to be classified as an instance of a highly variable group. However, because the group is perceived to be variable, inclusion of an atypical member has little effect on the overall group stereotype. In short, stereotypes create a Catch 22 situation. Once formed, they are highly resistant to change.

Fortunately, our previous discussion of generalization does raise one ray of hope for counteracting stereotypes. If people initially learn to view groups as heterogeneous in nature, they are less likely to apply group stereotypes to individual group members. In principle, at least, early training regarding the diversity within groups might lessen the tendency to make stereotype-based judgments about individuals.

PERCEIVED COVARIATION

A New Approach Focusing on Perceived Covariation

Exemplar Model of Perceived Covariation.   The predominant focus in the group variability literature has been on measures of group variability, especially on measures of variability with respect to individual features. We have begun thinking about these issues by using a new approach that focuses on perceived covariation among the features of group members. We assume that the mental representation of a group includes clusters of features representing exemplars of the group. These exemplars may be either individual members (e.g., Newt Gingrich) or subtypes (conservative Republican) of a group (Washington politicians). To give a simple example, the mental representation of the category *students* might include the subtypes *nerd*, *party animal*, and *athlete* (see Table 6.1). As argued earlier, feature patterns implicitly encode information about the variability of the group with respect to single features. In addition, feature patterns implicitly encode knowledge of covariation among features of group members. For instance, in Table 6.1, the traits *studious* and *sociable* are negatively correlated features for the category of students. To give a second simple example, the mental representation of types of people in business might include *fast-tracker*, *9-to-5er*, and *number cruncher* (see Table 6.1). Here, *analytical* and *hard-working* are positively correlated features of business types.

Research shows that people are sensitive to covariation information. Perceptions of covariation play a key role in inference, judgment, and prediction. Perceived covariation provides the basis for our implicit personality theories (IPT; Schneider, 1973), allowing us to infer one trait, attitude, or behavior from another, and inferring attributes from category membership. Perceived covariation also provides the basis for causal attributions (Kelley, 1967).

An interesting question is whether group membership or expertise affects perceptions of covariation. This brings together two relatively separate literatures — one on ingroup–outgroup differences and one on perceived covariation. Are there ingroup–outgroup differences in perceived covariation? What is the effect of experience? Does greater experience in a domain

TABLE 6.1
Examples of Types of Group Members

Types of College Students		
Nerd	*Party Animal*	*Athlete*
studious	sociable	sociable
unsociable	not studious	not studious
dress without style	dress stylishly	dress OK

Types of People in Business		
Fast Tracker	*9-to-5er*	*Number Cruncher*
analytical	nonanalytical	analytical
hard working	lazy	hard working
decisive	indecisive	indecisive

lead to stronger or weaker perceived covariation among features? In a recent article (Linville, Fischer, & Yoon, 1996), we suggested that, in the social world, people tend to overestimate the covariation of features describing other people. However, greater experience with a social group leads to lower perceived covariation among the features of group members.

Hypotheses. We made two predictions regarding perceived covariation among the features of group members (Linville et al., 1996). First, we predicted a *familiarity covariation effect*: Greater familiarity results in lower perceived covariation among the features of group members. Second, we predicted an *outgroup covariation effect:* Because people tend to be less familiar with their outgroups, they tend to perceive greater covariation among the features of outgroup members.

Linville et al. (1996) suggested several reasons why we might expect links among familiarity, group membership, and perceived covariation. First, people may start with a default expectation about the covariation among the traits of people. Prior research suggests that people overestimate the degree to which social features covary. In the extreme, people see correlations where none exists—the illusory correlation (Chapman & Chapman, 1967; Hamilton, 1981; Hamilton & Gifford, 1976). In other cases, they overestimate the magnitude of weak correlations (Berman & Kenny, 1976; D'Andrade, 1974). There is a particular tendency to overestimate the degree of evaluative consistency among features—positive features go with other positive features, and negative features go with other negative features. This is consistent with cognitive consistency theory and implicit personality theory (Abelson & Rosenberg, 1958; Rosenberg & Sedlak, 1972). Some person schemas do, however, reflect expectations of negative feature correlation (e.g., active persons are also seen as demanding, and warm persons are seen as dependent). With greater familiarity with a group, one may encounter a wider variety of types of group members displaying various pattern of traits, including counterexamples, whose feature patterns violate expectations of consistency. This weakens the perceived covariation among features.

Second, outgroup covariation is consistent with sampling theory. In small samples, correlation among features is too large in absolute terms (positive correlations are too positive, and negative ones are too negative). With a larger sample of exemplars, correlations among features will become weaker and closer to the population correlations.

Third, when familiarity with a group is low, a higher proportion of knowledge may be based on socially conveyed "second-hand exemplars." Such exemplars are frequently stereotypic, and may overestimate the actual covariation among the features of group members and subtypes (Linville et al., 1996).

An Implicit Approach to Measuring Perceived Covariation

Linville et al. (1996) developed a method for measuring implicit perceptions of covariation. First, participants generated different subtypes of a social group. They described each subtype by circling a set of feature values that best characterized that subtype. For each feature, they selected one of three levels (e.g., lazy, average, or motivated; indecisive, average, or decisive; In our current work, we use larger numbers of levels per feature). We used these subtype descriptions to compute two measures of perceived covariation for each participant. The first was the average absolute correlation ($Avg\ |R|$), computed by taking the absolute value of the correlation between each pair of features, then averaging across all pairs of features. This reflects degree of correlation, per se, positive or negative. The second measure was the average correlation ($Avg\ R$), computed by averaging the signed correlations between all pairs of features. This measure reflects evaluatively consistent correlation among features—the degree to which positive features go with positive features and negative features with negative features.

Both covariation measures are implicit in the sense that they are derived from subtypes created by the participant, not from direct judgments of covariation. Our implicit measures of perceived covariation have several advantages. First, they reflect a property of the knowledge structure guiding social judgments—the correlation among features in that structure—rather than metabeliefs about covariation. Second, people do not have to be consciously aware of feature correlation. Lewicki (1986) showed that knowledge of covariation affects other judgment, even when people are unable to consciously articulate the covariation. Finally, people find the implicit task more natural than making direct estimates of covariation.

Empirical Results: Familiarity, Group Membership, and Perceived Covariation

Age-Related Groups. Linville et al. (1996) tested the familiarity covariation and outgroup covariation hypotheses in three studies. In the first, young and old participants generated types of young and old people (e.g., grandmothers, golf buffs, sorority/fraternity types, pre-meds), from which we calculated the $Avg\ R$ and $Avg\ |R|$ measures. Three important findings emerged (Linville et al., 1996).

First, we found support for an *outgroup covariation effect*. Both young and old participants perceived greater covariation among features of their age outgroup. This was true for both types of covariation—$Avg |R|$ reflecting covariation per se and $Avg R$ reflecting evaluative consistency (see Fig. 6.1). This effect remained significant when controlling for number of subtypes generated, favorability of feature ratings, and whether the features were age-stereotypic. Note that the $Avg |R|$ measure was larger than $Avg R$. This implies that participants perceived some pairs of features to be negatively correlated. If all correlations were positive, the two measures would be equal.

Second, we found support for a *familiarity covariation effect*. Those more familiar with an age group perceived lower covariation among features. This result was supported for both measures of covariation and four measures of familiarity: number of acquaintances in the group, number of group members known well, contact hours per month with group members, and number of names of group members generated in a 3-minute listing.

Third, we found that familiarity acted as a mediator of the ingroup–outgroup difference in perceived covariation. As already noted, those more familiar with a group perceived less covariation among the features of group members. Further, if familiarity is a mediator, the outgroup covariation effect should be weaker when controlling for level of familiarity with the group. In fact, the effect was not significant when controlling for familiarity. Using these same criteria, the number of subtypes generated by a participant was not a mediator of the outgroup covariation effect. In short, we found support for both an outgroup covariation effect and a familiarity covariation effect for age-related ingroups and outgroups. Further, the outgroup covariation effect appears to be mediated in part by differential familiarity with the ingroup and outgroup.

Gender Groups. If familiarity is a mediator of ingroup–outgroup differences in perceived covariation, then gender may be a special case. Gender is an important and salient group membership, but students report high and approximately equal familiarity with both male and female college students. Thus, differences in perceived covariation for gender should be relatively small. To test this prediction, we asked male and female college students to generate types of male and female college students (e.g., preppie, artsie type, political radical; Linville et al., 1996). There were no significant gender differences in number of male and female friends or number of male and female close friends for either gender. Given this, it is not surprising that there were no ingroup–outgroup differences in perceived covariation (see Fig. 6.1). In short, with no group familiarity difference, there was no group covariation difference.

Professional Groups. In our final study, we looked at familiarity more directly, in terms of the amount of experience or expertise with a social

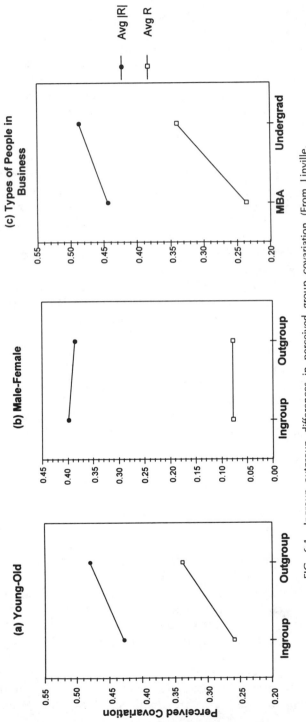

FIG. 6.1. Ingroup–outgroup differences in perceived group covariation (From Linville, Fischer, and Yoon, 1996.) Copyright 1996 by the American Psychological Association. Reprinted with permission.

domain—types of people in business. MBA students (who had an average of 3.4 years of business experience) and undergraduate business students (who averaged less than 1 year of business experience) generated types of people in business (e.g., team player, 9-to-5er) using a variety of features, including high to low analytical skill, verbal skill, and leadership ability. Here we had two measure of experience. At the individual level, students differed in their number of years of work experience; at the group level, MBA students had more years of work experience than undergraduates.

Because MBAs have several more years of business experience than undergraduates, they encounter more varied types in business settings, and should therefore perceive lower covariation among features. The results support this prediction (Linville et al., 1996). First, at the group level, MBA students perceived lower covariation among features of business types than did undergraduate business students. This was true for both $Avg\ |R|$, reflecting covariation per se, and $Avg\ R$, reflecting evaluative consistency (see Fig. 6.1). This group difference remained significant when controlling for number of types generated and favorability of ratings. Second, at the individual level, those with more years of work experience perceived less covariation among the features of business types. Finally, work experience acted as a mediator of covariation differences between MBA and undergraduate business. Controlling for the number of years of work experience eliminated the MBA–undergraduate difference in perceived correlation. Number of subtypes generated was not a mediator.

In summary, three studies supported the familiarity covariation hypothesis that greater familiarity leads to less perceived covariation. These studies also supported the outgroup covariation hypothesis. Because people tend to be less familiar with their outgroups, they perceive greater covariation among the features of outgroup members.

CONSEQUENCES OF PERCEIVED COVARIATION

Why should we care about perceived covariation? Our current research is examining consequences of perceived covariation, including judgment, inferences, generalizations, and behavior. We have found a *covariation extremity* effect—greater perceived covariation among features leads to more extreme evaluative judgment (Linville & Fischer, 1996). Why should perceived covariation be linked with judgmental extremity? Figure 6.2 provides a simple illustration. If one perceives high covariation among features, especially in the $Avg\ R$ sense, one will tend to perceive members of a group as having *evaluatively consistent* profiles of features. Thus, a new

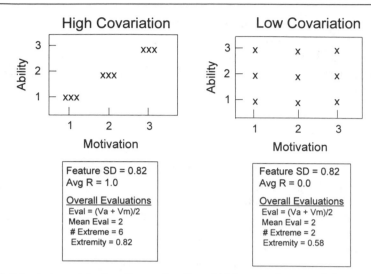

FIG. 6.2. Judgmental extremity as a function of high versus low covariation among features. The extremity measure used here is the standard deviation of the overall evaluations.

target may be encoded as more consistent—either good in most respects, bad in most respects, or average in most respects. The result is more extreme overall judgments about targets. However, if one perceives low covariation among features, it is more likely that a new target will be encoded as good in some respects but bad in others. The result is more moderate overall judgments (see Fig. 6.2). Note that this *covariation extremity* hypothesis results from evaluatively consistent correlations, not from correlation per se.

To test the covariation extremity hypothesis, we asked college students to generate subtypes of retired adults (Linville & Fischer, 1996). From these we calculated the *Avg R* and *Avg |R|* measures of perceived covariation. Students also constructed perceived frequency distributions over each feature. From these we calculated the standard deviation (*SD*) of their perceived distributions, a traditional measure of variability. Finally, participants read a series of vignettes, each a scenario describing a specific older person. After reading each vignette, they made an overall favorability rating of the target. Each vignette was generally positive (e.g., a target overcame a fear of heights to join friends on a picnic) or generally negative (e.g., a target was awkward and withdrawn at a dinner party). We used the judgments of these vignettes to calculate an evaluative extremity measure— the range (difference) between the evaluations of the positive and negative vignettes. Greater range indicates greater evaluative extremity.

Our results reveal a strong covariation extremity effect. Those perceiving higher covariation among features of a group were more extreme, displaying a greater range between evaluations of the positive and negative targets ($r = 0.33$). They judged a positive target more positively and a negative target more negatively. The covariation extremity effect was stronger for $Avg\ R$, reflecting evaluative consistency, as it should be according to the reasoning behind the hypothesis. We also found a strong negative relation between familiarity with a group and perceived covariation among features of its subtypes ($r = $ -0.58 for $Avg\ R$ and -0.41 for $Avg\ |R|$).

Finally, we found that familiarity was also negatively related to judgmental extremity. Those less familiar with a group were more extreme in judging individual group members ($r = -0.30$). Does perceived covariation mediate this link between familiarity and extremity? A simple path analysis suggests yes. The significant path between familiarity and judgmental extremity ($\beta = -0.30$) was weakened and became nonsignificant when perceived covariation was added to the model ($\beta = -0.16$). In contrast, perceived variability with respect to individual features was not a mediator of the familiarity extremity link. Adding it to the model did not weaken the familiarity extremity link.

In short, this new research suggests that perceived covariation may have at least as much impact as perceived variability on intergroup judgment and behavior. Greater familiarity with a group leads to lower perceived covariation and less extreme overall judgments about group members. Further, perceived covariation appears to be an important mediator of this link between familiarity and extremity of judgment.

CONCLUSION

We began this chapter by reviewing an extensive body of research on perceptions of group variability. We found important empirical regularities regarding its determinants. In most cases, ingroup members perceive greater variability among the members of a group than do outgroup members. This outgroup homogeneity effect has several causes, including greater familiarity with the ingroup, greater attention to individuating features of ingroup members, and greater exposure to stereotypic and second-hand exemplars of outgroups. We also noted two important exceptions to this pattern — when outgroup members are almost as familiar with a group as ingroup members (e.g., gender) and when group membership is central to self-identity. We also discussed how group variability research has contributed to recent advances in theories of how people represent and process information about social categories and to greater interest in multiple exemplar models. In each of these areas, much has been accomplished in the past two decades.

Although less is known regarding the consequences of perceived group variability, our review revealed several important judgmental consequences. First, perceiving a group as homogeneous leads people to generalize group stereotypes to individual members. This suggests that increasing the perceived variability of a group may lessen the tendency to apply group stereotypes to individual members. Second, when a group is homogeneous, people are more likely to generalize stereotype-consistent information about an individual to the group as a whole, but less likely to generalize counterstereotypic information about an individual to the group. Third, perceiving a group as homogeneous makes people less likely to classify an atypical exemplar as a member of the group. Thus, if a new exemplar is deviant enough from a group stereotype to require substantial change in it, the exemplar is unlikely to be treated as an instance of the group. This explains why exposing people to counterstereotypic exemplars of a group has little impact on the group stereotype. Finally, perceiving a group as less complex or differentiated leads people to make more extreme overall evaluations of group members. Because people tend to have less complex representations of their outgroups, they tend to make more extreme overall judgments about outgroup members. Thus, increasing people's complexity regarding their outgroups can lessen the tendency to make extreme judgments about outgroup members. In short, perceiving outgroups as low in variability facilitates stereotype formation, resilience, and application, and perceiving outgroups as less differentiated leads to more extreme overall evaluations of outgroup members.

Our recent work on perceptions of covariation among the features of group members and subtypes suggests that perceptions of covariation may be at least as important as variability perceptions. People perceive greater covariation among the features of outgroup members. Lack of familiarity with outgroups appears to mediate this outgroup covariation effect (Linville, Fischer, & Yoon, 1996). Finally, our new work suggests that perceived covariation has important judgmental consequences (Linville & Fischer, 1996). Greater perceived covariation among features leads to more extreme overall judgments about group members. Thus, lack of familiarity with a group contributes to greater perceived covariation, which in turn leads to more extreme judgments about individual group members.

These judgmental consequences of perceived variability and covariation are interesting and potentially important. However, many important questions regarding behavioral consequences remain unanswered. For example, how do perceptions of variability and covariation affect: prejudice and discrimination; decisions about whether to hire, promote, or fire group members; intergroup conflict; attraction and avoidance; resource-allocation decisions; competitive versus cooperative behavior; choice of power and persuasion strategies; and nonverbal behavior toward group members? Past research on perceived variability and covariation provides a rich empirical and theoretical basis for future research on these new behavioral questions.

REFERENCES

Abelson, R. P., & Rosenberg, M. J. (1958). Symbolic psycho-logic: A model of attitudinal cognition. *Behavioral Science, 3*, 1-13.

Bartsch, R. A., & Judd, C. M. (1993). Majority-minority status and perceived ingroup variability revisited. *European Journal of Social Psychology, 23*, 471-483.

Berman, J. S., & Kenny, D. A. (1976). Correlational bias in observer ratings. *Journal of Personality and Social Psychology, 34*, 263-273.

Brewer, M. B. (1991). The social self: On being the same and different at the same time. *Personality and Social Psychology Bulletin, 17*, 475-482.

Brewer, M. B. (1993). Social identity, distinctiveness, and in-group homogeneity. *Social Cognition, 11*, 150-164.

Brewer, M. B., & Kramer, R. M. (1985). The psychology of intergroup attitudes and behaviors. *Annual Review of Psychology, 36*, 219-243.

Brewer, M. B., & Lui, L. (1984). Categorization of the elderly by the elderly: Effects of perceiver's category membership. *Personality and Social Psychology Bulletin, 10*, 585-595.

Brown, R., & Wootton-Millward, L. (1993). Perceptions of group homogeneity during group formation and change. *Social Cognition, 11*, 126-149.

Chapman, L. J., & Chapman, J. (1967). Genesis of popular but erroneous psychodiagnostic observations. *Journal of Abnormal Psychology, 72*, 193-204.

D'Andrade, R. G. (1974). Memory and the assessment of behavior. In H. Blalock (Ed.), *Measurement in the social sciences* (pp. 159-186). Chicago: Aldine.

Dovidio, J., & Gaertner, S. L. (1986). *Prejudice, discrimination, and racism.* New York: Academic Press.

Estes, W. K. (1993). Concepts, categories, and psychological science. *Psychological Science, 4*, 143-153.

Ford, T. E., & Stangor, C. (1992). The role of diagnosticity in stereotype formation: Perceiving group means and variances. *Journal of Personality and Social Psychology, 63*, 356-367.

Fried, L. S., & Holyoak, K. J. (1984). Induction of category distributions: A framework for classification learning. *Journal of Experimental Psychology: Learning, Memory, and Cognition, 10*, 234-257.

Hamilton, D. L. (1981). Illusory correlation as a basis for stereotyping. In D. L. Hamilton (Ed.), *Cognitive processes in stereotyping and intergroup behavior* (pp. 115-144). Hillsdale, NJ: Lawrence Erlbaum Associates.

Hamilton, D. L., & Gifford, R. K. (1976). Illusory correlation in interpersonal perception: A cognitive basis of stereotypic judgments. *Journal of Experimental Social Psychology, 12*, 392-407.

Hamilton, D. L., & Sherman, J. W. (1994). Stereotypes. In R. S. Wyer, Jr. & T. K. Srull (Eds.), *Handbook of social cognition* (2nd ed., Vol. 2, pp. 1-68). Hillsdale, NJ: Lawrence Erlbaum Associates.

Haslam, S. A., & Oakes, P. J. (1995). How context-independent is the outgroup homogeneity effect? A response to Bartsch and Judd. *European Journal of Social Psychology, 24*, 469-475.

Hilton, J. L., & von Hippel, W. (1996). Stereotypes. *Annual Review of Psychology, 47*, 237–271.

Hintzman, D. L. (1986). "Schema abstraction" in a multiple-trace memory model. *Psychological Review, 93*, 411–428.

Islam, M. R., & Hewstone, M. (1993). Dimensions of contact as predictors of intergroup anxiety, perceived out-group variability, and out-group attitude: An integrative model. *Personality and Social Psychology Bulletin, 19*, 700–710.

Jones, E. E., Wood, G. C., & Quattrone, G. A. (1981). Perceived variability of personal characteristics in in-groups and out-groups: The role of knowledge and evaluation. *Personality and Social Psychology Bulletin, 7*, 523–528.

Judd, C. M., & Bartsch, R. A. (1995). Cats, dogs, and the OH effect: A reply to Simon and to Haslam and Oakes. *European Journal of Social Psychology, 25*, 477–480.

Judd, C. M., & Park, B. (1988). Out-group homogeneity: Judgments of variability at the individual and group levels. *Journal of Personality and Social Psychology, 54*, 778–788.

Judd, C. M., Park, B., Ryan, C. S., Brauer, M., & Kraus, S. (1995). Stereotypes and ethnocentrism: Diverging interethnic perceptions of African American and White American youth. *Journal of Personality and Social Psychology, 69*, 460–481.

Judd, C. M., Ryan, C. S., & Park, B. (1991). Accuracy in the judgments of in-group and out-group variability. *Journal of Personality and Social Psychology, 61*, 366–379.

Kelley, H. H. (1967). Attribution theory in social psychology. In D. Levine (Ed.), *Nebraska Symposium on Motivation* (Vol. 15, pp. 129–238). Lincoln, NE: University of Nebraska Press.

Kelly, C. (1989). Political identity and perceived intragroup homogeneity. *British Journal of Social Psychology, 28*, 239–250.

Kraus, S., Ryan, C. S., Judd, C. M., Hastie, R., & Park, B. (1993). Use of mental frequency distributions to represent variability among members of social categories. *Social Cognition, 11*, 22–43.

Krueger, J., & Rothbart, M. (1988). Use of categorical and individuating information in making inferences about personality. *Journal of Personality and Social Psychology, 55*, 187–195.

Kruschke, J. K. (1992). ALCOVE: An exemplar-based connectionist model of category learning. *Psychological Review, 99*, 22–44.

Lambert, A. J. (1995). Stereotypes and social judgment: The consequences of group variability. *Journal of Personality and Social Psychology, 68*, 388–403.

Lambert, A. J., & Wyer, R. S., Jr. (1990). Stereotypes and social judgment: The effects of typicality and group heterogeneity. *Journal of Personality and Social Psychology, 59*, 676–691.

Lewicki, P. (1986). Processing information about covariation that cannot be articulated. *Journal of Experimental Psychology: Learning, Memory, and Cognition, 12*, 135–146.

Linville, P. W. (1982). The complexity-extremity effect and age-based stereotyping. *Journal of Personality and Social Psychology, 42*, 193–211.

Linville, P. W. (1997). The heterogeneity of homogeneity. In J. Cooper & J. Darley (Eds.), *Attribution processes, person perception, and social interaction: The legacy of Ned Jones.* Washington, DC: American Psychological Association.

Linville, P. W., & Fischer, G. W. (1993a). Exemplar and abstraction models of perceived group variability and stereotypicality. *Social Cognition, 11*, 92–125.

Linville, P. W., & Fischer, G. W. (1993b, June). *Perceived variation, covariation, and extremity of judgment about group members.* Paper presented at the Duck Conference on Social Cognition, Duck, NC.

Linville, P. W., & Fischer, G. W. (1996). *Perceived variability, covariance, and judgments about group members.* Unpublished paper, Duke University, Durham, NC.

Linville, P. W., Fischer, G. W., & Salovey, P. (1989). Perceived distributions of the characteristics of ingroup and outgroup members: Empirical evidence and a computer simulation. *Journal of Personality and Social Psychology, 57,* 165–188.

Linville, P. W., Fischer, G. W., & Yoon, C. (1996). Perceived covariation among the features of ingroup and outgroup members: An outgroup covariation effect. *Journal of Personality and Social Psychology, 6,* 1–23.

Linville, P. W., & Jones, E. E. (1980). Polarized appraisals of out-group members. *Journal of Personality and Social Psychology, 38,* 689–703.

Linville, P. W., & Salovey, P. (1982). *The complexity-extremity effect: Age-based perceptions of the elderly.* Unpublished manuscript, Yale University, New Haven, CT.

Linville, P. W., Salovey, P., & Fischer, G. W. (1986). Stereotyping and perceived distributions of social characteristics: An application to ingroup–outgroup perception. In J. Dovidio & S. L. Gaertner (Eds.), *Prejudice, discrimination, and racism* (pp. 165–208). New York: Academic Press.

Lorenzi-Cioldi, F., Eagly, A. H., & Stewart, T. L. (1995). Homogeneity of gender groups in memory. *Journal of Experimental Social Psychology, 31,* 193–217.

Mackie, D. M., & Asuncion, A. G. (1990). On-line and memory-based modification of attitudes. *Journal of Personality and Social Psychology, 59,* 5–16.

Mackie, D. M., Sherman, J. W., & Worth, L. T. (1993). On-line and memory-based processes in group variability judgments. *Social Cognition, 11,* 44–69.

McClelland, J. L., & Rumelhart, D. E. (1985). Distributed memory and the representation of general and specific information. *Journal of Experimental Psychology: General, 114,* 159–188.

Medin, D. L. (1989). Concepts and conceptual structure. *American Psychologist, 44,* 1469–1481.

Messick, D. M., & Mackie, D. M. (1989). Intergroup relations. *Annual Review of Psychology, 40,* 40–45.

Mullen, B., & Hu, L. (1989). Perceptions of ingroup and outgroup variability: A meta-analytic integration. *Basic and Applied Social Psychology, 10,* 233–252.

Nisbett, R. E., Krantz, D. H., Jepson, C., & Kunda, Z. (1983). The use of statistical heuristics in everyday intuitive reasoning. *Psychological Review, 90,* 339–363.

Nisbett, R. E., & Kunda, Z. (1985). Perceptions of social distributions. *Journal of Personality and Social Psychology, 48,* 297–311.

Ostrom, T. M., Carpenter, S. L., Sedikides, C., & Li, F. (1993). Differential processing of in-group and out-group information. *Journal of Personality and Social Psychology, 64,* 21–34.

Ostrom, T. M., & Sedikides, C. (1992). Out-group homogeneity effects in natural and minimal groups. *Psychological Bulletin, 112,* 536–552.

Park, B., & Hastie, R. (1987). Perception of variability in category development: Instance-versus abstraction-based stereotypes. *Journal of Personality and Social Psychology, 53,* 621–635.

Park, B., & Judd, C. M. (1990). Measures and models of perceived group variability. *Journal of Personality and Social Psychology, 59,* 173–191.

Park, B., Judd, C. M., & Ryan, C. S. (1991). Social categorization and the representation of variability information. In W. Stroebe & M. Hewstone (Eds.), *European review of social psychology* (Vol. 2, pp. 211–245). Chichester, England: Wiley.

Park, B., & Rothbart, M. (1982). Perception of out-group homogeneity and levels of social categorization: Memory for the subordinate attributes of in-group and out-group members. *Journal of Personality and Social Psychology, 42,* 1051–1068.

Park, B., Ryan, C. S., & Judd, C. M. (1992). Role of meaningful subgroups in explaining differences in perceived variability for in-groups and out-groups. *Journal of Personality and Social Psychology, 63,* 553–567.

Payne, J. W., Bettman, J. R., & Johnson, E. J. (1993). *The adaptive decision maker.* Cambridge, England: Cambridge University Press.

Posner, M. I., & Keele, S. W. (1968). On the genesis of abstract ideas. *Journal of Experimental*

Psychology, 77, 353–363.

Quattrone, G. A. (1986). On the perception of a group's variability. In S. Worchel & W. Austin (Eds.), *The psychology of intergroup relations* (Vol. 2, pp. 25–48). Chicago: Nelson-Hall.

Quattrone, G. A., & Jones, E. E. (1980). The perception of variability within ingroups and outgroups: Implications for the Law of Small Numbers. *Journal of Personality and Social Psychology, 38,* 141–152.

Rehder, B., & Hastie, R. (1996). *The moderating influence of variability on belief revision.* Unpublished manuscript, Department of Psychology, University of Colorado, Boulder, CO.

Rosenberg, S., & Sedlak, A. (1972). Structural representations of implicit personality theory. In L. Berkowitz (Ed.), *Advances in experimental social psychology* (Vol. 6, pp. 235–297). New York: Academic Press.

Ryan, C. S., Judd, C. M., & Park, B. (1996). Effects of racial stereotypes on judgments of individuals: The moderating role of perceived group variability. *Journal of Experimental Social Psychology, 32,* 71–103.

Schneider, D. J. (1973). Implicit personality theory: A review. *Psychological Bulletin, 79,* 294–309.

Schneider, D. J. (1991). Social cognition. *Annual Review of Psychology, 42,* 527–561.

Sedikides, C. (1996). *Differential processing of ingroup and outgroup information: The role of familiarity.* Unpublished manuscript, University of North Carolina, Chapel Hill, NC.

Sedikides, C. (in press). Differential processing of ingroup and outgroup information: The role of relative group status in permeable boundary groups. *European Journal of Social Psychology.*

Sedikides, C., & Ostrom, T. M. (1993). Perceptions of group variability: Moving from an uncertain crawl to a purposeful stride. *Social Cognition, 11,* 165–174.

Sherman S. J., Judd, C. M., & Park, B. (1989). Social cognition. *Annual Review of Psychology, 40,* 281–326.

Simon, B. (1992a). The perception of ingroup and outgroup homogeneity: Re-introducing the intergroup context. In W. Stroebe & M. Hewstone (Eds.), *European review of social psychology* (Vol. 3, pp. 1–30). Chichester: Wiley.

Simon, B. (1992b). Intragroup differentiation in terms of in-group and out-group attributes. *European Journal of Social Psychology, 22,* 407–413.

Simon, B. (1995). The perception of ingroup and outgroup homogeneity: On the confounding of group size, level of abstractness and frame of reference: A reply to Bartsch and Judd. *European Journal of Social Psychology, 25,* 463–468.

Simon, B., & Brown, R. (1987). Perceived homogeneity in minority–majority contexts. *Journal of Personality and Social Psychology, 53,* 703–711.

Simon, B., & Pettigrew, T. F. (1990). Social identity and perceived group homogeneity: Evidence for the in-group homogeneity effect. *European Journal of Social Psychology, 20,* 269–286.

Smith, E. E., & Medin, D. L. (1981). *Categories and concepts.* Cambridge, MA: Harvard University Press.

Smith, E. R., & Zarate, M. A. (1992). Exemplar-based model of social judgment. *Psychological Review, 99,* 3–21.

Tajfel, H. (1978). *Differentiation between social groups.* San Diego, CA: Academic Press.

Tajfel, H. (1982). Social psychology of intergroup relations. In M. R. Rosenzweig & L. W. Porter (Eds.), *Annual review of psychology* (Vol. 33, pp. 1–39). Palo Alto, CA: Annual Reviews.

Wilder, D. A. (1986). Social categorization: Implications for creation and reduction of intergroup conflict. In L. Berkowitz (Ed.), *Advances in experimental social psychology* (Vol. 19, pp. 293–355). New York: Academic Press.

7

Judging and Behaving Toward Members of Stereotyped Groups: A Shifting Standards Perspective

Monica Biernat
University of Kansas

Theresa K. Vescio
University of Wales, College of Cardiff

Melvin Manis
University of Michigan

One of the authors of this chapter is an "excellent" athlete. This person is also a woman. She is accorded this label despite the fact that her male teammate, who can hit a softball just as far, throw just as hard, and run just as fast as she, is not. That is, considered "objectively," the man and woman in this example perform at the same level; at a "subjective" level, however, the woman is judged to be better than the man. It is argued here that this judgment phenomenon is based on the operation of stereotype-based shifting standards—the activation of within-category standards of evaluation to judge members of different groups on stereotype-relevant dimensions. In this example, the stereotype that men are more athletic than women presumably gives rise to the use of different standards or performance expectations to judge a man's versus a woman's athleticism. Given the lower (or less demanding) standard of athleticism for women than for men, it is easier for the woman to surpass the standard and, accordingly, to be judged an "excellent" athlete.

In fact, the behavior of the stereotyper may increase the likelihood that a female athlete will surpass the low standard for her gender. For example, a fielder who faces a female batter may move in, or play a shallow field; when facing a man, the fielder may step back. If each batter hits the ball 150 feet, it is the woman, not the man, who is more likely to get on base—her ball will sail over the fielder's head; his will be caught.

The interest in this chapter is in the implications of gender- and other social category-based judgment patterns on the behaviors directed toward individual group members. In the world of coed softball, for example, is the subjectively "excellent" female athlete more likely than her "good" male teammate to receive positive feedback from her teammates? Is she assigned to the better field position, or to a higher slot in the batting order? Our admittedly unscientific inquiry into these questions yields the answers of "yes" and "no." The woman in our example *does* receive more pats on the back, more smiles, and more cheers than the man. Yet she is less likely than he to play shortstop, or to bat in the clean-up slot. It appears, then, that some behaviors (cheers) are consistent with judges' subjective assessments, whereas others (position in the batting order) more closely follow from stereotyped representations.

This chapter explores these issues by asking the general question: How do stereotypes influence judgments of and behavior toward members of stereotyped groups? This question is approached using the framework of our "shifting standards" model (Biernat, 1995; Biernat & Manis, 1994; Biernat, Manis, & Nelson, 1991). This is a judgment model which articulates how cognitive representations of stereotyped groups are translated into verbal or written evaluations of individual group members, but one of the goals in this chapter is to examine the implications of standard-based judgments for intergroup behavior. *Intergroup behavior* refers here to a wide variety of actions (ranging from nonverbal conduct to important choice decisions) that are affected by a target individual's membership in a stereotyped group. In practice, both intergroup cognitions (beliefs and stereotypes about different groups) and intergroup behaviors are examined by comparing judgments of and actions toward members of one social category (e.g., men, Whites) versus another (women, African Americans). This chapter begins with a general overview of the shifting standards model, and then outlines a broader perspective on the links among judgment standards, target evaluations, and actions directed toward members of stereotyped groups.

THE SHIFTING STANDARDS MODEL

The shifting standards model posits that, when asked to make social judgments, the stereotypes that individuals hold about different social groups are activated, and these influence the judgmental standards that are called to mind. A standard, which incorporates a mean and range of expectations regarding the likely behaviors or attributes to be found among the members of a social group, is specific to that category of people; thus, judgmental standards differ from one social category to another. For example, individuals may believe that men are more athletic than women, and they may expect rather different ranges of athletic behavior from these two groups (e.g., the likely range of hitting distance for male softball players extends further than the expected range for female players).

Expectations of this sort affect perceivers' use of rating scales (most important, the subjective end anchors of these scales) when they evaluate individual targets. Most person perception and stereotyping research involves the use of "subjective," traitlike response scales (e.g., "rate this target on a 1 [*very unathletic*] to 7 [*very athletic*] continuum"), and such scales allow judges to adjust the meaning of rating points in a category-specific, category-appropriate manner. More specifically, raters routinely adjust the meaning of different rating scale endpoints or end anchors so as to reflect and accommodate the expected range of category members on the attribute being judged. For example, when judging the athleticism of a man, one might reserve the label *very athletic* for the truly outstanding performer, perhaps a professional; that same label, however, may apply to any woman who, say, works out regularly and plays intramural sports. In the softball example, a 150-foot hit may fall near the high end of the expected range of hitting distances for women, and would likely be labeled *excellent*, that same hit would fall nearer to the midpoint of a perceiver's expectations for men, and be labeled *average*. Analogously, research on height judgments has indicated that the label *tall* for a man is typically reserved for individuals with heights of about 6′ 3.5″, whereas *tall* for a woman translates into a height of about 5′ 9″ (Roberts & Herman, 1986).

What are the implications of this subjective, category-specific adjustment in the use of descriptive terms? It may render uninterpretable any direct comparison between the subjective evaluations of targets who come from different social categories (see Biernat & Manis, 1994; Biernat et al., 1991). For example, if a member from one group is judged (on a subjective scale) to be equivalent to a member of another group, this does not necessarily mean that stereotypes are inoperative, and that the two targets are mentally represented in equivalent terms. Rather, the mental representation may be consistent with social stereotypes, but equivalent ratings result because these stereotypes lead perceivers to evaluate the targets against different standards. For example, a man might be labeled *moderately aggressive* if he shoves someone aside; a woman might receive that same *moderately aggressive* label for interrupting a conversation. Despite the fact that the two actors have received the same subjective assessment, the man may still be regarded as more aggressive than the woman at a representational level.

The judgmental effects produced by the use of different subjective standards can be avoided, however, if evaluations are made on response scales that do not allow for meaning shifts. Such scales have been referred to as objective, common rule, or externally anchored in nature. For example, a perceiver who believes that men earn more money than women will normally adjust what is meant by a subjective label such as *financially successful* when judging a man versus a woman. However, if asked to estimate financial success in "dollars earned" — an objective unit of judgment — such adjustment of meaning cannot occur. A dollar is a dollar, an unchanging unit, regardless of who earns it. Consistent with this reasoning, in a study in which subjects judged the financial status of several male and female targets, those asked to render their judgments in dollars indicated that the men earned more money than the women; those asked to make financial success estimates in subjective terms (*very unsuccessful* to *very successful*), however, rated these same women as more financially successful than the men (Biernat et al., 1991, Study 2).

In general, subjective rating scales refer to any judgment format that allows the respondent to interpret and define the meaning of rating scale categories (e.g., Likert-type or semantic-differential scales). It has been argued that stereotypes lead perceivers to define these rating categories in distinctive ways when evaluating targets from different social groups. In contrast, "objective" scales are externally anchored or "common rule" in nature — measurement units have the same meaning regardless of the target's category membership. Thus, feet, inches, dollars, pounds, and seconds qualify as "objective" — their meaning does not shift when there is a change in the category membership of the target to be evaluated. Under the rubric of objective scales are included such judgments as estimated standardized test scores (to assess competence stereotypes) and rank orderings (which fit our conception of objectivity in that they involve direct comparisons among targets on a single, constant dimension).

Other researchers who have compared "objective" and "subjective" response scales have noted that objective scales are less sensitive to context (e.g., contrast) effects, precisely because they do not allow for semantic changes of meaning of the sort proposed here (Campbell, Hunt, & Lewis, 1958; Krantz & Campbell, 1961; Manis, 1967, 1971). In related work, Upshaw and Ostrom and their colleagues (Ostrom & Upshaw, 1968; Upshaw, 1978; Upshaw, Ostrom, & Ward, 1970) distinguished between the content of someone's attitude (e.g., his or her beliefs about the number of years in prison that would be appropriate for someone who had repeatedly been found guilty of drunk driving) and the rating this judge might produce if asked to indicate how stern versus lenient he or she would be in sentencing such a defendant. Note that years in prison would qualify as an "objective" (common rule) indicator of the judge's views on punishment severity, whereas his or her self-rating would constitute a "subjective" indicator. Empirical research in this area normally indicates a positive relationship between (objective) measures of attitude content and (subjective) self ratings of attitude, but this relationship is far from perfect, and is dependent on a perceiver's perspective (the end anchors that define the extremes of each judge's rating scale). A judge who sentences a guilty defendant to a 1-year term, and who feels that drunk-driving sentences should normally range between 6 months (a lenient minimum) and 1 year (a stern maximum) would regard a 1-year sentence as *more severe* than another judge who recommends the same 1-year jail term, while believing that drunk driving sentences should range between 1 and 2 years (see also Higgins & Lurie, 1983; Higgins & Stangor, 1988). Foreshadowing our own emphasis on the distinction between subjective and objective (common rule) scales, Campbell et al. (1958) wrote that:

> Terms like *heavy* and *light* are in their proper semantic usage situationally relative, i.e. they convey no absolute meaning apart from a specific comparative setting. We can speak of a heavy *truck*, a heavy *suitcase*, or a heavy *fishline*. In such usage, terms like heavy and light contrast with "absolute" terms like one ounce, ten pounds or three kilos, which, in dealing with the same attributes of physical objects, have become extricated from immediate comparisons and are understood to be invariant attributes of the object. . . . (pp. 220–221, italics in original).

The shifting standards model extends this theme by focusing on the susceptibility of subjective and objective judgments to the context created by social stereotypes. In general, stereotypes are assumed to activate category-specific standards of judgment, which affect the assignment of meaning to the rating points of subjective response scales. Objective scales, by virtue of their link to external reality, provide a more accurate reflection of perceivers' mental representations of members of stereotyped groups. That is, because objective scales are more clearly tied to a constant, external reality than are subjective scales, they require no context-specific interpretation that may disrupt the translation of a mental representation into a semantic judgment. Thus, subjective rating scales often mask the operation of stereotypes, whereas objective scales do not.

A MODEL OF STANDARD-BASED JUDGMENT AND BEHAVIOR

Figure 7.1 presents a general framework for describing work on shifting standards and social judgment; it also outlines some predictions regarding the behavioral implications of these judgments. The model begins with the premise that situational cues may trigger stereotype activation. These cues

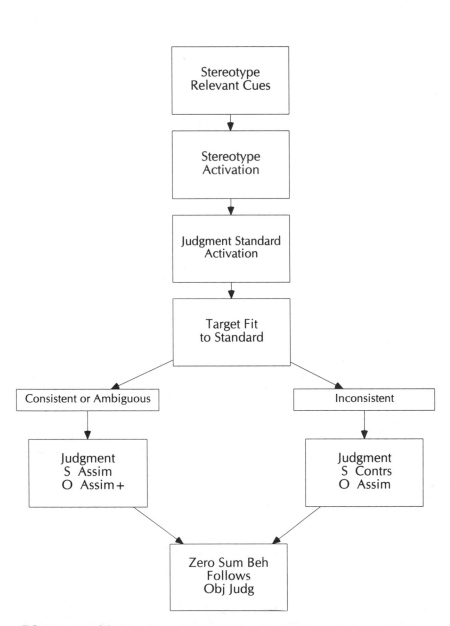

FIG. 7.1. A model of the effects of stereotype-based judgment standards on judgment of and behavior toward individual group members. S = Subjective scale, O = Objective scale, Assim = Assimilation, Contrs = Contrast.

may include the mere presence of a member of a stereotyped group (Brewer, 1988; Devine, 1989; Perduo & Gurtman, 1990), explicit instructions to use the stereotype, subtle primes, and other contextual variables. To return to the softball example, salient aspects of the situation (e.g., the field, the athletic context) and the actor (e.g., a female batter) may activate relevant dimensions of gender stereotypes (Trope, 1986).

Once activated, stereotypes may serve any number of functions for the perceiver (see Snyder & Miene, 1994), one of which is to provide useful information regarding category-specific standards (e.g., means and ranges of expected situation-relevant attributes or behavior from the members of one category vs. another). Thus, in a judgment situation, stereotype activation immediately leads to standard activation—the triggering of a comparative context to be used for evaluating members of different groups.

In this model, the stereotypes and activated standards described thus far are quantitative in nature (i.e., they reflect the perceiver's expectation that one category of people, on average, has more [or less] of some attribute than another: men are taller than women, women are more verbally able than men, African Americans are more athletic than Whites; McCauley, Stitt, & Segal, 1980). However, stereotypes and standards may also reflect the perception that category members (e.g., men vs. women) are qualitatively different from each other. Qualitative differences involve the perception that two categories of people vary in the kind or type of attributes they exhibit (Kunda & Sherman-Williams, 1993; Kunda, Sinclair, & Griffin, 1995). For example, men and women may be expected to engage in different forms or varieties of aggressive behavior; "good fathers" and "good mothers" may differ in the types of behaviors and skills they are expected to display. Quantitative differences probably reflect the most common way in which stereotypes are conceptualized, and indeed they characterize all of the work done thus far from the shifting standards perspective. However, the quantitative–qualitative distinction may be important in discussing judgment standards, in that the former representation allows individuals from different categories to be judged on the same dimensions, whereas the latter does not. This point is returned to later; for now the focus is on the judgment implications of using standards based on quantitative differences between social categories.

Effects of Stereotype-Based Standards on Judgment

Perceivers use their activated judgment standards to evaluate individual group members. In this model, it is assumed that perceivers know more than merely the category membership of these individual targets. Specifically, they have some individuating information about category members that can be described as either *ambiguous*, *consistent*, or *inconsistent* with regard to the relevant group stereotype. As can be seen in Fig. 7.1, it is predicted that when perceivers make judgments on subjective response scales, ambiguous and/or consistent targets will be *assimilated* to (i.e., judged congruently with) the group stereotype (Goldstone, 1995; Herr, Sherman, & Fazio, 1983; Hilton & von Hippel, 1990; Manis, Nelson, & Shedler, 1988; Schwarz & Bless, 1992). It is also assumed that ambiguous and stereotype-consistent information function similarly because both can be thought of as lying within or near the "latitude of acceptance" of a stereotyped belief (see Sherif & Hovland, 1961). In its recognition that stereotypes guide information processing, interpretation, and inference, this prediction characterizes many findings in the stereotyping literature (Hamilton & Sherman, 1994; von Hippel, Sekaquaptewa, & Vargas, 1995).

When targets display evidence that runs counter to stereotypes, however, the shifting standards model predicts that subjective judgments may reveal *contrast* from the group stereotype, due to the location of the relevant scale end anchors. For example, a highly competent woman may be judged as more competent than a highly competent man (Abramson, Goldberg, Greenberg, & Abramson, 1977), or an upper class, standard English-speaking African American may be judged more favorably (e.g., more intelligent and competent) than a White with similar speech characteristics (Jussim, Coleman, & Lerch, 1987). This view that targets who are discrepant from expectations are contrasted from these comparative standards is also consistent with the social judgment perspective of Sherif and Hovland (1961; Manis, 1960, 1961), and with a variety of other judgment models (Helson, 1964[1]; Manis et al., 1988; Parducci, 1965, Upshaw, 1969; see Wedell, Parducci, & Geiselman, 1987).

The shifting standards model additionally suggests, however, that when perceivers use objective/externally anchored response scales to evaluate individual targets, judgments will normally reflect assimilation to group stereotypes. That is, even when a group member engages in behavior that seemingly disconfirms a stereotype, assessments of that target (relative to

---

[1]The shifting standards model differs, however, from Helson's (1964) adaptation level theory in a number of important ways. Most important, Helson's model is primarily a theory of *contrast*, not assimilation, effects. Stimuli on opposite sides of one's adaptation level (AL) are displaced away, in opposite directions, from the AL; the quantitative formulations of AL theory do not adequately account for the assimilative trends that are predicted by the shifting standards model and other approaches. Furthermore, because AL theory assumes that judgment displacements reflect actual perceptual distortions, it cannot account for the scale effects (based on subjective and objective response wording) that are central to the shifting standards model, and that argue for a semantic interpretation of judgment displacements.

assessments of a target from a different category who displays that same behavior) will be stereotype-consistent.[2] This occurs because objective scales do not allow for category-specific shifts in meaning, and are therefore more likely to directly reflect perceivers' (stereotype-based) mental representations of targets. Perceivers will still be attentive to individuating information, such that, for example, a "highly athletic" woman would be judged more athletic than an "unathletic" woman; but within athleticism level (high or low), the model predicts that judgments in objective units will reveal a stereotype-assimilative pattern: An athletic woman will be judged less athletic than an athletic man, due to the operation of stereotyped expectations about the athleticism of women versus men.

From the shifting standards perspective, then, the patterns of judgment that are observed when raters use objective versus subjective response scales will differ most when targets display behavior that is inconsistent with stereotypes. In these cases, subjective scales will show evidence of contrast, and objective scales will show evidence of assimilation, to group stereotypes. When targets display stereotype-consistent or ambiguous behaviors, both subjective and objective judgments should show assimilation, but, as we previously observed (Biernat et al., 1991; Biernat & Manis, 1994), the assimilation effect is normally more striking on objective response scales: "Common rule response scales reveal clear stereotyping effects, but . . . subjective response scales — because they can be adjusted to fit different classes of exemplars — dilute and sometimes reverse these effects" (Biernat & Manis, 1994, p. 6).

It is important to add some clarification to these predictions regarding assimilation and contrast effects. Both of these judgment displacements occur relative to some reference point; in general, this reference point is the mean expectation for the target group. Thus, assimilation to a group stereotype or standard refers to a target judgment that is displaced *toward* the expected group mean, and contrast from a group stereotype or standard refers to a judgment that is displaced *away* from the expected group mean. Operationally, however, assimilation effects are typically said to occur when targets from contrasting social categories (who are otherwise identical) are judged in a stereotype-consistent direction *relative to each other.*

---

[2]Although we claim that objective measures will always show assimilation, even from targets who are inconsistent with group expectations, paired-comparison data from Manis, Paskewitz, and Cotler (1986) produced clear evidence of contrast when subjects were asked to choose the most "disturbed" of two patients (one from a generally high- and one from a generally low-disturbed hospital) who produced moderately disturbed vocabulary definitions. This pattern of contrast on an objective (paired-choice) scale may be limited, however, to situations in which "stereotypes" are experimentally induced. In our paired-comparison research involving a preexisting stereotype (beliefs about the relative heights of women and men), we have consistently found evidence of assimilation (Nelson et al., 1990).

This "between-target group" approach represents a somewhat different conception than the "group norm" approach to displacement effects. For example, the between-target approach focuses on whether Paul or Paula is thought to be more aggressive, given that each has been observed to "interrupt others." In contrast, the group norm approach asks if the aggression ratings awarded to Paula are displaced toward the ratings of the average woman (assimilation) or away from this standard (contrast). As a consequence, Paul may be rated as more aggressive than Paula (*assimilation*, as defined by the "between-target" approach), despite the fact that Paula's aggression ratings have been displaced away from the unaggressive behavioral standard that is normally set for women (i.e., she has been contrasted with respect to expectations for women as a group).

In research that compares the assessments of targets who have behaved identically, but who belong to different social categories, one target is generally stereotype-consistent (e.g., an aggressive man) and the other is stereotype-inconsistent (e.g., an aggressive woman). In such a case, this model suggests that the man's ratings should be assimilated to the male standard of aggressiveness (the mean of the male distribution), but the woman should be contrasted from the female standard of relative passivity. Hence, her ratings, like his, might be displaced toward the aggressive pole of the rating continuum. Will the man in this example therefore be judged more aggressive than the woman (an assimilation effect, as defined by the between-target criterion), or will the woman be judged more aggressive than the man (a between-target contrast effect)? The results that emerge will likely depend on several factors, including: (a) the degree of overlap that judges perceive between their subjective expectations for members of the two social categories, (b) the degree of stereotype inconsistency in the targets' actions, and (c) the relative salience of the individual targets.

With respect to the first point, if the judgment standards for the contrasting social categories are highly discrepant, the subjective aggressiveness ratings assigned separately to Paula and Paul are likely to show a contrastive pattern (i.e., Paula may be rated as quite aggressive with respect to other women, whereas Paul is rated as merely average in aggressiveness, for a man). This contrast effect is assumed to derive from the fact that Paul is being rated with respect to a more "demanding" standard than Paula. However, if judges were simply asked to indicate which of the two targets was the more aggressive, as a more direct, "objective" indication of the judges' mental representations, Paul would probably be regarded as the more aggressive of the two. In a similar vein, if both Paul and Paula are 5' 10" tall, Paula is more likely to be described as "tall" by those who know her (a subjective, contrastive assessment), despite the fact that she would be regarded as shorter than Paul in a paired-comparison format (see Nelson, Biernat, & Manis, 1990).

What might be expected when standards for different social categories are less discrepant than is the case in the prior gender and aggression example? For example, consider the case of a perceiver who sees only a small difference in aggression (and considerable overlap in aggression distributions) for women and men. Other things being equal, it may be anticipated that the subjective ratings assigned separately to Paul and Paula would show a contrastive pattern because the female standard for aggressiveness will still be less "demanding" than the male standard. However, because the male and female standards are less discrepant than in the earlier example, the contrastive effects that derive from this scaling/expectational difference should be less pronounced than before.

With respect to the second point, if the stereotype-inconsistent target's behavior or attributes are mildly, rather than wildly, inconsistent, assimilation is more likely to be obtained. For example, although an aggressive woman may represent a strong case of stereotype inconsistency, a passive man may not. Thus, subjective ratings of the aggressive woman, compared with those of the aggressive man, may produce an overall pattern of contrast (Paula rated as *more aggressive* than Paul). However, subjective ratings of a *passive* woman relative to a passive man may produce an overall pattern of assimilation (Paula rated as *more passive* than Paul). Finally, the salience of a target will likely determine which judgment pattern prevails (point c, previous page). In general, stereotype-disconfirming targets are likely to be highly salient, and more likely than stereotype-confirming targets to attract attentional and elaborative resources (Hastie, 1980; Srull & Wyer, 1989; Stangor & McMillan, 1992). This could intensify the contrastive tendency (relative to the assimilative tendency that affects judgment of the stereotype-consistent target) and produce a net between-target group contrast effect. Salience may also be heightened when judgments are made of outgroup rather than ingroup members, particularly when the outgroup is a numerical minority (e.g., Taylor, 1981). In this case, the attributes of the outgroup target may carry more weight in the judgment process than the attributes of the ingroup target, and therefore assimilation may predominate if the outgroup (rather than ingroup) target is stereotype consistent, and contrast may predominate if the outgroup (rather than ingroup) target is stereotype inconsistent (Linville, 1982; Linville & Jones, 1980).

Evidence From Our Lab. In much of our research on the shifting standards model, we have not explicitly manipulated the individuating characteristics of judgment targets, but rather have assumed that they are consistent or ambiguous with respect to relevant stereotypes. For example, in our studies on judgments of gender-relevant physical characteristics (e.g., height, weight; Biernat et al., 1991, Study 2), we have exposed perceivers to stimulus sets of male and female photographs that generally reflect the actual distributions of men and women on these attributes. In these cases, we have found support for the shifting standards prediction that objective judgments (e.g., feet and inches, pounds) reveal strong evidence of stereotype operation (e.g., men judged taller and heavier than women), and that subjective judgments (e.g., "short" to "tall," "light" to "heavy") reveal significant reductions of this effect, due to a shift in the judges' subjective anchors. Nonetheless, the subjective scales continue to produce patterns of assimilation to gender stereotypes. Similarly, when asked to judge the "athleticism" of an unsystematically chosen sample of African-American and White males (depicted in photographs), subjects using both an objective rank ordering procedure and a subjective trait rating procedure (*very unathletic* to *very athletic*) were stereotype consistent in their judgments. Thus, although both scaling procedures yielded an assimilative pattern, this effect was significantly stronger on the objective (rank order) index (Biernat & Manis, 1994, Study 4).

In the studies from our lab that have involved an explicit manipulation of target qualities, such that some targets show evidence of stereotype-inconsistent attributes, we have supported the prediction that objective judgments reveal assimilation to stereotypes, whereas subjective judgments reveal contrast. For example, in a height judgment study, in which perceivers were presented with stimulus photographs of female targets who were "objectively" taller than male targets, those who estimated heights in feet and inches nonetheless judged the men to be taller than the women. By contrast, those who estimated heights in subjective (*short* to *tall*) units judged the women taller than the men (Biernat & Kobrynowicz, 1997a). The female targets in this study were tall for women, and the male targets were short for men; subjective judgments revealed this contrastive pattern.

In a study focusing on the stereotype that Whites are more verbally skilled than African Americans, participants were asked to make judgments about the "verbal ability" of a series of African-American and White male targets (Biernat, Vescio, & Billings, 1997). Half of these targets showed evidence of high and half of low verbal ability (as indicated by the definitions they provided in an oral vocabulary test). Each target was first rated on a subjective response scale (*very low* to *very high* verbal ability), and later on an objective response scale (expected letter grade in high school English courses, a common rule scale, from A to F). The subjective judgments showed evidence of outgroup polarization (Linville & Jones, 1980): High-ability African-American targets were judged more positively than high-ability White targets, and low-ability African-American targets were judged more negatively than low-ability White targets. This pattern is consistent with the predicted patterns of assimilation and contrast on subjective scales: The stereotype-consistent African-American target (low verbal ability) was judged in a stereotype-consistent manner (lower in verbal ability than the comparable White), but the stereotype inconsistent African-American target (high verbal ability) was contrasted from the stereotype (judged higher in verbal ability than the comparable White).[3] In objective units, however, the African-American target was always judged to be less verbally able than the White, at each level of ability/stereotype consistency. This also provides strong support for the prediction that objective judgments normally reveal assimilation to stereotypes.

In an additional study that involved manipulations of stereotype fit, Biernat and Manis (1994, Study 1), asked participants to evaluate a male or female author of a masculine (e.g., bass fishing) or feminine (e.g., meal planning) magazine article. It was assumed that a woman who writes about feminine topics and a man who writes about masculine topics are stereotype consistent in their behaviors, but that individuals who write on topics relevant to the opposite gender are stereotype inconsistent. Following the usual paradigm, half of the participants judged the quality of the magazine article on objective response scales, and half on subjective scales. Objective judgments consisted of estimates of the monetary worth and letter grade that should be assigned to the article; subjective judgments were made on rating scales anchored by the words *very little money* and *lots of money,* and *excellent* and *terrible.* Results indicated that stereotype-inconsistent targets (i.e., female authors of masculine articles and male authors of feminine articles) were judged more negatively than stereotype-consistent targets among the judges who used objective response scales. However, these same stereotype-inconsistent targets were judged more positively than stereotype-consistent targets when the judges used subjective response scales. That is, on subjective judgment scales, stereotype-inconsistent targets were contrasted from the relevant stereotype (e.g., men were thought to be subjectively better at writing feminine articles than women), but on objective scales, the authors were assimilated to stereotyped expectations (e.g., male authors were thought to have produced feminine articles that were worth less money than those produced by the female authors).

More recently, a similar pattern was noted when subjects evaluated male and female applicants for a masculine (chief of staff) or feminine (secretary) job (Biernat & Kobrynowicz, 1997b). Once again, applicants for "gender-appropriate" jobs were conceptualized as stereotype consistent, and those applying for jobs typically occupied by the opposite gender as stereotype

---

[3] A White target with poor verbal skills may generally disconfirm the verbal ability stereotype, but as argued elsewhere, this individual is still likely to fall well within a perceiver's range of expectations for Whites' ability (see Biernat et al., 1997). Thus, although a White with poor verbal skills will be judged accordingly, this individual will not be judged as low in verbal ability as a stereotype-confirming, low-verbal African-American target.

inconsistent. Objective ratings (e.g., letter grades) revealed judgments consistent with stereotypes regarding the fit between gender and job — females were judged better than males at the feminine job, and males were judged better than females at the masculine job. However, subjective judgments indicated the opposite pattern. That is, subjective ratings suggested that male applicants would be better secretaries than females, and that female applicants would be better chiefs of staff than males. Consistent with the shifting standards perspective, these data suggest that the male applicant for the feminine job was perceived as "very good, *for a male*" (a relatively undemanding standard) and the female applicant for the masculine job as "very good, *for a female*" (again, an undemanding standard). Nonetheless, at the objective level, evaluations of these targets were consistent with stereotypes — men do not make good secretaries, and women do not make good chiefs of staff.

Behavior Follows From Judgment

It is assumed that perceivers generally behave toward individual group members in a manner consistent with their judgments (i.e., that behavior follows from judgment). From the shifting standards perspective, however, a critical question is whether perceivers behave in accordance with their subjective or objective judgments. These judgments are often in agreement, but the question becomes more important when subjective and objective judgments are discrepant. According to the model, this is most likely when targets display stereotype-inconsistent attributes. To return to the softball example, do individuals behave toward the female athlete in terms of her "excellent" subjective standing, or in terms of her lower objective (i.e., stereotypical) standing relative to that of her male teammate?

To answer this question, a distinction is made between two broad categories or forms of behavior — those that involve allocation of limited resources and those that do not. Included in the first category are behavioral choices (e.g., who gets promoted, who plays shortstop) and allocation of "valuable" assets (e.g., money, responsibilities), which have the following defining attribute: Behaving toward one individual restricts the behavioral options that are available toward another. Such behaviors have a "zero-sum" quality. This class of behavior is generally regarded as the more meaningful to the recipient, in that tangible resources are at stake. The second class of behaviors has a nonzero-sum nature, in that the same or similar actions can be bestowed on a limitless number of targets, without resource depletion. Falling under this rubric are such behaviors as non-verbal cues, verbal praise or punishment, and so on. Thus, a hiring decision is a zero-sum behavior — by hiring one individual, others are rejected. In contrast, a pleasant behavioral interaction style (e.g., smiling, making eye contact, etc.) is a nonzero-sum behavior—this may be displayed to many individuals without being expended.

It is suspected that zero-sum behaviors will generally follow from objective appraisals (i.e., directly from stereotypic representations), whereas nonzero-sum behaviors may follow from subjective judgments of group members. Thus, it is the male softball player, not the female, who is assigned to play shortstop and to bat in the clean-up position. Such behavioral choices are based on the stereotyped perception that men are better athletes than women. However, the reader will recall that the subjectively "excellent" female athlete is more likely than her "good" male counterpart to receive praise and pats on the back from her teammates. As limitless resources, praise and back pats may be more readily delivered to the subjectively better performer.

Zero-Sum Behaviors. Some empirical evidence that is consistent with the prediction regarding zero-sum behaviors can be found in a field study that examined gender effects on subordinate and supervisor cross-evaluations (Gupta, Jenkins, & Beehr, 1983). Using a sample of employees from a broad range of work settings, these researchers found an overall tendency for females (both supervisors and subordinates) to be subjectively evaluated more positively than males. At the same time, however, the behavior of employers toward the employees seemed more consistent with a stereotype-consistent objective representation of males as better than females—male subordinates were awarded more promotions and pay raises than the same females who were subjectively evaluated so positively. As the authors wrote about employers' treatment of women: "While opinions (evaluations) may be positive, actions (promotions) still follow tradition" (p. 183).

In the domain of race, Weitz (1972) studied the behavioral choices of White subjects who were led to believe that they would be interacting with either an African-American or a White partner. She found that, although some Whites reported extremely positive subjective feelings of "friendliness" toward their African-American partners, these same individuals engaged in the most negative behavioral responses to the partner (e.g., they were less likely to choose to wait with the partner during a break in the experiment, and chose to interact with the partner in only the least intimate of experimental tasks). We conceptualize these as "zero-sum" behaviors, in that they involve choices between alternatives: waiting with the partner (vs. alone), and selecting among seven tasks those three that one would prefer to do alone rather than with the partner. Again, behavior followed not from the subjective sense of friendliness, but from the stereotypical representation of African Americans as less desirable partners than Whites.

To this point, we have not collected behavioral data in our research on the shifting standards model. Nonetheless, one may further see the case for our claim that zero-sum behavior follows from objective judgment by playing out several scenarios based on our nonbehavioral findings. In a study on judgments of financial success (Biernat et al., 1991, Study 2), it was found that men were estimated to earn more money than women, whereas women were subjectively judged to be more financially successful than men. Had subjects been asked to choose someone (male or female) to solicit for funds, or to pay for a meal, our intuition is that, all else being equal, most people would choose a man. A male target from this sample is likely to *objectively* have more money than a woman, even if she has been rated as high in financial success (for a woman).

Similarly, in our research on judgments of male and female authors of masculine and feminine articles (Biernat & Manis, 1994, Study 1), it was found that the authors of "appropriately" gender-typed stories were objectively judged more positively than authors of cross-gender-typed stories, but that subjectively this pattern was reversed. If the subjects were magazine editors, deciding to whom a story should be assigned, our guess is that this editorial behavior would be consistent with objective representations — women would be assigned to feminine stories, and men to masculine stories. And if our subjects were employers, we suspect that their hiring decisions with respect to applicants for masculine versus feminine jobs would likely follow from the objective representation of women as better secretaries and men as better chiefs of staff (Biernat & Kobrynowicz, 1997b).

Finally, in the study of judgments of perceived verbal ability of African-American and White high school students, perceivers assigned higher (objective) grades to Whites than African Americans, but subjectively judged a high-ability African American more positively than a high-ability White (Biernat et al., 1997). If subjects in this study had been asked to choose a tutor for help on an English assignment, or to ask for assistance with a crossword puzzle, we would expect high-ability Whites to be chosen more frequently than high-ability African Americans, and low-ability Whites to be chosen more frequently than low-ability African Americans. Of course, these are merely speculations. Empirical work is sorely needed to test our predictions.

Nonzero Sum Behaviors and Patronizing Behavioral Standards.   The receipt of more cheers and more pats on the back by female than male softball players provides an anecdotal example of how nonzero-sum behaviors may follow from subjective judgments. These behaviors may also represent a "wow" effect — they are demonstrations of surprise that an

individual has surpassed an expected (low) performance standard. In her work on status characteristics theory, Foschi (1992) described such standards, and the reaction to their being surpassed, as "patronizing" in nature. Patronizing standards are evident in the setting of lower minimum thresholds for stereotyped group members to "qualify" for particular attributes. For example, in the case of coed softball, when a female batter steps up to the plate, stereotypes and activated standards may lead fielders to move in, thereby setting a lower threshold for successful hitting performance than would be the case for a male batter. That is, the distance the ball must travel before a hit is subjectively labeled as *good* is much shorter for the woman than the man.

The setting of lower standards for devalued groups was documented in the previously described employee evaluation study (Biernat & Kobrynowicz, 1997b). In that work, subjects were asked to indicate the number of job-relevant skills they would require of a male or female job candidate before they would feel confident that he or she "meets the minimum standard" to perform the skill. Both male and female "employers" set lower minimum requirements for women than for men. However, despite these lower minimum standards, the same study documented higher ability standards for women than for men. An *ability standard* refers to a threshold at which a perceiver is willing to make an inference that an observed performance is due to the ability of the performer (Foddy & Smithson, 1989; Foschi, 1992; Foschi, Lai, & Sigerson, 1994; Webster & Foschi, 1988). In this study, although "employers" reported setting lower minimum standards for women than for men, they also set higher ability standards (i.e., required more evidence to document ability) for women than for men.

The analog to this finding in the softball example is that, although outfielders may play a shallow field for a female batter, thereby increasing the likelihood of a successful at-bat (a "hit"), they may also set a much higher criterion for a female than a male batter to qualify as having true athletic ability. This higher criterion may take the form of requiring a longer hit or a longer sequence of repeated hits (e.g., the woman may need to hit the ball a certain distance a greater number of times) to make an inference or attribution of athletic skill to a woman. Thus, although the woman's "good" hit may be greeted with praise, that same woman will be required to do more than the man to be the recipient of behavior that counts (i.e., zero-sum behaviors), such as a favorable field position or slot in the batting order. Zero-sum behavioral choices are based not on the target's success in surpassing a lenient standard, but on the objective representation of devalued groups as being less good, able, competent, athletic, and so on than valued or high-status groups.

Qualitative Differences in Judgment Standards

To this point, we have focused on judgment and behavior based on standards that reflect quantitative differences between social categories (e.g., men are more athletic or aggressive than women). But category membership may also define *qualitative* differences as well, such that the members of one group may display an attribute in a manner that differs in kind from the way it is displayed among members of a contrasting group (Kunda & Sherman-Williams, 1993; Kunda et al., 1995). For example, the trait descriptor *athletic* may apply to both men and women, but its meaning may be substantively different for the two groups. It is not simply that the trait *athletic* translates into more athleticism for men than women (a quantitative difference), but that men and women exhibit their athleticism in qualitatively different ways (e.g., men play sports, women do aerobics). Similarly, shifting standards regarding gender and parenting may mean that the subjective evaluation *good parent* translates into more involvement in parenting activities for women than for men (Kobrynowicz & Biernat, in press), but it may also mean that women and men display their good parenting in substantively different ways (e.g., men are financial providers, women nurture and care give). This argument is similar to Dunning's (1993) point that subjective trait labels are "sponge words" that can take on idiosyncratic and context-specific meanings.

As previously noted, such qualitative differences in stereotype and standard representation have not been the subject of much empirical research. Nonetheless, some speculations are offered on their implications for judgment of and behavior toward stereotyped group members. With regard to judgment, we suspect that standards based on qualitative differences have somewhat different effects than those based on quantitative differences because they render the dimensions of judgment noncomparable across social categories. That is, because perceived qualitative group differences lead respondents to judge individual targets on substantively different dimensions, these ratings cannot be (and typically are not) directly compared across categories.

For example, a woman who does aerobics (stereotype-consistent behavior for women) may be judged to be "athletic," and a man who plays several competitive sports (stereotype-consistent behavior for men) may receive the same subjective *athletic* label. These judgments, however, are not equivalent in meaning; indeed, perceivers in real-world settings would not spontaneously engage in direct comparisons of the two targets. However, if forced to rank order these two individuals on a single, athletic dimension (an objective judgment), we suspect that the "men are more athletic than women" stereotype would be revealed. This may occur for at least two reasons: (a) the athleticism that males exhibit is more prototypical of the trait *athletic* than is the athleticism that females exhibit ("playing sports" is a better exemplar of the trait category than is "doing aerobics"), and (b) the athleticism of men is valued more than the athleticism of women.

This pattern should operate for other stereotypes as well. A mother who tucks her children in bed at night will be judged a "good parent," as will a father who works hard at his job so that his family lives well. Each parent is "good" in his or her own way, and perceivers are unlikely to engage in direct comparisons of the two. However, if forced to rank the mother and father on a single "good parenting" dimension, stereotypes are likely to lead to the woman being ranked higher than the man. Gender stereotypes in this domain mean that the behaviors mothers typically engage in are more prototypic of "good parenting," and more valued than the behaviors in which fathers typically engage.

In summary, our judgment predictions regarding standards that are based on qualitative group differences differ from those involving quantitative group differences, in that the judgment dimensions themselves may vary, such that targets from different categories are not normally compared. In fact, direct comparisons may only occur when directly prompted (as in a laboratory setting, or when one must make a concrete choice— who's the best athlete or the best parent?). Otherwise, one may readily refer to both males and females as "good athletes" or "good parents," but mean substantially, substantively different things by these labels.

What about behavior? As indicated earlier, zero-sum behavior is generally predicted to follow from objective, stereotype-congruent perceptions (e.g., the man is selected more quickly than the woman when choosing basketball teams; the mother is more likely than the father to have custody of the children following a divorce), but one real-world example reveals that such behavior may sometimes follow from subjective (perhaps stereotype-contrastive) evaluations. The example concerns child custody battles. As Chesler (1987) noted, the tendency for mothers to be assigned custody of children after divorce is only true in uncontested cases. When parents fight for custody, fathers tend to win out in about 70% of the cases. Furthermore, the courts appear to use gender-based "double standards" for judging parental worth, such that "mothers are expected to meet more stringent standards of parenting" than fathers (Chesler, 1991, p. 410). The result is that fathers may be awarded custody when their past parental performance is objectively equivalent to or less than that of mothers (but higher than that of "typical" fathers), or when they indicate their intent to be better fathers in the future. Presumably, this is based on the subjective perception that "he's really an involved parent, *for a man*." The mere act of requesting custody may also be perceived as counterstereotypic for a man, and may be taken as such a strong sign of parental interest that the subjective sense of the man as a "good father" guides the behavioral choice.

This example, then, provides at least suggestive evidence that zero-sum behavior toward stereotyped group members may occasionally follow from subjective perceptions, rather than from objective (stereotype-consistent) representations. Research is clearly needed to better understand the factors and conditions that might be responsible for such effects. It has been intimated here that this behavioral pattern is more likely when perceivers hold qualitatively different expectations for members of contrasting social groups, but the prediction has yet to be put to empirical test.

CONCLUDING COMMENTS

This chapter has suggested that category-specific judgment standards affect evaluations of, and behavior toward, individual group members. Stereotypes are assumed to activate these standards, which, in turn, influence both objective and subjective judgments in predictable ways. Research has documented that objective judgments tend to consistently reveal (assimilative) stereotyping effects, and that subjective judgments show a weakened form of this pattern (when targets have stereotype-consistent or stereotype-ambiguous attributes) or pattern reversals (i.e., contrast effects, when targets have stereotype-inconsistent attributes). Predictions regarding behavioral effects are more speculative, but in general zero-sum behavior (such as choices among candidates for a position, or allocation of resources) should follow from objective judgments. This is so because objective judgments more accurately reflect perceivers' mental representations of different targets, in comparison with the context-bound, category-specific nature of subjective judgments. Meaningful behaviors involving limited resources will follow from the representation, not from the semantic label.

Lower standards for a social group may also manifest themselves in "patronizing" behaviors—a fielder moves in to face a female batter, or an employer assigns less difficult tasks to an African-American than a White employee (Pettigrew & Martin, 1987). Such behaviors may make it easier for the devalued group member to surpass the low standards, resulting in a subjective "wow" effect: The fielder is visibly impressed when the woman hits a ball over his head, and the employer congratulates the African-American employee on his or her "good" performance. These behavioral reactions have a nonzero-sum quality, in that their display toward one target is independent of their display toward another. Although they may have some positive consequences for the recipient, such responses are unlikely to convince the perceiver that the female batter has athletic ability, or that the employee is truly competent. Instead, at the next opportunity, behavioral choices (i.e., zero-sum behaviors) will likely continue to follow from the perceiver's stereotyped representations—the fielder will again move in; the employer will again assign the African-American employee an easier or less important task. At some point, this behavioral pattern may change, but research suggests that devalued group members have a relatively difficult time documenting their ability in stereotyped domains (Biernat & Kobrynowicz, 1997b).

Further research is needed to test many of the predictions set forth in this chapter, particularly those regarding the judgment–behavior link. The shifting standards model and other stereotyping approaches have generated considerable evidence that intergroup cognitions (stereotypes) reliably affect judgments of individual targets, but the behavioral implications of stereotypes and judgments have received less empirical attention. This is unfortunate because intergroup behaviors of the sort described here (e.g., placement decisions, resource allocations, nonverbal interaction styles) are likely to have important implications for the daily lives of stereotyped group members. This chapter offers the unique predictions that intergroup behaviors vary in kind (some have a zero-sum and some have a nonzero-sum quality), that these behaviors follow from objective and subjective judgments, respectively, and that attributes of the individual target in combination with the kind or format of response determine whether both judgment and behavior reflect bias against or in favor of members of stereotyped groups. This recognition that stereotypes and the judgment standards they activate may have varied and complex effects on both judgment and behavior is necessary for a fuller understanding of intergroup interaction.

More fundamental issues regarding the shifting standards model require examination as well. For example, it seems important to develop good measures of category standards, and to explicitly test the mediational role that standards may play in judgment and behavior. By measuring standards, it will also be possible to examine several forms of assimilative and contrastive effects—those relative to within-category standards, and those based on the comparison between targets from contrasting social categories. Because individual targets belong to any number of categories simultaneously, it will also be critical in future research to address which category standard will be activated in a given situation (Zarate & Smith, 1990). For example, are African-American women evaluated against an African-American standard, a female standard, or some conjunctive representation? The model also has implications for perceivers' memory of individual group members. For example, when the coed softball team disbands, how will teammates recall the batting performance of the "excellent" female athlete? Will she be remembered as hitting further than 150 feet, as "excellent" in a harsh or stringent context may imply, or as less than 150 feet, as might be true of an excellent *female* performance? As Higgins' work on the "change of standard" effect suggests, perceivers may recreate the meaning of the label *excellent* in a manner that incorporates both the original and more recent contexts (Higgins & Lurie, 1983; Higgins & Stangor, 1988). We hope that the shifting standards model will prove a fertile ground for testing these and many other important research questions.

ACKNOWLEDGMENTS

The research reported in this chapter was supported by NIMH grant #R29MH48844. The authors are grateful to Laura Billings, Chris Crandall, Diane Kobrynowicz, Michelle Nario-Redmond, and the editors for their helpful comments on earlier drafts.

REFERENCES

Abramson, P. R., Goldberg, P. A., Greenberg, J. H., & Abramson, L. M. (1977). The talking platypus phenomenon: Competency ratings as a function of sex and professional status. *Psychology of Women Quarterly, 2*, 114–124.

Biernat, M. (1995). The shifting standards model: Implications of stereotype accuracy for social judgment. In Y. T. Lee, L. Jussim, & C. McCauley (Eds.), *Stereotype accuracy: Toward appreciating group differences* (pp. 87–114). Washington, DC: American Psychological Association.

Biernat, M., & Kobrynowicz, D. (1997a). *Shifting standards and the assimiliation and contrast of judgments to group stereotypes.* Manuscript submitted for publication.

Biernat, M., & Kobrynowicz, D. (1997b). Gender- and race-based standards of competence: Lower minimum standards but higher ability standards for devalued groups. *Journal of Personality and Social Psychology, 72*, 544–557.

Biernat, M., & Manis, M. (1994). Shifting standards and stereotype-based judgments. *Journal of Personality and Social Psychology, 66*, 5–20.

Biernat, M., Manis, M., & Nelson, T. E. (1991). Stereotypes and standards of judgment. *Journal of Personality and Social Psychology, 60*, 485–499.

Biernat, M., Vescio, T. K., & Billings, L. S. (1997). *Outgroup polarization and the shifting standards model.* Manuscript submitted for publication.

Brewer, M. B. (1988). A dual process model of impression formation. In T. K. Srull & R. S. Wyer (Eds.), *Advances in social cognition* (Vol. 1, pp. 1–36). Hillsdale, NJ: Lawrence Erlbaum Associates.

Campbell, D. T., Hunt, W. A., & Lewis, N. A. (1958). The relative susceptibility of two rating scales to disturbances resulting from shifts in stimulus contexts. *Journal of Applied Psychology, 42*, 213–217.

Chesler, P. (1987). *Mothers on trial: The battle for children and custody.* New York: Harcourt Brace.

Chesler, P. (1991). Mothers on trial: The custodial vulnerability of women. *Feminism and Psychology, 1*, 409-425.

Devine, P. G. (1989). Stereotypes and prejudice: Their automatic and controlled components. *Journal of Personality and Social Psychology, 56*, 5-18.

Dunning, D. (1993). Words to live by: The self and definitions of social concepts and categories. In J. Suls (Ed.), *Psychological perspectives on the self* (Vol. 4, pp. 99-126). Hillsdale, NJ: Lawrence Erlbaum Associates.

Foddy, M., & Smithson, M. (1989). Fuzzy sets and double standards: Modeling the process of ability inference. In J. Berger, M. Zelditch, Jr., & B. Anderson (Eds.), *Sociological theories in progress: New formulations* (pp. 73-99). London: Sage.

Foschi, M. (1992). Gender and double standards for competence. In C. L. Ridgeway (Ed.), *Gender, interaction, and inequality* (pp. 181-207). New York: Springer-Verlag.

Foschi, M., Lai, L., & Sigerson, K. (1994). Gender and double standards in the assessment of job applicants. *Social Psychology Quarterly, 57*, 326-339.

Goldstone, R. L. (1995). Effects of categorization on color perception. *Psychological Science, 6*, 298-304.

Gupta, N., Jenkins, G. D., Jr., & Beehr, T. A. (1983). Employee gender, gender similarity, and supervisor-subordinate cross-evaluations. *Psychology of Women Quarterly, 8*, 174-184.

Hamilton, D. L., & Sherman, J. W. (1994). Stereotypes. In R. S. Wyer & T. K. Srull (Eds.), *Handbook of social cognition* (Vol. 2, pp. 1-68). Hillsdale, NJ: Lawrence Erlbaum Associates.

Hastie, R. (1980). Memory for behavioral information that confirms or contradicts a personality impression. In R. Hastie, T. M. Ostrom, E. B. Ebbesen, R. S. Wyer, D. L. Hamilton, & D. E. Carlston (Eds.), *Person memory: The cognitive basis of social perception* (pp. 141-172). Hillsdale, NJ: Lawrence Erlbaum Associates.

Helson, H. (1964). *Adaptation-level theory: An experimental and systematic approach to behavior*. New York. Harper & Row.

Herr, P. M., Sherman, S. J., & Fazio, R. H. (1983). On the consequences of priming: Assimilation and contrast effects. *Journal of Experimental Social Psychology, 19*, 323-340.

Higgins, E. T., & Lurie, L. (1983). Context, categorization, and memory: The "change-of-standard" effect. *Cognitive Psychology, 15*, 525-547.

Higgins, E. T., & Stangor, C. (1988). A "change-of-standard" perspective on the relations among context, judgment, and memory. *Journal of Personality and Social Psychology, 54*, 181-192.

Hilton, J. L., & von Hippel, W. (1990). The role of consistency in the judgment of stereotype-relevant behaviors. *Personality and Social Psychology Bulletin, 16*, 430-448.

Jussim, L., Coleman, L. M., & Lerch, L. (1987). The nature of stereotypes: A comparison and integration of three theories. *Journal of Personality and Social Psychology, 52*, 536-546.

Kobrynowicz, D., & Biernat, M. (in press). Do the same traits imply the same behavior? Shifting standards in the interpretation of trait concepts. *Journal of Experimental Social Psychology*.

Krantz, D. L., & Campbell, D. T. (1961). Separating perceptual and linguistic effects of context shifts upon absolute judgments. *Journal of Experimental Psychology, 62*, 35-42.

Kunda, Z., & Sherman-Williams, B. (1993). Stereotypes and the construal of individuating information. *Personality and Social Psychology Bulletin, 19*, 90-99.

Kunda, Z., Sinclair, L., & Griffin, D. (1995). *Equal ratings but separate meanings: Stereotypes and the construal of traits*. Unpublished manuscript.

Linville, P. W. (1982). The complexity-extremity effect and age-based stereotyping. *Journal of Personality and Social Psychology, 42*, 193-211.

Linville, P. W., & Jones, E. E. (1980). Polarized appraisals of out-group members. *Journal of Personality and Social Psychology, 38*, 689-703.

Manis, M. (1960). The interpretation of opinion statements as a function of recipient attitude. *Journal of Abnormal and Social Psychology, 60*, 340–344.

Manis, M. (1961). The interpretation of opinion statements as a function of message ambiguity and recipient attitude. *Journal of Abnormal and Social Psychology, 63*, 76–81.

Manis, M. (1967). Context effects in communication. *Journal of Personality and Social Psychology, 5*, 326–334.

Manis, M. (1971). Context effects in communication: Determinants of verbal output and referential decoding. In M. H. Appley (Ed.), *Adaptation-level theory* (pp. 237–255). New York: Academic Press.

Manis, M., Nelson, T. E., & Shedler, J. (1988). Stereotypes and social judgment: Extremity, assimilation, and contrast. *Journal of Personality and Social Psychology, 55*, 28–36.

Manis, M., Paskewitz, J. R., & Cotler, S. (1986). Stereotypes and social judgment. *Journal of Personality and Social Psychology, 50*, 461–473.

McCauley, C., Stitt, C. L., & Segal, M. (1980). Stereotyping: From prejudice to prediction. *Psychological Bulletin, 87*, 195–208.

Nelson, T. E., Biernat, M., & Manis, M. (1990). Everyday base rates (sex stereotypes): Potent and resilient. *Journal of Personality and Social Psychology, 59*, 664–675.

Ostrom, T. M., & Upshaw, H. S. (1968). Psychological perspective and attitude change. In A. Greenwald, T. Brock, & T. Ostrom (Eds.), *Pschological foundations of attitudes* (pp. 217–242). New York: Academic Press.

Parducci, A. (1965). Category judgment: A range frequency model. *Psychological Review, 72*, 407–418.

Perdue, C. W., & Gurtman, M. B. (1990). Evidence for the automaticity of ageism. *Journal of Experimental Social Psychology, 26*, 199–216.

Pettigrew, T., & Martin, J. (1987). Shaping the organizational context for Black American inclusion. *Journal of Social Issues, 43*, 41–78.

Roberts, J. V., & Herman, C. P. (1986). The psychology of height: An empirical review. In C. P. Herman, M. P. Zanna, & E. T. Higgins (Eds.), *Physical appearance, stigma, and social behavior: The Ontario Symposium* (Vol. 3, pp. 113–140). Hillsdale, NJ: Lawrence Erlbaum Associates.

Schwarz, N., & Bless, H. (1992). Construing reality and its alternatives: An inclusion/exclusion model of assimilation and contrast effects in social judgment. In L. L. Martin & A. Tesser (Eds.), *The construction of social judgment* (pp. 217–245). Hillsdale, NJ: Lawrence Erlbaum Associates.

Sherif, M., & Hovland, C. I. (1961). *Social judgment: Assimilation and contrast effects in communication and attitude change.* New Haven, CT: Yale University Press.

Snyder, M., & Miene, P. (1994). On the functions of stereotypes and prejudice. In M. P. Zanna & J. M. Olson (Eds.), *The psychology of prejudice: The Ontario Symposium* (Vol. 7, pp. 33–54). Hillsdale, NJ: Lawrence Erlbaum Associates.

Srull, T. K., & Wyer, R. S., Jr. (1989). Person memory and judgment. *Psychological Review, 96*, 58–83.

Stangor, C., & McMillan, D. (1992). Memory for expectancy-congruent and expectancy-incongruent social information: A review of the social and social developmental literatures. *Psychological Bulletin, 111*, 42–61.

Taylor, S. E. (1981). A categorization approach to stereotyping. In D. L. Hamilton (Ed.), *Cognitive processes in stereotyping and intergroup behavior* (pp. 88–114). Hillsdale, NJ: Lawrence Erlbaum Associates.

Trope, Y. (1986). Identification and inferential processes in dispositional attribution. *Psychological Review, 93*, 239–257.

Upshaw, H. S. (1969). The personal reference scale: An approach to social judgment. In L. Berkowitz (Ed.), *Advances in experimental social psychology* (Vol. 4, pp. 315–371). New York: Academic Press.

Upshaw, H. S. (1978). Social influence on attitudes and on anchoring of congenile attitude scales. *Journal of Experimental Social Psychology, 14,* 327–339.

Upshaw, H. O., Ostrom, T. M., & Ward, C. D. (1970). Content versus self-rating in attitude research. *Journal of Experimental Social Psychology, 6,* 272–279.

von Hippel, W., Sekaquaptewa, D., & Vargas, P. (1995). On the role of encoding processes in stereotype maintenance. In M. P. Zanna (Ed.), *Advances in experimental social psychology* (Vol. 27, pp. 177–254). New York: Academic Press.

Webster, M., Jr., & Foschi, M. (1988). Overview of status generalization. In M. Webster, Jr. & M. Foschi (Eds.), *Status generalization: New theory and research* (pp. 1–20, 477–478). Stanford, CA: Stanford University Press.

Wedell, D. H., Parducci, A., & Geiselman, R. E. (1987). A formal analysis of ratings of physical attractiveness: Successive contrast and simultaneous assimilation. *Journal of Experimental Social Psychology, 23,* 230–249.

Weitz, S. (1972). Attitude, voice, and behavior: A repressed affect model of interracial interaction. *Journal of Personality and Social Psychology, 24,* 14–21.

Zarate, M. A., & Smith, E. R. (1990). Person categorization and stereotyping. *Social Cognition, 8,* 161–185.

8

The Role of Stereotypic Knowledge in the Construal of Person Models

Bernd Wittenbrink
University of Chicago

Bernadette Park
Charles M. Judd
University of Colorado

Never mind.
In the end she will manage to look just like it.
> —Pablo Picasso's reply to friends who
> thought his portrait of Gertrude Stein
> was not a good resemblance.
> (Penrose, 1981, p. 118)

One of the rather fundamental tasks in social life is the necessity of forming impressions of other people. Although most of us may lack the skills to communicate our impressions by means of a few brush strokes, we nevertheless rely in our daily social interactions on our ability to understand what other people are like. As a salesperson, we may try to judge what approach to take with a particular client; as a juror, we may have to decide whether the defendant is the person construed by the prosecution or the often quite different person construed by the defense. In fact, as social perceivers, we are particularly at ease in combining diverse sets of information into an overall judgment of what a given person is like. Of course, in doing so, we often go far beyond what is "objectively" known, constructing a person in our mind based as much on the inferences we draw from the available information as on this information itself. The fact that we encounter people in the context of their various group memberships, rather than as solitary individuals, allows us to enrich our impressions with the knowledge we hold about these groups. Indeed, the impressions we form of the people around us, the way we see their behaviors and, of course, our own behavioral choices are critically influenced by our stereotypic beliefs about what a given group of people is like.

Over the past decades, social-psychological research has accumulated ample evidence for the power of such stereotypic influences on the perceiver's construal of the social environment (Darley & Gross, 1983; Duncan, 1976; Linville & Jones, 1980; Sagar & Schofield, 1980; Word, Zanna, & Cooper, 1974). The goal of this chapter is to focus on a particular aspect of stereotypic functioning in social perception—the role stereotypes play in the perceiver's attempts to integrate social information into a coherent and subjectively meaningful representation of an individual. Specifically, it argues that stereotypes include, beyond assumptions about group attributes, beliefs about structural relations that link these attributes to each other and to the perceiver's external knowledge about the world. As such, stereotypes provide the perceiver with a relational structure that helps organize pieces of social information into an integrated representation of the social environment.

IMPRESSION FORMATION: THE AGGREGATION OF SOCIAL INFORMATION

The notion that social perceivers strive to obtain a subjectively coherent representation of a target person, that they attempt to form an impression that goes beyond mere lists of target attributes and that integrates the knowledge of such attributes into a subjectively meaningful entity, has a long tradition in the literature on impression formation. The classic work by Solomon Asch (1946) demonstrated how the observation of one target attribute influenced the interpretation given to other attributes of the target. In Asch's view, these effects indicate that, in forming an impression of another person, people actively combine the various pieces of information available about a given individual. In doing so, the perceiver arrives at an impression that is more than simply a list of attributes describing the person, a rather gestaltlike perception derived from the "particular form of relations between the traits" (p. 259).

Asch's argument that, in fact, perceivers actively integrate available information about a target into a coherent impression of the individual instead of forming evaluative judgments by collapsing across attributes finds additional support in a later study (Asch & Zukier, 1984). In this experiment, participants were simply asked to imagine a person for whom they were given two attributes, and to briefly describe what they thought such a person was like. Although some of the attribute pairs were clearly discordant (e.g., ambitious:lazy; dependent:hostile), participants had no difficulty describing these hypothetical target individuals, and easily offered explanations for why such rather incongruous attributes could characterize one and the same person. For example, one variant of the explanations given assumed one attribute to be the underlying cause for the presence of the other: "This person is *dependent* but is resentful of his dependence, and consequently becomes *hostile*" (Asch & Zukier, 1984, p. 1234; italics original). In contrast, an alternative explanation assumed the two attributes were both based on an additional common source: "A bully: is submissive to superiors and quite cruel to subordinates" (Asch & Zukier, 1984, p. 1236). As the two examples show, participants not only resolved the apparent contradiction between the two critical trait attributes, but their impressions also included crucial assumptions about possible interrelations among the attributes. In fact, these assumptions about attribute relations appeared to be crucial for a successful integration of the given trait attributes into a coherent impression.

Recently, Park, DeKay, and Kraus (1994) attempted to discern the underlying processes by which people integrate social information to an impression of another person. Specifically, Park et al. suggested that, in forming an integrated impression, people develop a narrative account or a "story" about the target person. Similar to recent developments in the social perception and social judgment literature (Fiske, 1993), this conception emphasizes the importance of causal "mental models" (Johnson-Laird, 1983) for the processing of social information and social judgments (Lalljee & Abelson, 1983; Miller & Read, 1991; Pennington & Hastie, 1988). Within this framework, the perceiver is thought to construct mental models of the available information by integrating the information with relevant world knowledge and assumptions about how events are causally related to each other. Complex social judgments (e.g., judicial decisions, evaluations of a given target) are based on such a modellike representation. That is, in the case of impressions about another person, the mental model in which information about a given target is represented, the "person model" (Park et al., 1994), allows the perceiver to generate attributions for observed target behaviors, and to simulate past or future behaviors, which, in turn, may serve as constraints for the perceiver's own behavior toward the target individual.

MODEL GENERATION AND STRUCTURAL ASPECTS OF STEREOTYPIC KNOWLEDGE

An important aspect of this approach to impression formation is that, in the resulting representational model available, information is intricately linked to the perceiver's background knowledge, determining what aspects of the information are relevant, and directing inferences regarding unobserved events and behaviors. This view is, of course, quite consistent with present theorizing in the social-cognition literature, and psychological experiments offer ample evidence for the use of confirmatory hypothesis-testing strategies (Skov & Sherman, 1986; Snyder & Cantor, 1979), as well as the perceiver's failure to differentiate between actual encountered information and spontaneously generated inferences (Bransford & Franks, 1971; Pennington & Hastie, 1988). Consistent with this general framework, similar effects have also been documented for the perceiver's expectation regarding stereotypic target attributes. Stereotypes have the potential to bias the perceiver's impression of another person, such that stereotype-consistent target attributes are more likely to be remembered (Bodenhausen, 1988; Cohen, 1981; Hilton, Klein, & von Hippel, 1991; Rothbart, Evans, & Fulero, 1979), and may falsely intrude the perceiver's representation of the target (Snyder & Uranowitz, 1978).

Yet besides generating stereotypic expectations about certain target attributes, stereotypes may serve an additional function in the generation of person models. Stereotypes may also provide important background information for the relational structure of the developed person model. That is, although stereotyping research has primarily focused on the influence of stereotypic group attributes on the processing of social information, it is clear that stereotypic knowledge is more complex than mere beliefs regarding the presence or absence of various group characteristics. In particular, our knowledge about social groups also contains knowledge of how these characteristics are related to one another, including explanations about the underlying causes of a group's characteristics. For instance, in the United States, people may hold the stereotype that African Americans tend to be poor. In addition, they may also hold beliefs about the underlying causes of this stereotypic attribute: Some people may think that African Americans are poor because of racial discrimination and blocked opportunities, whereas others may attribute their poverty to laziness or an inadequate value system.

In fact, the relevance of such causal explanations for Whites' stereotypic beliefs about African Americans has found increased attention among research directed at identifying sets of beliefs that predict various kinds of race-related social judgments and behaviors (i.e., voting behavior, hiring decisions; Bobo & Kluegel, 1993; Katz & Hass, 1988; Kinder & Sears, 1981; Kluegel, 1990; Sears, Citrin, & van Laar, 1995). Although this literature differs widely in its assumptions about the origins of existing belief differences (e.g., realistic group conflict, value differences, or social influence), it consistently identifies two opposing causal models for Whites' beliefs about African Americans. The first model identified holds that

African Americans are individually responsible for their economic failure and their current social status. African Americans are believed to lack the motivation and proper values to function successfully in society, and they are thought to use claims of discrimination in order to gain unfair advantages and escape their social responsibilities. In contrast, the alternative explanation assumes that their lower social status and economic failure is due to structural disadvantages with which African Americans are faced in U.S. society. These structural circumstances, such as lack of job opportunities or an inadequate education system, are thought to result from both discrimination and ignorance on the side of the White majority. At a more general level, these two models may be characterized by whether African Americans are perceived to be the victims or perpetrators of racial conflict (Ryan, 1976).

It is our argument that causal assumptions contained in stereotypic knowledge such as these help the perceiver in integrating available pieces of information about the social environment. That is, structural properties of stereotypic knowledge serve as a kind of causal blueprint or framework when a stereotype is applied to a given set of information. This blueprint aids the perceiver in integrating the information into a structure of underlying cause–effect relations. In other words, structural properties of stereotypic knowledge should provide constraints for the causal structure underlying the mental model the perceiver generates to integrate available social information.

For instance, in the experiment by Asch and Zukier (1984), participants used a variety of different explanations for their construal of the target individuals. Similarly, in the Park et al. (1994) studies, several different person models were construed for a given set of target information. Such ambiguity inherent in social information may be further reduced by relevant stereotypic knowledge as it provides additional constraints for the potential interrelations contained in the available information. For example, if the target described as dependent and hostile in the Asch and Zukier experiment is also said to be German, the target may indeed be more likely construed as a "bully." That is, applying the stereotypic assumption that Germans, as a result of their authoritarian upbringing, tend to be submissive to their superiors while being condescending and belligerent to their subordinates, may lead to a person model in which the attributes "dependent" and "hostile" are thought to be caused by a common variable—in this case, the person's authoritarian personality.

In our own work, we have pursued this idea that stereotypic knowledge guides the integration of social information by supplying a structure for the identification of cause–effect relations. For example, in a series of studies, participants' stereotypic knowledge about African Americans influenced their construal of trial-related events in the context of a jury decision-making experiment (Wittenbrink, Gist, & Hilton, 1997). In these experiments, participants were provided with written testimony regarding a trial in which a member of a high school basketball team was accused of having assaulted one of his teammates. The defendant's race was manipulated such that he was either an African-American student on a predominantly Caucasian team, or a Caucasian student on a predominantly African-American team. Except for the race and names of the defendant and his teammates, the actual trial information remained identical in both race conditions, with the defendant always belonging to the minority of the team and the victim always a member of the team majority. The testimony provided further information that the victim had recently replaced the defendant as a starter on the team, and described the more immediate conflict between the two. The defendant was said to have exchanged insults with the victim and an eye witness (who was a friend of the victim). During this exchange, the victim allegedly fell and hit his head; he consequently suffered a temporary coma and permanent hearing loss. The cause of the fall was in dispute. The prosecution argued that the defendant pushed the victim in the course of the argument, causing him to fall and be injured, whereas the defense argued that the victim simply tripped over a locker room bench. During the course of the testimony, it became clear that the defendant was not well integrated into the team, was friends only with the one other minority member of the team, and was having emotional problems stemming from his parents' divorce.

Following the trial materials, participants were asked to write a brief summary of what they believed had happened in the disputed events. Analysis of these accounts clearly indicate that participants' construal of the trial-related events varied with their stereotypic beliefs about African Americans. Participants who in a pretest unrelated to the experiment had been identified as holding beliefs of African Americans consistent with what we earlier referred to as a "victim" explanation were more likely to construe the available information in a way that perceived the African-American trial protagonists as the victims of racial discrimination. In contrast, participants who subscribed to a "perpetrator" account of African Americans were more likely to perceive the African-American participants as the initiating agents of the events. This differential construal of cause-effect relations was observed across experimental conditions, independent of whether the African-American target held the role of defendant or plaintiff in the trial.

It appears that the effects of participants' stereotypic knowledge on their construal of the trial events occurred upon integration of the trial information. In one experiment, interference with participants' ability to successfully integrate the trial information into a coherent representation of the disputed events led to an attenuation of the previously observed stereotyping effects. Specifically, this experiment presented participants with trial information piece by piece in individual sentences. For half the participants, these evidence items were presented in random order, thus increasing the difficulty to construe meaningful relations among the available pieces of information (Devine & Ostrom, 1985; Pennington & Hastie, 1992). The remaining participants received the items in an order that preserved the temporal sequence of events. Although participants in the two conditions did not differ in their overall recall of the trial information, and were also equally cognizant of the trial protagonists' race, "victim" and "perpetrator" participants in the random-order condition were less likely to differ in their construal of cause–effect relations underlying the disputed events.

Thus, participants' stereotypic knowledge was crucial for their integration of the available trial information, providing "a common theme" (Bodenhausen, 1988) around which the information could be organized. Just as the participants' preexisting knowledge about team sports and jealousy helped them understand what the defendant probably felt when the coach replaced him on the starting line-up, their pre-existing stereotypes helped them to understand why the assault occurred. Participants with a victim explanation for the situation of African Americans employed an understanding of racial relations in which discrimination exists, often causes conflict, and in which aggressive behavior on the part of African Americans is frequently a reaction to discriminatory behavior directed toward them. As one participant explained when the defendant was African American, " . . . it seems (the defendant) was being discriminated against by the team and was the object of racial slurs, . . . (the victim) goaded (the defendant) with racial slurs." In contrast, for participants who brought with them an understanding of African Americans as perpetrators of racial conflict, the African-American protagonists in the trial used references to discrimination to exploit liberal guilt and receive undeserved advantages. As summarized in one account from this participant group, " . . . (this was) a case of a black person that thinks he is being discriminated against all the time by everyone while in reality no one is discriminating against him. He is just trying to use racism to allow himself to get away with a crime."

THE ROLE OF STEREOTYPES IN IMPRESSION FORMATION

Our previous work showed that: (a) episodes of information about a target are interpreted in one of several ways in the process of developing a model of the person (Park et al., 1994), and (b) stereotypes can operate as background knowledge, enabling a causal analysis of why a particular event occurred (Wittenbrink et al., 1997). We wished to examine more directly the hypothesis that stereotypes can serve as an organizational tool for interpreting and combining information about an individual into a person model. We hypothesized that multiple episodes of behavior would be interpreted differently when they were considered as a unit, as opposed to individually, because the group of episodes would call to mind a particular role stereotype that would then suggest a different interpretation of the acts than when they were considered individually.

Our reasoning in designing this study was as follows. We began with four role stereotypes. These were a caring, but somewhat unmotivated and uninspired nurse, a hard-working lawyer who spends little time or energy on family, a "clinging vine" who cannot let go of a romantic relationship terminated by his or her partner, and a "gigolo" who is free-spirited and somewhat irresponsible in relationships. For each role, we generated eight behavioral episodes. When considered in isolation, most of these episodes were either positive or ambiguous in nature. When considered as a whole, however, the episodes suggested the moderately negative role stereotype from which they were derived. We expected that if participants judged each episode independently, they would view these in a somewhat positive manner. But when the episodes were considered as a set, we expected that the combination of episodes would call to mind the negative role stereotype, and this would be used to interpret and integrate the various episodes into a more negative person model than when the episodes were initially thought of as independent. As a result, participants would develop more negative person models and attribute more negative trait attributes in the integration condition than in the no-integration condition.

Note that two of the roles ("gigolo" and lawyer) are typically male role stereotypes, and two (nurse and "clinging vine") are typically female role stereotypes. Members of an outgroup generally hold stronger stereotypes of a target group than do the members of that group (i.e., the outgroup homogeneity effect; Park & Judd, 1990; Park & Rothbart, 1982; Quattrone & Jones, 1980). We hypothesized that the tendency to invoke the role stereotype under the integration instructions would be stronger for outgroup roles than for ingroup roles. Thus, the magnitude of the difference in impressions in the integration versus no-integration conditions should be larger for outgroup than for ingroup role stereotypes.

It may be that this larger difference for outgroup role stereotypes holds regardless of the gender of the target. That is, as a woman, I may hold particularly strong stereotypes of the gigolo type and the workaholic lawyer, and under the integration instructions I may use those strong stereotypes (more so than a male counterpart) *regardless* of whether the target who occupies that role is male or female. The stereotype applies to the role, and therefore the effects occur regardless of who occupies the role. Alternatively, the gender of the target may interact with the outgroup stereotype role prediction. We included target gender as a factor in the design to allow us to examine which of these possibilities would occur.

Each of the eight behavioral episodes developed for a given target were approximately three to five sentences long, and focused on a single event or revelation. Consider the following two episodes from the clinging vine target.

> I think that commitment in a relationship is extremely important and very much under-appreciated these days. My parents divorced when I was 7 years old. I still remember the lonely, empty feeling when my Dad left our house for the last time. I have vowed never to do that to my children. People are too quick to dismiss their feelings and their relationships. You cannot so easily undo what two people share. Instead, you should try to build on it, to strengthen it, and to keep it alive.

> Perhaps one of the most difficult times during my relationship with Steven (the target's former boyfriend) was when his father died of a prolonged illness (stomach cancer). It was very difficult for him and I tried to be by his side at all times and to offer whatever support I could.

The remaining six episodes for this target conveyed the following information:

> She is upset that her boyfriend of 2 years left her and is not willing to give him up.
> Stopped by his apartment after the break up and looked through his mail and called his home in the evenings to see who was there.
> Prior to the break-up, her partner had made plans to spend a weekend with coworkers at the beach after a work trip. She surprised him by flying out to join him and rented a place for just the two of them.
> Feels her sister is more like a roommate than a spouse with her husband because they give each other "space" such as a trip apart each year, and dinner or the theater with friends rather than the spouse.
> A month after the breakup, took a surprise picnic dinner to her ex's apartment where she found him with another woman. Threw the picnic dinner at her ex.
> Was offered a good position with a company about 1,000 miles away from her current home and turned it down even though she had no other job options because she could not accept that the relationship was over.

Although the first two episodes seem quite positive, in the context of the remaining information, they are given a new interpretation. The divorce comes to be seen as a critical event from which this person has never recovered. Her support for her partner during his father's illness takes on a smothering quality.

Each participant read about only one target. Participants in the integration condition were paced through the eight episodes and asked to use them to form an impression of the target. They first wrote an open-ended description of the target, and then rated the target on nine evaluatively laden trait attributes, using a 9-point Likert-type scale. The trait adjectives included *well adjusted, responsible, lazy, good natured, self-confident, intelligent, happy,* sincere, and *outgoing.* Following these trait ratings, participants received descriptions of two alternative "person models." One of these person models always capitalized on the positive interpretation of the behaviors (e.g., a caring and committed person who gives herself completely to a relationship; the kind of person romance novels are written about), and one focused on the negative interpretation (e.g., a pitiful person who needs to get on with life, not be so dependent, pick up the pieces, and move on). For each model, participants rated how well it fit their impression of the target on a 9-point scale (1 = *Not at all similar to my impression,* 9 = *Extremely similar to my impression*). Following these assessments of their overall impression, participants considered each episode individually and rated the target on the nine evaluative trait adjectives, separately for each episode.

In the no-integration condition, participants read each episode believing it was performed by a unique person. That is, different from the previous condition, these participants first wrote brief impressions and rated the target on the nine traits *following each episode.* After all eight episodes were presented (in random order), they were then told that all the behaviors had in fact been performed by a single person, to think of them in that manner, and to rate this person on the nine trait attributes. Finally, they completed the model rating task.

The design was a 2 (participant gender) X 2 (integration instructions) X 2 (gender of the role stereotype [with a replication for each gender]) X 2 (target gender) factorial, with all variables manipulated between participants. Three hundred and ten participants were recruited for the study.

For present purposes, we focus on the model ratings and trait measures. For all four targets, one model was evaluatively positive and the other negative. Our prediction was that the negative connotations associated with the role stereotype would become evident in the integration condition, but not in the no-integration condition. Therefore, we expected participants to be more likely to choose the negative model over the positive model in the integration condition. Similarly, we expected more negative trait ratings of the target in the integration condition. These differences as a function of the integration variable were expected to be stronger when the role was an outgroup stereotype role, rather than an ingroup stereotype role.

Model Ratings

Participants' ratings of how well their impression fit with the positive and negative person model were analyzed by treating the two ratings as a within-subjects factor. To simplify presentation of the results from this analysis, Table 8.1 contains the mean values for this model rating task as a difference between the positive and negative model ratings. That is, higher numbers indicate a better fit of the positive model relative to the negative model. Target gender had no reliable effects in the analyses, and results were therefore collapsed across male and female targets.

The predicted condition difference was quite evident. Participants rated the negative model as a poorer fit in the no-integration than in the integration condition, $F(1, 274) = 49.91, p < .001$. Moreover, as predicted, this difference depended on the gender of the role stereotype and participant gender, such that the condition difference was larger in the case of gender outgroup role stereotypes than for gender ingroup role stereotypes, $F(1, 274) = 9.98, p < .002$. This interaction did not depend on target gender. It appears that the stronger stereotypes held by outgroup members applied to the roles themselves, and were less affected by who occupied the roles.

Trait Ratings

Table 8.2 presents the parallel means for the global trait rating task – the trait ratings that took all eight behaviors into account. All ratings were scored such that higher numbers indicated a more positive impression; the ratings on the nine traits were averaged into a single measure, indicating the favorability of the trait impression. As for the model rating task, there was a substantial condition effect such that the target was seen much more positively in the no-integration than in the integration condition, $F(1, 276) = 27.71, p < .001$. This condition difference was moderated by the gender

TABLE 8.1
**Mean Difference in Ratings of Positive Minus Negative Model Fit
by Condition, Participant Gender, and Gender of the Stereotype Role**

Participants	Female Stereotype Role		Male Stereotype Role	
	No-Integration	Integration	No-Integration	Integration
Male	2.10	−4.40	−.37	−.94
Female	.89	−1.76	−.31	−2.32

Note. Ratings were made on a 9-point scale: 1 = *Not at all similar to my impression*, 9 = *Extremely similar to my impression.*

TABLE 8.2
Mean Trait Ratings of Target by Condition, Participant Gender,
and Gender of the Stereotype Role

Participants	Female Stereotype Role		Male Stereotype Role	
	No-Integration	Integration	No-Integration	Integration
Male	6.31	4.78	6.24	6.15
Female	5.80	5.15	6.55	5.88

Note. Ratings were made on a 9-point scale, with higher numbers indicating more positive trait impressions.

of the role and by participant gender, such that the condition difference was larger for gender outgroup roles than for gender ingroup roles, $F(1, 276) = 7.93, p < .005$. Again, this interaction was not qualified by target gender.

In addition to these global trait ratings, participants also considered each episode individually and rated the target in each episode in isolation. Thus, it was possible to use the average ratings across traits on an episode-by-episode basis in both the integration and the no-integration conditions to determine whether the effects of the global ratings replicated. The same effects were in fact obtained: $F(1, 276) = 43.47, p < .001$ for the condition effect, and $F(1, 276) = 5.44, p < .02$ for the condition by gender of the role by participant gender interaction.

In summary, we argued that stereotypes can operate as background knowledge that enables participants to comprehend and integrate information in a manner that is distinct from what would occur without the stereotype knowledge. Stereotypes permit a unique construal of the world, suggesting a particular pattern of causal relations that is derived from the stereotype knowledge. In this study, we predicted that a series of behaviors when considered in isolation would be viewed somewhat positively. But when considered as a whole, the pattern of behaviors suggested a particular "type" of person. Participants could successfully apply their stereotypes of this type of person in interpreting the behaviors, and doing so resulted in a more negative view of the target. This was evidenced both in the rated fit of the person models and in the target trait ratings. Thus, the rated fit of the positive person model over the negative person model was much larger for participants who read the behavioral descriptions as isolated episodes than for participants who integrated the episodes into a coherent impression. Similarly, the target was rated much more positively on the trait attributes by participants who did not integrate the behavioral episodes than by participants who did integrate the behavioral episodes. Consistent with past research showing that participants hold stronger stereotypes of outgroups than of ingroups, the integration versus no-integration difference was stronger for both of these measures for judgments of outgroup stereotype roles than for ingroup stereotype roles. The gender of the target, per se, was not important in determining model choice or trait ratings; rather, it was the gender associated with the role that mattered.

In their written impressions, integration participants often reasoned about why a behavior occurred in such a way as to make the behavior consistent with the negative model. For example, in the "clinging vine" target, the divorce of her parents was seen as a powerful event that caused her to become extremely dependent on relationships in her adult life. Her spontaneous trip to join her boyfriend for a weekend at the beach, when he had planned on spending it with coworkers, was then interpreted by integration participants as invasive and overbearing, caused by her fears about relationships ending. No-integration participants simply viewed this act as a demonstration of her affection for her boyfriend. Little causal analysis was present in the written impressions of no-integration participants, whereas this appeared to dominate the impressions of integration participants. In summary, participants' stereotypes were used to comprehend the set of behavioral episodes resulting in much different impressions than when the behaviors were considered in isolation, and the relevance of the stereotypes was therefore much less obvious.

ORGANIZATION AND REPRESENTATION OF STEREOTYPIC KNOWLEDGE

In our work, we have repeatedly found ourselves drawn to this very Aschian conception of both impression formation (Park et al., 1994) and stereotype use (Wittenbrink et al., 1997, the integration study just described). However, one frustrating feature of this approach is that, although it is conceptually appealing, it is fairly amorphous and ambiguous when one tries to make the arguments more concrete. Rather than flesh out the theory, the tendency, both in our own research and others', has been to present empirical demonstrations of differences that presumably derive from the operation of competing causal knowledge structures, or from the presence versus absence of this background knowledge. In Asch's (1946) original article, he talked about the forces the various bits of information exerted on one another, and the unique "whole" these pieces could produce when considered as a unit, rather than in isolation. Still, it is not clear how to conceptualize these "forces" or how this influence process takes place.

One means for making these conceptual proposals more tractable is to worry about the actual nature of the "background knowledge," and the process by which this information is accessed and used. We offer the following speculations about issues of organization and representation of stereotypic categorical knowledge. Keep in mind that our purpose in doing so is primarily to elucidate and make more concrete our conceptual arguments, rather than to offer definitive empirical evidence in support of these arguments.

A troublesome characteristic of the approach adopted here, and in Park et al. (1994) as well as Wittenbrink et al. (1997), is the potential for unlimited proliferation of person types or person models generated by the background knowledge. That is, we argued that stereotypes can be used to understand the reasons for the occurrence of particular events, and therefore can be used to develop a model of what a given target individual is like (as well as a model of the situation in which the behavior occurs). However, this position raises the question as to how background knowledge is matched with specific information about a given social situation. How can an infinite number of combinations of attributes possibly be matched with a finite set of knowledge?

One interpretation of this argument is that we have prestored knowledge structures corresponding to every possible person model, both those influenced by group stereotypes and those that are simply used for person perception. Thus, we have a model for a "gigolo" type, a "clinging vine" type, the overly ambitious professional who neglects his family, and the underachieving, somewhat insecure person who is barely making it. However, an infinite number of possible models exists, each one slightly different from the others due to some distinct attribute.

This problem was particularly apparent in the Park et al. (1994) study, where any given combination of attributes seemed to take on a unique personality, and yet it was clear that a large number of such unique combinations must exist. Likewise, social-psychology experiments are replete with examples in which participants readily utilize information that identifies a given target as a member of a category so idiosyncratic that, in all likelihood, participants had never given them much thought before entering the laboratory (e.g., experimental psychologists; Insko, Rall, & Schopler, 1972; Harvard-educated carpenters; Kunda, Miller, & Claire, 1990). Are we really to believe that we have prestored knowledge structures corresponding to every possible combination of characteristics that drives the person model formed? Are we to believe that we have prestored knowledge structures corresponding to every possible combination of attributes within a given stereotype that suggest each of the various "types" of group members we know to exist? On the one hand, we have the sense that each of these combinations has a psychological reality—that their meaning and importance are immediately available, in such a way that they appear to exist as independent, preformed knowledge structures. Yet the sheer number of such possible combinations makes this conceptualization implausible.

A related argument was made by Barsalou (1983), who pointed out that people are quite capable of generating assumptions about groupings in the environment on the fly For example, if people were asked to group their friends into those with whom they would like to go camping and those with whom they would not, most people could do so. Yet do we want to conclude that people necessarily hold a separately stored knowledge structure of a *good camping partner*?

More generally, as much as it seems highly unlikely that we have prestored structures corresponding to every possible person model or every social grouping one can conceive of in interpreting behavior, it is as difficult to decide what the dimensions are that people do use to partition their (social) environment. Thus, not surprisingly, social psychologists have debated over what exactly the attribute is by which people choose to organize their representation of other people: Gender and race (McCann, Ostrom, Tyner, & Mitchell, 1985), age (Brewer & Lui, 1989), social roles (e.g., professions; Bond & Brockett, 1987), relationships (Sedikides, Olsen, & Reis, 1993), attributes important for a person's own self-concept (Markus, Smith, & Moreland, 1985), or even the target's goals (Hoffman, Mischel, & Mazze, 1981; Trzebinski, McGlynn, Gray, & Tubbs, 1985) have all been suggested as organizing dimensions.

What is common to all of these arguments is that they point to a substantial flexibility with which our background knowledge can accommodate the complexity of social reality. This flexibility indeed seems to require a theoretical framework for the nature of conceptual knowledge that is less static.

In an attempt to address this issue, Murphy and Medin (1985) proposed that concepts are embedded in people's naive theories about the world. The perceiver's theories provide an explanatory principle that is believed to be shared by the category members. Such explanatory principles are thought to guide the detection of attribute covariations in the environment and organize existing knowledge relevant to the category.

Accordingly, Wittenbrink (1994) suggested that social knowledge is similarly organized by the perceiver's naive "theories" about the world. These theories provide subjective explanations that structure the social environment, defining the partitions the perceiver imposes on it. They explain what a given group of people is like, what attributes the group members share, and, more important, why they share these attributes. The perceiver's theories serve as constraints for the importance and, hence, salience of group attributes by defining the meaning of the attributes. In other words, rather than an objective feature structure of the stimulus environment, the perceiver's conceptual knowledge determines the level of abstraction at which stimulus features will be grouped, as well as the particular feature covariations that will be considered for this grouping. People's naive theories about the world will constrain the range of attributes considered for the representation of social concepts, and will determine the partitions people use to structure their social environment.

In this understanding, a stereotype can be thought of as a kind of shorthand for a more elaborate theory of what a group of people is like. Beyond beliefs about dimensional properties, these shorthands include a causal structure that allows the integration of knowledge about social groups. The rule knowledge on which the stereotype is based provides links among various aspects of world knowledge, and allows for the spontaneous generation of group attributes and causal links among those attributes. Thus, rather than being a fixed entity, stereotypes exist as a conglomerate of knowledge whose boundaries are fuzzy and that is held together by the perceiver's theory.

A possible way to actually implement such a theory-based organization of conceptual knowledge is suggested by recent work on knowledge representation — namely, work on connectionist models. Smith (1996) presented an extremely useful overview of connectionism for a social-psychological audience, and our analysis is drawn primarily from his work. The basic notion is that knowledge is represented in a distributed fashion, such that no one-to-one mapping exists between a concept and its location in the memory space. Instead, each psychological event is represented by a pattern, such as a series of 0s and 1s. Different segments of this pattern correspond to different attributes of the stimulus, so that, for example, one segment might code the person's intelligence, one his helpfulness, and one his physical appearance. These patterns are then stored in memory. When accessing memory to make some judgment, information from these past "events" is accumulated.

As applied to the stereotyping domain, the process might work something like the following. In the study presented earlier, each episode is encoded as a pattern. For example, for the "clinging vine" target, the episode describing her parents' divorce might be encoded 00101 11010, where the first block codes for the fact that her parents divorced, and the second fact codes for her reaction to the divorce — namely, that she felt lonely and empty. In the no-integration condition, this pattern is then compared against other events stored in memory that share similar sequence patterns. Thus, it might call to mind others whose parents have divorced, and, in particular, those who felt empty and lonely at the divorce. Then characteristics of these other exemplars can be used to draw inferences about this particular person. In a segment that codes for "success at adult relationships," if these other exemplars on average share the pattern of "insecure adult attachments," the inference might be drawn that this person too will have trouble with adult relationships.

In the integration condition, the divorce episode and the other seven episodes are simultaneously presented to the memory system. Hence, the fact that she threw a picnic dinner at her ex-boyfriend is encoded and used to construct knowledge about others who have thrown food at an ex (or behaved in a hostile manner toward an ex). This set of eight episodes or patterns will activate relevant past memory traces, and together they will generate a unique set of characteristics derived from the past memory traces. Thus, the system looks at what it knows about people whose parents divorce, who have a traumatic break-up as an adult, who throw food at their ex, who turn down a job in the hope of rekindling the old romance, and the culmination of information about all past memory traces who have one or more of these characteristics is produced. This derived memory trace will then suggest other characteristics of the target, such as overly dependent, unable to let go, and feels sorry for self. Importantly, these will be characteristics that *are not* derived from the consideration of each of the episodes in isolation. It is the ability of the system to simultaneously consider all the relevant past instances that produces the unique pattern of characteristics that we observed in the person models developed in the integration condition.

In the no-integration condition, each of the episodes is presented in isolation to the memory system, and each accumulates related information. Thus, the divorce episode will activate other divorce episodes, and the traumatic break-up episode will activate other similar break-up episodes. But the consideration by the memory system of each behavioral episode occurs discreetly because of the nature of the no-integration instructions. Even if after considering all eight episodes the participant then tries to pool the activated traces from each of the eight episodes (upon learning that all were performed by the same target), this pooled set will not be the same as the set of traces activated in the integration condition. Each set of traces was retrieved from an episode in isolation, and this set will not be the same as that generated when all the episodes are simultaneously considered.

From this perspective, an infinite number of "person models" or "person types" based on stereotypes are possible, but these are derived from knowledge in the system and do not exist as static knowledge structures per se. This is a much more tenable representation hypothesis. It is the unique combination of information presented to the system (that is derived from the behavioral descriptions of a given target) that generates the person model of this target. Again, the person model is a derived entity, and this derived entity can contain information on a whole host of dimensions, such as the likely causes of different types of behavior this person might engage in, an affective or likeability judgment, and expectation of future behavior.

Given the scope of the present chapter, our discussion of a connectionist approach to person and stereotype representation must necessarily remain sketchy. However, a number of authors have recently begun to offer more formal connectionist accounts for common phenomena in social judgment and impression formation (e.g., effects of individuating information in stereotype-based impressions; Kunda & Thargard, 1996; presentation order effects; Kashima & Kerekes, 1994; dissociation of memory for specific information and overall judgments; Weber, Goldstein, & Busemeyer, 1991; causal inferences in social judgments; Read & Marcus-Newhall, 1993). Clearly, this work has great potential for implementing some of the most important research questions in these domains.

BEHAVIORAL CONSEQUENCES OF STEREOTYPE-INDUCED PERSON MODELS

Implied in the close attention psychology has given to the question of how people form impressions of other people and how they construe the social world around them is the assumption that people's subjective construals will ultimately affect their actions. Likewise, it was stated earlier that a person model used for the integration of target information will serve as a constraint for the perceiver's own behavior toward the target individual. These behavioral effects can, in turn, constrain the behavior of the target, in the sense that he or she ends up acting differently as a function of the perceiver's construal (e.g., Jussim, 1986; Snyder, Tanke, & Berscheid, 1977). Thus, the final section of this chapter turns to the question of how behavior is affected by the person models derived from stereotype knowledge. It discusses a number of issues concerning behavioral effects, as well as a variety of behavioral consequences that follow from the particular model formed.

In considering the scope and magnitude of expected behavioral consequences, it is crucial to remember that behavior is multiply determined. Social psychologists have focused on perceptual consequences of stereotypes for a prolonged period because these occur in immediate proximity to the application of the stereotype. Examining behavioral consequences is at least one step removed from studying their perceptual consequences; accordingly, a number of other important influences affect behavior in addition to the stereotype. Such variables include situational factors like existing social norms (Ajzen & Fishbein, 1980), the extent to which the circumstances allow people to access stored knowledge from memory (Sanbonmatsu & Fazio, 1990), as well as personality factors such as self-monitoring (Snyder & Swann, 1976). As a result, the effect of the stereotype will often be subtle and perhaps difficult to detect. Nevertheless, stereotypic construal contributes in important ways to the final behavioral output of the perceiver, and documenting such effects constitutes an important goal for future research in this area.

Causal Attributions and Predictions of Future Behaviors

One sort of measure that falls somewhere in-between the assessment of pure "perceptual" effects of stereotypic knowledge and concrete behavioral outputs concerns judgments about the target, which are influenced by perceptions of the target and which influence the next link of the chain — behavioral outputs of the perceiver. Such judgments include causal attributions explaining the target's behavior and predictions about future behavior. Also, evaluative judgments of the target, such as how much one likes this person, presumably relate in a fairly direct manner to behavior on the part of the perceiver toward the target. Clearly these judgments are not "behavior" in the sense of concrete actions, but they are closer to behavior than, for example, the trait ratings of the targets.

The person model account argues that such judgments should depend on the particular model formed. The model should guide interpretation of acts performed by the target, and these interpretations will reinforce the model itself. Similarly, the model can be used to "play out" or simulate expected future behavior (Kahneman & Tversky, 1982), again in a manner consistent with the model.

To test these expectations within the gender role study described earlier, we asked participants in the experiment's integration condition about their interpretations of various acts performed by the target, and they were asked to make predictions regarding the target's future behavior. For each judgment, participants considered two explanations for a particular behavior, or two possible future behaviors, and rated on a 7-point scale how well each alternative fit their impression of the target (1 = *poor fit;* 7 = *excellent fit*). As an example, consider the "clinging vine" target. Participants were instructed to recall the behavior that the target flew out to spend the weekend with her boyfriend when he had planned to spend it with friends. They then considered two possible explanations for this behavior: that she "thought it would be a nice surprise for both of them to spend a weekend away together," or, alternatively, that she "is unable to let [him] go even for a weekend with his friends. She can't stand that he might enjoy others besides herself." Participants further predicted what the target would be like in 20 years, and rated the following two possibilities for fit to their impression: "She will be a devoted wife and mother who genuinely loves her relationships with her husband and kids," and "She will probably be single because no one could stand how overbearing she is. Either no one will marry her, or eventually they will leave her." Thus, each participant made four causal attributions and/or behavioral predictions. Participants made these judgments after they had read all eight episodes, and after they

TABLE 8.3
Mean Ratings of Fit of Positive and Negative Causal Explanations
and Future Behaviors by Model Choice

Measure	Positive Model (n = 33)	Negative Model (n = 117)
Positive causal options and behaviors	4.70	3.35
Negative causal options and behaviors	4.77	5.68

performed the trait ratings, but prior to completion of the model choice task.

Table 8.3 presents the mean ratings for the options consistent with the positive model, and consistent with the negative model, broken down by which model the participant rated as best fitting his or her impression. Note that only the integration participants performed this task.[1] As is clear from Table 8.3, participants rated the causal option and behavioral prediction consistent with their model as a better fit to their impression than the options consistent with the alternative model. Thus, participants who preferred the positive model over the negative model rated the causal explanation/behavioral prediction consistent with the positive model as a better fit to their impression than participants who preferred the negative model over the positive model, $F(1, 127) = 38.01, p < .001$. Similarly, the option that was more consistent with the negative model was rated as a better fit by participants who preferred the negative model than by participants who preferred the positive model, $F(1, 127) = 32.55, p < .001$.

In principal, participants were generating different explanations for the behaviors as they read about them. Moreover, in a real-world setting, whatever sorts of future behaviors might be anticipated in thinking about the target, the expectations would be driven by the model choice.

As with the causal attributions and predictions of future behavior, it is certainly reasonable that an evaluation of the target will be influenced by the person model formed. This evaluation should, in turn, have consequences for other judgments, such as whether to hire the person, how to evaluate the person in an interpersonal or business setting, or whether to date the person. We asked integration participants in our study to rate the overall likeability of the target (1 = *not at all likable;* 7 = *very likable*). Consistent with our expectation, participants who chose the positive over the negative model reported liking the target significantly more (*M* = 4.88) than participants who chose the negative over the positive model (*M* = 3.36), $F(1, 127) = 22.91, p < .001$.

---

[1]We thought this task would not make sense to the no-integration participants, but, on reflection, it likely would have been just fine.

These results nicely illustrate how the perceiver's stereotypic construal of a given target influences consecutive judgments related to the target's behaviors. Although, in the present study, we did not assess any specific actions towards the target, we would expect more direct behavioral measures to be influenced by the person model formed in similar ways. For example, if in our study we had told participants forming impressions of the "clinging vine" target about a "computer dance" function (Berscheid & Walster, 1974), giving them the opportunity to attend the dance with the target, we expect that participants forming the "clinging vine" model would have been much less likely to attend the dance with their partner than those who formed the romance novel model.

Stereotype-Induced Person Models and Behavioral Confirmation

An additional way in which person models are likely to influence behavior is through the expectations they induce about the behavior of others and the behavioral confirmation that often follows from such expectations. Thus, expectations about differences between physically attractive and unattractive people affect the perceiver's behavior toward a target individual who is thought to be either attractive or not, and these behavioral differences in turn influence the target's own behavior (Snyder et al., 1977). Expectations based on social categories such as gender and ethnicity have been shown to produce similar effects (e.g., Word et al., 1974; Zanna & Pack, 1975).

Recent work on behavioral confirmation as a result of social expectations has begun to identify factors that moderate the effect. One of the more interesting of these, from the point of view of the present argument, focuses on the perceiver's goals in a social interaction. Neuberg (1989) demonstrated that behavioral confirmation as a result of a perceiver's prior expectation is less likely to occur if the perceiver brings the goal of forming an accurate appraisal of the target individual to the interaction. However, Snyder and Haugen (1994) recently showed that if the perceiver is given instructions to "check out your first impression of (the target). Find out what she is like, what her personality traits are, and find out what someone with her personality can be expected to say and do" (p. 228), then behavioral confirmation is strengthened. Although the goals of accuracy and "checking out first impressions" may sound somewhat similar, they may have very different consequences in terms of the extent to which perceivers develop, elaborate, and act on the basis of category-based person models. Although this remains only speculation presently, an accuracy set may encourage a more tentative construction of person models on the part of the perceiver, whereas a set of instructions that encourages the participants to use and evaluate initial impressions may strengthen the integration of perceptual information into person models, thereby increasing the strength of behavioral expectations and behavioral confirmation.

Regardless of the validity of these speculations, the construction of person models that are, in part, based on stereotypic knowledge may not only affect the perceiver's own behavior vis-à-vis the target, but also the target's behavioral responses. Factors that strengthen the construction of these person models (such as the integration manipulation used in the gender role study described earlier) may thus affect the degree to which behavioral confirmation ensues.

Generalized Behavioral Consequences of Person Models

A further, more generalized effect of stereotypic person models is suggested by recent research on the consequences of stereotype activation. Specifically, Bargh, Chen, and Burrows (1996) argued that activation of a stereotype can affect not only perceptions of (and perhaps behavior toward) a target (as in the "Donald" paradigm; Bargh & Pietromonaco, 1982), but also the perceiver's behaviors that are unrelated to a given stereotype target. For example, in their Experiment 2, participants in the experimental condition unscrambled sentences relevant to stereotypes of the elderly; in the neutral priming condition, they unscrambled sentences containing age-nonspecific words. The speed with which the participant then walked down the hall to the elevator was timed, and those participants primed with the elderly stereotype walked significantly slower than those in the neutral prime condition.

Following this reasoning, it seems quite possible that activation of a previously formed person model could have similar implicit consequences on the perceiver's behavior, even if this behavior has no apparent connection to the relevant target person. For example, one might expect the impressions participants form of the "clinging vine" target in the gender model study to affect the way participants think about their own romantic relationships and their related behavior. Such a hypothesis could, of course, be easily tested within the paradigm of our initial study. For example, participants could again perform the gender model study using the "clinging vine" target, followed by an allegedly independent second study, introduced as an experiment concerned with romantic relationships. Participants would be asked to write a brief description of his or her current or most recent romantic relationship, its strengths and weaknesses, and any roles the two people appeared to adopt in the relationship.

In addition, such a study could present participants with scenarios in which different role expectations result in conflicting behavioral alternatives (e.g., watching a football game with friends vs. going on a date with partner). Following the argument that activation of a certain person model influences the construal of social situations even if they are not directly related to the target person, one would expect participants' descriptions and their behavioral choices to depend on their choice of person model in the initial impression-formation task. That is, the relationships should be construed in a more negative manner with issues of overdependence by those who form the "clinging vine" model, and as more romantic and other-worldly by those who form the romance novel model. Similarly, in the scenarios, participants with a "clinging vine" model should be more likely to choose behaviors inconsistent with their relationship role expectations.

In conclusion, although discussion of some of these issues still remains speculative, stereotype knowledge plays a fundamentally important role in one's construal of the social world. Moreover, one's construal has clear and important ramifications both for one's own behavior and for the behavior of the target. At present, a primary research goal is to explore these perception–behavior links in detail along the lines discussed earlier. Such research is critical to understand the behavioral consequences of stereotyping.

ACKNOWLEDGMENT

Preparation of this chapter was partially supported by NIMH grant R01 MH45049 to Bernadette Park and Charles M. Judd.

REFERENCES

Ajzen, I., & Fishbein, M. (1980). *Understanding attitudes and predicting social behavior.* Englewood Cliffs, NJ: Prentice-Hall.

Asch, S. E. (1946). Forming impressions of personality. *Journal of Abnormal and Social Psychology, 41,* 258–290.

Asch, S. E., & Zukier, H. (1984). Thinking about persons. *Journal of Personality and Social Psychology, 46,* 1230–1240.

Bargh, J. A., Chen, M., & Burrows, L. (1996). Automaticity of social behavior: Direct effects of trait construct and stereotype activation on action. *Journal of Personality and Social Psychology, 71,* 230–244.

Bargh, J. A., & Pietromonaco, P. (1982). Automatic information processing and social perception: The influence of trait information presented outside of conscious awareness on impression formation. *Journal of Personality and Social Psychology, 43,* 437–449.

Barsalou, L. W. (1983). Ad hoc categories. *Memory and Cognition, 11,* 211–227.

Berscheid, E., & Walster, E. (1974). Physical attractiveness. In L. Berkowitz (Ed.), *Advances in experimental social psychology* (Vol. 7, pp. 157–215). New York: Academic Press.

Bobo, L., & Kluegel, J. R. (1993). Opposition to race-targeting: Self-interest, stratification ideology, or racial attitudes? *American Sociological Review, 58,* 443–464.

Bodenhausen, G. V. (1988). Stereotypic biases in social decision making and memory: Testing process models of stereotype use. *Journal of Personality and Social Psychology, 55,* 726–737.

Bond, C. F., & Brockett, D. R. (1987). A social context-personality index theory of memory for social acquaintances. *Journal of Personality and Social Psychology, 52,* 1110–1121.

Bransford, J. D., & Franks, J. J. (1971). The abstraction of linguistic ideas. *Cognitive Psychology, 2,* 331–350.

Brewer, M. B., & Lui, L. N. (1989). The primacy of age and sex in the structure of person categories. *Social Cognition, 7,* 262–274.

Cohen, C. E. (1981). Person categories and social perception: Testing some boundaries of the processing effects of prior knowledge. *Journal of Personality and Social Psychology, 40,* 441–452.

Darley, J. M., & Gross, P. H. (1983). A hypothesis-confirming bias in labeling effects. *Journal of Personality and Social Psychology, 44,* 20–33.

Devine, P. G., & Ostrom, T. M. (1985). Cognitive mediation of inconsistency discounting. *Journal of Personality and Social Psychology, 49,* 5–21.

Duncan, B. L. (1976). Differential social perception and attribution of intergroup violence: Testing the lower limits of stereotyping of Blacks. *Journal of Personality and Social Psychology, 34,* 590–598.

Fiske, S. T. (1993). Social cognition and social perception. *Annual Review of Psychology, 44,* 155–194.

Hilton, J. L., Klein, J. G., & von Hippel, W. (1991). Attention allocation and impression formation. *Personality and Social Psychology Bulletin, 17,* 548–559.

Hoffman, C., Mischel, W., & Mazze, K. (1981). The role of purpose in the organization of information about behavior: Trait-based versus goal-based categories in person cognition. *Journal of Personality and Social Psychology, 40,* 211–225.

Insko, C.A., Rall, M., & Schopler, J. (1972). Role of inconsistency in mediating awareness of interaction processes. *Journal of Personality and Social Psychology, 24,* 102–107.

Johnson-Laird, P. N. (1983). *Mental models. Towards a cognitive science of language, inference, and consciousness.* Cambridge, England: Cambridge University Press.

Jussim, L. (1986). Self-fulfilling prophecies: A theoretical and integrative review. *Psychological Review, 93,* 429–445.

Kahneman, D., & Tversky, A. (1982). The simulation heuristic. In D. Kahneman, P. Slovic, & A. Tversky (Eds.), *Judgment under uncertainty: Heuristics and biases* (pp. 201–208). Cambridge, England: Cambridge University Press.

Kashima, Y., & Kerekes, A. R. Z. (1994). A distributed memory model of averaging phenomena in person impression formation. *Journal of Experimental Social Psychology, 30,* 407–455.

Katz, I., & Hass, R. G. (1988). Racial ambivalence and American value conflict: Correlational and priming studies of dual cognitive structures. *Journal of Personality and Social Psychology, 55,* 893–905.

Kinder, D. R., & Sears, O. R. (1981). Prejudice and politics: Symbolic racism versus racial threats to the good life. *Journal of Personality and Social Psychology, 40,* 414–431.

Kluegel, J. R. (1990). Trends in Whites' explanations of the Black–White gap in socioeconomic status, 1977–1989. *American Sociological Review, 55,* 512–525.

Kunda, Z., Miller, D. T., & Claire, T. (1990). Combining social concepts: The role of causal reasoning. *Cognitive Science, 14,* 551–577.

Kunda, Z., & Thargard, P. (1996). Forming impressions from stereotypes, traits, and behaviors: A parallel-constraint satisfaction theory. *Psychological Review, 103,* 284–308.

Lalljee, M., & Abelson, R. P. (1983). The organization of explanations. In M. Hewstone (Ed.), *Attribution theory: Social and functional extensions* (pp. 65–80). Oxford, England: Basil Blackwell.

Linville, P. W., & Jones, E. E. (1980). Polarized appraisals of out-group members. *Journal of Personality and Social Psychology, 38,* 689–703.

Markus, H., Smith, J., & Moreland, R. L. (1985). Role of the self-concept in the perception of others. *Journal of Personality and Social Psychology, 49,* 1494–1512.

McCann, C. D., Ostrom, T. M., Tyner, L. K., & Mitchell, M. L. (1985). Person perception in heterogeneous groups. *Journal of Personality and Social Psychology, 49,* 1449–1159.

Miller, L. C., & Read, S. J. (1991). On the coherence of mental models of persons and relationships: A knowledge structure approach. In G. J. O. Fletcher & F. Fincham (Eds.), *Cognitions in close relationships* (pp. 69–99). Hillsdale, NJ: Lawrence Erlbaum Associates.

Murphy, G. L., & Medin, D. L. (1985). The role of theories in conceptual coherence. *Psychological Review, 92,* 289–316.

Neuberg, S.L. (1989). The goal of forming accurate impressions during social interactions: Attenuating the impact of negative expectancies. *Journal of Personality and Social Psychology, 56,* 374–386.

Park, B., DeKay, M. L., & Kraus, S. (1994). Aggregating social behavior into person models: Perceiver-induced consistency. *Journal of Personality and Social Psychology, 66,* 437–459.

Park, B., & Judd, C. M. (1990). Measures and models of perceived group variability. *Journal of Personality and Social Psychology, 59,* 173–191.

Park, B., & Rothbart, M. (1982). Perception of out-group homogeneity and levels of social categorization: Memory for the subordinate attributes of in-group and out-group members. *Journal of Personality and Social Psychology, 42,* 1051–1068.

Pennington, N., & Hastie, R. (1988). Explanation-based decision making: Effects of memory structure on judgment. *Journal of Experimental Psychology: Learning, Memory, and Cognition, 14,* 521–533.

Pennington, N., & Hastie, R. (1992). Explaining the evidence: Tests of the story model for juror decision making. *Journal of Personality and Social Psychology, 62,* 189–206.

Penrose, R. (1981). *Picasso: His life and work* (3rd ed.). Berkeley, CA: University of California Press.

Quattrone, G., & Jones, E. E. (1980). The perception of variability within in-groups and out-groups. Implications for the law of small numbers. *Journal of Personality and Social Psychology, 38,* 141–152.

Read, S. J., & Marcus-Newhall, A. (1993). Explanatory coherence in social explanations: A parallel distributed processing account. *Journal of Personality and Social Psychology, 65,* 429–447.

Rothbart, M., Evans, M., & Fulero, S. (1979). Recall for confirming events: Memory processes and the maintenance of social stereotypes. *Journal of Experimental Social Psychology, 15,* 343–355.

Ryan, W. (1976). *Blaming the victim.* New York: Vintage.

Sagar, H. A., & Schofield, J. W. (1980). Racial and behavioral cues in black and white children's perceptions of ambiguously aggressive acts. *Journal of Personality and Social Psychology, 39,* 590–598.

Sanbonmatsu, D. M., & Fazio, R. H. (1990). The role of attitudes in memory-based decision making. *Journal of Personality and Social Psychology, 59,* 614–622.

Sears, D. O., Citrin, J., & van Laar, C. (1995, September). *Black exceptionalism in a multicultural society.* Paper presented at the joint meeting of the Society for Experimental Social Psychology and the European Association of Experimental Social Psychology, Washington, DC.

Sedikides, C., Olsen, N., & Reis, H. T. (1993). Relationships as natural categories. *Journal of Personality and Social Psychology, 64,* 71–82.

Skov, R. B., & Sherman, S. J. (1986). Information-gathering processes: Diagnosticity, hypothesis-confirmatory strategies, and perceived hypothesis confirmation. *Journal of Experimental Social Psychology, 22,* 93–121.

Smith, E. R. (1996). What do connectionism and social psychology offer each other? *Journal of Personality and Social Psychology, 70,* 893–912.

Snyder, M., & Cantor, N. (1979). Testing hypotheses about other people: The use of historical knowledge. *Journal of Experimental Social Psychology, 15,* 330–342.

Snyder, M., & Haugen, J.A., (1994). Why does behavioral confirmation occur? A functional perspective on the role of the perceiver. *Journal of Experimental Social Psychology, 30,* 218–246.

Snyder, M., & Uranowitz, S. W. (1978). Reconstructing the past: Some cognitive consequences of person perception. *Journal of Personality and Social Psychology, 36,* 941–950.

Snyder, M., & Swann, W. B. (1976). When actions reflect attitudes: The politics of impression management. *Journal of Personality and Social Psychology, 34,* 1034–1042.

Snyder, M., Tanke, E.D., & Berscheid, E. (1977). Social perception and interpersonal behavior: On the self-fulfilling nature of social stereotypes. *Journal of Personality and Social Psychology, 35,* 656–666.

Trzebinski, J., McGlynn, R. P., Gray, G., & Tubbs, D. (1985). The role of categories of an actor's goals in organizing inferences about a person. *Journal of Personality and Social Psychology, 48,* 1387–1397.

Weber, E. U., Goldstein, W. M., & Busemeyer, J. R. (1991). Beyond strategies: Implications of memory representation and memory processes for models of judgment and decision making. In W. E. Hockley & S. Lewandowsky (Eds.), *Relating theory and data: Essays on human memory in honour of Bennet B. Murdock* (pp. 75–101). Hillsdale, NJ: Lawrence Erlbaum Associates.

Wittenbrink, B. (1994). *Stereotypes as social concepts in a knowledge-based approach to categorization.* Unpublished doctoral dissertation, University of Michigan.

Wittenbrink, B., Gist, P. L., & Hilton, J. L. (1997). Structural properties of stereotypic knowledge and their influences on the construal of social situations. *Journal of Personality and Social Psychology, 72,* 526–543.

Word, C. O., Zanna, M. P., & Cooper, J. (1974). The nonverbal mediation of self-fulfilling prophecies in interracial interaction. *Journal of Experimental Social Psychology, 10,* 109–120.

Zanna, M. P., & Pack, S. J. (1975). On the self-fulfilling nature of apparent sex differences in behavior. *Journal of Experimental Social Psychology, 11,* 583–591.

IV

Processes Affecting Intergroup Cognition and Behavior: Motivational and Social Processes

9

A Systemic View of Behavioral Confirmation: Counterpoint to the Individualist View

Theresa Claire
Susan T. Fiske
University of Massachusetts at Amherst

Stereotypes of social groups are harmful not just because they are categorical, negative, or false, but because they guide the treatment of members of those groups. One of the most disturbing and intriguing consequences of stereotypic treatment is the self-fulfilling prophecy—when one person's stereotype induces another to act just as the stereotype predicts. Consider the following examples, which are loosely drawn from research on the topic: An African-American job candidate is treated with such distance and abruptness that he flounders in an interview (cf. Word, Zanna, & Cooper, 1974); a man expects a female coworker to enjoy "feminine" tasks, and after talking to him she chooses those very tasks when she and her colleagues negotiate who will do what (cf. Skrypnek & Snyder, 1982); and a man talking to an unattractive woman does so with such detachment and boredom that her responses in the conversation are also unfriendly and uninteresting (cf. Snyder, Tanke, & Berscheid, 1977).

These examples illustrate the complicated volley of thought and action that composes the self-fulfilling prophecy (Darley & Fazio, 1980). One individual (termed the *perceiver*) has a stereotypic (i.e., negative, generalized, and learned) conception of a group that influences his or her behavior toward a member of that group (the *target* of the stereotype). In responding to the perceiver's actions, the target confirms the perceiver's initial stereotyped view. Both the perceiver and target attribute meaning to the other's acts, and respond in the interaction based on their perceptions. Theoretical analyses and experimental demonstrations of the *self-fulfilling prophecy* (also known as *behavioral confirmation*) have captured this interplay of thought, behavior, and thoughts about behavior (e.g., Darley & Fazio, 1980; Miller & Turnbull, 1986; Snyder, 1984; Snyder & Swann, 1978). It is one of the few research traditions in social psychology to integrate the study of both social thought *and* action, so it is a topic uniquely suited for this book.

Research on behavioral confirmation of stereotypes has integrated the study of interpersonal cognition and behavior, but psychologists have often neglected the broader, intergroup context in which this interpersonal phenomenon occurs. We argue that this inattention to social context (due, in part, to researchers' ideological assumptions and, in part, to method-ological constraints) has led psychologists to underestimate the pressure on targets to confirm stereotypes of their group. This chapter broadens the focus from the single dyadic interaction to the target's experience across time, interactions, and perceivers. This framework emphasizes the socially shared nature of stereotypes and reveals some factors that increase the likelihood of behavioral confirmation. Taking a target's perspective also reveals the social nature of the factors that contribute to a target's *resistance* to negative stereotypes. This contextual analysis and many of the hypoth-eses derived from it can apply to positive generalizations of a group as well. Because targets of negative stereotypes experience a more unified concep-tion of their group, this chapter first focuses on stereotypes, and returns to positive generalizations later. To introduce the discussion of factors that promote or inhibit behavioral confirmation, an overview of research in the field and the philosophical assumptions of individualism that often accom-pany it are presented.

A REVIEW OF PERSPECTIVES
ON BEHAVIORAL CONFIRMATION

The early empirical demonstrations of behavioral confirmation exemplify social psychologists' extended fascination with the power of social influ-ence. In some of the field's most popularly discussed experiments, partici-pants either succumbed to small amounts of social pressure or did so in a way that was harmful to themselves or others (Prentice & Miller, 1992). For example, individuals gave depictions of their physical world that they knew to be incorrect when they observed others giving a false view (Asch, 1956). They failed to help someone in danger (Darley & Latané, 1968) or remove themselves from danger (Latané & Darley, 1968) because they followed others who failed to act. Most notably, they inflicted what they thought to be incredible physical suffering onto others because an authority told them to do so (Milgram, 1974). In each case, one of the reasons these results are counterintuitive and intriguing is their violation of an individualist view of human nature. The participants in these studies were simply more influenced by others than most people would have predicted. Into this tradition came behavioral confirmation, in which one person can influence another to behave in a stereotypic and often detrimental fashion. Like conformity, obedience, and other popular research topics, behavioral confirmation is antithetical to a prevailing view of people as relatively autonomous. This contradiction between the power of social influence and an individualist view of behavior is one cause of the continued surprise and interest in the behavioral confirmation effect.

In the course of almost 30 years of study, researchers have built on this interest by demonstrating behavioral confirmation in a variety of different experimental and field settings, using different types of expectancies (see Snyder, 1992, for a review). Once the influence of these expectancies on the target was demonstrated experimentally, some researchers directed their attention to the mechanisms that drive the effect, including verbal and nonverbal mediators (e.g., Chaikin, Sigler, & Derlega, 1974; Cooper & Baron, 1977; E. Jones & Cooper, 1971). Research on the persistence of the effect showed that, even when targets did not confirm perceivers' expectancies, perceivers sometimes believed they had (Dond, 1972; Farina & Ring, 1965; Iokes, Patterson, Rajecki, & Tanford, 1982; Swann & Snyder, 1980)—a phenomenon known as *perceptual confirmation*. In such cases, both perceivers' initial view of the target and their belief in the stereotype are supported. On the target side of the interaction, researchers found evidence that targets' expectancy-confirming behavior extended to new situations with different perceivers (Fazio, Effrein, & Falender, 1981; Snyder & Swann, 1978), implying that behavioral confirmation may influence the target beyond the time frame of the initial interaction.

A second wave of theory and research emphasized factors about the target that limit behavioral confirmation, including awareness of the stereotype (Hilton & Darley, 1985) and certainty of one's own self-concept (Swann, 1987; Swann & Ely, 1984). This research appropriately directed attention to the target of the stereotype as an active participant in the interaction, but the presence of these limiting conditions was interpreted as evidence that behavioral confirmation was uncommon. A number of theorists advocated the view that individuals resist social pressures to confirm, and that, outside of the laboratory, disconfirmation or even the verification of a target's preexisting self-concept are equally or more likely (e.g., Hilton & Darley, 1985; E. Jones, 1990; Jussim, 1989; Miller & Turnbull, 1986; Swann, 1987). In support of this view, Miller and Turnbull

(1986) correctly noted that a publishing bias favors confirmatory results over nonconfirmatory ones (i.e., those that support the null hypothesis).

These predictions about the everyday experience of targets advance the myth of the fully autonomous individual. In emphasizing aspects of the individual that limit behavioral confirmation, theorists have overlooked situational and societal variables that may increase the likelihood of the effect. Neglecting these social variables underestimates confirmatory pressure on targets, and may distort the overall prevalence of behavioral confirmation. In addition, even when targets have the personality or ability to disconform stereotyped expectancies, those very aspects of the individual may themselves be socially determined. Before developing these ideas, the following section addresses the methodological constraints that reinforce the prevailing individualist assumptions.

TAKING THE TARGET'S PERSPECTIVE

To understand the significance of the pressure on targets, one must take the perspective of a target across time and interactions. However, most behavioral confirmation experiments have studied a target's interaction with one perceiver over an extremely short period of time. These brief, controlled interactions have the advantage of demonstrating conclusively that it is the perceiver's expectancy that elicits the target's self-fulfilling behavior. In addition, this methodology is amenable to questions about one interaction, hence the advances in the study of verbal and nonverbal mediators, as well as motivational moderators of behavioral confirmation. But in constraining possible social influence to short-term, one-on-one interactions, the methodology itself necessarily reinforces an individualist view of behavior by ignoring the repetitiveness of a target's experience over time and across situations, and the cumulative effect of these interactions. Thus, existing research on behavioral confirmation begs questions about the frequency, importance, and consequences of such interactions in the life of the target (E. Jones, 1990; Jussim & Eccles, 1992).

Long-Term Relationships

Some researchers have stepped beyond the short-term relationship between perceiver and target to ask how extended contact would affect the target's behavior over time, but they see no need for concern about long-term expectancy effects. The consensus among theorists who have considered the duration of perceiver–target relationships is that behavioral confirmation is a phenomenon of initial acquaintanceship (e.g., Darley, Fleming, Hilton, & Schwann, 1988; Snyder, 1992; Snyder & Haugen, 1994). They noted that empirical demonstrations of behavioral confirmation take place in the first meeting between perceiver and target, and they predicted that the effect diminishes over time as targets have more opportunities to disconfirm stereotypes and more complicated goals for the interaction. As a result, Darley et al. (1988) suggested that the prevalence of confirmation is overestimated because studies of behavioral confirmation between strangers are overrepresented in the literature.

Nevertheless, it is not apparent that a longer relationship diminishes behavioral confirmation. More contact may just as easily provide more opportunities to confirm. After all, subsequent meetings between the perceiver and target are shaped by their memory of the first meeting. Perceivers' expectancies are likely to be even stronger if the target confirmed the stereotype in their first interaction (or if the perceiver merely interpreted the target's behavior as confirmation). The momentum from the first meeting is added pressure on the target, who must now violate an expectancy that was previously confirmed.

Although most of the empirical work on behavioral confirmation examines an extremely short-term relationship between perceiver and target, educational research on behavioral confirmation in the classroom provides some exceptions. Many of these studies assess teacher expectancy effects over repeated interactions. The work has yielded mixed results. Not all of the studies found teachers' expectancies to affect student performance over time (Conn, Edwards, Rosenthal, & Crowne, 1968; Claiborn, 1969; Mendels & Flanders, 1973; O'Connell, Dusek, & Wheeler, 1974). But the research generally supports the presence of behavioral confirmation (e.g., Crano & Mellon, 1978; Meichenbaum, Bowers, & Ross, 1973; Seaver, 1973; Zanna, Sheras, Copper, & Shaw, 1975; for a review, see Rosenthal & Rubin, 1978), especially on measures of academic performance.

Jussim approached the question of the long-term importance of expectancy effects in a quantitative manner. Using path-analytic techniques, he compared behavioral confirmation, perceptual confirmation, and accuracy of teachers' expectancies in two studies of math classes (Jussim, 1989, 1991). Finding evidence for all three, he concluded that there is support for a weak constructivist position. That is, perceivers' expectancies shape the behavior of targets (i.e., behavioral confirmation) and their own perceptions of target behavior (i.e., perceptual confirmation), but their perceptions reflect rather accurately targets' preexisting abilities, as measured by students' preexperimental test scores. This interpretation seems to oversimplify the issue of accuracy in two ways. The next two sections address these issues fully, but a brief summary is: (a) Behavior that reflects the perceiver's expectancy may have become a part of the target's behavioral repertoire as a result of interactions that occurred before the window of study. The perceiver's assessment of this behavior will be labeled by researchers as accuracy, although it originated in response to the perceiver's expectancy at an earlier point in time. (b) Targets interact with multiple perceivers. To the extent that others' expectancies match those of the perceiver under study (i.e., to the extent that perceivers share the same stereotyped expectancy of the targets), the perceiver's assessment of the target may accurately reflect the target's behavior. However, accuracy in this case is not due to detection of innate or essential qualities of the individual, but qualities that were shaped in response to a previous perceiver's expectancy.

Multiple Relationships

In experimental studies, targets of expectancies are often arbitrarily defined as such, and the expectancy is created by giving falsified information about their extroversion, competence, or some other trait to (also arbitrarily defined) perceivers. Although many of these studies use expectancies that are based on real social stereotypes of categories, such as race, gender, and physical attractiveness, the targets are not necessarily members of these categories (e.g., Skrypnek & Snyder, 1982; Snyder, Tanke, & Berscheid, 1977; Word, Zanna, & Cooper, 1974). For example, male perceivers in the Snyder et al. experiment saw a photo of an attractive or unattractive woman with whom they believed they were speaking, but the female target was not the woman in the photograph. Other studies use expectancies such as likability, which are not directly related to any one social group (Curtis & Miller, 1986; E. Jones & Panitch, 1971; Kelley & Stahelski, 1970). This method of assigning an expectancy in the laboratory provides the methodological control to interpret a change in targets as due solely to the perceiver's treatment of them, but it can draw a picture of self-fulfilling prophecies as quite ephemeral and random; individuals are pressured to behave this way or that, depending on the capricious notions that people may have received about them.

Outside of the laboratory, the pressure on targets is far from capricious. Because social stereotypes are widely known, discussed, and popularized (e.g., Devine, 1989), people who are members of a target group have many interactions with different people who share an identical conception of the target. This is particularly true for certain categories of targets, often those who are easily identified by noticeable physical characteristics. For example, in this society, being African American, physically disabled, or elderly often functions as a "master status" category (Goffman, 1963; E. Jones et al., 1984). Although the person belongs to other categories, perceivers from majority groups accord extreme importance to this one salient feature, and it influences both interpretations of the target's behavior and behavior toward the target. Thus, stereotypes are not only widely shared, but some are also pervasively applied in interactions with targets.

From the target's perspective, the pervasiveness of perceiver stereotypes about one's group means increased pressure to confirm stereotypes because of the sheer number of times the target must face the stereotypic conception. Snyder, Tanke, and Berscheid (1977) were explicit on this point in their pioneering study on the effects of men's beliefs about female participants' physical attractiveness: "For if there is any social-psychological process that ought to exist in 'stronger' form in everyday interaction than in the psychological laboratory, it is behavioral confirmation. In the context of years of social interaction in which perceivers have reacted to their actual physical attractiveness, our 10-minute getting-acquainted conversations over a telephone must seem minimal indeed" (p. 664). The methodology of behavioral confirmation draws attention away from the duration and number of relationships that targets have with perceivers, and it distorts the nature of perceivers' expectancies as arbitrary instead of systematically stereotypic. In doing so, it underestimates the pressure on targets to behaviorally confirm.

The Consequences of Shared Beliefs

Few studies have examined targets' experiences with multiple perceivers, but theorists have certainly recognized the importance of behavioral confirmation for a target's subsequent interactions with other people. For example, Snyder and his colleagues (Snyder, 1981; Snyder & Swann, 1978; Snyder, Tanke, & Berschcid, 1977) predicted that confirmatory behaviors would be "internalized and incorporated into the target's self-conception" (Snyder, 1981, p. 198) if the behaviors fall within a wide latitude of acceptance. Internalization is considered important because of the consequences for the target's future behavior—if the behaviors are internalized, the target will repeat them in new situations with different perceivers. Researchers have not explicitly studied the process of internalization, but there is some experimental evidence that targets will repeat behaviors that were elicited by perceivers in previous situations (Fazio, Effrein, & Falender, 1981; Snyder & Swann, 1978). Future research may help identify the conditions under which confirmatory behavior is internalized, but expectancies that are often repeated and those that do not appear negative to the target appear to be likely candidates for acceptance.

Internalization is indeed a potentially harmful consequence of stereotype confirmation, but it is not the only means by which a target can be harmed. In some cases, even one instance of confirmation may have extreme consequences for a target's material or intangible resources. For this reason, interviews for the purpose of dispensing a resource (e.g., a job, a scholarship) or deciding one's fate (e.g., custody of one's child, immigration status, a criminal sentence) can be hazardous for targets. Moreover, regardless of subsequent internalization, the experience of behavioral confirmation can be harmful to targets' emotional well-being or self-concept, particularly if targets are aware that their behavior supports a negative stereotype of their group (Steele, 1992). Finally, although internalization makes it more likely that targets will repeat stereotype-consistent behavior in future situations, it is not necessary for this behavior to be repeated. The shared and pervasive nature of stereotypes ensures that targets will encounter many different perceivers who treat them with the same expectancy. Thus, a target does not need to carry the behavior from one situation to the next because new perceivers with the identical stereotype may cause the target to repeat the confirmatory behavior by eliciting it again in new interactions.

BEHAVIORAL CONFIRMATION IN CONTEXT

When behavioral confirmation occurs in the context of a target's everyday relationships, the pressure on targets to confirm is likely to be great. Two such examples are considered: when a perceiver holds power over a target, and when a perceiver's expectancy is disseminated to a third party.

Power Relations

Social-psychology experiments not only present a misleading view of the content of expectancies as arbitrary instead of stereotypic; they also distort the context of that pressure. With some notable exceptions, most of the behavioral confirmation literature ignores the power hierarchy between perceiver and target, despite its omnipresence and importance in social life. Behavioral confirmation researchers are certainly not alone in neglecting power relations. Many theorists have called for social psychologists' consideration of contextual or structural factors generally and power specifically (Cartwright, 1959; Clark, 1974; Dépret & Fiske,1993; Kipnis, 1972; Ng, 1980). However, the inclusion of power is particularly important in this area because of the many reasons to suspect that power differences may determine when behavioral confirmation will occur.

When social psychologists examine stereotyping and behavioral confirmation, in empirical studies or in theory, they begin their analysis at a point before or during the first meeting of a dyad, and proceed by tracking the influence of a perceiver's stereotype through the course of the interaction. It is often recognized that *perceiver* and *target* are arbitrary terms, and that both interactants have expectancies and perceptions of the other that play out simultaneously (e.g., Darley & Fazio, 1980; E. Jones, 1989). The thesis of this section is: If a person has relatively more power over another in an interaction, this powerholder's expectancy of the one who is dependent is more likely to be confirmed behaviorally, and the powerholder is less likely to confirm the other's view. Power will determine whose view of the other is most influential. Or, to use researchers' terms of art, if a perceiver has power over the target, behavioral confirmation is more likely to occur than if it is the target who has power over the perceiver.

Delimiting the concepts of power and powerlessness is difficult because of the many ways people control, influence, or affect others, and the many reasons to need, care about, respect, or fear others. The president of the United States, one's supervisor, one's older brother, and one's romantic partner may have a great deal of power, but the sources, consequences, and nature of their power are varied. Emphasizing the commonalities among these different types of power, researchers have defined *power* as outcome control and *powerlessness* as outcome dependence (Dépret & Fiske, 1993; Kelley & Thibaut, 1978; Thibaut & Kelley, 1959). Because individuals may be simultaneously powerful and dependent in a relationship, people are said to hold power or to be powerful when they have relatively more power in the relationship, and to be dependent when they have relatively less power in the relationship (see Thibaut & Kelley's [1959] "usable power"). The present analysis is limited to relationships in which one person has control over material or intangible resources the other wants, but related concepts such as authority and status are expected to operate in much the same way as the more restricted definition of *power* as outcome control. For example, perceivers who hold status or situational authority as a result of their occupation or class background may be more successful in influencing lower status targets to confirm their stereotypes than if the perceiver and target are equal in status.

Evidence for the Influence of Power. Some authors have suggested that a power imbalance increases the likelihood of behavioral confirmation (Copeland, 1994; Darley & Fazio, 1980; Miller & Turnbull, 1986; Snyder, 1992), but few studies directly manipulate the power of interactants to examine this premise. However, it has a great deal of indirect support from behavioral confirmation research that confounds experimental role and power. In such studies, the person who holds or is given an expectancy of the other also has power over the one whose behavior is studied. *Perceiver* is assumed to be synonymous with *powerholder* and *target* with *dependent* (Copeland, 1994). Individuals in the roles of employer, teacher, and experimenter have power over job applicants, students, and experimental participants (e.g., Rosenthal, 1963; Rosenthal & Jacobson,1968; Word, Zanna, & Cooper, 1974). Studies of behavioral confirmation in which the target's power equals or betters the perceiver's are nonexistent.

In a study that did orthogonally manipulate expectancy role (i.e., perceiver or target) and power, Copeland (1994) found that behavioral confirmation is most likely to occur when a perceiver has power over a dependent target. In his study, participants believed that one (powerful) student could choose a partner for a lucrative game from among two (dependent) students. When the powerful participant was also given arbitrary information about the extroversion of the other person (i.e., when the powerholder was also the perceiver), the expectancy was behaviorally confirmed in a subsequent interaction. But when the dependent student received the expectancy (i.e., the target held power over the perceiver), behavioral confirmation did not occur. In the same vein, Vidrin and Neuberg (1990) found marginal support for their prediction that status differences would influence the likelihood of behavioral confirmation. Targets who interacted with supposedly high-status perceivers were more likely to confirm the perceiver's expectancy than those who interacted with purportedly equal- or low-status perceivers.

Copeland's study was the first to directly test the effects of power differences on behavioral confirmation, and the results support the prediction that behavioral confirmation is more likely when a power imbalance favors the perceiver. However, more studies are needed to substantiate these results and to extend them to different stereotyped expectancies and other operationalizations of power. Further research is also important because the procedure in Copeland's study may have created demand for behavioral confirmation. To investigate possible mediating effects of participant motivations on behavioral confirmation, participants in the study were asked to check their motives for the interaction from a list supplied by the experimenter. Because participants completed this list before the interaction, it may have biased their subsequent behavior, creating behavioral confirmation of the perceiver's expectancy *and* the experimenter's hypothesis.

Theorists have simplified the discussion of behavioral confirmation by dividing it into a sequence of thought and behavior (e.g., Darley & Fazio, 1980). A power hierarchy may facilitate each stage of confirmation. Each stage is considered in the following four sections.

Initial Expectancies.   Recent work in the area of stereotyping shows that, even before two people meet each other, a power imbalance shapes the interaction by altering their reliance on stereotypes about the other. Having power over another increases the likelihood of forming a stereotyped impression of the powerless person, and being dependent on another increases the chance of seeing the powerful person as an individual. For example, Goodwin and Fiske (1995) gave written information about high school students to undergraduates who evaluated them for a job. Undergraduates who anticipated having significant input into hiring decisions paid more attention to stereotype-consistent information and less attention to incidents in which targets violated the expectancy. Those with less power were more likely to attend to stereotype-inconsistent information that could lead to an idiosyncratic impression.

These results are corroborated by research on mutual outcome dependeneucy, in which participants who cooperated or competed with each other formed more individuated impressions than those who did not depend on each other (Erber & Fiske, 1984; Neuberg & Fiske, 1987; Ruscher & Fiske, 1990; Ruscher, Fiske, Miki, & Van Manen, 1991). As previously mentioned, stereotypes that color this first interaction are particularly important because of the possibility that behavioral confirmation becomes a script that grows increasingly demanding as it is repeated throughout the relationship between perceiver and target.

Perceivers' Actions. For behavioral confirmation to occur, a perceiver must not only hold an expectancy of the target, but must also act in a way that elicits the target's confirmation. In its most abrupt form, an individual may act on stereotypic expectancies by refusing to interact with the target (Darley & Fazio, 1980; Swann & Ely, 1984). For example, a social club president with no personal knowledge of a minority applicant may deny that person's membership. In this case, there is no behavioral confirmation, but neither does the target have the opportunity to disconfirm the president's expectancy. Ending the relationship is an option for perceivers only if they do not depend on targets, so the perceiver's power will influence whether the relationship is aborted.

Assuming that perceivers and targets do interact, there are a number of reasons why holding power increases the chance that perceivers will act on their stereotypes. First, because powerholders are, by definition, less dependent on others, the degree to which their behavior reflects their own attitudes should be stronger than for those who are more constrained by self-presentation concerns (Brown & Levinson, 1987; Ng & Bradac, 1993; Snodgrass, 1992). Powerholders are not as affected materially by what others think of them, so they are freer to act on their perceptions and attitudes. In other words, the powerful act on their stereotypes because they can. This is not to say that those in power never care what others think of them, but dependents have more reason to guard their behavior because of their vulnerability to others.

Second, many theorists have noted that individuals' goals for an interaction influence the likelihood of behavioral confirmation (Hilton & Darley, 1985; Miller & Turnbull, 1986; Neuberg, 1989, 1994). Research by Snyder and his colleagues (Copeland & Snyder, 1995; Snyder, 1992; Snyder & Haugen, 1994) demonstrated that holding power creates goals for the interaction that facilitate the expression of perceivers' stereotypes. Positions of power (e.g., supervisor, teacher, judge) often require the assessment of others. Perceivers' desire to predict the future behavior of targets motivates them to characterize targets' dispositional traits (Leyens, 1983). This contributes to stereotypic thoughts about the target, as well as corresponding expressive actions that lead to the target's confirmation of the stereotype. High-power roles, which create time pressure for the perceiver, may also contribute to this motivation to form a dispositional evaluation of the target (Fiske, 1993; Neuberg, 1994). A hurried perceiver who is motivated to evaluate the target can use a convenient stereotype as a proxy, and holds the power to treat the target accordingly.

A third cause of the powerholder's and the dependent's differential expression of stereotypes is conversational style. Power affords conversational privileges, and the conversational styles associated with having and lacking power may also serve to propagate the perceiver's view of the target. People who hold power are more likely to initiate conversation, take longer and more frequent conversational turns, interrupt others and dominate when others attempt to interrupt, and even control the content of the conversation with their directive style. Conversely, those who depend on others wait for their partner's lead, spend more conversational time listening, interrupt less often and allow others to interrupt, respond to the topics suggested by the powerholder, and use hesitating forms of speech (Deutsch, 1990; Erickson, Lind, Johnson, & O'Barr, 1978; Leffler, Gillespie, & Conaty, 1982; O'Barr, 1982). Regardless of whether these conversational styles are a result of the differing motivations of those in high- and low-power roles, or are simply a product of the social convention of the roles, they provide the opportunity for powerholders' stereotypes to be expressed (Ng & Bradac, 1993).

Targets' Responses. Once the perceiver treats the target as if the stereotype is true of that individual, the wheels of behavioral confirmation are set in motion, and the target may respond by confirming the stereotype. A dependent target is more likely to behaviorally confirm than is a powerful or equal-power target. Targets with low power simply have few opportunities to disconfirm stereotypes in a conversation that they do not control. In addition to conversational constraints, a dependent target is more motivated than an equal-power target to please and possibly agree with the content of statements or allusions made by the perceiver because of the peceiver's control over the target's outcomes (Copeland & Snyder, 1995; J.

Jones, 1986; Neuberg, 1994; Snodgrass, 1992; Snyder, 1992; Snyder & Haugen, 1995). This increased responsiveness to the perceiver should produce behavioral confirmation. However, the motivation to please a powerful perceiver also creates concern for the perceiver's approval. If aware of a perceiver's negative expectancy, dependent targets are in the contradictory position of wishing to accommodate the perceiver *and* to disprove the expectancy. Absent this awareness, dependence will increase targets' vulnerability to behavioral confirmation.

Interpretations of the Target's Actions. Determining whether targets have behaved stereotypically is the final stage in the behavioral confirmation sequence. Even the judgment that behavioral confirmation has occurred may be affected by the power relationship between the interactants. This section addresses the interpretations of target behavior made by observers, perceivers, and targets themselves.

To objectively assess behavioral confirmation, researchers have relied on observers' ratings of the target's behavior. Behavioral confirmation is said to have occurred when a group of target participants treated with one expectancy behave differently than those treated with another expectancy. In naturally occurring situations, the power relationships among the perceiver, target, and observer may influence what is a more straightforward process in the laboratory. Unlike research assistants/observers in a behavioral confirmation experiment (who typically see or hear only the targets' behaviors), observers of an interaction are able to watch the manner in which the perceiver treats the target. Their judgments may be influenced by the power relationship between perceiver and target. One could argue that an observer who sees a target confirm a perceiver's stereotype might take into account the role of the perceiver's influence, particularly in a situation where the perceiver clearly has the power to influence the target. However, a large body of research on correspondence bias shows that people rarely discount sufficiently for the external influences on others' behavior (e.g., Gilbert & Jones, 1986; E. Jones & Davis, 1965; E. Jones & Harris, 1967; Ross, Amabile, & Steinmetz, 1977). In fact, a power imbalance between perceiver and target may even increase the likelihood that the target will be viewed as behaving stereotypically, precisely because the observer will be more strongly influenced by a powerful perceiver's definition of the situation (and view of the target) than by a perceiver who is equal in power to the target. Similarly, if the perceiver has power over the observer, the observer will be motivated to take the powerholder's perspective, and may be more likely to interpret the target's behavior as confirmation of the stereotype.

In perceptual confirmation, it is the perceiver's judgment of the target's behavior, not the observer's judgment, that is the dependent measure of interest (Snyder, 1981, 1984). Just as a power imbalance is predicted to facilitate both behavioral confirmation and observers' judgments that confirmation has occurred, so too may a power imbalance affect the perceiver's judgment. The same motivational mediators that cause powerful perceivers to view targets stereotypically will affect their perceptions of targets after an interaction. In addition to these motivational and ability constraints on attention to the target's disconfirming behavior, research on perceiver-induced constraint testifies to people's difficulty in indentifying their own influence on a target (Gilbert & Jones, 1986). In fact, the literature shows that even perceivers who have complete control over another's responses believe that others' internal attitudes correspond with behaviors they were made to perform (E. Jones & Davis, 1965).

Curiously, targets' perceptions of their own behaviors are often neglected in the literature. Research has focused on the observer's objective and the perceiver's subjective appraisals of target confirmation, but it has neglected the issues of when targets judge their own behavior to be confirmatory, the factors that influence this judgment, and how these judgments compare to perceiver and observer perceptions. Actor–observer research shows that people look to the situation for causes of their own behavior, particularly when it is negative, but are less likely to make situational allowances for others (e.g., E. Jones & Nisbett, 1971; Watson, 1982). This research suggests that targets will be less likely than perceivers and observers to view their confirmatory behaviors as internally driven. The question of how power relations affect targets' interpretations of their own confirmation remains unexplored. Increasing targets' dependence may improve their awareness of perceivers' external influence on their behavior because the imbalance in their relationship is more salient, or it may simply cause them to adopt the powerful perceiver's view.

The Intersection of Power and Stereotyping.   Initial empirical and theoretical work suggest that a power hierarchy favoring the perceiver contributes to behavioral confirmation effects. This work is significant not only because it delineates the conditions that facilitate behavioral confirmation, but also because of the overall likelihood of these worst-case conditions in everyday interaction. It is not the case that people who are members of commonly stereotyped groups are equally distributed in positions of high and low power. People who tend to be targets of stereotypes are generally those who have less power in the workplace, the home, government, and education. For example, in the domain of professional relationships, income earned is a simple but consistent measure of power. Those who earn less tend to take orders from and depend on the hiring, promotional, salary, and resource-allocation decisions of those who earn more. Using this metric, a variety of stereotyped groups have been shown to earn less than others or suffer other economic disadvantages in the workplace (Crocker & Major, 1989; Crosby, 1984; J. Jones, 1986; Pettigrew, 1985). According to motivational theories of stereotyping, this negative relationship between target membership and power is no accident. Stereotypes are thought to serve the purpose of explaining, rationalizing, and maintaining power differences between groups (e.g., Fiske, 1993; Hoffman & Hurst, 1990; Jost & Banaji, 1994; Sidanius, 1993).

Of course, that does not mean that being a member of a stereotyped group is synonymous with low power. All individuals experience situations and relationships in which they have relatively more power than others, ones in which they are dependent on others, and ones that are equally interdependent. But in general, targets of stereotypes have less power and status in relationships than others because stereotyping is inherently a power-laden phenomenon (Fiske, 1993). From this perspective, the current research trend examining the effects of participants' interaction goals on the likelihood of behavioral confirmation is important not only because goals are derived from social roles, but also because social roles are unevenly distributed in society.

Third-Party Effects

Behavioral confirmation occurs in the context of the power relationship between perceiver and target, as well as in the context of perceivers' and targets' relationships with others outside the dyad. As described in a later section, targets' contact with others can provide a source of resistance to stereotype confirmation. In contrast, the perceiver's contact with others may provide stereotypic expectancies about the target. That is, a perceiver who interacts with the target may convey the expectancy to a new perceiver, who may then act on it in interactions with the target. This "third-party effect" is important because of the manner in which the stereotype is relayed to the third person.

The literatures on correspondence bias (i.e., dispositional attributions for another's actions) and perceptual confirmation (i.e., dispositional attributions for actions elicited by the perceiver) show that people fail to recognize outside influences on the target's behavior. Once a target has confirmed a perceiver's stereotype, the perceiver believes the target possesses the quality demonstrated, so that a target who raised his voice is aggressive and one who listened silently in conversation is timid. When ascribed trait information is passed on to a third person, by the perceiver's word or deed, the third party has even less ability to recognize the perceiver's influence on the target and the stereotypic source of the information. Thus, an expectancy that was originally category-based (ap-

plied to the target based on qualities attributed to his or he group)
masquerades as target-based (derived from the essence of that individual).
The information is customized to the target and stripped of its group-based
origin. Weisz and Jones (1993) showed that target-based, or individualized,
expectancies are stronger than category-based expectancies, or stereotypes
(see also E. Jones, 1990), and that people feel more confident relying on
them. In addition, an expectancy that is formed from individualized
comments about the target or modeled from the perceiver's behavior is
more difficult for the target to resist or even identify than one that is
obviously stereotypic.

When these third-party effects occur in the context of a power imbalance, the likelihood that the original perceiver's stereotype will influence the
target is still greater. If the third party is dependent on the original
perceiver, this third person is more likely to attend to and accept the
perceiver's views, including those about the target, setting the stage for
future actions toward the target. A power imbalance between the third
party and a dependent target increases the likelihood that views now held by
a powerful third party will be instantiated in interaction. In both cases, the
original perceiver's stereotyped view of the target is more likely to be
confirmed in subsequent interactions between the target and the third party.

A SYSTEMIC VIEW OF BEHAVIORAL CONFIRMATION

Targets of sterotypes have long-term and repeated interactions with multiple individuals who share and act on the same beliefs about the target. In
addition, targets often face this social pressure in contexts that facilitate
behavioral confirmation — in interactions with someone who has power over
the target or with one whose expectancy is tailored to the target. Because the
influence on targets is system wide, it is appropriate to reconsider popular
definitions of both behavioral confirmation and accuracy of expectancies.

Researchers frequently begin their analyses with Merton's (1957) classic
definition of behavioral confirmation: "The self-fulfilling prophecy is, in
the beginning, a false definition of the situation evoking a new behavior
which makes the originally false conception come true" (p. 423). By
emphasizing the absence of confirming behavior before the interaction, this
definition captures the notion that it is the perceiver's treatment that elicits
the target's confirming behavior. However, this focus on the change in an
initially false or erroneous stereotype (see also Snyder, 1992) limits unnec-
essarily the scope of behavioral confirmation.

To demonstrate the limits of this definition, consider one possible reaction to systemic stereotyping. If targets were exclusively confronted with an identical stereotypic expectancy across repeated situations, occasions, and interaction partners, they would repeatedly succumb to this treatment. Their stereotypic behavior would appear to show cross-situational consistency and temporal stability, "the calling cards of personality traits and dispositions" (Snyder & Swann, 1978, p. 199). But if they were merely responding to the identical constraining stereotype, repeated time and again, this cross-situational consistency would be an illusion. Using the target's initial behavior as a criterion for behavioral confirmation is problematic if that behavior was itself a product of others' stereotyped expectancies. Thus, defining behavioral confirmation in terms of the target's previous behavior neglects situations in which a target confirms in response to a perceiver's behavior and has always confirmed that stereotypic expectancy, *but would respond differently with different treatment.*

Swann (1987) described behavioral confirmation in terms of global and circumscribed accuracy. The perceiver's conception of the target is globally inaccurate, but because of its influence it accurately describes the target's behavior in the situation. This tension between "what is" and "what could have been" should be extended over a longer time period, to account for the nature of targets' experience with stereotypes. A perceiver's stereotype could be accurate in a circumscribed *and* a global fashion if the target has responded to repeated stereotyping with repeated confirmation. But in the same way that circumscribed accuracy is considered "false" (i.e., mutable) in the bigger picture of the target's other interactions, so may global accuracy be false in the bigger picture of how the target might have been treated and might have come to act. That is, an individual who repeatedly confirms stereotyped conceptions is no more displaying "true" behavior than is the target participant in a 1-hour behavioral confirmation experiment.

Of course, in one sense, an individual's existing tendency to behave with a certain personality or level of ability can certainly be viewed as accurate; what is a truer description of an individual if not the manner in which he or she behaves? However, if one understands behavior to have strong social influences, then the concept of a "true" personality or level of ability becomes meaningless. There is only the individual's behavior, which is largely the result of past treatment. One must question the validity of considering an individual's current personality or level of ability to be fated and fixed, especially when behavior was shaped by negative, group-based treatment. Even behaviors that have come to be internalized by targets would have differed with a different history of treatment, and in some cases may be altered with different future treatment.

In this view, the reason that behavioral confirmation is harmful is not because an originally false expectancy becomes true in any one situation, but because groups of people are treated with systematically different expectancies. Individuals who are members of majority groups are no less subject to social influences. They too are affected by a history of reinforcement and expectancies. As with negative stereotypes, once these socially desirable expectancies are behaviorally confirmed, they are viewed as a unique and essential part of that individual's true nature. What begins as differential conceptions of social groups may be created, at least in part, in the course of ongoing and repeated social interaction, and then viewed as natural and immutable differences between groups.

TARGETS' RESISTANCE TO CONFIRMATION

Despite the substantial pressures on targets to confirm social stereotypes, there is ample evidence that they can behaviorally *disconfirm*. Disconfirmation is apparent not only from experimental demonstrations in which situational conditions are created to produce both confirmation and disconfirmation (e.g., Hilton & Darley, 1985; Swann & Ely, 1984), but also from the empirical evidence comparing stereotypes of target groups with the actual behavior of their members (see Judd & Park, 1993, for a review). How is it that stereotyped targets are ever able to disconfirm the strong and uniform expectancies attached to their group? Three answers are rooted in targets' social relationships with others.

Behavioral Confirmation of Positive Expectancies

Targets resist stereotypes through the same process by which they sometimes exhibit them—through behavioral confirmation. People are not invariably treated in a manner consistent with the stereotype of their group. First, they are members of more than one social group. People's responses to them will often reflect the complexity of their membership in various types of groups (e.g., ethnicity, age, occupation, club membership, etc.) Even individuals who are members of master status groups will be treated according to other categories. To the extent that targets interact with people who treat them in a manner counter or irrelevant to the stereotype, they will behaviorally confirm those expectancies. Exposure to nonstereotypic expectancies gives targets a repertoire of behaviors to regard as possible—ones that they may repeat, remember, and internalize. These repeated nonstereotypic expectancies shape a target's long-term behavior to be individuated by the same process that repeated exposure to stereotypic expectancies elicits repeated stereotypic behavior.

In this view of social behavior, the extent to which manifest personalities or abilities are determined by stereotypes depends on the frequency and proportion of the stereotypic contact that targets receive, and on the attributions they make about that treatment. This analysis of stereotype-consistent and stereotype-inconsistent expectancies allows us to differentiate between target groups and individuals who may be more vulnerable to behavioral confirmation and those who are better able to resist confirmation. For example, individuals who are exposed to other members of their target group, particularly those people who reject the stereotype of the group, are more likely to be treated with stereotype-inconsistent expectancies. But targets who are isolated from others like them in social interactions will experience more pressure to confirm because of the relatively homogeneous (i.e., uniformly stereotypic) treatment they receive. Groups and individuals who are often treated stereotypically, those who have relatively few interactions in which they do not encounter stereotypes, and those who believe they have elicited the perceiver's stereotyped treatment will more readily confirm to stereotypes, and will suffer more corresponding psychological harm.

This contextualist view of personality can inform current discussions of personality stability and change. For example, Swann and his colleagues (Swann, 1983, 1987; Swann, Griffin, Predmore, & Gaines, 1987; Swann & Ely, 1984; Swann & Read, 1981) argued that individuals are motivated to self-verify by behaving in accordance with their own self-concept. Their empirical research demonstrates individuals' tenacity in maintaining their self-concepts. When perceivers' and targets' conceptions of targets conflicted, targets acted on their self-images, failing to confirm perceivers' expectancies (Swann & Ely, 1984). Targets who were more certain of their view were less likely to confirm the perceiver's expectancy (Swann & Ely, 1984).

These data are consistent with a contextualist view, if one assumes that targets' current self-conceptions were influenced by past interactions. Indeed, there may be a strong motivation to self-verify, but the next question becomes how one develops this accepted and verified "self." Swann (1987) noted that, "As children gather more and more evidence on which to base their self-conceptions, they begin to work to confirm these conceptions" (p. 1039). To the extent that members of a stereotyped group are consistently and repeatedly treated with stereotyped expectancies, this information and their own confirming behavior is one potential influence on their self-concepts. If individuals do not receive countervailing treatment that helps to form a robustly different self-view, some of the ways in which they have been induced to confirm stereotypes will either become a part of their self-concepts or at least a part of their repertoire of well-learned behaviors. Thus, the battle between self-verification and self-confirmation is properly understood only in the context of past interactions with others.

To predict the influence of stereotyped treatment, it is also important to consider targets' understanding and valuation of their own and others' behavior. Targets' perceptions of a perceiver's stereotyped overture and its context can result in concerted efforts to disconfirm (e.g., if targets are aware of its stereotyped nature) or in stereotype confirmation (e.g., if targets evaluate the expectancy positively). An unexplored alternative to confirmation is target behavior that is influenced by the expectancy without directly confirming it (Jones et al., 1984). For example, in response to a perceiver's stereotype, a target may avoid future interactions or become reserved and formal in conversation without confirming the stereotype. A target who is expected to perform poorly in an area may disidentify without a reduction in performance. Of course, continued lack of interest will eventually result in behavioral confirmation, as the target performs the task under the duress of the negative expectancy (Crocker & Major, 1979; Steele, 1992).

Awareness of the Stereotype

Targets need not be aware that a perceiver has a stereotypic expectancy to disconfirm it; but when they are aware, they are more likely to make attributions that protect the self and facilitate disconfirmation. In an experimental analogy to the importance of awareness, Hilton and Darley (1985) showed that participants who were correctly informed that another person might have a view of them as cold (all perceiver participants were in fact given this view) did not behaviorally confirm the expectancy, whereas participants who were ignorant of the expectancy did act more reserved. Although the expectancy in this experiment was not based on a stereotype about the individual's category membership, stereotyped expectancies are likely to function similarly.

However, awareness in real life is complicated by the variety of meanings that targets may give to stereotypic expectancies. First, targets can be aware that a stereotype of their group exists, and that there is a probability that any particular individual with whom they interact may endorse it. Groups that have a history of consciousness about their oppression will provide their members with the knowledge of negative stereotypes. To the extent that this knowledge helps individual targets interpret the perceiver's stereotype-consistent actions as such (cf. Ruggiero & Taylor, 1995), the target will be aided in disconfirmation. This implies that stereotyped groups that are well established and those that work to "raise the consciousness" of their members will assist targets in disconfirming stereotypes, whereas stereotyped individuals who do not think of themselves as full members of a stereotyped group — or those who do not believe that others like them compose a group — will be more likely to confirm. The awareness that one belongs to a stereotyped group may be partially responsible for self-esteem differences between target groups (Crocker, Luhtanen, Blaine, & Broadnax, 1994; Rosenberg, 1979). Although groups have other properties that aid their members, even the knowledge that others share their experience as a target of stereotyping may bolster individuals' ability to disconfirm.

In addition to an awareness that stereotypic expectancies can exist, a target may also be aware that an individual perceiver holds these beliefs. Targets can learn of perceiver attitudes from other people or from the perceiver's own obviously stereotyping actions. Ironically, extremely stereotypic behavior on the part of the perceiver may protect the target from behavioral confirmation (although such behavior probably signals an increased likelihood of perceptual confirmation). It is ambiguous behavior that is most difficult attributionally for the target (Ruggiero & Taylor, 1995).

An awareness that streotypes exist generally or situationally is not enough to ensure behavioral disconfirmation. Targets of stereotypes must also believe that the expectancies are negative and undeserved. Awareness of a stereotypic expectancy that is viewed positively simply facilitates confirmation. Even if targets believe that a stereotype is negative, they may endorse its application to the self (Crocker & Major, 1989). For example, resisting stereotypes is still very much an individual endeavor for people who are considered overweight. As a result, the stereotypes associated with being heavy are often endorsed by targets, despite the fact that they are obviously negative (Crocker, Cornwell, & Major, 1993). For awareness of an expectancy to aid targets, they must believe that the expectancy is negative, is undeserved, and can be overcome situationally.

Other Forms of Social Support

It may be obvious from the previous sections that it is difficult to talk about targets' resistance to stereotyping — in a particular situation and in the long term — without discussing the views of their group and the more local reactions of their peers. Social support can refer to a range of passive and active assistance that targets receive from others. Some of these types of support were outlined in the previous section: identifying that a stereotype exists, that it is undeserved, and that a particular perceiver holds stereotypic attitudes. There are other types of social support as well. Peers can give specific suggestions about how to handle perceivers' expectancies, especially ones that create a bind for targets (E. Jones et al., 1984). More indirectly, they may model these strategies for disconfirmation. Peers may support targets emotionally, giving them more confidence to fight stereotypes. In addition, providing material resources (or the information to acquire material resources) ensures that targets confront stereotypes minimally, and that when they are confronted, the target has as much power in the situation as possible.

CONCLUSION

This chapter's focus on the long-term experience of the target of stereotyping highlights the context in which intergroup cognitions (i.e., stereotypes) may be realized behaviorally in social interaction. Theorists of behavioral confirmation have neglected factors that are inherently social in nature: society's shared beliefs about the target, the relationship of the interactants, and the social knowledge that a target brings to the interaction. Emphasizing the context of behavioral confirmation reveals the extent of the pressure on targets to confirm stereotypes and the resources that targets have to resist this pressure. In addition, this systemic view allows one to predict which individuals and groups are most susceptible to confirmation.

ACKNOWLEDGMENTS

Preparation of this chapter was supported by National Institute of Mental Health Grants MH10585-01 to Theresa Claire and MH41801 to Susan Fiske, and by National Science Foundation Grant SBR92-21480 to Susan Fiske. For their insightful comments on earlier versions of this chapter, we thank Jennifer Eberhardt, Don Operario, Olivier Sultan, and the editors of this volume.

REFERENCES

Asch, S. E. (1956). Studies of independence and confirmity: A minority of one against a unanimous majority. *Psychological Monographs, 70* (9, Whole No. 416).

Bond, M. (1972). Effect of an impression set on subsequent behavior. *Journal of Personality and Social Psychology, 24,* 301–305.

Brown, P., & Levinson, S. C. (1987). *Politeness: Some universals in language usage.* Cambridge, England: Cambridge University Press.

Chaikin, A. L., Sigler, E., & Derlega, V. J. (1974). Nonverbal mediators of teacher expectancy effects. *Journal of Personality and Social Psychology, 30,* 144–149.

Cartwright, D. (1959). *Studies in social power.* Ann Arbor, MI: Research Center for Group Dynamics, Institute for Social Research.

Claiborn, W. (1969). Expectancy effects in the classrooms: A failure to replicate. *Journal of Educational Psychology, 60,* 377-383.

Clark, K. B. (1974). *Pathos of power.* New York: Harper & Row.

Conn, L. K., Edwards, C. N., Rosenthal, R., & Crowne, D. P. (1968). Perception of emotion and response to teachers' expectancy by elementary school children. *Psychological Reports, 22,* 27-34.

Cooper, H. M., & Baron, R. M. (1977). Academic expectations and attributed responsibility as predictors of professional teachers' reinforcement behavior. *Journal of Educational Psychology, 69,* 409-418.

Copeland, J. T. (1994). Prophecies of power: Motivational implications of social power for behavioral confirmation. *Journal of Personality and Social Psychology, 67,* 264-277.

Copeland, J. T., & Snyder, M. (1995). When counselors confirm: A functional analysis. *Personality and Social Psychology Bulletin, 21,* 1210-1220.

Crano, W. D., & Mellon, P. M. (1978). Causal influence of teachers' expectations on children's academic performance: A cross-lagged panel analysis. *Journal of Educational Psychology, 35,* 867-881.

Crocker, J., Cornwell, B., & Major B. (1993). The stigma of overweight: Affective consequences of attributional ambiguity. *Journal of Personality and Social Psychology, 64,* 60-70.

Crocker, J., Luhtanen, R., Blaine, B., & Broadnax, S. (1994). Collective self-esteem and psychological well-being among White, Black, and Asian college students. *Personality and Social Psychology, 20,* 503-513.

Crocker, J., & Major B. (1989). Social stigma and self-esteem: The self-protective properties of stigma. *Psychological Review, 96,* 608-630.

Crosby, F. (1984). The denial of personal discrimination. *American Behavioral Scientist, 27,* 371-386.

Curtis, R. C., & Miller, K. (1986). Believing another likes or dislikes you: Behaviors making the beliefs come true. *Journal of Personality and Social Psychology, 51,* 284-290.

Darley, J. M., & Fazio, R. H. (1980). Expectancy confirmation process arising in the social interaction sequence. *American Psychology, 35,* 867-881.

Darley, J. M., Fleming, J. H., Hilton, J. L., & Swann, W. B., Jr. (1988). Dispelling negative expectancies: The impact of interaction goals and target characteristics on the expectancy confirmation process. *Journal of Experimental Social Psychology, 24,* 19-36.

Darley, J. M., & Latané, B. (1968). Bystander intervention in emergencies: Diffusion of responsibility. *Journal of Personality and Social Psychology, 8,* 377-383.

Dépret, E. F., & Fiske, S. T. (1993). Social cognition and power: Some cognitive consequences of social structure as a source of control deprivation. In G. Weary, F. Gleicher, & K. Marsh (Eds.), *Control motivation and social cognition* (pp. 176-202). New York: Springer-Verlag.

Deutsch, F. M. (1990). Status, sex, and smiling: The effect of smiling in men and women. *Personality and Social Psychology Bulletin, 16,* 531-540.

Devine, P. G. (1989). Stereotypes and prejudice: Their automatic and controlled components. *Journal of Personality and Social Psychology, 56,* 5-18.

Erber, R., & Fiske, S. T. (1984). Outcome dependency and attention to inconsistent information. *Journal of Personality and Social Psychology, 47,* 709-726.

Erickson, B., Lind, A. E., Johnson, B. C., & O'Barr, W. M. (1978). Speech style and impression formation in a court setting: The effects of "powerful" and "powerless" speech. *Journal of Experimental Social Psychology, 29,* 288-298.

Farina, A., & Ring, K. (1965). The influence of perceived mental illness on interpersonal relations. *Journal of Applied Social Psychology, 70,* 47-51.

Fazio, R. H., Effrein, E. A., & Falender, V. J. (1981). Self-perception following social interation. *Journal of Personality and Social Psychology, 41,* 232–242.

Fiske, S. T. (1993). Controlling other people: The impact of power on stereotyping. *American Psychologist, 48,* 621–628.

Gilbert, D. T., & Jones, E. E. (1986). Perceiver-induced constraint: Interpretations of self-generated reality. *Journal of Personality and Social Psychology, 50,* 269–280.

Goffman, E. (1963). *Stigma: Notes on the management of spoiled identity.* Englewood Cliffs, NJ: Prentice-Hall.

Goodwin, S. A., & Fiske, S. T. (1995). *Power and motivated impression formation: How powerholders stereotype by default and by design.* Manuscript submitted for publication, University of Massachusetts at Amherst.

Hilton, J. L., & Darley, J. M. (1985). Constructing other persons: A limit on the effect. *Journal of Experimental Social Psychology, 21,* 1–18.

Hoffman, C., & Hurst, N. (1990). Gender stereotypes: Perception or rationalization? *Journal of Personality and Social Psychology, 58,* 197–208.

Ickes, W., Patterson, M. L., Rajecki, D. W., & Tanford, S. (1982). Behavioral and cognitive consequences of reciprocal versus compensatory responses to pre-interaction expectancies. *Social Cognition, 1,* 160–190.

Jones, E. E. (1989). Expectancies, actions and attributions in the interaction sequence. In J. P. Forgas & J. M. Innes (Eds.), *Recent advances in social psychology: An international perspective.* North-Holland: Elsevier.

Jones, E. E. (1990). *Interpersonal perception.* New York: Freeman.

Jones, E. E., & Cooper, J. (1971). Mediation of experimenter effects. *Journal of Personality and Social Psychology, 20,* 70–74.

Jones, E. E., & Davis, K. E. (1965). From acts to dispositions: The attribution process in person perception. In L. Berkowitz (Ed.), *Advances in experimental social psychology* (Vol. 2). New York: Academic Press.

Jones, E. E., Farina, A., Hastorf, A. H., Markus, H., Miller, D. T., & Scott, R. A. (1984). *Social stigma: The psychology of marked relationships.* New York: Freeman.

Jones, E. E., & Harris, V. A. (1967). The attribution of attitudes. *Journal of Experimental Social Psychology, 3,* 1–24.

Jones, E. E., & Nisbett, R. E. (1971). The actor and the observer: Divergent perceptions of the causes of behavior. In E. E. Jones, D. E. Ranouse, H. H. Kelley, L. E. Nisbett, S. Valins, & B. Weiner (Eds.), *Attribution: Perceiving the causes of behavior* (pp. 79–94). Morristown, NJ: General Learning Press.

Jones, E. E., & Panitch, D. (1971). The self-fulfilling prophecy and interpersonal attraction. *Journal of Experimental Social Psychology, 7,* 356–366.

Jones, J. M. (1986). *Prejudice and racism.* Reading, MA: Addison-Wesley.

Jost, J. T., & Banaji, M. R. (1994). The role of stereotyping in system-justification and the production of false consciousness. *British Journal of Social Psychology, 33,* 1–27.

Judd, C. M., & Park, B. (1993). Definition and assessment of accuracy in social stereotypes. *Psychological Review, 100,* 109–128.

Jusssim, L. (1989). Teacher expectations: Self-fulfilling prophecies, perceptual biases, and accuracy. *Journal of Personality and Social Psychology, 57,* 469–480.

Jussim, L. (1991). Social perception and social reality: A reflection-construction model. *Psychological Review, 98,* 54–73.

Jussim, L., & Eccles, J. S. (1992). Teacher expectations: II. Construction and reflection of student achievement. *Journal of Personality and Social Psychology, 63,* 947–961.

Kelley, H. H., & Stahelski, A. J. (1970). The social interaction basis of cooperators' and competitors' beliefs about others. *Journal of Personality and Social Psychology, 16,* 66–91.

Kelley, H. H., & Thibaut, J. W. (1978). *Interpersonal relations.* New York: Wiley.

Kipnis, D. (1972). Does power corrupt? *Journal of Personality and Social Psychology, 24,* 33–41.

Latané, B., & Darley, J. M. (1968). Group inhibition of bystander intervention in emergencies. *Journal of Personality und Social Psychology, 10,* 215-221.

Leffler, A., Gillespie, D. L., & Conaty, J. C. (1982). The effects of status differentiation on nonverbal behavior. *Social Psychology Quarterly, 45,* 153-161.

Leyens, J.-Ph. (1983). *Sommes-nous tous des psychologues? Approche psychosociale des théories implicites de personalité* [Are we all psychologists? A psychosocial approach to implicit personality theories.] Brussels: Mardaga.

Merton, R. K. (1957). *Social theory and social structure.* New York: The Free Press.

Meichenbaum, D. H., Bowers, K. S., & Ross, R. R. (1973). A behavioral analysis of the teacher expectancy effect. *Journal of Personality and Social Psychology, 13,* 306-316.

Mendels, G., & Flanders, J. P. (1973). Teachers' expectations and pupils' performance. *American Educational Research Journal, 10,* 203-212.

Milgram, S. (1974). *Obedience to authority; an experimental view.* New York: Harper & Row.

Miller, D. T., & Turnbull, W. (1986). Expectancies and interpersonal processes. *Annual Review of Psychology, 37,* 233-256.

Neuberg, S. L. (1989). The goal of forming accurate impressions during social interactions: Attenuating the impact of negative expectancies. *Journal of Personality and Social Psychology, 53,* 431-444.

Neuberg, S. L. (1994). Expectancy-confirmation process in stereotype-tinged social encounters: The moderating role of social goals. In M. P. Zanna & J. M. Olson (Eds.), *The psychology of prejudice: The Ontario symposium* (Vol. 7, pp. 103-130). Hillsdale, NJ: Lawrence Erlbaum Associates.

Neuberg, S. L., & Fiske, S. T. (1987). Motivational influences on impression formation: Outcome dependency, accuracy-driven attention, and individuating processes. *Journal of Personality and Social Psychology, 53,* 431-444.

Ng, S. H. (1980). *The social psychology of power.* San Francisco: Academic Press

Ng, S. H., & Bradac, J. J. (1993). *Power In language: Verbal communication and social influence.* Newbury Park, CA: Sage.

O'Barr, W. M. (1982). *Linguistic evidence: Language, power, and strategy in the courtroom.* New York: Academic Press.

O'Connell, E. J., Dusek, J. B., & Wheeler, R. J. (1974). A follow-up study of teacher expectancy effects. *Journal of Educational Psychology, 606,* 325-328.

Pettigrew, T. F. (1985). New black-white patterns: How best to conceptualize them? *Annual Review of Sociology, 11,* 329-349.

Prentice, D. A., & Miller, D. T. (1992). When small effects are impressive. *Psychological Bulletin, 112,* 160-164.

Rosenberg, M. (1979). *Conceiving the self.* New York: Basic Books.

Rosenthal, R. (1963). On the social psychology of the psychological experiment: The experimenter's hypothesis as an unintentional determinant of experimental results. *American Science, 51,* 268-283.

Rosenthal, R., & Jacobson, L. (1968). *Pygmalion in the classroom.* New York: Holt, Rinehart & Winston.

Rosenthal, R., & Rubin, D. B. (1978). Interpersonal expectancy effects: The first 345 studies. *Behavioral and Brain Sciences, 3,* 377-415.

Ross, L., Amabile, T. M., & Steinmetz, J. I. (1977). Social roles, social control, and biases in social perception processes. *Journal of Personality and Social Psychology, 3,* 485-494.

Ruggiero, K. M., & Taylor, D. M. (1985). Coping with discrimination: How disadvantaged group members perceive the discrimination that confronts them. *Journal of Personality and Social Psychology, 68,* 826-838.

Ruscher, J. B., & Fiske, S.T. (1990). Interpersonal competition can cause individuating processes. *Journal of Personality and Social Psychology, 58,* 832-843.

Ruscher, J. B., Fiske, S. T., Miki, H., & Van Manen, S. (1991). Individuating processes in competition: Interpersonal versus intergroup. *Personality and Social Psychology Bulletin,* *17,* 595–605.

Seaver, W. B. (1973). Effects of naturally induced teacher expectancies. *Journal of Personality Social Psychology, 28,* 333–342.

Sidanius, J. (1993). The psychology of group conflict and the dynamics of oppression: A social dominance perspective. In W. McGuire & S. Iyengar (Eds.), *Current approaches to political psychology* (pp. 183–219). Durham, NC: Duke University Press.

Skrypnek, B. J., & Snyder, M. (1982). On the self-perpetuating nature of stereotypes about women and men. *Journal of Experimental Social Psychology, 18,* 277–291.

Snodgrass, S. E. (1992). Further effects of role versus gender on interpersonal sensitivity. *Journal of Personality and Social Psychology, 62,* 154–158.

Snyder, M. (1981). On the self-perpetuating nature of social stereotypes. In D. L. Hamilton (Ed.), *Cognitive processes in stereotyping and intergroup behavior* (pp. 183–212). Hillsdale, NJ: Lawrence Erlbaum Associates.

Snyder, M. (1984). When belief creates reality. In L. Berkowitz (Ed.), *Advances in experimental social psychology* (Vol. 18, pp. 248–305). Orlando, FL: Academic Press.

Snyder, M. (1992). Motivational foundations of behavioral confirmation. In M. P. Zanna (Ed.), *Advances in experimental social psychology* (Vol. 25, pp. 67–114). San Diego, CA: Academic Press.

Snyder, M., & Haugen, J. A. (1994). Why does behavioral confirmation occur? A functional perspective on the role of the perceiver. *Journal of Experimental Social Psychology, 30,* 218–246.

Snyder, M., & Haugen, J. A. (1995). Why does behavioral confirmation occur? A functional perspective on the role of the target. *Personality and Social Psychology Bulletin, 21,* 963–974.

Snyder, M., & Swann, W. B., Jr. (1978). Behavioral confirmation in social interaction: From social perception to social reality. *Journal of Experimental Social Psychology, 14,* 148–162.

Snyder, M., Tanke, E. D., & Berscheid, E. (1977). Social perception and interpersonal behavior: On the self-fulfilling nature of social stereotypes. *Journal of Personality and Social Psychology, 35,* 656–666.

Steele, C. M. (1992, April). Race and the schooling of black Americans. *The Atlantic Monthly.*pp. 68–78.

Swann, W. B., Jr. (1983). Self-verification: Bringing social reality into harmony with the self. In J. Suls & A. G. Greenwald (Eds.), *Social psychological perspectives on the self* (Vol. 2, pp. 33–66). Hillsdale, NJ: Lawrence Erlbaum Associates.

Swann, W. B., Jr. (1987). Identity negotiation: Where two roads meet. *Journal of Personality and Social Psychology, 53,* 1038–1051.

Swann, W. B., Jr., & Ely, E. J. (1984). A battle of wills: Self-verification versus behavioral confirmation. *Journal of Personality and Social Psychology, 46,* 1287–1302.

Swann, W. B., Jr., Griffin, J. J., Predmore, S. C., & Gaines, B. (1987). The cognitive-affective crossfire: When self-consistency confronts self-enhancement. *Journal of Personality and Social Psychology, 52,* 881–889.

Swann, W. B., Jr., & Read, S. J. (1981). Self-verification processes: How we sustain our self-conceptions. *Journal of Experimental Social Psychology, 17,* 351–372.

Swann, W. B., Jr., & Snyder, M. (1980). On translating beliefs into action: Theories of ability and their application in an instructional setting. *Journal of Personality and Social Setting, 38,* 879–888.

Thibaut, J. W., & Kelley, H. H. (1959). *The social psychology of groups.* New York: Wiley.

Vidrin, L. M., & Neuberg, S. L. (1990, August). *Perceived status: A moderator of expectancy confirmation effects.* Paper presented at the 98th annual convention of the American Psychological Association, Boston.

Watson, D. (1982). The actor and the observer: How are their perceptions of causality divergent: *Psychological Bulletin, 92,* 682–700.

Weisz, C., & Jones, E. E. (1993). Expectancy disconfirmation and dispositional inference: Latent strength of target-based and category-based expectancies. *Personality and Social Psychology Bulletin, 19,* 563–573.

Word, C. O., Zanna, M. P., & Cooper, J. (1974). The nonverbal mediation of self-fulfilling prophecies in interracial interaction. *Journal of Experimental Social Psychology, 10,* 109–120.

Zanna, M. P., Sheras, P. L., Cooper, J., & Shaw, C. (1975). Pygmalion and Galatea: The interactive effects of teacher and student expectancies. *Journal of Experimental Social Psychology, 11,* 279–287.

10

Getting by With a Little Help From Our Enemies: Collective Paranoia and Its Role in Intergroup Relations

Roderick M. Kramer
Stanford University

David M. Messick
Northwestern University

"I take the view that this lack [of subversive activity] is the most ominous sign in our whole situation. It convinces me more than perhaps any other factor that the sabotage we are to get, the Fifth Column activities we are to get, are timed just like Pearl Harbor was timed. . . . I believe we are just being lulled into a false sense of security."
> —Governor Earl Warren, testifying at a 1942 congressional hearing regarding the absence of evidence of sabotage or espionage activity by Japanese Americans up to that time (cited in Dawes, 1988, p. 251, italics added).

"I distinctly heard it. He muttered under his breath, 'Jew!'"

"You're crazy."

"No, I'm not. We were walking off the tennis court and he was there with his wife and me. He looked at her, and then they both looked at me. And under his breath he said, 'Jew!'"

"Alvie, you're a total paranoid."

"How am I paranoid? I pick up on those kind of things."
> —Scene from Woody Allen's *Annie Hall* (italics added).

Fiske and Taylor (1991) characterized social cognition as the study of "how people make sense of other people and themselves" (p. 14). As such, social-cognitive theory and research attempts to clarify the role that cognitive processes play in social judgment and behavior. Application of the social-cognitive paradigm to the study of intergroup relations has proved an enormously fruitful enterprise. Over the past two decades, our understanding of the antecedents and consequences of intergroup cognitions has made impressive strides (see Brewer & Kramer, 1985; Hamilton, 1981; Messick & Mackie, 1989, for reviews).

As substantial as these gains have been, there remain important lacunae in our understanding of intergroup cognition and behavior. The study of distrust and suspicion between social groups is one such lacuna. Although few social psychologists would dispute the importance of distrust and suspicion as factors in intergroup relations, systematic theory and research on these topics remains surprisingly sparse (see Brewer, 1981; Insko, Schopler, & Sedikides, chap. 5, this volume, for notable exceptions). A primary aim in this chapter, accordingly, is to articulate a social-cognitive model of intergroup distrust and suspicion. To set the stage for our arguments, it may be helpful to begin with a brief overview of previous approaches to conceptualizing intergroup distrust and suspicion.

PREVIOUS CONCEPTIONS OF INTERGROUP DISTRUST AND SUSPICION

Over the past 40 years, a substantial scholarly literature on trust and distrust has accumulated (see Barber, 1983; Gambetta, 1987; Holmes, 1991; Kramer & Tyler, 1995, for overviews). Although trust theorists differ considerably with respect to the emphasis they afford to micro- versus macro-level determinants of distrust and suspicion, several points of convergence are discernible across these diverse perspectives. First, distrust and suspicion are generally conceptualized as psychological states that are closely linked to individuals' beliefs and expectations about other people. For example, the dispositional inferences individuals make regarding others' intentions and motives are presumed to influence judgments about their trustworthiness. Distrust and suspicion arise when individuals attribute such things as lack of credibility to others' claims or commitments, and hostile motives or deceptive intentions to their actions, especially in situations where uncertainty or ambiguity is present regarding the cause of their behavior (Deutsch, 1973; Lindskold, 1978). Further, most conceptions of distrust assume that psychological states such as fear of exploitation, lack of confidence, and low expectations of reciprocity are significant correlates of distrust (Deutsch, 1973; Messick et al., 1983; Tyler, 1993).

Suspicion has generally been treated as an important cognitive component of distrust. It has been defined as "a psychological state in which perceivers actively entertain multiple, possibly rival, hypotheses about the motives or genuineness of a person's behavior. Moreover, suspicion involves the belief that the actor's behavior may reflect a motive that the actor wants hidden from the target of his or her behavior" (Fein & Hilton, 1994, pp. 168–169).

In much of the experimental social-psychological literature, especially those studies grounded in game theoretic conceptions of choice behavior, these social inference and attributional processes have been construed as reasonably rational and orderly forms of social inference, consistent with the idea that social perceivers resemble "intuitive scientists" trying to make sense of the social and organizational worlds they inhabit (Kelley, 1973). For example, Rotter (1980) and Lindskold (1978) conceptualized distrust as a generalized expectancy or belief regarding the lack of trustworthiness of other individuals that is predicated on a specific history of interaction with them. According to this view, when people make judgments about others' trustworthiness (or lack of it), they act much like "intuitive Bayesians," whose inferences are updated on the basis of their prior experience. Research in this tradition has shed considerable light on the conditions under which such "history-based" forms of distrust and suspicion evolve. For example, it has been closely linked to patterns of exchange that involve repeated violations of reciprocity (Deutsch, 1973; Lindskold, 1978; Rotter, 1980). Thus, when individuals act on faith only to discover that their faith in another has been misplaced, trust declines.

While recognizing the importance of history-based forms of distrust, a number of researchers have noted that other forms of distrust and suspicion appear to be far less rational in their antecedents and origins (Barber, 1983; Deutsch, 1973; Luhman, 1979). For example, Deutsch (1973) proposed a form of pathological or irrational distrust that he characterized in terms of an "inflexible, rigid, unaltering tendency to act in a suspicious manner, irrespective of the situation or the consequences of so acting" (p. 171). The pathology of this form of distrust, he noted, is reflected in "the indiscriminateness and incorrigibility of the behavioral tendency" (p. 171). Irrational distrust reflects an exaggerated propensity toward distrust, which can arise even in the absence of specific experiences or interactional histories that justify or warrant it. Irrational distrust represents a form of presumptive distrust that is conferred *ex ante* on other social actors.

Initial evidence for the existence of this kind of distrust came from ethnographic and field research (Blake & Mouton, 1986; Brewer & Campbell, 1976; Sherif, Harvey, White, Hood, & Sherif, 1961; Sumner, 1906). Subsequent laboratory experiments on ingroup bias, using the minimal group paradigm, provided further evidence for it. For example, Brewer and her students (Brewer, 1979; Brewer & Silver, 1978) demonstrated that categorization of individuals into distinct groups, even when those group boundaries are based on arbitrary and transient criteria, can lead individuals to perceive outgroup members as less trustworthy, less honest, and less cooperative than other members of their own group. According to this perspective, trust often begins and ends at the social category or group boundary.

More recently, Insko, Schopler and Sedikes (chap. 5, this volume) explored differences between distrust that arises between individuals (interpersonal distrust) and distrust that arises between groups (intergroup distrust). Their findings suggest a basic "discontinuity" between individual and intergroup group distrust. This discontinuity, they noted, may reflect the existence of an outgroup schema.

While drawing on previous theory and research, we attempt next to articulate a different theoretical perspective on the social-cognitive determinants of intergroup distrust and suspicion. This conception derives from social information-processing perspectives on social judgment and behavior.

A SOCIAL INFORMATION-PROCESSING PERSPECTIVE ON DISTRUST AND SUSPICION

To understand the dynamics of intergroup distrust and suspicion from a social information-processing perspective, it is useful to start at the level of the individual social perceiver embedded in an intergroup context. We begin by introducing the notion of the intuitive social auditor.

Trust and the Intuitive Social Auditor

It was noted earlier that previous models have emphasized that individuals' judgments about others' trustworthiness are anchored, at least in part, on (a) their a priori expectations about others' behavior, and (b) the extent to which subsequent experience supports or discredits those expectations. Boyle and Bonacich's (1970) analysis of trust development is representative of such arguments: Individuals' expectations about trustworthy behavior tend to change "in the direction of experience and to a degree proportional to the difference between this experience and the initial expectations applied to it" (p. 123). The portrait of the social perceiver that emerges from this research is that of a interpersonal bookkeeper or "social auditor" who attempts to maintain an accurate accounting of past exchanges and transactions.

In their purest form, such models imply a rather straightforward "arithmetic" to trust, with some actions adding to the accumulation of trust and others subtracting from it. However, this simple picture is complicated by the fact that systematic biases in social information processing often corrupt the "mental accounting" of the intuitive social auditor. To see where these biases come from, as well as the effects they exert on social judgment, it is useful to consider how social information processing affects judgments about trust and distrust.

Salancik and Pfeffer (1978) provided a useful perspective on social information-processing theory. They posited that, to understand social behavior, it is essential to examine the "informational and social environment within which behavior occurs and to which it adapts" (p. 226). They also noted that one reason social context is so consequential is that it selectively directs individuals' attention to certain information, making that information more salient and sharpening its impact on individuals' expectations and interpretations of both their own and others' behavior.

Research shows that a variety of goals, not always compatible with each other, affect how people process social information about other people with whom they are interdependent. In some instances, individuals may be motivated to obtain accurate information about themselves and others, on the assumption that such information will be useful in making realistic assessments of how to manage their interdependence with others more effectively (Ashford, 1989; Kelley, 1973). In other situations, they may be primarily concerned with obtaining information that will reduce uncertainty regarding their standing in a social relationship (Tyler, 1993). In still other contexts, they may be concerned with obtaining evidence that will satisfy needs for self-protection (Wood & Taylor, 1991), self-enhancement (Brown, 1986; Taylor & Brown, 1988, 1994), reassurance (Kramer, 1994), or self-verification (Swann & Read, 1981).

In intergroup contexts, any or all of these motives can come into play when individuals from one group interact with members of another. In some situations, for example, it may be most important for individuals to accurately assess the nature of the relationship between their two groups. In the context of an intergroup negotiation, individuals may be most concerned with obtaining accurate information that will help them discern the other group's interests and forge an integrative agreement. In other settings, individuals' paramount concern may be knowing where they stand in the eyes of outgroup members, especially if that outgroup exercises significant "fate control" over them. For example, assembly line workers may be highly motivated to know what their managerial counterparts think of their group in general to gauge their prospects for promotion. In other contexts, such as those that threaten individuals' sense of self-esteem or self-efficacy vis-à-vis membership in a stigmatized or marginal group, individuals may be motivated to obtain reassuring or self-affirming information.

These divergent goals can affect social information processing via several distinct routes, including their impact on (a) the expectations with which individuals approach their intergroup interactions, (b) the information they find salient during those interactions, and (c) how they subsequently construe a given interaction and encode it in memory. This portrait of the motivated, vigilant social information processor is useful with respect to understanding what sort of information might affect judgments about trust and distrust. However, it does not help us understand how intergroup cognitions about distrust and suspicion become "decoupled" from actual interactional histories. To see this link, it is useful to introduce the concept of "paranoid social cognition."

Paranoid Social Cognition

Early theory and research on paranoid cognition focused almost exclusively on extreme forms of paranoia, such as are typically observed among psychiatric patients in clinical settings (Cameron, 1943). On the basis of such observations, Colby (1981) defined *paranoid cognitions* as "persecutory delusions and *false beliefs* whose propositional content clusters around ideas of being harassed, threatened, harmed, subjugated, persecuted, accused, mistreated, wronged, tormented, disparaged, vilified, and so on, by malevolent others, either specific individuals or groups" (p. 518, italics added).

In contrast to clinical theories, recent social-psychological research has focused on less extreme forms of paranoid cognition that arise in ordinary social and situational contexts (Fenigstein & Vanable, 1992; Kramer, 1994; Zimbardo, Andersen, & Kabat, 1981). This research proceeds from the intuition that, in milder form, paranoid cognitions appear to be quite prevalent and are often observed even among normal individuals, especially when people find themselves in what they perceive as awkward or threatening social situations. As Fenigstein and Vanable (1992) proposed, ordinary people

> in their everyday behavior often manifest characteristics — such as self-centered thought, suspiciousness, assumptions of ill will or hostility, and even notions of conspiratorial intent — that are reminiscent of paranoia . . . on various occasions, one may think one is being talked about or feel as if everything is going against one, resulting in suspicion and mistrust of others,

as though they were taking advantage of one or were to blame for one's difficulties. (pp. 130–133).

Integrating Colby's definition with this intuition, *collective paranoia* is defined as collectively held beliefs, either false or exaggerated, that cluster around ideas of being harassed, threatened, harmed, subjugated, persecuted, accused, mistreated, wronged, tormented, disparaged, or vilified by a malevolent outgroup or outgroups. According to this definition, the perceived source of threat (an outgroup or outgroups) and the object of threat (the ingroup to which an individual belongs) are both defined at the social group or category level.

It is possible to imagine situations in which a paranoid person maintains pathological suspicion of a personal nature against another person (it's him against me). There are situations including a group that becomes paranoid about a single individual. There are also situations in which social paranoia is of a personal nature against a group (them against me). Finally, there can be paranoia inputed to a group against another group (them against us) — the case considered at the heart of collective paranoia.

Several psychological phenomena may differentiate these forms of extreme distrust. In particular, the we–them sort that is identified as collective paranoia rests on the bedrock of ingroup–outgroup differentiation, which has been widely studied. When intuitive social auditors do the accounting of transactions that are between-group exchanges, they very likely code them differently from within-group encounters. There is evidence that ingroup members are more likely to give other members the benefit of the doubt, manifesting what Brewer (1996) termed a *leniency bias*.

Another factor that would tend to maintain and exacerbate distrust and suspicion, which might be called the *outgroup unitization* hypothesis, refers to the tendency to treat the outgroup as a single unit in the accounting scheme. Outgroup unitization reflects the tendency to differentiate less among outgroup members than among ingroup members when doing the social auditing. As a consequence, a breach of trust from one member of the outgroup can be repaid to any other member. If an outgroup member insults one, one can retaliate against any other outgroup member. The target of the retaliation naturally perceives the retaliatory act as gratuitous aggression, further enhancing distrust and suspicion. If an ingroup member insults one, one retaliates against that person.

Outgroup unitization influences the intuitive auditor's accounting with positive as well as negative exchanges. If an individual treats an outgroup member kindly, the social auditor records the act as a positive contribution — not only to their interpersonal relationship, but to the outgroup as a whole. One implication is that any member of the outgroup should be appropriately grateful, indebted, or appreciative of the act. In contrast, kind acts to ingroup members do not create the expectation that other ingroup members will be indebted to oneself. The unit for the ingroup will be the person; for the outgroup, it will be the group.

COLLECTIVE PARANOIA AND THE HIERARCHICAL INTERGROUP RELATION

Thus far, we have presented some general arguments regarding the impact of social information processing or intergroup distrust and suspicion. One approach to developing theory about complex social-psychological phenomena such as distrust and suspicion is to examine extreme instances of them. Extreme forms of a phenomenon often throw into bold relief important dynamics that remain obscure or hard to detect in more ordinary social contexts. For example, social psychologists have learned a great deal about the dynamics of helping behavior by studying individuals' collective reactions to unexpected emergency situations (Latane & Darley, 1968). In this spirit, we explore next an extreme form of distrust that arises in hierarchical contexts.

Hierarchical relationships—relationships characterized by asymmetries in the power and status of interdependent groups—are among the most important and prevalent forms of social organization (Kanter, 1977a; Miller, 1992). Hierarchy characterizes many forms of intergroup relation, including the relationship between management and labor groups within organizations; between dominant and token social groups; between majority groups in political power and marginal groups seeking power; and between religious and secular sectors in society. As is shown here, they are also a form of relationship in which the contours and features of collective paranoia are likely to loom particularly large.

The prevalence of hierarchy reflects its many virtues as a form of organizing—virtues that have been long noted by social and organizational theorists. As with many virtues, however, hierarchy enjoys its share of problems, the catalogue of which varies depending on where in the hierarchical relationship a group happens to be situated. From the perspective of groups that occupy positions of low power or status within a hierarchical social system, the fear of exploitation and the chronic suspicion that they are being treated unfairly by those above them are real and recurring concerns. In contrast, it is common for groups in high-status positions to fear that those below them seek to displace them and can't be trusted unless they are watched closely.

In conjunction, these divergent concerns about trust remind us of the elusive quality of trust in hierarchical relations, and the comparative ease with which distrust and suspicion roam over the hierarchical landscape (Barber, 1983; Hill, 1992; Kanter, 1977b; Miller, 1992; Sitkin & Roth, 1993; Tyler & Lind, 1992).

Antecedents of Collective Paranoia in Hierarchical Relations

Research on paranoid social cognition identifies several psychological factors that contribute to paranoid cognitions. Of particular relevance to this chapter is evidence that paranoid social cognitions are likely to arise in situations where individuals: (a) feel a heightened sense of self-consciousness, (b) perceive themselves to be under intense evaluative scrutiny, and/or (c) are uncertain of their status or standing within a social relation (Fenigstein, 1979, 1984; Fenigstein & Vanable, 1992; Kramer, 1994). We elaborate next on the role each of these psychological factors play in the emergence of paranoid social cognition.

Heightened Self-Consciousness. Studies have shown that heightened self-consciousness increases individuals' tendency to make overly personalistic attributions about others' intentions and motives (Buss & Scheier, 1976; Fenigstein & Vanable, 1992; Kramer, 1994). Fenigstein (1984) characterized this as the *overperception of self-as-target bias* and argued that, because of it, individuals tend to construe even relatively innocuous social encounters in unrealistically self-referential terms. According to this evidence, self-consciousness induces an exaggerated or "irrational" suspicion that other people are observing and evaluating them. Thus, ironically, an individual's own self-consciousness engenders the perception of being under intense social scrutiny. This tendency, of course, is one of the defining features of a paranoid style of cognition. As Colby (1981) noted, "Around the central core of persecutory delusions [that preoccupy the paranoid person] there exists a number of attendant properties such as suspiciousness, hypersensitivity, hostility, fearfulness, and self-reference that lead such individuals to interpret events that have nothing to do with them as bearing on them personally" (p. 518).

Within the context of intergroup relations, one important factor that can influence self-consciousness is the "relational demography" (Tsui, Egan, & O'Reilly, 1992) that characterizes the broader social context within which the intergroup relation is embedded. All humans possess membership in multiple social categories. As a consequence, they can categorize themselves — and be categorized by others in turn — in a variety of different ways.

These include categorizations based on physical attributes such as age, race, or gender; categorizations based on socially defined categories such as religion and social class; and organizationally defined attributes, such as institutional affiliations and departmental memberships. Recognizing their importance, researchers have afforded a great deal of attention in recent years to exploring how such categorization processes influence social perception within groups and organizations (Ashforth & Mael, 1989; Kanter, 1977a; Tsui, Egan, & O'Reilly, 1992; Wharton, 1992).

Several conclusions emerge from research on social categorization. First, social categorization often influences how individuals define themselves in a given social situation. Turner (1987) used the term *self-categorization* to refer to these processes and their effects. Self-categorization is affected by the particular social context within which individuals find themselves. In particular, there is evidence that individuals categorize themselves in terms of those attributes that are distinctive or unique in a given setting. For example, if an individual is the only female in a group, her distinctive gender status may be afforded disproportionate emphasis when explaining her behavior — affecting not only how she is seen by others, but also how she sees herself. Thus, one factor that can enhance self-consciousness is for a person to be unique or distinctive with respect to some obvious characteristic, like race or gender (Taylor, Fiske, Etcoff, & Ruderman, 1978). Indeed, it is hard to imagine a more potent way to increase the salience of a group boundary or social category than to have "solo status" as a lone woman in an otherwise all-male office. Not only is self-consciousness increased, but it is increased about the group characteristics that can lead to group-based attributions for others' behaviors and judgments.

From a cognitive standpoint, the enhanced distinctiveness of the category during social interaction makes gender-based attributions more available during social information processing. Intergroup differences become highly salient explanations for behavior, and the social auditor grows suspicious by crediting plusses and minuses to group, rather than individual, accounts. As a result, they tend to become more salient or "loom larger" during subsequent interactions as well, affecting both social inference processes and the behaviors that flow from them (Cota & Dion, 1986; Kanter, 1977a, 1977b; Taylor, 1981).

The argument that self-categorization on the basis of distinctive or exceptional status produces a heightened form of self-consciousness is consistent with a considerable body of evidence regarding the cognitive and social consequences of "being different" or standing out from other members of a group (Kanter, 1977a, 1977b; Tsui, Egan, & O'Reilly, 1992; Taylor, 1981). In social information-processing terms, one fairly immediate consequence of individuals' awareness of being different from others is that it prompts effortful attributional search for the causes of others' behavior toward them, while injecting considerable ambiguity in the social inference process. Such self-consciousness might be expected to be especially pronounced when individuals are uncertain about how much merely "being different" from others influences how they are evaluated and treated.

Perceived Evaluative Scrutiny. A second factor that contributes to paranoid social cognition is the perception of being under evaluative scrutiny. Research has shown that when individuals feel under moderate or intense evaluative scrutiny, they tend to overattribute others' behaviors to personalistic causes (Fenigstein & Vanable, 1992; Kramer, 1994). For example, to junior faculty members under review for tenure in an academic department, even casual and seemingly benign encounters can take on significant and potentially sinister import because they feel under continual evaluative scrutiny by more senior colleagues. Thus, the failure of a senior colleague to return a casual hello as they pass one another in the hall may prompt intense rumination on the part of the junior faculty member about the cause or "meaning" of the event ("Did I say something at the last faculty meeting that offended the person?" "Has he decided to vote against me for tenure and feels uncomfortable seeing me?"). The effect of perceiving themselves under evaluative scrutiny thus leads members of one group to attribute the behavior of others in overly personalistic and diagnostic terms (i.e., as having implications for their standing in the relationship). As a consequence, even when plausible nonpersonalistic accounts are available, individuals who feel under evaluative scrutiny tend to discount the credibility of such accounts in favor of those that are viewed as more self-relevant.

In many respects, token groups exemplify these cognitive dilemmas and difficulties. Token status in a hierarchy is based on "ascribed characteristics (master statuses such as gender, race, religion, ethnic group, and age) or other characteristics that carry with them a set of assumptions about culture, status, and behavior that are highly salient for majority category members" (Kanter, 1977b, p. 966). In discussing the effects of token status on social perception and interpersonal relations, Kanter (1977a, 1977b) noted that individuals who are members of token categories are likely to attract disproportionate attention from other groups, particularly those who enjoy dominant status in terms of numerical proportions. For example, she observed that females in many American corporations often feel as if they are in the "limelight" compared with their statistically more numerous male counterparts.

In support of these observations, Taylor (1981) demonstrated that observers often allocate disproportionate amounts of attention to individuals who have token status in groups, especially when making attributions about group processes and outcomes. Lord and Saenz (1985) provided an important extension of this early work by showing how token status affects the cognitive processes of tokens. Based on their findings, they concluded that, "Tokens feel the social pressure of imagined audience scrutiny, and may do so even when the 'audience' of majority group members treat them no differently from nontokens" (p. 919).

The model of the vigilant social auditor advanced earlier helps explain this pattern. From a social information-processing perspective, individuals in lower status groups in a social hierarchy are likely to be more hypervigilant and ruminative information processors compared with their higher status counterparts, especially members of those groups on whom they are evaluatively dependent. As a consequence of their enhanced vigilance and rumination, they tend to (over)construe others' behavior as diagnostic of trust-related concerns.

These arguments imply that individuals in lower status groups should develop, over time, more elaborate and differentiated mental accounting systems for tracking trust-related transactions. According to this cognitive elaboration hypothesis, we would expect individuals on the bottom of a hierarchical relation (those in the subordinate role) to be able to recall more trust-related incidents and behaviors compared with their superordinate counterparts. Fiske (1993) identified a number of factors involved in this asymmetry. Her research suggests that people are vigilant and careful information processors when they need to be, but often rely on stereotypes and other poorly articulated schemas of others when they can get away with it. She observed, "The power*less* are stereotyped because no one needs to, can, or wants to be detailed and accurate about them. The power*ful* are not so likely to be stereotyped because subordinates need to, can, and want to form detailed impressions of them. The powerless need to try to predict and possibly alter their own fates" (p. 624, italics in original).

Extrapolating from such evidence and arguments, one might expect that violations of trust will tend to "loom larger" than confirmations of trust for those in positions of low power or control in such situations. Several lines of research suggest this hypothesis. First, violations of trust are highly salient to victims, prompting intense ruminative activity and greater attributional search for the causes of the violation (Janoff-Bulman, 1992). Second, to the extent that violations of trust are coded as interpersonal losses, they should loom larger than "mere" confirmations of trust of comparable magnitude (e.g., failure to keep a promise should have more impact on judgments about trustworthiness than "merely" keeping it; Kramer, 1995b). Finally, cognitive responses to positive and negative events are often highly asymmetrical (Peeters & Czapinski, 1990; Taylor, 1993). As Taylor (1991) noted, "negative events produce more causal attribution activity than positive events, controlling for expectedness" (p. 70).

Uncertainty About Social Standing. A third factor that can contribute to the emergence of paranoid social cognition is the level of uncertainty about social standing that social perceivers possess. Recent research on the group value model suggests that people attach great psychological importance to their standing within social systems and social interactions (Lind & Tyler, 1988). *Standing* refers to the "information communicated to a person about his or her status with the group . . . communicated both by interpersonal aspects of treatment — politeness and/or respect — and by the attention paid to a person as a full group member" (Tyler, 1993, p. 148).

According to this model, individuals are motivated to determine whether they have been treated fairly and whether they are valued or respected by those on whom they are dependent (Tyler, 1993). Consequently, they try to diagnose their standing, using information from exchanges and encounters as clues to whether their standing in the relationship is "good" or "bad."

Because of their ongoing concerns about standing, individuals in lower status or less powerful groups tend to be proactive information seekers, searching for data that will help them make sense of their place in the social order (Ashford, 1989). In doing so, individuals are torn between their desire to obtain accurate information about where they stand in a social system and reassuring or self-enhancing information (Brown, 1991, 1995; Sedikides, 1993; Strube et al., 1986; Strube & Roemmele, 1985; Trope, 1983, 1986). As a result, when individuals find themselves in situations where their self-esteem or positive social identity is threatened, a conflict may arise between the desire to find out where they actually stand in the relationship and the desire to assuage their fears about poor standing or loss of standing.

CONSEQUENCES OF COLLECTIVE PARANOIA

Having described some of the antecedents of collective paranoia, we turn now to consideration of some of its consequences for intergroup cognition and behavior.

Cognitive Consequences

Hypervigilant Social Information Processing. One consequence of perceived threat about standing is to activate adaptive information search and appraisal. Moderate levels of threat often provoke vigilant information processing about the nature of the threat and the responses that might be taken to reduce it (Janis, 1989; Janoff-Bulman, 1992; Lazarus & Folkman,

1984). When a threat becomes too severe, however, individuals may experience a hypervigilant style of social information processing. This hypervigilant information processing can lead, in turn, to the misconstrual of social information, affecting judgments about another's trustworthiness (Kramer, 1995a).

Dysphoric Rumination. A second response individuals often have to threatening events is dysphoric rumination (Janoff-Bulman, 1992). *Dysphoric rumination* refers to the tendency for individuals to unhappily reimagine, rethink, and relive pleasant or unpleasant events. Research (Lyubomirsky & Nolen-Hoeksema, 1993; Kramer, 1994; Tesser, 1978) has indicated a number of reasons that dysphoric rumination might contribute to paranoid social cognitions. First, rumination following negative events has been found to increase negative thinking about those events and contribute to a pessimistic explanatory style when trying to explain them. Dysphoric ruminators appear to engage in "worse case" thinking about their troubles and the prospects for resolving them. Second, rumination can increase individuals' confidence in the interpretations and explanations they have generated to explain aversive or threatening events. This result is ironic and might, at first glance, seem counterintuitive. One might argue that the more individuals ruminate about the causes of their difficulties, the more likely they should be to generate numerous alternative, reasonable hypotheses, leading to decreased confidence in an especially implausible or "paranoid" account of their difficulties.

However, as Wilson and Kraft (1993) aptly noted, "Because it is often difficult to get at the exact roots of [many] feelings, repeated introspections may not result in better access to the actual causes. Instead, people may repeatedly focus on reasons that are plausible and easy to verbalize" (p. 410). Such results suggest the operation of an interesting "cognitive effort" heuristic (e.g., "Because I've thought so much about this, it must be true"). Along these lines, Kramer (1994) demonstrated support for the hypothesis that inducing dysphoric rumination about others' motives increases distrust and suspicion of them.

We posit that hypervigilance and dysphoric rumination can affect social information processing and threat perception between social groups in at least three ways.

Sinister Attribution Error. The sinister attribution error or bias reflects a tendency for individuals to overattribute hostile intentions and malevolent motives to others (Kramer, 1994). Individuals should discount the validity of any single causal explanation when multiple, competing explanations for that behavior are available (Kelley, 1973; Morris & Larrick, 1995). Thus, even when individuals suspect they may be the target or cause of another's behavior, they should discount this self-referential or personalistic attribu tion if other plausible reasons exist.

However, there is substantial evidence that people often make overly personalistic attributions of others' actions, even when competing explanations are readily available (Fenigstein, 1979; Fenigstein & Vanable, 1992; Heider, 1958; Hilton, Fein, & Miller, 1993; Kramer, 1994; Vorauer & Ross, 1993). Certain cognitive states, such as self-consciousness, increase this tendency to make such overly personalistic and negative attributions (Fenigstein & Vanable, 1992; Kramer, 1994).

Biased Punctuation of Interactional History. *Biased punctuation* of social interactions refers to a tendency for interdependent decision makers to organize their interpersonal histories in a self-serving fashion (Kahn & Kramer, 1990). Thus, in the case of an intergroup conflict, members of Group A are likely to construe the history of conflict with Group B as a sequence B–A, B–A, and B–A, in which the initial hostile or aggressive move was made by B, causing A to engage in defensive and legitimate retaliatory actions. However, Actor B punctuates the same history of interaction as A–B, A–B, and A–B, reversing the roles of aggressor and defender. The tendency to punctuate a behavioral sequence in a self-serving fashion is a type of social script called the *aggressor–defender* model (Pruitt & Rubin, 1986).

Because defiance is morally acceptable, whereas aggression is not, each party to a conflict will frame the interaction so as to make the other party the "prime mover"—the one who initiated the conflict. Considered in conjunction with the outgroup unitization hypothesis mentioned earlier, it is easy to see how an act is seen as a response by one side can be viewed as an initiation by the other.

The problem of biased punctuation of history may be considerably exacerbated by recall biases. Insko, Schopler, & Sedikes (chap. 5, this volume) review and integrate the results of a provocative set of recent experiments, suggesting that individuals tend to recall intergroup relations as relatively more competitive than interindividual relations (see also Pemberton, Insko, & Schopler, 1996).

Exaggerated Perceptions of Conspiracy. Exaggerated perceptions of conspiracy reflect a tendency for individuals to overestimate the extent to which their perceived outgroup enemies or adversaries are engaged in coordinated and concerted hostile or malevolent actions against them. Just as biased punctuation of interactional history entails an overperception of episodic or causal linkages between disparate or unconnected events, so the exaggerated perception of conspiracy entails an overperception of social linkages among outgroup actors. At the core of the exaggerated perception of conspiracy is the tendency to overperceive interdependent connections among the actions of individual outgroup members, even when their acts are, in actuality, independent. In the context of intergroup relations, these exaggerated perceptions of conspiracy center around the presumed intentionality of the outgroup's acts (i.e., actions are construed as coordinated attempts aimed at harming one's own group).

Exaggerated perceptions of conspiracy are likely to emerge later in a conflict, after issues have intensified. In these circumstances, group positions are likely to be extreme, with the resulting perception that anyone who is not with our group must be against it. Thus, both sides in an intense conflict may perceive objectively moderate positions to be more favorable to the other side (Dawes, Singer, & Lemons, 1972; Lord, Lepper, & Ross, 1979).

Affective and Behavioral Consequences of Collective Paranoia

Several affective and behavioral consequences of collective paranoia are posited here. First, collective paranoia contributes to a form of affective response that has been termed *moral aggression*. The term *moral aggression* has been used to refer to the intense negative reactions individuals sometimes experience when they feel they have been treated in an unfair, unjust, or untrustworthy fashion (see e.g., Brewer, 1981; Campbell, 1975; Trivers, 1971). The notion of moral aggression reflects a basic intuition about the phenomenology of injustice: People often have a very limited tolerance for other people or groups who are perceived to be dishonest or untrustworthy, especially when they believe that they themselves or the groups to which they belong are engaging in more cooperative, trustworthy behavior (Schelling, 1958; Wilson, 1978). There is evidence that moral aggression is associated with strong anger and desire for retribution (Bies, 1987). Such feelings have been linked to intergroup violence and revenge behaviors (Bies, Tripp, & Kramer, 1996).

A second form of behavior driven by collective paranoia is defensive noncooperation. Kramer and Brewer (1986) noted that one reason groups "defect" from preserving common resource pools shared with other groups is that they believe others are not doing their fair share. Thus, they construe their own noncooperative behavior as defensively motivated (i.e., designed to protect their own welfare), even if that means compromising the collective welfare. Such behavior is intended to minimize the risks of exploitation or getting the so-called "sucker's payoff." It thus constitutes a form of preemptive defense against the expectation that trust will be violated. Of course, to the extent that each group engages in such acts, the result is a series of reciprocal disappointments and self-justificatory acts that can exacerbate intergroup distrust and suspicion, creating a self-fulfilling prophecy.

CONTRIBUTIONS AND IMPLICATIONS

A major aim of this chapter was to suggest a new framework for thinking about the antecedents and consequences of intergroup distrust and suspicion. The arguments regarding the effects of heightened self-consciousness, the perception of being under evaluative scrutiny, and uncertainty about standing on social information suggest how exaggerated or irrational forms of distrust and suspicion can evolve from social information-processing tendencies that foster the misconstrual of others' actions and motives. The list of factors considered here obviously does not exhaust the possible factors that might contribute to the development of collective paranoia. Rather, it was merely intended to illustrate the kinds of cognitive, structural, and social relational factors that might intensify intergroup distrust and suspicion. However, it helps us converge on an important intuition about the psychological dynamics of collective paranoia. In each case, central issues include perceptions of vulnerability and lack of perceived control over important outcomes implied by the presence of powerful evaluative outgroups.

Much of this analysis has proceeded from the presumption that many of the social-cognitive correlates of collective paranoia reflect rather ordinary social information-processing goals and motives gone awry. Social and organizational life is an ongoing process of sense making and adaptation — individuals like to know where they fit in a complex social hierarchy. Moreover, when problems arise, they attempt to engage in effective reality testing and problem solving. Thus, we view group members in social contexts as intentionally rational, vigilant, and discerning social perceivers. They normally engage in constructive attempts to make sense of their environments, and vigilance and rumination are useful strategies for so doing. Thus, when occasions arise that threaten a group's security, status, esteem, or perceived control over events, group members engage in an active search for the sources and causes of their difficulties. During such search, other social groups with whom they are interdependent, especially those that are perceived as powerful and/or in control of important outcomes, will quite naturally attract attention. Such groups become objects of vigilant scrutiny and rumination.

Of course, all individuals routinely confront sense-making dilemmas.

However, as was shown here, for those groups who occupy certain disadvantaged social positions relative to other groups (i.e., those who perceive themselves as particularly vulnerable, are uncertain about their standing in the social order, and/or perceive themselves under evaluative scrutiny), these sense-making predicaments are more acute.

It is useful to raise a few caveats about this analysis. First, many of the conceptual labels employed in our model — such as *sinister attribution error, paranoid social cognition,* and *exaggerated perception of conspiracy* — may strike some readers as excessively pejorative. In effect, they seem to blame the victim by prejudging or assuming an objective reference point against which the cognitions of certain groups fall short. For example, character-izing the cognitive processes of individuals who happen to belong to relatively disadvantaged groups within a social system as "paranoid" might seem to minimize the legitimacy of their concerns or the validity of their plight.

This is far from the intent of this analysis. Rather, the spirit of the analysis is to suggest some deleterious cognitive and behavioral conse-quences that are sometimes correlated with certain locations within social hierarchies. To the extent that social locations influence the magnitude and direction of certain social information-processing biases, we have argued, they may contribute to a potentially debilitating pattern of misperception and misattribution. A better understanding of these irrational bases of distrust and suspicion is a first step in developing a set of more efficacious behavioral technologies for building and restoring trust in between groups.

Relatedly, the label *sinister attribution error* clearly implies a mistaken or flawed process of social inference, again seeming to cast aspersions on the cognitive competence of members of certain social groups. Insofar as research findings reviewed in this chapter document that psychological processes such as self-consciousness and dysphoric rumination lead to systematic distortions in the attribution and social inference process, the term *error* or *bias* seems quite appropriate. However, it is important not to misconstrue such cognitive errors as "errors" in a more existential sense. In highly competitive or political social contexts, for example, a propensity toward vigilance with respect to detecting the lack of trustworthiness of a powerful outgroup may be quite prudent and adaptive. In such environ-ments, it is often better to be "safe than sorry."

Such possibilities prompt consideration of other adaptive functions of collective paranoia. There are several ways in which the psychological processes associated with paranoid cognitions (i.e., heightened vigilance, self-consciousness, and rumination) may have adaptive consequences, especially for groups who are relatively disadvantaged with respect to their power or status within a social hierarchy. First, as noted, distrust is not always irrational. In the competition for scarce resources and attempt to gain social power, groups are almost certain to encounter other groups who wish to hold them back, rival groups who seek to displace them, and/or less powerful but equally ambitious groups seeking to curry favor or mislead them. Thus, although the fears and suspicions of some groups may sometimes seem exaggerated to outsiders, this does not mean that their distrust is necessarily without foundation or foolish. The expression, "Just because you're paranoid doesn't mean they *aren't* out to get you," often contains more than a kernel of truth.

When viewed from this perspective, psychological processes such as vigilance and rumination may be quite functional. In much the same way that defensive pessimism contributes to a form of adaptive preparedness when individuals anticipate challenging events (Norem & Cantor, 1986), so might paranoid cognitions help individuals maintain their motivation to overcome perceived dangers and obstacles within their social environments (even when those dangers and obstacles seem misplaced or inflated from the perspective of more neutral observers). Moderate levels of social paranoia, including a tendency toward hypervigilant and ruminative information processing, might help individuals make sense of the social situations they are in and help them determine appropriate forms of adaptive response.

ACKNOWLEDGMENTS

We are grateful to Bill Barnett, Jim Baron, Joe Bauman, Jane Dutton, Alice Isen, John Levine, Joanne Martin, Michael Morris, and Jeff Pfeffer for their thoughtful comments provided at various stages in the development of these ideas. We especially thank Chester Insko, John Schopler, and Constantine Sedikides for their extensive and constructive feedback on this chapter.

REFERENCES

Ashford, S. J. (1989). Self-assessments in organizations: A literature review and integrative model. In L. L. Cummings & B. M. Staw (Eds.), *Research in organizational behavior* (Vol. 11, pp. 133–174). Greenwich, CT: JAI.

Ashforth, B. E., & Mael, F. (1989). Social identity theory and the organization. *Academy of Management Review, 14,* 20–39.

Barber, B. (1983). *The logic and limits of trust.* New Brunswick, NJ: Rutgers University Press.

Bies, R. J. (1987). The predicament of injustice: The management of moral outrage. In L. L. Cummings & B. M. Staw (Eds.), *Research in organizational behavior* (Vol. 9, pp. 289–319). Greenwich, CT: JAI.

Bies, R. J., Tripp, T. M., & Kramer, R. M. (1996). At the breaking point: Cognitive and social dynamics of revenge in organizations. In J. Greenberg & R. Giacalone (Eds.), *Antisocial behavior in organizations.* Thousand Oaks, CA: Sage.

Blake, R. R., & Mouton, J. (1986). From theory to practice in interface problem solving. In S. Worchel & W. G. Austin (Eds.), *Psychology of intergroup relations (2nd ed., pp. 67–87). Chicago: Nelson-Hall.

Boyle, R., & Bonacich, P. (1970). The development of trust and mistrust in mixed-motives games. *Sociometry, 33,* 123–139.

Brewer, M. B. (1979). In-group bias in the minimal intergroup situation: A cognitive-motivational analysis. *Psychological Bulletin, 86,* 307–324.

Brewer, M. B. (1981). Ethnocentrism and its role in interpersonal trust. In M. B. Brewer & B. E. Collins (Eds.), *Scientific inquiry and the social sciences* (pp. 345–360). San Francisco: Jossey-Bass.

Brewer, M. B. (1996). In-group favoritism: The subtle side of intergroup discrimination. In D. M. Messick & A. Tenbrunsel (Eds.), *Codes of Conduct* (pp. 160–170). New York: Russell Sage.

Brewer, M. B., & Campbell, D. T. (1976). *Ethnocentrism and intergroup attitudes: East African evidence.* New York: Halsted.

Brewer, M. B., & Kramer, R. M. (1985). Intergroup relations. *Annual Review of Psychology, 36,* 219–243.

Brewer, M. B., & Silver, M. (1978). Ingroup bias as a function of task characteristics. *European Journal of Social Psychology, 8,* 393–400.

Brown, J. (1986). Evaluation of self and others: Self-enhancement biases in social judgment. *Social Cognition, 4,* 343–353.

Brown, J. D. (1991). Accuracy and bias in self-knowledge. In C. R. Snyder & D. F. Forsyth (Eds.), *Handbook of social and clinical psychology: The health perspective* (pp. 158–178). New York: Pergamon.

Brown, J. D. (1995). Truth and consequences: The costs and benefits of accurate self-knowledge. *Personality and Social Psychology Bulletin 21,* 1288–1298.

Buss, D. M., & Scheier, M. F. (1976). Self-consciousness, self-awareness, and self-attribution. *Journal of Research in Personality, 10,* 463–468.

Cameron, N. (1943). The development of paranoiac thinking. *Psychological Review, 50,* 219–233.

Campbell, D. T. (1975). On the conflict between biological and social evolution and between psychology and moral tradition. *American Psychologist, 30,* 1103–1126.

Colby, K. M. (1981). Modeling a paranoid mind. *The Behavioral and Brain Sciences, 4,* 515–560.

Cota, A. A., & Dion, K. L. (1986). Salience of gender and sex composition of ad hoc groups: An experimental test of distinctiveness theory. *Journal of Personality and Social Psychology, 50,* 770–776.

Dawes, R. (1988). *Rational choice in an uncertain world.* New York: Harcourt Brace.

Dawes, R. M., Singer, D., & Lemons, F. (1972). An experimental analysis of the contrast effect and its implications for intergroup communication and the indirect assessment of attitude. *Journal of Personality and Social Psychology, 21,* 281–295.

Deutsch, M. (1973). *The resolution of conflict.* New Haven, CT: Yale University Press.

Fenigstein, A. (1979). Self-consciousness, self-attention, and social interaction. *Journal of Personality and Social Psychology, 37,* 75–86.

Fenigstein, A. (1984). Self-consciousness and self as target. *Journal of Personality and Social Psychology, 47,* 860–870.

Fenigstein, A., & Vanable, P. A. (1992). Paranoia and self-consciousness. *Journal of Personality and Social Psychology, 62,* 129–138.

Fein, S., & Hilton, J. L. (1994). Judging others in the shadow of suspicion. *Motivation and Emotion, 18,* 167–198.

Fiske, S., & Taylor, S. (1991). *Social cognition* (2nd ed.). New York: Random House.

Fiske, S. T. (1993). Controlling other people: The impact of power on stereotypes. *American Psychologist*, 48, 621-628.

Gambetta, D. (1987). *Trust: Making and breaking cooperative relations*. New York: Oxford University Press.

Hamilton, D. L. (1981). *Cognitive processes in stereotyping and intergroup behavior*. Hillsdale, NJ: Lawrence Erlbaum Associates.

Heider, F. (1958). *The psychology of interpersonal relations*. Hillsdale, NJ: Lawrence Erlbaum Associates.

Hill, L. A. (1992). *Becoming a manager*. Cambridge, MA: Harvard Business School.

Hilton, J. L., Fein, S., & Miller, D. T. (1993). Suspicion and dispositional inference. *Personality and Social Psychology Bulletin*, 19, 501-512.

Holmes, J. G. (1991). Trust and appraisal in close relationships. *Advances in Personal Relationships*, 2, 57-104.

Janis, I. L. (1989). *Crucial decisions*. New York: The Free Press.

Janoff-Bulman, R. (1992). *Shattered assumptions: Towards a new psychology of trauma*. New York: The Free Press.

Kahn, R. L., & Kramer, R. M. (1990). Untying the knot: De-escalatory processes in international conflict. In R. L. Kahn & M. N. Zald (Eds.), *Organizations and nation-states: New perspectives on conflict and cooperation* (pp. 139-180). San Francisco: Jossey-Bass.

Kanter, R. (1977a). *Men and women of the corporation*. New York: Basic Books.

Kanter, R. (1977b). Some effects of proportions on group life: Skewed sex rations and responses to token women. *American Journal of Sociology*, 82, 965-990.

Kelley, H. H. (1973). Causal schemata and the attribution process. *American Psychologist*, 28, 107-123.

Kramer, R. M. (1994). The sinister attribution error: Origins and consequences of collective paranoia. *Motivation and Emotion*, 18, 199-230.

Kramer, R. M. (1995a). In dubious battle: Heightened accountability, dysphoric cognition, and self-defeating bargaining behavior. In R. M. Kramer & D. M. Messick (Eds.), *Negotiation in its social context* (pp.151-172). Thousand Oaks, CA: Sage.

Kramer, R. M. (1995b). Divergent realities, convergent disappointments: Trust and the intuitive auditor. In R. M. Kramer & T. R. Tyler (Eds.), *Trust in organizations* (pp. 216-245). Thousand Oaks, CA: Sage.

Kramer, R. M., & Brewer, M. B. (1986). Social group identity and the emergence of cooperation in resource conservation dilemmas. In H. Wilke, C. Rutte, & D. M. Messick (Eds.), *Experimental studies of social dilemmas* (pp. 187-233). Frankfurt, GER: Lang.

Kramer, R. M., & Tyler, T. R. (1995). *Trust in organizations*. Thousand Oaks, CA: Sage.

Latane, B., & Darley, J. M. (1968). *The unresponsive bystander*. New York: Appleton-Century-Crofts.

Lazarus, R. S., & Folkman, S. (1984). *Stress, appraisal, and coping*. New York: Springer.

Lind, E. A., & Tyler, T. R. (1988). *The social psychology of procedural justice*. New York: Plenum.

Lindskold, S. (1978). Trust development, the GRIT proposal, and the effects of conciliatory acts on conflict and cooperation. *Psychological Bulletin*, 85, 772-793.

Lindskold, S. (1986). GRIT: Reducing distrust through carefully introduced conciliation. In S. Worchel & W. G. Austin (Eds.), *Psychology of intergroup relations* (pp. 137-154). Chicago: Nelson Hall.

Lord, C. G., Lepper, M., & Ross, L. (1979). Biased assimilation and attitude polarization: The effects of prior theories on subsequently considered evidence. *Journal of Personality and Social Psychology*, 37, 2098-2109.

Lord, C. G., & Saenz, D. S. (1985). Memory deficits and memory surfeits: Differential cognitive consequences of tokenism for tokens and observers. *Journal of Personality and Social Psychology*, 49, 918-926.

Luhmann, N. (1979). *Trust and power*. New York: Wiley.

Lyubomirksy, S., & Nolen-Hoeksema, S. (1993). Self-perpetuating properties of dysphoric rumination. *Journal of Personality and Social Psychology, 65*, 339–349.

Messick, D. M., & Mackie, D. (1989). Intergroup relations. *Annual Review of Psychology, 40*, 45–81.

Messick, D. M., Wilke, H., Brewer, M. B., Kramer, R. M., Zemke, P., & Lui, L. (1983). Individual adaptations and structural changes as solutions to social dilemmas. *Journal of Personality and Social Psychology, 44*, 294–309.

Miller, G. J. (1992). *Managerial dilemmas: The political economy of hierarchies*. New York: Cambridge University Press.

Morris, M. W., & Larrick, R. P. (1995). When one cause casts doubt on another: A normative analysis of discounting in causal attribution. *Psychological Review, 102*, 331–355.

Norem, J. K., & Cantor, N. (1986). Defensive pessimism: Harnessing anxiety as motivation. *Journal of Personality and Social Psychology, 51*, 1208–1217.

Peeters, G., & Czapinski, J. (1990). Positive-negative asymmetry in evaluations: The distinction between affective and informational negativity effects. *European Review of Social Psychology, 1*, 33–60.

Pemberton, M. J., Insko, C. A., & Schopler, J. (1996). Experience of and memory for differential distrust of individuals and groups. *Journal of Personality and Social Psychology*.

Pruitt, D. G., & Rubin, J. Z. (1986). *Social conflict: Escalation, stalemate, and settlement*. New York: Random House.

Rotter, J. B. (1980). Interpersonal trust, trustworthiness, and gullibility. *American Psychologist, 35*, 1–7.

Salancik, G. R., & Pfeffer, J. (1978). A social information processing approach to job attitudes and task design. *Administrative Science Quarterly, 23*, 224–253.

Schelling, T. C. (1958). The strategy of conflict: Prospectus for a reorientation of game theory. *Journal of Conflict Resolution, 2*, 203–264.

Sedikides, C. (1993). Assessment, enhancement and verification determinants of the self-evaluation process. *Journal of Personality and Social Psychology, 65*, 317–338.

Sherif, M., Harvey, O. J., White, B. J., Hood, W. R., & Sherif, C. W. (1961). *Intergroup cooperation and competition: The Robbers' Cave Experiment*. Norman, OK: University Book Exchange.

Sitkin, S. B., & Roth, N. L. (1993). Explaining the limited effectiveness of legalistic "remedies" for trust/distrust. *Organizational Science, 4*, 367–392.

Strube, M. J., Lott, C. L., Le-Xuan-Hy, G. M., Oxenberg, J., & Deichmann, A. K. (1986). Self-evaluation of abilities: Accurate self-assessment versus biased self-enhancement. *Journal of Personality and Social Psychology, 51*, 16–25.

Strube, M. J., & Roemmele, L. A. (1985). Self-enhancement, self-assessment, and self-evaluative task choice. *Journal of Personality and Social Psychology, 49*, 981–993.

Sumner, W. G. (1906). *Folkways*. Lexington, MA: Ginn.

Swann, W., & Read, S. (1981). Self-verification processes: How we sustain our self-conceptions. *Journal of Experimental Social Psychology, 17*, 351–372.

Taylor, S. E. (1981). A categorization approach to stereotyping. In D. L. Hamilton (Ed.), *Cognitive processes in stereotyping and intergroup behavior* (pp. 83–114). Hillsdale, NJ: Lawrence Erlbaum Associates.

Taylor, S. E. (1991). Asymmetric effects of positive and negative events: The mobilization-minimization hypothesis. *Psychological Bulletin, 110*, 67–85.

Taylor, S. E., & Brown, J. D. (1988). Illusion and well-being: A social psychological perspective on mental health. *Psychological Bulletin, 103*, 193–210.

Taylor, S. E., & Brown, J. D. (1994). Positive illusions and well-being revisited: Separating fact from fiction. *Psychological Bulletin, 116*, 21–27.

Taylor, S. E., Fiske, S. T., Etcoff, N. L., & Ruderman, A. (1978). Categorical bases of person memory and stereotyping. *Journal of Personality and Social Psychology, 36*, 778–793.

Tesser, A. (1978). Self-generated attitude change. In L. Berkowitz (Ed.), *Advances in experimental social psychology* (Vol. 11, pp. 289–338). San Diego, CA: Academic Press.

Trivers, R. L. (1971). The evolution of reciprocal altruism. *Quarterly Review of Biology, 46*, 35–57.

Trope, Y. (1983). Self-assessment in achievement behavior. In J. M. Suls & A. G. Greenwald (Eds.), *Psychological perspectives on the self* (Vol. 2, pp. 93–121). Hillsdale, NJ: Lawrence Erlbaum Associates.

Trope, Y. (1986). Self-enhancement and self-assessment in achievement behavior. In R. M. Sorrentino & E. T. Higgins (Eds.), *Handbook of motivation and cognition: Foundations of social behavior* (Vol. 1, pp. 350–378). New York: Guilford.

Tsui, A. S., Egan, T. D., & O'Reilly, C. (1992). Being different: Relational demography and organizational attachment. *Administrative Science Quarterly, 37*, 549–579.

Turner, J. (1987). *Rediscovering the social group: A self-categorization theory.* Oxford, England: Basil Blackwell.

Tyler, T. R. (1993). The social psychology of authority. In J. K. Murnighan (Ed.), *Social psychology in organizations: Advances in theory and practice* (pp. 141–160). Englewood Cliffs, NJ: Prentice-Hall.

Tyler, T. R., & Lind, E. A. (1992). A relational model of authority in groups. In M. Snyder (Ed.), *Advances in experimental social psychology* (Vol. 25), pp. 115–192). New York: Academic Press.

Vorauer, J. D., & Ross, M. (1993). Making mountains out of molehills: An informational goals analysis of self- and social perception. *Personality and Social Psychology Bulletin, 19*, 620–632.

Wharton, A. S. (1992). The social construction of gender and race in organizations: A social identity and group mobilization perspective. In *Research in the sociology of organizations* (Vol. 1, pp. 55–84). Greenwich, CT: JAI.

Wilson, E. O. (1978). *On human nature.* New York: Bantam.

Wilson, T. D., & Kraft, D. (1993). Why do I love thee? Effects of repeated introspections about a dating relationship on attitudes towards the relationship. *Personality and Social Psychology Bulletin, 19*, 409–418.

Wood, J. V., & Taylor, K. L. (1991). Serving self-relevant goals through social comparison. In J. Suls & T. A. Wills (Eds.), *Social comparison: Contemporary theory and research* (pp. 101–127). Hillsdale, NJ: Lawrence Erlbaum Associates.

Zimbardo, P. G., Anderson, S. M., & Kabat, L. G. (1981). Induced hearing deficit generates experimental paranoia. *Science, 212*, 1529–1531.

11

Individuals, Groups, and Social Change: On the Relationship Between Individual and Collective Self-Interpretations and Collective Action

Bernd Simon
Westfälische Wilhelms-Universität, Münster, Germany

Divide et Impera! (Divide and Rule!). This adage suggests that everybody who has power over other people and wants to preserve that status quo should prevent those others from uniting (Apfelbaum, 1979). It also accords with the common observation that it is united individuals or, in other words, groups that are the typical agent of change in the social power structure, and not single, isolated individuals. Accordingly, social movements have been defined — from a social-psychological perspective — as "efforts by large numbers of people, who define themselves and are also often defined by others as a *group*, to solve *collectively* a problem they feel they have in *common*, and which is perceived to arise from their relations with other groups" (Tajfel, 1981, p. 244; italics added).

This chapter argues that an understanding of the social-psychological determinants of individuation and group formation is crucial for any theory of collective action and social change. The main aim here is to bring together theorizing and research from two hitherto rather strictly separated domains. These are the more social-psychologically oriented domain of group processes and intergroup relations, on the one hand, and the more sociologically oriented domain of social movement participation, on the other hand (for a similar attempt, see Kelly, 1993). Such an approach is especially intriguing because it combines social psychologists' expertise in the field of intergroup cognition (e.g., categorization and stereotyping) with social movement researchers' expertise in the field of actual intergroup behavior (e.g., social movement participation).

The focus of the present chapter is on people, who by virtue of their membership in some group or social category find themselves in a low-status (subordinated or dominated) segment within the wider social context. Membership in low-status groups leads—in addition to objective or material disadvantages—also to a psychological predicament, in that it is incompatible with a positive self-concept and thus poses a threat to one's self-respect (Tajfel & Turner, 1986). Consequently, members of low-status groups face, among others, the psychological problem of low self-respect, and should be motivated to search for adequate solutions. Hypothetically, solutions can range from individual strategies of social mobility to collective strategies of social change. The former rests on the person's belief "that he can improve in important ways his position in a social situation, or more generally move from one social position to another, *as an individual*" (Tajfel, 1981, p. 246; italics in the original). Thus, social mobility strategies aim to leave a low-status—hence, unattractive ingroup physically or at least psychologically. In contrast, social change strategies should be adopted to the extent that a person believes that "the only way for him to change these [disadvantageous] conditions (. . .) is *together with his group as a whole*" (Tajfel, 1981, p. 247; italics added). Social change strategies include such "classic" militant forms of intergroup behavior or collective action as revolts and strikes, but also more moderate forms such as signing a petition or attending a group meeting.

Following Tajfel (1981; Tajfel & Turner, 1986), this chapter builds on the premise that a person's preference for either individual (social mobility) strategies or collective (social change) strategies depends on his or her self-interpretation as either a unique individual (the individual self) or an interchangeable group member (the collective self). Therefore, the first major part of this chapter elaborates on the distinction between the individual self and the collective self, as well as their social-cognitive determinants. The second part then deals more directly with a particular form of intergroup behavior or collective action—namely, social movement participation.

ON THE DISTINCTION BETWEEN THE INDIVIDUAL SELF AND THE COLLECTIVE SELF

It has long been acknowledged, by both lay persons and social scientists, that people behave differently in interpersonal settings than in collective or group settings. There is indeed ample empirical evidence for what appears to be a "discontinuity" between the perception and behavior of people acting as individuals, on the one hand and the perception and behavior of people acting as group members, on the other hand (e.g., R. W. Brown, 1954; R. J. Brown & Turner, 1981; Schopler & Insko, 1992). Accordingly, the relationship between the individual and the group has been declared a "master problem" of social psychology (F. Allport, 1962; R. J. Brown & Turner, 1981).

In dealing with this master problem, Tajfel and Turner (1979, 1986) initiated a most influential approach that was first known as social identity theory (Tajfel & Turner, 1979) and was later further developed into self-categorization theory (Turner, Hogg, Oakes, Reicher, & Wetherell, 1987). The social identity or self-categorization approach has directed researchers' attention to the role of self-interpretation processes in mediating the transition from individual (interpersonal) perception and behavior to collective or group perception and behavior, and vice versa. A key element of that approach is the distinction between personal identity or the individual self, on the one hand, and social identity or the collective self, on the other hand (Turner, Oakes, Haslam, & McGarty, 1994). The individual self and the collective self have been conceptualized as two different forms of self-interpretation, with each being responsible for particular types of perceptual and behavioral phenomena. Representing self-interpretation as a unique individual, the individual self is viewed as the psychological basis of individual phenomena (i.e., patterns of perception and behavior characterized by interindividual variation). The collective self refers to self-interpretation at a higher level of abstraction or inclusiveness, which implies depersonalization of individual self-perception (e.g., Simon & Hamilton, 1994). In other words, the collective self represents self-interpretation as an interchangeable group member, and is viewed as the psychological basis for collective or group phenomena (that is, patterns of perception and behavior characterized by interindividual uniformity).

From such a perspective, the occurrence of individual and group phenomena then depends on the relative weighting of the individual self and the collective self in people's self-concepts. That is, the likelihood of individual phenomena (e.g., individual social mobility or "exit") increases relative to the likelihood of group phenomena (e.g., social movement participation or "voice"), to the extent that the individual self has stronger impact on people's current self-concepts than the collective self, and vice versa (as to the distinction between "exit" and "voice," see Tajfel, 1981).

A Self-Aspect Model of the Individual and Collective Selves

The analysis presented in this chapter is deeply rooted within the social identity or self-categorization approach (Tajfel & Turner, 1979, 1986;

Turner et al., 1987). Still, a modified conceptualization of the individual self and collective self is presented here, which goes beyond earlier conceptualizations in several respects. Most important among these are the implications that follow from the self-aspect model (SAM) proposed later for the relationship between the individual self and the collective self in modern society (for a more detailed description, see Simon, 1997; Simon & Mummendey, 1997).

A basic premise of the model is that people engage in self-interpretation, which refers to the cognitive process whereby a person gives meaning to his or her own experiences, including the reactions of his or her social environment toward him or her. Through self-interpretation, people achieve an understanding of themselves or, in other words, a self-concept, which in turn influences their subsequent perception and behavior. The individual self and the collective self are conceptualized as two different variants of self-interpretation. The individual self stands for self-interpretation as a unique individual ("I" or "me"), whereas the collective self stands for self-interpretation as an interchangeable group member ("we" or "us"). The individual self and the collective self can, among other variants of self-interpretation, determine a person's phenomenal or working self-concept (Markus & Kunda, 1986; Sherman, Judd, & Park, 1989). Before the individual self and collective self can be defined more precisely, another concept needs to be introduced — namely, the concept of "self-aspect."

Borrowing from Linville (1985, 1987), a *self-aspect* is viewed here as a cognitive category or concept that serves to process information and organize knowledge about the own person. Self-aspects can refer, among others, to generalized psychological characteristics or traits (e.g., introverted), physical features (e.g., red hair), roles (e.g., father), abilities (e.g., bilingual), tastes (e.g., preference for strawberry ice cream), attitudes (e.g., against the death penalty), and explicit group or category membership (e.g., member of the communist party). The development of self-aspects is a function of a person's experiences in various social roles, relationships, and situations.[1] Moreover, each self-aspect can be experienced as socially shared, and therefore has the potential to define a social category or group membership. As argued at great length elsewhere (Simon, 1997), there is no reason to assume that social categories are defined with reference to specific "social" types of self-aspects (e.g., nationality, gender, race). In fact, all

---

[1]There is clearly some overlap between the concepts of self-aspect and self-schema (Markus, 1977). However, according to Markus (1977), self-schemas develop only for such self-aspects that a person ascribes to the self to an extreme degree, and that at the same time are highly important to the person. Thus, all self-schemas are based on self-aspects, but not every self-aspect develops into a self-schema. In this sense, the notion of self-aspect represents the more general concept.

self-aspects are social, in that they acquire their meaning and significance only within a context of social relations among people. Self-aspects are never absolute features of an isolated monad, but always relational features (e.g., "young" versus "old") of interdependent social beings. More important, for each self-aspect, it is possible that, under appropriate social conditions, the fact that it is shared with other people can become relevant, and thus lay the foundation for meaningful social categorization. Take, for example, the self-aspect "wearing glasses." It does not need too much social-scientific sophistication to assume that, for most readers to whom this self-aspect applies, "wearing glasses" is not a likely platform for the perception of socially significant similarities (and differences). But now imagine that all people who wear glasses were suddenly singled out for the same special treatment (perhaps because they were considered literate and therefore dangerous). The situation would change dramatically. "Wearing glasses" would suddenly constitute a socially significant similarity (and "not wearing glasses" a socially significant difference), and thus provide the basis for meaningful group membership. In such a situation, all other self-aspects that are not related to "wearing glasses" would lose in importance. A collective self as "people who wear glasses" would be likely to dominate the working self-concept of people possessing the respective self-aspect.

Applying the concept of self-aspect as introduced here, the concepts of individual and collective self can now be defined more precisely. A collective self is activated whenever people interpret their own experiences, perceptions, and behaviors, as well as the (re)actions of other people toward them primarily in terms of a particular self-aspect they share with other (but not all other) people in the relevant social context. That is, a collective self is a specific self-interpretation that is centered on a single dominant, socially shared self-aspect (e.g., "First and foremost, I am a communist"). At this point, it should then also become evident that it is somewhat misleading to speak of *the* collective self. At least hypothetically, a person can have as many different collective *selves* as he or she has different self-aspects, as each self-aspect can provide the criterion for meaningful social self-categorization under appropriate social conditions.[2]

However, the individual self should be activated to the extent that self-interpretations are based on a more comprehensive set or configuration of different (i.e., independent or nonredundant) self-aspects (e.g., "I am female, a physician, extraverted, politically active, a mother, have red hair, etc."). The more comprehensive that set, the more complex that configuration, and the less likely it is that another person possesses the identical set of aspects (see also Simmel, 1955). Consequently, activation of the indi-

---

[2]In a similar vein, James (1910) argued that a person has "as many different social selves as there are distinct groups of persons about whose opinion he cares" (p. 294).

vidual self implies that one's own uniqueness moves into the foreground. Note that, as with the collective self, a person can have more than just one individual self. Different subconfigurations or subsets of the entire ensemble of possible self-aspects may be processed and used for self-interpretation in different situations. Accordingly, it is also justified to speak of different individual selves of a person.

Finally, it should be reiterated that it is not argued here that the individual self and the collective self are based on inherently different types of self-aspects. On the contrary, the same self-aspect (e.g., "German") can provide the basis for a collective self at one time ("We, the Germans"), whereas at another time it may be construed as simply one component, among many others, of the individual self ("I am a psychologist, male, German, have brown eyes, etc."). In other words, there is no difference in the quality of the self-aspects as such, but a difference in the function they serve in the particular social context. For example, during a soccer game between the Netherlands and Germany, the self-aspect "German" is likely to function as a social category of which one is a member together with about 80 million other people. However, during a job interview, this self-aspect represents one of many features, the ensemble of which represents one as a unique individual (i.e., one's individual self). The distinction between the individual self and the collective self is therefore not so much a distinction in terms of the content of one's self-interpretation as one in terms of its structure or complexity.

Self-Interpretation and Social Context

From an ontological point of view, there is certainly no reason to grant a priori either the individual self (selves) or the collective self (selves) a privileged position (i.e., greater weight) in people's working self-concepts. Neither of these two major variants of self-interpretation can be regarded as intrinsically and invariably more valid or authentic than the other. Both reflect accentuation processes. The individual self is grounded in an accentuation of intrapersonal relative to interpersonal similarities, whereas the collective self is grounded in an accentuation of intragroup relative to intergroup similarities (for an excellent discussion of this issue, see Oakes, Haslam, & Turner, 1994).

From a phenomenological point of view, it must be acknowledged that the individual self and the collective self can indeed be *experienced* as differentially valid or authentic. This differential experience or relative weighting of the individual self and the collective self in people's working self-concepts is by no means arbitrary. It can systematically be tied to the social context, both at the macro- and microlevels.

At the macrolevel, sociological theory and research indicates that, in the course of modernization (conceptualized as functional differentiation), traditional collectives (e.g., social class, ethnicity, family) lose their capacity to sustain close social ties among people (Beck, 1994; Esser, 1988; Schimank, 1985; see also Marx, 1978; Weber, 1978). Collectives or social circles intersect to a greater extent—they become increasingly permeable and lose in permanence. Consequently, the social fabric, and thus the system of social coordinates necessary to locate each person, increases in complexity (Elias, 1988; Simmel, 1955). Because "a complexly differentiated and organized society requires a parallel view of the self" (Stryker & Serpe, 1982, p. 206), one important outcome of modernization is individualization of self-interpretation. In other words, the complex social positioning of the own person in modern society results in a correspondingly complex matrix of self-aspects thereby expanding the basis for the individual self. In his sociohistorical analysis of changes in people's self-concepts, Elias (1988, 1990) identified such a trend toward an increasing prepotency of the individual self ("I-identity") relative to the collective self ("we-identity").

So far, this macrolevel analysis suggests that, in modern society, "the general climate" favors the individual self. This conclusion also accords with much social-psychological theorizing and data on the self originating in Western societies (Markus & Kitayama, 1991; Triandis, 1989). Interestingly, the phenomenal prepotency of the individual self is also reflected in an assumption that underlies much current research on social stereotyping. That is the assumption that the individual self and its consequences represent some kind of objective standard against which to judge the validity or accuracy of the collective self and its various consequences, including social stereotyping (e.g., Judd & Park, 1993; for a critique of this assumption, see Oakes et al., 1994; Oakes & Reynolds, 1997). The fact that this assumption is widely shared within the mainstream of (Western) social psychology can be seen as evidence for the powerful impact of the "general climate" explicated earlier.

Metaphorically speaking, both research participants and researchers are fish in the same ocean, and both take the water for granted. Both research participants and researchers tend to take for granted the general climate prevailing in their common habitat. Yet there is also life outside that habitat, and it is equally valid and authentic. What is more, even within the same habitat and the same general climate, there are variable "weather conditions." It is the impact that these "weather conditions" exert, against the backdrop of the "general climate," on self-interpretation to which this chapter now turns. More specifically, it explores how, on the microlevel, the immediate social context influences the relative weighting of the individual self and the collective self in modern society.

Some Social Contextual Determinants of the Individual and Collective Selves

Although it is assumed here that modern society favors the individual self over the collective self, this is not to say that the collective self has simply been rendered obsolete in modern society. Both real-life examples and research tell us that this is not the case. People do not always act solely in terms of their individual selves. They also act in terms of their collective selves under specifiable circumstances because modern society is not void of opportunities for self-interpretation in terms of collective selves. In fact, as modern society gives access to additional (nonredundant) self-aspects, and because each self-aspect can at least hypothetically provide the basis for a collective self, the number of potential or latent collective selves increases. At the same time, however, the ensuing pluralism of potential collective selves makes each of them rather fragile, and allows the activation of each particular collective self only within the limits of specific social conditions.

Quite a body of social-psychological research conducted mainly within the framework of self-categorization theory is now available; it demonstrates the role of social contextual variables in determining when a collective self (and which) supersedes the individual self, at least temporarily (e.g., Simon & Hamilton, 1994; Simon, Pantaleo, & Mummendey, 1995; Turner et al., 1994). Some of that research is discussed in more detail here because it is directly relevant to the question of whether or when members of low-status or unattractive groups will interpret themselves as group members rather than as individuals. The specific focus is on three social contextual variables — namely, group status or attractiveness, relative group size, and common fate. These variables are also directly relevant to social movement research because many, if not all, social movements are rooted in or start out as minority groups, either in terms of numbers or social status or both (e.g., the civil rights movement, the women's movement, or the gay and lesbian movement). Similarly, the experience or construction of common fate (e.g., shared experience of unjust treatment) is another important social-psychological antecedent of social movement participation (Ferree & Miller, 1985; Neidhardt & Rucht, 1993; Tajfel, 1981).

Group Status.   Group membership is rarely, if ever, value-free. Groups are embedded in a structured system of intergroup relations, in which some groups hold higher status positions than others. Consequently, different groups (and the respective memberships) have different value connotations, and therefore different attractiveness. Following the social identity or self-categorization approach (Tajfel & Turner, 1986; Turner et al., 1987), people strive to maintain or achieve a positive self-concept (or, more fundamentally, positive self-esteem). As value connotations associated with one's group memberships impact on the positivity or negativity of one's self-concept, positive value connotations should increase and negative value connotations should decrease the positivity of the self-concept. Thus, the collective self should be more acceptable if the value connotations associated with the particular ingroup are positive rather than negative. In more general terms, people should be more willing to engage in collective self-interpretations and view themselves as interchangeable group members, to the extent that the particular group membership is (based on) a positively valenced self-aspect. If the critical self-aspect (group membership) is negatively valenced, however, self-interpretation as a unique individual (the individual self) should be more likely because it dilutes the impact of the unattractive self-aspect (group membership).

There exists a body of empirical evidence that supports these assumptions. For example, in a series of studies, Simon et al. (1995) predicted and found that the relative emphasis on the individual or collective self varied systematically as a function of the value connotations associated with group membership. In the first two studies, the critical value connotations were manipulated simply by asking participants to list either positively or negatively valenced attributes that they thought were typical of their fellow ingroup members (i.e., their compatriots), as well as of themselves. Accentuation of perceived intragroup similarities (i.e., higher estimates of within-ingroup and self-ingroup similarities) relative to differences served as an indicator of the collective self. De-accentuation (i.e., lower estimates) of intragroup similarities relative to differences was viewed as indicative of the individual self. As expected, the emphasis on the collective self relative to the individual self increased when value connotations (of temporarily accessible ingroup attributes) were positive as opposed to negative. Similar, although somewhat weaker, results were found in a third study, in which the impact of the more stable or chronic attractiveness of membership in two real-life groups (i.e., gay men vs. straight men) was examined (see also Jackson, Sullivan, Harnish, & Hodge, 1996).

So far, these results do not allow one to formulate a favorable prognosis as to the chances of low-status groups to provide its members with an adequate basis for collective self-interpretation, and thus collective action. It appears that low-status, and thus negatively valenced, group membership is not conducive to the establishment of a collective self. However, there is some other research that suggests that this conclusion needs to be qualified in some interesting way. Before turning to that research, I need to highlight that the dependent measures used by Simon et al. (1995) contained some reference to the participants as individual persons (e.g., "How much do you agree? 'In many respects, I am like most of my compatriots.' "). It is possible that such reference (further) increased the accessibility of the individual self so that it was readily available as an alternative form of self-interpretation when needed (i.e., when group membership was carrying negative value connotations).

That interpretation was supported in an experiment conducted most recently (Simon & Hastedt, in press, Experiment 1). That experiment also investigated the impact of value connotations (positive vs. negative) associated with group membership on the emphasis people put on the collective self relative to the individual self. As a basis for collective self-categorization, after careful pretesting, we selected participants' preference for urban life ("prefer to live in the city") or rural life ("prefer to live in the country"). Value connotations associated with group membership were manipulated using the Simon et al. (1995) attribute-listing procedure described earlier. The main dependent measure was derived from an adaptation of Taylor, Fiske, Etcoff, and Ruderman's (1978) error rate paradigm (see also van Knippenberg, van Twuyver, & Pepels, 1994). Participants first read 12 statements together with the alleged speakers' names and group memberships (i.e., preference for urban or rural life). Subsequently, each statement was presented again without the speaker's name, and participants had to pick the correct speaker from a list with the names and group memberships of all 12 speakers. The material used in this memory task was carefully pretested. It ensured equal levels of attractiveness and intragroup similarity for both ingroup and outgroup, and a sufficient overall (normative and comparative) fit between content of statements and group membership (see Oakes, Turner, & Haslam, 1991). As an indicator of the collective self, the number of confusion errors within the ingroup was used. This measure reflects how often participants ascribed a statement allegedly made by an ingroup member erroneously to another ingroup member. Therefore, it is directly indicative of the degree to which ingroup members were seen or remembered as interchangeable (Brewer, Weber, & Carini, 1995). Before turning to the results, two more pieces of information need to be provided.

First, it should be emphasized that this memory task did not contain any direct reference to the participants as individual persons. In fact, it did not contain any reference to the own person at all. This "remoteness" ensured that the individual self was not made particularly accessible. Second, to examine the influence of the accessibility of the individual self more directly, a second independent variable was introduced. Besides the value connotations associated with group membership, we also manipulated whether participants were led to think about themselves individually before data collection. This was accomplished by administering a free-format self-description task before the memory task or not. Remember, the memory task did not contain any direct reference to the own individual person, but ample information as to whether the stimulus persons shared or did not share group membership with self. Moreover, there was a reasonable fit between group membership and content of statements, so that categorization into ingroup and outgroup was indeed meaningful (Oakes, Turner, & Haslam, 1991). This offset any gross accessibility advantage of the individual self relative to the collective self, at least as long as participants were not led to think about their own individuality (i.e., their various self-aspects) by the experimenter's instruction to describe themselves. When a self-description task preceded the memory task, however, the situation more closely resembled that in Simon et al. (1995, Studies 1 and 2); hence, these findings were expected to be replicated. However, without prior self-description (i.e., when the individual self was less accessible as an alternative self-interpretation), negative value connotations were expected to be less likely to undermine the collective self.

Our major hypothesis was confirmed by a significant interaction between the two independent variables — value connotations and accessibility of individual self (i.e., insertion of self-description task). Given high accessibility of the individual self (insertion of self-description before the memory task), more within-ingroup errors were found when value connotations associated with group membership were positive than when they were negative (4.1 vs. 3.5), thus replicating the Simon et al. (1995, Studies 1 and 2) findings. Given low accessibility of the individual self (no prior self-description), however, that difference was not only reduced, but reversed (3.4 vs. 3.9).

Because both differences were only marginally significant, these findings have to be interpreted cautiously. Nevertheless, they do suggest that positive value connotations or high-group status are not the *conditio sine qua non* of collective self-interpretation. Instead, there may exist circumstances under which even members of low-status groups emphasize the collective self and regard group solidarity ("closing ranks"), and not individual separation from the group or social mobility, as the more viable coping strategy (see also Doosje, Ellemers, & Spears, 1995). One could speculate that members of low-status groups rely more on the collective self and group-level coping strategies, when they have or believe to have additional resources at their disposal that could compensate for their status disadvantage. For instance, it is possible that people think there is "strength" or "safety" in numbers (Sachdev & Bourhis, 1984; Sherif, 1966; Simon, 1992; see also Taylor & Brown, 1988). Although relative group size was not manipulated, and in fact not even mentioned in the experiment just discussed, people often overestimate the size of their ingroup relative to that of the outgroup (Simon & Mummendey, 1990; see also Ross, Greene, & House, 1977). Thus, one possibility is that research participants assigned to low-status groups may have implicitly assumed that their ingroup was in a majority position vis-à-vis the outgroup. Therefore, they may have found the collective self derived from low-status group membership more acceptable, at least as long as the individual self was not an immediately accessible alternative (i.e., when no self-description preceded the memory task). These considerations are certainly speculative and need more direct empirical testing in future. Still, they point to an intriguing interactive impact on self-interpretation of relative group size and group status. This interaction is discussed more systematically in the following section.

The Interaction Between Relative Group Size and Group Status.   The preceding section focused primarily on group status (or value connotations associated with group membership). In real life, however, intergroup contexts, and especially those in which social movements emerge, are typically characterized by both status and size asymmetries (Farley, 1982; Tajfel, 1981). Consequently, the joint influence of those asymmetries on individual and collective self-interpretation is now discussed.

Ellemers, Doosje, van Knippenberg, and Wilke (1992) compared the attractiveness of low- and high-status minority and majority groups. They found that a minority ingroup with high status was more attractive than a minority ingroup with low status, whereas high- and low- status majority ingroups did not differ in attractiveness. Similarly, Simon and Hamilton (1994, Experiment 2) found that (collective) self-categorization and self-stereotyping on ingroup attributes were more pronounced in high-status than in low-status minority groups. For majority groups, the respective status effects were not significant. The pattern of means actually revealed a slight reversal, such that members of low-status majorities self-categorized and self-stereotyped slightly more than members of high-status majorities (see Simon & Hamilton, 1994, Figs. 1 and 2). Interestingly, this reversal was most clearly visible on those measures that contained no direct reference to the participant as an individual person (i.e., on the ingroup homogeneity measure; see Simon & Hamilton, 1994, Table 2).

The latter observation is clearly in line with the interpretation of Simon and Hastedt's (in press, Experiment 1) findings discussed in the preceding section. Again, it appears that low-status group membership is not neces-sarily incompatible with an emphasis on the collective self. Low-status group members may indeed emphasize their collective self, provided they can rely on the strength of their group in term of numbers (size), and the individual self is not an immediately accessible alternative.

This interpretation was further substantiated in an additional experiment by Simon and Hastedt (in press, Experiment 2). The paradigm in the prior experiment was used (Simon & Hastedt, in press, Experiment 1). More specifically, the identical memory task was used. This time, however, the experimental design included relative group size (minority vs. majority ingroup) as a third independent variable in addition to value connotations associated with group membership (positive vs. negative) and accessibility of the individual self (low vs. high). Relative group size was manipulated by providing participants with false feedback as to the numbers (percentages) of people sharing or not sharing their preference for urban or rural life. All independent variables were manipulated between participants. It is again the number of within-ingroup errors in the memory task that is the relevant dependent measure here.

Overall, the three-way interaction was statistically significant. More important, the simple interaction between relative group size and value connotations was highly significant when accessibility of the individual self was low (no prior self-description). As expected, the number of within-ingroup errors then indicated that minority group members placed greater emphasis on the collective self when the value connotations associated with their group membership were positive as opposed to negative (3.7 vs. 2.6). But the opposite was true for majority members (2.5 vs. 3.5). Both simple effects were significant. Given high accessibility of the individual self (with prior self-description), only a significant main effect of value connotations was obtained. In that condition, all group members placed greater emphasis on the collective self when value connotations were positive than when they were negative, irrespective of group size (3.8 vs. 3.1).

In summary, one context has been identified in which group members placed greater emphasis on a collective self derived from a negatively connoted group membership than on one derived from a positively connoted group membership. It is a situation in which group members can rely on the strength of their group in terms of numbers, and in which the individual self is not an immediately accessible self-interpretation alternative. However, the latter specification indicates that, even for members of low-status majorities, the collective self (or group solidarity) may be rather fragile, especially in modern individualistic societies. The collective self seems to evaporate as soon as the individual self is in sight (or comes to mind) as an alternative self-interpretation. Turning to minority groups, prior work showed that cognitive salience or accessibility factors may prompt members of numerical minorities to interpret themselves in terms of their collective self (Mullen, 1991; Sedikides & Skowronski, 1991; Simon & Hamilton, 1994). But the present results suggest that minority members may be eager to reject collective self-interpretations as soon as status inferiority comes into play. Under such circumstances, minority membership may simply be too risky so that the individual self is eagerly accentuated instead (see also Simon, Glässner-Bayerl, & Stratenwerth, 1991; Simon et al., 1995, Study 3).

So far, this social-psychological analysis does not permit a favorable prognosis for low-status groups in general, and low-status minority groups in particular, as to the chances of providing their members with an acceptable collective self. A similarly unfavorable prognosis should then result as to the willingness of people to participate in (collective actions of) social movements to the extent that those movements are associated with low-status (minority) groups. Certainly one important reason for these unfavorable prognoses is that, in modern individualistic societies, the individual self emerges as a likely alternative to the collective self. This alternative is especially eagerly embraced when the collective self is socially devalued, and hence unattractive. Individual social mobility should be particularly appealing as a coping strategy under such circumstances. Still, it cannot be denied that people feel, think, and act in terms of socially devalued or unattractive collective selves (Tajfel, 1981). People join social movements even when they entail socially devalued collective selves (e.g., the gay and lesbian movement; see Adam, 1987; Taylor & Whittier, 1992). To be sure, not all people do so all the time, but enough people do so some of the time to warrant further investigation.

Writing on the social psychology of minorities, Tajfel (1981) suggested that even members of low-status minority groups often come to interpret themselves in terms of a collective self. Most likely, that would be the case not because they freely choose to do so, but because they are denied an individual self, even in modern societies. Instead, a collective self is thrust on them by virtue of their collective or common fate. The next section focuses on that factor.

Common Fate.   No one is an island; how we are seen and treated by others impacts on how we see ourselves (Mead, 1934). A group of people may thus come to see each other as one (i.e., as interchangeable) because they are treated as one. In other words, "a common identity is thrust upon a category of people because they are at the receiving end of certain attitudes and treatment from the 'outside' " (Tajfel, 1981, p. 315). Members of stigmatized minorities (e.g., Jews, African Americans, gays) may be a case in point. It has indeed been argued that what may be construed as a common (say Jewish, African-American, or gay) identity (e.g., similar lifestyles, shared attributes) reflects and/or developed to a large extent as a response to the common or categorical treatment of members of stigmatized groups by the outside world (e.g., G. Allport, 1979; Simon et al., 1991). In a nutshell, common treatment or common fate may breed common identity.

Building on these insights, Simon et al. (1995, Study 4) hypothesized that gay men would view themselves in terms of their collective self to the extent that they are (made) aware of their ingroup as the recipient of special treatment by the outside world (i.e., the heterosexual majority). This should be so because awareness of such treatment highlights common fate, and thus provides a meaningful basis for collective self-interpretation. Simon et al. (1995, Study 4) manipulated awareness of special treatment of the ingroup experimentally by asking gay men either to recall pertinent episodes (e.g., episodes of hostile treatment) or simply to answer some irrelevant filler questions. In addition, the effect of the quality of the treatment inflicted on the ingroup was examined. In one treatment condition, participants were instructed to recall a situation in which gays encountered hostile treatment, whereas participants in another condition were to recall a situation in which gays were treated in a particularly friendly and fair way. It was expected that a hostile treatment of gay men relative to a friendly treatment would further promote the emphasis on the collective self because the threatening nature of hostile treatment would muster additional feelings of solidarity among ingroup members. Accentuation of perceived intragroup similarities versus differences (i.e., the extent to which estimates of within-ingroup and self-ingroup similarities exceeded estimates of corresponding differences) served as the main dependent variable. Increasing emphasis on the collective self relative to the individual self was expected to manifest itself as an increase of perceived intragroup similarities relative to differences (and vice versa).

The results confirm the main hypothesis. When not made aware of their ingroup as the recipient of special treatment by the outside world (no treatment condition), gay participants clearly accentuated intragroup differences relative to intragroup similarities. In other words, they stressed their individual selves. However, that tendency was significantly reduced or even (nonsignificantly) reversed when participants were made aware of special treatment of their ingroup. Interestingly, the quality of the treatment (hostile vs. friendly) did not influence the tendency of gay men to view themselves in terms of their individual or collective self. The collective self was not further accentuated by an additional "solidarity effect" in the hostile treatment condition. Further inspection of the data suggests that the failure to find such a solidarity effect may have been due to reduced personal involvement in the hostile treatment condition. Only a minority of the participants in that condition reported that they had experienced the recalled incident personally, whereas in the friendly treatment condition all participants except one had recalled a personal experience.

Still, considering the rather modest strength of the experimental manipulation employed by Simon et al. (1995, Study 4), the results are quite encouraging. They demonstrate that awareness of common fate is an important step, although certainly not the only one, toward increased prominence of the collective self relative to the individual self. Thus, highlighting or construing a common fate for its constituency may be one important step each social movement (or leader thereof) has to undertake to promote collective self-interpretation ("consciousness raising"), and thus ultimately participation in collective action. The following turns to a more thorough discussion of the necessary steps toward social movement participation and the role of the collective self in that process.

STEPS TOWARD SOCIAL MOVEMENT PARTICIPATION

This part of the chapter focuses on social movement participation as a particular form of intergroup behavior or collective action. More specifically, social-psychological principles of movement participation are reviewed here, and an attempt is made to link the distinction between the individual self and the collective self up with these principles of movement participation. Before doing so, it must be emphasized that I deal here with the social-psychological question of how people come to participate in a social movement. This is not to deny or diminish the importance of a sociostructural analysis of social movements. On the contrary, any analysis that aims to explain of the emergence of a specific social movement needs to identify the frictions and contradictions inherent in the respective society, as well as their structural basis (Smelser, 1962). Thus, the origins of the labor movement have been traced back to the contradictions of a society structured by social class, whereas the roots of the feminist movement are seen in the integrative problems arising for women in modern, functionally differentiated societies (Neidhardt & Rucht, 1993). Moreover, the ability of any social movement to mobilize sufficient resources (including people) certainly depends, to a large extent, on structural factors (McCarthy & Zald, 1973, 1977; Oberschall, 1973; Tilly, 1978).

However, a social-psychological analysis is necessary to understand how the social structure translates into or manifests itself in concrete experiences and actions of people (which may then feed back again on social structure). The social-psychological analysis presented in the remainder of this chapter focuses on the role of collective versus individual self-interpretations at various steps in the process toward movement participation. For that purpose, a model of movement participation developed by Klandermans and colleagues (Klandermans, 1997; Klandermans & Oegema, 1987) is adopted, which includes four steps: (a) becoming a part of the mobilization potential, (b) becoming a target of mobilization attempts, (c) becoming motivated to participate, and (d) overcoming barriers to participation. Klandermans and Oegema (1987) substantiated the relevance of these four steps empirically in research on mobilization and participation in the Dutch peace movement. They showed that different factors come into play at different steps, so that at each step another group of people drops out of the mobilization/participation process. In the following, each step is specified in more detail, and the role of the collective self at each particular step is elaborated.

Becoming Part of the Mobilization Potential

Someone is considered part of the mobilization potential to the extent that he or she sympathizes with or has a positive attitude toward the movement. More specifically, the mobilization potential consists of members of society who share a "collective action frame" vis-à-vis the movement's cause. Collective action frames consists of shared sets of beliefs that serve to interpret and explain social issues, as well as to suggest appropriate collective (re)actions (Gamson, 1992). Three specific components can be distinguished according to Gamson (1992). First, collective action frames provide people with interpretations and explanations of personal grievances in terms of injustice (e.g., interpretation of lower salary of women relative to men as discrimination against women), which in turn result in moral indignation. Second, they possess an identity component, in that they suggest interpretations of self and others in terms of an "us versus them" antagonism (e.g., "They, the men, discriminate against us women"). Third, collective action frames have an agency component. They suggest that social change is possible, and that the movement is actually capable of bringing about the desired change.

The generation and adoption of collective action frames is a function of a multifaceted social influence process operating against the background of individual dispositions and cultural themes and counterthemes (Klandermans, 1997). Notwithstanding these complexities, there is reason to assume that people are more willing to construct and adopt collective action frames if such frames relate to preexisting (or chronically accessible) group memberships or collective selves. In general, research has shown that social influence is more readily accepted if the target shares a relevant group membership with the source (Kelly, 1993; Mackie & Cooper, 1984; Turner, 1991).

It follows that social movements that can build on preexisting group memberships (e.g., the women's movement, which can build on the male–female categorization) should be particularly successful in disseminating collective action frames. This is most obvious with respect to the identity ("us vs. them") component of such frames. But the collective self appears to play a facilitating role also in adopting the injustice and agency components. For instance, Smith, Spears, and Oyen (1994) reported that members of a collectively deprived group tended to accentuate experienced deprivation and perceived injustice most strongly when shared group membership was highlighted. Thus, it appears that personal grievances are particularly likely to be interpreted as injustice if they systematically affect "people like us" (Smith et al., 1994).[3]

Finally, there is some correlational evidence consistent with the assumption that collective self-interpretation is also conducive to the adoption of the agency component of collective action frames. That evidence stems from a questionnaire study conducted in 1993 (i.e., after the unification of Germany) with 188 employees of an East German city.[4] These respondents indicated on 5-point scales that they perceived more similarities than differences between self and other East Germans (3.6 vs. 2.5; all contrasts and correlations reported in this section are statistically significant), but less similarities than differences between self and West Germans (2.7 vs. 3.4). They also perceived more similarities than differences within the ingroup (East Germans) as a whole (3.7 vs. 2.9), thus highlighting ingroup homogeneity. In short, their collective self as East Germans was highly accessible.

This was further corroborated by another measure on which respondents indicated that their East German identity would make up about 78% of their total identity (correlation with accentuation of self-ingroup similarities relative to differences was .40). What is more, respondents evaluated ingroup homogeneity, but not ingroup heterogeneity, as a strength of the ingroup (0.7 vs. 0.0 on a 5-point scale, ranging from *weakness* [−2] to *strength* [+2)). The evaluation of ingroup homogeneity as a strength increased with the emphasis on the collective self, as indicated by the relative accentuation of self-ingroup similarities ($r = .33$). These results suggest that an emphasis on the collective self implies the accentuation of perceived ingroup homogeneity and the evaluation of ingroup homogeneity as an asset that strengthens the ingroup's position in the struggle for social change ("United we stand, divided we fall"). Thus, collective self-interpretations appear to bolster the belief in the ingroup as an efficacious social agent.

Although necessary, the adoption of a collective action frame—with its injustice, identity, and agency components—is not a sufficient condition for movement participation. Further steps need to be taken to turn sympathizers into participants.

---

[3]Interestingly, experienced deprivation and perceived injustice were drastically reduced if the particular group member was not personally deprived. This specific finding testifies again to the fragility of the collective self or group solidarity.

[4]I am grateful to Amélie Mummendey and Rosemarie Mielke, who enabled me to include the respective questions in one of their questionnaires distributed as part of a research project supported by the Deutsche Forschungsgemeinschaft (Mu 511/13-1,2,3).

Becoming a Target of Mobilization Attempts

Sympathy with a social movement and its cause is not enough. People must be reached to inform them about specific actions (e.g., sit-ins or demonstrations) and to influence their willingness to take part in those actions. The mass media and direct mailing are two routes through which people can be reached. In addition, research has shown that recruitment networks based on friendship ties and ties with organizations play a critical role in this process (for an overview, see Klandermans & Oegema, 1987). Targeting organizations or friendship networks, instead of single individuals, is particularly efficient because it makes "en bloc recruitment" possible. The collective self may come into play here in at least two ways. First, if it is rooted in a social group, which provides group members with a relevant collective self, the social movement can more easily gain access to the organizations of that group and its friendship networks by stressing that "we are all one." The civil rights movement, which drew heavily on church organizations in the African-American community is a case in point (Friedman & McAdam, 1992). Second, targeted organizations (e.g., churches) or friendship networks (e.g., peer groups) may themselves constitute important bases for collective self-interpretations. Consequently, as soon as representatives of organizations or central figures (leaders or prototypes) of friendship networks show interest in the social movement's cause, such interest is likely to become normative within the respective circles. This in turn should lead to increased information-seeking behavior and better information flow within the targeted circles.

To be sure, social movement activists strive to provide targets with information that increases targets' willingness to participate in specific actions. However one-sided that information may be, being informed about specific actions is not tantamount to being motivated to participate. This brings us to the third step.

Becoming Motivated to Participate

Following an expectancy value or rational choice framework (Klandermans, 1984), the motivation to participate in a specific collective action of the social movement is typically viewed as a function of the perceived costs and benefits of participation (for an overview over pertinent research, see Klandermans & Oegema, 1987). At this point, it is important to note that the goal of the movement, if achieved, is a "collective good." All people sympathetic to the movement's cause will benefit from goal achievement, regardless of whether they personally participated in collective action, and thus contributed to goal achievement. For example, all factory workers benefit from improvement in working conditions successfully fought for in a strike, regardless of whether they personally participated in the strike. It follows that the collective good or collective benefit (which is conceptualized as a multiplicative function of the value of the action goal and the expectation that the action goal will be reached) may be insufficient as a motivating force because people can hope for a "free ride." In addition to the collective benefit, potential "free riders" need selective incentives to participate, which have to do with social or nonsocial costs and benefits (e.g., ridicule/admiration by significant others or losing/winning money, respectively; Olson, 1977). To summarize in terms of Ajzen and Fishbein's (1980) theory of reasoned action, collective benefits and nonsocial incentives determine together the attitude toward participation in collective action, whereas social incentives represent the subjective norm component. Attitude and subjective norm then codetermine the intention to participate in collective action.

Research by Klandermans (1984) and Klandermans and Oegema (1987) on the intention or motivation to participate in collective action corroborated especially the importance of collective benefits and social incentives. However, the conceptualization of the potential participator as someone who weights up costs and benefits has been criticized as atomistic or individualistic, and lacking an adequate theory of the values on which people base their cost–benefit analyses (Friedman & McAdam, 1992; Kelly, 1993). According to those critics, researchers have failed to acknowledge the social or collective origin of values. Instead, they seem to assume, at least implicitly, that values are intrinsic properties of individuals, and thus result in rather fixed self-interests. In contrast, self-categorization theory (Turner et al., 1987), explicitly acknowledges the variable nature of self-interests, stating that "To the degree that the self is depersonalized, so too is self-interest" (p. 65).

Drawing directly on self-categorization theory, Kelly and coworkers (Kelly, 1993; Kelly & Kelly, 1994) highlighted the role of the collective self in the process of becoming motivated to participate in collective action. They hypothesized and found greater willingness to participate in collective action, regardless of individual self-interest, when respondents (members of a trade union in Britain) placed strong emphasis on their collective self (as unionists). Similarly, in the context of gender relations, Kelly and Breinlinger (1995) found that women's willingness to participate in collective action increased with the emphasis on their collective self (as women). What is more, emphasis on the collective self as women, and especially as feminist activists, was positively related to actual participation, as reported retrospectively by respondents.

These findings are encouraging, and will hopefully inspire more people to work on the role of the collective self in motivating participation in collective action. Several directions for future research can be suggested here. They all relate to the question of how the calculation of costs and benefits may be affected by a shift from the individual to the collective self, and vice versa. First, the relative importance of collective benefits and selective incentives may change because egoistic, nonsocial (selective) incentives (e.g., losing or winning money for oneself) may become unimportant as soon as greater emphasis is placed on the more inclusive collective self. Second, it is also possible that the meaning of nonsocial incentives (e.g., the risk to be beaten up) changes because "What is painful at the individual level becomes a source of pride at the group level" (Brewer, 1991, p. 481). Third, the basis of social (selective) incentives could change with greater emphasis placed on the collective self because it may then be primarily ingroup members who are regarded as significant others. Fourth, new costs and benefits may enter the equation if group membership, or the collective self for that matter, entails commitment to a movement as one of its obligations (e.g., "To be African American means to get involved in the struggle for civil rights"). Verification of the collective self or identity may then become an incentive or benefit, and potential disconfirmation or even loss of the collective self a cost (Friedman & McAdam, 1992). Finally, the usefulness of the differentiation between the collective self as a member of the broader social category (say women, gays, or African Americans) and the collective self as a member of the less inclusive group of (say feminist, gay, or African-American) activists needs to be examined. For instance, Friedman and McAdam (1992) suggested that, "The more inclusive the collective [self or] identity, the harder it is to control [its adoption], and thus the less powerful it is as a selective incentive" (p. 165). The chapter now turns to the last step toward social movement participation.

Overcoming Barriers to Participation

Even if someone is highly motivated to participate in collective action, obstacles or barriers beyond his or her control (e.g., illness or lack of transportation) can prevent him or her from actually participating. It is unlikely that an emphasis on the individual or collective self has much direct influence on the occurrence or nonoccurrence of barriers that are not under the volitional control of potential participators. Yet to the extent that an emphasis on the collective self strengthens one's motivation to participate, people may actually try harder to overcome barriers when they place strong emphasis on the collective self. By the same token, people may then also try harder to anticipate and prepare for potential barriers, thus increasing their (actual and perceived) "behavioral control" (Ajzen & Madden, 1986).

SUMMARY AND CONCLUDING REMARKS

This chapter first elaborated on the distinction between the individual self and the collective self and their respective roles as the psychological bases of individual or collective perception and behavior. It was then suggested that members of low-status minorities are especially hesitant about interpreting themselves in terms of their collective self, and thus decrease their chances of bringing about social change through collective action. One important reason for this reluctance seems to be that, in modern society, the individual self is a likely alternative form of self-interpretation, which encourages the adoption of individual social mobility strategies. Still, real life teaches that, under certain conditions, even members of low-status minorities emphasize their collective self and engage in collective action, such as joining social movements. Research discussed in this chapter suggests that awareness of common fate may be one important prerequisite for this to occur, but more research along these lines is needed in the future.

The second part of the chapter focused on a particular form of intergroup behavior or collective action – namely, social movement participation. The formation of social movements is one route, among others, through which low-status (minority) groups can work toward social change (which is not to say that all social movements originate in low-status groups). The chapter showed how the incorporation of the collective self and its social-cognitive determinants can enrich theorizing and research on social movement participation. More generally, this chapter discussed the integration of theorizing and research on intergroup cognition and intergroup behavior – two areas that are all too often investigated separately.

ACKNOWLEDGMENTS

Part of the research reported in this chapter was supported by a grant from the Deutsche Forschungsgemeinschaft (Si 428/2-1). I am grateful to Claudia Hastedt and the editors for their thoughtful comments on an earlier version of this chapter.

REFERENCES

Adam, B. D. (1987). *The rise of a gay and lesbian movement* (Twayne's social movements series). Boston: Twayne.

Ajzen, I., & Fishbein, M. (1980). *Understanding attitudes and predicting social behavior.* Englewood Cliffs, NJ: Prentice-Hall.

Ajzen, I., & Madden, T. J. (1986). Prediction of goal directed behavior: Attitudes, intentions, and perceived behavioral control. *Journal of Experimental Social Psychology, 22,* 453–474.

Allport, F. H. (1962). A structuronomic conception of behaviour: Individual and collective. *Journal of Abnormal and Social Psychology, 64,* 3–30.

Allport, G. W. (1979). *The nature of prejudice.* Reading, MA: Addison-Wesley.

Apfelbaum, E. (1979). Relations of domination and movements for liberation: An analysis of power between groups. In W. G. Austin & S. Worchel (Eds.), *The social psychology of intergroup relations* (pp. 188–204). Monterey, CA: Brooks/Cole.

Beck, U. (1994). Jenseits von Stand und Klasse? [Beyond class?]. In U. Beck & E. Beck-Gernsheim (Eds.), *Riskante Freiheiten* (pp. 43–60). Frankfurt: Suhrkamp.

Brewer, M. B. (1991). The social self: On being the same and different at the same time. *Personality and Social Psychology Bulletin, 17,* 475–482.

Brewer, M. B., Weber, J. G., & Carini, B. (1995). Person memory in intergroup contexts: Categorization versus individuation. *Journal of Personality and Social Psychology, 69*(1), 29–40.

Brown, R. J., & Turner, J. C. (1981). Interpersonal and intergroup behaviour. In J. C. Turner & H. Giles (Eds.), *Intergroup behaviour* (pp. 33–65). Oxford: Basil Blackwell.

Brown, R. W. (1954). Mass phenomena. In G. Lindzey (Ed.), *Handbook of social psychology* (pp. 833–876). Reading, MA: Addison-Wesley.

Doosje, B., Ellemers, N., & Spears, R. (1995). Perceived intragroup variability as a function of group status and identification. *Journal of Experimental Social Psychology, 31,* 410–436.

Elias, N. (1988). *Die Gesellschaft der Individuen (The society of the individuals).* Frankfurt am Main: Suhrkamp.

Elias, N. (1990). *Über den Prozeß der Zivilisation (The civilizing process).* Frankfurt am Main: Suhrkamp.

Ellemers, N., Doosje, B., van Knippenberg, A., & Wilke, H. (1992). Status protection in high status minority groups. *European Journal of Social Psychology, 22,* 123–140.

Esser, H. (1988). Ethnische Differenzierung und moderne Gesellschaft [Ethnic Differentiation and Modern Society]. *Zeitschrift für Soziologie, 17,* 235–248.

Farley, J. (1982). *Majority-minority relations.* Englewood, NJ: Prentice-Hall.

Ferree, M. M., & Miller, F. D. (1985). Mobilization and meaning: Toward an integration of social psychological and resource perspectives on social movements. *Sociology Inquiry, 55,* 38–61.

Friedman, D., & McAdam, D. (1992). Collective identity and activism: Networks, choices, and the life of a social movement. In A. D. Morris & C. M. Mueller (Eds.), *Frontiers in social movement theory* (pp. 156–173). New Haven, CT: Yale University Press.

Gamson, W. A. (1992). *Talking politics.* Cambridge, England: University of Cambridge Press.

Jackson, L. A., Sullivan, L. A., Harnish, R., & Hodge, C. N. (1996). Achieving positive social identity: Social mobility, social creativity, and permeability of group boundaries. *Journal of Personality and Social Psychology, 70,* 241–254.

James, W. (1910). *Psychology: The briefer course.* New York: Holt, Rhinehart & Winston.

Judd, C. M., & Park, B. (1993). Definition and assessment of accuracy in social stereotypes. *Psychological Review, 100,* 109–128.

Kelly, C. (1993). Group identification, intergroup perceptions and collective action. In W. Stroebe & M. Hewstone (Eds.), *European review of social psychology* (Vol. 4), pp. 59–83). Chichester: Wiley.

Kelly, C., & Breinlinger, S. (1995). Identity and injustice: Exploring women's participation in collective action. *Journal of Community and Applied Social Psychology, 5,* 41–57.

Kelly, C., & Kelly, J. E. (1994). Who gets involved in collective action? Social psychological determinants of individual participation in trade unions. *Human Relations, 47*(1), 63–87.

Klandermans, B. (1984). Mobilization and participation: Social psychological expansions of resource mobilization theory. *American Sociological Review, 49,* 583–600.

Klandermans, B. (1997). *The social psychology of protest.* Oxford: Basil Blackwell.

Klandermans, B., & Oegema, D. (1987). Potentials, networks, motivations, and barriers: Steps towards participation in social movements. *American Sociological Review, 52,* 519–531.

Linville, P. W. (1985). Self-complexity and affective extremity: Don't put all your eggs in one cognitive basket. *Social Cognition, 3,* 94–120.

Linville, P. W. (1987). Self-complexity as a cognitive buffer against stress-related illness and depression. *Journal of Personality and Social Psychology, 52,* 663–676.

Mackie, D., & Cooper, J. (1984). Attitude polarization: Effects of group membership. *Journal of Personality and Social Psychology, 46,* 575–585.

Markus, H. (1977). Self-schemata and processing information about the self. *Journal of Personality and Social Psychology, 35,* 63–78.

Markus, H., & Kunda, Z. (1986). Stability and malleability of the self-concept. *Journal of Personality and Social Psychology, 51,* 858–866.

Markus, H. R., & Kitayama, S. (1991). Culture and the self: Implications for cognition, emotion, and motivation. *Psychological Review, 98,* 224–253.

Marx, K. (1978). The German ideology/manifest of the communist party. In R. C. Tucker (Ed.), *The Marx-Engels Reader* (2nd ed., pp. 473–483). New York: Norton.

McCarthy, J. D., & Zald, M. N. (1973). *The trend of social movements in America: Professionalization and resource mobilization.* Morristown, NJ: General Learning Press.

McCarthy, J. D., & Zald, M. N. (1977). Resource mobilization and social movements: A partial theory. *American Journal of Sociology, 82,* 1212–1241.

Mead, G. H. (1934). *Mind, self and society.* Chicago: University of Chicago Press.

Mullen, B. (1991). Group composition, salience, and cognitive representations: The phenomenology of being in a group. *Journal of Experimental Social Psychology, 27,* 297–323.

Neidhardt, F., & Rucht, D. (1993). Auf dem Weg in die "Bewegungsgesellschaft"? Über die Stabilisierbarkeit sozialer Bewegungen (On the way to a "movement society"?). *Soziale Welt, 44,* 305–326.

Oakes, P. J., Haslam, S. A., & Turner, J. C. (1994). *Stereotyping and social reality.* Oxford: Basil Blackwell.

Oakes, P. J., & Reynolds, K. J. (1997). Asking the accuracy question: Is measurement the answer? In R. Spears, P. J. Oakes, N. Ellemers, & S. A. Haslam (Eds.), *The social psychology of stereotyping and group life* (pp. 51–71). Oxford: Basil Blackwell.

Oakes, P. J., Turner, J. C., & Haslam, S. A. (1991). Perceiving people as group members: The role of fit in the salience of social categorizations. *British Journal of Social Psychology, 30,* 125–144.

Oberschall, A. (1973). *Social conflict and social movements.* Englewood Cliffs, NJ: Prentice-Hall.

Olson, M. (1977). *The logic of collective action. Public goods and the theory of groups.* Cambridge, MA: Harvard University Press.

Ross, L., Greene, D., & House, P. (1977). The false consensus effect: An egocentric bias in social perception and attribution processes. *Journal of Experimental Social Psychology, 13,* 279–301.

Sachdev, I., & Bourhis, R. Y. (1984). Minimal majorities and minorities. *European Journal of Social Psychology, 14,* 35–52.

Schimank, U. (1985). Funktionale Differenzierung und reflexiver Subjektivismus: Zum Entsprechungsverhältnis von Gesellschafts- und Identitätsform (Functional differentiation and reflexive subjectivism: On the correspondence between society and identity). *Soziale Welt, 4,* 447–465.

Schopler, J., & Insko, A. (1992). The discontinuity effect in interpersonal and intergroup relations: Generality and mediation. In W. Stroebe & M. Hewstone (Eds.), *European review of social psychology* (pp. 121–151). Chichester: Wiley.

Sedikides, C., & Skowronski, J. J. (1991). The law of cognitive structure activation.

Psychological Inquiry, 2(2), 169–184.

Sherif, M. (1966). *The psychology of social norms.* New York: Harper Torchbook.

Sherman, J. S., Judd, C. M., & Park, B. (1989). Social cognition. *Annual Review of Psychology, 40,* 281–326.

Simmel, G. (1955). *The web of group-affiliations* (R. Bendix, Trans.). New York: The Free Press.

Simon, B. (1992). The perception of ingroup and outgroup homogeneity: Re-introducing the intergroup context. In W. Stroebe & M. Hewstone (Eds.), *European review of social psychology* (Vol. 3, pp. 1–30). Chichester: Wiley.

Simon, B. (1997). Self and group in modern society: Ten theses on the individual self and the collective self. In R. Spears, P. J. Oakes, N. Ellemers, & S. A. Haslam (Eds.), *The social psychology of stereotyping and group life* (pp. 318–335). Oxford: Basil Blackwell.

Simon, B., Glässner-Bayerl, B., & Stratenwerth, I. (1991). Stereotyping and self-stereotyping in a natural intergroup context: The case of heterosexual and homosexual men. *Social Psychology Quarterly, 54,* 252–266.

Simon, B., & Hamilton, D. L. (1994). Self-stereotyping and social context: The effects of relative ingroup size and ingroup status. *Journal of Personality and Social Psychology, 66,* 699–711.

Simon, B., & Hastedt, C. (in press). When misery loves categorical company: Accessibility of the individual self as a moderator in category-based representation of attractive and unattractive ingroups. *Personality and Social Psychology Bulletin.*

Simon, B., & Mummendey, A. (1990). Perceptions of relative group size and group homogeneity: We are the majority and they are all the same. *European Journal of Social Psychology, 20,* 351–356.

Simon, B., & Mummendey, A. (1997). Selbst, Identität und Gruppe: Eine sozialpsychologische Analyse des Verhältnisses von Individuum und Gruppe. In A. Mummendey & B. Simon (Eds.), *Identität und Verschiedenheit: Zur Sozialpsychologie der Identität in komplexen Gesellschaften.* Bern: Huber.

Simon, B., Pantaleo, G., & Mummendey, A. (1995). Unique individual or interchangeable group member? The accentuation of intragroup differences versus similarities as an indicator of the individual self versus the collective self. *Journal of Personality and Social Psychology, 69,* 106–119.

Smelser, N. J. (1962). *A theory of collective behavior.* New York: The Free Press.

Smith, H., Spears, R., & Oyen, M. (1994). "People like us": The influence of personal deprivation and group membership salience on justice evaluations. *Journal of Experimental Social Psychology, 30,* 277–299.

Stryker, S., & Serpe, R. T. (1982). Commitment, identity salience, and role behavior: Theory and research example. In W. Ickes & E. S. Knowles (Eds.), *Personality, roles, and social behavior* (pp. 199–218). New York: Springer.

Tajfel, H. (1981). *Human groups and social categories: Studies in social psychology.* Cambridge, England: Cambridge University Press.

Tajfel, H., & Turner, J. C. (1979). An integrative theory of intergroup conflict. In W. G. Austin & S. Worchel (Eds.), *The social psychology of intergroup relations* (pp. 33–47). Monterey, CA: Brooks/Cole.

Tajfel, H., & Turner, J. C. (1986). The social identity theory of intergroup behavior. In S. Worchel & W. G. Austin (Eds.), *Psychology of intergroup relations* (pp. 7–24). Chicago: Nelson Hall.

Taylor, S. E., & Brown, J. D. (1988). Illusion and well-being: A social psychological perspective on mental health. *Psychological Bulletin, 103,* 193–210.

Taylor, S. E., Fiske, S. T., Etcoff, N. L., & Ruderman, A. J. (1978). Categorical and contextual bases of person memory and stereotyping. *Journal of Personality and Social Psychology, 36,* 778–793.

Taylor, V., & Whittier, N. E. (1992). Collective identity in social movement communities. In A. D. Morris & C. M. Mueller (Eds.), *Frontiers in social movement theory* (pp. 104–129). New Haven, CT: Yale University Press.

Tilly, C. (1978). *From mobilization to revolution.* Reading, MA: Addison-Wesley.

Triandis, H. C. (1989). The self and social behavior in differing cultural contexts. *Psychological Review, 96,* 506–520.

Turner, J. C. (1991). *Social influence.* Pacific Grove, CA: Brooks/Cole.

Turner, J. C., Hogg, M. A., Oakes, P. J., Reicher, S. D., & Wetherell, M. S. (1987). *Rediscovering the social group. A self-categorization theory.* Oxford: Basil Blackwell.

Turner, J. C., Oakes, P. J., Haslam, S. A., & McGarty, C. (1994). Self and collective: Cognition and social context. *Personality and Social Psychology Bulletin, 20,* 454–463.

van Knippenberg, A., van Twuyver, M., & Pepels, J. (1994). Factors affecting social categorization processes in memory. *British Journal of Social Psychology, 33,* 419–431.

Weber, M. (1978). The disintegration of the household: The rise of the calculative spirit and of the modern capitalist enterprise. In G. Roth & C. Wittich (Eds.), *Max Weber: Economy and society* (Vol. 1). Berkeley, CA: University of California Press.

12

Group Socialization and Intergroup Relations

John M. Levine
Richard L. Moreland
Carey S. Ryan
University of Pittsburgh

Intergroup relations has been an important area of social-psychological research for decades (see Brewer & Brown, in press; Mackie & Hamilton, 1993; Macrae, Stangor, & Hewstone, 1996; Oakes, Haslam, & Turner, 1994). Although much has been learned about how people relate to ingroup versus outgroup members, theoretical and empirical work in this area can be criticized on two grounds. First, most researchers have oversimplified the social environment in which intergroup relations occur (Levine & Moreland, in press). In general, they have focused on only two groups (an ingroup and an outgroup) and assumed that (a) those groups have competitive and often hostile relations with one another; (b) an individual can belong to only one of the groups; and (c) outsiders, who do not belong to either group, are indifferent to what happens between the groups. Although intergroup situations of this kind certainly occur, they are by no means universal. There are many cases in which three or more groups interact; these groups can have cooperative and even cordial relations; an individual can belong to more than one group; and outsiders often care deeply about how the groups behave toward one another (e.g., Insko et al., 1994; Ryan, 1995).

A second criticism is that many researchers have either ignored causal connections between intergroup and intragroup processes or (when such connections are analyzed) focused on how relations between groups affect relations within groups. The latter approach is illustrated by research on realistic group conflict theory, which demonstrates that conflict between groups can produce psychological and social changes within groups, including greater solidarity and more hierarchical status relations among members (e.g., Dion, 1979; Sherif, Harvey, White, Hood, & Sherif, 1961; Staw, Sandelands, & Dutton, 1981). Also relevant is self-categorization theory, which posits that psychological group formation occurs when people categorize themselves as members of an ingroup that is distinct from some outgroup (Turner, Hogg, Oakes, Reicher, & Wetherell, 1987). Self-categorization, in turn, influences several intragroup phenomena, including cohesion, majority and minority influence, and group polarization (e.g., Abrams & Hogg, 1990; Hogg, 1992).

Although much less attention has been given to how relations within groups affect relations between groups, some suggestions have been offered. For example, it has been suggested that the process of ingroup formation, the content of ingroup norms, and the character of ingroup members can all affect hostility toward an outgroup (see Sherif & Sherif, 1969). It has also been argued that ingroup cohesion may produce outgroup depreciation (Dion, 1979; Wilder, 1986) and that social identity processes within groups may produce conflict between groups (Ashforth & Mael, 1989; Kramer, 1991). Finally, it has been suggested that intragroup support for greed contributes to intergroup conflict (Schopler et al., 1993).

In natural groups that exist outside the psychological laboratory, intergroup and intragroup processes are inextricably linked, and neither can be adequately explained without considering the other. Thus, to understand how the members of Group A relate to the members of Group B, we must also understand how they relate to others in their own group. And to understand how the members of Group A relate to others in their own group, we must also understand how they relate to the members of Group B.

GROUP SOCIALIZATION

In seeking to clarify the reciprocal relations between events that occur within and between groups, a number of intragroup processes might be examined. This chapter focuses on *group socialization*, which involves temporal changes in the relationship between a group and each of its members. Moreland and Levine (1982; Levine & Moreland, 1994) developed a model of group socialization that is unique in emphasizing both temporal change and reciprocal influence. That is, the model assumes that individual–group relationships change in systematic ways over time and that both parties are potential sources and recipients of influence. Both the group and the individual thus change as a function of the socialization process. Although the model is applicable to many kinds of groups, it is meant to apply primarily to small, autonomous, voluntary groups, whose members interact on a regular basis, have affective ties with one another, share a common frame of reference, and are behaviorally interdependent. In this chapter, we are especially concerned with "open" groups (Ziller, 1965), which devote considerable time and energy to recruiting new members and retaining old ones.

Group socialization depends on three psychological processes: *evaluation, commitment*, and *role transition*. Evaluation, which is basically a cognitive process, involves efforts on the part of the group and the individual to assess the rewardingness of their relationship. During evaluation, the group seeks to determine how much an individual contributes to the achievement of its goals, and the individual seeks to determine how much the group contributes to the satisfaction of his or her needs. In addition to evaluating the present rewardingness of their relationship, the group and the individual may also remember how rewarding it was in the past and predict how rewarding it will be in the future. Both parties may also evaluate the past, present, and future rewardingness of their alternative relationships. These six evaluations combine to produce feelings of commitment on the part of the group and the individual. Commitment, which is basically an affective process, is high to the extent that both parties believe (a) their past relationship was more rewarding than previous alternative relationships, (b) their present relationship is more rewarding than current alternative relationships, and (c) their future relationship will be more rewarding than future alternative relationships. A more extensive discussion of commitment can be found in Moreland, Levine, and Cini (1993; see also Dutton, Dukerich, & Harquail, 1994; Farrell & Rusbult, 1981; Meyer & Allen, 1991).

Commitment has a number of consequences for the individual and the group. For example, the more committed a group is to an individual, the more the group will accept the individual's needs and values, feel positive affect toward the individual, attempt to fulfill the individual's expectations, and try to gain or retain the individual as a group member. Perhaps the most important consequence of commitment is role transition, which is basically a behavioral process. Both the group and the individual develop decision criteria, or specific levels of commitment indicating that a qualitative change in their relationship is warranted. When either party's commitment level reaches its decision criterion, that party will try to initiate a role transition, and when the commitment levels of both parties reach their respective decision criteria, the role transition will occur. Following a role transition, the group's expectations for the individual and the individual's expectations for the group will change, stimulating a new round of evaluations, which may lead to further changes in commitment and subsequent role transitions. In this way, the individual can pass through five phases of group socialization (investigation, socialization, maintenance, resocialization, and remembrance), separated by four role transitions (entry, acceptance, divergence, and exit). Figure 12.1 illustrates how the relationship between a group and an individual might change over time.

During the *investigation* phase, when the individual is a prospective member, the group engages in recruitment, looking for people who will contribute to the attainment of its goals. Similarly, the individual engages in reconnaissance, looking for groups that will contribute to the satisfaction of his or her needs. If evaluation causes both parties' commitment levels to rise to their respective entry criteria (EC), then the role transition of *entry* will occur, and the individual will become a new member.

During the *socialization* phase, the group attempts to change the individual so that he or she contributes more to the attainment of group goals, and the individual attempts to change the group so that it contributes more to the satisfaction of personal needs. To the extent the group is successful, the individual undergoes assimilation, and to the extent the individual is successful, the group undergoes accommodation. If evaluation causes both parties' commitment levels to rise to their respective acceptance criteria (AC), then the role transition of *acceptance* will occur, and the individual will become a full member.

During the *maintenance* phase, the group and the individual engage in role negotiation, seeking a specialized role for the individual (e.g., treasurer) that fulfills both the group's goals and the person's needs. If this negotiation succeeds, then the commitment levels of both parties will remain high. If it fails, then their commitment levels will fall, perhaps dropping to their respective divergence criteria (DC). This decline in commitment will precipitate the role transition of *divergence*, and the individual will become a marginal member.

During the *resocialization* phase, the group tries to restore the individual's contributions to the attainment of group goals, and the individual tries to restore the group's contributions to the satisfaction of personal needs. If assimilation and/or accommodation are successful, then both parties' commitment levels may rise to their respective divergence criteria, producing a special role transition (convergence) that returns the individual to full membership. But if both parties' commitment levels fall to their respective exit criteria (XC), then the role transition of *exit* will occur, and the individual will become an ex-member (as depicted in Fig. 12.1).

Finally, during the *remembrance* phase, both parties engage in a retrospective evaluation of their past relationship. The group recalls its experiences with the individual, and these memories become part of the group's tradition. Similarly, the individual engages in reminiscence about

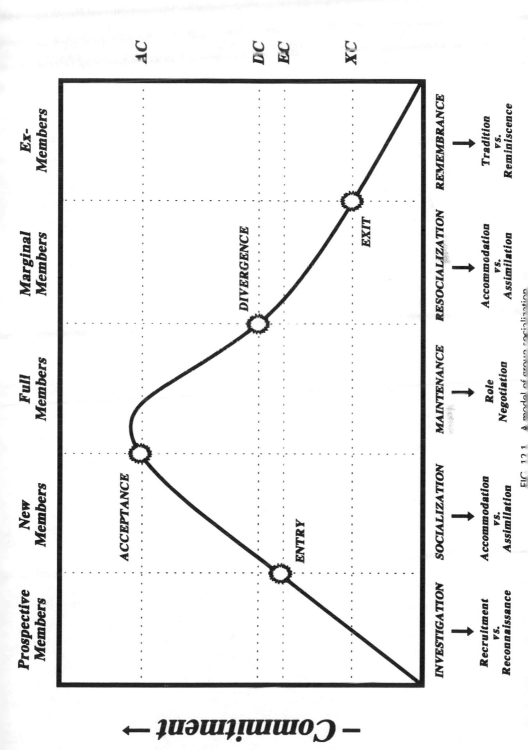

FIG. 12.1. A model of group socialization.

his or her experiences with the group. If the parties continue to influence one another's outcomes, then they also engage in an ongoing evaluation of their current relationship. Over time the commitment levels of both parties eventually stabilize at some level.

Figure 12.1 is a simplified representation of how the relationship between a group and an individual might change over time. Moreland and Levine (1982) discussed several ways in which passage through a group might diverge from the pattern shown in the figure. For example, group and individual commitment levels may change abruptly rather than gradually, perhaps because the individual performs some heroic act on the group's behalf. And the group and the individual may not always be equally committed to one another or share the same set of decision criteria, which can produce conflict between them. Elaborations and extensions of the original group socialization model, as well as research on the model's early phases, are summarized by Levine and Moreland (1994).

In this chapter, we will use the group socialization model to clarify some important relationships between intragroup and intergroup processes. In particular, we will focus on how a group's desire to gain new members and retain old ones, which is based on the evaluation and commitment mechanisms discussed earlier, affects the group's behavior toward people who might join or who already belong. To the extent the group wants these people as members, it will seek to alter their thoughts, feelings, and actions. Moreover, to the extent the group is competing with other groups for members, its treatment of prospective and current members may influence the cognitions, emotions, and behaviors of its competitors, which in turn may have important consequences for intergroup relations.

INTRAGROUP AND INTERGROUP RELATIONS: EXCLUSIVE MEMBERSHIPS

As noted earlier, most of the theoretical and empirical work on intergroup relations assumes that a person can belong to only one group at a time, so we will begin our discussion by considering this "exclusive membership" case. And we will make a second simplifying assumption, namely that the social environment is composed of only two groups—A and B.

A venerable theoretical framework for understanding intergroup conflict is realistic group conflict theory (RCT; D. Campbell, 1965; Jackson, 1993; Sherif et al., 1961). According to RCT, groups have real conflicts of interest concerning the acquisition and retention of rewards, and these conflicts promote intergroup competition and hostility. The rewards underlying conflicts of interest are generally scarce resources, such as land, or economic opportunities, such as jobs. In many situations, however, groups also find themselves competing for members, and this competition can have important implications for both intra- and intergroup relations.

According to population ecology models, which are based loosely on natural selection principles, groups compete with one another and only the strongest survive (Freeman & Hannan, 1983). This perspective has been elaborated by McPherson (1983, 1988), who argued that every group occupies a particular "niche" in its social environment. The size of this niche depends on the characteristics that the group wants its members to have, the presence of other groups that want members with the same characteristics, and the number of such people in the community. To the extent that two groups want the same kinds of people and there are not enough of these people to staff both groups, competition over prospective members will occur. Thus, even groups that are not negatively interdependent in obvious ways (e.g., a volunteer fire department and an Elks Club) will compete for members if there are not enough people in the community to make both groups viable. As McPherson and Smith-Lovin (1988) noted, "The functional requirements and goals of the organizations may be completely compatible (or unrelated). All that is required for competition is that limited resources (the time of a limited number of people) in a given social domain are sought by two or more types of organizations" (p. 89).

McPherson's analysis suggests an important way in which intragroup processes (a group's efforts to recruit new members) can affect intergroup processes (conflict with other groups over members). Moreover, once intergroup conflict concerning members begins, it can have a reciprocal impact on the internal dynamics of each group, for example, by changing the group's recruiting goals and techniques (McPherson & Ranger-Moore, 1991). We now turn to a discussion of the strategies that Group A might use to increase its competitive advantage over Group B in a war for members and the impact that these strategies might have on the relations between the groups.

Prospective Members Who Belong to Neither Group

Many prospective members are people who currently do not belong to either Group A or Group B. In an effort to recruit such people, Group A can try to make itself sufficiently attractive so that their commitment levels rise to their entry criteria. When this happens, prospective members will want to undergo the role transition of entry and begin the socialization phase of group membership. One way for Group A to increase commitment among prospective members is by convincing them that the group has many attractive qualities and they will benefit from belonging to it. Alternatively, Group A can engage in "anticipatory accommodation," which involves changing itself to better satisfy prospective members' personal needs (Levine & Moreland, 1985). Anticipatory accommodation can involve immediate changes in the group and/or promises that changes will occur later, after people have actually joined the group. Such promises may not be believed, of course, if the group does not seem to have either the ability to fulfill its promises (e.g., because it lacks the necessary resources) or the motivation to do so (e.g., because it tends to forget its promises after it makes them).

Anticipatory accommodation can have effects that go well beyond attracting members. For example, a group that exaggerates the benefits of membership may later be the target of disenchantment and even anger if new members decide that the silk purse they were promised was actually a sow's ear (Wanous, 1980; Wanous, Poland, Premack, & Davis, 1992). And even if the group keeps its promises to new members, doing so may deplete resources that the group will later need to induce these people to stay or others to join. Finally, anticipatory accommodation to prospective members may produce resentment and jealousy in oldtimers, who will then feel less committed to the group and expend less effort on its behalf.

Anticipatory accommodation assumes that prospective members' entry criteria are stable, and therefore the group's task is to raise their commitment levels to those criteria. Another strategy, of course, is to persuade prospective members to lower their entry criteria for the group (Moreland & Levine, 1984). To accomplish this, the group might claim that prior prospective members, who were later quite successful in the group, had relatively low entry criteria when they joined. Or the group might signal that its own entry criterion is both lower than the individual's entry criterion and lower than its own commitment level, indicating that the group is ready to extend an offer of membership and implying that the person has an unreasonable standard for joining. This strategy would be strengthened if the group also threatened to raise its entry criterion and/or lower its commitment level if the individual did not adopt a more reasonable standard.

So far, we have focused on how Group A might alter prospective members' commitment levels or their decision criteria for entry. These strategies would be sufficient if no other group were involved and prospective members simply had to choose between joining Group A and joining no group. However, when prospective members have the option of joining either Group A or Group B, an additional recruiting strategy becomes available to Group A. Specifically, Group A might try to alter prospective members' commitment to Group B rather than (or in addition to) their commitment to Group A, or their entry criteria for that group. Of course, a critical difference exists: Group A wants to make itself as attractive as possible, whereas it wants to make Group B as unattractive as possible.

A common technique for accomplishing this latter goal is to transmit negative information about Group B to prospective members. This can also strengthen commitment among current group members (cf. Campbell, 1987; Johnson & Rusbult, 1989; Kanter, 1968). However, prospective members are often suspicious of blatant attempts to denigrate other groups. So it is in Group A's interest to transmit negative information about Group B in subtle ways that disguise its true intentions. Several strategies might be used to accomplish this goal. One strategy is to "damn with faint praise," extolling Group B's trivial virtues while ignoring its important ones (e.g., "Oh, you're considering joining Phi Gamma Gamma? They make terrific Mother's Day cards, and their cook does a wonderful job with organ meats"). A second strategy is to sharply criticize Group B while feigning ignorance about their search for members (e.g., "Those Phi Betas are really a bunch of drunks and liars. Oh my gosh, you're not being rushed by them are you? I'm terribly sorry. Some of their members are great guys"). A third strategy is to persuade prospective members that the dimensions on which Group A outranks Group B are the most important criteria for evaluating the groups. This strategy is most effective if Group A does not immediately compare itself to Group B, but rather arranges for prospective members to learn about its superiority in some other manner. Finally, because prospective members may be suspicious of anything that Group A says about Group B, a useful strategy is to induce someone with no apparent links to Group A to transmit negative information about Group B. This is particularly effective if the person is an ex-member of Group B and thus can provide an insider's view of its weaknesses.

There are additional risks associated with giving prospective members negative information about Group B, at least when that information can be attributed to Group A. The prospective members may share the information with Group B (e.g., "I suppose I shouldn't be telling you this, but the Delta Lambdas said you guys have the worst graduation rate on campus"). Such unpleasant revelations may cause Group B to retaliate by spreading even worse stories about Group A. This sequence of events illustrates how behavior designed to further one group's goals (recruiting new members) can negatively affect relations between that group and other groups. Being the target of Group B's retaliatory stories also can force Group A to confront unpleasant truths about itself, which in turn raise self-doubts (cf. Feldman, 1994; Sutton & Louis, 1987).

Prospective Members Who Belong to the Other Group

Some prospective members are people who currently belong to Group B. In one sense, Group A's goal for these people is identical to its goal for people who do not belong to either group, namely to increase their commitment to Group A until it reaches their entry criteria for that group. But in order for members of Group B to enter Group A, something else has to happen. These people must also leave Group B, and that will only occur if their commitment to Group B falls to their exit criteria for that group. So, Group A must lower their commitment to Group B while simultaneously raising their commitment to itself. The second half of this task involves anticipatory accommodation, as discussed earlier. If there is a history of negative relations between the two groups, however, then members of Group B may find it hard to believe positive things about Group A, reducing the likelihood that anticipatory accommodation will be successful.

In addition to having a hard time raising prospective members' commitment to itself, Group A may also have trouble lowering their commitment to Group B. Several factors may contribute to this difficulty. First, because members of Group B are committed (at some level) to their group, they may resist negative information about it, regardless of whether that information comes from Group A or a supposedly disinterested third party (Bond & Kwok-Venus, 1991). This resistance is likely to vary directly with members' commitment to Group B. Because commitment is lower in the socialization and resocialization phases of group membership than in the maintenance phase, new members and marginal members should be more receptive than full members to negative information about Group B (see Fig. 12.1). Second, even if prospective members have relatively low commitment to Group B, they may be reluctant to commit "treason" by joining Group A. This reluctance may stem from fear of retaliation by Group B, as in the extreme case where members of a criminal gang believe that defectors will be hunted down and killed. Or it may derive from an internalized code of values that forbids defection to a competing group under any circumstances. In either case, even people who have very low commitment to Group B will refuse to consider joining Group A. Finally, to the extent Group B is aware that its members are in danger of being stolen, it may strongly oppose Group A's efforts to lower its members' commitment. The threat that Group B feels will increase its hostility to Group A and lead it to retaliate in some way, perhaps by trying to steal Group A's members. This retaliation, in turn, may elicit a counterattack from Group A, producing an upward spiral in intergroup tension.

In seeking to recruit members of Group B, Group A may also attempt to increase their exit criteria for their current group. The more these criteria can be raised, the less members' commitment to Group B must be lowered for exit to occur. Group A could use several strategies for raising members' exit criteria. For example, Group A might claim that ex-members of Group B who had high exit criteria, and therefore left quickly when their commitment began to decline, were subsequently happier than ex-members who had low exit criteria, and therefore remained in the group for a long time despite low commitment. Or Group A might imply that Group B's exit criterion is extremely high, which puts current members in danger of expulsion regardless of their own commitment levels and exit criteria. These and similar communications should lead the members of Group B to adopt higher exit criteria, thereby raising the probability that they will leave the group.

Current Members of One's Own Group

We have focused so far on Group A's attempts to recruit prospective members. But to win the war for members, Group A must also retain its current members, some of whom may be tempted to defect to Group B. To accomplish this, Group A can (a) raise the commitment of its current members to itself, (b) lower their exit criteria, (c) lower the commitment of its current members to Group B, or (d) raise their entry criteria. All of these strategies will be pursued more vigorously if Group A feels strongly committed to the potential defectors. Thus, Group A will expend more energy to retain full members than either new members or marginal members (see Fig. 12.1).

Compared with the task of recruiting outsiders, retaining insiders is easier in some ways and harder in others. Factors that facilitate retention include current members' disinclination to commit treason; their willingness to believe negative information about a traditional outgroup; their inability to predict with certainty what life in Group B will be like; and their attachment to particular members of Group A and/or outsiders who have ties with these members (cf. Moreland, Levine, & Cini, 1993; Stryker, 1968, 1987). Factors that inhibit retention include current members' belief that openness to change is a positive characteristic; their feeling of "betrayal" by a group to which they were once highly committed; their knowledge about hidden weaknesses in Group A; and their ignorance about such weaknesses in Group B (cf. Wilsnack, 1980).

One might expect that Group A's efforts to retain its own members would be less likely to exacerbate intergroup tension than would its efforts to steal Group B's members. But this may not always be the case. For example, even if Group A is not actively trying to produce defection from Group B, Group B may assume that Group A's attempts to retain members are designed to increase its ability to prevail in intergroup conflict. Group B may also assume (often correctly) that Group A's efforts to retain members involve some derogation of Group B. Finally, Group B may obtain evidence that Group A is in fact telling its members negative things about Group B. Regardless of the source (or veracity) of Group B's beliefs that it is being derogated, Group B is likely to retaliate. This retaliation might involve making pro-B and anti-A comments to members of Group A, Group B, or both. And to the extent that Group A's behavior was not originally motivated by hostile impulses, its belief that Group B is engaging in unprovoked retaliation is likely to produce a counterattack and subsequent escalation of conflict between the groups.

The Impact of Intergroup Conflict Over Other Resources

In cases where groups compete for resources other than members (e.g., access to jobs), intergroup conflict concerning members is likely to be exacerbated. One could expect to see all of the prior strategies carried out with increased vigor, and other strategies might be used as well. For example, in an effort to weaken Group B, Group A may seek to reduce Group B's ability to recruit new members and retain old ones, even if these people are *not* expected to join Group A. If intergroup conflict is sufficiently high, this "strategy of denial" may occur even when there are enough potential members for both groups to carry out their internal functions. In this situation, Group A would not try to raise prospective members' commitment to itself, but instead would try to lower their commitment to Group B (and raise their exit criterion if they already belong to Group B). To the extent that prospective or current members of Group B see Group A as a disinterested party that is not trying to recruit them, they may be relatively open to negative information about Group B. In addition, Group A might lower its own decision criteria (entry, acceptance, divergence, or exit) to increase the likelihood that people will enter the group and remain in it.

INTRAGROUP AND INTERGROUP RELATIONS: SIMULTANEOUS MEMBERSHIPS

It is possible for a person to be a member of two or more groups at the same time. In fact, simultaneous group memberships are the norm for most people, rather than the exception (e.g., Curtis & Zurcher, 1973; Davis & Stern, 1981; Vanbeselaere, 1991; Wong-Rieger & Taylor, 1981). To simplify our discussion of this case, we will assume that the person simultaneously belongs to just two groups — A and B. Here Group A's goal is not simply to retain the person as a member, but also to capture enough of the person's time and energy to achieve group goals. Thus, in contrast to exclusive memberships, simultaneous memberships stimulate realistic group conflict over the person's commitment level, but not his or her membership per se.

According to the group socialization model (Levine & Moreland, 1994; Moreland & Levine, 1982), a person's willingness to devote time and energy to a group is a direct function of his or her commitment to that group. Thus, Group A's goal concerning a member who also belongs to Group B is to ensure that the person's commitment to Group A rises to or stays above whatever level is necessary for that person to work hard on Group A's behalf. Because determining this level is often quite difficult, Group A may simply try to raise the member's commitment as high as possible, on the assumption that too much commitment does not present a problem, whereas too little does. Moreover, because Group A will probably assume an inverse relationship between a shared member's commitment to it and to Group B, Group A may seek to minimize the latter commitment while maximizing the former. A current example is the feeling among some African-American males that African-American females' concern about women's issues necessarily weakens their concern about racial issues. As with exclusive memberships, intra- and intergroup processes are often reciprocally linked in the case of simultaneous memberships.

One factor that can affect how Group A responds to a shared member's perceived commitment to it and to Group B is the *relative magnitude* of these two commitment levels. To the extent that Group A views a member's commitment to Group B as greater than his or her commitment to itself, Group A will feel anxious. This anxiety, in turn, may cause Group A to take steps to increase the member's commitment to it and decrease his or her commitment to Group B. These steps might include accommodating to the member by working harder to satisfy his or her needs and trying to convince the member that commitment to Group B will not pay off in the long run. Similar, but less intense, efforts may occur if Group A believes that the shared member is equally committed to the two groups. If Group B learns about Group A's efforts, of course, then conflict between the groups can escalate.

Another factor that can affect how Group A responds to a shared member's perceived commitment to it and to Group B is *changes* in these two commitment levels. To the extent that the person seems to be gaining commitment to Group B and/or losing commitment to Group A, Group A will feel anxious. Increased commitment to Group B might be inferred from the person's verbal statements (e.g., praise for Group B) or behavior (e.g., strong efforts to help Group B achieve its goals). Similarly, decreased commitment to Group A might be inferred from the person's verbal statements (e.g., complaints about Group A) or behavior (e.g., weak efforts to help Group A achieve its goals). However, not all commitment changes are likely to be equally troubling. Group A should feel anxious to the extent that commitment changes are large, happen quickly, and cannot be attributed to transient events. Group A's anxiety should elicit efforts to increase the member's commitment to itself and decrease the member's commitment to Group B. As before, Group B's responses to these actions may exacerbate intergroup conflict.

Anxiety can turn to anger when Group A believes that a shared member's shifting commitment will seriously undermine the attainment of group goals. This belief is particularly likely when (a) the person is a key member of Group A, such as a leader; (b) other members of Group A seem likely to follow the person's example by decreasing their commitment to Group A and/or increasing their commitment to Group B; and (c) the person is suspected of telling Group B about Group A's secrets. Unlike anxiety, which stimulates efforts to bring the errant member back into the fold, anger may cause Group A to punish the member and expel him or her from the group (Levine, 1989). These reactions are likely to be especially harsh when the member's commitment change is defined as treason. And if Group B is believed to have purposely undermined the person's commitment to Group A, then various forms of retaliation may occur. These in turn are likely to provoke counterattacks and escalation of intergroup conflict.

Of course, the opposite pattern of responses by Group A would be expected if a shared member seemed to be gaining commitment to Group A and/or losing commitment to Group B. Again, commitment changes might be inferred from the person's verbal statements and/or behavior concerning the groups. The larger these changes are, the more quickly they happen, and the less they can be attributed to transient events, the more reassured Group A should feel. This reassurance will cause Group A to expend less energy trying to increase the member's commitment to itself or decrease the member's commitment to Group B. These responses by Group A should produce a de-escalation of intergroup conflict, because Group B is likely to perceive Group A's behavior as a sign of friendship (or at least tolerance) rather than hostility.

The preceding predictions seem plausible in most intergroup contexts, but there are some special circumstances where they may not hold. For example, if Group A's initial commitment to a shared member is low, because it does not view him or her as particularly helpful at attaining group goals, then it may respond quite differently. That is, Group A may react *positively* to information that the person's commitment is rising in Group B and falling in Group A (because this signals that the person will soon leave Group A for Group B) and *negatively* to information that the person's commitment is falling in Group B and rising in Group A (because this signals that the person will never leave Group A for Group B). And even if

Group A's commitment to a shared member is high, the group may sometimes respond negatively to information that the person's commitment to Group B is falling. This might occur if the information were interpreted to mean that the person is capable of treason, which could someday be directed toward Group A.

The consequences of belonging to two groups simultaneously are also affected by the relations between the groups. It is unlikely that a person could gain or retain membership in two groups that have strongly negative relations (e.g., street gangs battling over turf). Leaving aside such extreme cases, individuals can simultaneously belong to groups whose relations run the gamut from strongly positive to moderately negative. Regarding the former, a person might be a member of a fundamentalist religious denomination and a conservative political group that seeks to ban abortion (Curtis & Zurcher, 1973). Regarding the latter, a person might be a member of a group that seeks to reduce taxes and an organization that supports increased government spending on social services. As the relations between groups become more polarized (in either a negative or positive direction), those groups will probably become more sensitive to the commitment levels of shared members and more inclined to respond behaviorally to "commitment problems." For example, as intergroup relations become more negative, Group A should work harder to ensure that shared members have high commitment to it and low commitment to Group B. In contrast, as intergroup relations become more positive, Group A should work harder to ensure that shared members have high commitment both to it and Group B.

In cases where groups want positive relations with one another, they should encourage, rather than discourage, joint memberships. Thus, Group A might recruit members of Group B with the understanding that they will not have to give up their current affiliation when they join. Or Group A might suggest that some of its own members enter Group B with the same understanding. Joint members are quite useful to groups, because they can function as "boundary spanners" who facilitate intergroup communication and reduce the likelihood of misunderstandings and conflicts (Nelson, 1989; Tushman & Scanlan, 1981). For example, Ancona and Caldwell (1988) found that work groups in organizations often benefit from both "emigration" (encouraging members of their own group to participate in other groups) and "immigration" (allowing members of other groups to participate in their own group). Of course, intergroup relations can also be improved by people who belong to one group, but interact extensively with other groups. Ancona and Caldwell also found that some work groups develop specialized roles designed to facilitate interactions with other groups in the same organization. These roles include the "scout," who imports information and resources that the group needs, the "ambassador," who exports information and resources to outsiders, and the "sentry," who controls information and resources that outsiders want to send into the group.

CREATING AND MAINTAINING SHARED BELIEFS ABOUT THE SOCIAL WORLD

Regardless of whether group memberships are exclusive or simultaneous, a critical component of belonging to a group is sharing beliefs about the social world with fellow members (cf. Bar-Tal, 1990; Farr & Moscovici, 1984; Levine & Moreland, 1991). It seems especially important for people to have shared views of how ingroup members are similar to one another and different from outgroup members. According to Turner et al. (1987), people categorize themselves as a group to the extent that "the subjectively perceived differences between them are less than the differences perceived between them and other people (psychologically) present in the setting" (p. 51). A number of important consequences flow from this self-categorization. For example, people evaluate others on the basis of their "prototypicality," or the degree to which they exemplify the stereotypical attributes that differentiate the ingroup from the outgroup (Hogg, Cooper-Shaw, & Holzworth, 1993). Thus, ingroup members who seem highly prototypical of their group are strongly liked, whereas outgroup members who seem highly prototypical of their group are strongly disliked.

In addition to viewing their own group as better than the outgroup on stereotypical attributes that maximize within-group similarities and between-group differences, people also view ingroups and outgroups differently in other ways. For example, information about outgroup members is represented in a simpler fashion than is information about ingroup members, and the outgroup is usually (although not always) viewed as more homogeneous than the ingroup (e.g., Judd & Park, 1988; Linville, Fischer, & Salovey, 1989; Mullen & Hu, 1989; Park, Ryan, & Judd, 1992; Simon, 1992). Moreover, people show a preference for information indicating that they are similar to the ingroup and different from the outgroup (Wilder & Allen, 1978).

If Group A and Group B are competing for members, then Group A will try to shape prospective members' views about both groups to match its own views. Group A will differentiate the ingroup and the outgroup on a variety of dimensions, such as competence, friendliness, and trustworthiness, that emphasize the ingroup's superiority to the outgroup. And Group A will also suggest other ways in which the two groups differ. For example, it may claim that ingroup members show substantial variability in their personalities and behaviors, whereas outgroup members do not (cf. Ryan, Park, & Judd, 1996). These efforts, if successful, should make prospective members more anxious to join Group A and less anxious to join Group B. To the extent that prospective members come to view the social world through Group A's eyes, they will perceive Group A as more positive, complex, heterogeneous, and similar to themselves than Group B (cf. Brown & Wootton-Millward, 1993; Levine, Bogart, & Zdaniuk, 1996).

Group A's ability to elicit these perceptions depends on both its commitment to prospective members and their commitment to it. To the exent that Group A is highly committed to prospective members (perhaps because they possess special skills), it will be motivated to ensure that prospective members accept its version of reality. This motivation should influence how Group A behaves toward prospective members, which in turn should affect how receptive they are to Group A's views. For example, the more committed Group A feels toward prospective members, the harder it should work to convince them to adopt its views regarding differences between Group A and Group B. As a consequence, prospective members will be more likely to accept the views of a group that has high, rather than low, commitment to them.

Similarly, to the extent that prospective members are more highly committed to Group A than to Group B, they will be motivated to accept Group A's version of reality. This motivation should influence how prospective members behave toward Group A, which in turn should affect how receptive they are to Group A's views. For example, if prospective members are more committed to Group A than to Group B, then they should spend more time interacting with Group A and learning about its perspective. As a consequence, prospective members will be more likely to accept Group A's version of reality than Group B's version. Of course, if Group A's description of itself does not seem accurate (e.g., it claims to be heterogeneous, but appears homogeneous), then prospective members who interact extensively with Group A may become less, rather than more, inclined to accept its views.

So far, we have focused on Group A's efforts to convince *prospective* members to adopt its views of the social world. However, Group A is also motivated to convince *current* members that its views are valid. In particular, it wants people who have not yet attained full member status (new members) and people who once held this status but later lost it (marginal members) to view the ingroup and the outgroup in "proper" ways. In the former case, the group wants the socialization phase of membership to be successful, that is, for the new member to undergo the role transition of acceptance and become a full member for the first time (cf. Levine & Moreland, 1991; Moreland & Levine, 1989). In the latter case, the group wants the resocialization phase of membership to be successful, that is, for the marginal member to undergo the role transition of convergence and become a full member once again.

Although the group's goal during both socialization and resocialization is to produce assimilation in the individual, this goal may be easier to achieve in the former membership phase. Even when a new member and a marginal member are equally committed to the group, the new member is likely to be more optimistic about the future. After all, the typical new member not only recently experienced a positive role transition (entry), after a period of rising individual and group commitment, but also expects the commitment levels of both parties to rise further and anticipates making another positive role transition (acceptance). In contrast, the typical marginal member not only recently experienced a negative role transition (divergence), after a period of declining individual and group commitment, but also expects the commitment levels of both parties to decline further and fears making another negative role transition (exit). Given their different orientations toward the future, it would not be surprising if new members were more susceptible than marginal members to persuasive messages from the group on just about any topic, including differences between the ingroup and outgroup.

This line of reasoning suggests that new members may be particularly prone to stereotypic as well as ethnocentric thoughts and behaviors. Anecdotal evidence for these tendencies can be found in the statements of new converts to religious and political groups, who often make extreme claims about ingroup virtues and outgroup vices. One possible explanation for new members' willingness to accept Group A's views is that they want to demonstrate their group loyalty to *oldtimers* in Group A, which causes them to adopt (or even exaggerate) oldtimers' arguments about the differences between the ingroup and outgroup. Of course, new members may also want to demonstrate their group loyalty to *themselves*. Deciding to join and actually joining a group are stressful experiences that can produce cognitive dissonance (e.g., Aronson & Mills, 1959; Gerard & Mathewson, 1966). To reduce that dissonance, new members may selectively attend to or distort information about the ingroup and outgroup to make the ingroup seem more positive and the outgroup more negative. Thus, one would expect people who have recently entered the socialization phase of group membership to exhibit more ethnocentrism than those who have been in that phase for some time. Presumably, people who have just become new members are more motivated to prove their loyalty and reduce dissonance than are those who have been new members longer. (Note that this prediction deviates from our general assumption that greater commitment on the part of prospective and current members leads to more assimilation.)

That new members are more likely than marginal members to accept Group A's views of the social world does not mean, of course, that marginal members are immune from this tendency. As Noel, Wann, and Branscombe (1995) recently demonstrated, people who feel insecure about their status within a desirable group respond by derogating an outgroup, particularly if they believe that ingroup members will learn about their behavior (see also Breakwell, 1979). The fact that these marginal members seem attentive to the reactions of ingroup members suggests that outgroup derogation is a self-presentational strategy designed to regain acceptance from the ingroup. Thus, one would expect people who have recently entered the resocialization phase of group membership to exhibit more ethnocentrism than those who have been in that phase for some time. Presumably, people who have just become marginal members are more optimistic that a demonstration of loyalty will produce convergence (and avoid exit) than are those who have been marginal members longer.

In the case of simultaneous memberships, Group A's task becomes much more complicated. From the member's perspective, both groups are now ingroups *and* outgroups. That is, when Group A is the ingroup, Group B is the outgroup, and when Group B is the ingroup, Group A is the outgroup. This has important implications for Group A's efforts to convince a shared member to view the social world through its eyes (rather than through Group B's eyes). First, to the extent that the person is more committed to Group A than to Group B, he or she will be more likely to adopt Group A's perspective. This means that Group A should try to increase the person's commitment to it and decrease the person's commitment to Group B. Second, to the extent that Group A is more salient than Group B to the person, he or she will be more likely to adopt Group A's perspective. This means that Group A should try to increase its own salience and decrease Group B's salience (e.g., by encouraging the person to wear clothing bearing Group A's name). Efforts to raise individual commitment are generally more effective than efforts to raise group salience, because heightened commitment is more stable than heightened salience (unless the group manages to make itself permanently salient, for example, by convincing the person to get a large tattoo bearing its name). Although the commitment strategy is typically more effective than the salience strategy, it is also much harder to implement.

We have assumed to this point that Group A's views about itself and Group B are stable, so that Group A's task is simply to convince prospective and current members that these views are valid. However, ingroup and outgroup perceptions may change over time as a function of both intra- and intergroup processes. Particularly important are shifts in the membership composition of each group and alterations in the level of conflict between the groups.

Regarding shifts in membership composition, the entry of new members into one or both groups, and the exit of old members from those groups, are likely to alter how the groups view themselves and each other. If one assumes that Group A's views of itself and Group B are influenced (although not completely determined) by the actual characteristics of the people who belong to the two groups (Judd, Ryan, & Park, 1991), then changes in these characteristics should affect how Group A perceives the groups. For example, if Group A loses athletes and gains musicians while Group B does the reverse, then Group A's views of the two groups are likely to change. This change, of course, might occur on some dimensions (e.g., the major attributes on which the groups are perceived to differ), but not on others (e.g., the perceived homogeneity of the groups). Moreover, because Group A has more information about itself than about Group B, changes in its own membership are more likely to shift its views about both groups than are changes in the other group's membership. In this context, it is important to recall a basic tenet of self-categorization theory (Turner et al., 1987), namely that the critical attributes used to differentiate the ingroup from the outgroup are those that simultaneously maximize within-group similarities and between-group differences. Any composition changes in the groups that alter the distributions of these critical attributes are thus likely to have profound effects on ingroup and outgroup perceptions.

In addition to changes that occur within groups, such as the entry and exit of members, changes that occur between groups, such as increases or decreases in conflict, can also affect how Group A perceives itself and Group B. For example, if intergroup conflict escalates, then Group A should come to see itself in (even) more positive terms and Group B in (even) more negative terms (Brewer, 1979). Heightened conflict may also have other perceptual effects, such as greater ingroup–outgroup differences in perceived variability (Ryan, 1996). A different pattern of perceptual changes would be expected if intergroup conflict de-escalates. Here, Group A should come to see Group B as both more positive and more heterogeneous than before (cf. Levine et al., 1996). As an example, consider the changes that have occurred in Americans' views of Russians since the end of the cold war.

The likelihood that intergroup conflict will escalate versus de-escalate may be affected by Group A's beliefs about how it is viewed by Group B (cf. Bond, 1986; Brigham, 1973; Lieberson, 1985; Rettew, Billman, & Davis, 1993). If Group A makes inaccurate and overly negative assumptions about Group B's views, then its hostility toward Group B should increase. But accurate assumptions on the part of Group A do not necessarily solve the problem. If Group B's stereotype of Group A is in fact very negative, then Group A's (accurate) knowledge of this stereotype should also increase its hostility toward Group B. In contrast, if events lead Group A to make more positive assumptions about Group B's views, then its hostility to Group B should decrease, regardless of the accuracy of these assumptions. This is not to say, of course, that Group B is totally helpless in this process. If Group B believes that Group A's assumptions about its views will have important consequences for intergroup relations, Group B may seek to influence these assumptions by publicizing true or false information about its views.

CONCLUSIONS

In this chapter, we discussed some of the ways in which intergroup processes can influence intragroup processes, and vice versa. We focused on the case in which two groups are in competition for members and examined (a) how this intergroup context affects each group's efforts to recruit and retain members and (b) how these activities within groups modify the relations between groups. We relied heavily on a model of group socialization that explains temporal changes in the relationships between groups and their members (Levine & Moreland, 1994; Moreland & Levine, 1982). In particular, we used the three psychological processes underlying the model (evaluation, commitment, and role transition) to help explain causal connections between inter- and intragroup events. Our analysis illustrates the complexity, and we hope the utility, of simultaneously considering how cognition, affect, and behavior operate in inter- and intragroup contexts.

Although our discussion was fairly broad, we did not analyze all of the ways in which group socialization and intergroup relations might be related. One important question that deserves attention is the degree to which our analysis is applicable to cases involving three or more groups. In discussing how people who plan to join a particular group alter their views about that group and other groups prior to entry, Levine et al. (1996) suggested that a gradient of perceptual change might occur. Consider the case of prospective members who expect to join Group A and believe that this group has negative relations with Group B and positive relations with Group C. How these people perceive Group B and Group C should depend on the relations between these groups and Group A. According to Levine et al., prospective members' perceptions of Group C will shift away from their perceptions of Group B and toward (but not all the way to) their perceptions of Group A. That is, Group C will come to be seen as more positive and heterogeneous than Group B, but as less positive and heterogeneous than Group A. These changes may be due, at least in part, to assimilation-contrast effects that derive from comparisons among the three groups (Wilder, 1986).

Although this example suggests that our analysis of the two-group case is easily generalized to the three-group case, an important difference between the two cases is worth noting. A substantial amount of research using the "minimal group paradigm" has demonstrated that simply categorizing people into two groups using some arbitrary criterion (e.g., one group ostensibly prefers paintings by Klee, the other group ostensibly prefers paintings by Kandinsky) reliably produces ingroup bias concerning the allocation of rewards (see Diehl, 1990; Mullen, Brown, & Smith, 1992). These results have often been interpreted to mean that social categorization is not only a necessary, but also a sufficient, condition for intergroup discrimination (cf. Bornstein et al., 1983). However, recent evidence suggests that the minimal group paradigm may fail to produce ingroup bias when three, rather than just two, groups are involved (Hartstone & Augoustinos, 1995). The ineffectiveness of the paradigm with three groups may be attributable to how subjects construe this intergroup situation. That is, subjects may be much less likely to view intergroup relations as an "us versus them" struggle in the three-group than in the two-group case. Although negative relations among three (or more) groups certainly exist in the real world (e.g., the hostility among Serbs, Croats, and Muslims in the former Yugoslavia), such relations may be less common than data from the traditional minimal group paradigm would lead us to believe (but see Insko et al., 1994). Moreover, when these negative relations do occur, they probably stem from strong realistic group conflict, rather than simple social categorization. If so, then those aspects of our analysis based on realistic group conflict theory may be especially relevant to situations involving three or more groups.

REFERENCES

Abrams, D., & Hogg, M. A. (1990). Social identification, self-categorization, and social influence. In W. Stroebe & M. Hewstone (Eds.), *European review of social psychology* (Vol. 1, pp. 195–228). Chichester, England: Wiley.

Ancona, D. G., & Caldwell, D. F. (1988). Beyond task and maintenance: Defining external functions in groups. *Group and Organization Studies, 13,* 468–494.

Aronson, E., & Mills, J. (1959). The effect of severity of initiation on liking for a group. *Journal of Abnormal and Social Psychology, 59,* 177–181.

Ashforth, B. E., & Mael, F. (1989). Social identity theory and the organization. *Academy of Management Review, 14,* 20–39.

Bar-Tal, D. (1990). *Group beliefs: A conception for analyzing group structure, processes, and behavior.* New York: Springer-Verlag.

Bond, M. H. (1986). Mutual stereotypes and the facilitation of interaction across cultural lines. *International Journal of Intercultural Relations, 10,* 259–276.

Bond, M. H., & Kwok-Venus, C. (1991). Resistance to group or personal insults in an ingroup or outgroup context. *International Journal of Psychology, 26,* 83–94.

Bornstein, G., Crum, L., Wittenbraker, J., Harring, K., Insko, C. A., & Thibaut, J. (1983). On the measurement of social orientations in the minimal group paradigm. *European Journal of Social Psychology, 13,* 321–350.

Breakwell, G. M. (1979). Illegitimate group membership and inter-group differentiation. *British Journal of Social and Clinical Psychology, 18,* 141–149.

Brewer, M. B. (1979). In-group bias in the minimal intergroup situation: A cognitive-motivational analysis. *Psychological Bulletin, 86,* 307–324.

Brewer, M., & Brown, R. (in press). Intergroup relations. In D. Gilbert, S. Fiske, & G. Lindzey (Eds.), *The handbook of social psychology* (4th ed.). Boston: McGraw-Hill.

Brigham, J. C. (1973). Ethnic stereotypes and attitudes: A different mode of analysis. *Journal of Personality, 41,* 206–233.

Brown, R., & Wootton-Millward, L. (1993). Perceptions of group homogeneity during group formation and change. *Social Cognition, 11,* 126–149.

Campbell, A. (1987). Self-definition by rejection: The case of gang girls. *Social Problems, 34,* 451–466.

Campbell, D. T. (1965). Ethnocentric and other altruistic motives. In D. Levine (Ed.), *Nebraska symposium on motivation* (Vol. 13, pp. 283–301). Lincoln, NE: University of Nebraska Press.

Curtis, R. L., Jr., & Zurcher, L. A., Jr. (1973). Stable resources of protest movements: The multi-organizational field. *Social Forces, 52,* 53–61.

Davis, P., & Stern, D. (1981). Adaptation, survival, and growth of the family business: An integrated systems perspective. *Human Relations, 34,* 207–224.

Diehl, M. (1990). The minimal group paradigm: Theoretical explanations and empirical findings. In W. Stroebe & M. Hewstone (Eds.), *European review of social psychology* (Vol. 1, pp. 263–292). Chichester, England: Wiley.

Dion, K. L. (1979). Intergroup conflict and intragroup cohesiveness. In W. G. Austin & S. Worchel (Eds.), *The social psychology of intergroup relations* (pp. 211–224). Monterey, CA: Brooks/Cole.

Dutton, J. E., Dukerich, J. M., & Harquail, C. V. (1994). Organizational images and member identification. *Administrative Science Quarterly, 39,* 239–263.

Farr, R., & Moscovici, S. (Eds.). (1984). *Social representations.* Cambridge, England: Cambridge University Press.

Farrell, C., & Rusbult, C. E. (1981). Exchange variables as predictors of job satisfaction, job commitment, and turnover: The impact of rewards, costs, alternatives, and investments. *Organizational Behavior and Human Performance, 27,* 78–95.

Feldman, D. C. (1994). Who's socializing whom? The impact of socializing newcomers on insiders, work groups, and organizations. *Human Resource Management Review, 4,* 213–233.

Freeman, J., & Hannan, M. T. (1983). Niche width and the dynamics of organizational populations. *American Journal of Sociology, 88,* 1116–1145.

Gerard, H. B., & Mathewson, G. C. (1966). The effects of severity of initiation on liking for a group: A replication. *Journal of Experimental Social Psychology, 2,* 278–287.

Hartstone, M., & Augoustinos, M. (1995). The minimal group paradigm: Categorization into two versus three groups. *European Journal of Social Psychology, 25,* 179–193.

Hogg, M. A. (1992). *The social psychology of group cohesiveness: From attraction to social identity.* New York: New York University Press.

Hogg, M. A., Cooper-Shaw, L., & Holzworth, D. W. (1993). Group prototypicality and depersonalized attraction in small interactive groups. *Personality and Social Psychology Bulletin, 19,* 452–465.

Insko, C. A., Schopler, J., Graetz, K. A., Drigotas, S. M., Currey, D. P., Smith, S. L., Brazil, D., & Bornstein, G. (1994). Interindividual-intergroup discontinuity in the Prisoner's Dilemma Game. *Journal of Conflict Resolution, 38,* 87–116.

Jackson, J. W. (1993). Realistic group conflict theory: A review and evaluation of the theoretical and empirical literature. *Psychological Record, 43,* 395–413.

Johnson, D. J., & Rusbult, C. E. (1989). Resisting temptation: Devaluation of alternative partners as a means of maintaining commitment in close relationships. *Journal of Personality and Social Psychology, 57,* 967–980.

Judd, C. M., & Park, B. (1988). Out-group homogeneity: Judgments of variability at the

individual and group levels. *Journal of Personality and Social Psychology, 54,* 778–788.
Judd, C. M., Ryan, C. S., & Park, B. (1991). Accuracy in the judgment of in-group and out-group variability. *Journal of Personality and Social Psychology, 61,* 366–379.
Kanter, R. M. (1968). Commitment and social organization: A study of commitment mechanisms in Utopian communities. *American Sociological Review, 33,* 499–517.
Kramer, R. M. (1991). Intergroup relations and organizational dilemmas: The role of categorization processes. In B. M. Staw & L. L. Cummings (Eds.), *Research in organizational behavior* (Vol. 13, pp. 191–228). Greenwich, CT: JAI.
Levine, J. M. (1989). Reaction to opinion deviance in small groups. In P. Paulus (Ed.), *Psychology of group influence* (2nd ed., pp. 187–231). Hillsdale, NJ: Lawrence Erlbaum Associates.
Levine, J. M., Bogart, L. M., & Zdaniuk, B. (1996). Impact of anticipated group membership on cognition. In R. M. Sorrentino & E. T. Higgins (Eds.), *Handbook of motivation and cognition: Vol. 3. The interpersonal context* (pp. 531–569). New York: Guilford.
Levine, J. M., & Moreland, R. L. (1985). Innovation and socialization in small groups. In S. Moscovici, G. Mugny, & E. Van Avermaet (Eds.), *Perspectives on minority influence* (pp. 143–169). Cambridge, England: Cambridge University Press.
Levine, J. M., & Moreland, R. L. (1991). Culture and socialization in work groups. In L. B. Resnick, J. M. Levine, & S. D. Teasley (Eds.), *Perspectives on socially shared cognition* (pp. 257–279). Washington, DC: American Psychological Association.
Levine, J. M., & Moreland, R. L. (1994). Group socialization: Theory and research. In W. Stroebe & M. Hewstone (Eds.), *European review of social psychology* (Vol. 5, pp. 305–336). Chichester, England: Wiley.
Levine, J. M., & Moreland, R. L. (in press). Small groups. In D. Gilbert, S. Fiske, & G. Lindzey (Eds.), *The handbook of social psychology* (4th ed.). Boston: McGraw-Hill.
Lieberson, S. (1985). Stereotypes: Their consequences for race and ethnic interaction. *Research in Race and Ethnic Relations, 4,* 113–137.
Linville, P. W., Fischer, G. W., & Salovey, P. (1989). Perceived distributions of characteristics of in-group and out-group members: Empirical evidence and a computer simulation. *Journal of Personality and Social Psychology, 57,* 165–188.
Mackie, D. M., & Hamilton, D. L. (Eds.). (1993). *Affect, cognition, and stereotyping: Interactive processes in group perception.* San Diego, CA: Academic Press.
Macrae, C. N., Stangor, C., & Hewstone, M. (Eds.). (1996). *Stereotypes and stereotyping.* New York: Guilford.
McPherson, J. M. (1983). An ecology of affiliation. *American Sociological Review, 48,* 519–532.
McPherson, J. M. (1988). A theory of voluntary organization. In C. Milofsky (Ed.), *Community organizations* (pp. 42–76). New York: Oxford University Press.
McPherson, J. M., & Ranger-Moore, J. R. (1991). Evolution on a dancing landscape: Organizations and networks in dynamic Blau space. *Social Forces, 70,* 19–42.
McPherson, J. M., & Smith-Lovin, L. (1988). A comparative ecology of five nations: Testing a model of competition among voluntary organizations. In G. R. Carroll (Ed.), *Ecological models of organizations* (pp. 85–109). Cambridge, MA: Ballinger.
Meyer, J. P., & Allen, N. J. (1991). A three-component conceptualization of organizational commitment. *Human Resource Management Review, 1,* 61–89.
Moreland, R. L., & Levine, J. M. (1982). Socialization in small groups: Temporal changes in individual–group relations. In L. Berkowitz (Ed.), *Advances in experimental social psychology* (Vol. 15, pp. 137–192). New York: Academic Press.
Moreland, R. L., & Levine, J. M. (1984). Role transitions in small groups. In V. L. Allen & E. van de Vliert (Eds.), *Role transitions: Explorations and explanations* (pp. 181–195). New York: Plenum.
Moreland, R. L., & Levine, J. M. (1989). Newcomers and oldtimers in small groups. In P.

Paulus (Ed.), *Psychology of group influence* (2nd ed., pp. 143-186). Hillsdale, NJ: Lawrence Erlbaum Associates.

Moreland, R. L., Levine, J. M., & Cini, M. A. (1993). Group socialization: The role of commitment. In M. Hogg & D. Abrams (Eds.), *Group motivation: Social psychological perspectives* (pp. 105-129). London: Harvester Wheatsheaf.

Mullen, B., Brown, R., & Smith, C. (1992). Ingroup bias as a function of salience, relevance, and status: An integration. *European Journal of Social Psychology, 22,* 103-122.

Mullen, B., & Hu, L. (1989). Perceptions of ingroup and outgroup variability: A meta-analytic integration. *Basic and Applied Social Psychology, 10,* 233-252.

Nelson, R. E. (1989). The strength of strong ties. *Academy of Management Journal, 32,* 377-401.

Noel, J. G., Wann, D. L., & Branscombe, N. R. (1995). Peripheral ingroup membership status and public negativity toward outgroups. *Journal of Personality and Social Psychology, 68,* 127-137.

Oakes, P. J., Haslam, S. A., & Turner, J. C. (1994). *Stereotyping and social reality.* Oxford, England: Blackwell.

Park, B., Ryan, C. S., & Judd, C. M. (1992). Role of meaningful subgroups in explaining differences in perceived variability for in-groups and out-groups. *Journal of Personality and Social Psychology, 63,* 553-567.

Rettew, D. C., Billman, D., & Davis, R. A. (1993). Inaccurate perceptions of the amount others stereotype: Estimates about stereotypes of one's own group and other groups. *Basic and Applied Social Psychology, 14,* 121-142.

Ryan, C. S. (1995). Motivations and the perceiver's group membership: Consequences for stereotype accuracy. In Y. Lee, L. J. Jussim, & C. R. McCauley (Eds.), *Stereotype accuracy: Toward appreciating group differences* (pp. 189-214). Washington, DC: American Psychological Association.

Ryan, C. S. (1996). Accuracy of black and white college students' in-group and out-group stereotypes. *Personality and Social Psychology Bulletin, 22,* 1114-1127.

Ryan, C. S., Park, B., & Judd, C. M. (1996). Assessing stereotype accuracy: Implications for understanding the stereotyping process. In C. N. Macrae, C. Stangor, & M. Hewstone (Eds.), *Stereotypes and stereotyping* (pp. 121-157). New York: Guilford.

Schopler, J., Insko, C. A., Graetz, K. A., Drigotas, S., Smith, V. A., & Dahl, K. (1993). Individual-group discontinuity: Further evidence for mediation by fear and greed. *Personality and Social Psychology Bulletin, 19,* 419-431.

Sherif, M., Harvey, O. J., White, B. J., Hood, W. R., & Sherif, C. W. (1961). *Intergroup conflict and cooperation: The Robbers Cave experiment.* Norman, OK: University of Oklahoma Press.

Sherif, M., & Sherif, C. W. (1969). *Social psychology.* New York: Harper & Row.

Simon, B. (1992). The perception of in-group and out-group homogeneity: Reintroducing the intergroup context. In W. Stroebe & M. Hewstone (Eds.), *European review of social psychology* (Vol. 3, pp. 1-30). Chichester, England: Wiley.

Staw, B. M., Sandelands, L. E., & Dutton, J. E. (1981). Threat-rigidity effects in organizational behavior: A multi-level analysis. *Administrative Science Quarterly, 26,* 501-524.

Stryker, S. (1968). Identity salience and role performance: The relevance of symbolic interaction theory for family research. *Journal of Marriage and the Family, 30,* 558-564.

Stryker, S. (1987). Identity theory: Developments and extensions. In K. Yardley & T. Honess (Eds.), *Self and identity: Psychosocial perspectives* (pp. 89-103). New York: Wiley.

Sutton, R. I., & Louis, M. R. (1987). How selecting and socializing newcomers influences insiders. *Human Resource Management, 26,* 347-361.

Turner, J. C., Hogg, M. A., Oakes, P. J., Reicher, S. D., & Wetherell, M. S. (1987). *Rediscovering the social group: A self-categorization theory.* New York: Basil Blackwell.

Tushman, M. L., & Scanlan, T. J. (1981). Boundary spanning individuals: Their role in information transfer and their antecedents. *Academy of Management Journal, 24,* 289–305.

Vanbeselaere, N. (1991). The different effects of simple and crossed categorizations: A result of the category differentiation process or of differential category salience? In W. Stroebe & M. Hewstone (Eds.), *European review of social psychology* (Vol. 2, pp. 247–278). Chichester, England: Wiley.

Wanous, J. P. (1980). *Organizational entry: Recruitment, selection, and socialization of newcomers.* Reading, MA: Addison-Wesley.

Wanous, J. P., Poland, T. D., Premack, S. L., & Davis, K. S. (1992). The effects of met expectations on newcomer attitudes and behaviors: A review and meta-analysis. *Journal of Applied Psychology, 77,* 288–297.

Wilder, D. A. (1986). Social categorization: Implications for creation and reduction of intergroup bias. In L. Berkowitz (Ed.), *Advances in experimental social psychology* (Vol. 19, pp. 291–355). Orlando, FL: Academic Press.

Wilder, D. A., & Allen, V. L. (1978). Group membership and preference for information about others. *Personality and Social Psychology Bulletin, 4,* 106–110.

Wilsnack, R. W. (1980). Information control: A conceptual framework for sociological analysis. *Urban Life, 8,* 467–499.

Wong-Rieger, D., & Taylor, D. M. (1981). Multiple group membership and self-identity. *Journal of Cross Cultural Psychology, 12,* 61–79.

Ziller, R. C. (1965). Toward a theory of open and closed groups. *Psychological Bulletin, 64,* 164–182.

V

On the Reduction of Unwanted Intergroup Cognition and Behavior

13

Stereotypes in Thought and Deed: Social-Cognitive Origins of Intergroup Discrimination

Galen V. Bodenhausen
Northwestern University

C. Neil Macrae
University of St. Andrews

Jennifer Garst
Ohio State University

Discrimination based on social group membership is ubiquitous in human cultures (LeVine & Campbell, 1972). Despite an increase in people's awareness of, and concern about, discrimination based on race, gender, and other demographic categories, such biases are still ubiquitously evident in personal behavior and institutional practices. Examples abound in the popular media as well as the scientific literature. A national restaurant chain was recently required to pay more than $50 million to African-American customers who had been systematically mistreated by the company's employees (Kohn, 1994). A careful investigation of automobile dealerships in the Chicago area revealed a consistent pattern of bias against African-American and female customers in retail car sales negotiations (Ayres, 1991). Observation of the classroom behavior of school teachers has revealed alarming disparities in the treatment of boys and girls, consistently putting the girls at an educational disadvantage (Sadker & Sadker, 1994). The litany of such injustices is extensive. The present chapter considers the role played by stereotypic beliefs in the development of such patterns of discrimination.

In examining the connections between intergroup cognition and intergroup behavior, fairly broad conceptions of both phenomena are adopted. On the cognitive side, the focus here is on the mental processes involved in evaluating individual members of social groups, and particularly the role played by beliefs about group-typical characteristics in such evaluative analysis. The range of processes fitting under this general description includes implicit, automatic cognition, as well as explicit, effortful cognition (Bargh, in press; Devine, 1989; Greenwald & Banaji, 1995). On the behavioral side, the focus here is on any observable response involving or directed at outgroup members. Phenomena of interest include decisions made about outgroup members, verbal and nonverbal interaction patterns, and so on.

The existence of shared stereotypic beliefs about the social groups that are subjected to discrimination is indisputable. However, whether such beliefs play a causal role in the production of discrimination is a question worth considering. *Stereotypes* consist of specific descriptive beliefs attributed to a social group, whereas *prejudice* refers to a general evaluation (usually negative) of the group. It might be the case that general prejudice (i.e., dislike of stigmatized groups) rather than specific stereotypes (i.e., specific descriptive beliefs about the group) account for the negative treatment that group members receive (Jussim, Nelson, Manis, & Soffin, 1995). Although animus per se might be an important factor in producing discrimination, there are several reasons to believe that stereotypic beliefs can play an important role as well. The real-life examples cited earlier are illustrative. The restaurant employees who treated African-American customers rudely or even refused to served them at all had specific beliefs about these customers (e.g., how they would behave, how they would tip, whether they would leave without paying) that informed their reactions to the customers (Kohn, 1994). Sadker and Sadker (1994) found that teachers who provided girls with less useful and less diagnostic feedback in the classroom did so, in part, because of their stereotypic assumptions about the fragility of girls: "I don't like to tell a girl anything is wrong, because I don't like to upset her" (p. 55). In fact, cultural gender-role stereotypes result in teacher behavior that trains girls to "defer to boys; to avoid math and science as male domains; to value neatness and quiet more than assertiveness and creativity; to emphasize appearance and hide intelligence. Through this curriculum in sexism they are turned into educational spectators instead of players, but education is not a spectator sport" (Sadker & Sadker, 1994, p. 13).

Ayres (1991) explicitly compared different theoretical models of the mediation of car salespersons' bias against female and African-American customers, and found that animus alone was not sufficient to explain the dealers' discriminatory practices. Specific beliefs about negotiating savvy played an important role. Sales pitches also often followed a stereotypic course. For example, salespersons emphasized economy of operating expenses to African-American customers and attractiveness of the car's color and upholstery to female customers. Whether such stereotypes represent beliefs about interests and abilities that are accurate to a significant degree is an empirical question (Judd & Park, 1993; Ottati & Lee, 1995). One might expect that dealers would not rely on such stereotypes if they did not "pay off" (but see Ayres, 1991). Regardless of whether stereotypes are truly accurate, people who hold them often assume that they are and act accordingly. Most important, the car dealers' descriptive beliefs about African-American and female customers are likely to be central in accounting for the disparate treatment.

Perhaps the most elementary and insidious form of discrimination is segregation: social arrangements that minimize contact with the members of other groups. Yet even this primitive form of discrimination is not simply a byproduct of animus or xenophobia. Recent studies of residential segregation emphasize the important role of stereotypic beliefs in guiding segregated housing choices (Farley, Steeh, Krysan, Jackson, & Reeves, 1994; Massey & Denton, 1993). Thus, a variety of instances of real-world discrimination appear fundamentally to involve the operation of stereotypes. Controlled laboratory studies also point to this conclusion. For example, antiminority biases in mock juror decision making tend to occur only against defendants who are accused of stereotypic offenses (e.g., Bodenhausen & Wyer, 1985; Gordon, 1990; for a meta-analytic review, see Mazzella & Feingold, 1994). Similar laboratory findings have been offered in accounting for discrimination in employment opportunities (Krieger, 1995). But if stereotypes do play a role in producing discrimination, what is the nature of their role? Under what conditions does the activation of social stereotypes lead to discriminatory judgments and behavior? How can these effects be circumvented or counteracted? It is these questions that this chapter seeks to address.

STEREOTYPE ACTIVATION: SOWING THE SEEDS OF DISCRIMINATION

Although there are many pathways to discrimination, the focus here is on the process that begins when the social perceiver notices a target's membership in a stereotyped group, and, as a consequence, concepts that are associated with the group become activated in the perceiver's mind. From this starting point, this section traces what are considered to be some of the most important steps on the path to discrimination (or its avoidance).

Quite obviously, stereotypes will not lead to discrimination if they are never activated. Thus, it is logical to begin this consideration by examining the factors that determine whether stereotype activation will in fact occur. Many of the social stereotypes that have attracted great attention in recent years are ones that are linked to group memberships that can be discerned from even a cursory visual inspection of another person. For example, physical appearance is often marked in ways that readily reveal a person's gender, ethnicity, and age group, and clothing (e.g., style, uniforms) may indicate socioeconomic status (SES), occupation, religion, and other group memberships. As such, people may routinely and rather automatically categorize others into groups based on these cues (e.g., Brewer, 1988; Fiske & Neuberg, 1990). But is simply detecting membership in such groups sufficient to elicit mental activation of the stereotypes associated with the group? This question has been the subject of much debate in recent years.

Devine (1989) proposed that racial stereotypes are indeed activated automatically upon detection of racial group membership. She argued that, because people are inevitably exposed to the pervasive cultural representation of stereotypic ideas during socialization, social category membership comes to be inextricably associated with stereotypic notions that spring to mind without any intention on the perceiver's part. As evidence for this claim, Devine demonstrated that even preconscious presentation of racial group labels produced activation of stereotypic concepts. Specifically, after exposure to preconscious primes pertaining to the category "African Americans," participants later judged an ambiguous target person in ways that were more consistent with stereotypes about African Americans, compared with unprimed control participants, in keeping with the assumption that stereotypes about this group had been automatically and unintentionally activated. In more recent research, preconscious category activation has also been found to result in automatic stereotype activation in the domains of gender (Klinger & Beall, 1992), age (Perdue & Gurtman, 1990), and occupation (Macrae, Milne, & Bodenhausen, 1994; for reviews, see Bargh, 1997; Hilton & von Hippel, 1996).

One provocative feature of Devine's (1989) analysis is the presumption that the automatic activation of stereotypes remains in place even among individuals who do not endorse the stereotypic beliefs. Arguing that cultural conditioning makes stereotype activation a habitual phenomenon, she asserted that only by the deployment of conscious, effortful processes can low-prejudice persons counter the unavoidable activation of stereotypic notions. Essentially, then, she argued that automatic stereotype activation (at least with respect to highly conditioned stereotypes, such as those pertaining to race) is not subject to individual differences, although conscious resistance to these automatic effects is likely to vary across individuals. More recent findings, however, have raised the possibility that there may be individual differences in the automatic activation of stereotypic beliefs (Locke, MacLeod, & Walker, 1994; Wittenbrink, Judd, & Park, 1997). As Bargh (1997) put it, "As with all preconscious processes, what determines whether the stereotype becomes automatically activated in this way [upon just the mere presence of a group member] is whether it has been frequently and consistently active in the past in the presence of relevant social group features" (p. 14). To the extent that Devine is correct in viewing racial stereotypes as pervasively active in most individuals' cultural environments, her claim that such stereotypes are inevitably activated in the presence of group members is likely to be largely correct. If there is meaningful variation in the frequency and consistency of people's exposure to such ideas, however, there may be variation in the automatic component of stereotype activation as well (see also Fazio, Jackson, Dunton, & Williams, 1995).

In addition to the possibility that individual differences may moderate the automaticity of stereotype activation, other recent research suggests that activation may also be constrained by perceivers' level of attentional resources. Most notably, Gilbert and Hixon (1991) reported evidence suggesting that stereotype activation may not occur when perceivers are cognitively busy. In their experiments, participants viewed a videotape depicting an Asian woman. Simultaneously, the participants were asked to complete a series of word fragments, many of which could be completed as words that reflect concepts stereotypically associated with Asians (e.g., completing "_ I C E" as *rice* rather than *mice*). In fact, participants tended to choose stereotypic word completions under baseline conditions, but when they were cognitively busy (e.g., mentally rehearsing a digit string for subsequent recall), their word completions were not significantly more likely to reflect stereotypic concepts. Gilbert and Hixon concluded that stereotype activation is *conditionally* automatic, in that it depends on the availability of sufficient mental resources to be accomplished.

Following up on Gilbert and Hixon's (1991) findings, other researchers have developed evidence suggesting that perceivers' goals may be a more important moderator of stereotype activation than processing resources per se. For example, Spencer and Fein (1994) proposed that sufficiently motivated perceivers might be able to activate social stereotypes even under conditions of busyness. They examined busy people who either had or had not experienced a threat to their self-esteem. Previous research suggests that one motivation for engaging in stereotyping is to bolster one's self-esteem when under threat (e.g., Crocker, Thompson, McGraw, & Ingerman, 1987; Hogg & Abrams, 1988). Perhaps this motivation is sufficient to produce stereotype activation even among busy people. This pattern is exactly what Spencer and Fein found. The resource demands of stereotype activation may be fairly minimal, so that even busy perceivers can accomplish it if they have some reason to do so.

Evidence for goal-directed categorization can also be found in a recent study by Pendry and Macrae (1996). Confirming the theorizing of Brewer (1988) and Fiske and Neuberg (1990), Pendry and Macrae demonstrated that the extent of stereotype activation is moderated by perceivers' level of involvement with a target. When relatively uninvolving processing objectives are in place, stereotype activation occurs only at the broadest level (i.e., superordinate) of category representation. However, when involving interactional goals are operating (e.g., accountability, outcome-dependence), a target is categorized both in terms of a higher order representation (e.g., woman) and a more differentiated category subtype (e.g., business woman). That the categorization process operates in such a manner should come as no real surprise. Almost four decades ago, Bruner (1957) and Jones and Thibaut (1958) alerted us to the importance of goal-directed social categorizations. Whether, when gazing into the eyes of stranger, we see a potential dream date or a patient in need of a cataract operation depends on the goals, motives, and expectations we bring to bear on social interaction.

Thus, it appears that the activation of stereotypes on the mere detection of a categorizable social target is a fairly commonplace occurrence, although not a universal one. As is the case in so many social-psychological domains, the nature of stereotype activation seems to critically depend on the pattern of chronic and recent activation and use of these concepts (Bargh, 1997; Higgins, Rholes, & Jones, 1977; Sedikides & Skowronski, 1991; Srull & Wyer, 1979), as well as the perceivers' current motivation and attentional resources (Chaiken, Liberman, & Eagly, 1989; Fazio, 1990; Fiske & Neuberg, 1990; Petty & Cacioppo, 1986).

Of course, when a perceiver encounters another person, it is almost always the case that multiple bases for categorization (and hence, for stereotyping) exist (Stangor, Lynch, Duan, & Glass, 1992). An important question that has not yet received much empirical attention concerns the factors that determine which of the possible stereotypes will be activated. For instance, an elderly African-American woman could be the victim of sexist, ageist, and/or racist discrimination. In any given situation, are all of the stereotypes associated with these demographic categories likely to be activated? If only a subset is activated, which will it be? In some cases, there may be well-established subtypes that represent the conjunction of various possible social categories. In such cases, it is the unique subtype (rather than both superordinate categories) that is most likely to be activated. In cases where no well-established subtype applies, Macrae, Bodenhausen, and Milne (1995) argued that there is likely to be a cognitive competition among the various possible categorizations. The stereotypes associated with the category that "wins" the competition become activated, whereas the "losing" stereotypes are actively inhibited. Thus, in an effort to confer coherent meaning to the current situation, social perceivers appear to prefer relatively simple, well-structured impressions based on a single, dominant categorization, rather than the potential hodgepodge of mental associations that could ensue if all relevant stereotypes were to be activated.

The studies reported by Macrae et al. (1995) confirm that the intercategory competition is affected by a number of factors, including the recency of category activation (more recently activated or "primed" categories tend to dominate), as well as the presence of cues signaling the contextual appropriateness of one categorization or another. For example, participants exposed to a Chinese woman tended to activate stereotypes about women (and inhibit stereotypes about Asians) when the target was seen applying makeup, but they tended to activate stereotypes about Asians (and inhibit stereotypes about women) when she was seen eating noodles with chopsticks. The contextual salience of a given categorical identity (e.g., the only woman in a room otherwise filled with men) also seems to be important in its activation (Biernat & Vescio, 1993; McGuire, McGuire, Child, & Fujioka, 1978; Taylor, Fiske, Etcoff, & Ruderman, 1978).

Moreover, prejudicial attitudes in certain domains may make relevant social categories chronically likely to be activated (Stangor et al., 1992). A hard-core racist may always categorize the African Americans he or she encounters in terms of their race, rather than any of the vast array of other possible bases for categorizing any particular member of this group. Thus, although stereotype activation often occurs automatically, a variety of factors regulate which of the possibly applicable stereotypes are selected for activation.

As noted at the outset, stereotypes will not produce discrimination if they are not activated. But it appears reasonable to assume that stereotypes are indeed activated under a variety of common circumstances. Once activated, how do stereotypes impinge on information processing to bias judgment and behavior? If they are activated, do they inevitably produce biases of this sort? The remaining sections of the chapter consider in some detail the questions of how and when activated stereotypes are likely to produce discriminatory responses.

NOTHING BUT THE FACTS? SOCIAL CONSTRUAL THROUGH A STEREOTYPIC LENS

One of the most fundamental assumptions of social-psychological theory is the view that perceivers actively impose meaning and coherence on the social stimuli to which they are exposed (Asch, 1946; Bruner, 1957; Ross & Nisbett, 1991). Much research has addressed the role played by attitudes (e.g., Fazio, 1990), expectancies (e.g., Neuberg, 1996; Olson, Roese, &

Zanna, 1996), scripts and schemas (e.g., Taylor & Crocker, 1981), recently activated exemplars (e.g., Smith, in press), and other sorts of preexisting knowledge structures on this process of construing the social milieu. To make sense of the raw, often ambiguous social stimuli that they encounter, perceivers must inevitably make use of their prior knowledge, and stereotypic knowledge has been shown to affect this process in numerous systematic ways (Hamilton & Sherman, 1994).

From Hastorf and Cantril's (1954) classic demonstrations of team allegiances differentially affecting perceptions of football games, to Latané and Darley's (1968) studies of how people respond to ambiguous emergencies, to more recent research on reactions to the performance and/or outcomes of minority group members (Major & Crocker, 1993), social psychologists have long assumed that the way people construe the social situation is critically important in shaping their judgments and behavioral reactions. The identical situation can provoke radically different responses if it is given radically different interpretations. In keeping with this long-standing tradition, we believe that stereotypes affect overt responses, producing discriminatory judgments and behaviors, via their impact on the construal of social targets and the immediate social situation (Fazio, 1990). Once activated, stereotypes affect which stimuli people notice and how they interpret them, as well as whether and how they remember the information later.

Consider a classroom teacher who must instruct and otherwise manage a collection of energetic school children. In all likelihood, there will often be times when a lot of behavior is happening simultaneously. Given the challenges of monitoring such a variety of behavioral displays, the teacher may have to be selective in allocating attention to the children. Under taxing mental circumstances such as these, stereotypic expectancies may be especially likely to guide attention (Bodenhausen & Lichtenstein, 1987; Macrae, Hewstone, & Griffiths, 1993; Pratto & Bargh, 1991; Stangor & Duan, 1991). Thus, for example, if the teacher believes that minority children are more disruptive or rambunctious, he or she may be more likely to notice such displays when they are performed by the minority group while tending to overlook them in others. If such displays elicit rebukes and punishments with greater frequency when they are performed by the minority group, then discrimination has occurred. Analogously, studies of mock juror decision making have shown that jurors are more likely to notice and remember incriminating evidence when it fits with stereotypic preconceptions, leading them to harsher judgments, compared with cases in which the same evidence is attributed to a nonstereotyped target (e.g., Bodenhausen, 1988). Like the teacher's impression of child conduct in the classroom, the juror's construal of the evidence is not simply a product of the facts per se, but rather is filtered through a stereotypic lens.

In addition to the problem of allocating limited attentional resources to the range of available environmental stimuli, perceivers are also confronted with the task of disambiguating the stimuli to which they attend. Human behavior is often complex and ambiguous, and therefore open to multiple plausible interpretations. Stereotypic expectancies provide one way of selecting among competing interpretations (Kunda & Sherman-Williams, 1993). Is a child who pokes another child with a pencil being playful or hostile? According to research done by Sagar and Schofield (1980), it all depends on the race of the child. African-American children who do so are much more likely to be viewed as hostile, compared with White children performing identical actions. If the same behavior provokes a harsher or more punitive response when performed by an African-American versus a White child, then discrimination has occurred, based on differential construal of the situation (see also Duncan, 1976).

So far the story developed here is relatively straightforward. Stereotypes are frequently activated, typically automatically, in the presence of out-group members. Once in mind, these concepts color people's interpretations of ambiguous stimuli, much as any accessible concept tends to do when the available stimuli can be assimilated to it (Wyer & Srull, 1989). Moreover, stereotypic expectations guide attention to the subset of available stimuli to which they are relevant. In so doing, they can bias the interpretations placed on a target and his or her behavior. It is these biased interpretations that give rise to discriminatory responses.

This picture captures the essential processes connecting stereotypic knowledge and discrimination. However, the Activation → Construal → Discrimination pathway sketched here is obviously subject to qualifications and modifications. For example, there are some circumstances that exacerbate the impact of stereotypic knowledge on judgment and memory, including (a) mental busyness (e.g., Macrae, Hewstone, & Griffiths, 1993), (b) information overload (e.g., Pratto & Bargh, 1991; Rothbart, Fulero, Jenson, Howard, & Birrell, 1978), (c) time pressure (e.g., Kruglanski & Freund, 1983), (d) low levels of circadian arousal (Bodenhausen, 1990), and (e) certain emotional states, including happiness, anger, and anxiety, although not sadness (Baron, Inman, Kao, & Logan, 1992; Bodenhausen, Kramer, & Süsser, 1994; Bodenhausen, Sheppard, & Kramer, 1994). These factors probably do not typically affect stereotype activation (but see Gilbert & Hixon, 1991); rather, they seem to confer greater importance to the activated stereotypic concepts in the process of forming a construal of the target by undermining more evidence-based or "bottom-up" processing of the stimulus field.

Like many other investigators (e.g., Brewer, 1988; Chaiken et al., 1989; Fiske & Neuberg, 1990; Petty & Cacioppo, 1986), we assume that the systematic assessment of stimulus features requires both motivation and sufficient attentional resources. Each of the factors listed earlier seems to involve some constraint of these processing resources, thereby enhancing the desirability of a quick, heuristic response to the target in lieu of a more thorough assessment. Some bottom–up processing of the stimulus information is still likely to occur, but it will tend to be biased and incomplete (Chaiken, Giner-Sorolla, & Chen, 1996; Chaiken & Maheswaran, 1994). Under such conditions, discriminatory responses to the target are even more likely because the construal of her or him is more likely to be stereotypically biased.

Just as there are situations where stereotype activation is likely to have a greater impact on construal processes, there may be a variety of circumstances under which the activation of stereotypic beliefs has little if any impact on construal, and consequently does not lead to discrimination. Thus, to fully understand the social-cognitive origins of discrimination, one also needs to understand the processes that may constrain, undermine, or prevent stereotype activation from having its biasing sequelae.

One limiting condition of stereotype application that has received considerable research attention is the presence of target information that is incompatible with stereotypic construals. When the target does not appear to fit the social category well, and this disconfirmatory information is not easily overlooked, he or she may not be subject to stereotypic impressions or discriminatory reactions (for reviews, see Brewer, 1996; Fiske & Neuberg, 1990). Similarly, if diagnostic and nonstereotypic information about a target is readily available and perceivers are motivated and able to process this information, its influence may often dominate construals of the target, thereby minimizing stereotypic influences (for a review, see Kunda & Thagard, 1996). Another set of limiting conditions that has only recently begun to receive empirical scrutiny concerns the ways that perceivers may attempt to compensate for stereotypic biases, often in an explicit effort to avoid unfairly biased or discriminatory responses. When do perceivers attempt to avoid biased construals of outgroup targets? How do they go about doing this? How successful are they in accomplishing this goal? These questions will be considered in some detail in the next section.

THE ELIMINATION OF DISCRIMINATION: CAN STEREOTYPES BE STOPPED?

The simple Activation → Construal → Discrimination model developed so far captures the fundamental elements of the social-cognitive underpinnings of intergroup discrimination. The abundant and growing literature on social stereotyping suggests the need for many additional considerations if we are to capture adequately the complexity and flexibility of the cognitive system. Figure 13.1 presents a more articulated version of the model, incorporating several moderator variables that recent research has shown to be important in determining whether perceivers can effectively regulate their own cognition and behavior in the service of avoiding discriminatory responses to outgroup members. The following sections consider in detail how these factors interact to produce successful avoidance of stereotyping and discrimination, or not.

Awareness

For perceivers to initiate efforts to avoid or make adjustments for possible influences of activated stereotypes, they must be aware that such influences are a possibility in the first place. If they do not entertain even the possibility of such influences, they will of course take no steps to avoid or mitigate stereotypic biases (Strack & Hannover, 1996). Moreover, there are several reasons to believe that perceivers may often be unaware that their perceptions and reactions have been affected by their stereotypes and prejudices.

A growing body of research has documented the occurrence of *implicit* stereotyping effects (Banaji & Greenwald, 1995; Greenwald & Banaji, 1995). This term refers to cases in which people show evidence of being influenced by activated stereotypes, although they have no conscious recollection of the triggering experience. Cognitive psychologists have produced an impressive array of evidence showing that experiences of which people have no conscious recollection can exert marked influences on their performance on a variety of tasks (e.g., Jacoby, 1991; Schacter, Chiu, & Ochsner, 1993). Greenwald and Banaji (1995) showed that these processes have direct relevance to phenomena of interest to social psychologists as well (see also Bornstein & Pittman, 1992; Seamon, Williams, Crowley, & Kim, 1995). In one series of studies, Banaji and her colleagues found that activating gender-based expectations affected ratings of subsequently encountered male and female targets, independent of participants' explicit memory for the priming episode (Banaji, Hardin, & Rothman, 1993). Because of its automaticity, stereotype activation can thus occur without perceivers' awareness or intent; unless they have some reason to be on their guard about the possibility of such influences, these biases may well go undetected. Awareness of a possible influence may only arise in cases in which the perceiver has acquired some sensitivity to the possibility of bias. For example, because racial bias has been such a widely discussed and debated phenomenon in America, many Americans may have cultivated an awareness of the potential for such bias, and this issue may come to mind frequently when members of racial minorities are encountered. However, prejudice and discrimination based on social

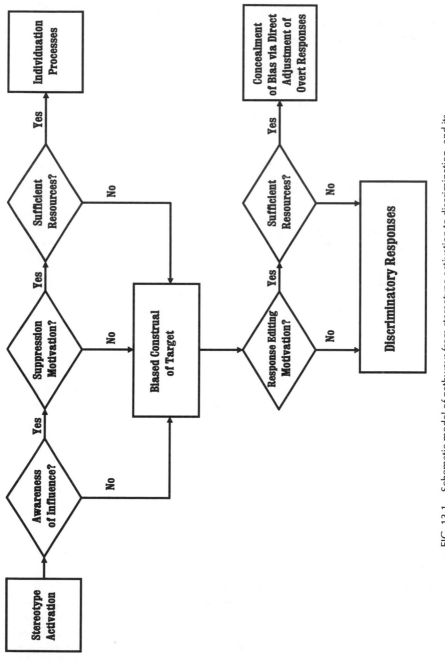

FIG. 13.1. Schematic model of pathways from stereotype activation to discrimination, and its avoidance. Moderator variables are depicted in diamond-shaped boxes.

class has not received much attention or concern in American society, so the average perceiver may have little tendency to be vigilant for the possible impact of unfair class-related preconceptions.

Even when people are aware of the general possibility that stereotypes and prejudice may have influenced them, they may be skilled at deceiving themselves about their own susceptibility to such influences. In their theory of aversive racism, Gaertner and Dovidio (1986) posited that, although most people are socialized to possess negative feelings and beliefs about minorities, they also aspire to be egalitarian and fair-minded. As a result, such persons are unlikely to express negative reactions to minority targets if such reactions might appear to be based on prejudice. Crucially, however, their research shows that when situational factors present an ostensible excuse for a negative response, reactions to minority targets are indeed discriminatory. For example, participants in baseline conditions were just as likely to offer help to an African-American as to a White confederate. However, when a situational excuse for failing to help was present (specifically, the presence of other bystanders who could assume the responsibility for helping; see Darley & Latané, 1968), African Americans were offered far less help than Whites under otherwise identical circumstances (Gaertner & Dovidio, 1977). It is possible that this occurrence of biased reactions to minority targets only in the presence of contextual justification factors reflects a conscious self-presentational strategy, but it is equally plausible that such justifications represent a form of self-deception, whereby individuals convince themselves that the target's race has played no role in their decision not to help. These experiments raise the sobering possibility that even sensitive individuals who aspire to egalitarian ideals may underestimate their own vulnerability to discriminatory reactions. Unless they can admit to that susceptibility, they are unlikely to initiate any attempt to avoid stereotypic influences. Such individuals are then likely to follow the path to biased construals that leads on to discrimination.

Motivation for Suppressing Stereotypes

Assuming that a person is aware of the possibility of stereotypic bias, does he or she care about it? This is the question of suppression motivation. As Dovidio and Gaertner (1986) observed, concerns about egalitarianism and fairness toward minority groups have been on the rise in recent decades. Public opinion polls now reveal nearly universal endorsement of the general principles of equal opportunity and equal treatment under the law (Schuman, Steeh, & Bobo, 1985), although agreement with these principles does not always produce support for specific programs and policies designed to implement them (e.g., Sears & Kinder, 1985). What is quite clear, however, is that historical events of recent decades (e.g., the Holocaust in Nazi

Germany, racial conflict and the struggle for civil rights in the United States) have made many people sensitive to the potential evils of discrimination. Discrimination has been exposed and examined in employment, education, housing, criminal justice, and other domains of daily life.

Increased awareness of these problems has had several important consequences. First, the social climate is now one where public endorsement of discrimination, assertion of the superiority or inferiority of one group or another, and general expressions of stereotypic beliefs are unlikely to be tolerated. Individuals who espouse such views may be subjected to scorn, rebuke, and other forms of punishment. Moreover, equal opportunity principles have been codified into law, and those who engage in discrimination are subject to criminal and civil penalties, as in the case of the restaurant chain described at the outset of this chapter (see also Fiske, Bersoff, Borgida, & Deaux, 1991). In this climate, the social perceiver may be motivated to avoid stereotypic thinking if only to avoid the sanctions that may ensue if such thoughts leak out in the form of prejudicial judgments and/or actions.

More optimistically, many social perceivers may be motivated to avoid stereotypic thoughts because their own personal standards dictate that stereotypic preconceptions are an inadequate basis for interpersonal responses. Devine and her colleagues (Monteith, Devine, & Zuwerink, 1993; Devine, Monteith, Zuwerink, & Elliot, 1991) conducted an interesting program of research examining the struggle such individuals engage in to overcome conditioned, habitual prejudices and stereotypes. Because they view stereotypic thoughts and prejudicial feelings as unacceptable and unfair, these individuals are highly motivated to avoid the influence of such reactions. Devine et al. demonstrated that when low-prejudice individuals experience stereotypic inclinations, the discrepancy between the inclination and their egalitarian personal standards creates an uncomfortable feeling of compunction that motivates them to work to bring their reactions more in line with their ideal standards.

Whether such motivation arises from personal or normative sources, there may be many conditions in which social perceivers desire to avoid the influence of stereotypes in their perceptions, judgments, and overt reactions. In the absence of such motivation, stereotypic biases may operate unchecked (see Fig. 13.1).

Willing, But Able? Attentional Requirements of Mental Control

So far, the horizontal pathway across the top of Fig. 13.1 depicts the case of a perceiver who is aware of the possibility that stereotypes may be having some influence on him or her, and who is motivated to avoid this influence. The ultimate goal, as the figure indicates, is to reach an assessment of the target (and to make corresponding behavioral choices) based on person-specific factual data, rather than category-based preconceptions. If successful, the perceiver would achieve the goal of avoiding discrimination by effectively ignoring stereotypic influences. But once the process of construing the target has begun, can the influence of activated stereotypes be reduced or eliminated simply because the perceiver desires it to be? This question has been the focus of several recent investigations.

Stopping unwanted thoughts turns out to be a common human goal (Wegner & Pennebaker, 1993). As a result, a sizable literature has addressed the processes and consequences of mental control. After examining processes of mental control in many different domains, Wegner (1994) developed a general theoretical model of thought suppression. The model postulates that when people desire to avoid a certain type of thought (e.g., stereotypes), this goal is realized by the joint operation of two processes. The first is a monitoring process that scans the mental environment looking for signs of the unwanted thought. If detected, a second operating process is initiated that directs consciousness away from the unwanted thought by focusing on a suitable distracter. Crucially, the monitoring process is assumed to operate in a relatively automatic fashion (see Bargh, 1989), whereas the operating process is postulated to be effortful and to require adequate cognitive resources for successful execution. Thus, detecting the presence of stereotypic ideas can be readily accomplished, relatively independently of the amount of attentional capacity currently available, but replacing these thoughts with more suitable material when they do arise can happen only when sufficient resources are present.

To detect unwanted thoughts, one must keep in mind what it is one is trying to avoid. Thus, the monitoring process, although relatively automatic, must involve at some level the mental activation of the to-be-avoided concept(s). Otherwise, there would be no criterion on which to conduct the search of consciousness. One of the ironic things about mental control that is apparent from this theoretical perspective is that trying to avoid a particular thought actually may result in its hyperaccessibility (Wegner & Erber, 1993). That is, the very act of trying not to think in stereotypic terms may actually increase the extent of stereotype activation. Of course, as long as the perceiver has adequate resources, the operating process may be able to keep the focus of attention away from the stereotypic material. But if the perceiver is busy, distracted, or under time pressure, or his or her motivation for suppression slacks off, the hyperaccessibility created by suppression efforts may not be checked by the operating process. As a result, the intention to avoid biased judgments and reactions may actually backfire, producing even more biased construals than might otherwise have been the case.

Macrae, Bodenhausen, Milne, and Jetten (1994) documented the accuracy of these ironic predictions in a series of experiments. In one study, participants were asked to write a passage about a skinhead depicted in a photograph (the category "skinhead" was selected to minimize the possibility of spontaneous stereotype suppression motivation because few people are concerned about unfairly discriminating against this group). Half of the participants were instructed to avoid the influence of stereotypes in writing their passages, whereas the remainder received no instructions in this regard. When this instruction was fresh in mind and participants had ample resources to devote to its pursuit, those individuals who had been instructed to avoid stereotypic influences were able to write less stereotypic passages. However, when the same people were subsequently asked to write a passage about a different skinhead, but without any reinstatement of the suppression instructions, the former stereotype suppressers showed clear evidence of a *rebound effect*. That is, they furnished passages that were even more stereotypic than those composed by the participants who had never been asked to suppress their stereotypes.

Another study confirmed that the suppression instruction did result in greater mental accessibility of stereotypic concepts. With stereotypic concepts highly accessible and no operating process in place to direct attention away from them, it appears that construals of social targets are likely to be biased, often to a degree that is greater than if they had never sought to suppress the stereotype in the first place. Converging evidence has been provided by Wegner, Erber, and Bowman (cited in Wegner, 1994), who showed that participants could comply with instructions to avoid sexist pronouncements in a sentence-completion task, but only when they had ample time to do so. If they were required to respond immediately, they ironically tended to form even more sexist sentences than did participants who had not been instructed to avoid sexist thoughts. More recent work has shown that stereotype suppression occurs in the absence of explicit instructions from an experimenter (Macrae, Bodenhausen, & Milne, 1995b), and that self-awareness plays an important role in the regulation of stereotypical thinking.

It is one thing to demonstrate that stereotype suppression can have unintended mental consequences, but what about its implications for overt behavior? Can social discrimination result from perceivers' good-faith attempts to avoid stereotypic influences? Macrae et al. (1994, Experiment 2) showed that the rebound effect is not limited to impressions and judgments, but also finds behavioral expression. In this study, participants again wrote passages about a skinhead target, either with or without an explicit instruction to suppress stereotypic influences. Afterward, they were told that, in the next phase of the experiment, they would be meeting the person about whom they had written (i.e., the skinhead). They were escorted to another lab room, where the meeting was ostensibly to take place. Arriving there, each participant found the room to be empty, but one of several chairs contained the personal belongings of the skinhead. The experimenter indicated that the person would be right back, so the participant should have a seat and wait for him. Of key interest is the distance perceivers chose to sit from the skinhead's seat. Social distance, as argued previously, reflects one of the most primitive elements of intergroup relations, and preference for greater distance and intergroup segregation constitutes one of the most insidious forms of discrimination. Our prediction was that the hyperaccessibility of the skinhead stereotype that results from stereotype suppression would lead to more negative construals of the target, after the suppression instructions had dissipated. As a result, suppressers may ironically prefer to maintain a greater distance between themselves and the skinhead. This pattern was exactly what was found. These findings collectively indicate that the road to discrimination may be paved with good intentions. Without consistent motivation and processing capacity, these laudable goals may go unmet (see also Fazio, 1990; Fiske, 1989; Pendry & Macrae, 1994).

To Reveal or Conceal? Making Private Reactions Fit for Public Consumption

It would seem sometimes that perceivers are hard-pressed to avoid the influence of stereotypic notions in their construals of social targets. However, biased construals do not inevitably lead to biased actions. For one thing, the current situation may not afford perceivers any opportunity to express in behavior the implications of their subjective impressions. However, if an overt judgment (e.g., a hiring decision or a criminal verdict) is required, or if interpersonal interaction with the target is expected (e.g., a car sales negotiation or classroom instruction), these significant social behaviors may well be tainted by the biased construals perceivers have formed. The social perceiver may have one last line of defense against discriminatory reactions, however. If (and presumably only if) perceivers are aware that bias is of potential concern, they can take steps to modify their overt responses. Naturally, this self-regulatory activity would also require motivation and sufficient capacity.

As with the motivation to suppress stereotypes during earlier stages of information processing, the desire to edit out stereotypic influences prior to the commission of public behavior can have more than one origin. For

example, a high-prejudice individual may form a negative, highly stereotypic construal of a target and feel convinced that this perception is
accurate and justified. Yet he or she might also be aware that overt
expression of this impression could lead to censure. Thus, although
prejudiced individuals may not attempt to avoid stereotypic thoughts, they
may often want to avoid doing anything that would betray these subjective
feelings publicly. As such, they would simply conceal their true feelings and
take steps to adjust their overt judgments and behaviors to mask their
prejudice. However, if they lack any concern about the disapprobation of
others (e.g., if the immediate public audience is known to share their
prejudicial views), then no response editing will occur, and discriminatory
responses will be highly likely to ensue (see Fig. 13.1). Moreover, even if
they are motivated to conceal their negative reactions, they may not be able
to do so if the situation requires a rapid response or otherwise constrains
their cognitive resources.

Low-prejudice individuals may face a different set of concerns. Even if
these persons have attempted to avoid stereotypic inferences while evaluating the target, they may continue to be concerned about the possibility of
unfair biases. As such, they may often assume that whatever their initial
construal of a target might be, it is likely to contain some element of unfair
stereotypic bias. For these individuals, concealment is not the issue. Rather,
they want to make allowances for what they assume (perhaps often
correctly) to be a biased initial assessment. How do they go about correcting
for these presumed biases? A good deal of interesting research has
addressed this question recently (Baumeister & Newman, 1994; Petty &
Wegener, 1993; Schwarz & Bless, 1992; Strack & Hannover, 1996; Wilson
& Brekke, 1994). When people have an explicit theory about the likely
directional nature of the bias (e.g., the negative influence of outgroup
stereotypes), they can make adjustments to their overt responses in the
opposite direction (Wegener & Petty, 1995). Thus, if a teacher is concerned
about the appearance of prejudice in his or her dealings with a minority
student, then interpersonal behavior may be highly controlled to present
only unambiguously positive signals. Similarly, evaluations of female or
minority job candidates may be adjusted to be more positive.

To the extent that there is real stereotypic bias in one's initial construals
of a target, such corrective action represents a positive step toward
combating unfair discrimination. However, some caveats are in order.
First, to sound a now-familiar theme, the execution of corrections can occur
only when people are both motivated and able to engage in the necessary
cognitive effort (Martin, Seta, & Crelia, 1990; Wegener & Petty, 1995). In
their absence, any biases present in their construals will go unchecked, and
discriminatory actions may occur if the situation calls for an overt response.
Second, there is no guarantee that the correction that is applied to

judgments or behavior will be adequate to eliminate the original bias; by the same token, it is possible that the adjustments might actually overcompensate for the bias (e.g., Hatvany & Strack, 1980), potentially resulting in reverse discrimination. The appropriate calibration of adjustments that are intended to compensate for presumed biases is obviously a subjective matter, and therefore prone to its own distortions.

Whether corrective or concealment strategies are deployed may be affected by a number of contextual factors. For example, some situations create a sense of accountability (Tetlock, 1991) that may engender a general wariness about the scrutiny of one's public reactions. This concern may provide an extra motivational impetus for the work required to adjust or hide stereotypic biases. Any factor that raises concerns about social desirability could have similar effects. The heightened sensitivity that surrounds bias directed at some minority groups may create a general posture of concern about bias that arises in many or most situations in which group members are encountered. However, other negatively stereotyped groups that have not benefited from enhanced awareness of past injustices may be more prone to unchecked discrimination.

SUMMARY AND CONCLUSIONS

The connections between intergroup cognition and intergroup behavior are complex, and it is quite obvious that overt behavior directed at the members of outgroups is multiply determined. Nevertheless, this chapter attempted to sketch out a picture of some of the most basic elements of the path from stereotypes to discrimination. From the considerations raised here, a few fairly general conclusions seem warranted.

First, the seeds of discriminatory reactions often (although certainly not universally) lie in stereotypic beliefs about outgroups. These beliefs (as well as more affective reactions; see Jussim et al., 1995) can be activated without intent and without the perceiver's awareness. Once activated, a variety of processes are instigated that can lead to a biased and incomplete assessment of the data that are available about outgroup targets. If the meaning that is imposed on the target and his or her behavior is biased, ensuing reactions are also likely to be biased. Hence, discrimination can result.

Second, the avoidance of discriminatory responses is possible, but the prerequisites are considerable. The perceiver must be aware of the potential for bias, must care about the possibility of bias, and must have adequate cognitive resources to do something about it. Perceivers who are genuinely motivated to avoid stereotypic bias may attempt to suppress stereotypic thoughts, but as has been seen, this noble goal may have counterintentional consequences. Sometimes suppression activity may actually increase the extent of discriminatory responses (Macrae et al., 1994). These persons may also attempt to correct their initial judgments to eliminate potential biases, but it is difficult to know how to calibrate these adjustments appropriately. Other perceivers may have few qualms about harboring stereotypic ideas, yet they may be motivated to avoid public expression of their biased views. For them, the avoidance of discrimination amounts to little more than concealment and subterfuge. Furthermore, they may be especially likely to find apparently satisfactory situational justifications for discriminatory responses that can be used to deflect accusations of prejudice (Gaertner & Dovidio, 1986).

These findings indicate that intentions to avoid discrimination, whether they are internally or externally motivated, may often meet with failure. Although awareness and concern about discrimination have increased, it is premature to assume that its evils can be avoided simply by the formation of good intentions. Of course, not everyone has good intentions. To avoid discrimination, situations where intergroup contact occurs and where consequential decisions about outgroup members are being made need to be structured in a way that fosters (a) awareness of potential biases, (b) motivation to avoid such bias, and (c) ample time and freedom from distractions and other factors that limit attentional capacity to implement bias-minimizing strategies. Unfortunately, the classroom, the courtroom, the boardroom, and the other arenas of intergroup interaction are often not characterized by these features. Strong emotions, complex and demanding tasks and interaction patterns, time pressures, and distractions can undermine the effectiveness of these strategies.

Combating discrimination undoubtedly requires institutional commitments, but it also requires a personal commitment to look beyond one's preconceptions in constructing a mental model of the social world. Although difficult and fraught with perils, attempting to avoid the influence of erroneous and overgeneralized stereotypic beliefs is an essential ingredient in the complex recipe for social justice.

REFERENCES

Asch, S. (1946). Forming impressions of personality. *Journal of Abnormal and Social Psychology, 41*, 258–290.

Ayres, I. (1991). Fair driving: Gender and race discrimination in retail car negotiations. *Harvard Law Review, 104*, 817–872.

Banaji, M. R., & Greenwald, A. G. (1995). Implicit gender stereotyping in judgments of fame. *Journal of Personality and Social Psychology, 68*, 181–198.

Banaji, M. R., Hardin, C., & Rothman, A. J. (1993). Implicit stereotyping in person judgment. *Journal of Personality and Social Psychology, 65*, 272–281.

Bargh, J. A. (1989). Conditional automaticity: Varieties of automatic influence in social perception and cognition. In J. S. Uleman & J. A. Bargh (Eds.), *Unintended thought* (pp. 3–51). New York: Guilford.

Bargh, J. A. (1997). The automaticity of everyday life. In R. S. Wyer, Jr. (Ed.), *The automaticity of everyday life: Advances in social cognition* (Vol. 10, pp. 1–61). Mahwah, NJ: Lawrence Erlbaum Associates.

Baron, R. S., Inman, M. L., Kao, C. F., & Logan, H. (1992). Negative emotion and superficial social processing. *Motivation and Emotion, 16,* 323–346.

Baumeister, R. F., & Newman, L. S. (1994). Self-regulation of cognitive inference and decision processes. *Personality and Social Psychology Bulletin, 20,* 3–19.

Biernat, M., & Vescio, T. K. (1993). Categorization and stereotyping: Effects of group context on memory and social judgment. *Journal of Experimental Social Psychology, 29,* 166–202.

Bodenhausen, G. V. (1988). Stereotypic biases in social decision making and memory: Testing process models of stereotype use. *Journal of Personality and Social Psychology, 55,* 726–737.

Bodenhausen, G. V. (1990). Stereotypes as judgmental heuristics: Evidence of circadian variations in discrimination. *Psychological Science, 1,* 319–322.

Bodenhausen, G. V., Kramer, G. P., & Süsser, K. (1994). Happiness and stereotypic thinking in social judgment. *Journal of Personality and Social Psychology, 66,* 621–632.

Bodenhausen, G. V., & Lichtenstein, M. (1987). Social stereotypes and information-processing strategies: The impact of task complexity. *Journal of Personality and Social Psychology, 52,* 871–880.

Bodenhausen, G. V., Sheppard, L. A., & Kramer, G. P. (1994). Negative affect and social judgments: The differential impact of anger and sadness. *European Journal of Social Psychology, 24,* 45–62.

Bodenhausen, G. V., & Wyer, R. S., Jr. (1985). Effects of stereotypes on decision making and information-processing strategies. *Journal of Personality and Social Psychology, 48,* 267–282.

Bornstein, R., & Pittman, T. (Eds.). (1992). *Perception without awareness.* New York: Guilford.

Brewer, M. B. (1988). A dual process model of impression formation. In R. S. Wyer, Jr., & T. K. Srull (Eds.), *Advances in social cognition* (Vol. 1, pp. 1–36). Hillsdale, NJ: Lawrence Erlbaum Associates.

Brewer, M. B. (1996). When stereotypes lead to stereotyping: The use of stereotypes in person perception. In N. Macrae, M. Hewstone, & C. Stangor (Eds.), *Foundations of stereotypes and stereotyping* (pp. 254–275). New York: Guilford.

Bruner, J. S. (1957). Going beyond the information given. In H. Gruber, K. Hammond, & R. Jessor (Eds.), *Contemporary approaches to cognition* (pp. 41–69). Cambridge, MA: Harvard University Press.

Chaiken, S., Giner-Sorolla, R., & Chen, S. (1996). Beyond accuracy: Defense and impression motives in heuristic and systematic information processing. In P. M. Gollwitzer & J. A. Bargh (Eds.), *The psychology of action: Linking cognition and motivation to behavior* (pp. 553–578). New York: Guilford.

Chaiken, S., Liberman, A., & Eagly, A. H. (1989). Heuristic and systematic information processing within and beyond the persuasion context. In J. S. Uleman & J. A. Bargh (Eds.), *Unintended thought* (pp. 212–252). New York: Guilford.

Chaiken, S., & Maheswaran, D. (1994). Heuristic processing can bias systematic processing: Effects of source credibility, argument ambiguity, and task importance on attitude judgment. *Journal of Personality and Social Psychology, 66,* 460–473.

Crocker, J., Thompson, L. L., McGraw, K. M., & Ingerman, C. (1987). Downward comparison, prejudice, and evaluation of others: Effects of self-esteem and threat. *Journal of Personality and Social Psychology, 52,* 907–916.

Darley, J. M., & Latané, B. (1968). Bystander intervention in emergencies: Diffusion of responsibility. *Journal of Personality and Social Psychology, 8,* 377–383.

Devine, P. G. (1989). Stereotypes and prejudice: Their automatic and controlled components. *Journal of Personality and Social Psychology, 56,* 5–18.

Devine, P. G., Monteith, M. J., Zuwerink, J. R., & Elliot, A. J. (1991). Prejudice with and without compunction. *Journal of Personality and Social Psychology, 60,* 817–830.

Dovidio, J. F., & Gaertner, S. L. (1986). Prejudice, discrimination, and racism: Historical trends and contemporary approaches. In J. F. Dovidio & S. L. Gaertner (Eds.), *Prejudice, discrimination, and racism* (pp. 1–34). Orlando, FL: Academic Press.

Duncan, B. L. (1976). Differential social perception and attribution of intergroup violence: Testing the lower limits of stereotyping of blacks. *Journal of Personality and Social Psychology, 34,* 590–598.

Farley, R., Steeh, C., Krysan, M., Jackson, T., & Reeves, K. (1994). Stereotypes and segregation: Neighborhoods in the Detroit area. *American Journal of Sociology, 100,* 750–780.

Fazio, R. H. (1990). Multiple processes by which attitudes guide behavior: The MODE model as an integrative framework. In M. P. Zanna (Ed.), *Advances in experimental social psychology* (Vol. 23, pp. 75–109). Orlando, FL: Academic Press.

Fazio, R. H., Jackson, J. R., Dunton, B. C., & Williams, C. J. (1995). Variability in automatic activation as an unobtrusive measure of racial attitudes: A bona fide pipeline? *Journal of Personality and Social Psychology, 69,* 1013–1027.

Fiske, S. T. (1989). Examining the role of intent: Toward understanding its role in stereotyping and prejudice. In J. S. Uleman & J. A. Bargh (Eds.), *Unintended thought* (pp. 253–286). New York: Guilford.

Fiske, S. T., Bersoff, D. N., Borgida, E., & Deaux, K. (1991). Social science on trial: Use of sex stereotyping research in *Price Waterhouse v. Hopkins. American Psychologist, 46,* 1049–1060.

Fiske, S. T., & Neuberg, S. L. (1990). A continuum model of impression formation from category-based to individuating processes: Influences of information and motivation on attention and interpretation. In M. P. Zanna (Ed.), *Advances in experimental social psychology* (Vol. 3, pp. 1–74). San Diego, CA: Academic Press.

Gaertner, S. L., & Dovidio, J. F. (1977). The subtlety of white racism, arousal, and helping behavior. *Journal of Personality and Social Psychology, 35,* 691–707.

Gaertner, S. L., & Dovidio, J. F. (1986). The aversive form of racism. In J. F. Dovidio & S. L. Gaertner (Eds.), *Prejudice, discrimination, and racism* (pp. 61–89). Orlando, FL: Academic Press.

Gilbert, D. T., & Hixon, J. G. (1991). The trouble of thinking: Activation and application of stereotypic beliefs. *Journal of Personality and Social Psychology, 60,* 509–517.

Gordon, R. A. (1990). Attributions for blue-collar and white-collar crime: The effects of subject and defendant race on juror decisions. *Journal of Applied Social Psychology, 20,* 971–983.

Greenwald, A. G., & Banaji, M. R. (1995). Implicit social cognition: Attitudes, self-esteem, and stereotypes. *Psychological Review, 102,* 4–27.

Hamilton, D. L., & Sherman, J. W. (1994). Stereotypes. In R. S. Wyer, Jr., & T. K. Srull (Eds.), *Handbook of social cognition* (2nd ed., Vol. 2, pp. 1–68). Hillsdale, NJ: Lawrence Erlbaum Associates.

Hastorf, A. H., & Cantril, H. (1954). They saw a game: A case study. *Journal of Abnormal and Social Psychology, 49,* 129–134.

Hatvany, N., & Strack, F. (1980). The impact of a discredited key witness. *Journal of Applied Social Psychology, 10,* 490–509.

Higgins, E. T., Rholes, W. S., & Jones, C. R. (1977). Category accessibility and impression formation. *Journal of Experimental Social Psychology, 13,* 141–154.

Hilton, J. L., & von Hippel, W. (1996). Stereotypes. *Annual Review of Psychology, 47,*

237-271.

Hogg, M. A., & Abrams, D. (1988). *Social identifications: A social psychology of intergroup relations and group processes*. London: Routledge & Kegan Paul.

Jacoby, L. L. (1991). A process dissociation framework: Separating automatic from intentional uses of memory. *Journal of Memory and Language, 30*, 513-541.

Jones, E. E., & Thibaut, J. W. (1958). Interaction goals as bases of inference in interpersonal perception. In R. Taguiri & L. Petrullo (Eds.), *Person perception and interpersonal behavior* (pp. 151-178). Stanford, CA: Stanford University Press.

Judd, C. M., & Park, B. (1993). Definition and assessment of accuracy in social stereotypes. *Psychological Review, 100*, 109-128.

Jussim, L., Nelson, T. E., Manis, M., & Soffin, S. (1995). Prejudice, stereotypes, and labeling effects: Sources of bias in person perception. *Journal of Personality and Social Psychology, 68*, 228-246.

Klinger, M. R., & Beall, P. M. (1992, May). *Conscious and unconscious effects of stereotype activation*. Paper presented at the annual meeting of the Midwestern Psychological Association, Chicago.

Kohn, W. (1994, Nov. 6). Service with a sneer. *New York Times Magazine*, pp. 43-47, 58, 78, 81.

Krieger, L. H. (1995). The content of our categories: A cognitive bias approach to discrimination and equal employment opportunity. *Stanford Law Review, 47*, 1161-1248.

Kruglanski, A. W., & Freund, T. (1983). The freezing and unfreezing of lay inferences: Effects on impressional accuracy, ethnic stereotyping, and numerical anchoring. *Journal of Experimental Social Psychology, 19*, 448-468.

Kunda, Z., & Sherman-Williams, B. (1993). Stereotypes and the construal of individuating information. *Personality and Social Psychology Bulletin, 19*, 90-99.

Kunda, Z., & Thagard, P. (1996). Forming impressions from stereotypes, traits, and behaviors: A parallel constraint satisfaction theory. *Psychological Review, 103*, 284-308.

Latané, B., & Darley, J. M. (1968). Group inhibition of bystander intervention in emergencies. *Journal of Personality and Social Psychology, 10*, 215-221.

LeVine, R. A., & Campbell, D. T. (1972). *Ethnocentrism: Theories of conflict, ethnic attitudes, and group behavior*. New York: Wiley.

Locke, V., MacLeod, C., & Walker, I. (1994). Automatic and controlled activation of stereotypes: Individual differences associated with prejudice. *British Journal of Social Psychology, 33*, 29-46.

Macrae, C. N., Bodenhausen, G. V., & Milne, A. B. (1995a). The dissection of selection in person perception: Inhibitory processes in social stereotyping. *Journal of Personality and Social Psychology, 69*, 397-407.

Macrae, C. N., Bodenhausen, G. V., & Milne, A. B. (1995b). *Saying no to unwanted thoughts: The role of self-awareness in the regulation of mental life*. Manuscript submitted for publication.

Macrae, C. N., Bodenhausen, G. V., Milne, A. B., & Jetten, J. (1994). Out of mind but back in sight: Stereotypes on the rebound. *Journal of Personality and Social Psychology, 67*, 808-817.

Macrae, C. N., Hewstone, M., & Griffiths, R. J. (1993). Processing load and memory for stereotype-based information. *European Journal of Social Psychology, 23*, 77-87.

Macrae, C. N., Milne, A. B., & Bodenhausen, G. V. (1994). Stereotypes as energy-saving devices: A peek inside the cognitive toolbox. *Journal of Personality and Social Psychology, 66*, 37-47.

Major, B., & Crocker, J. (1993). Social stigma: The consequences of attributional ambiguity. In D. M. Mackie & D. L. Hamilton (Eds.), *Affect, cognition, and stereotyping: Interactive processes in group perception* (pp. 345-370). San Diego, CA: Academic Press.

Martin, L. L., Seta, J. J., & Crelia, R. A. (1990). Assimilation and contrast as a function of people's willingness and ability to expend effort in forming an impression. *Journal of Personality and Social Psychology, 59,* 27–37.

Massey, D., & Denton, N. (1993). *American apartheid: Segregation and the making of the underclass.* Cambridge, MA: Harvard University Press.

Mazzella, R., & Feingold, A. (1994). The effects of physical attractiveness, race, socio-economic status, and gender of defendants and victims on judgments of mock jurors: A meta-analysis. *Journal of Applied Social Psychology, 24,* 1315–1344.

McGuire, W. J., McGuire, C. V., Child, P., & Fujioka, T. (1978). Salience of ethnicity in the spontaneous self-concept as a function of one's ethnic distinctiveness in the social environment. *Journal of Personality and Social Psychology, 36,* 511–520.

Monteith, M. J., Devine, P. G., & Zuwerink, J. R. (1993). Self-directed versus other-directed affect as a consequence of prejudice-related discrepancies. *Journal of Personality and Social Psychology, 64,* 198–210.

Neuberg, S. L. (1996). Expectancy influences in social interaction: The moderating role of social goals. In P. M. Gollwitzer & J. A. Bargh (Eds.), *The psychology of action: Linking cognition and motivation to behavior* (pp. 529–552). New York: Guilford.

Olson, J. M., Roese, N. J., & Zanna, M. P. (1996). Expectancies. In E. T. Higgins & A. W. Kruglanski (Eds.), *Social psychology: Handbook of basic principles* (pp. 211–238). New York: Guilford.

Ottati, V., & Lee, Y.-T. (1995). Accuracy: A neglected component of stereotype research. In Y.-T. Lee, L. Jussim, & C. McCauley (Eds.), *Stereotype accuracy: Toward appreciating group differences* (pp. 29–59). Washington, DC: American Psychological Association.

Pendry, L. F., & Macrae, C. N. (1994). Stereotypes and mental life: The case of the motivated but thwarted tactician. *Journal of Experimental Social Psychology, 30,* 303–325.

Pendry, L. F., & Macrae, C. N. (1996). What the disinterested perceiver overlooks: Goal-directed social categorization. *Personality and Social Psychology Bulletin, 22,* 249–256.

Perdue, C. W., & Gurtman, M. B. (1990). Evidence for the automaticity of ageism. *Journal of Experimental Social Psychology, 26,* 199–216.

Petty, R. E., & Cacioppo, J. T. (1986). The elaboration likelihood model of persuasion. In L. Berkowitz (Ed.), *Advances in experimental social psychology* (Vol. 19, pp. 124–203). New York: Academic Press.

Petty, R. E., & Wegener, D. T. (1993). Flexible correction processes in social judgment: Correcting for context-induced contrast. *Journal of Experimental Social Psychology, 29,* 137–165.

Pratto, F., & Bargh, J. A. (1991). Stereotyping based upon apparently individuating information: Trait and global components of sex stereotypes under attention overload. *Journal of Experimental Social Psychology, 27,* 26–47.

Ross, L., & Nisbett, R. E. (1991). *The person and the situation: Perspectives of social psychology.* New York: McGraw-Hill.

Rothbart, M., Fulero, S., Jensen, C., Howard, J., & Birrell, B. (1978). From individual to group impressions: Availability heuristics in stereotype formation. *Journal of Experimental Social Psychology, 14,* 237–255.

Sadker, M., & Sadker, D. (1994). *Failing at fairness: How our schools cheat girls.* New York: Touchstone.

Sagar, H. A., & Schofield, J. W. (1980). Racial and behavioral cues in black and white children's perceptions of ambiguously aggressive acts. *Journal of Personality and Social Psychology, 39,* 590–598.

Schacter, D. L., Chiu, C.-Y. P., & Ochsner, K. N. (1993). Implicit memory: A selective review. *Annual Review of Neuroscience, 16,* 159–182.

Schuman, H., Steeh, C., & Bobo, L. (1985). *Racial attitudes in America: Trends and interpretations.* Cambridge, MA: Harvard University Press.

Schwarz, N., & Bless, H. (1992). Constructing reality and its alternatives: An inclusion/ exclusion model of assimilation and contrast effects in social judgment. In L. L. Martin & A. Tesser (Eds.), *The construction of social judgments* (pp. 217–245). Hillsdale, NJ: Lawrence Erlbaum Associates.

Seamon, J. G., Williams, P. C., Crowley, M. J., & Kim, I. J. (1995). The mere exposure effect is based on implicit memory: Effects of stimulus type, encoding conditions, and number of exposures on recognition and affect judgments. *Journal of Experimental Psychology: Learning, Memory, and Cognition, 21*, 711–721.

Sears, D. O., & Kinder, D. R. (1985). Whites' opposition to busing: On conceptualizing and operationalizing group conflict. *Journal of Personality and Social Psychology, 48*, 1141–1147.

Sedikides, C., & Skowronski, J. J. (1991). The law of cognitive structure activation. *Psychological Inquiry, 2*, 169–184.

Smith, E. R. (in press). Mental representation and memory. In D. Gilbert, S. T. Fiske, & G. Lindzey (Eds.), *Handbook of social psychology* (4th ed.). New York: McGraw-Hill.

Spencer, S. J., & Fein, S. (1994, April). *Effect of self-image threats on stereotyping.* Paper presented at the annual meeting of the Eastern Psychological Association, Providence, RI.

Srull, T. K., & Wyer, R. S., Jr. (1979). The role of category accessibility in the interpretation of information about persons: Some determinants and implications. *Journal of Personality and Social Psychology, 37*, 1660–1672.

Stangor, C., & Duan, C. (1991). Effects of multiple task demands upon memory for information about social groups. *Journal of Experimental Social Psychology, 27*, 357–378.

Stangor, C., Lynch, L., Duan, C., & Glass, B. (1992). Categorization of individuals on the basis of multiple social features. *Journal of Personality and Social Psychology, 62*, 207–218.

Strack, F., & Hannover, B. (1996). Awareness of influence as a precondition for implementing correctional goals. In P. M. Gollwitzer & J. A. Bargh (Eds.), *The psychology of action: Linking cognition and motivation to behavior* (pp. 579–596). New York: Guilford.

Taylor, S. E., & Crocker, J. (1981). Schematic bases of social information processing. In E. T. Higgins, C. P. Herman, & M. P. Zanna (Eds.), *Social cognition: The Ontario symposium* (Vol. 1, pp. 89–134). Hillsdale, NJ: Lawrence Erlbaum Associates.

Taylor, S. E., Fiske, S. T., Etcoff, N. L., & Ruderman, A. (1978). Categorical bases of person memory and stereotyping. *Journal of Personality and Social Psychology, 36*, 778–793.

Tetlock, P. E. (1991). An alternative metaphor in the study of judgment and choice: People as politicians. *Theory & Psychology, 1*, 451–475.

Wegener, D. T., & Petty, R. E. (1995). Flexible correction processes in social judgment: The role of naive theories in corrections for perceived bias. *Journal of Personality and Social Psychology, 68*, 36–51.

Wegner, D. M. (1994). Ironic processes of mental control. *Psychological Review, 101*, 34–52.

Wegner, D. M., & Erber, R. (1993). Social foundations of mental control. In D. M. Wegner & J. W. Pennebaker (Eds.), *Handbook of mental control* (pp. 36–56). Englewood Cliffs, NJ: Prentice-Hall.

Wegner, D. M., & Pennebaker, J. W. (Eds.). (1993). *Handbook of mental control.* Englewood Cliffs, NJ: Prentice-Hall.

Wilson, T. D., & Brekke, N. (1994). Mental contamination and mental correction: Unwanted influences on judgments and evaluations. *Psychological Bulletin, 116*, 117–142.

Wittenbrink, B., Judd, C. M., & Park, B. (1997). Evidence for racial prejudice at the implicit level and its relationship with questionnaire measures. *Journal of Personality and Social Personality, 72*, 262–274. .

Wyer, R. S., Jr., & Srull, T. K. (1989). *Memory and cognition in its social context.* Hillsdale, NJ: Lawrence Erlbaum Associates.

14

Positive Affect, Cognition, and the Reduction of Intergroup Bias

John F. Dovidio
Colgate University

Samuel L. Gaertner
University of Delaware

Alice M. Isen
Cornell University

Mary Rust
University of Delaware

Paula Guerra
Colgate University

Within the context of the contact hypothesis (Allport, 1954; Cook, 1984), researchers have identified a range of independent factors in intergroup situations, such as equal status, personal interaction, cooperative interdependence, and supportive norms, that are critical for reducing bias and conflict. Recent approaches to reducing intergroup bias have extended this work by focusing on potentially unifying frameworks involving fundamental cognitive, affective, and social processes (Brewer & Miller, 1984; Miller, Brewer, & Edwards, 1985; Stephan & Stephan, 1984, 1985). One such approach is the Common Ingroup Identity Model (Gaertner, Dovidio, Anastasio, Bachman, & Rust, 1993), a guiding framework in the present chapter that is based on the social categorization perspective of intergroup behavior (Brewer, 1979; Brown & Turner, 1981; Tajfel & Turner, 1979). The model proposes that intergroup bias and conflict can be reduced by influencing the ways in which group members conceive of group boundaries.

Previous research has demonstrated that techniques that decrease the salience of intergroup boundaries, such as individuating members of the outgroup by revealing variability in their opinions (Wilder, 1978) or personalizing interactions on the basis of more intimate, personally relevant information (Brewer & Miller, 1984; Miller et al., 1985), reduce bias toward members of other groups. Criss-crossing category memberships by forming new subgroups composed of members from both former subgroups also may reduce intergroup bias by either decreasing the salience of the earlier categorization schemas (decategorization) or by producing new, counter-acting social categories (i.e., recategorization; Brewer, Ho, Lee & Miller, 1987; Deschamps & Doise, 1978; Hewstone, Islam, & Judd, 1993; Miller, Urban, & Vanman, chap. 16, this volume; Vanbeselaere, 1987). In general, *decategorization* refers to individuation—thinking of the outgroup not as a social category, but rather in terms of individual group members; *recategorization* refers to using an alternative, superordinate social category to think about both the ingroup and the outgroup.

THE COMMON INGROUP IDENTITY MODEL

The Common Ingroup Identity Model recognizes the central role of social cognition—specifically social categorization—in ameliorating and creating intergroup bias. In particular, the model proposes that *re*categorization, in contrast to *de*categorization, may also provide an effective strategy to reduce intergroup bias. Recategorization is not designed to reduce or eliminate categorization, but rather to structure a definition of *group categorization* in ways that reduce intergroup bias and conflict. Specifically, if members of different groups are induced to conceive of themselves as a single group, rather than as two separate groups, attitudes toward former outgroup members will become more positive through processes involving pro-ingroup bias (Brewer, 1979; Mullen, Brown, & Smith, 1992; Tajfel & Turner, 1979). For example, categorization of a person as an ingroup member, rather than as an outgroup member, has been demonstrated to: (a) produce greater perceptions of shared beliefs (Brown, 1984; Brown & Abrams, 1986; Hogg & Turner, 1985; Stein, Hardyck, & Smith, 1965; Wilder, 1984); (b) facilitate empathic arousal, whereby a person's motiva-tional system becomes coordinated to the needs of another (Hornstein, 1976; Piliavin, Dovidio, Gaertner, & Clark, 1981); (c) enhance memory for positive information about others (Howard & Rothbart, 1980); and (d) reduce blame for an accident or other negative outcomes (Hewstone, Bond, & Wan, 1983; Wang & McKillip, 1978). Thus, by redefining original outgroup members as ingroup members, the cognitive and motivational processes that initially contributed to intergroup bias and conflict may be redirected toward establishing more positive intergroup relations.

The model, as it applies to the present chapter, is summarized schemat-ically in Fig. 14.1 (see also Gaertner et al., 1993). On the left, situational factors and interventions, such as interdependence and perceptual similar-ity, are hypothesized to influence cognitive representations of the member-ships (center) as one group (recategorization), as two groups (categoriza-tion), or as separate individuals (decategorization). In addition, affect can moderate the impact of these contextual factors on social cognition and

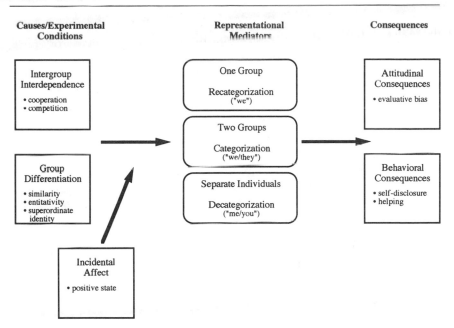

FIG. 14.1. The Common Ingroup Identity Model: The hypothesized effects of situational and affective manipulations on recategorization and on subsequent intergroup evaluative biases, self-disclosure, and helping.

categorization (Isen, 1993). Within the model and this chapter, intergroup cognition involved in social categorization is the critical mediator of subsequent intergroup attitudes and behavior. These resulting cognitive representations (i.e., one group, two group, or separate individuals) are then proposed to produce specific attitudinal and behavioral consequences. In particular, the present chapter examines the effects of situational and affective manipulations on recategorization and on subsequent intergroup evaluative biases, self-disclosure, and helping.

Consistent with this model, evidence indicates that aspects of intergroup contact that are designed to promote an inclusive one-group representation, rather than a representation of two groups, decreases intergroup bias. In one experiment (Gaertner, Mann, Murrell, & Dovidio, 1989), members of two original subgroups who shared a common group name, were cooperatively interdependent, and were spatially integrated perceived themselves more like one group, felt less like two groups, exhibited lower levels of intergroup bias than did members who retained their subgroup names, were competitively interdependent, and were segregated spatially. There were two additional aspects of the findings that were directly supportive of the model. Bias was reduced primarily by more positive evaluations of outgroup members; also, the impact of the manipulations on increasing positive evaluations of outgroup members and decreasing bias was mediated by group representations. Other research has indicated that spatial arrangements that influence perceptions of entitativity (i.e., perceptions of groupness; Gaertner & Dovidio, 1986; see also Campbell, 1958) and factors identified by the contact hypothesis, such as cooperation (Gaertner, Mann, Dovidio, Murrell, & Pomare, 1990) as well as perceptions of equal status, supportive norms, and interpersonal interaction (Gaertner, Rust, Dovidio, Bachman, & Anastasio, 1994), also improve evaluations of outgroup members and decrease intergroup bias by changing members' representations of the aggregate from two groups to one group.

The present chapter first explores how temporary and sometimes incidental interventions that create positive affect can influence intergroup perceptions and evaluations in ways outlined by the Common Ingroup Identity Model. Then the chapter examines how these hypothesized changes in intergroup cognitions relate to intergroup behaviors. The next section considers how inducing positive affect can influence perceptions and evaluations of individuals, and of members of temporary groups and ecologically meaningful social entities.

AFFECT AND SOCIAL CATEGORIZATION

This section reports three studies that have investigated how affect can shape intergroup relations. The first experiment presented in this chapter examined the effects of positive affect on self-categorization and the social categorization of others. The second experiment explored the influence of positive affect on the relations between temporary, laboratory-formed groups. The third experiment tested how interventions that emphasize a common ingroup identity can substantially and productively alter the impact of manipulated positive affect on intergroup relations between members of meaningful entities.

Positive affect and its influence on nonsocial categorization was initially investigated by Isen and Daubman (1984). In their study, participants were given the name of neutral objects (e.g., belt), and were asked to rate how well these objects fit into neutral categories (e.g., clothing), for which they were nontypical but plausible exemplars. Those authors found that people experiencing positive affect were more likely to include the nontypical exemplars as members of associated categories than were people in an affect control condition. This effect was not thought to represent "sloppy" or irrational categorization, but rather flexibility in thinking about the material—for several reasons. First, regardless of the affect condition, people identified typical exemplars as clear members of the categories. Categorization did not become random or irrational in the positive affect condition.

Second, Isen and Daubman (1984) proposed that positive affect promotes the use of more material, particularly positive material (which is more diverse information), thereby establishing a larger cognitive context in which more connections between nontypical exemplars and the categories can be identified. Third, for material that is at least neutral in valence, which means that it has some potentially positive features to be primed, positive affect can cue those positive aspects. Because of the shared positive aspects and valence that have been primed, this process leads to the material seeming more similar to categories that are neutral or positive in valence.

Theoretically, these findings are consistent with Isen's (1987) hypothesis that positive affect influences the organization of cognitive material. Positive affect increases the accessibility of diverse ideas and produces a more complex cognitive context than normally occurs (Isen, Johnson, Mertz, & Robinson, 1985). As Tversky and Gati (1978) found, when people have more information and ideas about concepts, they are more likely to report similarities when they are motivated to perceive similarities, and to report differences when they are motivated to perceive dissimilarities. Thus, when framed appropriately, positive affect can increase categorization breadth for neutral as well as positive stimuli, and can result in more perceived similarity or difference, depending on the rest of the context (see also Murray, Sujan, Hirt, & Sujan, 1990). Murray et al. (1990) also reported that the "default" value for positive affect was toward increased perception of similarity, unless something in the context specifically primed the person to look for differences.

Isen, Niedenthal, and Cantor (1992) extended these findings to social categorization. Isen et al. hypothesized that positive affect would facilitate broader social categorization of neutral-to-positive persons by leading people to associate what is usually seen as a neutral target with a positive category. Because positive affect primes positive material in memory, it facilitates a connection between the target and the positive category by cueing the positive material associated with the target. As a consequence, people experiencing positive affect would be expected to include nontypical exemplars into socially desirable categories, but they would not be expected to include nontypical exemplars into socially undesirable categories. For instance, a grandmother and a bartender could both be considered examples of "nurturant people," but a bartender would be considered a nontypical (and relatively neutral) exemplar, whereas a grandmother would be a typical (and very positive) exemplar. The results supported the predictions and the proposed mechanism. Positive affect increased the extent to which a nontypical exemplar was associated with a positive category. Also as predicted, positive affect did not increase the extent to which nontypical exemplars were associated with negative categories (i.e., "genius" for the category of emotionally unstable or pretentious people), presumably because positive affect does not activate negative material, and thus no additional connections are made. Again, this asymmetry in the influence of positive affect, which depends on the material under consideration, suggests that this effect is not just one of response bias or sloppy thinking. If it were, negative material would be affected similarly, or good exemplars of the category would be rated as poor exemplars.

In general, the research on positive affect suggests that its influence on category breadth is moderated by the valence (positive or negative) of the category and by the valence and the strength (nontypical or typical) of the exemplars being considered. For example, Isen (1993) posited that positive affect has its effect by reminding people of the positive aspects of the object, which then make the object seem more similar to the positive category being considered. As a consequence, with respect to the valence of the category, greater inclusiveness in categorization may be more likely to occur for more favorable social categories for which more positive connections exist. In contrast, positive affect would not be expected to increase the inclusiveness of categorization for negative categories, for which positive connections are rare or nonexistent (Isen et al., 1992). Thus, this effect occurs only for positive or neutral targets, for which potential positive connections exist, but not for negative targets, for which associations are fundamentally unfavorable (Isen et al., 1992; Murray et al., 1990). Positive affect may facilitate categorization of neutral targets into positive categories because, as Isen et al. (1992) explained, "people who are feeling good may recognize aspects of ideas (especially neutral or ambiguous ones) that they do not normally think of, and these features will tend to be more positive than usual, as well" (p. 67). Then, the more positive valence of the target or the additional positive features that are recognized can result in an increased sense of similarity between the target and the positive category.

In terms of intergroup attitudes, within minimal intergroup paradigms and with temporary laboratory groups, intergroup bias may primarily be related to ingroup favoritism rather than outgroup derogation (Brewer, 1979). Under these conditions, attitudes toward outgroup members are generally neutral; thus, positive affect may be effective at producing the broader, more inclusive social categorizations that are hypothesized in the Common Ingroup Identity Model to be critical in reducing bias. In contrast, positive affect would not be expected to facilitate superordinate representations or reduce intergroup bias between groups whose relations are dominated by hatred or serious threat — for which positive connections are unlikely to exist or to be activated. Nonetheless, there are many instances of group rivalries that have not yet reached the stage of hatred (e.g., subgroups or areas within an organization, such as marketing and manufacturing), for which improved affect may facilitate positive intergroup perceptions.

Although the present chapter examines intergroup relations among meaningful social entities as well as groups assembled in the laboratory, the intense level of intergroup conflict is not represented. Preliminary assessment of attitudes (1 = *very unfavorable attitude*, 5 = *neutral*, and 9 = *very favorable attitude*) revealed the range of initial intergroup attitudes that characterized our population of research participants. Arbitrarily assigned overestimators/underestimators demonstrated intergroup bias that was characterized primarily by ingroup favoritism ($M_{ingroup}$ = 5.56 vs. $M_{outgroup}$ = 4.87). Members of meaningful social entities used in the research presented in this chapter and related studies generally exhibited both ingroup favoritism and outgroup derogation, although ingroup favoritism was consistently stronger than outgroup derogation, and outgroup attitudes were not intensely negative (e.g., liberals/conservatives, $M_{ingroup}$ = 7.00 vs. $M_{outgroup}$ = 4.00; democrats/republicans, $M_{ingroup}$ = 6.86 vs. $M_{outgroup}$ = 4.21; profraternity/antifraternity, $M_{ingroup}$ = 6.40 vs. $M_{outgroup}$ = 4.37). Thus, many meaningful social groups are not yet so contemptuous as to derogate each other strongly. In addition, even in the absence of situations of intense conflict, the range of intergroup attitudes investigated in the present chapter can illuminate the nature of key processes in social cognition that shape intergroup attitudes and behavior in fundamental ways. Furthermore, by eliminating the foundation of intergroup bias and fostering a perceived common identity and ways of relating to each other, positive affect intervention at this stage of group relations may help to prevent the subsequent development of deep, intense hatred between groups.

Positive Affect and the Categorization of Others and Oneself

The goal of the first experiment (Rust, 1995) described in this chapter was to determine whether these cognitive processes that are activated by positive affect can be utilized to facilitate the recategorization of others into common ingroups. In particular, it was hypothesized that individuals experiencing positive affect would be more inclusive in associating themselves and others with the same positive social categories. Participants (n = 60) were randomly assigned into positive affect and control conditions. Affect was manipulated using a technique that resembles the Velten (1968) procedure, involving reading a series of affectively positive or neutral statements (Siebert & Ellis, 1991). Next, participants were asked to rate (0–9) how well they fit into a range of social categories, and then how well a range of other people (professors, local residents, engineering majors, and graduate teaching assistants) fit into these categories. Half of the categories were positive (e.g., Americans, intellectual people) and half were negative (e.g., nonconformists, political activists). In general, the positive and negative categories were not significantly different in the extremity of their valences. On a 7-point scale (1 = *negative*, 4 = *neutral*, and 7 = *positive*), the positive categories had a mean of 5.69 and the negative categories had a mean of 2.77.

The categorization ratings were generally supportive of predictions: People experiencing positive affect rated themselves and tended to rate others more strongly as members of the positively valenced categories and less strongly as members of the negatively evaluated categories. The multivariate Affect x Category Valence interaction was statistically significant ($p < .02$). This two-way interaction effect, illustrated in the left panel of Fig. 14.2, was significant for the measure of self-categorization ($p < .05$). A similar pattern, illustrated in the right panel of Fig. 14.2, was obtained for the ratings of a range of others for positive and negative categories. Although this interaction was not statistically reliable by itself ($p = .157$), participants in the positive affect condition rated targets as somewhat better examples of socially desirable categories and somewhat worse examples of socially undesirable categories than did participants in the control condition.

In general, these results extend earlier work demonstrating that positive affect produces more favorable evaluations of oneself (Isen, Shalker, Clark, & Karp, 1978) and more inclusive categorization (Isen et al., 1992). Positive affect can enhance the inclusiveness of social categorization, but it does so in specific ways. Consistent with the processes proposed by Isen et al. (1992), positive affect increases the association between positively or neutrally valenced exemplars and positive social categories, but does not

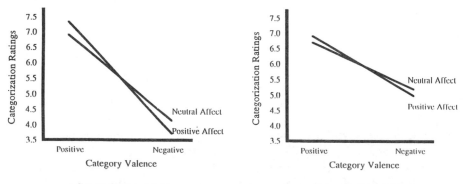

FIG. 14.2. Participants in the positive affect condition, compared with those in the neutral affect condition, tended to categorize self and others more strongly as members of positively valenced groups and less strongly as members of relatively negatively valenced groups.

facilitate the connection of these targets to negative social categories. These effects applied not only to categories such as "intellectuals" or "artistic," which could be construed as adjectives, but also to more conventional social categories, such as "Americans" or "middle-class people." Furthermore, of direct relevance to the Common Ingroup Identity Model, stronger perceptions of membership in these positive categories occurs both for the self and a range of other target persons — from professors to members of the local community. Therefore, positive affect may support the recategorization of members from different groups into a common, valued, superordinate group and potentially facilitate the reduction of intergroup bias. The experiment described next explored these implications in a more explicitly intergroup context.

Positive Affect and Laboratory Groups

This experiment specifically investigated how positive affect can influence intergroup perceptions and evaluations among members of laboratory groups in ways outlined by the Common Ingroup Identity Model (Dovidio, Gaertner, Isen, & Lowrance, 1995). Although the design was more complicated, this chapter focuses on the affect manipulation. In particular, it was hypothesized that positive affect would influence intergroup attraction by affecting the salience of group boundaries. This hypothesis is based on the convergence of several findings. Murray et al. (1990) found that positive affect increased participants' cognitive flexibility in approaching categorization tasks (about types of television programs) and representations. Isen and her colleagues (Isen, 1987; Isen & Daubman, 1984; Isen et al., 1992) demonstrated that positive feelings can facilitate broader and more inclusive positive categorization and reduce intergroup distinctions. In addition, Stroessner, Hamilton, and Mackie (1992) concluded (although for a different reason) that positive affect can interfere with processes, such as illusory correlation, that can contribute to intergroup stereotyping. Thus, it was predicted that participants in positive feeling states would be more likely to develop a more inclusive, superordinate representation of the aggregate than would participants in the affect control condition.

Participants in this experiment first formed a group and worked together on a problem-solving task. Then in preparation for a combined-group interaction, they saw a videotape, ostensibly of the other group. The experimenter asked the participants to "try to get to know the group as well as its solution [because] you will be interacting with them later." The videotape portrayed three confederates performing a similar problem-solving task. An affective manipulation was intended to create positive feelings. After the small-group interaction and before viewing the videotape of the other group, participants in the condition designed to produce positive affect were given a gift of candy, as has been done in previous research (e.g., Isen & Daubman, 1984); in the control condition, no mention of candy bars was made. Research on interpersonal behavior indicates that simply the association of positive events, which may elevate one's mood, with another person enhances attraction (Veitch & Griffitt, 1976) through social conditioning (Byrne & Clore, 1970; Lott & Lott, 1974). In intergroup situations, rewards associated with pleasant, cooperative interaction or success may similarly directly create more positive impressions of outgroup members (Worchel, Andreoli, & Folger, 1977). Positive affect has also been found to increase helping and generosity, which might also reflect a more favorable orientation to others engendered by positive feelings (Isen, 1970; Isen & Levin, 1972). It was hypothesized that positive affect can also influence intergroup attraction *indirectly* by affecting the salience of group boundaries, facilitating broader and more inclusive categorization and reducing intergroup distinctions. Thus, it was predicted that participants in positive feeling states would be more likely to develop a more inclusive, superordinate representation of the aggregate than would participants in the control condition. The measure of this superordinate representation reflected stronger ratings of the extent to which the total aggregate would feel like one group, and weaker ratings of the extent to which it would feel like two groups, in later interaction. Furthermore, it was hypothesized that more inclusive representations of the aggregate would, in turn, predict lower levels of intergroup bias.

The results support the predictions. As expected, positive affect increased the extent to which participants formed inclusive group representations, anticipating that the members of two groups would feel more like one, superordinate group and less like two separate groups. Moreover, as anticipated, stronger superordinate group representations, in turn, predicted lower levels of intergroup bias. Path analysis revealed a significant indirect path from the manipulation of positive affect, through more inclusive representations of the groups, to reduced bias in evaluations. The direct path from the affect manipulation to intergroup bias was nonsignificant. In addition, the reduction of bias occurred in the way proposed by the Common Ingroup Identity Model: Bias was reduced primarily by the more favorable ratings of the outgroup produced as a consequence of being recategorized from members of the outgroup to members of the superordinate ingroup.

Although consistent with the predictions, the findings of this experiment may be limited in both practical and conceptual ways. In particular, the intergroup situation involved laboratory groups with an intergroup relationship that was not clearly defined. That is, the groups were not in either explicit cooperation or competition with one another, factors that can have a profound impact on intergroup dynamics (Sherif, Harvey, White, Hood, & Sherif, 1954). Relatedly and pragmatically, this research also did not involve groups with enduring or meaningful boundaries or with current or past conflicts. The nature of intergroup bias may be quite different for ecologically meaningful social entities from what it is for laboratory groups (Mullen et al., 1992). Conceptually, the manner in which affect influences cognitive processes may also vary as a function of the context of decision making (Isen, 1993). That is, if positive affect facilitates elaborative processing, then the nature of information available can moderate the influence of positive affect on attitudes and behavior. Thus, the effects obtained in this experiment may not necessarily generalize to situations involving explicit competitive relations between groups or strong and meaningful intergroup boundaries, particularly when outgroup membership is associated with negative attitudes and feelings. Therefore, the experiment described next investigated the influence of positive affect on bias in the context of relations between meaningful entities.

Affect and the Context of Intergroup Contact

As previously noted, extremely hostile relations between groups or a long history of antagonism and competition between groups may mitigate the beneficial influence of positive affect that has been observed in intergroup perceptions. Similarly, other details of the relationship between the groups or the contexts in which the evaluation is being considered may influence the impact that positive affect has on these evaluations.

However, positive affect may moderate the influence of the historical or contemporary intergroup context on the nature of the groups' relations. For example, several studies have investigated the influence of positive affect on stereotyping. This work assumes that positive affect increases the use of the heuristic type of thinking, and that stereotyping represents heuristic processing. For example, Bodenhausen (1993) reported two studies (Bodenhausen & Kramer, 1990a, 1990b) that demonstrated that positive affect increased negative stereotypic judgments of outgroup members. However, more recent research indicates that this effect does not universally occur (Bodenhausen, Kramer, & Süsser, 1994).

Another line of research suggests that responsiveness to contextual cues may represent another form of heuristic thinking that is influenced by positive affect. Although responsiveness to the environment is not necessarily or even usually interpreted as heuristic thinking, this literature implies that overresponsiveness to environmental cues can reflect heuristic processes. Two different theoretical interpretations have been proposed in this work. One position, posited by Mackie and her colleagues, suggests that

positive affect may reduce the capacity for deliberative information processing, and thereby increase reliance on heuristic cues (Mackie et al., 1989;
Mackie & Worth, 1989; Worth & Mackie, 1987). An alternative position
(see Bodenhausen, 1993; Schwarz, Bless, & Bohner, 1991) is that positive
affect may increase people's use of heuristic cues, not because of reduced
cognitive capacity, but rather because of reduced motivation to process
information systematically.

However, it should be noted that greater influence of contextual cues
does not necessarily represent heuristic processing, nor does it necessarily
imply that positive affect interferes with systematic processes either through
the depletion of cognitive capacity or for motivational reasons. In fact, the
increased influence of contextual cues may reflect greater flexibility and
adaptivity. Recent work has recognized that these effects of positive affect
may reflect choices by participants, rather than inevitable consequences of
the affective state. For instance, Bodenhausen et al. (1994, Study 3)
demonstrated that positive affect does not promote stereotype use when the
task is described as important. These findings (see also Forgas, 1995a) are
compatible with the position proposed by Isen and her colleagues—that
positive affect enables systematic thinking as it enhances flexibility and
responsiveness to environmental contingencies, in the context of the
person's goals in the situation (Isen, 1984, 1987, 1993; Isen et al., 1978).

Specifically, Isen suggested that positive affect facilitates elaborative
processes (i.e., increased processing rather than decreased; Isen, Daubman,
& Nowicki, 1987; Isen et al., 1985; Lewinsohn & Mano, 1993; Smith &
Shaffer, 1991). Greater elaborative processing, in turn, could mediate
greater responsiveness to the intergroup context. Notably, because positive
affect promotes elaboration and flexibility in thinking, it could not only
increase the perception of similarity, as it does usually, but also could
increase perception of difference between groups when people are motivated to look for distinctions (e.g., Isen, 1987; Murray et al., 1990).
Furthermore, when groups have competitive or antagonistic relations,
positive mood could increase sensitivity to threat and risk (Isen & Geva,
1987; Isen, Nygren, & Ashby, 1988; Isen & Patrick, 1983) and increase
perceptions of difference and distrust, thereby promoting avoidance of risk
and enhancing bias. However, when group interactions involve cooperative,
friendly, or even neutral relations (as in Dovidio et al., 1995), positive affect
may increase the inclusiveness of one's group boundaries, and consequently
lead to more openness and thus reduce bias. Therefore, the conclusion of
researchers (e.g., Mackie et al., 1989; Schwarz et al., 1991) that positive
affect increases responsiveness to superficial cues in the environment, and
the research of Isen and her colleagues and others, which indicates that the
influence of positive affect on bias may be moderated by the nature of the
context, both suggest that positive affect may exacerbate intergroup bias

between directly competing groups or meaningful entities with traditionally competing vested interests. However, Isen's view suggests that increases in group biases may be mediated by group representations; in addition, these increases may occur substantially in other ways as well (e.g., increasing self-protection and sensitivity to threat, independent of the recognition of separate group identities).

To examine these issues, an experiment was conducted involving ecologically meaningful social entities, rather than arbitrarily composed groups. The groups were composed of students who described themselves as politically liberal or conservative, or as profraternity or antifraternity. The experiment examined the hypothesis that positive affect would increase bias between meaningful entities with generally conflicting interests, and explored the role that emphasizing a common ingroup identity could have in reducing this bias. Normally, as was found with laboratory groups with no history of conflict (Dovidio et al., 1995), positive affect readily cues common connections and identity. However, in the context of relations characterized by competition or conflict, positive affect would not play this role by itself, but rather would have this effect once this commonality was introduced by some other means.

Positive Affect and Meaningful Social Entities

This experiment partially replicated the procedures of Dovidio et al. (1995), except that it involved social categories of some importance to participants' identity (liberals, conservatives; profraternity, antifraternity). Participants ($n = 180$) first interacted in three-person groups on a problem-solving task. Then in preparation for a combined-group interaction, they saw a videotape of another group. The videotape portrayed three confederates, ostensibly representing a historically competitive group (e.g., liberals, if participants were conservatives) performing a similar problem-solving task. Affect and the salience of group membership were manipulated in a 2 x 2 design. The affect manipulation was intended to create positive feelings. After the small-group interaction and before viewing the videotape of the other group, participants in the conditions designed to produce positive affect were either given candy bars or viewed a comedy videotaped segment; in the control conditions, either no mention of candy bars was made or participants viewed a "neutral" videotape. The salience of group membership was varied by the labels participants used to refer to the two groups and themselves throughout the experiment. In a condition designed to reinforce existing group boundaries, participants referred to others in terms of their separate group memberships (e.g., liberals or conservatives). In a condition that emphasized the superordinate connection between the groups (the common identity condition) and their interconnection, the participants' common identity as a student of the university prefaced the references to their group membership (e.g., *Colgate* liberals, *Colgate* conservatives). This condition in which subgroup and superordinate identities were salient simultaneously was found in an earlier field study to relate to reduced levels of intergroup bias in a multiethnic high school (Gaertner et al., 1994).

The primary dependent measures were cognitive representations of the aggregate and group evaluations. Because of the possible interdependence among the group participants in each session, the unit of analysis throughout all statistical analyses was the mean for each three-person group ($n = 60$), rather than each individual's ratings. The primary analyses were based on a 2 (Context: two groups vs. common identity) x 2 (Affect: positive vs. neutral) design. Overall, participants demonstrated intergroup bias in their evaluations ($p < .01$). This bias generally reflected less liking for the outgroup relative to the ingroup ($Ms = 5.03$ vs. 5.76, on a 7-point scale), rather than strong dislike, in absolute terms, of the outgroup.

The analysis of intergroup evaluative bias (i.e., favoring the ingroup over the outgroup in evaluations) demonstrated the predicted interaction ($p < .01$). Both tests of simple effects produced significant results. As expected, in the two groups context, participants in the positive affect condition exhibited higher levels of bias than did those in the control (i.e., neutral affect) condition ($Ms = 1.04$ vs. 0.51; $p < .05$). However, in the common identity condition, positive affect participants showed lower levels of bias than did neutral affect participants ($Ms = 0.48$ vs. 0.86; $p < .02$). From an alternative perspective, emphasizing a common ingroup identity did not assuage bias in the control (neutral affect) condition; it did, however, in the positive affect condition. This overall pattern is strongly supportive of the hypothesized influence of positive affect on intergroup relations. Furthermore, consistent with earlier work, attitudes toward the outgroup contributed primarily to intergroup bias. The analysis of outgroup evaluations demonstrated a similar two-way interaction ($p < .01$), whereas the analysis of ingroup evaluations did not produce this interaction ($F < 1$). As in the previous studies, stronger superordinate group ratings were substantially correlated overall with lower levels of bias ($r = -.55$, $p < .001$) and more favorable evaluations of the outgroup ($r = +.55$, $p < .001$). Consistent with earlier work, superordinate group ratings were not significantly correlated with ingroup evaluations ($r = +.12$, $p > .35$).

To evaluate the hypothesized processes contributing to reduced bias in the superordinate group condition and increased bias in the two groups condition, path analyses were computed separately for each condition. In particular, for the superordinate group condition, the manipulation of positive affect was hypothesized to produce more inclusive group categorization (i.e., higher superordinate group ratings), which in turn was predicted to lead to reduced bias. As illustrated in the top panel of Fig. 14.3, the obtained results were highly consistent with the hypothesized pattern (Goodness of-Fit Index = .99, $\chi^2(2)$ = 0.01, $p < .95$). The manipulation of positive affect created higher levels of self-reported positive affect. Self-reported positive affect predicted, as expected, more inclusive group representations, which then significantly predicted lower levels of inter-group bias. The direct path from manipulated affect to bias was not significant. In general, these results conceptually replicate the processes demonstrated by the path analysis reported in Dovidio et al. (1995).

The path analysis for the two groups condition, which is represented in the lower panel of Fig. 14.3, also demonstrates a pattern of results that generally conforms to the predictions. Specifically, it was hypothesized that for groups with meaningful social boundaries under conditions in which

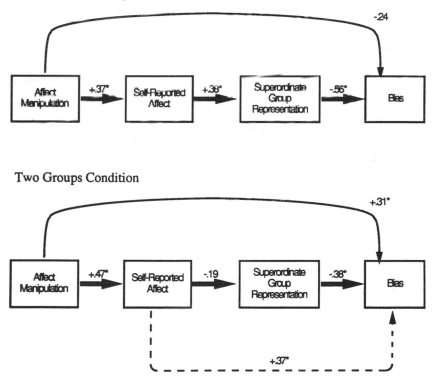

Superordinate Group Condition

Two Groups Condition

* indicates significant path (p < .05)

FIG. 14.3. Path analyses for the superordinate group condition and the two groups condition reveals potential ways by which positive affect predicts lower levels of bias in the superordinate group condition and higher levels of bias the two groups condition.

differences are salient, positive affect would lead to less inclusive group representations, and therefore greater levels of bias. Although the significant chi-square value suggests that the originally proposed model (identified by solid-line paths) fits the obtained data marginally (Goodness-of-Fit Index = .91, $\chi2(2)$ = 6.18, p < .046), the inclusion of an additional path from self-reported positive affect to bias (.37) significantly improves the fit of the model (Goodness-of-Fit Index = .99, $\chi2(2)$ = 0.06, p < .82). The direct paths from the affect manipulation and from self-reported affect to bias suggest that positive affect may influence bias by increasing the degree to which participants perceived the groups as separate entities, as well as more directly by enhancing the salience and impact of different group identities on intergroup attitudes. In addition, directly supportive of the differential impact of positive affect, comparison of the paths between the two models revealed a significant difference (+.38 vs. −.19, p < .05) between the superordinate group and two groups conditions for the paths from self-reported affect to superordinate group representations.

Overall, the results of this experiment demonstrate the predicted effect for positive affect on intergroup evaluations. When group boundaries are distinct and meaningful, positive affect may increase intergroup bias. Nevertheless, when a positive superordinate identity is made salient, positive affect can help reduce intergroup bias. These results are consistent with propositions of the Common Ingroup Identity Model and with the hypothesized processes by which positive affect influence cognitive processing (Isen et al., 1992). In the absence of other salient information about the relationship between groups (as with laboratory groups; Dovidio et al., 1995), affect may serve as information for defining intergroup evaluations and as a cue for guiding intergroup relations (Clore & Parrott, 1994). However for meaningful social entities, affect may influence the salience of features of the social context or the existing relationship that are involved in the analysis of the situation and in shaping one's reactions. For example, Isen proposed that, through enhanced deliberative processing, positive affect may increase sensitivity to threat. As a result, positive affect may tend to produce more segregated group representations (i.e., representations of the aggregate as two groups, rather than as one group), and may make the potential consequences of that intergroup relation more salient (relating to the direct paths, independent of superordinate representations, from manipulated affect and self-reported affect to bias). This interpretation follows from the findings reported by Isen et al. (1988), which showed that positive affect increased the negative utility (i.e., disutility) of possible negative consequences.

The next section examines some behavioral consequences of the recategorization processes proposed in the Common Ingroup Identity Model. As demonstrated, these consequences can be produced by the induction of positive affect in intergroup contexts. The extension from evaluative bias to intergroup behavior is not a trivial one. For example, in a recent review of the literature regarding the relationship between racial prejudice and racial discrimination by Whites, Dovidio, Brigham, Johnson, and Gaertner (1996) found that the correlation was significant, but relatively modest in magnitude ($r = .32$, $p < .01$). Also, Struch and Schwartz (1989) demonstrated that intergroup bias and intergroup aggression may have different antecedents. Thus, the next section further explores the consequences of promoting a common ingroup identity on behavioral interactions between groups.

COMMON INGROUP IDENTITY AND INTERGROUP BEHAVIOR

Support for the assumptions and implications of our model does not contradict or invalidate other models, such as those involving decategorization by providing personalizing and individuating information. In fact, these approaches are complementary. Creating a common ingroup identity may decrease intergroup anxiety (Stephan & Stephan, 1985) and enhance the quality of interactions between the memberships in ways that encourage the exchange of personalizing (Brewer & Miller, 1984) and individuating information (Wilder, 1978). The induction of a common ingroup identity is viewed primarily as a catalyst that can facilitate processes that have additional consequences for reducing intergroup bias. Understanding the interrelationships among the diverse factors that are associated with reduced bias and the various underlying processes proposed by different frameworks could lead to the type of theoretical elaboration that may substantially contribute to more effective applied interventions.

The last experiment described in this chapter examined the consequences of recategorization on two different types of intergroup behaviors: helping and self-disclosure (Dovidio, Gaertner, Validzic, Matoka, Johnson, & Frazier, in press). Because this experiment was an initial test of the influence of the processes outlined in the Common Ingroup Identity Model on these behaviors, group representations were manipulated by a series of interventions used by Gaertner et al. (1989) that have a reliable and strong impact on these perceptions. Future research will extend the causal sequence to include the often more subtle complexities of positive affect.

It was hypothesized that recategorizing the former outgroup members as members of a superordinate ingroup would facilitate helping toward these individuals. Theoretically, several factors could contribute to this effect. As noted at the beginning of this chapter, categorization of a person as an ingroup member increases perceptions of shared beliefs (e.g., Brown, 1984;

Wilder, 1984). The perception of greater interpersonal similarity, in turn, typically facilitates helping (see Dovidio, 1984). Furthermore, intergroup processes, as well as interpersonal processes, can promote helping. Hornstein and his colleagues (Flippen, Hornstein, Siegal, & Weitzman, 1996; Hornstein, 1976; Hornstein, Masor, Sole, & Heilman, 1971) demonstrated that recognition of common group membership increases helping beyond the mere effects of interpersonal similarity. Both interpersonal similarity and group identification might operate through empathic arousal and concern, which motivate helpful and sometimes altruistic actions (see Batson, 1991). Furthermore, if generalization is a function of stimulus similarity and association, it is also possible benefits to additional outgroup members who are not present during the interaction may occur, particularly when the revised superordinate representation and the earlier group identities are salient simultaneously (i.e., the perception of two subgroups within one group) or alternately (Gaertner et al., 1993). This is when positive affect may be especially helpful, too.

Perception of greater similarity, more favorable attributions, greater recognition of individual qualities, and greater empathy toward people categorized as ingroup rather than outgroup members could also facilitate the exchange of more self-disclosing information among members of the recategorized superordinate group. Self-disclosure increases as the closeness of the relationship between interactants increases (Dindia & Allen, 1992) and reflects interest in greater involvement with the other person (Davis, 1976; Derlega & Chaikin, 1976; Shaffer, Pegalis, & Bazzini, 1996). Thus, it was hypothesized that recategorization from two groups to one superordinate group would increase both helping and self-disclosure between members of former outgroups.

The procedure used for developing a common superordinate representation or reinforcing a two-group representation was similar to that used by Gaertner et al. (1989, 1990). Participants ($n = 144$) initially met in two 3-person groups, ostensibly composed of overestimators or underestimators, in a study of group decision making. Following the three-person group discussions, participants were informed of their upcoming contact with the other group. Aspects of the intergroup contact situation were manipulated to vary participants' cognitive representations as one group or two separate groups (e.g., integrated vs. segregated seating, common group name vs different subgroup names, similar vs. different dress; see Gaertner et al., 1989, 1990). Under the conditions representing the one- or two-group manipulations, the six participants worked again on the decision task, and then completed questionnaires that assessed their cognitive representations of the aggregate and the impressions of the interaction and interactants. Next participants were introduced to the final phase of the experiment, which purportedly involved examining one- and two-way interactions.

These tasks provided the cover stories for assessing self-disclosure and helping.

To investigate self-disclosure, two pairs of participants were brought to separate cubicles. One dyad was composed of an overestimator and an underestimator; the other was composed of two members from the same original subgroup (i.e., two overestimators or two underestimators). Two different experimenters, unaware of dyad members' original subgroup identities, informed participants that they would be involved in an examination of "conversation preferences and interactions." Dyad members were asked to discuss a moderately disclosing topic: "What are you most afraid of?" These conversations were audiorecorded and subsequently coded for level of intimacy (1–10).

To examine helping, the remaining two participants were escorted to separate rooms; they were informed that they had been chosen for the one-way communication condition, and that they would be listening to a videotape of one of the previous participants in the two-way communication condition. One participant was informed that the person on the videotape was a member of their original subgroup category (e.g., an overestimator), whereas the other participant was told that the other person was from the opposite group. The audiotape presented a situation, modeled after that used by Dovidio, Allen, and Schroeder (1990) in their study of altruism, that involved the inability of the student to complete an important project because of illness. To provide the helping opportunity, following the procedure of Dovidio et al. (1990), at the conclusion of the session the experimenter handed the participant an envelope, explaining, "Because the person let us use his information, he asked us to distribute this note." The note contained an appeal to help by placing posters recruiting volunteers in various locations across campus. To help, participants were asked to identify the locations in which they would be willing to hang the posters. The dependent measure of helping was the number of locations indicated.

As expected, the one-group manipulation produced more inclusive, one-group perceptions than did the two-group manipulation ($p < .05$). Furthermore, this manipulation had the predicted effect on the patterns of results for self-disclosure and helping. For self-disclosure, a significant one-group versus two-group manipulation x intragroup versus intergroup conversation interaction ($p < .05$) was obtained on the level of intimacy displayed by the dyads. As illustrated in Fig. 14.4, when separate group identities were reinforced by the two-group manipulation, simple effects analyses demonstrated that dyads composed of members of initially different groups exhibited less intimate self-disclosure than did dyads composed of members of the same original group ($p < .05$). As predicted, however, the one-group manipulation eliminated this difference ($p > .15$). In fact, as represented in Fig. 14.4, under these conditions, members of

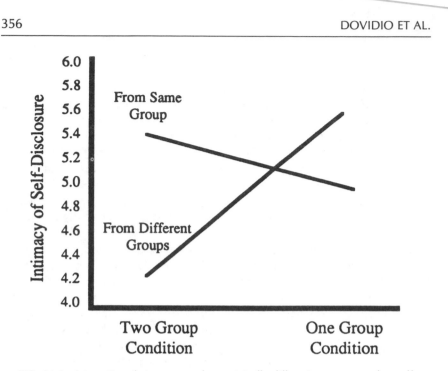

FIG. 14.4. Interactions between members originally different groups were less self-disclosing than interactions between members of the same group in the two-group condition; however, in the one-group condition, interactions between members of different groups and between members of the same group were equivalently self-disclosing.

initially different groups were somewhat more intimately self-disclosing than were members of the same original groups.

Furthermore, consistent with the prediction of the Common Ingroup Identity Model, the recategorization manipulation primarily affected behavior toward individuals who were initially members of the outgroup. Self-disclosure was significantly greater ($p < .05$) in dyads involving an original outgroup member (intergroup dyads) in the one-group manipulation than in the two-group manipulation condition. There was no significant difference in self-disclosure between members of the same original groups (intragroup dyads) as a function of the one-group versus two-group manipulation ($p > .30$). Therefore, as hypothesized by the Common Ingroup Identity Model, establishing a superordinate identity reduces intergroup bias primarily by improving response to the outgroup.

The pattern of results for helping was similar but weaker and less fully consistent with the predictions. The one-group versus two-group manipulation x intragroup versus intergroup helping opportunity interaction was only marginally significant ($p < .10$). As anticipated, with the two-group manipulation, participants were less helpful toward an original outgroup member than toward an original ingroup member (Ms = 2.25 vs. 4.83 locations; p < .10. In contrast, with the one-group manipulation, there was no significant intergroup bias in helping (p > .50). Paralleling the results for self disclosure, participants were slightly more helpful to an original outgroup member than to an original ingroup member under these conditions (Ms = 3.92 vs. 3.08 locations). However, unlike the results for self-disclosure and inconsistent with predictions, participants were not significantly more helpful to original outgroup members as a consequence of recategorization: The difference in helping toward an original outgroup member was somewhat but not significantly (p < .20) greater in the one-group than in the two-group condition. Overall, although less clear and strong than the findings for self-disclosure, this pattern of results for helping is generally consistent with — although not unequivocally supportive of — the processes and consequences proposed in the Common Ingroup Identity Model.

CONCLUSION

The research presented in this chapter illustrated complex but systematic interrelationships among social context, affect, cognition, intergroup evaluations, and intergroup behavior. In particular, the first three experiments reported in this chapter demonstrated the impact of positive affect on interpersonal perception and intergroup representations and bias. These experiments support the substantial literature on the effects of temporarily induced affect on how people evaluate objects, view social issues, see themselves, make social choices, and perceive and interpret social behaviors (Carnevale & Isen, 1986; Clark & Williamson, 1989; Forgas, 1991; Forgas & Bower, 1987; Isen, 1987; Isen et al., 1978; Mayer, Gaschke, Braverman, & Evans, 1992; Salovey, O'Leary, Stretton, Fishkin, & Drake, 1991; Sedikides, 1992). Whereas previous research has persuasively shown the significant impact of positive affect on interpersonal perception (Forgas, 1995b) and on evaluations of one's own intimate relations (Forgas, Levinger, & Moylan, 1994), this work focused on the *intergroup* consequences of positive affect.

In this respect, the research presented in this chapter complements the works of Bodenhausen (1993) and Forgas and Fiedler (1996), which also demonstrate that incidental affect, which is generated by factors that are not integral to the intergroup contact or interaction, can shape intergroup representations, attitudes, and behaviors in critical ways. As Mackie and Hamilton (1993) observed, "This affect, which in principle is unrelated to intergroup issues, may nevertheless carry over and influence the way information about groups and group members is processed" (p. 372). The present chapter focused on positive affect, whereas other research has demonstrated the important role of negative affect (Bodenhausen, 1993). For example, Forgas and Fiedler (1996) recently found that, under personally relevant conditions emphasizing intergroup conflict, sadness increased intergroup discrimination. However, the findings for negative mood are not entirely consistent. Bodenhausen (1993) concluded that negative states such as anxiety and anger increase negative stereotyping, but, contrary to the findings of Forgas and Fiedler (1996), that sadness does not. As Forgas and Fiedler (1996) and Bodenhausen (1993) proposed, future research needs to focus more fully on the potential moderators and mediators of these effects. The research presented in this chapter, which was confined to the influence of positive affect, suggests that the nature of the intergroup context may be a critical factor (see also Forgas & Fiedler, 1996).

This work could not definitively identify the operation of deliberative or heuristic processes as a consequence of positive affect. However, the overall pattern of results is generally consistent with memory-based, affect-priming theories that characterize models such as those of Bower (1991), Forgas (1995a), Lewinsohn and Mano (1993), and Isen (1993), which propose systematic thinking under conditions of positive affect. According to Bower (1981), within an associative network framework, "activation of an emotion node also spreads activation throughout the memory structures to which it is connected" (p. 135). Although aspects of Bower's spreading activation model (such as the cue-overload position of the model, and symmetry between negative and positive affect in impact; see Isen, 1984, 1987 for discussion) have not been supported by the accumulating evidence, propositions from a more general priming model have repeatedly been confirmed. As proposed by Isen et al. (1992), positive affect is most likely to facilitate the positive evaluation of objects and people and the inclusion of these objects and people into positive superordinate categories primarily when these objects and people have potential positive associates in memory (i.e., when they are evaluatively positive or neutral). When positive associates are not accessible (e.g., for negatively evaluated people and objects), positive affect would not be expected to produce more favorable feelings or attitudes; under conditions of threat, it could produce more negative reactions. Consistent with this perspective, that positive affect was related to increased favorability of outgroup evaluations and reduced intergroup bias when intergroup relations were relatively neutral and ambiguous between temporary groups. However, when the relations between the groups were historically competitive, positive affect tended to be associated with less favorable outgroup evaluations.

The focus here on intergroup processes, rather than on just the interpersonal consequences of positive affect, identified an additional mechanism by which positive affect might influence judgments of others. The evidence highlighted the potential importance of positive affect facilitating more inclusive social categorization and cognitive representations of the aggregate as mediators of changes in intergroup attitudes. In particular, the studies outlined in this chapter provided further support for the Common Ingroup Identity Model (Gaertner et al., 1993). The model asserted that intergroup bias and conflict can be reduced by factors that transform members' cognitive representations of the memberships from two groups to one group. This change in members' perceptions of group boundaries enables some of the cognitive and motivational processes that may initially contribute to intergroup bias and conflict being redirected toward establishing more harmonious intergroup relations. In the study with laboratory groups involving ambiguous or potentially cooperative relations, positive affect was related to more inclusive, superordinate conceptions of the aggregate, which, in turn, predicted lower levels of intergroup bias. In addition, for meaningful entities with histories of competition and conflict, positive affect enhanced the impact of a manipulation designed to increase the salience of a common identity in reducing intergroup bias. Given that many group activities lead to positive affect, and that people normally strive to achieve happiness, it is important to identify ways in which positive affect can be used to improve intergroup relations. Taken together, these findings offer continuing support for basic propositions of the Common Ingroup Identity Model, but also identify new, intergroup processes by which positive affect can influence perceptions of social relationships.

The focus on cognitive representations as key mediators of intergroup relations permits a parsimonious theoretical explanation for the effects of diverse contextual factors, and can also inform practical interventions designed to reduce bias. For example, over the past 40 years, the contact hypothesis has represented a promising and popular strategy for reducing intergroup bias and conflict. It proposes that, under certain prerequisite conditions, intergroup contact promotes the development of more harmonious intergroup relations. Among these conditions are equal status between the groups (optimally within and outside the contact situation), cooperative intergroup interaction, opportunities for personal acquaintance between outgroup members, and norms outside of the contact setting that support egalitarian intergroup interaction (Amir, 1969; Cook, 1985). Structurally, the contact hypothesis has represented a list of loosely connected, diverse conditions, rather than a unifying conceptual framework that explains how these prerequisite features achieve their effects. However, the Common Ingroup Identity Model offers a potentially integrating framework. Gaertner et al. (1994) found that many of these features operate through the common cognitive mechanism of producing a more inclusive, superordinate categorization of the memberships. By under-

standing these underlying dynamics, if political, socioeconomic, or structural circumstances prevent the introduction of some features of the contact
hypothesis, alternative interventions may be effectively identified and
substituted. Thus, explicating the links between intergroup cognition and
intergroup relations has valuable practical and theoretical benefits.

As research has demonstrated, however, the nature of intergroup
relations must be considered a critical factor in selecting appropriate
alternative interventions. It was found that positive affect reduced bias
between laboratory groups that were not in direct conflict and whose initial
outgroup attitudes were generally neutral. In contrast, for competing
groups and for meaningful social entities for which outgroup attitudes were
somewhat negative, the research indicated that positive affect tended to be
related to higher levels of bias unless connections to a positive superordinate
category were made salient. Among groups with intensely negative relations — relations beyond the scope of the work presented in the present
chapter — positive affect may be ineffective at reducing bias and may
potentially exacerbate conflict. Nevertheless, positive affect would be useful
in situations in which people could view other groups as competitors, but
they need not see them this way. For instance, marketing and production
units in organizations may perceive their groups as competitors for internal
resources; however, they may alternatively conceive of their groups as
interdependent units of a superordinate organization working cooperatively
toward a common goal. Thus, a theoretical understanding of the complex
relationships among potential interventions, key elements of the contact
situation and the relations between the groups, and psychological processes
involved is fundamental for selecting appropriate pragmatic strategies for
reducing conflict and bias.

Finally, the present research extends previous work on the Common
Ingroup Identity Model by demonstrating the effect of manipulations of
cognitive representations of the aggregate on intergroup behaviors, as well
as evaluations. Although Struch and Schwartz (1989) demonstrated that
different factors may predict intergroup attitudes and behavior, the central
mechanism of our model — the development of a superordinate identity — is
hypothesized to affect both attitudes and behavior. Supportive of this
hypothesis, the last experiment described in this chapter found that the
manipulation of cognitive representations of the aggregate facilitated
self-disclosing interactions between members of originally different groups
and tended to increase intergroup helping. These behaviors are particularly
significant ones because both self-disclosure and helping typically produce
reciprocity. More intimate self-disclosure by one person normally encourages more intimate disclosure by the other (Archer & Berg, 1978). As Miller,
et al. (1985; Miller, Urban, & Vanman, chap. 16, this volume) demon-

strated, personalized and self-disclosing interaction can be a significant factor in reducing intergroup bias.

Considerable cross-cultural evidence also indicates the powerful influence of the norm of reciprocity on helping (Schroeder, Penner, Dovidio, & Piliavin, 1995). According to this norm, people should help those who have helped them, and they should not help those who have denied them help for no legitimate reason (Gouldner, 1960). Thus, the development of a common ingroup identity can motivate interpersonal behaviors between members of initially different groups that can initiate reciprocal actions and concessions (see Deutsch, 1993; Osgood, 1962), which in turn will reduce immediate tensions and produce more harmonious intergroup relations beyond the contact situation.

As proposed earlier (Gaertner et al., 1993), although finely differentiated impressions of outgroup members may not be an automatic consequence of forming a common ingroup identity, these more elaborated, differentiated, and personalized impressions can quickly develop because the newly formed positivity bias is likely to encourage more open communication. The development of a common ingroup identity creates a motivational foundation for constructive intergroup relations, which can act as a catalyst for positive reciprocal interpersonal actions. Thus, the recategorization strategy proposed in our model and decategorization strategies, such as individuating (Wilder, 1984) and personalizing (Brewer & Miller, 1984) interactions, can potentially operate complementarily and sequentially to improve intergroup relations in lasting and meaningful ways.

ACKNOWLEDGMENTS

The work presented in this chapter was supported by NIMH Grant MH 48721. We are grateful to the editors for their helpful comments and constructive suggestions on an earlier draft of this chapter. In addition, we express our appreciation to Diane Mackie for providing videotapes that were used to manipulate affect in experiments presented in the chapter, and to Regina Conti for her assistance with the LISREL analyses.

REFERENCES

Allport, G. W. (1954). *The nature of prejudice*. Reading, MA: Addison-Wesley.
Amir, Y. (1969). Contact hypothesis in ethnic relations. *Psychological Bulletin, 71*, 319–342.
Archer, R. L., & Berg, J. H. (1978). Disclosure reciprocity and its limits: A reactance analysis. *Journal of Experimental Social Psychology, 14*, 527–540.

Batson, C. D. (1991). *The altruism question: Toward a social-psychological answer.* Hillsdale, NJ: Lawrence Erlbaum Associates.

Bodenhausen, G. V. (1993). Emotions, arousal, and stereotypic judgments: A heuristic model of affect and stereotyping. In D. M. Mackie & D. L. Hamilton (Eds.), *Affect, cognition, and stereotyping: Interactive processes in group perception* (pp. 13–37). San Diego, CA: Academic Press.

Bodenhausen, G. V., & Kramer, G. P. (1990a, June). *Affective states trigger stereotypic judgments.* Paper presented at the annual convention of the American Psychological Society, Dallas, TX.

Bodenhausen, G. V., & Kramer, G. P. (1990b). *Affective states and the heuristic use of stereotypes in social judgment.* Unpublished manuscript, Michigan State University, East Lansing, MI.

Bodenhausen, G. V., Kramer, G. P., & Süsser, K. (1994). Happiness and stereotypic thinking in social judgment. *Journal of Personality and Social Psychology, 66,* 621–632.

Bower, G. H. (1981). Mood and memory. *American Psychologist, 36,* 129–148.

Bower, G. H. (1991). Mood congruity effects in social judgments. In J. P. Forgas (Ed.), *Emotion and social judgments* (pp. 31–53). Elmsford, NY: Pergamon.

Brewer, M. B. (1979). Ingroup bias in the minimal intergroup situation: A cognitive-motivational analysis. *Psychological Bulletin, 86,* 307–324.

Brewer, M. B., Ho, H., Lee, J., & Miller, N. (1987). Social identity and social distance among Hong Kong school children. *Personality and Social Psychology Bulletin, 13,* 156–165.

Brewer, M. B., & Miller, N. (1984). Beyond the contact hypothesis: Theoretical perspectives on desegregation. In N. Miller & M. B. Brewer (Eds.), *Groups in contact: The psychology of desegregation* (pp. 281–302). Orlando FL: Academic Press.

Brown, R. J. (1984). The effects of intergroup similarity and cooperative vs. competitive orientation on intergroup discrimination. *British Journal of Social Psychology, 21,* 21–33.

Brown, R. J., & Abrams, D. (1986). The effects of intergroup similarity and goal interdependence on intergroup attitudes and task performance. *Journal of Experimental Social Psychology, 22,* 78–92.

Brown, R. J., & Turner, J. C. (1981). Interpersonal and intergroup behavior. In J. C. Turner & H. Giles (Eds.), *Intergroup behavior* (pp. 33–64). Chicago, IL: University of Chicago Press.

Byrne, D., & Clore, G. L. (1970). A reinforcement model of evaluative responses. *Personality: An International Journal, 1,* 103–128.

Campbell, D. T. (1958). Common fate, similarity and other indices of the status of aggregates of persons as social entities. *Behavioral Science, 3,* 14–25.

Carnevale, P. J. D., & Isen, A. M. (1986). The influence of positive affect and visual access on the discovery of integrative solutions in bilateral negotiation. *Organizational Behavior and Human Decision Processes, 37,* 1–13.

Clark, M. S., & Williamson, G. M. (1989). Moods and social judgments. In H. Wagner & A. Manstead (Eds.), *Handbook of social psychophysiology* (pp. 347–370). Chichester: Wiley.

Clore, G. L., & Parrott, G. (1994). Cognitive feelings and metacognitive judgments. *European Journal of Social Psychology, 24,* 101–116.

Cook, S. W. (1984). Cooperative interaction in multiethnic contexts. In N. Miller & M. B. Brewer (Eds.), *Groups in contact: The psychology of desegregation* (pp. 291–302). Orlando, FL: Academic Press.

Cook, S. W. (1985). Experimenting on social issues: The case of school desegregation. *American Psychologist, 40,* 452–460.

Davis, J. D. (1976). Self-disclosure in an acquaintance exercise: Responsibility for level of intimacy. *Journal of Personality and Social Psychology, 33,* 787–792.

Derlega, V. J., & Chaikin, A. L. (1976). Norms affecting self-disclosure in men and women. *Journal of Consulting and Clinical Psychology, 44*, 376–380.

Deschamps, J. C., & Doise, W. (1978). Crossed category membership in intergroup relations. In H. Tajfel (Ed.), *Differentiation between social groups* (pp. 141–158). London: Academic Press.

Deutsch, M. (1993). Educating for a peaceful world. *American Psychologist, 48*, 510–517.

Dindia, K., & Allen, M. (1992). Sex differences in self-disclosure: A meta-analysis. *Psychological Bulletin, 112*, 106–124.

Dovidio, J. F. (1984). Helping behavior and altruism: An empirical and conceptual overview. In L. Berkowitz (Ed.), *Advances in experimental social psychology* (Vol. 17, pp. 361–427). New York: Academic Press.

Dovidio, J. F., Allen, J., & Schroeder, D. A. (1990). The specificity of empathy-induced helping: Evidence for altruism. *Journal of Personality and Social Psychology, 59*, 249–260.

Dovidio, J. F., Brigham, J. C., Johnson, B. T., & Gaertner, S. L. (1996). Stereotyping, prejudice, and discrimination: Another look. In C. N. Macrae, C. Stangor, & M. Hewstone (Eds.), *Foundations of stereotypes and stereotyping* (pp. 276–319). New York: Guilford.

Dovidio, J. F., Gaertner, S. L., Isen, A. M., & Lowrance, R. (1995). Group representations and intergroup bias: Positive affect, similarity, and group size. *Personality and Social Psychology Bulletin, 8*, 856–865.

Dovidio, J. F., Gaertner, S. L., Validzic, A., Matoka, A., Johnson, B., & Frazier, S. (in press). Extending the benefits of recategorization: Evaluations, self-disclosure, and helping. *Journal of Experimental Social Psychology.*

Flippen, A. R., Hornstein, H. A., Siegal, W. E., & Weitzman, E. A. (1996). A comparison of similarity and interdependence as triggers for ingroup formation. *Personality and Social Psychology Bulletin, 22*, 882–893.

Forgas, J. P. (1991). Mood effects on partner choice: Role of affect in interpersonal decisions. *Journal of Personality and Social Psychology, 61*, 208–220.

Forgas, J. P. (1995a). Mood and judgment: The affect infusion model (AIM). *Psychological Bulletin, 117*, 39–66.

Forgas, J. P. (1995b). Strange couples: Mood effects on judgments and memory about prototypical and atypical targets. *Personality and Social Psychology Bulletin, 21*, 747–765.

Forgas, J. P., & Bower, G. H. (1987). Mood effects on person perception judgments. *Journal of Personality and Social Psychology, 53*, 53–60.

Forgas, J. P., & Fiedler, K. (1996). Us and them: Mood effects on intergroup discrimination. *Journal of Personality and Social Psychology, 70*, 28–40.

Forgas, J. P., Levinger, G., & Moylan, S. J. (1994). Feeling good and feeling close: Affective influences on the perception of intimate relationships. *Personal Relationships, 2*, 165–184.

Gaertner, S. L., & Dovidio, J. F. (1986). Prejudice, discrimination, and racism: Problems, progress and promise. In J. F. Dovidio & S. L. Gaertner (Eds.), *Prejudice, discrimination, and racism* (pp. 315–332). Orlando, FL: Academic Press.

Gaertner, S. L., Dovidio, J. F., Anastasio, P. A., Bachman, B. A., & Rust, M. C. (1993). The Common Ingroup Identity Model: Recategorization and the reduction of intergroup bias. In W. Stroebe & M. Hewstone (Eds.), *European review of social psychology* (Vol. 4, pp. 1–26). London: Wiley.

Gaertner, S. L., Mann, J., Murrell, A., & Dovidio, J. F. (1989). Reducing intergroup bias: The benefits of recategorization. *Journal of Personality and Social Psychology, 57*, 239–249.

Gaertner, S. L., Mann, J. A., Dovidio, J. F., Murrell, A. J., & Pomare, M. (1990). How does cooperation reduce intergroup bias? *Journal of Personality and Social Psychology, 59*, 692–704.

Gaertner, S. L., Rust, M. C., Dovidio, J. F., Bachman, B. A., & Anastasio, P. A. (1994). The contact hypothesis: The role of a common ingroup identity in reducing intergroup bias. *Small Group Research*, *25*, 224–249.

Gouldner, A. (1960). The norm of reciprocity: A preliminary statement. *American Sociological Review*, *25*, 161–178.

Hewstone, M., Bond, M. H., & Wan, K. (1983). Social facts and social attributions: The explanation of intergroup differences in Hong Kong. *Social Cognition*, *2*, 142–157.

Hewstone, M., Islam, M. R., & Judd, C. M. (1993). Models of crossed categorization and intergroup relations. *Journal of Personality and Social Psychology*, *64*, 779–793.

Hogg, M. A., & Turner, J. C. (1985). Interpersonal attraction, social identification and psychological group formation. *European Journal of Social Psychology*, *15*, 51–66.

Hornstein, H. A. (1976). *Cruelty and kindness: A new look at aggression and altruism*. Englewood Cliffs, NJ: Prentice-Hall.

Hornstein, H. A., Masor, H. N., Sole, K., & Heilman, M. (1971). Effects of sentiment and completion of a helping act on observer helping: A case for socially-mediated Ziergarnik effects. *Journal of Personality and Social Psychology*, *17*, 107–112.

Howard, J. M., & Rothbart, M. (1980). Social categorization for in-group and out-group behavior. *Journal of Personality and Social Psychology*, *38*, 301–310.

Isen, A. M. (1970). Success, failure, attention, and reaction to others: The warm glow of success. *Journal of Personality and Social Psychology*, *15*, 294–301.

Isen, A. M. (1984). Towards understanding the role of affect in cognition. In R. S. Wyer & T. K. Srull (Eds.), *Handbook of social cognition* (Vol. 3,pp. 179–236). Hillsdale, NJ: Lawrence Erlbaum Associates.

Isen, A. M. (1987). Positive affect, cognitive processes, and social behavior. In L. Berkowitz (Ed.), *Advances in experimental social psychology* (Vol. 20, pp. 203–253). Orlando, FL: Academic Press.

Isen, A. M. (1993). Positive affect and decision making. In M. Lewis & J. M. Haviland (Eds.), *Handbook of emotion* (pp. 261–277). New York: Guilford.

Isen, A. M., & Daubman, K. A. (1984). The influence of affect on categorization. *Journal of Personality and Social Psychology*, *47*, 1206–1217.

Isen, A. M., Daubman, K. A., & Nowicki, G. P. (1987). Positive affect facilitates creative problem solving. *Journal of Personality and Social Psychology*, *52*, 1122–1131.

Isen, A. M., & Geva, N. (1987). The influence of positive affect on acceptable level of risk: The person with a large canoe has a large worry. *Organizational Behavior and Human Decision Processes*, *39*, 145–154.

Isen, A. M., Johnson, M. M. S., Mertz, E., & Robinson, G. F. (1985). The influence of positive affect on the unusualness of word associations. *Journal of Personality and Social Psychology*, *48*, 1413–1426.

Isen, A. M., & Levin, P. F. (1972). Effect of feeling good on helping: Cookies and kindness. *Journal of Personality and Social Psychology*, *21*, 384–388.

Isen, A. M., Niedenthal, P. M., & Cantor, N. (1992). An influence of positive affect on social categorization. *Motivation and Emotion*, *16*, 65–78.

Isen, A. M., Nygren, T. E., & Ashby, F. G. (1988). The influence of positive affect on the subjective utility of gains and losses: It is just not worth the risk. *Journal of Personality and Social Psychology*, *55*, 710–717.

Isen, A. M., & Patrick, R. (1983). The effect of positive feelings on risk-taking: When the chips are down. *Organizational Behavior and Human Performance*, *31*, 194–202.

Isen, A. M., Shalker, T. E., Clark, M., & Karp, L. (1978). Affect accessibility of material in memory: A cognitive loop? *Journal of Personality and Social Psychology*, *36*, 1–12.

Lewinsohn, S., & Mano, H. (1993). Multi-attribute choice and affect: The influence of naturally occurring and manipulated moods on choice processes. *Journal of Behavioral*

Decision Making, 6, 33–51.

Lott, A. J., & Lott, B. E. (1974). The role of reward in the formation of positive interpersonal attitudes. In T. Huston (Ed), *Foundations of interpersonal attraction* (pp. 171–189). New York: Academic Press.

Mackie, D. M., & Hamilton, D. L. (1993). Affect, cognition, and stereotyping: Concluding comments. In D. M. Mackie & D. L. Hamilton (Eds.), *Affect, cognition, and stereotyping: Interactive processes in group perception* (pp. 371–383). San Diego, CA: Academic Press.

Mackie, D. M., Hamilton, D. L., Schroth, H. A., Carlisle, C. J., Gersho, B. F., Meneses, L. M., Nedler, B. F., & Reichel, L. D. (1989). The effects of induced mood on expectancy-based illusory correlations. *Journal of Experimental Social Psychology, 25,* 524–544.

Mackie, D. M., & Worth, L. T. (1989). Processing deficits and the mediation of positive affect in persuasion. *Journal of Personality and Social Psychology, 57,* 27–40.

Mayer, J. D., Gaschke, Y. N., Braverman, D. L., & Evans, T. W. (1992). Mood congruent judgment is a general effect. *Journal of Personality and Social Psychology, 63,* 119–132.

Miller, N., Brewer, M. B., & Edwards, K. (1985). Cooperative interaction in desegregated settings: A laboratory analog. *Journal of Social Issues, 41,* 63–75.

Mullen, B., Brown, R., & Smith, C. (1992). Ingroup bias as a function of salience, relevance, and status: An integration. *European Journal of Social Psychology, 22,* 103–122.

Murray, N., Sujan, H., Hirt, E. R., & Sujan, M. (1990). The influence of mood on categorization: A cognitive flexibility interpretation. *Journal of Personality and Social Psychology, 59,* 411–425.

Osgood, C. E. (1962). *An alternative to war or surrender.* Urbana, IL: University of Illinois Press.

Piliavin, J. A., Dovidio, J. F., Gaertner, S. L., & Clark, R. D. III. (1981). *Emergency intervention.* New York: Academic Press.

Rust, M. C. (1995). *Effects of mood on categorization.* Unpublished master's thesis, Department of Psychology, University of Delaware, Newark, DE.

Salovey, P., O'Leary, A., Stretton, M., Fishkin, S., & Drake, C. A. (1991). Influence of mood on judgments about health and illness. In J. P. Forgas (Ed.), *Emotion and social judgments* (pp. 241–262). Elmsford, NY: Pergamon.

Schroeder, D. A., Penner, L. A., Dovidio, J. F., & Piliavin, J. A. (1995). *Psychology of helping and altruism: Problems and puzzles.* New York: McGraw-Hill.

Schwarz, N., Bless, H., & Bohner, G. (1991). Mood and persuasion: Affective states influence the processing of persuasive communications. In M. P. Zanna (Ed.), *Advances in experimental social psychology* (Vol. 24, pp. 161–199). Orlando, FL: Academic Press.

Sedikides, C. (1992). Changes in the valence of the self as a function of mood. *Review of Personality and Social Psychology, 14,* 271–311.

Shaffer, D. R., Pegalis, L. J., & Bazzini, D. G. (1996). When boy meets girl (revisited): Gender, gender-role orientation, and prospect of future interaction on self-disclosure among same- and opposite-sex acquaintances. *Personality and Social Psychology Bulletin, 22,* 495–506.

Sherif, M., Harvey, O. J., White, B. J., Hood, W. R., & Sherif, C. (1954). *Experimental study of positive and negative intergroup attitudes between experimentally produced groups: Robbers Cave experiment.* Norman, OK: University of Oklahoma Press.

Siebert, P. S., & Ellis, H. C. (1991). A convenient self-referencing mood induction procedure. *Bulletin of the Psychonomic Society, 29,* 121–124.

Smith, S. M., & Shaffer, D. R. (1991). The effects of good moods on systematic processing: "Willing but not able, or able but not willing?" *Motivation and Emotion, 15,* 243–279.

Stein, D. D., Hardyck, J. A., & Smith, M. B. (1965). Race *and* belief: An open and shut case. *Journal of Personality and Social Psychology, 1,* 281–289.

Stephan, W. G., & Stephan, C. W. (1984). The role of ignorance in intergroup relations. In N. Miller & M. B. Brewer (Eds.), *Groups in contact: The psychology of desegregation* (pp. 229–257). Orlando, FL: Academic Press.

Stephan, W. G., & Stephan, C. W. (1985). Intergroup anxiety. *Journal of Social Issues, 41*, 157–175.

Stroessner, S. J., Hamilton, D. L., & Mackie, D. M. (1992). Affect and stereotyping: The effect of induced mood on distinctiveness-based illusory correlations. *Journal of Personality and Social Psychology, 62*, 564–576.

Struch, N., & Schwartz, S. H. (1989). Intergroup aggression: Its predictors and distinctness from ingroup bias. *Journal of Personality and Social Psychology, 56*, 364–373.

Tajfel, H., & Turner, J. C. (1979). An integrative theory of intergroup conflict. In W. G. Austin & S. Worchel (Eds.), *The social psychology of intergroup relations* (pp. 33–47). Monterey, CA: Brooks/Cole.

Tversky, A., & Gati, I. (1978). Studies of similarity. In E. Rosch & B. B. Lloyd (Eds.), *Cognition and categorization* (pp. 79–98). Hillsdale, NJ: Lawrence Erlbaum Associates.

Vanbeselaere, N. (1987). The effects of dichotomous and crossed social categorization upon intergroup discrimination. *European Journal of Social Psychology, 17*, 143–156.

Veitch, R., & Griffitt, W. (1976). Good news—bad news: Affective and interpersonal effects. *Journal of Applied Social Psychology, 6*, 69–75.

Velten, E. (1968). A laboratory task for induction of mood states. *Behavioral Research and Therapy, 6*, 473–482.

Wang, H., & McKillip, J. (1978). Ethnic identification and judgements of an accident. *Personality and Social Psychology Bulletin, 4*, 296–299.

Wilder, D. A. (1978). Reduction of intergroup discrimination through individuation of the out-group. *Journal of Personality and Social Psychology, 36*, 1361–1374.

Wilder, D. A. (1984). Predictions of belief homogeneity and similarity following social categorization. *British Journal of Social Psychology, 23*, 323–333.

Worchel, S., Andreoli, V. A., & Folger, R. (1977). Intergroup cooperation and intergroup attraction: The effect of previous interaction and outcome of combined effort. *Journal of Experimental Social Psychology, 13*, 131–140.

Worth, L. T., & Mackie, D. M. (1987). Cognitive mediation of positive affect on persuasion. *Social Cognition, 5*, 76–94.

15

Changing Intergroup Cognitions and Intergroup Behavior: The Role of Typicality

Miles Hewstone
University of Wales, Cardiff

Charles G. Lord
Texas Christian University

In the final of the 1995 Rugby World Cup, the "Springboks" of South Africa, against all expectations, defeated the New Zealand "All Blacks." Their match-winning points were scored by Joel Stransky, the one Jew on the team, who in fact scored all his team's points. With postmatch hyperbole, a journalist in the British newspaper *The Independent* wrote that, "he probably killed off once and for all the residual anti-Semitism that has long lingered in many Afrikaner – and some black – hearts" (26 June, 1995). Such an outcome is pretty unlikely, although many social-psychological interventions to defeat prejudice and improve intergroup relations seem to have been based on a similar logic.

Because stereotypical perceptions of outgroups are often negative and homogeneous, rationalizing discrimination and making cooperative intergroup interaction less likely, there is widespread agreement about the need for interventions that can bring about stereotype change. The classic form of intervention is aimed at encouraging contact, under appropriate conditions, among individuals from different groups (the so-called "contact hypothesis"; Allport 1954/1979; Amir, 1969; Cook, 1962). Yet a much-lamented failure of this intervention is that its results – at best, a positive change in attitudes toward the outgroup – do not generalize either "across situations" (i.e., one may be positive toward an outgroup member in one situation, but not others) or "across persons" (i.e., one may be positive toward one member of the outgroup, encountered under carefully constructed conditions, but this view does not extend to the group as a whole).

This chapter is concerned primarily with the latter form of generalization, which has been termed the main shortcoming of the contact hypothesis (Hewstone & Brown, 1986). It is argued that the failure to generalize positive attitudes promoted by the contact experience ("specific attitude change") to include other members of the outgroup not actually present in the contact situation ("generalized change in outgroup attitudes") can be overcome, in part, by basing interventions on a more sophisticated approach to exemplar-category relations that focuses on the key role of typicality (Rothbart & John, 1985; Smith, 1992; see Hewstone, 1996). Specifically, it is argued that social interventions aimed at changing stereotypes are more likely to be successful if they present stereotype-disconfirming information in the context of typical members of the outgroup. This typicality, whether manipulated by group-relevant information, priming, or otherwise, facilitates generalization from specific individuals to the outgroup as a whole. This generalization can be demonstrated both cognitively and behaviorally, with interesting implications for how to explore links between intergroup cognitions and intergroup behavior.

Like all the chapters in this volume, this one is concerned with "intergroup cognition," "intergroup behavior," and the link(s) among them; the "social-cognition" approach provides a valuable perspective on these issues. *Social cognition* can be defined as the study of social knowledge (its content and structure) and cognitive processes (including acquisition, representation, and retrieval of information), and how they provide a key to understanding social behavior and its mediating factors. From this perspective, we agree with the editors that *intergroup cognitions* should include "perceptions, memories, stereotypes, impressions, judgments, evaluations, and behavioral intentions pertaining to the ingroup and/or outgroup" (i.e., they refer to phenomena occurring "inside the heads" of social perceivers). *Intergroup behavior*, in contrast, is overt action directed at the ingroup and/or the outgroup as a whole, or against specific individual representatives of the group. In adopting these definitions, however, we do not wish to argue that either cognition or behavior is paramount. On the one hand, behavioral evidence is crucial data for supporting the claim that (intergroup) cognitions mediate behavior; on the other hand, higher level (intergroup) cognitions are more likely to improve behavioral prediction across a range of settings than are "one-off" behaviors.

INTERGROUP COGNITIONS

Rothbart and John's (1985) cognitive analysis of intergroup contact is based on principles of categorization. If one accepts that objects, or exemplars, differ in the degree to which they are viewed as prototypical examples of a category (what Barsalou [1987] called *graded structure*), then one should accept that it is the goodness-of-fit to the category prototype, and not just a few defining features, that determines whether a person becomes associated with a given category. Rothbart and Lewis (1988) showed that as prototypicality increased, the degree of inference from member to group increased. From this view, disconfirming attributes are most likely to become associated with the stereotype if they belong to an individual who is otherwise a good fit to the category.

Rothbart and John's (1985) view implies that the more a particular episode disconfirms a stereotypic category of which it is an instance, the more likely it is to be associated with a different, possibly counterstereotypical, category. This process enhances the tendency of stereotypic beliefs to confirm themselves. Thus, individuating information can "release" an exemplar from the attributes of a superordinate category, and at the same time render the stereotype immune from the attributes of the exemplar. Somewhat counterintuitively, stereotype-disconfirming information should therefore be linked to typical outgroup members.

Typicality and Stereotype Change

Evidence in support of the key role we ascribe to typicality comes from experimental studies investigating three cognitive models of stereotype change: bookkeeping, conversion, and subtyping (Weber & Crocker, 1983). The bookkeeping model (Rothbart, 1981) proposes a gradual modification of stereotypes by the additive influence of each piece of disconfirming information. Any single piece of disconfirming information elicits only a minor change in the stereotype; major change occurs gradually, and only after the perceiver has accumulated many disconfirming instances that deviate systematically from the stereotype. The conversion model (Rothbart, 1981) envisages a radical change in response to dramatic disconfirming information, but no change in response to minor disconfirming information. Finally, the subtyping model of stereotype change views stereotypes as hierarchical structures, in which discriminations can be created in response to disconfirming information (Ashmore, 1981; Brewer, Dull, & Lui, 1981; Taylor, 1981). This process leads to the formation of subtypes, which constitute exceptions unrepresentative of the group as a whole. One serious consequence of subtyping is that it may insulate the superordinate stereotype from change (Weber-Kollmann, 1985).

These models were tested in a series of studies that compared stereotype change in response to different patterns of disconfirming information: concentrated and dispersed. In the concentrated condition, disconfirming information was concentrated in a few group members, each of whom strongly disconfirmed the stereotype. In the dispersed condition, the same amount of disconfirming information was dispersed across several group members, each of whom only slightly disconfirmed the stereotype. Weber and Crocker (1983) found that stereotypes of occupational groups (librarians and lawyers) changed more when the disconfirming information was dispersed than when it was concentrated, but ony under large-sample conditions (30 vs. 6 members). They also showed that "disconfirmers" with high representativeness (e.g., White, middle-class, high-earning lawyers) were more successful at bringing about stereotype change than were disconfirmers with low representativeness (e.g., African-American lawyers). Overall, Weber and Crocker provided very strong support for subtyping, some support for bookkeeping, and none for conversion. Generally, stereotype-disconfirming information had greater impact on perceptions of the group as a whole (generalization) when it was associated with a group member who was perceived as typical of the group.

The results from a series of studies by Hewstone and coworkers also strongly support the subtyping model (although there is some scattered support for the mother models; see Hewstone, 1994, for a review). Our research also provided more direct support for the role of typicality by specifying the cognitive processes underlying stereotype change. Johnston and Hewstone (1992, Study 1) showed, first, that weak disconfirming members (in the dispersed condition) were rated more typical than strong disconforming members (in the concentrated condition). Moreover, this perceived typicality was the only dependent measure that mediated the relatively weaker stereotyping in the dispersed condition. This mediating role of perceived typicality has also been demonstrated in three other independent studies, generalizing across manipulations, subject groups, and target groups (Hantzi, in press; Hewstone, Hassebrauck, Wirth, & Waenke, 1995; Maurer, Park, & Rothbart, 1995).

Reactions to Stereotype-Disconfirming Exemplars: Subtyping and Typicality

Stereotype change is generally effected via the perceived typicality, or goodness-of-fit, of mild disconfirmers in the dispersed condition; it is generally impeded by the atypicality, or badness-of-fit, of strong disconfirmers in the concentrated condition. We suggest that, on the basis of perceived (a)typicality, extreme disconfirmers are "subtyped" or set apart from the rest of the group (see Weber-Kollmann, 1985). In this way, extreme disconfirming group members have little or no impact on perceptions of the group as a whole.

Our research has provided evidence of, or at least strongly consistent with, a subtyping process using a variety of measures. Perhaps the most impressive measure of subtyping, because unforced, is based on clustering in free recall. If participants do subtype disconfirmers more in the concentrated than the dispersed condition, they should organize their recall more in terms of the two subcategories: confirmers and disconfirmers. This is exactly what was found (Hewstone, Macrae, Griffiths, Milne, & Brown, 1994, Study 1).

In our most recent research, we explored the development and consequences of subtyping, and the results again reveal the key role of perceived typicality. First, we tested the idea that any condition(s) that impede encoding/storage of information by persons and linking together of similar group members will rule out subtyping (Hewstone et al., 1994, Study 2). It was reasoned that, when information is encountered in the standard "blocked" format (several sentences about each group member in turn), participants should find it quite easy to store information by person and form subtypes. In contrast, when information is presented "unblocked" (i.e., a random series of 48 sentences, varying from member to member across trials), participants should have great difficulty in keeping track of information, forming a coherent impression of each person, and constructing subtypes such as "confirmers" and "disconfirmers." This is exactly what was found. Apparently, blocking is a necessary condition for subtyping because the concentrated/dispersed effect was only significant when information was blocked. The clustering measure of subtyping was also only significant in the concentrated/blocked-by-person condition. But blocking is also a crucial condition for the dispersed pattern to produce stereotype change; unless information is blocked, participants will be unable to perceive the goodness-of-fit of disconfirmers in this condition, and that is the route to stereotype change. Thus, for perceptions of typicality to play their crucial, mediating role, information must be presented in a format that allows perceivers to distinguish between typical and atypical group members.

Our final study (Hewstone et al., 1994, Study 3) manipulated the number of subtypes in an attempt to demonstrate the role of subtyping in insulating stereotypes from change. If subtyping is a negative process, there should be more stereotyping in a two- versus one-subtype condition. We crossed concentrated/dispersed with number of subtypes and found that this was indeed the case. Stereotyping was weaker in dispersed than concentrated conditions, and in one- versus two-subtype conditions. The recall-clustering measure of subtyping showed exactly the same pattern of results. Because we formed the two subtypes in this study on the basis of unique disconfirming behaviors, we may have made the disconfirming members in this condition even less typical than in the one-subtype condition (we did not assess perceived typicality in this study). This explanation fits well with our typicality-based account of the subtyping model. If perceived typicality mediates stereotype change, then rendering disconfirmers less typical should have a negative impact on change (recall that Weber & Crocker's [1983] third study showed that representative members were more effective agents of change).

Hence, where an intervention such as intergroup contact allows, or worse facilitates, subtyping, generalized change in outgroup attitudes will tend to be blocked. But the key variable is perceived typicality. Although subtyping occurs, we have been unable to demonstrate that it mediates stereotype change (Hewstone et al., 1995). In contrast, two different studies have revealed that the perceived typicality of disconfirmers mediates stereotype change — when perceived typicality is controlled for, the different impact of concentrated and dispersed conditions disappears. This finding suggests a reevaluation of the nature of subtyping. Atypical disconfirmers are subtyped on the basis of perceived typicality, which may rule out their impact in the short and long term, but it is perceived typicality, not subtyping, that mediates stereotype change.

Intergroup Contact With Typical Outgroup Members

Further evidence of the importance of typicality comes from Hewstone and Brown's (1986) intergroup perspective on the contact hypothesis and related research. Hewstone and Brown (1986) contended (based on Brown & Turner, 1981) that, to be successful in changing outgroup evaluations, "favourable contact with an outgroup member must be defined as an intergroup encounter. A weak association between the contact-partner and the outgroup (i.e., if the target is an atypical outgroup member) will define the contact situation as an interpersonal, rather than an intergroup, encounter" (p. 18). Even where some interpersonal aspects are emphasized, category memberships must be clear (typicality must be evident) if gener-alization is to occur. Hewstone and Brown are neither alone nor the first to argue for "intergroup" contact.

There is now considerable support for the view that outgroup attitudes are generalized when memberships are clear in the contact situation. Wilder (1984, Study 1) varied systematically the typicality of the outgroup member in a simulated intergroup contact situation. The nature of the contact was also varied in line with traditional theorizing on contact. Thus, the contact person behaved either in a pleasant and supportive way toward the real participants, or in a less pleasant and more critical fashion. The interaction took place over a cooperative task. Wilder predicted that only in the combined conditions where the interaction was pleasant and the partner could be seen as typical of her college would ratings of the outgroup college become more favorable. Wilder's results were exactly in line with his prediction. Wilder (1984, Study 3) also demonstrated that the more positive evaluation of the outgroup following contact with the typical member could be interpreted in terms of ease of generalization. Participants judged the typical outgroup member's personality and behavior to be more indicative of how others in the outgroup would act in the same setting.

Although the participants in Wilder's (1984) study never actually came into contact with each other, this limitation was rectified in a realistic study by Desforges et al. (1991). They tested the specific hypothesis that contact affects attitudes, in part, by eliciting a more positive portrait of the typical group member. In the first stage of their experiment, student participants experienced contact for about 50 minutes with someone they believed to be a former mental patient. This contact involved either some form of cooperative interaction, or merely studying in the same room. When their attitudes and perceptions were re-tested 1 month later, those participants who initially had negative attitudes had more positive impressions of the former mental patient than those who had merely studied together. They also held more positive portraits of the typical former mental patient and more positive general attitudes toward former mental patients. Most supportive of our emphasis on typicality, changes in portraits of the typical mental patient were significantly correlated with changes in attitudes.

These findings were replicated and extended in a recent study by Vivian, Brown, and Hewstone (1995), which again manipulated typicality experimentally. In a cooperative work situation, British participants were led to believe that their German partner (a confederate) was either typical or atypical of his national group (Germans). Although there was no difference between conditions in rating German partners (who were viewed positively as a function of cooperation), only in the typicality conditions was this person explicitly associated with the German outgroup as a whole, leading to most positive ratings of the outgroup as a whole.

In a second survey study, Vivian et al. (1995, Study 2) found that dimensions of membership salience moderated the impact of traditional contact variables on European students' generalized attitudes toward a European outgroup For example, consistent with the intergroup contact model, typicality moderated the effect of amount of contact on desire to live in Germany. The association between contact and attitude was much higher for those respondents who reported having had contact with a German individual whom they perceived to be typical or his or her national group.

Taken together, these studies on intergroup contact illustrate the role of perceived typicality. They show that encountered members of the outgroup need to be perceived as having outgroup membership as an attribute, that the associative link between individual members and the outgroup as a whole cannot be broken altogether, or any change of attitude will not generalize beyond those particular individuals. Unless this is the case, people tend to react to stereotype-disconfirming information not with generalization, but with what Allport (1954/1979) called *re-fencing,* or what has more recently been called *subtyping.* The consequence of this process is that the "special case" is excluded and the category is held intact (see also Williams, 1964).

BEHAVIORAL ATTITUDES

All of the studies reviewed so far have focused on intergroup cognitions — primarily outgroup stereotypes. In trying to bridge cognitions and behavior, we first consider the intermediate construct *behavioral attitudes* because the main focus of social-psychological work linking cognition and behavior has been attitudes, and this area above all should have lessons to teach us. This section reviews evidence suggesting that generalization may be impaired by specific, person-based attitudes — attitudes based on personal or individuating information, and attitudes that are incidental versus integral to a contact setting.

Contact and Changing Specific Versus Abstract Category Exemplars

Another possibility raised by a categorization process analysis of intergroup contact is that some social category attitudes might be easier to change than others. Specifically, individuals who have in mind a specific person as their category prototype (i.e., a person or exemplar is used as the standard against which other category members are judged) might be less amenable to attitude change than might individuals who have in mind merely a vague abstraction. If a voter thinks of only a vague abstraction when he or she assesses his or her negative attitude toward politicans, for instance, he or she might have positive contact with a state senator whom he or she has not previously met. The next time he or she thinks about his or her attitude toward politicians, he or she might visualize the likable state senator, rather than a vague abstraction, so he or she might express a more positive attitude. A different voter, however, might picture a specific exemplar such as Bill Clinton or Bob Dole whenever he or she assesses his or her attitude toward politicians. Even if he or she had positive contact with the likable state senator, it might be more difficult for the state senator to supplant a specific person such as Clinton or Dole in the voter's cognitive representation of the category than it would be for the state senator to supplant a mere abstraction.

To test this possibility, Werth and Lord (1992) assessed students' attitudes before and after they met (as part of a classroom demonstration) a very likable person with AIDS. Students who had earlier said they thought of some abstract figure as the "typical" person with AIDS changed their attitudes toward the group more after this contact experience than did students who had earlier said that they thought of (and named) a specific person. This is exactly the result that would be predicted if the cognitive representation that accompanies an attitude also affects the likelihood of changing that attitude through intergroup contact.

Contact and Individuating Information

A related principle is that contact must be with a member who is closely associated with the cognitive representation connected with the initial attitude toward a social group or category. In their pioneering categorization approach to the contact hypothesis, Rothbart and John (1985) noted the seemingly paradoxical effect of individuating information. Considerable research has established that people like others better when the latter disclose personal information about themselves. At first glance, then, one might expect contact with a member of a negatively stigmatized group to be most beneficial when the group member discloses personal information than when he or she does not because self-disclosure enhances liking. The problem, however, is that personal information gives the target person an individual identity. When one knows enough about another person, one comes to view that person as a distinct individual (the ultimate subtype), and not as a category member. Personal or individuating information breaks the link between the target person and is or her group or category. The target person no longer represents the category. The contact is no longer perceived as intergroup contact, but rather as contact with an individual, who has little or no connection with the category. Liking that specific individual, then, cannot possibly generalize to ameliorated attitudes toward the group as a whole. The counterintuitive result suggested by Rothbart and John's (1995) categorization analysis, Allport's (1954) refencing idea, Abelson's (1983) differentiation concept, and other theoretically derived predictions, is that contact with a group member who discloses personal information will not produce generalization to a more positive attitude toward the group as a whole.

In the first direct empirical test of this counterintuitive proposition, the investigators led students who had expressed negative attitudes toward homosexuals on an earlier questionnaire to believe that they were holding a cooperative learning session with a male partner (a confederate) who was gay (Scarberry, Ratcliff, Lanicek, Scott, & Lord, in press). The 50-minute session was the same as used by Desforges et al., in which the student and the confederate took turns teaching each other segments of a text passage. The nongay confederate, who was blind to the experimental hypothesis, used factual analogies (e.g., "Like when someone tries to squeeze every last bit of toothpaste out of the tube") when his turn came to teach some randomly selected students. For the others, he used exactly the same analogies, except in the first person (e.g., "Like when I try to squeeze every last bit of toothpaste out of the tube"). The confederate, then, was equally cooperative and imparted exactly the same information in the two conditions, except the use of first-person pronouns in one condition made it appear that he was revealing aspects of his own personality, preferences, and experiences, all of which was intended to identify him as an individual, rather than as a representative of the homosexual category.

As predicted, students liked the confederate more (but not significantly more) when he used personal analogies. According to a subsequent memory test, they also learned the material equally well, regardless of whether the confederate used personal or impersonal analogies. However, when a different experimenter had students complete the initial attitude questionnaire for a second time, students were approximately twice as likely to express more positive attitudes toward homosexuals as a group when they had recently studied cooperatively with a gay man who used impersonal analogies than when they had recently studied cooperatively with the same gay man who used equivalent but personal analogies. Apparently, learning personal information about the member impaired generalization of liking from that group member to the group as a whole, just as a categorization analysis of the contact hypothesis had predicted.

Incidental Versus Integral Attitudes

A categorization process analysis of the contact hypothesis also predicts that generalization of liking to the group as a whole will be more likely when the specific member with whom contact occurs is perceived as a *representative* of the group. A crucial element of generalization, as Pettigrew (1979) and others have suggested, is "ensuring that in some way the participants in the contact encounters see each other as representatives of their group and not merely as 'exceptions to the rule' " (Hewstone & Brown, 1986, p. 18). One way to emphasize a group member's representativeness might be to portray group membership as the reason for his or her having been included in the contact situation. Positive contact with someone who merely happens to belong to a negatively stigmatized group is one thing. Positive contact with someone who has been chosen for the interaction because of belonging to a negatively stigmatized group is phenomenologically different. In the former case ("incidental" attitudes), the cognitive association between the specific person and the group might be weak. In the latter case ("integral" attitudes), it might be strong enough that the specific person's unexpectedly positive characteristics might generalize to the group as a whole. In other words, if liking for the specific members were somehow held constant, attitudes toward the group would still be ameliorated more if the specific person were perceived as being in the situation to represent the group.

The key to testing this representativeness hypothesis lies in holding specific liking constant. One instance in which specific liking is held constant occurs when contact is with a target person who belongs to not one but *two* negatively stigmatized social groups or categories. In the relevant study, students who had equally negative attitudes toward two social groups, such as former mental patients and homosexuals, shared a cooperative learning experience with another person (a confederate) who was said to belong to both categories (Desforges et al., in press). In a control condition, nothing more was said about the target person's participation in the study. In the reason condition, the experimenter volunteered that Daniel (the confederate) was chosen from among many nonstudents who wanted to earn a generous payment for participating because he belonged to one of his two groups. For instance, he was chosen either because he was a former mental patient or because he was gay. After interacting with Daniel for 50 minutes, students in both conditions liked Daniel more than they had expected.

Next, a second experimenter had students complete the same attitude questionnaire they had completed earlier in the semester, on which they provided their current attitudes toward many different social groups and categories, including the two to which Daniel belonged. As predicted, specific liking for Daniel generalized equally to ameliorated attitudes toward Daniel's two groups in the control condition. In contrast, in the reason condition, specific liking for Daniel generalized significantly more to the group that was the reason for his being included in the contact situation than to his other group. This greater generalization to the integral attitude group ran directly counter to a "preferential treatment" prediction that participants might resent Daniel's group getting preference for the coveted payment.

Interestingly, although everyday contact situations often involve contact with members of two or more negatively stigmatized group, the Desforges et al. (in press) study was the first direct study of cooperative contact with a person said to belong to two groups. The two-group paradigm seems ideal for testing further hypotheses about the generalization part of Allport's (1954) contact hypothesis because it clearly holds everything about the situation and the participant's reactions constant, from the beginning of contact through increased liking for the specific group member, so that only generalization to the group is free to vary in response to experimental manipulations. By using the two-group paradigm, it should be possible to test further the predicted effects of perceived category representativeness, typicality, mere category salience, perceived category variance, and many other factors that might affect only the generalization part of contact, without affecting specific liking.

Intergroup Behavior

Rothbart and John's (1985) review of the link between social categorization and behavioral episodes made two important and prescient points. First, social groups are represented cognitively by the characteristics of their most typical members. In Rothbart and John's words, "impressions of groups are heavily influenced by the attributes of those group members most strongly associated with the group label" (p. 101). Second, stereotypes of and attitudes toward social groups change when impressions of groups change. In Rothbart and John's words, "If stereotypic impressions are to change, disconfirming information must become associated with the group label" (pp. 101–102).

The first section of this chapter reviewed research relevant to Rothbart and John's first point about how groups are represented. Much research published since Rothbart and John's review supports their insight that people cognitively represent groups by thinking about the attributes they associate with what they regard (whether correctly or incorrectly) as the most typical group members. This section reviewed research relevant to Rothbart and John's second point about how stereotypes and attitudes change. Considerable recent work on the contact hypothesis supports Rothbart and John's model of change, in which either characteristics of the contact person or exogenous sources of category activation (or both) facilitate the association of disconfirming events with the stereotypic category.

A Matching Representations Hypothesis

This section of the chapter describes the next logical step in the chain of events related to social groups or categories—the translation of intergroup cognitions and attitudes into behavior toward members of stigmatized groups. If social categories are represented by their most typical members and attitude change involves changing that representation, it follows the attitude–behavior consistency is highest when the cognitive representation that informs the attitude matches the cognitive representation that informs the behavior.

This "matching representations" hypothesis is similar to Ajzen and Fishbein's (1977, 1980) specificity matching hypothesis for predicting and explaining attitude–behavior consistency. According to Ajzen and Fishbein, attitudes toward entire groups or categories predict behavior better when the attitude and behavior involve the same level of specificity. Attitudes toward an entire group or category might predict overall behavior across many different types of behavioral opportunities and targets, but they are unlikely to predict behavior in a specific setting, toward a specific target, under specific circumstances. To predict so specifically, the researchers would need to measure attitudes at a level every bit as specific as the behavior that the attitude is supposed to affect. Ajzen and Fishbein's models of reasoned action and planned behavior specify the precise parameters that must be measured if attitude–behavior consistency is to be anything but minimal (Ajzen, 1985; Ajzen & Fishbein, 1980). The matching representations hypothesis might be viewed as either a logical extension or a mirror image of Ajzen and Fishbein's approach. Instead of measuring attitudes that involve specific settings, targets, and circumstances, the matching representations hypothesis relies on general attitudes toward entire social groups or categories, but predicts reduced attitude–behavior consistency when the cognitive representation that informs the attitude is meaningfully different from the cognitive representation that informs the behavior.

The matching representations hypothesis is also similar to Millar and Tesser's (1992) matching hypothesis for predicting and explaining attitude–behavior consistency. According to Millar and Tesser, some attitudes involve more of a cognitive component and others involve more of an affective component. Affectively based attitudes predict consummatory behaviors (such as which soft drink to consume), in which behavioral decisions are informed more by affective than by cognitive considerations. Cognitively based attitudes, in contrast, predict instrumental behaviors (performed as a means to an end), in which behavioral decisions are informed more by cognitive than by affective considerations. The matching representations hypothesis is more specific than Millar and Tesser's matching hypothesis because it addresses only matches that occur within the cognitive component of attitudes — matches in the typical members, typical characteristics, and subtypes that come to mind when individuals contemplate either their attitudes toward a social category or their behavior toward a member or members of that category.

Finally, the matching representations hypothesis relies on many precepts of Smith and Zárate's (1990) social judgment model. According to this model, people evaluate and make decisions about new instances of a social category by comparing each new instance to a known category exemplar, which is generated spontaneously to represent the category. The generation of specific exemplars can occur without conscious awareness. It is sometimes more efficient than trying to conceptualize the entire category. It depends on the perceiver's goal of the moment, as well as on goals made salient by the ever-changing social context. Finally, it is influenced by the perceiver's past experiences (Smith, 1992; Zárate & Smith, 1990). Smith and Zarate's model presumably describes how people represent a social group or category when they initially assess their attitudes. It also presumably describes the way that contact experiences alter the cognitive representation so that different exemplars come to mind to represent the category, sometimes carrying with them a different set of attributes.

The matching representations hypothesis — that attitude–behavior consistency is highest when the cognitive representation that informs the attitude matches the cognitive representation that informs the behavior — makes several predictions that have been supported empirically. First, attitude–behavior consistency should involve a "typicality effect," in which attitudes toward social groups predict behavior better toward specific category members who match rather than mismatch what the attitude holder conceives as the typical category representative at the time when attitudes are measured. Second, attitude–behavior consistency should be greater when the typical member who comes to mind to represent the category is the same one at the time the behavior is measured as came to mind at the time the attitude was measured. Third, attitude–behavior consistency should be greater when the attitude holder is reminded (or "primed with") a typical rather than an atypical category member at the time when behavior is measured. The following sections describe research on these three corollaries of the matching representation hypothesis.

Typicality Effects in Attitude–Behavior Consistency

In some circumstances, the category member who represents the category at the time of behavior might be ambiguous. An individual who holds a negative attitude toward a particular minority group, for instance, might decide whether to vote for or against an affirmative action program that would benefit members of that group. Alternatively, the individual might be asked to decide which of several job applicants to hire and have only sketchy information about each applicant, including the (presumably salient) fact that one of them belongs to the despised group. In either of these cases, the attitude holder is free to imagine that the people affected by his or her actions have the attributes that he or she associates with typical group members. In other circumstances, however, the category member who represents the category at the time of behavior is not ambiguous. It is a specific person who is known to belong to the category. It may be a member of a physically distinctive racial group, a woman, or someone who (for whatever reason) is undeniably "one of them," yet is also a specific person. At such times, according to the matching representations hypothesis, the individual's attitude toward the entire category will predict the individual's behavior toward that specific person more when the specific person seems typical (matches the individual's category representation when attitude was measured) rather than atypical (mismatches the individual's category representation when attitude was measured).

In one test of the predicted "typicality effect" in attitude–behavior consistency, male college students provided their attitudes toward male homosexuals (Lord, Lepper, & Mackie, 1984). They also described the personality traits that they attributed to the typical homosexual, which were moderately idiosyncratic. For instance, many students described the typical male homosexual as sensitive, artistic, and nonathletic. Other students had different personality profiles in mind, such as perfectionist and ostentatious. One month later, the same students participated in an "unrelated" study, in which they were asked to cooperate with a new college program by agreeing to interact socially with visiting prospective transfer students. They read background information on several prospective transfer students, one of whom was openly gay. For each prospective transfer student, they indicated how willing they would be to meet him, show him around campus, introduce him to professors, and help with other activities. When the background information about the gay transfer student made him appear typical (by ascribing to him the same characteristics that the individual student ascribed to the typical homosexual), students' attitudes toward the general category of homosexuals predicted very well their willingness to interact with the specific gay student. When the background information about the gay transfer student made him appear atypical (by ascribing to him some characteristics opposite to those that the individual student had ascribed to the typical homosexual), students' attitudes did not predict their willingness to interact with him. The typicality effect, then, is that attitudes predict behavior better toward members who match rather than mismatch what the attitude holder had in mind when his or her attitude was initially measured.

Since the initial demonstration, other studies have examined typicality effects in greater detail. These studies suggest that the typicality effect applies even when the characteristics that make a member typical or atypical are not personality traits, but rather physical characteristics, or the specific subtype within the larger category. Furthermore, novices at thinking about a social category display a greater typicality effect than do "experts." For those familiar with a category, whether they like it or hate it, the criteria for category inclusion are many and diverse (Lusk & Judd, 1988). Experts look beyond inconsequential surface characteristics such as physical appearance and recognize that category members come in all shapes and sizes (Larkin, McDermott, Simon, & Simon, 1980). Experts do not need a perfect match to their prototypical category exemplar to justify acting in line with their (positive or negative) attitudes. (Think of racial bigots, for instance!) Novices, in contrast, have a more simplistic and less confident cognitive representation of the category, in which they can only be confident when a category member closely resembles their prototypical exemplar (Fiske, Kinder, & Larter, 1983). Thus in a relevant study, participants who knew several former mental patients displayed high attitude–behavior consistency toward both a typical member and an atypical member of that category. In contrast, participants who did not know even one former mental patient personally displayed high attitude–behavior consistency toward a typical member, but not toward an atypical member (Lord, Desforges, Ramsey, Trezza, & Lepper, 1991, Study 2).

In an extension of the typicality effect to category subtypes, students provided their attitudes toward former mental patients (Ramsey, Lord, Wallace, & Pugh, 1994). They also described what they thought of as the typical mental patient. Blind raters coded these free-response descriptions to determine which subtype of mental patient each student had in mind. Interrater reliability was high. For instance, it was easy to tell the difference between a description of a typical mental patient as someone who had low self-esteem and was suicidal (depression) and a description of a typical mental patient as someone who was constantly on guart against poison and other attacks (paranoia). Students who had easily recognizable subtypes in mind later participated in an "unrelated" study, in which they thought they were going to meet and interact with another student who "happened" to be a former mental patient. The students also read a brief description that the other student had been "treated last year" for a specific mental problem that either matched or mismatched the subtype the student had described 1 month earlier when attitudes were measured. The experimenter then escorted the student to a laboratory room, in which the other student (the former mental patient) had evidently left some books to mark his or her place at one end of a bench. The experimenter asked the student to take a seat on the bench, left the room long enough for the student to sit down, and returned to measure how far the student chose to sit from where the former mental patient was presumably sitting. As predicted, students' attitudes toward former mental patients as a whole predicted very well how far they chose to sit from where a specific former mental patient was presumably sitting, but only when the specific former mental patient belonged to the subtype that they had described when they had earlier provided their attitudes.

These studies of the typicality effect fit well with Rothbart and John's (1985) assumption that people judge social categories by recalling a typical, rather than an atypical, category member. When the specific member that they must behave toward matches the typical member that they had in mind when they provided their attitudes (in personality traits, demographic characteristics, physical features, or even the subtype within a larger social category), general attitudes predict behavior toward the specific member very well. When the specific member seems atypical or different from what they had in mind, attitude–behavior consistency is significantly reduced.

Stability of Category Exemplars

Another corollary of the matching representation hypothesis is that attitude–behavior consistency should be greater when the typical member who comes to mind to represent the category is the same one at the time the behavior is measured as came to mind at the time the attitude was measured. This corollary is reminiscent of early work in social psychology by LaPiere (1934) and Asch (1940). As early as 1934, LaPiere suggested that attitude–behavior consistency might depend, in part, on how a social category is represented. LaPiere toured the southwestern United States with a Chinese couple at a time when the media were reporting intense anti-Asian attitudes. To LaPiere's surprise, his Chinese friends were served courteously at all but 1 of 251 restaurants and hotels.

Subsequently, LaPiere sent an attitude questionnaire to the proprietors of these and other establishments. Of the respondents, including those at 128 of the places that LaPiere and his friends had visited, over 90% said they had such negative attitudes that they would refuse to serve "members of the Chinese race." In commenting on this striking example of attitude–behavior *inconsistency*, LaPiere (1934) noted that answers on an attitude questionnaire constitute a "verbal response to a symbolic situation" (p. 230) that might not correspond with the actual situation in which behavior occurs. Notwithstanding oft-repeated methodological shortcomings of this research, we find interesting LaPiere's speculation that the proprietors did not behave in line with their attitudes, at least in part, because his well-dressed, cultured friends did not match what the proprietors had in mind as "members of the Chinese race" when they completed the attitude questionnaire.

Six years later, in 1940, Asch addressed the "symbolic situation" more explicitly. Asch had students rank the intelligence, social usefulness,, conscientiousness, stability of character, and idealism of 10 professions, 1 of which was politics. To influence these rankings, Asch led some students to believe that 500 of their peers had, on average, ranked politics 10th (last) on all five dimensions. He led other students to believe that the 500 peers had ranked politics first. The purported peer rankings had a large influence on students' own rankings. For instance, those who thought peers had ranked politics last ranked politics between eighth and ninth on social usefulness, whereas those who thought peers had ranked politics first gave it a rank of fourth among professions that included business, engineering, law, music, teaching, and medicine.

When Asch interviewed the students, they claimed that they had not been swayed by or conformed to the peer ratings. Instead, Asch discovered that students in the different experimental conditions had different politicians in mind. When they learned that peers had ranked politics first, they thought about intelligent, idealistic statespersons such as Franklin D. Roosevelt. When thy learned that peers had ranked politics last, they thought about corrupt party hacks such as Boss Tweed, who ran the infamous Tammany Hall. Asch concluded that the students had been influenced indirectly rather than directly. When the peer rankings brought Roosevelt and other statespersons to mind, it seemed reasonable to call politics a noble profession. When the peer rankings brought Boss Tweed and others of his type to mind, it seemed just as reasonable to disparage the profession. The students were not aware that they might have had different politicians come to mind had they been in the other condition, so they explicitly denied that their attitudes had been influenced. As Asch observed, "the process under investigation entails *a change in the object of judgment, rather than in the judgment of the object*" (1940, p. 458, italics original).

A recent study tested whether changes in the object of judgment (the category member than comes to mind) between the time of attitude measurement and the time of behavior measurement might predict not only attitude–behavior consistency, but also the direction in which attitudes would be inconsistent (Sia, Lord, Blessum, & Lepper, 1997). Students provided their attitudes toward various social groups and categories, one of which was politicians. They also named the first politician they thought of to represent each category (e.g., Bill Clinton or Bob Dole), after which they named up to four more politicians that they thought might come to mind on other occasions. Two weeks later, the same students participated in an "unrelated" study, in which they rated how much they liked 150 people, objects, and events, a handful of which "happened" to be their own politician exemplars. Two weeks after that, the students again provided a first exemplar of the category (research on natural object categories shows that individuals have approximately a .44 probability of naming a different first exemplar for a category 1 month apart; Bellezza, 1984). Then, in another "unrelated" study, a different experimenter asked students to sign a petition and agree to send letters to the university administration in favor of bringing more politicians to speak on campus.

As predicted, students who named the same first exemplar to represent the politican category 1 month apart also displayed greater attitude–behavior consistency than did students who named different first exemplars to represent the category. Beyond that, it was possible to predict the direction of attitude–behavior inconsistency from knowing how much the individual student liked or disliked the category exemplars involved. Students who named a politician exemplar that they liked more than the first exemplar named 1 month earlier behaved more positively (or less negatively) than their earlier attitudes would have predicted. Students who named a category exemplar that they liked less than the first exemplar named 1 month earlier behaved less positively (or more negatively) than their earlier attitudes would have predicted.

These effects of exemplar stability on attitude–behavior consistency fit well with theoretical suggestions about the nature of attitudes and the conditions under which they predict behavior. First, the findings for attitude stability support and extend Wilson and Hodges' (1992) suggestions about the consequences of introspecting on reasons for holding an attitude. In a program of studies, Wilson and his associates have amassed considerable evidence that some attitudes are "temporary constructions," related to whichever piece of relevant information comes to mind (see also Tesser, 1978). For instance, Wilson, Kraft, and Dunn (1989) had students introspect about their reasons for liking or disliking various politicians; afterward, some students reported more positive attitudes than they previously expressed, whereas others reported more negative attitudes than they previously expressed.

Across such studies, students who spontaneously generate predominant reasons for holding a positive attitude adopt a more positive attitude, whereas those who spontaneously generate predominant reasons for holding a negative attitude adopt a more negative attitude (Wilson, et al., 1993). The present studies suggest as well that people who have more positive exemplars come spontaneously to mind are likely to adopt more positive attitudes, whereas people who have more negative exemplars spontaneously come to mind are likely to adopt more negative attitudes. The general principle supported by both Wilson's and the present studies is that attitudes often fluctuate according to which part of the large, and sometimes conflicting, "database" is salient at the time.

It would be interesting to investigate the factors that determine whether and which category exemplars come to mind when people consider their attitude toward and/or have an opportunity to behave toward a social category. In Asch's (1940) study, the deciding factor was probably peer opinion. When they learned that 500 peers had rated politicians positively, for instance, students may have inferred that their peers took "politicians" to mean "statesmen" (or "statespersons," had the study been conducted today), whereas when they learned that 500 peers had rated politicians negatively, they may have inferred that their peers took politicians to mean "party hacks." Another important factor in making one rather than another social category exemplar salient might be frequency of exposure, perhaps via media coverage.

In 1984, Lord et al. speculated that "this is one way in which a Martin Luther King, for example, can have a positive effect on race relations. Sufficient exposure to King may have caused millions of Americans to picture him, perhaps in the act of delivering his famous 'I have a dream' speech, whenever they thought of blacks" (p. 1264). In 1993, Graham, Weiner, Giuliano, and Williams showed that public opinion toward people with AIDS changed for the better immediately after Magic Johnson announced that he had the deadly disease. Thus, the present studies and the Graham et al. study suggest at least one mechanism through which a specific part of the database relevant to an attitude might change from one time to the next, with predictable consequences for attitude stability and attitude–behavior consistency. The mechanism involves adding a new member to a category who receives such widespread publicity that he or she becomes the most salient category member "overnight." Along these lines, it is also interesting to speculate on what happens when a previously salient exemplar (such as Pete Rose for baseball players or Jim Bakker for televangelists) changes greatly in likability. Do people have the same exemplar come to mind but change their attitude toward the category, or do they have a different exemplar come to mind and retain their initial attitude?

Priming Typical Exemplars

One way to examine issues about the role of cognitive representatives in attitude–behavior consistency toward social groups or categories is to manipulate which exemplar comes to mind. Rothhbart and John (1985) maintained, and much of the research reviewed in this chapter supports, that people make judgments about social categories, in part, by calling to mind an example of the category. What might happen if we could somehow intervene in the cognitive process and influence the probability of calling to mind a specific examplar? More specifically, would attitudes toward social categories better predict behavior toward those categories if we could increase the probability of a typical, rather than an atypical, category member coming to mind when the individual has to decide on a positive or negative behavior?

In a relevant study, college students provided their attitudes toward several social groups and categories, one of which was business leaders (Ratcliff et al., 1995). The students also listed all the famous business leaders that came to mind, and then rated how typical each was of the category. Later in the semester, the same students participated in two "unrelated" studies. The first was a "word find" experiment, in which they had to find 20 words and names that were embedded either vertically, horizontally, or diagonally in a large matrix of letters. Students were randomly assigned to conditions in which the third name that they had to find was one of the famous business leaders that the individual student had earlier named—one that the student had rated as either typical or atypical. In a control condition, no business leaders appeared on the list of names to find.

After they finished the "word find" experiment, students participated in a "separate" study, in which they learned that the university administration was considering awarding honorary degrees to business leaders such as Jerry Jones, owner of the Dallas Cowboys football team. The administration was supposedly collecting student opinions before reaching a final decision about awarding such honorary degrees. A questionnaire asked students how much they supported or opposed instituting such degrees, and how much they would encourage other students to support the practice.

After competing both the "word find" study and the "university administration questionnaire," the experimenter asked students to guess what the hypotheses of the two studies had been. No student expressed thoughts even close to the actual hypothesis—that priming them with category exemplars of different typicality would differentially affect attitude–behavior consistency. Nonetheless, priming had the predicted effect. Attitude–behavior consistency (correlation between initial attitude and the behavioral measure) was .26 with no prime, .07 with an atypical prime, and .70 with a very typical prime. Presumably, the cognitive accessibility of a typical versus atypical category representative increased the probability that students would be thinking about that typical or atypical exemplar at the time when they had to make their behavioral decisions, which affected attitude–behavior consistency.

CONCLUDING REMARKS

Based on the literature reviewed here on social categorization processes, five tentative prescriptions are offered for ameliorating an individual's negative intergroup cognitions, attitudes, and behaviors. First, the individual must become aware of a *typical*, not an atypical, category member who has positive attributes or behaves positively. If an anti-Semitic Afrikaner perceived Joel Stransky, who almost single-handedly won the Rugby World Cup for South Africa, as a typial Jew in many respects (whether in his physical appearance, attire, orthodox diet, or whatever), the Afrikaner would be more likely to adopt less negative intergroup cognitions, attitudes, and behaviors than if Joel Stransky seemed atypical in many ways.

Second, the specific category member in question must be perceived as *representing* the category (especially a category that is thought to be homogeneous), so that the connection between the specific member and the category is salient and beyond doubt. The probability of ameliorating an individual Afrikaner's cognitions, attitudes, and behavior toward Jews would be more likely, for instance, if the announcer at the Rugby World Cup frequently referred to Joel Stransky's role in representing other Jewish people.

Third, the specific category member must not fit easily into an unusual category subtype that is easily dismissed as "those few exceptions." Instead, the specific category member must be *difficult to cluster into a recognizable subtype*. Alternatively, the specific category member must obviously belong to a predominant subtype that is readily associated with the category — one that is accessible in the sense that it comes easily to mind. For Joel Stransky's exploits to change a prejudiced Afrikaner's cognitions, attitude, and behavior toward Jews, Joel must either be difficult to subtype as "one of the few Rugby-playing Jews, who are different from the rest," or must fit perfectly into what the Afrikaner has always regarded as the major subtype of Jews (e.g., perhaps he is also a banker or entrepreneur).

Fourth, the individual who has negative intergroup cognitions, attitudes, and behavior must not be *aware of individuating information* that would allow him or her to regard the positive specific category member as a unique individual or "subtype of one." It would be better for ameliorating an Afrikaner's anti-Semitic cognitions, attitudes, and behaviors, for instance, if the announcer constantly reminded the audience that Joel Stransky was a Jew and never mentioned individuating information about Joel's family, hobbies, or unusual interests.

Finally, the specific category member will ameliorate an individual's negative intergroup cognitions, attitudes, and behavior to the extent that the individual begins to *have that specific member come to mind* when contemplating the category. A previously anti-Semitic Afrikaner might be less likely to vote against a bill guaranteeing Jews fair treatment in employment and housing, for instance, if the hero Joel Stransky came to mind when he or she entered the polling booth.

To conclude, research on the contact hypothesis and attitude–behavior consistency suggests that we might design better interventions to avert intergroup cognitions, attitudes, and behavior if we took a more sophisticated approach to exemplar category relations. Specifically, our approach to changing intergroup cognitions and behavior suggests a number of lessons we have learned concerning the cognition–behavior interface in this context. These lessons owe much to Fishbein and Ajzen's (1975) pioneering work on specificity, allied to Rothbart and John's (1985) cognitive analysis of intergroup contact. Change in intergroup cognitions is more likely to be brought about by stereotype-disconforming information that is associated with typical members of the outgroup; any factors that weaken the link between member and category will impede generalization from the individual to the group as a whole. Change in behavior toward individual members of the outgroup is more likely to be brought about when the cognitive representation that informs the attitude matches the cognitive representation that informs the behavior. Evidently different aspects of an atittude may be salient at different times or in different settings, just as different categorizations of an individual may vary. To the extent that interventions manipulate, prime, or otherwise ensure that typical group members come to mind when attitudes are assessed, and that behavior toward typical members of outgroups is measured, then intergroup cognitions will be more likely to guide intergroup behavior.

ACKNOWLEDGMENT

The writing of this chapter was supported, in part, by a grant to Miles Hewstone from the Cardiff Research Initiative and NIMH Grant #MH49983 to Charles G. Lord.

REFERENCES

Abelson, R. P. (1983). Whatever became of consistency theory? *Personality and Social Psychology Bulletin, 9,* 37–54.

Ajzen, I. (1985). From intentions to actions: A theory of planned behavior. In J. Kuhl & J. Beckman (Eds.), *Action-control: From cognition to behavior* (pp. 11–39). Heidelberg: Springer.

Ajzen, I., & Fishbein, M. (1977). Attitude-behavior relations: A theoretical analysis and review of empirical research. *Psychological Bulletin, 84,* 888–918.

Ajzen, I., & Fishbein, M. (1980). *Understanding attitudes and predicting social behavior.* Englewood Cliffs, NJ: Prentice-Hall.

Allport, G. W. (1954/1979 ed.). *The nature of prejudice.* Cambridge/Reading, MA: Addison-Wesley.

Amir, Y. (1969). Contact hypothesis in ethnic relations. *Psychological Bulletin, 71,* 319–342.

Asch, S. E. (1940). Studies in the principles of judgments and attitudes: II. Determination of judgments by group and ego standards. *The Journal of Social Psychology, S.P.S.S.I. Bulletin, 12,* 433–465.

Ashmore, R. D. (1981). Sex stereotypes and implicit personality theory. In D. L. Hamilton (Ed.), *Cognitive processes in stereotyping and intergroup relations* (pp. 37–81). Hillsdale, NJ: Lawrence Erlbaum Associates.

Barsalou, L. W. (1987). The instability of graded structure: Implications for the nature of concepts. In U. Neisser (Ed.), *Concepts and conceptual development* (pp. 101–140). New York: Cambridge University Press.

Bellezza, F. S. V. (1984). Reliability of retrieval from semantic memory: Common categories. *Bulletin of the Psychonomic Society, 22,* 324–326.

Brewer, M. B., Dull, V., & Lui, L. (1981). Perceptions of the elderly: Stereotypes as prototypes. *Journal of Personality and Social Psychology, 41,* 656–670.

Brown, R., & Turner, J. C. (1981). Interpersonal and intergroup behaviour. In J. Turner & H. Giles (Eds.), *Intergroup behaviour* (pp. 33–65). Oxford: Basil Blackwell.

Cook, S. W. (1962). The systematic analysis of socially significant events: A strategy for social research. *Journal of Social Issues, 18,* 66–84.

Desforges, D. M., Lord, C. G., Pugh, M. A., Sia, T. L., Scarberry, N. C., & Ratcliffe, C. D. (in press). The role of group representativeness in the generalization part of the contact hypothesis. *Basic and Applied Social Psychology.*

Desforges, D. M., Lord, C. G., Ramsey, S. L., Mason, J. A., Van Leeuwen, M. D., Cox, L., & Lepper, M. R. (1991). Effects of structured cooperative contact on attitude prototypes and attitude change. *Journal of Personality and Social Psychology, 60,* 531–544.

Fishbein, M., & Ajzen, I. (1975). *Belief, attitude, intention and behavior: An introduction to theory and research.* Reading, MA: Addison-Wesley.

Fiske, S. T., Kinder, D. R., & Larter, M. (1983). The novice and the expert: Knowledge-based strategies in political cognition. *Journal of Experimental Social Psychology, 19,* 381–400.

Graham, S., Weiner, B., Guiliano, T., & Williams, E. (1993). An attributional analysis of reactions to Magic Johnson. *Journal of Applied Social Psychology, 23,* 996–1010.

Hantzi, A. (in press). Change in stereotypic perceptions of familiar and unfamiliar groups: The pervasiveness of the subtyping model. *British Journal of Social Psychology.*

Hewstone, M. (1994). Revision and change of stereotypic beliefs: In search of the elusive subtyping model. In W. Stroebe & M. Hewstone (Eds.), *European review of social psychology* (Vol. 5, pp. 69–109). Chichester: Wiley.

Hewstone, M. (1996). Contact and categorization: Social psychological interventions to change intergroup relations. C. N. Macrae, C. Stangor, & M. Hewstone (Eds.), *Foundations of stereotypes and stereotyping* (pp. 323–368). New York: Guilford.

Hewstone, M., & Brown, R. J. (1986). Contact is not enough: An intergroup perspective on the "contact hypothesis." In M. Hewstone & R. J. Brown (Eds.), *Contact and conflict in intergroup encounters* (pp. 1–44). Oxford: Blackwell.

Hewstone, M., Hassebrauck, M., Wirth, A., & Waenke, M. (1995). *Mediation of stereotype change via perceived typicality of disconfirmers.* Unpublished manuscript, Universities of Cardiff, Wales, and Mannheim.

Hewstone, M., Macrae, C. N., Griffiths, R., Milne, A., & Brown, R. (1994). Cognitive models of stereotype change: (5). Measurement, development, and consequences of subtyping. *Journal of Experimental Social Psychology, 30,* 505–526.

Johnston, L., & Hewstone, M. (1992). Cognitive models of stereotype change: (3) Subtyping and the perceived typicality of disconfirming group members. *Journal of Experimental Social Psychology, 28,* 360–386.

LaPiere, R. T. (1934). Attitudes versus actions. *Social Forces, 13,* 230–237.

Larkin, J., McDermott, J., Simon, D. P., & Simon, H. A. (1980). Expert and novice performance in solving physics problems. *Science, 208,* 1335–1342.

Lord, C. G., Desforges, D. M., Ramsey, S. L., Trezza, G. R., & Lepper, M. R. (1991), Typicality effects in attitude-behavior consistency: Effects of category discrimination and category knowledge. *Journal of Experimental Social Psychology, 27*, 550–575.

Lord, C. G., Lepper, M. R., & Mackie, D. (1984). Attitude prototypes as determinants of attitude-behavior consistency. *Journal of Personality and Social Psychology, 46*, 1254–1266.

Lusk, C. M., & Judd, C. M. (1988). Political expertise and structural mediators of candidate evaluations. *Journal of Experimental Social Psychology, 24*, 105–126.

Maurer, K. L., Park, B., & Rothbart, M. (1995). Subtyping versus subgrouping processes in stereotype representation. *Journal of Personality and Social Psychology, 60*, 812–824.

Millar, M. G., & Tesser, A. (1992). The role of beliefs and feelings in guiding behavior: The mismatch model. In L. L. Martin & A. Tesser (Eds.), *The construction of social judgments* (pp. 277–300). Hillsdale, NJ: Lawrence Erlbaum Associates.

Pettigrew, T. F. (1979). The ultimate attribution error: Extending Allport's cognitive analysis of prejudice. *Personality and Social Psychology Bulletin, 5*, 461–476.

Ramsey, S. L., Lord, C. G., Wallace, D. S., & Pugh, M. A. (1994). The role of subtypes in attitudes toward superordinate social categories. *British Journal of Social Psychology, 33*, 387–403.

Ratcliff, C. D., Hiller, M. L., Cherry, L., Broome, K., Sia, T. L., & Lord, C. G. (1995). *Priming category exemplars and attitude-behavior consistency.* Unpublished manuscript, Texas Christian University.

Rothbart, M. (1981). Memory processes and social beliefs. In D. L. Hamilton (Ed.), *Cognitive processes in stereotyping and intergroup behavior* (pp. 145–181). Hillsdale, NJ: Lawrence Erlbaum Associates.

Rothbart, M., & John, O. P. (1985). Social categorization and behavioral episodes: A cognitive analysis of the effects of intergroup contact. *Journal of Social Issues, 41*, 81–104.

Rothbart, M., & Lewis, S. (1988). Inferring category attributes from exemplar attributes: Geometric shapes and social categories. *Journal of Personality and Social Psychology, 55*, 861–872.

Scarberry, N. C., Ratcliff, C. D., Lanicek, D. L., Scott, K., & Lord, C. G. (in press). Effects of individuating information on the contact hypothesis. *Personality and Social Psychology Bulletin.*

Sia, T. L., Lord, C. G., Blessum, K. A., & Lepper, M. R. (1997). Is a rose always a rose? The role of social category exemplar change in attitude stability and attitude-behavior consistency. *Journal of Personality and Social Psychology, 72*, 501–514.

Smith, E. R. (1992). The role of exemplars in social judgment. In L. L. Martin & A. Tesser (Eds.), *The construction of social judgments* (pp. 107–132). Hillsdale, NJ: Lawrence Erlbaum Associates.

Smith, E. R., & Zárate, M. A. (1990). Exemplar and prototype use in social categorization. *Social Cognition, 8*, 243–262.

Taylor, S. E. (1981). A categorization approach to stereotyping. In D. L. Hamilton (Ed.), *Cognitive processes in stereotyping and intergroup behavior* (pp. 83–114). Hillsdale, NJ: Lawrence Erlbaum Associates.

Tesser, A. (1978). Self-generated attitude change. In L. Berkowitz (Ed.), *Advances in experimental social psychology* (Vol. 11, pp. 289–338). New York: Academic Press.

Vivian, J., Brown, R., & Hewstone, M. (1995). *Changing attitudes through intergroup contact: The effects of group membership salience.* Unpublished manuscript, Universities of Kent and Cardiff, Wales.

Weber, R., & Crocker, J. (1983). Cognitive processes in the revision of stereotypic beliefs. *Journal of Personality and Social Psychology, 45*, 961–977.

Weber-Kollmann, R. (1985). *Subtyping: The development and consequences of differentiated categories for stereotyped groups.* Unpublished doctoral dissertation, Northwestern University.

Werth, J. L., & Lord, C. G. (1992). Previous conceptions of the typical group member and the contact hypothesis. *Basic and Applied Social Psychology, 13,* 351–370.

Wilder, D. A. (1984). Intergroup contact: The typical member and the exception to the rule. *Journal of Experimental Social Psychology, 20,* 177–194.

Wilder, D. A. (1986). Cognitive factors affecting the success of intergroup contact. In S. Worchel & W. G. Austin (Eds.), *Psychology of intergroup relations* (pp. 49–66). Chicago: Nelson-Hall.

Williams, R. M. (1964). *Strangers next door: Ethnic relations in American communities.* Englewood Cliffs, NJ: Prentice-Hall.

Wilson, T. D., & Hodges, S. D. (1992). Attitudes as temporary constructions. In L. L. Martin & A. Tesser (Eds.), *The construction of social judgments* (pp. 37–65). Hillsdale, NJ: Lawrence Erlbaum Associates.

Wilson, T. D., Kraft, D., & Dunn, D. S. (1989). The disruptive effects of explaining attitudes: The moderating effect of knowledge about the attitude object. *Journal of Experimental Social Psychology, 25,* 379–400.

Wilson, T. D., Lisle, D. J., Schooler, J. W., Hodges, S. D., Klaaren, K. J., & LaFleur, S. J. (1993). Introspecting about reasons can reduce post-choice satisfaction. *Personality and Social Psychology Bulletin, 19,* 331–339.

Zárate, M. A., & Smith, E. R. (1990). Person categorization and stereotyping. *Social Cognition, 8,* 161–185.

16

A Theoretical Analysis of Crossed Social Categorization Effects

Norman Miller
Lynn M. Urban
Eric J. Vanman
University of Southern California

In flexible social structures, multiple conflicts crisscross each other and thereby prevent basic cleavages along one axis. The multiple group affiliations of individuals makes them participate in various group conflicts so that their total personalities are not involved in any single one of them. Thus segmental participation in a multiplicity of conflicts constitutes a balancing mechanism within the structure.

—Coser, 1956, pp. 153–154

In accord with Coser's statement, several social scientists have suggested that the pluralistic nature of our society, in which people belong to a variety of overlapping groups, helps reduce the conflict between groups (e.g., Brewer & Miller, 1984; LeVine & Campbell, 1972; Messick & Mackie, 1989; Murphy, 1957; Simmel, 1955; Vanbeselaere, 1991). The cognitive processes involved in self-categorization can produce a self-definition that is split among one's multiple group memberships, resulting in behavior that avoids benefit to any single group among one's group memberships. For example, when compared with other Republicans in the United States, a prochoice Republican may feel less animosity toward Democrats because many Democrats are members of the person's "prochoice" ingroup. Thus, the conflicting loyalties felt when faced with one's membership in two distinct groups may prevent one from completely favoring a single category.

393

Consequently, it has been suggested that if the crossed nature of category memberships can be made salient in schools, work settings, and other environments characterized by a diversity of groups, intergroup conflict will be reduced (Brewer & Miller, 1984).

Crossed categorization research conducted during the past two decades should speak on whether these benefits are to be expected. Unfortunately, however, an answer has not come easily, as experimental work has produced a variety of outcomes. For example, in some of the earliest research conducted on this subject, Deschamps and Doise (1978) found no bias between groups when crossed categories were present. However, in more recent work, Hewstone, Islam, and Judd (1993) found consistently large differences in ratings between particular crossed category targets, reflecting real bias between groups. To date, studies have shown an elimination of bias (Deschamps & Doise, 1978), a reduction in bias (Vanbeselaere, 1991), as well as an increase in bias (Eurich-Fulcher & Schofield, 1995) between groups after the introduction of crossed categories. To fully illustrate the inconsistency that characterizes the literature on crossed categorization research, Table 16.1 names and describes six distinct patterns of results that have been obtained in prior research.

The lack of explanation for this heterogeneity of results is troublesome for two reasons. First, it shows that researchers do not yet have a good overall understanding of the intergroup cognitions that occur in crossed categorization situations. Rather, we are left with disjointed, post hoc explanations for each individual set of results. Second, it undermines the confidence of those who wish to apply the principle of crossed categorization to classrooms, organizations, or communities for the purpose of improving intergroup behavior, and leaves them without guidelines for its appropriate application. This chapter attempts to provide a theoretical understanding of the processes that affect an individual's intergroup cognition in crossed categorization situations, and thereby enable more appropriate application of the crossed categorization principle for the purpose of reducing conflictual integroup behavior.

This task is approached from the perspective that intergroup cognition is an important factor in guiding intergroup behavior. In particular, the self-categorizations made by an individual with respect to distinct social categories, as well as the social categorization of others, determine how that individual will behave with respect to those others. Shared group memberships lead to more positive interactions than unshared group memberships. The routine occurrences of ingroup favoritism and outgroup derogation are well established, but the investigation of how social categorizations are made, altered, and influenced warrants continued attention. Factors other than sheer categorization affect intergroup behavior. Motivation obviously is important. For example, social desirability concerns or demand may cause one to behave in a manner not predictable

TABLE 16.1
Patterns of Crossed Categorization Results

Name of Pattern	Evaluative Ordering	Empirical Evidence	Notes*
Equivalence	II = IO = OI = OO	Deschanps & Doise (1978)	
		Brown & Turner (1979)	Condition 5
		Vanbeselaere (1987)	Performance ratings Future performance Friendship ratings
Additivity	II > IO = OI > OO	Vanbeselaere (1991)	General evaluations
		Hagendoorn & Henke (1991)	High-caste Hindus Upper class, high-caste Hindus
		Hewstone, Islam, & Judd (1993)	Study 1
Conjunction Dissimilarity	II > IO = OI = OO	Vanbeselaere (1987) Eurich-Fulcher & Schofield (1995)	Membership ratings
Conjunction Similarity	II = IO = OI > OO	Brown & Turner (1979)	Conditions 2–4
		Vanman (1990)	
		Vanbeselaere (1991)	Performance evaluations
Category Dominance**	Ii = Io > Oi = Oo il = oI > iO = oO	Arcuri (1982)	[Academic role over sex]
		Hagendoorn & Henke (1991)	High-caste Hindus Upper class Muslims Low-caste Hindus [Religion over class/caste]
		Stangor, Lynch, Duan, & Glass (1992)	[Sex over race]
		Hewstone, Islam, & Judd (1993)	Studies 1–2 [Religion over nationality]
		Urban (1997)	Liking measures Familiarity measures [Greek over university]
Hierarchical**	Ii > Io > Oi = Oo Ii = Io > Oi > Oo	Triandis & Triandis (1960)	White subjects [Race over all]
		Triandis & Triandis (1962)	[Race and religion over all]
		Brewer, Ho, Lee, & Miller (1987)	[Sex over nationality]
		Hewstone, Islam, & Judd (1993)	Study 2 [Religion over nationality]

*Entries in this column indicate the special circumstances within the cited reference that provide support for the named pattern.

**Use of the lower case (i or o) indicates a nondominant category.

by categorization per se. This chapter focuses primarily on the importance of category salience in affecting intergroup behavior, but will acknowledge other factors when appropriate.

OUTCOMES FROM PAST RESEARCH

In principle, the number of dimensions on which there are cues for shared ingroup membership, or instead outgroup status, is almost infinite. In keeping with the research on this topic, the focus here is on the paradigmatic case in which two orthogonal ingroup–outgroup distinctions are completely crossed to form four target groups: double-ingroup (II), ingroup–outgroup (IO), outgroup–ingroup (OI), and double-outgroup (OO). For example, if one considers the category dimensions of race and sex for a White female, the resulting target groups would be: White females (II), White males (IO), Black females (OI), and Black males (OO).

As indicated, Table 16.1 presents idealized forms of six obtained patterns. The Equivalence pattern reflects equivalent evaluation of the four target groups (II, IO, OI, OO). Three levels of evaluation characterize the Additivity pattern, with the double-ingroup rated as most positive, crossed groups evaluated as equivalently neutral, and the double-outgroup evaluated negatively. In both the Conjunction Dissimilarity and Conjunction Similarity patterns, there are two levels of evaluation. In the Dissimilarity case, double-ingroup targets are rated positively, whereas the crossed and double-outgroup targets are evaluated equally negatively. By contrast, in the Similarity pattern, double-ingroup and crossed target groups are seen as equally positive, but double-outgroup targets are rated negatively. The Category Dominance pattern also has two levels of evaluation. In this case, one of the two category dimensions is dominant (the nondominant category is indicated in Table 16.1 by the use of the lower case when referring to the ingroup or outgroup category). All targets possessing ingroup representation on the dominant dimension are positively evaluated, whereas all targets possessing an outgroup representation on the dominant dimension are negatively evaluated. Dominance may be found in a strong form, in which the weaker category dimension is completely ignored, or a weak form, in which the weaker category dimension is used to a lesser degree than the stronger one. Finally, the Hierarchical pattern describes an interaction between the two category dimensions. The effect of one category distinction depends on prior categorization on the second. First, as in the Category Dominance pattern, one category dimension must be dominant. On this dimension, ingroup and outgroup members are differentially evaluated. Ingroup or outgroup status on the other dimension is ignored unless the target is an ingroup member on the dominant dimension. Only then will ingroup versus outgroup status on the nondominant category affect evaluations. Obviously, Table 16.1 does not present all conceivable or plausible evaluative orderings of the four types of targets, but rather the most simplified and meaningful relationships between the target evaluations. Additional derivatives from these basic patterns can be conceived and empirically confirmed, such as a combination of the Category Dominance and Additivity patterns, in which the evaluative ordering is as follows: $Ii > Io > Oi > Oo$ (Urada & Miller, 1997). The six basic patterns were chosen because they have been suggested by published empirical work.

As previously indicated, prior research not only is inconsistent in its outcomes, but also has failed to provide an overarching theoretical integration that might account for such empirical inconsistency. In an effort to fill this gap, this chapter first presents a general theoretical model that, in principle, can yield many of the patterns shown in Table 16.1, but also suggests additional predictions. Then it describes a laboratory investigation that led us to rethink our initial theoretical interpretation of prior work and amend our model. Next, it presents aspects of a quantitative literature review that buttress our amended theoretical analysis. Finally, it suggests possibilities for using the model to improve intergroup behavior.

A THEORETICAL FRAMEWORK

Underlying our theoretical approach to understanding multiple crossed categorization effects is the salience, or activation, of the relevant social categories in the perceiver. The magnitude of bias toward target groups will depend on the salience of the relevant categories at the time of judgment. A highly salient category dimension (e.g., race) is more likely to be used to categorize people into ingroup and outgroup status than is a less salient dimension (e.g., shoe size). Such differences in salience lead to unequal strengths of categorization, which, in turn, are likely to affect judgments of liking and similarity.

At least two components have been suggested as determinants of category salience or activation (Bruner, 1973; Higgins & Brendl, 1995; Oakes, 1987). First, a category must be cognitively accessible to the perceiver. This accessibility is the result of a history of category priming experienced by the perceiver. This priming can vary in how directly, strongly, and frequently it occurs, and, consequently, variation in priming history can lead to differing levels of category accessibility.

A second factor suggested as a determinant of salience is "fit" or "applicability" (Higgins & Brendl, 1995; Oakes, 1987). Thus, even if a category is chronically used and highly accessible to a perceiver, it will not be invoked unless the stimulus to be judged "fits" the category, or at least does not contradict it (Higgins & Brendl, 1995). For example, although the racial category Black may be chronically accessible, if a fair-skinned, blond person with no Black characteristics is presented, the racial category of Black will not fit and will not be used in the situation. When considering the criterion of fit in conjunction with crossed categorization research, however, it is clear that researchers routinely use experimental procedures that make target group memberships well understood by the perceiver, thereby ensuring that the "fit" part of category salience is satisfied. Therefore, in developing our theoretical model, on first thought, it seemed likely that in experimental research the major difference between category dimensions lies in their relative accessibility to participants. In turn, differences in accessibility will lead to differing levels of category salience and, ultimately, differing patterns of intergroup judgment and behavior.

One problem in proposing that category salience, or activation, mediates experimentally obtained effects is that an a priori determination of its level is difficult. Oakes (1987) described a salient group membership as, "one which is functioning psychologically to increase the influence of one's membership in that group on perception and behavior, and/or the influence of another person's identity as a group member on one's impression of and hence behavior towards that person" (p. 118). To assess category salience by its influence, however, is circular. Moreover, heightened category salience does not always increase bias between groups. For example, when the salience of race is increased, in some circumstances it may actually reduce group differentiation as a consequence of social desirability concerns (Gaertner & Dovidio, 1986). In developing our theoretical model, this chapter focuses on two broad classes of antecedent factors that affect category salience: cognition and affect.

Cognitive Influence

The factors that function to create, reinforce, or diminish cognitions about social categories may either be chronic or contextual, and may either be conscious or implicit to the perceiver. The resulting category salience will drive thoughts about and behaviors toward people who are members of a social category.

Chronic, Conscious Activation.   One way in which categories become salient is by repeated exposure to category-related information (Bargh, Bond, Lombardi, Tota, 1986; Higgins, King, & Mavin, 1982; Srull & Wyer,

1979, 1980, 1989; Wyer & Srull, 1986). This may include exposure to historical, cultural, biological, and developmental information. In a family in which both parents strongly and consistently endorse the same religious values and behavior, religion is likely to be an important part of a child's identity. For others, cultural influences may work to make national identity salient. Secondary sex characteristics typically make gender a salient category dimension. Certain developmental stages also may make age differences salient. These influences can be widespread, as seen in the importance of religion in some geographic areas, such as Northern Ireland. When one category dimension has become highly accessible to a person, that dimension may dominate others in a crossed categorization situation and lead to the Category Dominance pattern shown in Table 16.1. For example, as a result of the history of protracted conflict that characterizes Northern Ireland, the Catholics and Protestants in that region may routinely ignore most category information other than religion when encountering someone new.

Although entire populations may be affected by repeated exposure to a class of information, individuals may have unique experiences with certain types of category information, such that individual differences arise with respect to the levels of category salience. For example, Fiske and Taylor (1991) suggested that some people may be especially prone to categorizing others in terms of intelligence, race, or other categories that seem to hold special importance for a given individual. In fact, Stangor, Lynch, Duan, and Glass (1992) found that highly prejudiced participants more often used race to categorize a set of strangers than did unprejudiced participants. Similarly, anti-Semitic persons, although not more accurate in detecting Jews, are more vigilant, and hence have higher base rates for "seeing" Jewish names in a list or Jewish faces in a photo display (Scodel & Freedman, 1956; Secord & Saumer, 1960). Clearly, individuals will differ in the extent to which particular categorizations are chronically accessible and frequently used to organize their social environment. Such chronic accessibility may also work to cause Category Dominance in crossed categorization situations.

Contextual Activation

Implicit. Some influences on cognitions are less obvious both to perceivers and outside observers and are present in automatic processing. For example, categories may be primed subliminally, or other tasks may temporarily take one's attention away from category processing without one realizing it. In the former case, category membership can be nonconsciously primed by certain aspects of the environment. Linguistic cues can function in this fashion (Perdue, Dovidio, Gurtman, & Tyler, 1990). When the word *we* was suboptimally paired with a subsequent nonsense syllable, that syllable was rated more positively than one paired with the word *they*. Furthermore, reaction times to positive person descriptors were facilitated by the *we* prime. If subtle factors such as pronoun choice can influence which category membership will be salient and how the person will be evaluated, crossed targets that are preceded by the word *we* (ingroup priming) should be seen as more like the double-ingroup, yielding a Category Conjunction Similarity pattern. By contrast, when preceded by *they* (outgroup priming), crossed targets should be seen as more like the double-outgroup, yielding a Category Conjunction Dissimilarity pattern.

Other situational influences on automatic category perception, although not subliminal, have unanticipated effects on one's perceptions. Cognitive load may increase or decrease the use of categories when perceiving others. For a category dimension to be salient, the perceiver must have sufficient cognitive resources to activate the relevant group information or stereotype. Under certain circumstances, one can be made sufficiently cognitively busy to impede stereotype accessibility (Bodenhausen & Lichtenstein, 1987; Gilbert & Hixon, 1991; Macrae, Milne, & Bodenhausen, 1994). Extrapolating to a crossed categorization situation, a heavy cognitive workload should diminish the distinctiveness of the categories and, in turn, produce outcomes more like the Equivalence pattern, as described in Table 16.1. This prediction may apply more strongly to situations in which category membership must be induced from more subtle cues, as when religion or political party affiliation must be inferred from a conversation, as opposed to situations wherein the existence of natural category distinctions such as race or sex makes the "fit" aspect manifest (Rosch, 1978). From this perspective, the category-inhibiting effects of cognitive load may also be more likely, for instance, in situations in which group membership is defined by assignment to distinct social roles (Brown & Wade, 1987; Marcus-Newhall, Miller, Holtz, & Brewer, 1993), rather than by the manifestly obvious physical differences that distinguish groups defined by race or sex.

As previously indicated, however, in some cases, cognitive load can also increase the use of categories in the judgment of people (Bodenhausen & Lichtenstein, 1987; Gilbert & Hixon, 1991; Martell, 1991). If a target's category membership is clear, cognitive load may cause one to automatically rely on it, rather than processing unique attributes about the target person. If so, increased load should augment differentiation between double-ingroup and double-outgroup targets, with evaluations of the crossed targets falling in-between (i.e., Additivity pattern).

Conscious.   Specific features of the crossed categorization setting may act to increase the salience of category distinctions. These include, among other factors, the degree to which the setting encourages an intergroup as opposed to an interpersonal focus, the nature of the groups, and the type of task to be performed. When features of the setting focus interaction at an interpersonal level, as opposed to invoking group loyalties and thereby inducing category-based responding, the magnitude of the difference between the two types of convergent targets, I-I and O-O, will be reduced, leading to outcomes that more closely approach the Equivalence pattern (Bettencourt, Brewer, Croak, & Miller, 1992). Situations wherein category members act as individuals rather than as groups or representatives of groups (Insko et al., 1987; Insko, Schopler, Hoyle, Dardis, & Graetz, 1990) will also push evaluations toward the Equivalence pattern. Similarly, when groups are formed on the basis of some arbitrary criterion, as in the minimal group situation (Mullen, Brown, & Smith, 1992), or when they are based on a common role assignment, rather than group memberships that are distinct for historical, cultural, or biological reasons (Marcus-Newhall et al., 1993), this same direction of effect can be expected.

Variation in the type of task assigned to the group is another situational feature that can make a particular social category dimension salient. For instance, in school settings, for various historical/cultural reasons, Blacks and Whites differ in their average level of academic performance (Coleman et al., 1966; Gerard & Miller, 1975; Wilson, 1987). Hence, were the group task an academic one, the racial dimension may be more salient than the sex dimension. By contrast, were the task an athletic one (e.g., baseball, 100-yard dash), the sex dimension would be more salient because the performance of males typically exceeds that of females.

Finally, features of society that act to create variation in the stability of status and the opportunity for individual social mobility will also have impact on the degree of evaluative bias toward convergent and crossed category targets. With the availability of individual mobility, social category distinctions are seen as less permanent, and identification with groups defined by them is reduced (Wright, Taylor, & Moghaddam, 1990). The effects of these factors may apply more strongly to members of low-status groups than to those in higher status groups because there is less to gain from identifying with a low-status group (Ellemers, Wilke, & Van Knippenberg, 1993). Thus, in the face of viable opportunities for individual upward mobility, members of two high-status groups may be unaffected, showing an Additivity pattern of evaluations, whereas evaluations by members of low-status groups may more closely approximate the Equivalence model. That is, the presence or absence of opportunity for mobility should not affect evaluations by high-status group members. By contrast, if low-status group members see their groups as resources for rebellion and collective action for gaining higher status, they too may show a strong Additivity pattern in their evaluations (Wright et al., 1990). Finally, if one is a member of one high-status group and one low-status group, a Category

Dominance pattern is expected because the benefits conferred by ingroup membership in the high-status category provide a strong basis for identification.

The roles of chronic and contextual priming have been discussed without acknowledging that they may conflict. When they do, recent, contextual primes will often predominate in the short-term; but in their absence, chronic primes will consistently predominate (Higgins, Bargh, & Lombardi, 1985; Wyer & Srull, 1980, 1986).

Affective Influences

The predictions regarding cognitive factors were made assuming a neutral mood. Affective arousal can also be expected to play a role in determining when each of the patterns enumerated in Table 16.1 will receive support. Three aspects of affect are relevant: (a) its valence, (b) its source, and (c) the specific emotion or mood state that accompanies affective arousal.

Valence. The positivity or negativity of one's affective state has important general consequences for the perception of people, as well as for targets in the crossed categorization situation. A negative affective state will have cueing and attentional consequences. Additionally, its guiding functions may decrease attraction toward others and result in avoidance and devaluation of them. The priming function of an antecedent negative emotional state will direct attention toward negatively valenced stimuli (Higgins & King, 1981). Because negative affect is associated with outgroups (Dijker, 1987; Jackson & Sullivan, 1989; Stephan & Stephan, 1989; Vanman & Miller, 1993), when it is strongly induced in the convergent/ crossed categorization setting, the outgroup-defining features of targets will be noted. Their presence, in conjunction with the strong mood congruity effects that are especially likely in judgments (Bower, 1991; Ellis & Ashbrook, 1991; Forgas, 1990), will combine to augment the negativity of evaluations of them. These mood congruity effects may be particularly likely for the typical targets in crossed categorization research for which only vague, if any, information is given other than the relevant group memberships (Sedikides, 1992).

Thus, the attentional cueing induced by a strong, negatively valenced emotional state will make each of the outgroup components of the crossed category targets salient, and in turn increase the negativity of evaluations of both crossed category targets as well as the double-outgroup target. This outcome corresponds to the Conjunctive Dissimilarity pattern. By contrast, when a strongly positive emotional state has been elicited in the perceiver, the same priming and mood congruity principles predict instead the

Conjunctive Similarity pattern. In addition, broader categorization characterizes positive mood (Isen, 1987; Isen & Daubman, 1984; Schwarz, 1990). This may reduce differential preference among all four types of target. Nevertheless, because the crossed categories share an ingroup membership with the actor on one of the two dimensions, it seems more likely that, in comparison with the double-outgroup, the two crossed categories will be assimilated to the double-ingroup.

Source.   As indicated, an arousal of irritation or anger can be general and unlinked to the particular social categories being evaluated. Alternatively, anger or irritation can be linked to a particular specifiable source, such as the experimenter, a confederate, or, in the case of crossed categorization research, a person who is an outgroup member on one of the two category dimensions. For instance, an insult from an outgroup member on Dimension A will increase the category salience of that dimension, as well as heighten antagonism toward others who are members of that particular outgroup category (Lewicki, 1986, p.200). Therefore, general, negatively valenced arousal is likely to yield support for the Category Conjunction Dissimilarity pattern, whereas when it is linked to one of the two outgroup categories in the crossed category situation, it is likely to produce a Category Dominance pattern.

Specific Emotion.   Specific negative experiential states, such as anger and sadness, may well share common negative components (Berkowitz, 1993; Clore, Ortony, Dienes, & Fujita, 1993). Nevertheless, they also have distinct attentional and guiding functions (Blaney, 1986; Niedenthal & Setterlund, 1994), as well as distinct information feedback functions (Carver & Scheier, 1990). Consequently, general valence effects will be moderated by the specific nature of the emotion that is elicited (E. Smith, 1993). This seems particularly likely for negatively valenced affect because the emotional states that accompany it show more differentiation than those associated with positively valenced affect (Bodenhausen, 1993). For instance, anxiety is associated with a stronger accentuation of differences between categories (Wilder, 1993), and thus might strengthen departures from the Equivalence pattern, as well as induce Dominance outcomes with respect to crossed groups.

Likewise, the arguments in the preceding section concerning the relation between general negative affect and the Conjunctive Dissimilarity pattern should be particularly likely to receive support when the negative arousal state is anger. A key feature of the anger that results from an insult or attack is that it directs attention to its source, producing an external orientation. This is seen in the tit-for-tat behavior commonly found in research on aggression (Borden, Bowen, & Taylor, 1971; Dengerink & Myers, 1977;

Ohbuci & Kambara, 1985) and competitive experimental games (Axelrod, 1984; Axelrod & Hamilton, 1981), in which attack produces retaliation. Thus, prior attacks or insults by outgroup members of both social category dimensions are likely to produce support for the Conjunctive Dissimilarity pattern, and attacks from outgroup members of one social category are likely to produce support for the Category Dominance pattern.

E. Smith (1993) suggested that five specific emotions are most likely to be aroused in intergroup situations: fear, disgust, contempt, anger, and jealousy. Of these, fear and disgust can be distinguished as emotions that imply avoidance or movement away from the outgroup, whereas contempt and anger imply movement against the outgroup. Attitudes that are driven by the former emotional states are likely to have different cognitive contents and behavioral implications than those associated with the latter forms of emotion (Kovel, 1970). The difference between the two forms of negative affect toward outgroups may be a function of the degree of conflict of interest that is perceived to exist between the outgroup and ingroup. As perceived conflict increases, avoidant emotions such as anxiety and disgust may be replaced by active hostility and aggression.

Sadness is a negative affective state that is associated with internal physiological responses that differ markedly from those associated with anger (Henry, 1986). Moreover, subjectively felt anger and sadness elicit very different self-reports about internal bodily states (Shields, 1984). Sadness or depression is more likely to elicit an internal self-focus, rather than an other-focus (meta-analysis: Carlson & Miller; 1987; see also Wood, Saltzberg, & Goldsamt, 1990). In impression-formation studies, sadness and depression have been associated with greater accuracy of judgments (Coyne, 1976; Fiedler & Forgas, 1988; Schwarz, 1990), but also less certainty about them (Campbell & Fehr, 1990; Herskovic, Kietzman, & Sutton, 1986; Pietromonaco, Rook, & Lewis, 1992). Less certainty is associated with less evaluative extremity (Gross, Holtz, & Miller, 1995; Johnson, 1940) and less impetus for action (Gerard & Orive, 1987). This suggests that a state of depression will reduce evaluative and behavioral bias. Thus, in contrast to the negative affective state of anger, which is expected to produce a Conjunctive Dissimilarity pattern among crossed and convergent category targets, sadness is more likely to yield outcomes closer to the Equivalence pattern.

SOME EMPIRICAL TESTS OF THE MODEL

In an investigation of category salience in crossed categorization, facial electromyography (EMG) was used as a measure of bias (Vanman, Kaplan,

& Miller, 1995). Although research in intergroup relations has relied largely largely on verbal measures of bias or affect, some early studies did incorporate measures of autonomic nervous system (ANS) activity, but with limited success (e.g., Cooper, 1959; Porier & Lott, 1967; Rankin & Campbell, 1955). In multiple category contexts that include naturally occurring social groups, wherein demand characteristics can be particularly troublesome, the measurement of facial activity may provide a more promising alternative to traditional self-report measures. For instance, if prejudice on one category dimension is subject to demand (e.g., "it's not appropriate for me to show bias against Blacks") but on another dimension, such as fatness (Crandall, 1994), it is not, then the sole use of verbal response measures may produce false confirmation of a Category Dominance pattern.

In the first experiment, White, non-Hispanic undergraduate females at the University of Southern California who did not belong to a sorority viewed 40 slides of other White students. To avoid problems of demand facial EMG was used as a measure of affective responding. Muscles in the cheek and brow regions typically exhibit increased activity during periods in which the participant later reports having experienced positive or negative affect respectively, even when no overt expression is observable (e.g., Cacioppo, Petty, Losch, & Kim, 1986; Fridlund, Schwartz, & Fowler, 1984; Smith, McHugo, & Lanzetta, 1986). Surface EMG activity was recorded with electrodes placed over these two regions. Prior to each slide exposure, each participant read two or three sentences of bogus information about the target, which included university affiliation (USC vs. UCLA) and whether or not the target belonged to a fraternity or sorority (Greek vs. non-Greek). Both category dimensions have had a long history of rivalry at USC. Facial EMG was then recorded while the participant viewed the slide. Following the slide presentation, the participant rated the likability of the target. The non-Greek participants exhibited the lowest level of liking toward the O-O targets (i.e., UCLA Greeks), whereas the O-I, I-O and I-I targets were liked equally — a Conjunction Similarity pattern. EMG activity from cheek muscle followed this same pattern — namely, less smiling for the O-O targets and equal liking for the crossed and I-I targets. (In this study, activity from the brow muscle failed to differentiate the targets.) These data are consistent with the notion that when participants are in a mildly positive mood, which is the typical baseline state for most persons during their daily life (cf. Sears, 1986), they make broader categorizations (Isen, 1987; Schwarz, 1990). Consequently, because crossed category targets share an ingroup membership with the experimental participants, the Conjunction Similarity pattern emerges.

An important feature of this first study is that the experimental procedures contained no features specifically intended to make category distinctions salient to the participants. If instead, both category dimensions are made highly salient, participants might be more likely to use category memberships in their evaluations and evidence an Additivity, rather than a Conjunctive Similarity, pattern. Therefore, in the second experiment, we attempted to make both category dimensions highly salient by requiring participants to write essays for approximately 3 minutes each about their own group memberships. This procedure was derived from other empirical work, in which questionnaires were administered to increase the salience of particular constructs (Effler, 1985; Goodhart, 1985; Stangor et al., 1992). The open-ended questions were chosen because they required more thought about relevant groups than simple questionnaires, thus making them stronger manipulations of salience. One essay task asked participants to explain why they had chosen not to join a fraternity or sorority. A second asked them to indicate what they would tell a high school student who might be considering attending USC instead of UCLA. A third essay on campus security issues was required as a filler task. After writing all three essays (with order of essay counterbalanced), our male and female White, non-Hispanic USC participants read information indicating the category identity of each of 32 targets and then viewed a slide of that target. Facial EMG was recorded during each slide presentation, after which participants made likability ratings.

Contrary to our expectation of an outcome closer to an Additivity pattern, the results again showed a Conjunction Similarity pattern: O-O targets were liked the least, whereas the crossed category and I-I targets were rated equally higher. In this study, both the brow and the cheek regions showed this pattern. More smiling occurred during the presentation of the crossed category and I-I targets, and more frowning occurred during the presentation of the O-O targets. Apparently, the imposition of the essay task, designed to heighten category salience, did not alter the effect of the apparently positive mood that participants brought to the experimental setting.

As indicated, the essay task was expected to increase the salience of the two relevant social category dimensions, and thereby produce greater differentiation between the two crossed category targets and the double-ingroup target. Having routinely assumed that the salience manipulation would predictably alter the pattern of evaluations, we had planned to conduct a third experiment, in which the essay task was varied across participant groups (i.e., fraternity/sorority essay, USC/UCLA essay, and neutral essay vs. three neutral essays) so as to confirm the between-study difference that was expected to emerge from the first two experiments. However, the failure to find the expected between-study difference led us to abort the planned Study 3, and to reconsider the experimental procedures, as well as our theoretical position.[1]

---

[1]The style chosen to present the theoretical model is somewhat atypical, in that authors do not usually make evident the empirical stumbling blocks and blind alleys that cause them to

In retrospect, it seemed likely that any potential effects of an essay task on category salience were underout by the measurement features that typify the experimental paradigms used in our own and other crossed categorization research. Specifically, the experimental procedures used to induce the "fit," or "applicability," aspect of salience may create a sufficiently high level of category salience to preclude any effect of manipulated accessibility. For instance, in our own studies, for each target the relevant category information for the two dimensions of interest (and little else) was manifestly presented on every trial. Therefore, the effects of the essay task in raising accessibility might be negligible due to the near asymptotic salience imposed by the procedures for target presentation. Moreover, this feature characterizes virtually all prior crossed categorization studies. Standard experimental procedures used throughout the crossed categorization literature routinely and consistently make each target's identity, with respect to the two dimensions of interest, virtually the only information known about them, and thus make them absolutely unambiguous.

This interpretation of the results seems consonant with recent findings from another study of multiple categories (Stangor et al., 1992). In a series of experiments, these researchers examined how category accessibility affected the use of race and sex as methods of categorizing target persons. Accessibility was manipulated either by having participants fill out questionnaires about racial or sexual discrimination, or by explicitly directing them to pay attention to one dimension or the other. The failure of their accessibility manipulation to affect their outcomes suggests that race and sex are highly, if not asymptotically, salient as a result of the manifest cues available for such differentiation and the extensive attention and practice given to categorizing people in these ways. Consequently, any temporary attempt to change these habitual patterns of categorization has little effect. In a study involving a less practiced and less salient category — namely, style of dress — an accessibility manipulation did yield the predicted effect (Stangor et al., 1992).

If this evaluation of our own experimental procedures is correct, as indicated, previously published crossed categorization research must also have similarly induced high category salience and near asymptotic category accessibility. Even in between-group designs, in which participants evaluate only a single target, the experimental procedures make each of the two dimensions (and the participant's position with respect to them) the only relevant information on which to base category perceptions. Yet what can account for the heterogeneity in outcomes depicted in Table 16.1? Our post

---

modify their theoretical models. Nevertheless, it may be valuable for some readers to see in a first-hand sense that theory development proceeds in a piecemeal fashion from the original ideas to subsquent ideas when data do not fit as expected.

hoc thinking led us to hypothesize that, with category salience always high, participants may be more affected by the relative importance of the social category dimensions, rather than by their differential salience. We do not mean to imply that category salience should be abandoned as a crucial variable in determining crossed categorization outcomes. Rather, category importance is viewed as an additional conceptual variable that needs to be incorporated into the theoretical model. To test the role of this motivational variable, a meta-analytic synthesis of data collected in crossed categorization paradigms was conducted.

META-ANALYTIC EXAMINATION OF PAST FINDINGS

Our research synthesis is based on approximately 26 effect sizes extracted from 12 studies (see Urban & Miller, 1997, for full details). Four separate types of effect sizes were coded from the studies: mean evaluation of double-ingroup compared with the combined crossed groups (II vs. IO & OI); combined crossed groups vs. double-outgroup (IO & OI vs. OO); the double-ingroup versus the double-outgroup (II vs. OO); and one crossed group versus the other (IO vs. OI). The latter effect size — IO versus OI — was calculated as the absolute value of the effect size. Thus, rather than attempting to determine a priori which category dimension in the IO and OI configurations was dominant, we assessed it in a post hoc manner by noting the magnitude of the difference between these two crossed groups, independent of the sign of the effect. Therefore, a small effect size signifies Equivalence for the two crossed categories, whereas a larger effect size can be considered indicative of Category Dominance.

Combined across studies, the mean effect sizes for each of these four comparisons are presented in Table 16.2. All of them fall within the medium range, as described by Cohen (1969). Inspection shows that crossed groups tend to lie somewhere between the double-ingroup and the double-outgroup, conforming to an Additivity pattern. However, one can also see

TABLE 16.2
Mean Effect Sizes Across Studies

Comparison	Mean ES (d+)	95% CI
II vs. IO&OI	.41	.33/.49
IO&OI vs. OO	.30	.22/.38
IO vs. OI (absolute value)	.28	.19/.37
II vs. OO	.48	.40/.56

that, across studies, one of the two category dimensions tends to dominate the other, as indicated by the absolute magnitude of difference between the two crossed groups.

Our synthesis of these data suggests that crossing categories does have beneficial effect, in that crossed targets are not seen as negatively as double-outgroup members. More important to our theoretical concern, however, the significant heterogeneity among effect sizes for each of the four types of comparison supported our intention to examine the importance of the relevant dimensions as a moderator variable.

We turn now to this more critical theoretical aspect of our meta-analysis. Given our failure to manipulate salience effectively in Vanman et al. (1995), along with our post hoc analysis of the nature of the typical crossed categorization research paradigm, we next examined variation in the importance of category dimensions as a moderator of the effect sizes. Borrowing from the definition used by Boninger, Krosnick, Berent, and Fabrigar (1995), *importance* is a subjective sense of concern, caring, or significance attached to a category dimension. Conforming to our emphasis on its motivational properties, importance stems from such sources as self-interest, social identification, or personal values (Boninger et al., 1995).[2] Therefore, the degree to which one social category is linked to another by a history of antagonism was expected to contribute to its importance. For members of a category that is linked to another category by a history of antagonism, category membership is likely to be associated with important self-interests, potent feelings of identification with one's social group, and strong personal values.

When the levels of antagonism or importance differ between category dimensions within a study, the more important category is likely to have greater influence in evaluations of target persons. Therefore, larger differences in the comparison between IO and OI were expected to emerge when the category dimensions differed in importance — an effect consonant with the Category Dominance pattern outlined in Table 16.1.

Category importance can differ between studies, as well as within studies. For example, in a study that used religion and nationality as the two category dimensions, the overall level of importance should exceed that found in one that used university campus organizations to categorize targets, primarily because the latter have little or no history of antagonism. Higher levels of category importance were expected to be associated with

---

[2]Although it is important to examine the factors that cause antagonism between groups and heighten the importance of category dimensions, the issue is beyond the scope of this chapter and meta-analysis. Moreover, the information available in the method sections of the studies included in the meta-analysis was not adequate for exploring this topic. For a general treatment of this issue at a theoretical level, see LeVine and Campbell (1972).

larger effect sizes overall. This effect was particularly expected in the II versus OO comparison, reflecting stronger departures from the Equivalence pattern.

These predictions parallel those made for high category salience or activation. Nevertheless, although importance may empirically covary with salience to a moderate degree, from our theoretical perspective we view them as conceptually distinct. Even when salience is asymptotic, we still expect to find differences in crossed categorization patterns when importance is varied. That is, when an important, real category is crossed experimentally with an unimportant, artificial category, even if both dimensions are made maximally salient, we expect a Category Dominance pattern in which the important category is dominant.

To empirically assess the potential theoretical role of the importance, judges who were blind to our hypothesis were asked to rate each of the two category dimensions in each study. Based on information in the method section of each study, they rated: (a) the degree to which each dimension was likely to be important to the participants, and (b) the level of historical antagonism between the groups on that dimension. Both ratings were included because, although we felt that historical antagonism is a major factor in determining importance, there are other factors (e.g., status) that can increase one's identification with the ingroup. In addition, because little variation was anticipated in the low levels of importance associated with artificial categories, their inclusion in the analyses was only likely to decrease the sensitivity, and thus they were excluded. In fact, a test for equality of variances revealed that the studies of artificial groups had significantly smaller variance than the studies of real groups on a measure of overall importance, $s^2_{artificial} = .004$, $s^2_{real} = .142$, $F = 19.99$, $p < .001$.

As expected, the correlation between the two coded variables was highly significant, ($r = .91$, $p < .001$). Therefore, these ratings were then combined as follows. First, a discrepant importance index was formed by subtracting the codings of one category dimension from the other (e.g., discrepant importance = importance of religion − importance of nationality), taking the absolute value and then adding differences between the two codings to obtain an overall discrepancy between group dimensions for each study (e.g., discrepant importance + discrepant antagonism). Next, an index of overall importance was formed by adding the codings for the two dimensions (e.g., overall importance score = importance of religion + importance of nationality) and then combining the sums of the two types of codings (overall importance + overall antagonism).

To assess the moderating role of discrepant importance on the effect size between the IO and OI groups, the index was entered into a univariate regression, for which the IO versus OI effect size was the dependent variable. As expected, discrepant importance was found to be a significant predictor of the IO versus OI effect size ($\beta = .27, p < .05$). Next, the moderating effect of overall importance was examined. As mentioned previously, greater overall importance was expected to be associated with larger effect sizes for the II versus OO comparison. The overall importance index was also entered into a univariate regression equation, for which the II versus OO effect size was the dependent variable. It was found to be a marginal predictor of the II versus OO effect size ($\beta = .17, p = .07$). These results support the following ideas: (a) the greater the discrepancy between the importance of two category dimensions within a study, the greater the likelihood that Category Dominance patterns will occur; and (b) the greater the importance of the category dimensions within a study, the less likely it is that an Equivalence pattern will be found. This preliminary evidence supports the general notion that the absolute (between studies) and relative (within studies) importance of category dimensions contribute to patterns of crossed categorization evaluations.

Finally, a factor that reduces the intergroup focus in the experimental setting should reduce the importance of category distinctions, and thus be expected to reduce the differentiation made between groups (Schopler & Insko, 1992). Consequently, variation in whether the setting emphasized intergroup versus interpersonal aspects of the relation between self and the targets should affect the magnitude of the effect sizes. To test this notion, crossed categorization studies were coded for whether participants were asked to judge broad groups (e.g., American girls, or a typical American girl) or instead, specific persons who also happened to be members of particular groups (e.g., Susan, who at some point was also identified as an American girl). We predicted that bias would be more prevalent, and effect sizes larger, when participants were focused on the intergroup nature of the experiment, as when rating broad groups. This is indeed what was found. As seen in Table 16.3, for all four comparisons of crossed and convergent category targets, the effect sizes were larger when the research paradigms emphasized intergroup, rather than interpersonal, relations.

TABLE 16.3
Categorical Comparison of Mean Effect Sizes for Group Versus Individual Ratings

Comparison	Group Rating	Individual Rating	Probability
II vs. IO & OI	.5474	.2209	$p < .0001$
IO & OI vs. OO	.4244	.2173	$p < .05$
IO vs. OI	.3730	.1739	$p < .05$
II vs. OO	.5890	.3325	$p < .01$

TESTING CATEGORY SALIENCE EFFECTS
IN THE LABORATORY

It has been argued that the experimental paradigm used in crossed categorization research undermined our attempt to test directly hypotheses regarding the accessibility component of category salience. Typically, experimental procedures only provide information about the target's identity with respect to the two dimensions that are crossed or made convergent with the participants identity, thereby making them highly salient. The within-subjects design that is typically used in crossed categorization studies, requiring comparison of the four combinations of targets, acts to further maximize the accessibility of the social category information. Moreover, some studies, such as those of Vanman et al. (1995), used multiple presentations of the four combinations of targets, thereby further increasing making the clarity or distinctiveness of the relevant dimensions to the participants.

Future research on the effect of category salience must use instead convergent and crossed cues regarding category identity, along with response measurement procedures that do not spontaneously provide strong category salience. For instance, requiring participants to induce the relevant social category memberships of targets will increase ambiguity and reduce the salience of the two critical category dimensions. To illustrate, a White participant might view a video of a short scene about Bill, manifestly Black, seen leaving a car with a Republican Party bumper sticker while wearing a UCLA T-shirt. On leaving the car, he might be heard striking up a conversation with a friend in which he talks about how his plans to join his family for a Christmas celebration will not disrupt his plans to represent Jamaica in the world track events. In this example, at least eight potentially important category dimensions may be relevant: sex, school, race, political party affiliation, religion, language, athlete/nonathlete, and nationality. Consequently, the information-processing task confronting the respondent is a complex one. Within this context, subconscious priming (Bargh, 1992) of the categories race and political party, for instance, could be imposed for half of the White and Black participants selected for the study. Mood manipulations can be superimposed on the priming manipulations. In either a between- or within-subjects design, other targets would be similar to Bill on all dimensions other than race and political party, making targets vary only with respect to the four combinations of race and party affiliation. The effect of the importance of the social category dimensions also can be studied within this more complex paradigm by (a) selecting dimensions pretested as differing in their importance, or (b) experimentally manipulating the perceived importance of the category dimension (e.g., choice of partner for a competitive political debate).

PROSPECTS FOR INTERGROUP CHANGE

The start of this chapter noted that crossed categorization has been proposed as a method for reducing intergroup conflict and discrimination (Brewer & Miller, 1984). The inconsistency of past research suggests that simply introducing crossed categories will not predictably reduce intergroup bias. One must look at the many influences on intergroup cognitions that may facilitate or diminish the positive effects of crossed categorization. It is useful to remind ourselves that intergroup behaviors do not occur in a vacuum. Rather, factors such as cognitive load, moods, or chronic activation, which are known to have potent effects on individual behavior, must be expected to influence intergroup behavior as well. We believe that intergroup behavior is preceded by changes that these, and other variables, impose on the nature of intergroup cognitions. Therefore, theoretical variables such as those proposed in our model must be considered to successfully use crossed categorization to promote harmony between groups.

For example, a schoolteacher who wants to employ the theoretical promise of crossed categorization to reduce intergroup conflict in his or her classroom should consider cognitive factors present in the setting. If two social groups divide the classroom (e.g. Blacks and Whites), the teacher should introduce at least one other category dimension into the situation (e.g., eagle team and tiger team) to create some shared memberships among those who were originally in opposing groups. In addition, the teacher should introduce activities that make the new team category dimension more important, as well as salient, to subjects. This will help prevent a Category Dominance effect, in which the original social grouping remains dominant. This may be achieved by creating classroom activities that emphasize the new groups and provide opportunities for within-team interactions and shared tasks. At the same time, efforts to reduce cognitive load (reduce noise and unnecessary stress) will help prevent students from falling back on old heuristics involving the two original categories.

In addition, the teacher should consider the affective tone of the classroom when employing these procedures. If students are routinely in a good mood following recess and a poor mood following a math test, the team categories are more likely to be effective after recess when mood is elevated. In this way, teachers can create and use classroom situations to maximize the beneficial impact of crossed categorization.

Some shared dimensions of categorization that cross-cut racial/ethnic dimensions, such as the distinction between children and adults, may, in fact, be more important to children than racial/ethnic differences. All children share common problems in their interactions with parents and teachers. The relative importance of such cross-cutting dimensions as age and authority can be made more salient to children in classroom discussions, thereby diminishing the relative importance and behavioral consequences of racial/ethnic distinctions (Miller & Harrington, 1990, 1992).

Another strategy that can be derived from crossed categorization principles and used by a teacher to improve intergroup relations is to educate students directly about psychological effects. Students can be made to realize that people are members of many different groups, not only those that are most obvious. It can be demonstrated that most people have at least something in common with every other individual. In addition, children can be taught about how moods may affect their judgment and behavior, and how to protect themselves against its negative effects.

SUMMARY

The opening section of this chapter presented a theoretical analysis outlining how cognitive and affective factors might moderate category salience and category processing to produce many of the crossed categorization patterns that have emerged in prior research. In addition, it presented two recent crossed categorization studies, in which we attempted to alter the pattern of liking across the persons representing the four combinations of ingroup–outgroup attributes by varying category salience between studies. However, the results, in combination with those of others (Stangor et al., 1992), led us to the view that many social category dimensions are routinely highly accessible, and that the typical measurement procedures used in prior research induced high salience for the relevant category dimensions of each experimental study. By consistently making the location of targets on the two dimensions of interest manifest to the respondent, any additional manipulation of category accessibility, such as that intended by our essay task, becomes irrelevant. Moreover, as indicated, such near-asymptotic salience of the relevant dimensions routinely is maintained in the response measurement phase of crossed categorization research; it is done so by having participants only evaluate respondents whose major identifying attributes correspond to the previously induced categories. We therefore proposed that a motivational variable—the relative importance of the category dimensions—might provide a better account for the variation among outcomes of previous studies than does category salience per se.

In a meta-analysis of crossed categorization studies, it was confirmed that the relative importance of the category dimensions does moderate the effect sizes that reflect differential evaluations of the crossed categorization targets. We view our introduction of category importance as an additional variable that reflects the operation of motivational factors within the crossed categorization setting. Additionally, ways in which future research in crossed categorization might better address the role of category salience were suggested — namely, by utilizing procedures that do not spontaneously elicit high category salience. With the use of measurement settings that more strongly require participants to induce the relevant category dimensions, our theorizing about category salience, and the moderating roles of accessibility and affect, is more likely to find confirmation. Finally, we proposed some applications for our extended model of crossed categorization that might function to reduce conflict between social groups.

ACKNOWLEDGMENT

Preparation of this chapter was facilitated by National Science Foundation Grant SBR 9319752, Norman Miller, Principal Investigator.

REFERENCES

Arcuri, L. (1982). Three patterns of social categorization in attribution memory. *European Journal of Social Psychology, 12,* 271–282.

Axelrod, R. (1984). *The evolution of cooperation.* New York: Basic Books.

Axelrod, R., & Hamilton, W. D. (1981). The evolution of cooperation. *Science, 211,* 1390–1396.

Bargh, J. A. (1992). Does subliminality matter to social psychology? The awareness of the stimulus versus the awareness of its influence. In R. Bornstein & T. S. Pittman (Eds.), *Perception without awareness: Cognitive, clinical, and social perspectives* (pp. 236–255). New York: Guildford.

Bargh, J. A., Bond, R. N., Lombardi, W. L., & Tota, M. E. (1986). The additive nature of chronic and temporary sources of construct accessibility. *Journal of Personality and Social Psychology, 50,* 869–879.

Berkowitz, L. (1993). Towards a general theory of anger and emotional aggression: Implications of the cognitive neoassocianistic perspective for the analysis of anger and other emotions. In R. S. Wyer and T. K. Srull (Eds.), *Perspectives on anger and emotion* (pp. 1–46). Hillsdale, NJ: Lawrence Erlbaum Associates.

Bettencourt, B. A., Brewer, M. B., Croak, M. R., & Miller, N. M. (1992). Cooperation and reduction of intergroup bias: The role of reward structure and social orientation. *Journal of Experimental Social Psychology, 28,* 301–319.

Blaney, P. H. (1986). Affect and memory — a review. *Psychological Bulletin, 99,* 229–246.

Bodenhausen, G. V. (1993). Emotions, arousal, and stereotypic judgements: A heuristic model of affect and stereotyping. In D. M. Mackie & D. L. Hamilton (Eds.), *Affect, cognition, and stereotyping: Interactive processes in group perception* (pp. 13–38). San Diego: Academic Press.

Bodenhausen, G. V., & Lichtenstein, M. (1987). Social stereotypes and information-processing strategies: The impact of task complexity. *Journal of Personality and Social Psychology, 52,* 871–880.

Boninger, D. S., Krosnick, J. A., Berent, M. K., & Fabrigar, L. R. (1995). The causes and consequences of attitude importance. In R. E. Petty & J. A. Krosnick (Eds.), *Attitude strength: Antecedents and consequences* (pp. 159-189). Hillsdale, NJ: Lawrence Erlbaum Associates.

Borden, R. J., Bowen, R., & Taylor, S. P. (1971). Shock setting as a function of physical attack and extrinsic reward. *Perceptual and Motor Skills, 33*, 563-568.

Bower, G. H. (1991). Mood congruity of social judgments. In J. P. Forgas (Ed.), *Emotion and social judgments* (pp. 31-54). Oxford: Pergamon.

Brewer, M. B., Ho, H. K., Lee, J., & Miller, N. (1987). Social identity and social distance among Hong Kong schoolchildren. *Personality and Social Psychology Bulletin, 13*, 156-165.

Brewer, M. B., & Miller, N. (1984). Beyond the contact hypothesis: Theoretical perspectives on desegregation. In N. Miller & M. B. Brewer (Eds.), *Groups in contact: The psychology of desegregation* (pp. 281-302). Orlando, FL: Academic Press.

Brown, R. J., & Turner, J. C. (1979). The criss-cross categorization effect in intergroup discrimination. *British Journal of Social and Clinical Psychology, 18*, 371-383.

Brown, R. J., & Wade, G. (1987). Superordinate goals and intergroup behavior: The effect of role ambiguity and status on intergroup attitudes and task performance. *European Journal of Social Psychology, 17*, 131-142.

Bruner, J. S. (1973). *Beyond the information given*. New York: Norton.

Cacioppo, J. T., Petty, B. E., Losch, M. E., & Kim, H. S. (1986). Electromyographic activity over facial muscle regions can differentiate the valence and intensity of affective reactions. *Journal of Personality and Social Psychology, 50*, 250-260.

Campbell, J. D., & Fehr, B. (1990). Self-esteem and perceptions of conveyed impression: Is negative affectivity associated with greater realism? *Journal of Personality and Social Psychology, 58*, 122-133.

Carlson, M., & Miller, N. (1987). Explanation of the relation between negative mood and helping. *Psychological Bulletin, 102*, 91-108.

Carver, C. S., & Scheier, M. F. (1990). Origins and functions of positive and negative affect: A control process view. *Psychological Review, 97*, 19-35.

Clore, G. L., Ortony, A., Dienes, B., & Fujita, F. (1993). Where does anger dwell? In R. S. Wyer & T. K. Srull (Eds.), *Perspectives on anger and emotion* (pp. 57-88). Hillsdale, NJ: Lawrence Erlbaum Associates.

Cohen, J. (1969). *Statistical power analysis for the behavioral sciences*. New York: Academic Press.

Coleman, J. S., Campbell, E. Q., Hobson, C. J., McPartland, J., Mood, A. M., Weinfield, F. D., & York, R. L. (1966). *Equality of educational opportunity*. Washington, DC: Office of Education, U.S. Government Printing Office.

Cooper, J. B. (1959). Emotion in prejudice. *Science, 130*, 314-318.

Coser, L. A. (1956). *The functions of social conflict*. New York: The Free Press.

Coyne, J. C. (1976). Depression and the response of others. *Journal of Abnormal Psychology, 85*, 186-193.

Crandall, C. S. (1994). Prejudice against fat people: Ideology and self-interest. *Journal of Personality and Social Psychology, 66*, 882-894.

Dengerink, H. A., & Myers, J. D. (1977). Three effects of failure and depression on subsequent aggression. *Journal of Personality and Social Psychology, 35*, 88-96.

Deschamps, J. C., & Doise, W. (1978). Crossed category memberships in intergroup relations. In H. Tajfel (Ed.), *Differentiation between social groups* (pp. 141-158). Cambridge, England: Cambridge University Press.

Dijker, A. J. M. (1987). Emotional reactions to ethnic minorities. *European Journal of Social Psychology, 17*, 305-325.

Effler, M. (1985). The influence of salience in causal attributions for scholastic and academic performance. *Archiv fur Psychologie, 137*, 233-240.

Ellemers, N., Wilke, H., & Van Knippenberg, A. (1993). Effects of the legitimacy of low group or individual status on individual and collective status enhancement strategies. *Journal of Personality and Social Psychology, 64*, 766-778.

Ellis, H. C., & Ashbrook, P. N. (1991). The "state" of mood and memory research: A selective review. In D. Kuiken (Ed.), *Mood and memory: Theory, research, and applications* (pp. 1-21). Newbury Park, CA: Sage.

Eurich-Fulcher, R., & Schofield, J. W. (1995). Correlated versus uncorrelated social categorizations: The effect on intergroup bias. *Personality and Social Psychology Bulletin, 21*, 149-159.

Fiedler, K., & Forgas, J. (1988). *Affect, cognition, and social behavior*. Toronto: Hogrefe.

Fiske, S. T., & Taylor, S. E. (1991). *Social cognition* (2nd ed.). New York: McGraw Hill.

Forgas, J. P. (1990). Affective influences on individual and group judgments. *European Journal of Social Psychology, 41*, 197-214.

Fridlund, A. J., Schwartz, G. E., & Fowler, S. C. (1984). Pattern recognition of self-reported emotional state from multiple-site facial EMG activity during affective imagery. *Psychophysiology, 21*, 622-637.

Gaertner, S. L., & Dovidio, J. F. (1986). The aversive form of racism. In J. F. Dovidio & S. L. Gaertner (Eds.), *Prejudice, discrimination, and racism* (pp. 61-89). San Diego: Academic Press.

Gerard, H. B., & Miller, N. (1975). *School desegregation: A long-range study*. New York: Plenum.

Gerard, H. B., & Orive, R. (1987). The dynamics of opinion formation. *Advances in Experimental Social Psychology, 20*, 171-202.

Gilbert, D. T., & Hixon, J. G. (1991). The trouble of thinking: Activation and application of stereotypes. *Journal of Personality and Social Psychology, 60*, 509-517.

Goodhart, D. E. (1985). Some psychological effects associated with positive and negative thinking about stressful event outcomes: Was Pollyanna right? *Journal of Personality and Social Psychology, 48*, 216-232.

Gross, S., Holtz, L., & Miller, N. (1995). Attitude certainty. In R. E. Petty & J. A. Krosnick (Eds.), *Attitude strength: Antecedents and consequences* (pp. 215-246). Hillsdale, NJ: Lawrence Erlbaum Associates.

Hagendoorn, L., & Henke, R. (1991). The effect of multiple category membership on intergroup evaluations in a north Indian context: Class, caste, and religion. *British Journal of Social Psychology, 30*, 247-260.

Henry, J. P. (1986). Neuroendocrine patterns of emotional response. In R. Plutchik & H. Kellerman (Eds.), *Emotion: Theory, research, and experience* (pp. 37-60). Orlando, FL: Academic Press.

Herskovic, J. E., Kietzman, M. L., & Sutton, S. (1986). Visual flicker in depression: Response criteria, confidence ratings, and response times. *Psychological Medicine, 16*, 187-197.

Hewstone, M., Islam, M. R., & Judd, C. M. (1993). Models of crossed categorization and intergroup relations. *Journal of Personality and Social Psychology, 64*, 779-793.

Higgins, E. T., Bargh, J. A., & Lombardi, W. (1985). The nature of priming effects on categorization. *Journal of Experimental Psychology: Learning, Memory, and Cognition, 11*, 59-69.

Higgins, E. T., & Brendl, C. M. (1995). Accessibility and applicability: Some "activation rules" influencing judgment. *Journal of Experimental Social Psychology, 31*, 218-243.

Higgins, E. T., & King, G. (1981). Accessibility of social constructs: Information-processing consequences of individual and contextual variability. In N. Cantor & J. F. Kihlstrom (Eds.), *Personality, cognition, and social interaction* (pp. 69-121). Hillsdale, NJ: Lawrence Erlbaum Associates.

Higgins, E. T., King, G. A., & Mavin, G. H. (1982). Individual construct accessibility and subjective impressions and recall. *Journal of Personality and Social Psychology, 43*, 35-47.

Insko, C. A., Punkley, R. L., Hoyle, R. H., Dalton, B., Hong, G., Slim, R., Landry, P., Holton, B., Riffin, P. F., & Thibaut, J. (1987). Individual-group discontinuity: The role of intergroup contact. *Journal of Experimental Social Psychology, 23*, 250–267.

Insko, C. A., Schopler, J., Hoyle, R. H., Dardis, G. J., & Graetz, K. A. (1990). Individual-group discontinuity as a function of fear and greed. *Journal of Personality and Social Psychology, 58*, 68–79.

Isen, A. M. (1987). Positive affect, cognitive processes, and social behavior. In L. Berkowitz (Ed.), *Advances in experimental social psychology* (pp. 203–253). San Diego: Academic Press.

Isen, A. M., & Daubman, K. A. (1984). The influence of affect on categorization. *Journal of Personality and Social Psychology, 47*, 1206–1217.

Jackson, L. A., & Sullivan, L. A. (1989). Cognition and affect in evaluations of stereotyped group members. *The Journal of Social Psychology, 129*, 659–672.

Johnson, D. M. (1940). Confidence and expression of opinion. *The Journal of Social Psychology, Society for the Psychological Study of Social Issues Bulletin, 12*, 221–242.

Kovel, J. (1970). *White racism, a psychohistory*. New York: Pantheon.

LeVine, R. A., & Campbell, D. T. (1972). *Ethnocentrism: Theories of conflict, ethnic attitudes, and group behavior*. New York: Wiley.

Lewicki, P. (1986). *Nonconscious social information processing*. Orlando, FL: Academic Press.

Macrae, C. N., Milne, A. B., & Bodenhausen, G. V. (1994). Stereotypes as energy-saving devices: A peek inside the cognitive toolbox. *Journal of Personality and Social Psychology, 66*, 37–47.

Marcus-Newhall, A., Miller, N., Holtz, R., & Brewer, M. B. (1993). Cross-cutting category membership with role assignment: A means of reducing intergroup bias. *British Journal of Social Psychology, 32*, 125–146.

Martell, R. F. (1991). Sex bias at work: The effects of attentional memory demands on performance ratings of men and women. *Journal of Applied Social Psychology, 21*, 1939–1960.

Messick, D. M., & Mackie, D. M. (1989). Intergroup relations. *Annual Review of Psychology, 40*, 45–81.

Miller, N., & Harrington, H. J. (1990). A situational identity perspective on cultural diversity and teamwork in the classroom. In S. Sharan (Ed.), *Cooperative learning: Theory and research* (pp. 39–76). New York: Praeger.

Miller, N., & Harrington, H. J. (1992). Social categorization and intergroup acceptance. In R. Hertz-Lazarowitz & N. Miller (Eds.), *Interaction in cooperative groups: The theoretical anatomy of group learning* (pp. 203–227). New York: Cambridge University Press.

Mullen, B., Brown, R., & Smith, C. (1992). Ingroup bias as a function of salience, relevance, and status: An integration. *European Journal of Social Psychology, 22*, 103–122.

Murphy, R. F. (1957). Intergroup hostility and social cohesion. *American Anthropologist, 59*, 1018–1035.

Niedenthal, P. M., & Setterlund, M. B. (1994). Emotion congruence in perception. *Personality and Social Psychology Bulletin, 20*, 401–411.

Oakes, P. (1987). The salience of social categories. In J. C. Turner, M. A. Hogg, P. J. Oakes, S. D. Reicher, & M. S. Wetherell (Eds.), *Rediscovering the social group* (pp. 117–141). Oxford: Basil Blackwell.

Ohbuci, K., & Kambara, T. (1985). Attacker's intent and awareness of outcome, impression management, and retaliation. *Journal of Experimental Social Psychology, 21*, 321–330.

Perdue, C. W., Dovidio, J. F., Gurtman, M. B., & Tyler, R. B. (1990). "Us" and "Them": Social categorization and the process of intergroup bias. *Journal of Personality and Social Psychology, 59*, 475–486.

Pietromonaco, P. R., Rook, K. S., & Lewis, M. A. (1992). Accuracy in perceptions of interpersonal interactions: Effects of dysphoria, friendship, and similarity, *Journal of Personality and Social Psychology, 63,* 247-259.

Porier, G. W., & Lott, A. J, (1967). Galvanic skin responses and prejudice. *Journal of Personality and Social Psychology, 5,* 253-259.

Rankin, R. E., & Campbell, D. T. (1955). Galvanic skin response to Negro and white experimenters. *Journal of Abnormal and Social Psychology, 51,* 30-33.

Rosch, E. (1978). Principles of categorization. In E. Rosch & B. B. Loyd (Eds.), *Cognition and categorization* (pp. 87-116). Hillsdale, NJ: Lawrence Erlbaum Associates.

Schopler, J., & Insko, C. A. (1992). The discontinent effect in interpersonal and intergroup relations: Generality and mediation. In W. Stroebe & M. Hewstone (Eds.), *European Review of Social Psychology* (Vol. 3, pp. 121-152). Chicester: Wiley.

Schwarz, N. (1990). Feelings as information: Informational and motivational functions of affective states. In E. T. Higgins & R. M. Sorrentino (Eds.), *Handbook of motivation and cognition* (pp. 527-561). New York: Guilford.

Scodel, A., & Freedman, M. L. (1956). Additional observations on the social perceptions of authoritarians and non-authoritarians. *Journal of Abnormal Social Psychology, 52,* 92-95.

Sears, D. O. (1986). College sophomores in the laboratory: Influences of a narrow data base on social psychology's view of human nature. *Journal of Personality and Social Psychology, 51,* 515-530.

Secord, P. F., & Saumer, Z. (1960). Identifying Jewish names: Does prejudice increase accuracy? *Journal of Abnormal and Social Psychology, 52,* 329-337.

Sedikides, C. (1992). Changes in the valence of the self as a function of mood. In M. S. Clark (Ed.). *Emotion and Social Behavior: Review of Personality and Social Psychology, 14,* 271-311.

Shields, S. A. (1984). Reports of bodily changes in anxiety, stress, and anger. *Motivation and Emotion, 8,* 1-21.

Simmel, G. (1955). *Conflict* (K. H. Wolff, Trans.) Glencoe, IL: The Free Press.

Smith, C. A., McHugo, G. J., & Lanzetta, J, T (1986). The facial muscle patterning of posed and imagery-induced expressions of emotion by expressive and non-expressive posers. *Motivation and Emotion, 10,* 133-157.

Smith, E. R. (1993). Social identity and social emotions: Toward new conceptualizations of prejudice. In D. M. Mackie & D. L. Hamilton (Eds.), *Affect, cognition, and stereotyping: Interactive processes in group perception* (pp. 297-316). San Diego: Academic Press.

Srull, T. K., & Wyer, R. S. (1979). The role of category accessibility in the interpretation of information about persons. *Journal of Personality and Social Psychology, 37,* 1660-1672.

Srull, T. K., & Wyer, R. S. (1980). Category accessibility and social perception: Some implications for the study of person memory and interpersonal judgments. *Journal of Personality and Social Psychology, 38,* 841-856.

Srull, T. K., & Wyer, R. S. (1989). Person memory and judgment. *Psychological Review, 96,* 58-83.

Stangor, C., Lynch, L., Duan, C., & Glass, B. (1992). Categorization of individuals on the basis of multiple social features. *Journal of Personality and Social Psychology, 62,* 207-218.

Stephan, W. G., & Stephan, C. W. (1989). Antecedents of intergroup anxiety in Asian-Americans and Hispanic-Americans. *International Journal of Intercultural Relations, 13,* 203-219.

Triandis, H. C., & Triandis, L. M. (1960). Race, social class, religion, and nationality as determinants of social distance. *Journal of Abnormal and Social Psychology, 61,* 110-118.

Triandis, H. C., & Triandis, L. M. (1962). A cross-cultural study of social distance. *Psychological Monographs: General and Applied, 76,* 1-21.

Urada, D. I., & Miller, N. (1997). *The effect of positive affective arousal on the crossed categorization effect.* Manuscript in preparation.

Urban, L. M. (1997). *Judgments of persons from crossed social categories: Psychological importance of categories and insult.* Unpublished master's thesis, University of Southern California, Los Angeles.

Urban, L. M., & Miller, N. M. (1997). *A meta-analysis of crossed categorization effects.* Manuscript submitted for publication.

Vanbeselaere, N. (1987). The effects of dichotomous and crossed social categorizations upon intergroup discrimination. *European Journal of Social Psychology, 17*, 143–156.

Vanbeselaere, N. (1991). The different effects of simple and crossed categorization: A result of the category differentiation process or of differential category salience? In W. Stroebe & M. Hewstone (Eds.), *European review of social psychology* (pp. 247–278). Chichester: Wiley.

Vanman, E. J. (1990). *Multiple social categories: Differentiating affective reactions between natural groups using facial electromyography.* Unpublished master's thesis, University of Southern California, Los Angeles.

Vanman, E. J., Kaplan, D. L., & Miller, N. (1995). *Assessment of crossed categorization effects on intergroup bias with facial electromyography.* Manuscript submitted for publication.

Vanman, E. J., & Miller, N. (1993). Applications of emotion theory and research to stereotyping and intergroup relations. In D. M. Mackie & D. L. Hamilton (Eds.), *Affect, cognition, and stereotyping: Interactive processes in group perception* (pp. 213–238). San Diego: Academic Press.

Wilder, D. A. (1993). Freezing intergroup evaluations: Anxiety fosters resistance to counter-stereotypic information. In M. S. Hogg & D. Abrams (Eds.), *Group motivation: Social psychological perspectives* (pp. 68–86). New York: Harvester Wheatsheaf.

Wilson, W. J. (1987). *The truly disadvantaged: Inner city, the underclass, and public policy.* Chicago: The University of Chicago Press.

Wood, J. V., Saltzberg, J. A., & Goldsamt, L. A. (1990). Does affect induce self-focused attention? *Journal of Personality and Social Psychology, 58*, 899–908.

Wright, S. C., Taylor, D. M., & Moghaddam, F. M. (1990). Responding to membership in a disadvantaged group: From acceptance to collective protest. *Journal of Personality and Social Psychology, 58*, 994–1003.

Wyer, R. S., Jr., & Srull, T. K. (1980). The processing of social stimulus information: A conceptual integration. In R. Hastie, T. M. Ostrom, E. B. Ebbesen, R. S. Wyer, D. Hamilton, & D. E. Carlston (Eds.), *Person memory: The cognitive basis of social perception* (pp. 227–300). Hillsdale, NJ: Lawrence Erlbaum Associates.

Wyer, R. S., Jr., & Srull, T. K. (1986). Human cognition in its social context. *Psychological Review, 93*, 322–359.

VI

Concluding Commentary

17

Intergroup Cognition and Intergroup Behavior: Crossing the Boundaries

Diane M. Mackie
University of California, Santa Barbara

Eliot R. Smith
Purdue University

In 1934, Richard LaPiere accompanied a Chinese-American couple of his acquaintance on an extended trip in the southwestern United States (LaPiere, 1934). Along the way, the trio visited over 200 hotels and restaurants. At only one were they offered anything less than courteous service. This fact was of considerable importance to LaPiere, who had earlier contacted these establishments only to be repeatedly told that Chinese Americans would not be welcome as customers or guests. As every social psychologist knows, this lack of consistency between expressed attitudes and actual behavior became oft-cited evidence in the debate over whether and how attitudes guided behavior (e.g., Blumer, 1955; Wicker, 1969). Given the attitude objects involved, however, the study generated surprisingly little theoretical debate in the domain of intergroup relations. Few similar questions appear to have been raised about whether prejudice can or does guide discrimination.

Indeed, despite the existence of studies like LaPiere's, intergroup researchers have by and large assumed consistency among stereotypes, prejudice, and discrimination (Dovidio, Brigham, Johnson, & Gaertner, 1996). Beliefs about groups' characteristic qualities are assumed to dictate how much the groups are liked and, in turn, how they are treated. More than being merely unproblematic, consistent relations among these three constructs have been foundational assumptions of many of the main approaches to understanding intergroup relations (this term is used to subsume both intergroup cognitions and intergroup behavior, as those terms are defined by the editors). For example, social identity theory assumes that the cognitions and evaluations derived from group memberships drive discrimination (Hogg & Abrams, 1988, 1990; Tajfel & Turner, 1979). Similarly, the recent explosion of research on the social and cognitive processes that underlie stereotypes is typically justified on the basis that it is cognitions, even more than "reality," that influence social behavior (Bodenhausen, Macrae, & Garst, chap. 13, this volume; Fiske, 1993; Hamilton & Trolier, 1986; Schneider, 1996). The cognition–behavior link is also the defining mechanism in self-fulfilling prophecies (Darley & Fazio, 1980; Jussim, 1991; Merton, 1948), where a perceiver's beliefs result in treatment of the target that actually encourages confirmation of those beliefs. Finally, the contact hypothesis, social psychology's major theory of how intergroup relations might be improved, also assumes that changes in knowledge will produce changes in intergroup behavior (Allport, 1954; Amir, 1969; Cook, 1978).

Despite its popularity, this traditional view has not been without its critics (Brigham, 1971). The assertion that prejudice determines stereotypes, rather than the other way around, has been made quite frequently (Dovidio et al., 1996; Jussim, Nelson, Manis, & Soffin, 1995; Schaller & Maass, 1989). Like Allport (1954) before them, some theorists have argued that prejudice and stereotypes result from attempts to justify discrimination, rather than serving as prerequisites to such behavior (Fiske, 1993; Hoffman & Hurst, 1990; Jost & Banaji, 1994)

The empirical waters are similarly muddied. There is considerable evidence that beliefs influence both evaluations (for examples and reviews, see Dovidio et al., 1996; Hamilton & Gifford, 1976; Schaller & Maass, 1989) and behaviors (Ayres, 1991; Dovidio et al., 1996; Sadker & Sadker, 1994; Farley, Steeh, Krysan, Jackson, & Reeves, 1994; Massey & Denton, 1993). At the same time, some studies find that cognitive measures of beliefs are basically unrelated to measures of prejudice (Esses, Haddock, & Zanna, 1993) or behavior (Brigham, 1971; Stangor et al., 1991). Other research has shown that measures of evaluations are no better predictors of intergroup behavior (Struch & Schwartz, 1989).

Thus, the time is ripe for social psychologists to look more closely at the relations between intergroup cognitions and intergroup behavior, and their implications for intergroup relations. This volume is thus particularly timely in its attempt to resolve some of the theoretical and empirical discrepancies in the literature by encouraging contributors to focus on the interface between intergroup cognitions and behaviors. This commentary chapter focuses on challenges to the traditionally assumed relation between cognitions and behaviors. When the cognition–behavior link first came under empirical and theoretical fire in the attitudes domain, several well publicized calls for elimination of the concept of attitudes were made (e.g., Wicker, 1969). However, researchers soon turned to the more theoretically enriching task of trying to understand why and how such discrepancies arose (Fazio, 1990; Fazio & Zanna, 1981; Fishbein & Ajzen, 1974, 1975; Lord, Lepper, & Mackie, 1984; Snyder & Ickes, 1985). This is the approach we believe will also be most fruitful for progress in understanding intergroup relations.

The chapter first looks at three possible reactions to the appearance of dissociations between intergroup cognitions and intergroup behaviors: specifying the conditions under which consistency should occur, considering alternative aspects of intergroup cognitions that have effects on behavior, and rethinking the causal order of the cognition–behavior sequence. Under each of these headings, relevant work from this volume is considered, as are other possibilities for explaining inconsistencies from that perspective. Finally, we draw some general conclusions and notes some areas for future theoretical and empirical attention.

ACCOUNTING FOR DISSOCIATIONS BETWEEN INTERGROUP COGNITIONS AND BEHAVIOR

This section considers three general developments in thinking about intergroup relations that help shed light on when and why intergroup cognitions will and will not show a predictable relation to intergroup behavior.

Clarifying Conditions Under Which Intergroup Cognitions Determine Behavior

The most obvious solution to apparent lapses in the consistent relationship between intergroup cognitions and intergroup behaviors is that specific conditions must obtain before cognitions can guide behaviors. This approach has proved especially illuminating in the attitudes domain. Researchers rising to the challenge that attitudes were ineffective predictors of behavior, for example, have mapped out both the mechanisms by which and the conditions under which attitudes do in fact have a powerful influence on behavior. This same approach is currently the most well developed in the intergroup literature and in this volume as well.

For example, this approach is taken in chapter 13 by Bodenhausen, Macrae, and Garst. These authors make a strong claim that stereotypic thought causally impacts discrimination, provided the processes necessary to mediate that impact occur. Thus, specific beliefs about a group's ability (say to negotiate a deal) will affect how they are treated by a car salesperson (what they will be told, how tough the bargaining stance will be) if several processes occur under the right conditions. Basically, stereotypic beliefs must first be activated (and thus the cognitive and motivational conditions for activation must be met) and then influence the interpretation or construal of information. This process can be facilitated or inhibited by a number of cognitive and motivational factors, but in some cases will produce biased perceptions with the potential to cause stereotype-consistent behavior. However, this perception–behavior sequence can be short-circuited if people recognize and attempt to compensate for bias. These authors discuss conscious suppression of stereotypic views as the main compensatory mechanism, providing empirical evidence for the capacity and motivational prerequisites for such redress to occur. One of the more fascinatingly ironic implications of such attempts is their unintended side effects, such as a heightened accessibility of the suppressed stereotype and overcompensation. The first may result in greater application of the stereotype in later intergroup encounters, whereas the latter leads to the "bending over backward" effect, and perhaps reverse discrimination.

Wittenbrink, Park, and Judd (chap. 8) also propose that intergroup behavior will be better understood when the nature of intergroup cognition is better understood. They argue that stereotypes are more complex cognitive structures than traditional views have led researchers to believe. Specifically, they suggest that stereotypes include not only group attributes, but also beliefs about structural relations that link those attributes together and theories about the world that provide causal explanations about stereotype content. Thus, discrete pieces of information processed in different combinations can produce emergent impressions of social types that could not be predicted from mere aggregation of the information. For example, in one experiment they demonstrate that eight pieces of information about a target resulted in quite different stereotypes if they were processed configurally, rather than in a piecemeal fashion. Similarly, they show that perceivers who believe that African Americans' attributes reflect victim status have quite different evaluative and behavioral reactions to that group than do perceivers who see the same characteristics as indicating that African Americans are instigators of aggression.

Behavior, of course, is predicted to follow from expectations generated by the emergent stereotype, rather than any individual piece of information in it. Although the authors do not produce any empirical behavioral evidence for their claims, they do demonstrate that perceivers' expectations about the targets' future behavior differed as a function of the emergent stereotype, thus providing a basis for behavioral confirmation. Thus, the emergence of derived social types could help explain apparent dissociations between more traditional assessment of stereotype content and subsequent behavior. That is, the emergent stereotype, rather than unconnected aspects of the stereotype's content, will predict intergroup behavior.

The conditions under which cognitions will impact consequent responses are also central to Miller, Urban, and Vanman's (chap. 16) contribution to the volume. The program of research they describe is of particular note because its dependent measures are, for the most part, covert assessments of positive or negative reactions measured via facial electromyography — measures that are argued to be relatively immune to social and self-presentational concerns. As these authors note, research on cross categorization (situations in which others are ingroup members on one dimension and outgroup members on another) has produced almost every conceivable pattern of results. They set out to delineate the conditions under which members of cross-cutting categories will be favored as much as those who are ingroups members on both dimensions, or liked less than true ingroup members but more than those who are outgroup members on both dimensions, and so forth. They start by listing the conditions necessary for crossed categorization to be activated, and in particular the conditions that will make one or more of the cross-cutting categories salient, and thus drive the particular pattern of intergroup liking that results. To the extent that categorization situations outside the laboratory also make one or both multiple categories dominant, different intergroup evaluations and behavior will ensue.

Simon's (chap. 11) chapter on the relation between self-interpretations and participation in collective action also makes the case for more clearly outlining the kinds of intergroup cognitions that will predict intergroup behavior. His chapter is particularly intriguing because it attempts to relate the literature on social movements (surely a quintessential intergroup behavior) to the mainstream social cognition literature about categorization, and particularly Linville's (1985) work on multiple self-aspects. The basic idea is that only collective representations of the self will prompt participation in social movements (i.e., collective cognitions are necessary for collective behavior). A collective sense of self is activated when people interpret their own experiences and behaviors, as well as others' reactions to them, in terms of a self-aspect that they share with others. Group status, group size, common fate, and their interactions are just some of the conditions that determine the development, strength, and activation of such collective selves. It is the activation of a collective self that then becomes the prerequisite for social action, which depends on perceptions of the world in terms of *we* versus *them*, perceptions of personal grievances in terms of group injustice, as well as agency beliefs that suggest that social change is possible and attainable. This idea is reminiscent of earlier analyses of stability (e.g., Tajfel, 1978). Intergroup or collective behavior is to be expected then only when appropriate intergroup or collective cognitions are present.

Hewstone and Lord (chap. 15) also take the approach of specifying more carefully the conditions under which cognitions have impact on behavior. Their chapter focuses on resolving inconsistencies in the impact of intergroup contact on intergroup relations. They note that although contact with a member of a different group under appropriate conditions can result in more positive evaluations of the interactant, this view does not typically extend to the group as a whole. They argue that generalized change in outgroup attitudes and consequent behavior can be achieved by focusing on the role of the interactant's typicality. Extending Fishbein and Azjen's (1974, 1975) work on specificity of measurement and Rothbart and John's (1985) ideas about category structure, they demonstrate that generalization of positive attitudes to an outgroup as a whole depends on encountered outgroup members being perceived both *as* outgroup members and as *typical* outgroup members. In a series of studies, they show that generalization of positive attitudes is easier when perceivers have abstract rather than specific category representations, when the interactant is personalized, and when the interactant has been chosen because of his or her group membership.

Hewstone and Lord's analysis goes further, however, in arguing that these attitudes will result in consistent behavior only when the target of behavior is also typical of the attitude object. That is, unless the person to whom action is directed is similar to the currently accessed cognitive representation of the group, intergroup cognitions will not dictate intergroup behavior. Empirical results confirm that intergroup attitudes predict behavior toward category members who match rather than mismatch the perceiver's category representation—that attitude–behavior consistency is greater when the target of behavior is similar to the exemplar that comes to mind to represent the category at the time of behaving, and that attitude–behavior consistency is greater when the actor is primed with or reminded of a typical rather than an atypical category member when behavior occurs. This work is particularly useful because of its equal concern for the cognition–behavior link and for the antecedents of cognition, and because the authors assess actual behavior (such as seating distance and petition signing) rather than behavioral intention measures alone.

Given Hewstone and Lord's assertion that abstract intergroup representations might facilitate change through contact, Wilder and Simon (chap. 2) make an interesting distinction between two types of groups and the cognitions that represent each one. Categorically defined groups are determined by abstraction of the properties that members share, and so group properties adhere to any individual identified as a member. In contrast, dynamically defined groups are determined by interaction among members. From this perspective, membership is defined by fit with the group's organization, rather than by similarity, and groups can have emergent properties.

More important, dynamic group perceptions are more the result of "bottom-up" processing than the "top-down" processing that guides perceptions of category groups. For example, fans with categorical views of baseball teams are more likely to attribute individual player's behaviors to their internal characteristics, whereas those with dynamic representations are more likely to attribute behavior to the social context in which it happens (i.e., as a matter of strategy, determined by previous actions of the own team or the rival team). The authors make the same argument regarding discrimination: Whether one has a mental representation of a group that is category based or dynamic has implications for behavior toward the group and individual group members. In fact, they argue that categorical representations may be harder to change because they direct biased information processing more clearly than dynamic representations. Such a distinction obviously deserves greater empirical validation, not only because of the apparent discrepancy between Wilder and Simon's and Hewstone and Lord's views on the issue, but also as a possible explanation for disassociation between intergroup cognitions and intergroup behavior. Not only may there be differences across perceivers and across target groups in the ways groups are perceived, but cognitions about groups may change with time and experience, rendering the timing of dependent measure assessment crucial to whether cognitions and behavior are related.

Hamilton, Sherman, and Lickel (chap. 3) pick up the same theme of differences among types of groups with their discussion of the "entitativity continuum." Groups with features such as internal organization and structure, like Wilder and Simon's dynamic groups, are likely to be seen as highly entitative units by both their own members and outsiders. In contrast, groups featuring similarity, akin to Wilder and Simon's categorical groups, are moderate in entitativity, whereas groups with only proximity are low in entitativity. Hamilton and Sherman take the view that high entitativity leads to expectations of coherence and consistency, so that (for instance) observers will draw online dispositional inferences about the group from members' behaviors. Stereotypes and also presumably prejudice and discrimination will be more well defined and clear-cut in the case of more entitative groups.

However, it may not be true that all cognitions and intergroup behaviors follow the same pattern. For example, stereotypic inferences that group members share the group's general characteristics (and intergroup behaviors corresponding to these inferences) may be most readily and confidently produced for categorical groups, especially if they are viewed as "natural kinds." Blanket stereotyping might be less likely for a dynamic group because internal structure and organization may imply heterogeneity (at least of roles and functions) within the group. On the other hand, inferences of coherence, organization, or interdependence (and intergroup behaviors following from these properties) may be more likely for more entitative and "dynamic" groups possessing internal structure. Thus, it may not be that all types of intergroup cognitions and behavior are simply stronger or more pronounced for more entitative groups. Instead, levels of entitativity may interact with the specific nature of inferences made and related intergroup behaviors. Nevertheless, the distinctions among different types of groups made by Wilder and Simon as well as Hamilton et al. are important reminders that all groups are not the same.

Linville and Fischer (chap. 6) also underline this point by suggesting that a perceiver's familiarity with a group is the key variable that influences judgments and behavior. Familiarity, with its obvious causal link to group membership (i.e., the fact that people will generally be more familiar with ingroups than with outgroups), has been linked to perceptions of group heterogeneity in earlier work. Now Linville and Fischer demonstrate that it also influences perceptions of covariation among group members' features and extremity of judgments. One plausible suggestion is that more extreme judgments are more likely to lead to corresponding behaviors toward group members, so that cognitive–behavioral consistency would be more likely for groups with which the perceiver was relatively less familiar. Outgroups (as opposed to ingroups) would generally fit this description. However, this chapter (like most in the literature) does not offer any studies with actual behavioral dependent measures that test this seemingly reasonable hypothesis.

Biernat, Vescio, and Manis (chap. 7) also discuss conditions under which intergroup cognitions will affect intergroup behaviors, drawing on their earlier work on shifting standards of judgment. They note that when a judgment is to be made about a member of a particular group, a group stereotype may activate not only expectancies about the member, but also standards for judgment. Thus, a woman who is 5 feet 11 inches in height may be called "tall" on the basis of gender-specific standards, although a man of the same height would not be so labeled. Past research, summarized in this chapter, has tested and confirmed various predictions of the model. Most important is a distinction between "subjective" judgment scales (such as "short . . . tall") and "objective" scales (such as estimated height in feet and inches). Group-specific standards are much more likely to affect judgments on subjective than on objective scales.

The key conceptual advance in this chapter is consideration of whether group-specific standards or more absolute judgments will affect behavior. The authors suggest that the answer has much to do with whether the behavior is zero-sum. That is, when competitive rankings or allocation of limited resources are at stake, absolute standards must be used because members of different groups must be compared side by side on a common scale. In contrast, when praise, blame, or more generally ratings of different individuals' performances are being handed out, group-specific standards may come into play. The most significant message of this chapter, then, is that the relations between intergroup cognitions (such as privately held or overtly expressed evaluations of performances by members of different groups) and intergroup behaviors will depend on the nature of the behaviors.

This dependence has been theoretically unexplored in social psychology in general, let alone within the field of intergroup relations. Past studies have included behavioral measures of both types: allocation of points in Tajfel matrices (e.g., Tajfel, Billig, Bundy, & Flament, 1971) represent zero-sum or choice behaviors, whereas assessments of smiling, petition signing, helping, seating distance, and the like represent nonzero-sum or ratinglike behaviors. After all, lending aid or sitting close to a member of one group does not diminish one's ability to do the same to someone else. Despite the use of both types of behavioral measures, however, theories have not distinguished between them, and have generally made similar predictions for both (Messick & Mackie, 1989). In analyzing behavioral dependent measures conceptually, social psychologists might well take account of the literature in decision theory on preference reversals (Slovic, 1995)—another important example of dissociations between ratings and rankings or choices. Studies in this area have found conditions under which people who rate Alternative A as superior to Alternative B nevertheless select B over A when offered the choice. Because this pattern of behavior violates basic assumptions, much theoretical and empirical effort has been devoted to explaining it. Some of this work might well be useful in understanding differences among different types of intergroup behavior that correspond conceptually to ratings (such as avoidance or helping) versus rankings (such as hiring or firing decisions).

Thus, the majority of chapters in the volume share the approach of specifying the nature of intergroup cognitions in more detail and assuming that these more differentiated cognitions will allow better prediction of intergroup behavior. Although the processes that produce these differentiated intergroup cognitions are increasingly well specified, the processes necessary to translate those cognitions into behavior remain relatively underresearched. Indeed, many chapters mentioned in this section do not include actual behavioral measures but assume that behavior will follow quite unproblematically from the "right" cognitions. The chapter by Dovidio et al. (chap. 14) is unique in this volume by virtue of its careful analysis of the complex relation between intergroup cognition and intergroup behavior. In their contribution, they argue that a mental representation of two or more formerly discrete groups as a common ingroup will promote positive intergroup behavior. Thus, when cognitions are changed so that members of different groups conceive of themselves as a single group, behavior changes such that former outgroup members are now treated to the benefits usually reserved for ingroup members. In their preliminary research on this issue, they focus on the impact of common group identity representations on helping and self-disclosive behavior. Members of two three-person groups learned they were to work together under conditions that either made their common superordinate group membership or their two distinct group memberships salient. Some members of each group were then given the opportunity to self-disclose to a member of the other group. Other members of each group received a request for help from a member of the other group. As expected, more inclusive group perceptions were induced when the superordinate group was made salient, and both self-disclosure and helping (albeit to a lesser extent) also increased compared with the condition in which the two groups remained distinct. Thus, the authors are able to conclude that their experiments provide considerable support for the idea that cognitive representations are a key mediator of intergroup behavior, as long as the exact nature of that cognitive representation is properly understood.

In summary, much more needs to be done along these lines to rectify the lack of knowledge about the gap between intergroup cognitions and intergroup behavior. The most generally useful model of this translation in the attitude domain is Fazio's (1990) MODE model, which posits both a direct and indirect route by which attitudes influence behaviors. Attitudes influence behaviors directly by changing perceptions of the attitude object, which in turn trigger attitude-consistent behaviors. This is the process path on which most intergroup researchers in this volume have focused. The MODE model's indirect route builds on Fishbein and Ajzen's (1975) concern with behavioral intentions: Cognitions produce conscious intentions, which in turn guide behaviors. The indirect route is thus more deliberative and resource-intensive.

Consideration of Fazio's incorporation of the theory of reasoned action in the MODE model makes clear several glaring omissions in thinking about the relation between intergroup cognitions and intergroup behavior. First, one central but relatively neglected component of the theory of reasoned action is the important role attributed to social norms. Intergroup researchers' focus on the more individualistic concept of attitudes, rather than the collective concept of norms, is particularly ironic given the subject matter, and the area of intergroup relations is perfectly suited to redressing this imbalance. For example, it may turn out that certain types of intergroup behavior are actually strongly attitude-driven, but that other behaviors are more norm-driven. Indeed, awareness of the impact of normative cognitions on intergroup behavior is now reemerging, as is discussed in more depth in the next section.

A second omission in much theory regarding intergroup relations is the dimension of behavioral and attitudinal specificity. Intergroup behaviors may relate to a single individual (e.g., hiring a group member for a job) or the entire group (e.g., supporting or opposing governmental policies that benefit or harm the group). Similarly, attitudes may relate to individual members or to a group as a whole. As much of Fishbein and Ajzen's work on the correspondence principle makes clear, attitudes and behaviors at different levels of specificity may not relate to each other, but this insight has largely been lacking in thinking about intergroup attitudes and behavior, with certain outstanding exceptions (e.g., Hewstone & Lord, chap. 15, this volume; Fazio et al., 1995).

A third omission is the distinction between relatively deliberate behaviors for which Fazio's indirect, intention-mediated route will be expected to apply, and relatively unthinking or automatic behaviors that should be driven by Fazio's direct route. Focusing on the intention-driven route might lead social psychologists to reconsider their perhaps too easy assumption that most people do not want to be prejudiced. Considering the role of prejudice-driven intentional behavior may also throw more light on the occurrence of "hot" forms of discrimination, such as hate crimes. Again, researchers in intergroup relations have investigated behaviors that may be driven by the direct or indirect route, but with little attention to the theoretical distinction. Except for investigators who emphasize the possibility of conscious suppression of automatic stereotypic responses (see Bodenhausen et al., chap. 13, this volume), predictions for both types of behaviors have often been identical.

Finally, as noted earlier, Biernat and her associates developed the theme that zero-sum or choice behaviors (such as rankings) and nonzero-sum evaluative behaviors (such as ratings) may differ systematically in their relations to cognitions and judgmental standards. Decision theorists have also found preference reversals and other types of dissociation between these types of behaviors in their own investigations, suggesting the importance of the distinction.

In these four respects and no doubt others as well, it seems likely that more specific and detailed applications of sophisticated theories of attitude–behavior relations, such as Fazio's MODE model, could enrich the field of intergroup relations. Distinguishing between attitudes and behaviors that are relatively norm-driven versus attitude-driven, that are general versus specific, that are directly versus indirectly related, and that are zero-sum versus nonzero-sum can only increase our ability to predict and understand the connections between cognitions and behaviors. Dealing with such issues is not only theoretically important, but may also make clear how to promote the impact of positive intergroup cognitions and interfere with negative cognitions.

Considering Alternate Causal Influences on Intergroup Behavior

In focusing on the cognition–behavior interface, the editors of this volume define *intergroup conditions* quite broadly: "perceptions, memories, stereotypes, impressions, judgments, evaluations, and behavioral intentions" — anything that happens inside the perceiver's head. Nevertheless, some researchers have made progress in understanding intergroup relations by considering other factors represented "in the perceiver's head," but not included specifically in this definition. Reflecting trends in the social psychology literature more generally, chapters in this volume suggest the value of considering three additional determinants of behavior: affect, social relations among groups, and norms.

Affect. In particular, there has been a general resurgence of interest in distinguishing between cognition and affect, and a renewed focus on intergroup affect and emotion (see Mackie & Hamilton, 1993, for overviews). Research on this topic has reflected one of two general approaches, both of which are represented in the contributions to this volume.

First, some researchers have focused on the impact of affect on group-relevant cognitive processing. This approach, taken by Dovidio et al., for example, assumes that intergroup cognitions are the forerunners of intergroup behaviors. However, ongoing affective or emotional states are, in turn, assumed to influence those cognitions in significant ways. For example, affective states can facilitate or inhibit the restructuring of representations that occurs when members of two different groups start to see themselves as members of a single group. Building on Isen's (Isen & Daubman, 1984) demonstrations that positive affect increases category inclusion for mildly positive and mildly nontypical exemplars, the authors argue that positive affect can promote categorization of outgroup members into the ingroup (as long as severe intergroup hostility is not present). They demonstrate that individuals experiencing positive affect were more likely to consider themselves and perhaps also members of other groups to be members of positively valenced categories. They were also more likely to think that members of their own group and another group they would encounter later would see themselves as one superordinate group, and were less likely to show intergroup bias toward a competitive outgroup with whom they shared a common group affiliation. In general, more inclusive representations of the two groups as one were directly related to reduced ingroup bias.

Although cognitive representations remain the key mediator of intergroup behavior in this approach, affect can be seen to have a significant impact on those cognitive representations. Further research is also required to see if affect has a direct effect on behavior (as well as an indirect effect through cognitive representations), although this was not the case for dependent measure like evaluative ratings. Whatever the outcome of such studies, Dovidio and his colleagues' research clearly shows that including the role of affect will allow better understanding of the relation between intergroup cognition and intergroup behavior.

Kramer and Messick (chap. 10) take a similar approach, but bring a new perspective to the study of affect in intergroup relations by focusing on distrust and suspicion rather than the so-called "basic" emotions. As they point out, despite the importance of these two affective reactions to intergroup dealings, there has been little systematic research on the topic (although Insko, Schopler, & Sedikides' and Levine et al. chapters in this volume are exceptions). Distrust arises when attributions about lack of credibility and hostile or deceptive intent are made in the context of fear or insecurity, and suspicion is felt when there is ambiguity about the possible presence of these states. Distrust and suspicion are intergroup cognitions to the extent that they are based in expectancies, inferences, and attributions that guide and often bias information processing. But they can also have a motivational and emotional dimension—a dimension that Kramer and Messick label *collective paranoia*. Collective paranoia reflects false or exaggerated beliefs or feelings that one and one's group is likely to be "harassed, threatened, harmed, subjugated, persecuted, accused, mistreated, wronged, tormented, disparaged, or vilified by a malevolent out-group or out-groups." Basic cognitive processes support such paranoia. For example, group categorization produces a leniency bias toward the ingroup (or, conversely, a harshness bias about the outgroup); perceived homogeneity makes it seem as if the outgroup is acting with a single unified purpose; and increased self-consciousness, the pressure of evaluative scrutiny, and ambiguity about one's social standing promote biased or conflicted information seeking.

What are the consequences of such collective paranoia? According to Kramer and Messick, influences on intergroup cognition include hypervigilant information processing and dysphoric rumination, which in turn increase errors of over personalism (or, in this case, overgroupism), group-serving biases in the attribution process, and exaggerated perceptions of conspiracy. More important, these processes can culminate in an affective reaction that has been termed *moral aggression* or *moral outrage*. *Moral aggression* refers to intense negative reactions to the feeling of being treated unfairly or unjustly, and involves strong anger and the desire for retribution (Bies, 1987). Although they are disappointingly vague about the details of their empirical evidence, Kramer and his colleagues find that this affective reaction is closely linked to intergroup violence and intergroup revenge—the kind of "hot" discriminatory behaviors that are largely missing from social researchers' repertoire of dependent variables. These consequences of collective paranoia can also result in preemptive defensive noncooperation of the type often seen in prisoner dilemma games and social dilemmas. As the authors note, such behavior often results in ongoing reciprocal aggression which creates both confirmation of the original suspicion and distrust and a strong self-fulfilling prophecy. Thus, they identify an important affective determinant of intergroup behavior that arises from and contributes to intergroup cognitions, but that has its own independent influence on behavior.

The idea that affect may also be an antecedent of intergroup relations—independent of cognitions—reflects the second general approach that has been taken in the literature. For example, in Miller and his colleagues' (chap. 16) analysis of the effects of cross categorization, the importance of cognitive factors is supplemented by acknowledgment of the independent influences of affect. These authors note that specific emotions are as important in this regard as the mere valence of experienced affect, and that the effect of emotional arousal can also depend on awareness of its source (Schwarz & Clore, 1983). Thus, if either of the crossed categories differ in valence, the valence of any incidental mood state that either precedes or accompanies the intergroup encounter can draw attention to one or the other, undermining a truly crossed effect. If the source of emotion is a member of one of the cross-cut categories or is related to an insult aimed at one of the categories (what Bodenhausen, 1993, termed *integral affect*), this too can result in the dominance of one, rather than the other, of the categories. Finally, the authors note social psychologists' increasing awareness of and information about the distinct effects that may be associated with discrete emotions. Although anger, sadness, fear, and anxiety are all considered negative emotions, they can have different cognitive and motivational consequences, as well as distinct informational feedback functions. Although predictions about the impact of these specific emotions in cross categorization and intergroup research more generally await further empirical evaluation, Miller and his colleagues reflect an important trend in the literature of trying to incorporate these variables into models of intergroup encounters.

The importance of affect is also recognized in a theory recently proposed by Smith (1993). This theory reconceptualizes prejudice as a group-based emotion, felt on behalf of an ingroup that becomes part of the perceiver's self (as proposed by social identity and self-categorization theories) and based on appraisals of an outgroup's standing in relation to the ingroup. Thus, an outgroup might be regarded with fear, anger, disgust, or other discrete emotions. One important consequence of this view is that behavioral discrimination against an outgroup (viewed as emotionally driven action tendencies) may be of qualitatively different sorts for groups that are targets of distinct emotions. Pettigrew (1996) advanced preliminary evidence that is consistent with this theory, finding in surveys of several European nations that people who are most apt to identify with and feel emotions on behalf of their ingroups—specifically, people who feel pride on behalf of ingroups—are also most likely to harbor prejudice against outgroups. This theory, in emphasizing the importance of discrete emotions (as Miller and colleagues and Kramer and Messick also do in different ways), supplements the more traditional analyses of affect that focus more narrowly on positive versus negative valence, and may point the way toward additional theoretical and empirical considerations relevant to intergroup relations.

Relations Among Groups as Context. As mentioned earlier, early research traditions in intergroup relations focused fairly narrowly on cognitive determinants. They also simplified matters in another way: by considering groups isolated from historical circumstances and societal context. Current research, including some represented in this volume, has begun to remedy this deficiency, particularly by considering the power and status relations of groups as key determinants of the shape and outcomes of intergroup relations.

For example, Kramer and Messick's (chap. 10) analysis of intergroup distrust acknowledges that typical forms of distrust are shaped by groups' relative power positions. Upper groups in a hierarchy worry about revolution from below; lower groups worry about exploitation from above. These typical correlates of power position will obviously have implications for the ways that groups in different positions think about and treat each other.

Power relations are also a central component of Simon's (chap. 11) model of collective intergroup cognitions and collective action. As noted, group status and group size are both important determinants of whether collective self-representations will form and make collective action possible. Although socially determined group status is not always internalized, group status has a disproportionate effect on the valence of the contents of self-aspects, and thus on willingness to engage in collective self-interpretations. Thus, members of a low-status group might be less likely to form collective self-interpretations around that group membership, and consequently less likely to engage in collective action. However, low-status groups might form collective intergroup cognitions if they can rely on the group to provide "safety" or "strength" in numbers. They may also be forced to do so by the social context, as when they are faced with a common fate or common treatment. Being treated alike may make group members think of themselves as alike. Thus, the intergroup cognitions that facilitate intergroup behavior are directly influenced by the power relations between groups, defined both in terms of resources and numbers.

The most detailed treatment of power relations in this volume is provided by Claire and Fiske (chap. 9). They discuss the way power relationships affect processes of stereotype use and behavioral confirmation. They note that although behavioral confirmation research was spawned by practical concerns, such as when a job interviewer's expectations might shape the behaviors of an interviewee, typical research paradigms have omitted the element of differential power that gave those concerns particular weight. Claire and Fiske provide an initial theoretical framework for the analysis of effects of relative power — of the social or organizational context of the intergroup encounter — on the behavioral confirmation of stereotypes. Their argument recognizes that the relation of power to stereotypes is complex; not only does relative power increase the likelihood that stereotypes will become self-fulfilling, but the content of those stereotypes often rationalizes and justifies those power relations.

Perhaps the most intriguing part of Claire and Fiske's chapter is their discussion of the conceptual definition of *self-fulfilling prophecy*. The traditional definition involves a perceiver's initially false stereotype that comes to affect the target's behavior. But Claire and Fiske note that if the stereotype is shared, particularly by powerful groups in society, so that target persons or groups are repeatedly and stably influenced by it, it becomes difficult to say in what sense the expectation is "initially false." In other words, when an expectancy is widely shared and has lasting effects on a target, the resulting transsituational and temporal consistency in the target's behavior fulfills naive criteria for declaring the expectancy to be "true." Thus, the basis for declaring that a self-fulfilling prophecy has occurred cannot be "the target behaves differently for perceivers who hold different expectancies" because such perceivers may not even exist. Instead, the basis becomes "the target would have behaved differently had perceivers treated the target differently."

This discussion brings up deep epistemological and ontological issues, including criteria for declaring a stereotype "true" or "false" and definitions of causality. Research on stereotyping has only recently begun to grasp the important implications of the Cronbach argument about an "accuracy" criterion (e.g., Ryan, Park, & Judd, 1996). Claire and Fiske shift from a covariational definition of causation — from "X (the perceiver's expectancy) causes Y (the target's conforming behavior) because Y is present when X is present and absent when X is absent" — to a counterfactual definition. These considerations regarding the accuracy of an impression and the definition of causation illustrate some of the nonobvious considerations that come up when one attempts to place intergroup relations conceptually into the context of a society with a history, power structures, and consistency across multiple perceivers. As Claire and Fiske's work makes apparent, this process involves more than just adding another one or two independent variables to the equation.

Levine, Moreland, and Ryan (chap. 12) take account of group relationships as a context in a different way, focusing on the implications of intergroup competition for members. In a situation of competition, intragroup processes of socialization and seeking commitment from members will affect intergroup attitudes and behavior. The chapter makes a plausible case that groups' needs for relative uniformity in their members' beliefs, as well as for commitment from their members, can spur intergroup conflict. This can occur whether group memberships are exclusive or potentially overlapping, for even in the latter case each group demands loyalty or commitment above and beyond mere nominal membership. One conceptually important point is that this chapter assumes that the groups in question are small, face to face, and voluntary in nature. This assumption contrasts with the social categories that have most often been the focus of the intergroup relations literature, which is largely driven by enduring concerns with ethnic and national conflicts (related issues arise in the Wilder and Simon [chap. 2] and Hamilton, Sherman, & Lickel [chap. 3] chapters). However, as the authors note, at least parts of their analysis also apply to the situation of social categories; in their example, an African-American woman may feel pressures from African-American men to increase commitment to her ethnic group at the expense of commitment to women as a group. The chapter thus identifies a new dynamic stemming from intragroup needs for member commitment, with potentially important effects on intergroup cognition and behavior.

Norms. Besides affect and the context of relations among groups, a third oft-neglected variable with a potent impact on intergroup cognitions and behavior is norms. As noted earlier, the normative component in classic attitude theories (e.g., Fishbein & Ajzen, 1975) has often been ignored or downplayed in applications of those theories to intergroup behavior. Yet the impact of norms in this area may be pervasive, as several of the chapters in the volume suggest.

Although they do not use the term, Insko, Schopler, and Sedikides' chapter (chap. 5) on the discontinuity between individuals and groups makes implicit reference to the concept of norms. Specifically, the first two of their three hypotheses, involving differential fear of groups and social support for greed, invoke norms. The schema-based expectation that groups will be more hostile and competitive than individuals can be viewed as a norm, a general expectation about the way people typically do (and perhaps should) act. As Insko et al. make clear, this expectation pervasively influences both the way people think about and act toward group versus individual opponents in games with moderately noncorrespondent outcomes. The idea that groups offer social support for greed—so that people can justify exploitation of opponents as being for the good of the ingroup, rather than as naked selfishness—also rests on a norm. In fact, two norms are evident here: the idea that what benefits the ingroup is right, and the idea that selfish exploitation of an opponent is wrong. Thus, both descriptive and prescriptive norms are inherent components of the Insko et al. explanation for differential distrust of individuals and groups.

Schaller, Rosell, and Asp (chap. 1) also discuss the impact of norms, also without using the term. The "context" or cultural setting in which intergroup cognition and behavior takes place exerts its influence largely through norms. This chapter's discussion of the mutual influences of cognition, behavior, and norms is particularly useful. Norms affect the self-concept, as well as the categorization of others and behavior toward those others. In turn, patterns of cognition and behavior that recur and stabilize acquire the force of norms, influencing even more individuals. The evolutionary emphasis of the Insko et al. chapter yields much the same picture. Selective forces at both the individual and group levels shape individual thought and behavior and also group-level patterns. As Insko et al. note, the outcomes of evolution need not be identical at the individual and group levels, and typical results might include interpersonal cooperation within a group paired with intergroup distrust and suspicion. Oft-repeated patterns of cognition and behavior become effective within a given group as norms, and they contribute to shaping such outcomes as differential distrust of groups and individuals. The overall picture of an "evolving social landscape" affected by (and in turn affecting) both intrapersonal and interpersonal processes is a compelling one, although as always one must remain aware of the conceptual and methodological difficulties of actually working at such an inclusive theoretical level.

In conclusion, the recent emphasis on norms as influences on intergroup behavior should be carried even further than it is in these chapters. As argued elsewhere (Mackie & Smith, 1996), there are several reasons to expect norms to be more effective than individual attitudes in shaping behavior. Furthermore, behaviors that are norm-driven will often have qualitatively different consequences from attitude-driven behaviors. In the field of intergroup relations, Steele (1992; Steele & Aronson, 1995) demonstrated that the sharedness of stereotypes has important consequences for targets. Being treated in a particular way (on the basis of a stereotypic expectation) by one individual has quite different effects from being so treated consistently across time by a wide range of other individuals and groups. The same point comes up in Claire and Fiske's chapter (chap. 9) in this volume. In a somewhat different arena, Devine and her colleagues (Devine, Monteith, Zuwerink, & Elliot, 1991) showed that normatively shared prejudice (their term is *prejudice without compunction*) gives rise to different cognitive and perhaps behavioral consequences than prejudice that is counternormative, and therefore subject to concealment and suppression. In these and other ways, effects of norms need to be carefully distinguished, at both the conceptual and empirical levels, from effects of attitudes. Particularly when intergroup relations are at issue, a much more energetic focus on the effects of norms on both cognitions and behavior seems likely to prove fruitful.

As noted at the beginning of this section, research on intergroup relations began with a strong focus on the cognitive determinants of intergroup behavior. This was true in both the North American (e.g., Hamilton, 1981) and European traditions (e.g., Tajfel & Turner, 1979). Now the focus is broadening to consider the effects of other important variables—most notably, affect, social and structural variables such as size and power relations among groups, and norms. This change in focus is welcome. Certainly the recent emergence of significant bodies of cross-cultural research on intergroup relations suggests the immense importance of the social and normative context of intergroup relations: the groups' histories, relative sizes, cultural similarities and differences, and norms regarding intergroup cognitions and behaviors. Not all intergroup situations around the world exactly resemble African-American–White relations in the United States, which much existing research has implicitly or explicitly taken as a model. As Schaller et al. (chap. 1) effectively argue, once we take this broader view, an overemphasis on the principle of parsimony seems misplaced. Arguing that a certain factor can (and therefore should) be omitted from theory because it seems unnecessary to explain a particular instance of intergroup relations makes no sense if the same factor is demonstrably important in a different cultural and normative context. Contexts affect cognitions, behaviors, and also the nature of the links between cognitions and behaviors, and researchers are only beginning to grasp the widespread implications of that fact.

Rethinking the Causal Relations Between Intergroup Cognitions and Behavior

In their opening chapter, Schaller and Stangor point out that intergroup researchers must expand their theorizing to encompass multiple demonstrations that the traditional direction of causality from cognitions to attitudes to behavior can be stood on its head. Evaluative attitudes can dictate cognitions (Schaller, 1992; Schaller & Maass, 1989). Behavior can determine both cognitions and evaluations, as when stereotypes and prejudice exist to justify discrimination (Jost & Banaji, 1994). Despite empirical demonstrations of this "reversed" causality, social psychologists have been slow to develop, or even borrow, the kind of theorizing that Schaller and Stangor suggest. None of the contributions to this volume take as their starting point that intergroup behavior can influence intergroup cognitions. This is particularly surprising given the often close relations between theoretical and research work in the attitudes domain and the intergroup relations domain. For example, in the attitudes domain, both self-perception theory and dissonance theory have been well developed as mechanisms by which behavior causes cognitions.

Self-perception processes operate when unconstrained behavior is attributed to one's underlying dispositions (Bem, 1963). Little is known about the possible role of self-perception processes in the relation between intergroup attitudes and behavior. Are positive and negative behaviors equally likely to be attributed internally, for example, making attributions of prejudice or lack thereof equally likely? Are active intergroup behaviors (such as aggression) and passive behaviors (such as avoidance) equally likely to be the target of self-perception processes? The other main mechanism by which intergroup behavior might influence intergroup cognitions is cognitive dissonance (Festinger, 1957). Given the evidence that social roles, socioeconomic and political conditions, and compliance with social norms often dictate the treatment that people receive, discriminating against others with only minimal "insufficient" justification—indeed without much thought at all—may be a frequent occurrence. If so, negative intergroup attitudes may often be developed and maintained through dissonance reduction processes.

Most of the time, self perception and dissonance processes are likely to result in intergroup cognitions and intergroup behaviors that are consistent. This is not always the case with dissonance reduction processes, however. Festinger (1957) suggested several means other than attitude change by which any tension aroused by inconsistent behavior might be resolved, and more recent reformulations of dissonance indicate many other pathways by which inconsistencies can be explained away. Thus, any dissonance caused by poor treatment of outgroup members could be resolved through reaffirmation of one's values, for example. That is, a situation might arise in which tension associated with discrimination against a member of another group was ironically dealt with by reaffirming one's conviction that one is egalitarian. In this case, measurement of values ("I treat everyone fairly") and assessment of behavior ("I treated him unfairly") would clearly produce a dissociation. Only consideration of the direction of causality between behavior and cognition would allow a principled understanding of this apparent discrepancy.

Another perspective on the causal relations between intergroup cognitions and behavior may come from the idea that behavior often reflects aspects of the psychological self. For example, social identity and self-categorization theory hold that viewing the self as a group member leads to social influence, conformity to group norms, and other types of behavior. If we accept this idea, intergroup cognition may be identified as what we think about them, whereas intergroup behavior follows from what we and they each think about *ourselves*. For example, if the ingroup perceives the outgroup as a group and attributes particular stereotypes to them, but the outgroup does not see themselves as a unitary group, behavior is unlikely to line up directly with cognitions (see Hamilton, Sherman, & Lickel's [chap. 3] discussion of degrees of entitativity). In effect, dissociations among cognitions and behaviors may come about because things do not always look the same from the inside as from the outside.

This perspective would allow researchers and theorists to bring to bear the vast body of literature on similarities and differences between self-perception and other-perception, and also the literature on relations between self-perception and behavior (through such processes as self-perception, self-expression, self-verification, and self-enhancement). These literatures would clearly suggest that the relations of intergroup cognition (loosely, perceptions of others) to intergroup behavior (which depends on one's own and others' self-perceptions) will not be simple, direct, and causally unidirectional.

Accepting the idea that various types of individual cognitions, social norms, and intergroup behaviors can all cause each other may lead us in some novel theoretical directions. Traditional approaches within social psychology (such as Fishbein and Ajzen's classic attitude theory) have specified a causal ordering, with (for example) beliefs and perceived norms causing attitude, attitude causing behavioral intention, and intention causing behavior. However, as Schaller et al. and Claire and Fiske emphasize, as soon as one's perspective is broadened to a longer time frame and a social group or society rather than an individual, it is clear that causal influences are not unidirectional. Recurring patterns of behavior become norms, for example, and people then rationalize them by adopting or changing relevant attitudes.

In this regard, one important trend is the emergence of a new type of psychological theory, termed *connectionism*, which holds that thought and behavior are the outcome of interactions among massive numbers of interconnected simple computational units inspired by biological neurons (see Smith, 1996, for an overview). Connectionism offers the prospect of a more principled theoretical treatment of non-unidirectional causation, compared with traditional psychological theories that assume cognition and behavior flow from processes of the construction and manipulation of languagelike symbols. For example, connectionist models show how multiple forms of mental representation (e.g., beliefs, attitudes, norms, affect, personal goals) all influence each other as the overall system "settles" into a final state that can guide behavior and become accessible to consciousness. Theorists no longer are constrained to line different types of cognitions and behaviors up in a unidirectional sequence for reasons of theoretical tractability. Of course, individual minds are not the only systems that operate in this fashion. Indeed, the presence of multiple causal interactions among a set of variables is the very definition of the term *system*. Groups, societies, and various other entities also constitute systems in this sense, making an adequate theoretical treatment of complex patterns of mutual causation an urgent goal.

CONCLUSIONS AND PROSPECTS

In explaining their motivation for assembling this book, the editors note that the time is right to ask hard questions about the complex and multifaceted ways in which intergroup cognition and intergroup behavior are related. By and large, the contributions to the volume fulfill this mission, in particular specifying ways in which intergroup cognition influences intergroup behavior, and detailing the mediational roles played by affective, motivational, and social context processes. The cumulative effect of the chapters in the volume is to make great progress in closing an unnecessary and unhelpful gap in social psychology's approach to intergroup relations. On the one hand, theorists and researchers, especially in the social cognition tradition, have developed sophisticated analyses of the mental representations that are thought to be relevant to intergroup relations. As a result, our understanding of stereotyping, group and intergroup impressions, and perceptions of variability and homogeneity has increased dramatically (Hamilton & Sherman, 1994; Messick & Mackie, 1989; Mackie & Hamilton, 1993; Macrae, Stangor, & Hewstone, 1996; Park & Judd, 1990; Sedikides & Ostrom, 1993). On the other hand, there has been a parallel growth in attention to issues of ingroup bias, patterns of resource allocation between groups, and systematic discrimination (Brewer, 1979, 1991; Crosby, Bromley, & Saxe, 1980; Jost & Banaji, 1994; Opotow, 1990). Yet this volume represents one of the first attempts to bridge the distance between these two literatures, and to integrate what is known about intergroup cognition and intergroup behavior in a comprehensive way.

The benefits of such an attempt go far beyond theoretical development.

Social psychologists' concern with intergroup relations has always had a practical bent: How can prejudice and discrimination be reduced? Thus, a better understanding of the antecedents and consequences of these forms of intergroup cognition and intergroup behavior becomes a weapon in the war against them. Knowing the conditions under which cognitions direct behavior suggests practical means for facilitating those conditions when cognitions are favorable and for intervening when they are not. Specifying the role of affect and motivation similarly indicates ways in which their beneficial consequences can be exploited and their insidious consequences inhibited. Understanding the multiple influences that social context has on intergroup perceptions and intergroup action prompts recognition that changes in social systems, as well as the impact of social systems on social thinking, need to be addressed. Bringing the impact of norms into the behavioral equation seems particularly likely to spawn new and more effective means of changing and controlling prejudice and discrimination.

Many of the positive contributions made in this volume mirror growing research trends in the discipline as a whole. By the same token, however, much of what is missing here is also reflective of the state of our discipline. In particular, we need as a discipline to "get behavioral." We need to know that our assumptions about cognition and evaluations are true—that they really do make a difference for social behavior, which after all is the social psychological bottom line. Although a lack of attention to behavioral dependent variables is characteristic of the field as a whole, this lack is particularly damning in the study of intergroup relations (Messick & Mackie, 1989; Schneider, 1996). For example, it is telling that, in a volume dedicated to the interface between intergroup cognition and intergroup behavior, only three of the chapters reported studies in which actual behavior (rather than evaluations, predictions about behavior, or behavioral intentions) was studied (e.g., Dovidio et al., chap. 14; Hewstone & Lord, chap. 15; Insko, Schopler, & Sedikides, chap. 5). Thus, although many of the chapters presented sound theoretical reasons to suggest that the cognitions investigated would guide social behavior, there was little empirical verification of those assumptions.

The kinds of dependent measures used in this domain are problematic for a second reason. Many of the measures that are currently used in intergroup work attempt to reflect actual social interactions. For example, allocation measures are intended to reflect distributions of social and material resources, whereas seating distance and helping measures reflect acceptance of social engagement and interaction with outgroup members. However, as noted earlier, there are strong reasons to believe that not all behaviors are the same from a theoretical point of view: Some are more attitude-driven and some more normatively driven, some are specific and some more general, some are zero-sum and some not, and so forth. It is far from clear that behavioral measures employed in research to date have covered this whole spectrum.

For example, research has typically come up short on measures that typify what is meant by discrimination in everyday life—redlining, focused suspicion of minority customers or clients, differences in negotiation strategies used against women and minorities, and differential encouragement given to boys and girls in classrooms. Perhaps even more important, given the national and international climate, social psychologists have avoided—no doubt for many solid practical and ethical reasons—measures of "hot hate," the kinds of measures that bridge the gap between mere dislike of an outgroup and hate crimes, ethnic cleansing, pogroms, enslavement, and genocide (see Opotow, 1990; Staub, 1990). Despite the difficulties, we will need to develop some means of testing the relevance of our models for just such situations if our promise to elucidate social relations is to be fulfilled. For example, Kramer and Messick provide plausible reasons why suspicion and distrust might trigger moral aggression, and thus virulent intergroup interaction. But without some means of assessing the extremity of the behavioral part of the equation, this plausibility cannot be assessed empirically.

In conclusion, much progress toward a better understanding of intergroup cognitions and intergroup behavior can come from integrating work from other research domains. Theory and research on attitudes and impression formation have had an obvious impact on the study of intergroup relations. But consideration of relevant literatures on the self, relationships, emotions, aggression and altruism, and norms would also enrich intergroup theory (Mackie & Smith, 1996). Such an integrative exercise is important beyond any benefits that might accrue to our understanding of intergroup relations. By "crossing the boundaries" between areas of research interest, social psychologists further the pursuit of general principles that underlie the diversity of social psychological phenomena. It is the identification of such basic unifying principles that will best mark scientific progress in the discipline.

ACKNOWLEDGMENTS

Preparation of the manuscript was supported, in part, by National Science Foundation grant SBR-9209995 to Diane M. Mackie, and by National Institute of Mental Health Grants R01 MH46840 and K02 MH01178 to Eliot R. Smith. We thank Tracy Phal and Holly Unruh for help in preparing the manuscript.

REFERENCES

Allport, G. W. (1954). *The nature of prejudice*. Reading, MA: Addison-Wesley.

Amir, Y. (1969). Contact hypothesis in ethnic relations. *Psychology Bulletin, 71*, 319–342.

Ayres, I. (1991). Fair driving: Gender and race discrimination in retail car negotiations. *Harvard Law Review, 104*, 817–872.

Bem, D. J. (1963). An experimental analysis of self-persuasion. *Journal of Experimental Social Psychology, 1*, 199–218.

Bies, R. J. (1987). The predicament of injustice: The management of moral outrage. In L. L. Cummings & B. M. Staw (Eds), *Research in organizational behavior* (Vol. 9, pp. 289–319). Greenwich, CT: JAI.

Blumer, H. (1955). Attitudes and the social art. *Social Problems, 3*, 59–65.

Bodenhausen, G. V. (1993). Emotions, arousal, and stereotypic judgments: A heuristic model of affect and stereotyping. In D. M. Mackie & D. L. Hamilton (Eds.), *Affect, cognition, and stereotyping: Interactive processes in group perception* (pp. 13–37). San Diego, CA: Academic Press.

Brewer, M. B. (1979). Ingroup bias in the minimal intergroup situation: A cognitive-motivational analysis. *Psychological Bulletin, 86*, 307–324.

Brewer, M. B. (1991). The social self: On being the same and different at the same time. *Personality and Social Psychology Bulletin, 17*, 475–482.

Brigham, J. C. (1971). Ethnic stereotypes. *Psychological Bulletin, 76*, 15–38.

Cook, S. W. (1978). Interpersonal and attitudinal outcomes in cooperating interracial groups. *Journal of Research and Development in Education, 12*, 97–113.

Crosby, F., Bromley, S., & Saxe, L. (1980). Recent unobtrusive studies of black and white discrimination and prejudice: A literature review. *Psychological Bulletin, 87*, 546–563.

Darley, J. M., & Fazio, R. H. (1980). The origin of self-fulfilling prophecies in a social interaction sequence. *American Psychologist, 35*, 867–881.

Devine, P. G., Monteith, M. J., Zuwerink, J. R., & Elliot, A. J. (1991). Prejudice with and without compunction. *Journal of Personality and Social Psychology, 60*, 817–830.

Dovidio, J. F., Brigham, J. C., Johnson, B. T., & Gaertner, S. L. (1996). Stereotyping, prejudice, and discrimination: Another look. In C. N. Macrae, M. Hewstone, & C. Stangor (Eds.), *Foundations of stereotypes and stereotyping* (pp. 276–319). New York: Guilford.

Esses, V. M, Haddock, G., & Zanna, M. P. (1993). Values, stereotypes, and emotions as determinants of intergroup attitudes. In D. M. Mackie & D. L. Hamilton (Eds.), *Affect, cognition, and stereotyping: Interactive processes in group perception* (pp. 137–166). San Diego, CA: Academic Press.

Farley, R., Steeh, C., Krysan, M., Jackson, T., & Reeves, K. (1994). Stereotypes and segregation: Neighborhoods in the Detroit Area. *American Journal of Sociology, 100*, 750–780.

Fazio, R. H. (1990). Multiple processes by which attitudes guide behavior: The MODE model as an integrative framework. In M. Zanna (Ed.), *Advances in experimental social psychology* (Vol. 23, pp. 75–109). San Diego, CA: Academic Press.

Fazio, R. H., Jackson, J. R., Dunton, B. C., & Williams, C. J. (1995). Variability in automatic activation as an unobtrusive measure of racial attitudes: A bona fide pipeline? *Journal of Personality and Social Psychology, 69*, 1013–1027.

Fazio, R. H., & Zanna, M. P. (1981). Direct experience and attitude consistency. In L. Berkowitz (Ed.), *Advances in experimental social psychology* (Vol. 1, pp. 161–202). San Diego, CA: Academic Press.

Festinger, L. (1957). *A theory of cognitive dissonance*. Stanford, CA: Stanford University Press.

Fishbein, M., & Ajzen, I. (1974). Attitudes toward objects as predictors of single and multiple behavioral criteria. *Psychological Review, 81*, 59-74.

Fishbein, M., & Ajzen, I. (1975*). Belief, attitude, intention, and behavior: An introduction to theory and research*. Reading, MA: Addison-Wesley.

Fiske, S. T. (1993). Social cognition and social perception. *Annual Review of Psychology, 44*, 155-194.

Hamilton, D. L. (1981). Stereotyping and intergroup behavior: Some thoughts on the cognitive approach. In D. L. Hamilton (Ed.), *Cognitive processes in stereotyping and intergroup behavior* (pp. 333-354). Hillsdale, NJ: Lawrence Erlbaum Associates.

Hamilton, D. L., & Gifford, R. K. (1976). Illusory correlation in interpersonal perception: A cognitive basis of stereotypic judgments. *Journal of Experimental Social Psychology, 12*, 392-407.

Hamilton, D. L., & Sherman, J. W. (1994). Stereotypes. In R. S. Wyer, Jr. & T. K. Srull (Eds.), *Handbook of social cognition* (Vol. 2, pp. 1-68). Hillsdale, NJ: Lawrence Erlbaum Associates.

Hamilton, D. L., & Trolier, T. K. (1986). Stereotypes and stereotyping: An overview of the cognitive approach. In J. F. Dovidio & S. L. Gaertner (Eds.), *Prejudice, discrimination, and racism* (pp. 127-163). Orlando, FL: Academic Press.

Hoffman, C., & Hurst, N. (1990). Gender stereotypes: Perception or rationalization. *Journal of Personality and Social Psychology, 58*, 197-208.

Hogg, M. A., & Abrams, D. (1988). *Social identifications: A social psychology of intergroup relations and group processes*. London: Routledge Kegan Paul.

Hogg, M. A., & Abrams, D. (1990). Social motivation, self esteem and social identity. In D. Abrams & M. A. Hogg (Eds.), *Social identity theory: Constructive and critical advances* (pp. 28-47). London: Harvester Wheatsheaf.

Isen, A. M., & Daubman, K. A. (1984). The influence of affect on categorization. *Journal of Personality and Social Psychology, 52*, 1122-1131.

Jost, J. T., & Banaji, M. R. (1994). The role of stereotyping in system-justification and the production of false consciousness. *British Journal of Social Psychology, 33*, 1-27.

Jussim, L. (1991). Social perception and social reality: A reflection-construction model. *Psychological Review, 98*, 54-73.

Jussim, L., Nelson, T. E., Manis, M., & Soffin, S. (1995). Prejudice, stereotypes, and labeling effects: Sources of bias in person perception. *Journal of Personality and Social Psychology, 68*, 228-246.

LaPiere, R. T. (1934). Attitudes vs. actions. *Social Forces, 13*, 230-237.

Linville, P. W. (1985). Self-complexity and affective extremity: Don't put all of your eggs in one cognitive basket. *Social Cognition, 3*, 94-120.

Lord, C. G., Lepper, M. R., & Mackie, D. (1984). Attitude prototypes as determinants of attitude-behavior consistency. *Journal of Personality and Social Psychology, 46*, 1254-1266.

Mackie, D. M., & Hamilton, D. L. (Eds.). (1993). *Affect, cognition, and stereotyping: Interactive processes in group perception*. San Diego, CA: Academic Press.

Mackie, D. M., & Smith, E. R. (1996). *Intergroup relations: Insights from a theoretically integrative approach*. Unpublished manuscript, University of California, Santa Barbara.

Macrae, C. N., Stangor, C., & Hewstone, M. (Eds.). (1996). *Stereotypes and stereotyping*. New York: Guilford.

Massey, D. S., & Denton, N. A. (1993). *American apartheid: Segregation and the making of the underclass*. Cambridge, MA: Havard University Press.

Messick, D. M., & Mackie, D. M. (1989). Intergroup relations. *Annual Review of Psychology, 40*, 45-81.

Merton, R. (1948). The self-fulfilling prophecy. *Antioch Review, 8*, 193–210.

Opotow, S. (1990). Moral exclusion and injustice: An introduction *Journal of Social Issues, 46(1)*, 1–20.

Park, B., & Judd, C. M. (1990). Measures and models of perceived group variability. *Journal of Personality and Social Psychology, 59*, 173–191.

Pettigrew, T. F. (1996). The affective component of prejudice: Empirical support for the new view. In S. A. Tuch & J. K. Martin (Eds.), *Racial attitudes in the 1990s: Continuity and change.* Westport, CT: Praeger.

Rothbart, M., & John, O. P. (1985). Social categorization and behavioral episodes: A cognitive analysis of intergroup contact. *Journal of Social Issues, 41*, 81–104.

Ryan, C. S., Park, B., & Judd, C. M. (1996). Assessing stereotype accuracy: Implications for understanding the stereotyping process. In C. N. Macrae, C. Stangor, & M. Hewstone (Eds.), *Stereotypes and stereotyping* (pp. 121–157). New York: Guilford.

Sadker, M., & Sadker, D. (1994). *Failing at fairness: How schools cheat girls.* New York: Touchstone.

Schaller, M. (1992). Ingroup favoritism and statistical reasoning in social inference: Implications for formation and maintenance of group stereotypes. *Journal of Personality and Social Psychology, 63*, 61–74.

Schaller, M., & Maass, A. (1989). Illusory correlation and social categorization: Toward an integration of motivation and cognitive factors in stereotype information. *Journal of Personality and Social Psychology, 56*, 709–721.

Schneider, D. (1996). Unfinished business. In C. N. Macrae, C. Stangor, & M. Hewstone (Eds.), *Stereotypes and stereotyping* (pp. 419–453). New York: Guilford.

Schwarz, N., & Clore, G. L. (1983). Mood, misattribution, and judgments of well-being: Informative and directive functions of affective states. *Journal of Personality and Social Psychology, 45*, 513–523.

Sedikides, C., & Ostrom, T. M. (Eds.). (1993). Perceptions of group variability [Special Issue]. *Social Cognition, 11*, 1–175.

Slovic, P. (1995). The construction of preference. *American Psychologist, 50*, 364–371.

Smith, E. R. (1993). Social identity and social emotions: Toward new conceptualizations of prejudice. In D. M. Mackie & D. L. Hamilton (Eds.), *Affect, cognition, and stereotyping: Interactive processes in group perception* (pp. 297–315). San Diego, CA: Academic Press.

Smith, E. R. (1996). What do connectionism and social psychology offer each other? *Journal of Personality and Social Psychology, 70*, 893–912.

Snyder, M., & Ickes, W. (1985). Personality and social behavior. In G. Lindzey & E. Aronson (Eds.), *Handbook of social psychology* (3rd ed., Vol. 2, pp. 883–947). New York: Random House.

Stangor, C., Sullivan, L. A., & Ford, T. E. (1991). Affective and cognitive determinants of prejudice. *Social Cognition, 9*, 359–380.

Staub, E. (1990). Moral exclusion, personal goal theory, and extreme destructiveness. *Journal of Social Issues, 46*(1), 47–64.

Steele, C. M. (1992, April). Race and the schooling of black Americans. *Atlantic Monthly*, pp. 68–78.

Steele, C. M., & Aronson, J. (1995). Stereotype threat and the intellectual test performance of African Americans. *Journal of Personality & Social Psychology, 69*, 797–811.

Struch, N., & Schwartz, S. H. (1989). Intergroup aggression: Its predictors and distinctness from intergroup bias. *Journal of Personality and Social Psychology, 56*, 364–373.

Tajfel, H. (1978). Intergroup behaviour: II. Group perspectives. In H. Tajfel & C. Fraser (Eds), *Introducing social psychology* (pp. 144–167). Oxford: Blackwell.

Tajfel, H., Billig, M. G., Bundy, R. P., & Flament, C. (1971). Social categorization and intergroup behavior. *European Journal of Social Psychology, 1*, 149–178.

Tajfel, H., & Turner, J. C. (1979). An integrative theory of intergroup conflict. In W. G. Austin & S. Worchel (Eds.), *The social psychology of intergroup relations* (pp. 33–47). Monterey, CA: Brooks/Cole.

Wicker, A. W. (1969). Attitude versus actions: The relationship of verbal and overt behavior responses to attitude objects. *Journal of Social Issues, 25(4),* 41–78.

Author Index

Subject Index